Everard (E Tresidder
1871-1944

Elsie Annie Garden
1871-1950

Thomas Burton
1884-1925

Annie Machen
1885-1952

Arthur Morley
1888-1961

Edith Helen Lee
1895-1959

Paul Denison Haskins
1905-1996

Jean J F M Tresidder
1904-1976

Nancy [A Burton
1910-1977

Ken [Burton BA
1924-Living

Renee Faith Morley
1926-2017

Reg [M Morley
1922-1998

Bram [B Morley
1932-

Eric Alfred Morley
1935-2002

Robert James Haskins
1948-Living

Carolyn Burton BSc
1957-Living

Michael Ian Burton BA
1960-Living

Margaret Aspinall MEd
1962-Living

Naomi Delia Simpson BA
1977-Living

Jonathan Neil Haskins
1986-Living

Christopher J Haskins
1989-Living

Rowan M Burton BA
1991-Living

Lois Margaret Burton
1993-Living

Quarter Cornish

My Family and Other Oddities

One family's experience
of Britain's impact on the world

ROBERT HASKINS

TREGERTHA IMPRINTS
BEDFORD

Published by Tregertha Imprints, Tree Garth, Ravensden, Bedford MK44 2RP
01234 772745
Further copies may be obtained from the publisher or by emailing
Quarter.Cornish@gmail.com
Front cover picture is from an original painting by the author

"Writing a book is an adventure. To begin with, it is a toy and an amusement. Then it becomes a mistress; then it becomes a master; then it becomes a tyrant. The last phase is that just as you are about to be reconciled to your servitude, you kill the monster, and fling him out to the public."

Winston Churchill

to the next generation

Contents

Haskins Family Tree..2

Introduction 10

1. Tinkers, Tailors and Golf Club Makers 13

2. Scriveners of Falmouth 25

3. Scarborough and the Silver Spoons 39

4. Happiest Days of our Lives 49

5. Oxford Life 63

6. Indian Empire 77

7. Spoonful of Sugar 115

8. Vanity 123

9. Garden Gates 133

10. China 147

11. Eyelids of the Morning 163

12. African Adventures 175

13. Disaster 191

14. Twirling Twenties 199

15. The Minotaur 211

16. The Banker 221

17. Northern Lights 233

18. The Grocer's Son 247

19. I Love Driving West 261

20. The Lost House of Heligan 267

21. Cauldron of History 269

Credits 275

Bibliography 276

Index..282

Introduction

'What are you like?' some folk will ask. They think I'm quirky, hard to categorise, non-conformist, even wacky. They don't even know when I am joking. So why am I like this? It's not deliberate. Was I made that way?

This book may explain why I am like what I am – is it nature or nurture? Under the cloth of conformity, you're probably not so different from some of the characters in these stories about me and my idiosyncratic family. Many of the people in these stories played a small part in Britain's influence on the world, before Brexit, before the European Community, during the Victorian era and before, when Britain ruled the waves, was developing world trade, was exporting more than it imported, and when it inspired emerging civilisations to adopt its Christian values.

My Cornish connection comes from my mother's side, the Tresidders. Cornwall, Falmouth in particular, became the hub of Britain's maritime and trading connections. Latterly, Cornwall has been an inspiration for artists and writers – including one or two in my family. Parts of this book have been written in my cottage on the south coast of Cornwall. Oddly, or maybe not so oddly, most of the village of Pentewan seemed to know about my intentions before I did. Those who've known me there for 30 years or so asked what the book was about. Well, my family comes from all over Britain – Haskins from London; Wiggins from Oxfordshire; Garden from Scotland, and Tresidder from Cornwall. Many trod pathways round the world in the days of the Empire. But then my wife Carolyn's side comes from Yorkshire, with a family life and experience mostly satisfied without moving away from their birthplace[1]. When I started my research for this book I had little inkling of any Yorkshire connections on my side.

The local villagers in Pentewan, however, always knew I had a right to live in Cornwall – as I'm a quarter Cornish. "Quarter Cornish?" my village friends said, with their accents betraying their origins. "Why don' you call the book that then? ' Quarter Cornish'."

The main incentives for putting pen to paper? The study of history was an interest of my father, not so much mine until now. I'd researched some interesting relations in the 1970s before the internet made it easy and my nephew Luke asked for more[2]. Then I'd found a Yorkshire link – what was the history behind a seaside home in Scarborough? A business trip to Calcutta fired me up to find out about an Indian connection – my grandfather was born there[3]. So, finally, as Robert Baden-Powell once said, "If you have ever seen the play 'Peter Pan' you will remember how the pirate chief was always making his dying speech because he was afraid that possibly, when the time came for him to die, he might not have time to get it off his chest – it is much the same with me."

✳ ✳ ✳ ✳

---

1.   *Carolyn Burton (b1957) married the author in 1985.*
2.   *Luke David Simpson (b1970).*
3.   *Dr Morton Everard Tresidder (1872-1944).*

As far as I was concerned, Yorkshire was a foreign country but, after moving to Wetherby and researching my family, there were some surprises. It was a surprise to discover that both my Durham-born sister-in-law Margaret Burton (née Aspinall) and my Liverpudlian brother-in-law Ian Simpson have Cornish blood. It was a surprise to find that my nephew, Hugh Simpson, is directly related to his wife Kate, going back umpteen generations. But more surprising was to find family links between me and my adopted Yorkshire town. A Cornish first cousin (3 times removed) on my mother's side married a girl from Wetherby[4]. She left her Yorkshire milling family to teach in Cornwall and married the local pharmacist. Yet another branch of my family, who made their fortune in Naples, had first kept a shop in Wetherby.

Name-dropping can be pompous, and whilst the Haskins frowned on it and the Wiggins revelled in it, there are names from history that have cropped up. One name, though, I have to say quietly: I am related to a family of Bastards …. 'Admonition Bastard' must be the most atrocious name in any family anywhere. Sums some of my family up, I suppose, particularly those cousins from Devon (or was it Cornwall?) called the Pollexfens – buccaneers as well as bastards.

People in my family, like most others, are a mixture of the good, bad and indifferent. Some commanded all that they surveyed; others did not. One or two had excessive charm although most of the time it was a sham. Some had integrity and compassion, others had feet of clay. I haven't mentioned the many with a humble faith who modestly followed their Christian upbringing but I do mention some who, in the carefully phrased language of one writer, put 'personal inclination ahead of public duty'. Some were given opportunities and took them. Others squandered their chances out of caution, cowardice or carelessness. Most were just caught in their circumstances and lived out their days without stressing over the wider world, like I do. Yet in one way or another they contributed to the course of history and, whether culturally significant or simply salacious, their story pays for the telling.

Let's start with Haskins, my surname. If you ask the genealogical 'experts' – the ones who make you up a coat of arms and print out a parchment, they'll tell you that the Haskins name comes from the old Norse 'Asketil' – Danish princes – one of whom crops up later. Breaking that down into its individual parts, 'Oss means God; and Ketil means cauldron: God's cauldron? Very romantic. The actual story is rather more unconventional, if the first Chapter of this book is anything to go by.

Nevertheless, let's pretend the "Hobby 'Oss," which dances round Padstow on May Day, is dancing round the ketil of this family's history. Let's follow the dance and discover the places and events that helped to make Britain great, and me the way I am, and let's see where that takes us.

---

4. *Thomas John Tresidder Corfield (1816-1887) married Marcia Clarke Burnley (1830-1912) in 1855. He was a pharmacist in St Day, Cornwall. Her first cousin (3x removed) David Farrar (1782-1839) and John Greenwood (also a relation) bought the corn mill by the River Wharfe at Wetherby when the 6th Duke of Devonshire auctioned off the whole of Wetherby in 1824 to pay for his parents' gambling debts. Marcia's father Jonathan Burnley (1800-1870) was a miller in Kirk Deighton and owned freehold houses and land in Linton, villages close to Wetherby. Jonathan Burnley was baptised at St James, Wetherby; Marcia at the Methodist chapel Boston Spa.*

Tinkers, Tailors and Golf Club Makers

A ship slips through the groynes of Constance (Konstanz), a stop on the lake on the border of Switzerland and Germany. Those on board will stare at the statue of Imperia. She stands with her legs a-cock, scantily clad, holding a naked Pope in one hand and a naked King in the other. Imperia is said to have shamelessly controlled the Council of Constance 1414-18 using her physical charms – persuading the Cardinals to commit cardinal sins[i]. The Council successfully sorted out who should be Pope – there were three fighting it out – but it also played a part in the origins of the Haskins family.

Imperia, Lake Constance

Family folklore, oral history passed down the through the generations, by word of mouth, disagrees with the geneological industry's fictional theory of our origins. It gives a different answer. It says the name Haskins derives from *Huss kins*, i.e. the family of **John Huss**[ii].

John Huss was the main topic on the lips of Imperia and her Cardinals in 1414 – he'd stirred them all up, the church hierarchy, by criticising them and no one likes criticism. The church was in a parlous state; cardinals who were more interested in worldly success than in eternal salvation.

Huss, based at Prague University, had translated the writings of the English pastor John Wycliffe into Czech in an effort to bring the church back to its senses[1]. Principles of living meant more to Huss than pandering to licentious leadership[iii]. He denounced – from the pulpit – fellow clergy who didn't live by their vows of poverty, chastity and obedience. It wasn't perhaps the best way to win friends – yet he influenced many people.

Good King Wenceslas (not the one in the carol) looked out for him but, in the end, Huss was condemned by the Council of Constance. He was handed over to the authorities and burnt at the stake. John Huss was to sow the seeds of the Reformation – Erasmus, Luther and Cromwell: the 'Reformation', the break with Rome, the dissolution of the monasteries, the dissenting Christians and the rise of the 'non-conformist' church[2].

Male DNA, father to father, doesn't alter from one generation to another – my Y-chromosome Haplogroup, M223, is pretty rare (4%), the database small. The gene is found today around the Baltic in Eastern Sweden, Denmark and the Netherlands plus Scotland and Germany[iv]. According to some writers, it may have come from the *Vandals*, the nomadic race who helped wipe out the Roman Empire, or from the Lazyges, another nomadic race from Romania who lent Emperor Hadrian an army of 5,000 to guard England from the unruly Picts in Scotland[v]. Judging from their behaviour, the Huss kins (family) possessed the *Vandal* gene.

The furthest back the family name of Haskins can be traced with certainty is no further than 1800, from when two hard-up jewellers lived in the London area of Islington, Clerkenwell and Shoreditch, an area still known as St Luke's, north-west of London's Old Street tube station, sometimes known as 'Silicone Roundabout' or, more traditionally, St Agnes Well.

John Huss (1369-1415)

---

1. *Rev John Wycliffe (c1329-1384) [NR], known as the 'Morning Star of the Reformation', vicar and philosopher who wrote about lordship and grace – all who believe have grace, whilst the corrupt church didn't and therefore couldn't be lords – essentially it is the philosophy of the priesthood of all believers.*
2. *Rev Desiderius Erasmus (1466-1536) [NR]; Rev Martin Luther (1483-1546) [NR].*

St Mary Islington was bombed in the last war but the tower and steeple remained intact

Could it be that the Haskins family came across the Channel at about the time when Protestant traders were pouring over from the Low Countries? Migrants, following their Protestant king, William of Orange, who'd landed in Brixham in Devon to take up the English crown on Guy Fawkes Day, 1688?

✳ ✳ ✳ ✳

The Bobbin Makers

In 1797, the Times advertised the sale of a library of law books plus bedsteads, sideboard, table, pier glasses (mirror), girandoles (candlesticks), curtains and carpets[vi]. **William Haskins**, brother of my great-great-great grandfather Joseph, was declared bankrupt; there was a court case about unpaid wages[3]. Joseph's son Arthur (who we'll meet later) was called to give evidence. Of the two brothers, Joseph if not William, seemed to have learnt a lesson; the Haskins family has been better at counting out its money ever since.

Joseph and William Haskins worked in the lower end of the Jewellery trade – the manufacture of glass beads. **Joseph Haskins** was born 1779 in Shoreditch, London[4]. He married **Catherine Church** at St Mary's, Islington on 4 Aug 1800 and until that point had been in business with his brother William first in Ironmonger Lane and then in Richmond Street. Whether or not he was related to John Huss, Joseph was a 'non-conformist', baptising at least one of his children (Robert) in the Upper Street Independent Church in Islington and burying the dead in Bunhill boneyard[vii].

Window at the Bunyan Meeting, Mill Street, Bedford.

Who would true valour see,
Let him come hither;
One here will constant be,
Come wind, come weather
There's no discouragement
Shall make him once relent
His first avowed intent
To be a pilgrim.

Whoso beset him round
With dismal stories
Do but themselves confound;
His strength the more is.
No lion can him fright,
He'll with a giant fight,
He will have a right
To be a pilgrim

1800 was a time of extremes: showy wealth for the rich (see Chapter 3) and dire hardship for the poor. There was a general ferment of unrest right across the land. England was being held together by a collection of motivated immigrants who kept their heads down and worked hard – optimists; self-starters like the Haskins brothers.

Joseph and Catherine moved their family from London to Bedfordshire, first to Maulden, nine miles from Bedford town. This was about 1814, which had one of the coldest winters, a year when the Thames froze over, or it could have been in 1815, the year of the Battle of Waterloo[viii]. Joseph would have wanted to explore new business opportunities as many London artisans were doing, but as a non-conformist, he may have been attracted to Bedford for other reasons[ix]. Perhaps he was seeking out his connections with John Bunyan who'd led worship in the town a hundred years earlier[5].

[3.] *William Haskins (1773-?)*

[4.] *Joseph Haskins (1779-1855) married Catherine Church (1777-1865) in 1800*

[5.] *John Bunyan (1628-1688).*

Family folklore also suggests that the Haskins family is related to John Bunyan, though I have no direct evidence[x]. Nevertheless, John Bunyan has been a hero of mine ever since reading *'Pilgrim's Progress'* when I was eleven[xi]. I had no trouble with mastering the old-fashioned language. It uses simple word pictures to tell a moral tale: something all children should read; it would probably do them more good than Shakespeare. I also like the hymn *'Who would true valour see,'* especially the line about fighting lions. Bunyan was a well-liked preacher who wrote over 60 books and inspired a wide circle of people including William Blake[6].

John Bunyan first preached at St John's Bedford. Some of the third generation of Haskins were baptised there. Joseph's eldest son, **Joseph John**, married **Phoebe Bowler** from Bunyan's birthplace, Elstow – maybe she was the family link[7].

Joseph described himself as a 'lapidary'. He not only sold glass beads but also crafted them, stringing them together as necklaces. Beads, or spangles as they were called, were used to weight lace bobbins to keep the lace taut. In the German tradition, they were melted off from a stick of glass and twirled on copper wire to make the hole, and pressed on the sides to make a square shape with markings on the surface. The glass might come from old decanter tops and be melted down using tallow candles. The colouring was added when the glass was soft[xii].

Lace-making was the salvation for home-workers in Bedfordshire and Northampton. Almost all women made extra money that way and Joseph found a ready market for his bobbins. He used his creative instincts to make 'luxury' bobbins, bought to give as presents for the women who made lace for a living – as practically all of them did. From parts of the shin bone of cattle, sheep and pigs he carved intricate grooves, inlayed with coloured tinsel, pewter or beads, sometimes incised with loose rings or with 'windows' in which appeared 'baby' bobbins each neatly turned, hollowed out from the main body. He also produced bobbins to be given away by parliamentary candidates at elections to win votes[8]. Joseph produced 'the finest and most elaborate bobbins of the century'[xiii]. Bobbins made by Joseph usually had a bead at the tail (and a line around its 'equator') with a projection drilled to take the spangles. There'd be tinsel on the shank, a ridged collar, a tapered neck and a completely flat surface at the top of the rim.

Out of Joseph and Catherine's 10 children (see the tree at the end of the chapter), **William Haskins**, their third child, was my great-great grandfather[9]. He was about 10 years old when they moved from London. As the second son, his job was sales and distribution, attending markets and fairs, selling the bobbins at a shilling each. William was a hawker, and in a way, he was following in John Bunyan's footsteps – Bunyan had been a tinker. William took over the bead and bobbin manufacturing side in his fifties, when his father and eldest brother Joseph John had both died.

The bobbin making and jewellery trades carried on through a couple of brothers for a generation or two; although the sixth son, **James Ebenezer**[10] used his skills with glass in a different way, learning how to make spectacles.

Bobbins for lace making, with 'spangles' to weight the end (50p shows the size) Luton Museum

A lace maker at work

---

6. *William Blake (1757-1827) [NR].*
7. *Joseph John Haskins (1803-1868) married Phoebe Bowler (1804-1877) in 1826.*
8. *'Robinson for ever' supported Sir George Robinson, 6th Bt (1766-1833) [NR] MP for Northampton 1820-32.*
9. *William Haskins (1804-1879) married (1) Eleanor Wright (1806-1831) in 1824 and (2) Ann Clifton (1804-1880) in 1834.*
10. *James Ebenezer Haskins (1816-1884) married Hannah Haskins (1817-1890) in Holborn in 1836 and they lived in Clerkenwell, London.*

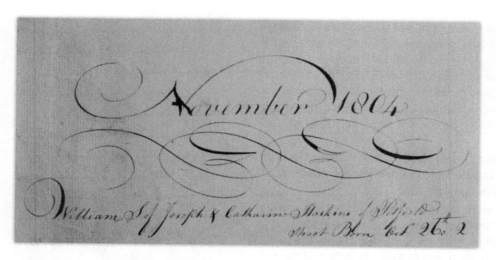

William Haskins, the author's great great grandfather, son of Joseph and Catherine, born 26 Oct 1804, baptised at St Leonard's Shoreditch, 2 Nov 1804

The fifth son Robert married a girl whose father, a watch gilder from Penge, taught him about gold so he could decorate his bobbins, though he branched out into dentistry – gold fillings[11]. Both he and his eldest son were married in Islington and lived for years in London, before each moved back to Bedford in later life[12].

Joseph John, Joseph's eldest son, might have been expected to carry on the business down the generations but it wasn't easy with six girls and an only son, **John Haskins**, wanting to become a hairdresser[13]. John moved to Leighton Buzzard, where he met his wife through his uncle David who'd retired there – their two wives came from the same Sussex family. He built the business up with four hairdressers working for him, a tobacconist shop on the side. John grew to be quite a force to be reckoned with; he became a Director of the Bedfordshire and Buckingham Building Society and, liking his flowers, was a committee member of both the local Chrysanthemum Society and the Horticultural Society. Gardening was both a relaxation and supplemented the dinner table in 1900[xiv].

✳ ✳ ✳ ✳

Cornish Smugglers

William's brothers, **David** and **Arthur** (Arthur gave evidence when his Uncle William went bankrupt), escaped the family business by becoming Excise Officers for the Inland Revenue[14].

On duty in Sussex, David met and married a girl from Framfield, Mary Tanner[15]. He lived into his nineties, boasting that he'd lived through the reigns of six monarchs, being one year old when George III had died[xv]. He is the first Haskins with a Cornish connection. Almost as soon as David was married, the authorities posted him to Camelford and all three of their children were born in Cornwall.

To say that Excise men were not popular in Cornwall was an understatement. They were employed along with the Customs to raise taxes and stop fraud. Smuggling had become a way of life in Cornwall and no one there wanted to pay taxes. During the Napoleonic Wars, France had blockaded British ports and cut off supplies from the outside world. My cottage in Cornwall, which was once an alehouse, was said to have had an illegal gin 'still' out the back under the cliff and out of the Exciseman's view. The government had to send in a tough team of outsiders from 'up country' to reinforce Customs duty, as it helped pay for the war. *Jamaica Inn*, immortalised in Daphne du Maurier's well-known story, was on David's patch[16].

11. *Robert Haskins (1813-1883) married Mary Ann Stillwell (1817-1910) in 1836. Her father was Richard Stilwell (1797-1877)/*

12. *An elder son died at the age of four. Julia was from Eversholt, Bedfordshire.*

13. *John Haskins (1834-1915) married Betsy Tanner (1835-1913) in 1867.*

14. *Arthur Haskins (1810-1863) married Jane Springham (1811-?) in 1837.*

15. *David Haskins (1819-1912) married Mary Tanner (1838-1912) in 1855.*

16. *Daphne du Maurier, Lady Browning DBE (1907-1989) [NR] wrote the novel Jamaica Inn in 1936.*

A Smuggler's Song

If you wake at midnight, and hear a horse's feet,
Don't go drawing back the blind, or looking in the street,
Them that asks no questions they isn't told a lie.
Watch the wall, my darling, while the Gentlemen go by!

Five-and-twenty ponies, trotting through the dark
With brandy for the Parson and 'baccy for the Clerk.
Laces for a lady and letters for a spy,
And watch the wall, my darling, while the Gentlemen go by!

If you meet King George's men, dressed in blue and red,
You be careful what you say, and mindful what is said.
If they call you "pretty maid," and chuck you 'neath the chin,
Don't you tell where no one is, nor yet where no one's been!

Five-and-twenty ponies, trotting through the dark
Brandy for the Parson, 'baccy for the Clerk.
Them that asks no questions isn't told a lie
So watch the wall, my darling, while the Gentlemen go by!

Rudyard Kipling - *abridged*

David was in Camelford at the same time as the unusual Parson Hawker, Vicar of Morwenstow, 25 miles up the coast. Hawker was an eccentric clergyman, first marrying at the age of 19 to a woman twice his age; and when he was 60 he wed a 21 year-old Polish girl, who bore him three children[17]. He used to pinch babies' bottoms after baptising them to make sure they 'yelled the devil out'. His fisherman's jersey, long sea boots, pink hat and yellow poncho probably helped in a 'Where's Wally?' situation. This was the 1840s and it was a long way from Oxford University where he'd won the prestigious Newdigate Prize for poetry.

Shipwrecks still occur in Cornwall. Underwater rocks can easily slice open a wooden hull. The villagers of Morwenstow were given to a spot of deliberate 'wrecking'. They wouldn't wait for ships to toss up on the rocks. They waited for stormy weather and then, in the dead of night would set up a light up on the cliffs to tempt them in. A law passed in 1735 had made it a criminal offence, but it didn't stop them – *"Who was to know, my han'some? A single candle-lantern, 'tis all it took"* [xvi]. Guided by a light, ships unfamiliar with the coastline headed towards what they thought was a harbour, and ended up intertwangled on the rocks. The contents washed up onto the shore-line, the villagers would then do some beachcombing – picking up the flotsam and jetsam washed up on the beach. It is said they cared little about the human cost: 'They would not take the hand of a drowning man.' [xvii] Excisemen like David? They'd have no qualms about doing them in.

Many thought Hawker was the mastermind behind the enterprise, though his aim was actually to save the drowning sailors. He had a look-out hut on the cliffs – now the smallest listed building in England, and owned by the National Trust.

A SHIP HAS BEEN SIGHTED
in this quarter
ENGAGING IN THE UNLAWFUL ACT OF
SMUGGLING
whosoever can lay information leading to the capture of this ship or its crew
will receive a reward of
£500
From His Majesty's Government
This 19th day of October 1782

Parson Hawker's hut

He used it for poetry writing. He could compose there, inspired by the sea, the sun shining through the irised rain. *"Oh, an' did I tell 'e 'bout his smoking habit?"* A little opium inspired his poetry but he wasn't alone. Samuel Taylor Coleridge wrote his best works under the influence[18]. Thomas De Quincey confessed to it. Collins, Shelley, Poe – even Keats took to it [xviii].

Men like David Haskins, drafted in from outside Cornwall, were less likely to be bribed. The government built rows of cottages in villages around the Cornish coast. Her Majesty's Excisemen were in the community but not of it. According to the stories Hawker told, some took bribes – gold coins left in cloth purses wedged between rocks. When one of the smugglers said to an Exciseman, 'Sir, Your pocket's unbuttoned,' he'd reply, 'Ay but never mind, my man, my money's safe enough.' [xix]

David may have known Mr Parminter, the subject of one of Hawker's tales. Parminter was a bold and determined Exciseman. People knew that no threats would deter him and no bribes would he take. Careful where he walked, he carried arms – he even trained his dauntless dog, Satan, to carry a loaded gun in his mouth, though one day the two of them went too far. At a cove six miles down the coast from Bude, there was a cave stashed with contraband. Parminter and his dog sniffed it out and hid, ready to pounce. When the first boat came in, Parminter, cutlass in hand, sprung down amongst the smugglers – sadly, Satan didn't follow. The crew's blood was up and, in the heat of the moment; the smugglers pulled Parminter down, held his neck over the gunwale and chopped off his head. Not an easy profession.

The straight row of terraced cottages above the chapel were built for the 'coastguards' at Portloe

Will you hear of the Cruel Coppinger?
He came from a foreign kind;
He was brought to us by the salt water,
He was carried away by the wind.

David Haskins was up against men like the Danish desperado 'Cruel Coppinger' [xx]. His motley gang had 'small active horses shaved from forelock to tail ... well soaped or greased from head to foot, so as to slip easily out of any hostile grasp.' Their revelry 'appalled the neighbourhood day and night'. Strange vessels would appear on the coast; signals would flash from headlands leading them into a safe creek. If the ground-swell was too strong, the ships would anchor outside the surf, and dinghies would row out to collect the spoil. David's colleagues must have had a few near misses with death. Near Port Isaac, one set of smugglers lured a Revenue cutter (a single-masted ship) through a treacherous channel and forced it aground – all on board perished.

---

18. *Samuel Taylor Coleridge (1772-1834) [NR]; William Collins (1721-1759) [NR]; Percy Bysshe Shelley (1792-1822) [NR]; Edgar Alan Poe (1809-1949) [NR]; Thomas De Quincey (1785-1859) [NR] wrote Confessions of an English Opium-Eater in 1823; John Keats (1795-1851) [NR].*

The locals were terrified of Coppinger's gang. No one moved at night over 'Coppinger's tracks'. These paths met on a headland called Steeple Brink. Two hundred feet down was 'Coppinger's Cave'. They say Coppinger whipped the Vicar and tormented his tailor, abducted men and enslaved them on board his ship. They say he paid for a farm – *Trewhiddle Manor*, in the Pentewan valley on the South coast – in 'Dollars and ducats, doubloons and pistoles, guineas – the coinage of every foreign country' [xxi].

Smuggling was still alive in the living memory of the people I knew in my youth on the south coast around the Dodman Point, (the inspiration for one of the Quiller-Couch[19] stories.) There's the story that John Grose and his daughter Betty told me, when they were on the cliffs about Vault Beach, a notorious rendezvous. They were half-way up with one or two other local folk who paused for a pipe. Suddenly they spotted the coastguards inching their way down the cliffs in order to catch them red-handed. The Groses fell down that cliff rather faster than they'd come up. Then there was Granny Nott, as a child at *Penare* when the Battle of Waterloo was raging, sitting on a barrel of rum, hiding it with her skirts when the 'Gaugers' came a-coming.

But then Cornwall (Kernow) was always out on a limb, a country within a country, separated by the Tamar, off the beaten track, the 'land of the saints', begrudging the interference of outside governments, whether it be English or European. The Cornish voted for 'Brexit' even though Europe granted it more money, officially recognised its language (Kernowek) – once spoken universally by those in the west – and awarded it 'National Minority status', as a separate European 'region' [xxii].

It was Parson Hawker who wrote the Cornish 'National Anthem', *The Song of the Western Men*. Hawker's song tells about the Trelawnys from Trelawne Manor, behind Looe. Squire Trelawny took 15-20,000 Cornishmen to Blackheath, marching in protest against excessive taxation imposed by Henry VII. The song is also about Bishop Trelawny, one of seven bishops arrested by James II because they wouldn't sign up to a law allowing Roman Catholicism[20]. Trelawny was taken off to the Tower but three weeks later was acquitted, to much rejoicing in Cornwall [xxiii]. When King James lost his throne he was succeeded by William of Orange – the Glorious Revolution; the reason, maybe, for the Haskins family first to set foot in England.

So here you have two generations of Haskins, the first generation from London, the second from Bedford. We'll leave them there and discover what happened to one of them, William, my great-great grandfather,

Vault Beach looking towards the Dodman Point

And shall Trelawny Live?
And shall Trelawny Die?
Here's twenty thousand Cornishmen
Will know the reason why.

Song of the Western Men

Dodman Point is notorious for shipwrecks. For example, in 1966 the Darlwyne sank with 29 passengers and 2 crew on a day out returning from Fowey to Mylor. The author, left in a pink hat, is standing next to the granite cross at the end of the Dodman Point. It was erected by the Vicar of Caerhays in 1896, 'In the firm hope of the second coming of our Lord Jesus Christ and for the encouragement of those who strive to serve him.' Also standing are the author's niece Bridget and nephew Simon Gates. Sitting: his sister Ann and father Paul Haskins. April 1972. The Dodman is the highest headland on the South Coast of Cornwall. It is often the first land that sailors see when sailing home to England.

---

19. *Sir Arthur Thomas Quiller-Couch (1863-1944) [NR].*
20. *Rt Rev Sir Jonathan Trelawny Bt DD (1650-1721) [NR], Bishop of Bristol and subsequently Exeter and Winchester. He was born near Pelynt near Looe, Cornwall. The 1687 Declaration of Indulgence allowed Roman Catholics the freedom to worship openly. James II was a Roman Catholic and was eventually driven to exile after the protestant William of Orange landed in England and took over the throne. With William of Orange came many of his Flemish countrymen.*

A stitch in time saves nine.

See a pin and pick it up, all the day you'll have good luck. See a pin and let it lie, bad luck you'll have until you die.

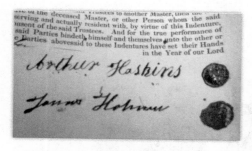

Ravensden in the 1900s.
George Haskins lived here in 1871.

Frith map of Bedford – red spots show where the Haskins's lived, in St Peter's Quarter: Harpur St, Chandos St, Adelaide Place, Wellington St, Balsall St, Tavistock St.

and his children.

* * * *

The Apprentices

My great-great grandfather, **William Haskins** married twice, first to **Eleanor (or Elinor) Wright**, from whom my family is descended, and then to **Ann Clifton**. Theirs was an unpretentious existence in Bedford but they sought to better themselves by finding apprenticeships for their sons. It wasn't cheap but it was the route to a secure livelihood.

William's first wife Eleanor was possibly the most keen for their sons to move up in the world. William was to apply for financial help from the Bedford charity, the Harpur Trust. Apprenticeships started at the age of about 13 and lasted 7 years after which they became fully qualified master craftsmen [xxiv]. It cost £30, £15 at the start and £15 half way through. The Master had to feed and accommodate the pupil – 'meat, drink, clothing, washing and lodging'.

Two of William's sons were apprenticed to tailors. **William Thomas Haskins**, the eldest child of William's first marriage, was my great grandfather. It was quite a common thing in those days to give your eldest child your same name. He was given another name to avoid any mix-up with his father William, so I'll call him William Thomas to save confusion. His story is in Chapter 4.

The whole family retained their cockney accent. When Sir Herewald Wake first met William Thomas and asked his name, William replied "Askins."[21] And how do you spell that? "Haitch, Hay, Hess, Kay, Hie, Hen, Hess!" [xxv] The whole Haskins family was the same. His brother Arthur was named 'Askins' in the 1861 Census.

The family lived in the streets around St Peter's church, near the non-conformist churches – all in walking distance. Some worshipped at the Wesleyan Chapel in Harpur Street, the street where William was born, and some at the Bunyan Meeting Room.

Of the other children, **Arthur Robert Haskins**, found an apprenticeship in London with James Holman who was an upholsterer (or 'upholder'.)[22] They were the interior designers of their day, dealing with gentlefolk who wanted soft furnishings: stuffed chairs, cushions and curtains – in an earlier age upholders had acted as funeral directors (see Chapter 11) [xxvi].

George Haskins carved out a good career as a machine maker and wheelwright at Ravensden, employing 3 men and 4 apprentices in 1871.

The girls were destined for service prior to marriage. **Emma** ('Askins) did not marry and set up with her sister **Ellen** a laundry in later life[23]. Ellen's only son George was disabled, like Tiny Tim in Dickens' *A Christmas Carol* – in the blunt language of the time, 'a cripple'. Emma's other sister **Louisa** was the lucky one[24]. She married someone whose father owned a 366 acre farm in North Wales.

There's one stranger in the family. Ann Clifton appears to have had another son outside wedlock, before William and she married – while Eleanor was still alive – had William been playing away from home? She went away to Moulton in Northamptonshire to give birth. **Benjamin Clifton** was apprenticed as a tailor with Joseph John, but when he was 21 he emigrated to Australia, which was probably a relief all round.

---

21. Sir Herewald Craufurd Wake (1852-1916), 12th Baronet [NR].
22. Arthur Robert Haskins (1828-1900) married Hannah Haskins (1827-1899). He was apprenticed at Stamford Street (near Waterloo), Stainforth Street and Blackfriars Road. Arthur and Hannah set up shop at 64 Nelson Square, not far from Southwark Cathedral.
23. Ellen Haskins (1837-1923) married George Armold (1837-1914) in 1860.
24. Louisa Haskins (1846-1924) married William Hutchings (1850-1933) in 1872. They moved to Llandrillo yn Rhos in Denbighshire, above Colwyn Bay. William was an Agricultural implement maker. Their two sons, Thomas Ewart Hutchings (1876-1907) and Ernest William Hutchings (1879-1953) went into farming.

✳ ✳ ✳ ✳

The Golfers

'Haskins & Son' golf club

Joseph John Haskins, William's second son, was apprenticed to the tailor Daniel Witherow, the local churchwarden, along with his half-brother Benjamin Clifton[25]. Whilst Benjamin was preparing to emigrate, Joseph John was stepping out with his boss's niece, **Susan Witherow**, ending up with her in the family way. When he married her in 1850, the bulge just showing, it was not too uncommon – his father had done the same thing[26]. Joseph John and Susan moved to Fenstanton, Huntingdonshire, and ran a tailor's shop.

One of their sons, **Arthur**, moved to Leighton Buzzard, most likely to learn the hairdressing trade from his father's first cousin, John Haskins. There he met and married **Mary Heley**[27]. Arthur and Mary set up their hairdressing businesses first in Woburn and then in Hoylake, West Kirby, at the tip of the Wirral, first at Albert Road and then at Market Street. Liverpool was a thriving place. Hoylake had just acquired a railway link from Liverpool and was becoming the playground of yuppies of the day. When the golf links opened, Arthur saw a new business opportunity. His children helped in the making and selling of sports equipment, particularly golf clubs and golf balls, which are still exchanged on the internet as sought-after items.

The 'Haskins' shop' was famous in its day and they made enough money to live in a semi-detached house near the golf course, so no longer 'over the shop'. The whole Hoylake Haskins family were mad about golf. *Arthur's fourth son,* **Thomas**, took a job at a newly opened course in Northern Ireland at Bangor and later moved down the road to the Holywood course[28]. When the First World War started, Thomas joined up and *Arthur's youngest son,* **Fred**, too young to enlist, took over. At 17, he was the youngest golf pro in the British Isles[29].

Arthur's eldest son **Bert** was also a golfing pro. He manufactured clubs and balls and married into a golfing family. His wife's niece, **Bunty Stephens**, captained England[30]. *Arthur's second son* **Joseph John**, who looked after the shop, was winning golfing competitions despite losing an arm[31].

In 1916, Fred joined up as a machine gunner. *Arthur's fifth son,* **George** had enlisted in the Denbighshire Yeomanry (part of the Royal Welch Fusiliers), the same regiment my father was to join in the Second World War[32]. George, a hairdresser like his father, became the regimental barber and, though small in stature, he developed a large personality.

Fred Haskins (1898-1981)

25. *Daniel Witherow (1807-1886) married Elizabeth Beechino (1806-1888) in 1827. His brother Samuel Witherow (1802-1857), a miller, married Sarah Whybrow (1797-1877). Susan Witherow (1828-1913) married Joseph John Haskins (1826-1863) in 1850.*

26. *William's eldest son, William Thomas, was born 28 Jul 1834, 6 months after his parents married on 13 Jan 1824.*

27. *Arthur Haskins (1855-1940) married Mary A Heley (1856-1940) in 1874.*

28. *Thomas William Haskins (1882-1946).*

29. *Frederick Haskins (1898-1981) married Lena (Magdalen) Strecker (1893-1984) in 1923.*

30. *Albert Henry Haskins (1875-1945) married Cissie (Mary Elizabeth) Stephens (1877-1924). Her niece Bunty (Frances) Stephens OBE (1924-1978) captained England in the Curtis Cup 1950-60.*

31. *Joseph John Haskins (1880-1961) married Ann Lyons in 1903*

32. *George Haskins (1892-1971).*

33. *Lucy Haskins (1877-1945) married Walter Hermann Schreyer in 1900. The Philadelphia left Liverpool on 11 Sep 1915 (2nd class) with their three children Gertrude, Theodor and Rosa.*

25 countries visited by Alison and Louise Bradshaw before the age of 25

Belgium
Borneo
Canada
Cambodia
Chile
China & Hong Kong
Costa Rica
Croatia
France
Germany
Indonesia
Japan
Malawi
Malaysia
Morocco
Philippines
Poland
Portugal
Singapore
South Africa
Spain
Sri Lanka
Sweden
Thailand
United   States

Arthur's eldest daughter **Lucy** married a German import/export salesman in 1900. When the war with Germany began, they set sail, with their three children, to start an import / export business in the USA[33].

When the war finished, her brother Fred followed her to the USA in 1919 [xxvii]. The business soon failed, and Fred found himself back on the street. He turned to the skill he knew best, finding golfing jobs in New York – making golf clubs and teaching. He found a summer job at the *Grosse Isle Club* near Detroit and then got his big break at Atlanta, where the weather was good enough to play golf all year. His English accent helped – Americans still like tuition from an English 'expert'.

East Lake Golf Club, Atlanta was wealthy. It was where the golfing legend Bobby Jones trained[34]. In 1922, Jones suggested Fred apply for the post of chief professional at the Country Club of Columbus, Georgia, a hundred miles away. Successful, Fred held that post until 1952, building it up from nothing. In 1948, he was asked to replace his East Lake boss Stewart Maiden, who'd died soon after taking on the prestigious new Peachtree course at Atlanta[35]. Fred went to take a look with his wife Lena, but when they were told that professionals had to go in by the servants' entrance, he promptly turned the job down. Whilst not that well-off, he was comfortable and well-respected at Columbus, having rebuilt the greens and started competitive tournaments [xxviii]. When Fred retired, he stayed on as its Greens Keeper until 1971, designing courses and still making golf clubs.

Fred was an excellent teacher of junior golfers. He charged a nickel, which he'd give to the caddie – he preferred to take a salary. He told the parents "If your child comes home early you will know they weren't behaving" – he did not put up with misbehaviour. His students won over 150 championships. In recognition of his achievements, he is remembered by the annual Fred Haskins Award, for the most outstanding collegiate golfer in the United States [xxix]. Tiger Woods was the 1996 winner[36].

❋ ❋ ❋ ❋

The Wanderers

Old William had four children with his first wife, Eleanor, and four (or five) with his second wife, Ann. Of these, only four remained in Bedford. The Victorian age of steam made travel more possible but the Haskins's appear to have been nomadic since the days of Roman Empire – something in the family's genes?

My own family has moved about more than many over the years, yet we all seem to return to our roots. I wanted to return from Hong Kong after three happy years there in the 1980s, even though I liked the place and its people. My son Jonathan Haskins has moved back to where his great great great great grandparents lived. My grandfather Charles Haskins (see Chapter 4) lived in five or six different parts of the country. My father, Paul Haskins (see Chapter 16) saw most of Britain before he was twenty-five, and half of Europe during the war and never wanted to go abroad after that, living his entire married life in the one house. Then there's me. I travelled to the other side of the world before I was 25 and have circled the globe (both hemispheres) since. Yet I, too, have owned the same place in Cornwall all my married life. My nieces and nephews have travelled more than me. My great-nieces, Alison and Louise, stepped foot in least 25 countries before the age of 25, yet each of them has still to visit Constance and Constantine[37].

34. *Robert Tyre Jones Jr. (1902-1971) [NR].*
35. *Stewart Maiden (1886-1948) [NR]*
36. *Eldrick Tont "Tiger" Woods (b1975) [NR].*
37. *Alison Rachel Bradshaw (b1989), Dr Louise Fiona Bradshaw (b1991).*

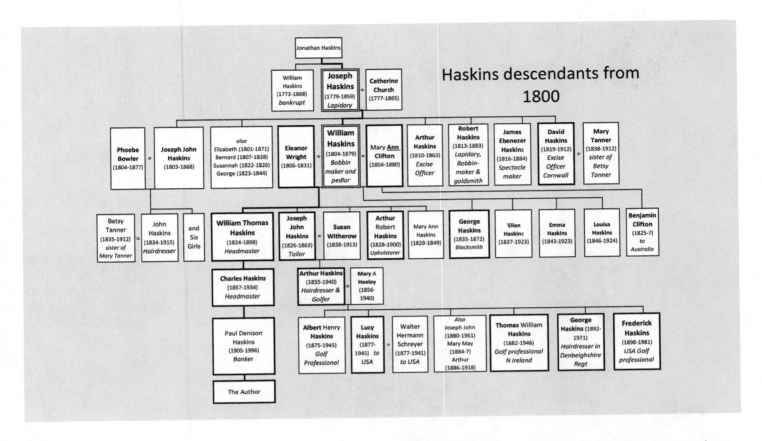

Haskins descendants from 1800

Other Notes and References

i.   16th Ecumenical Council.

ii. email David Wright 16 Jan 2015. There is no direct evidence.

iii. Principles still matter more than poor leadership to the Haskins family.

iv. Athey & Nordveldt, and http://en.wikipedia.org/wiki/Haplogroup_I-M438

v.   http://en.wikipedia.org/wiki/Iazyges. Publius Aelius Hadrianus Augustus [76-138 AD] [NR].

vi. Times 16 May 1797. David Wriight email 15 Jan 2015: Before William was declared bankrupt, there was a court case in the Old Bailey about unpaid wages. According to the trial transcript, William called his nephew, Arthur Haskins, to give evidence. The only Arthur Haskins in London of the correct age is Joseph Haskins's son born 1810. There are Trade Directories dating from 1805-1812 listing William & Joseph as bead-makers in St Luke's parish - Ironmonger's Row and later Richmond Street. The 1812 entry states "Business at Richmond Street now run by a relative – J Haskins."

vii. David Wright email 15 Jan 2015.

viii. Letter to Daily Telegraph 29 Dec 2013 – letter dated 9 Feb 1814 told of a 'Frost Fair' with 'nearly a thousand on the ice at one time' including a 'fine elephant'.

ix. Bruce W Clifton email 10 Nov 2013,: William Haskins and his second wife were buried vertically at Bedford's Foster Hill Road Cemetery; William in F9, grave 15, Ann in F10, grave 235. The Moravians arrived in Bedford in 1742 as protestant refugees and set up a congregation within St Peter's Church before acquiring a site in St Peter's Street in 1749 for work and worship. Moravians were buried vertically so they were ready for Judgement Day.

x.   David Wright email 15 Jan 2015.

xi. Author's 1960 diary aged 11 – 'Very holy - second part gets a bit boring'.

xii. Bedfordshire Times and Independent 10 May 1912.

xiii. Springett p32.

xiv. Bucks Herald 27 Feb 1915, Obituary.

xv. Bucks Herald 11 Jun 1910.

xvi. BBC Coast 2005 conducted an experiment to prove it could be done.

xvii. O'Connor, Chapter 29.

xviii. Roe pp307-8.

xix. Hawker p40. 'The Gauger's Pocket' was first printed in Household Words in 1853. Vol vi pp515-7.

xx. Hawker p123ff.

xxi. www.copinger.org.uk/1John28.html accessed 19 Feb 2015: around 1795.

xxii. European Union's NUTS2 areas – Nomenclature of Territorial Units for Statistics – which decide regional grant funding, were changed in 2007. National Minority Status was agreed in 2014.

xxiii. Strickland pp68, 382-3.

xxiv. Modern apprenticeships do not entitle the apprentices to assume the status of 'Masters of their Trade'. They are not even qualifications in their own right. People have to work towards NVQ Level 2 or beyond. They can start at any age from 16. It is up to them to establish a career thereafter.

xxv. Gordon. p223.

xxvi. Bedford Records Office , Ref X171/62/114.

xxvii. On the Mauritania, from Southampton – New York, Nov 1919.

xxviii. Hyatt p79: Donald Ross, the golf pro at Pinehurst and founder of the American Society for Golf Architects, designed the course but whether he personally visited Columbus is unclear. The South Eastern Amateur tournament was started by Fred Haskins in 1922.

xxix. The Haskins Award was established in 1971, 10 years before Fred's death. Selection is based on a national poll of commentators, writers, coaches and collegiate golfers, and is administered by the grandly titled 'Haskins Commission.'

Boats in Harbour by Elsie Tresidder

Scriveners of Falmouth

In the village of Constantine, a mile from the Helford River, amongst the swirling sea fret and the deep blue hydrangeas, Nycholas Tresyder was called to 'muster' in 1569[i]. 450 years later, Constantine churchtown is still hidden in the countryside behind Falmouth, still difficult for a stranger to find on a dark night. Many of the road signs haven't been updated since the Second World War – they were removed or turned round to confuse Germans. Nycholas was preparing to fight a different enemy – the Spanish Armada.

Constantine, like Constance in Southern Germany, has connections with the Roman Emperor, Constantine the Great. Constantine's mother was possibly English; and he was crowned Emperor in York in AD 306. Cornwall was on the very edge of his Empire, which stretched across the Mediterranean to Turkey and Egypt. The first Emperor to convert to Christianity, Constantine made Sunday a day of rest, humanised the criminal law and the law of debt, mitigated the conditions of slavery, gave grants to support poor children, and tolerated religious freedom across his Empire.

The parish church is one of only two in Britain dedicated to St Constantine. St Constantine lived a hundred years after the Emperor. A noble prince, a wild and violent soldier, the son of Cador, Duke of Cornwall, this nephew of King Arthur had been nominated as his successor[ii]. When this Constantine became a Christian like his namesake, he put away his sword and became a monk. They say that St Constantine helped St Petroc to build a monastery near Padstow – at 'Constantine' Bay.

In 1569, Queen Elizabeth I was worried about war with Spain. She'd called for a list of all those ready and able to fight. **Nycholas Tresyder** or Tresuder (spellings were erratic) was declared 'A' class, with his bow and twelve arrows[1]. He is the earliest verifiable Tresidder in my family.

Pronounced in the Cornish way with the accent on the second syllable – Tre-sidder, as spelt by the last nine generations. One s and two dds – the British Library has it wrong in their reference books. It's a true Cornish word – '*Tre, Pol and Pen, the three Cornishmen.*' *Tre* means settlement or farm and *seder* may mean archer; or is it a reference to the Jewish Passover?[iii] One thing not picked up from the written page, is how to pronounce it. The family were taught a rhyme: '*Please to consider/my name is Tresidder.*'

There are Tresidders in the graveyard in Constantine churchyard but my branch of the family moved to Falmouth almost as soon as it began. Falmouth is only 360 years old. Budock, where Nycholas's great grandson lived, was the closest village. The hamlet of Smithick, 'down under', contained a single manor house and a couple of cottages in his day. The nearest town was Penryn.

The Cornish are said by Herodotus and others to be descended from what let us loosely call the 'Syro-Phoenicians'. These 'Sea Peoples', whether Jew, Minoan, Mycenaean or Philistine, traded right across the Mediterranean, settled in Crete and the Carthage of Hannibal and his elephants, traded in North Africa and learnt enough astronomy to sail up the coastline of Spain, France and Britain. They settled on the edge of the Levantine coast, what we now call Lebanon, with Israel to the south and Syria to the north, a tall, strong, courageous, wealthy people. Syro simply means 'Syrian'. A Syrian friend, who comes from Damascus, says they eat 'Cornish' cream just like us, made in the traditional way, left overnight on a low heat on the hob. Perhaps it was the Cornish who taught the Syro-Phoenicians how to do it, but I'd like to think it was the other way round. The Syro-Phoenicians feature in Chapter 15.

Emperor Constantine (274?-337)

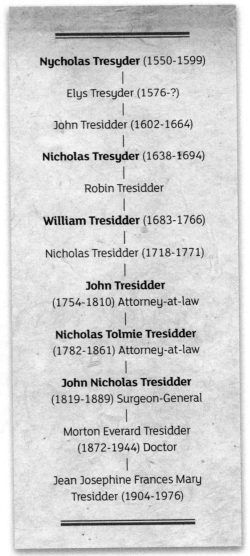

Nycholas Tresyder (1550-1599)
|
Elys Tresyder (1576-?)
|
John Tresidder (1602-1664)
|
Nicholas Tresyder (1638-1694)
|
Robin Tresidder
|
William Tresidder (1683-1766)
|
Nicholas Tresidder (1718-1771)
|
John Tresidder
(1754-1810) Attorney-at-law
|
Nicholas Tolmie Tresidder
(1782-1861) Attorney-at-law
|
John Nicholas Tresidder
(1819-1889) Surgeon-General
|
Morton Everard Tresidder
(1872-1944) Doctor
|
Jean Josephine Frances Mary Tresidder (1904-1976)

---

1.   *Nycholas Tresyder or Trusder (1550-1599).*

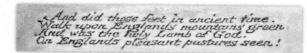

And did those feet in ancient time.
Walk upon Englands mountains green
And was the holy Lamb of God.
On Englands pleasant pastures seen!

Part of William Blake's original preface
for 'Milton a poem'

Ladies of Spain

Farewell and adieu to you Spanish Ladies
Farewell and adieu to you, Ladies of Spain
For we've received orders for to sail for old England
But we may never see you fair ladies again

Chorus: For we'll rant and we'll roar like true British sailors
We'll rant and we'll roar on all the salt seas
Until we strike soundings in the channel of old England
From Ushant to Scilly is thirty-five leagues

The first land we sighted was called the Dodman
Next Rame Head off Plymouth Start, Portland and Wight;
We sailed by Beachy, by Fairlight and Dover
And then we brought to the South Foreland Light

Chorus...

Joseph of Arimathea, the rich man who offered his sepulchre as Jesus's tomb, was a tin trader, or so they say. It was a period when most of the Roman Empire's iron was sourced from the British Isles, and almost all the tin[iv]. The Romans needed tin to make bronze – bronze statues decorated the rich houses of ancient Rome; the swords borne by the Roman Army were bronze. Tin was on a par with gold and silver, a precious metal and to find large quantities of tin they went to Cornwall. Did Joseph of Arimathea, the tin trader, trade in Cornwall? Did he bring his nephew, Jesus, with him as his apprentice? Did they touch land at St Just-in-Roseland near St Mawes? Ancient tradition handed down by word of mouth through the generations says some of this is true. Christianity was evident in Cornwall much earlier than the rest of England; some say as early as the first century. The Council of Arles in 314 was attended by four Bishops from Britain, one from Caerleon (Carlyon) in Monmouthshire[v]. There's a Carlyon in my family. Emperor Constantine's mother was probably a Caerlyon.

'Caer' (derivation 'Car') is indeed considered a Phoenician word[vi]. Evidence of tin working in Pentewan valley goes back to as early as 3015-2415 BC, "uncomfortably early," says R D Penhallurick[vii]. "It suggests that tin streaming in Cornwall began much earlier than hitherto suspected." A Bronze Age rapier was discovered in Caerhays valley. The land behind Caerhays beach, Porthluney, was an estuary in Roman times[viii].

The real Cornish folk have dark curly hair and swarthy Mediterranean features. My hair curls when it's going to rain – better than seaweed for predicting the weather. Is that the Syro-Phoenician in me? Some say the dark hair and blue eyes are because of the marriages made with men of the sunken Armada or the Spanish girls of that sea shanty in the box on the left, but I suspect our features go back at least to the Bronze Age.

Women pirates

Pendennis Castle from the South West

Falmouth was essentially founded on smuggling. The Killigrew family were responsible. They lived at *Arwenack Manor*, a few yards from the shoreline – the house is still there, near Falmouth's Maritime Museum. The Killigrews helped Henry VIII build *Pendennis Castle* and the smaller one at St Mawes on the opposite bank, defending the entrance to the Carrick Roads, the fourth deepest natural harbour basin in the world.

Smuggling started in earnest when Henry VIII's tussle with Europe over his divorce meant trading with Europe became difficult. Henry VIII had broken with the Catholic Church on account of his lust for Anne Boleyn. He'd divorced his Spanish Catholic Queen, Catherine of Aragon against the wishes of the Pope, who was under the cosh of her nephew, the Holy Roman Emperor Charles V. When Henry gave up trying to be nice to win them over and set up the Church of England instead, the rest of Europe cut off their trading relationships. Today we call it 'sanctions.'

Trade could only be done by smuggling. The gentry who owned estates along on the coast came into their own, renting out their harbours to the highest bidder. Local officials, possibly the Tresidders, would be in on the scheme, helping the smugglers sell their goods to market – ledgers and books are still in existence.

During the reign of Elizabeth I, England was in a tense stand-off with Spain. The Spaniards were shipping Mayan gold back across the Atlantic. It was all too tempting. Piracy was an obvious call. 'No Cornish jury would convict a man of piracy,' they used to say. Queen Elizabeth wanted her cut, so gave free rein to her admirals to plunder the Spanish galleons; the profits were large. Sir Francis Drake, a distant relation of mine through the Pollexfens and the Bastards, was 'commissioned to commit acts of war against Spain'. Having burnt Portobello, sacked Venta Cruz, reduced Rathlin, plundered Valperaiso, torched Iago and pillaged Vigo, mainly for his own ends, Spain put a bounty of 20,000 ducats on Drake's head – about £2 million in today's money[ix]. It was a way of life in Cornwall. John Rashleigh from Fowey, also related, is known to this day by pubs in St Austell, Charlestown and Polkerris[2]. There was no sex discrimination – women were at it too.

Elizabeth, wife of John Killigrew, who stored the stolen goods, was arrested and sentenced to death[3]. After her sons paid a substantial bribe, she was let off with a pardon. Her daughter-in-law, Lady Mary, lavished hospitality on visiting seamen and whipped their treasure from under their noses[4]. If a ship came into the bay to shelter for the night, she would invite the Captain to stay at *Arwenack Manor*. She'd slip out of the dinner party, taking her manservants, and row out to the ship in the thick of the night. Wielding her cutlass, with the help of her men, she'd slit the crew's throats. Then it really was a skeleton crew. Whilst her trusty men spirited the ship away, Mary would reappear at the party as if nothing had happened.

The stolen vessel would sail to the west coast of Ireland where it and its contents were sold – jewels, doubloons and 'pieces of eight'. People like the Pollexfens, based in Sligo or Galway, would buy it all[x]. By the 19th century the Pollexfen family was central to Sligo's economy.

By 1584, *Arwenack Manor* was the finest house in Cornwall, standing in bucolic isolation – the Killigrews owned land from Helford to Mylor. When Sir Walter Raleigh visited eleven years later, there was only one house in Smithick for his men to stay. Raleigh was full of good ideas and it was probably him more than anyone who encouraged the Killigrews to develop the place commercially[5].

In 1613, they began to build some houses[6]. Inevitably, other towns in Cornwall complained: a new town would take away their trade but by 1664 there were 200 houses[xi]. Nicholas Tresidder, the great grandson of Nycholas the archer, was on the scene from the start[7].

Sir Francis Drake (1540-1596)

2.   *John Rashleigh (1554-1624) built Menabilly, the residence of Daphne du Maurier, Lady Browning, DBE (1907-1989) [NR] and the setting for her book Rebecca. Rashleigh's father came from Barnstable. His grandson John Rashleigh (1621-1651) married Joan Pollexfen (1620-1668) in 1640. John senior owned the 140 ton, 60-man, Francis of Foy which went in 1573 to the West Indies with Sir Francis Drake (1540-1596). and was part of the fleet against the Spanish Armada in 1588 commanded by Drake, by then a Vice-Admiral. Charlestown was created in 1799. It was named after its builder, Charles Rashleigh (1747-1823).*

3.   *John Killigrew (1514-1567) [NR] first Governor of Pendennis Castle married Elizabeth Trewinnard (1518-after 1582) [NR].*

4.   *Mary Wolverston (c1535-1617) [NR].*

5.   *Sir Walter Raleigh (1554-1618) [NR].*

6.   *The third generation John, Sir John Killigrew (?-1633) [NR], initiated the scheme.*

7.   *Nicholas Tresyder (1638-1694).*

Falmouth harbour

Tregoneggie, Falmouth, home of the Tresidders

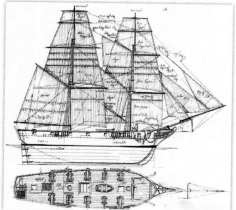

A Falmouth Packet ship

The Developers

✳ ✳ ✳ ✳

The commercial development of Falmouth was a priority for Sir Peter Killigrew[8]. Sir Peter was a man who'd successfully kept both sides happy in the Civil War (1642-51), though he lost his house in the process – it was blown up[xii]. During the Commonwealth period that followed, he moved the Customs House from Penryn and obtained a Charter for a market under the official name of Falmouth[xiii]. A mayor, aldermen, and burgesses were created. Some of the Tresidder family were to fill those shoes.

Soon after Charles II reclaimed the throne, he authorised a quay and a church at the new town. The church was dedicated to his father, 'Charles the Martyr'[xiv]. Charles II stumped up the money and Sir Peter the land[9]. In 1664, an Act of Parliament created the separate parish of Falmouth. Another enabled excise duties to be raised on ships and cargos. It must have helped that one of Sir Peter's cousins, Elizabeth Killigrew, had been with Charles in exile and was now keeping the king's bed warm in London[10].

We don't know where the Tresidders were living in Falmouth before Sir Peter died in 1668. We know Sir Peter's son bought up several large farmhouses including *Tregoneggie* and that a hundred years later the freehold was sold to the Tresidders probably when Samuel Tresidder came into money.

Falmouth of 1688 was the place to be. Those other jealous Cornish towns had been correct: Falmouth had outstripped them. As Britain became more international (for instance Charles II's Portuguese wife gave Bombay (Mumbai) to Britain as part of her dowry), Cornwall became the open window upon the world[xv]. The quays were full of ships and Falmouth was appointed the General Post Office's (GPO) nerve centre. 'Packet' ships circled the world with cargoes for people living in the countries that Britain had acquired – India, Canada, America, West Indies. They started out from Falmouth. The brigantines were each able to carry 150 tons of cargo, manned by as many as thirty men. Although the ships were privately owned, on a share basis, they were contracted to the GPO on a secure basis. In 1705, five were plying to and fro between Falmouth and the West Indies. By 1764 they went to Lisbon, New York, Corunna in Spain, Gibraltar (by then British), South Carolina, Florida and the Gulf of Mexico. The Killigrews' influence diminished and citizens like the Tresidders were in charge of the town[xvi].

✳ ✳ ✳ ✳

Falmouth Quays and Founding Fathers

The Tresidders grew wealthy. In 1774, **Samuel Tresidder**, my great (x5) uncle, as the master of the Killigrew quays, had charge of 'All matters at the Quay, to receive all Duties for Quayage, Cellarage, and Groundage.'[xvii] By 1793, he was squire of *Tregoneggie* for in that year he'd made enough money to own this house, its outbuildings, and 'the whole town and fields'[11]. He spent a further £180 on two grist mills and cottages at Restronguet, where the Pandora Inn is today. He rented out *Penannce Mills* (above Swanpool) and *Trevenne* or *Trevence*, and a whole load of other properties – effectively a Cornish millionaire[xviii].

---

8.   *Sir Peter Killigrew (c1593-1668) [NR].*

9.   *1662 foundations; 1663 opened; 1664 consecrated. Charles II also paid for the parsonage.*

10. *Elizabeth Killigrew (1622-80) [NR], Viscountess Shannon, maid of Honour to Queen Henrietta Maria, gave birth to a daughter Charlotte Jemima Henrietta Fitzroy by Charles II in 1650.*

11. *Samuel Tresidder (1730-1800),*

Tregoniggie (as it is currently spelt) is now a large industrial estate off the Bickland Water Road covering everything from food to a music school. There's even a Tresidder Close. His original domain would have stretched down to the Bickland Stream, with good views over Falmouth and the Carrick Roads estuary behind [xix].

The Tresidder fortune passed to my great (x3) grandfather **John Tresidder**[12]. Although Samuel had two sons, the elder drowned in the harbour and, as neither had children, John inherited the lion's share [13]. John became a wealthy man, what with this, his own land, and that inherited from his own father [xx]. 'Gentleman' John decided to become a solicitor. His name appeared in the law list as early as 1790 – 'attorney-at-law', as they said in those days, like American lawyers. The older word was Scrivener. John was the first of three generations of solicitors[xxi].

Nicholas Tolmie Tresidder (1782-1861)

The Arsenic Sandwich

Falmouth's increase in trade and wealth developed in line with the number of ships. There were scheduled services to South America and the Far East and by the time of the Battle of Waterloo (1815), over 40 packet ships connected the world. The next twenty years saw the start of private shipping with six steam-driven ships based in Falmouth by 1834.

As well as customs and excise, bills of lading and the buying and selling of property, there were men wealthy enough to bother about writing wills – so the lawyers had their hands full. By 1844, there were twelve solicitors' firms in Falmouth [xxii]. Freemasonry in Cornwall was first established in Falmouth, the *Love and Honour* Lodge opening in 1751. John Tresidder was inducted as a member at the age of 28 in 1783.

NOTICE is hereby given, that the Partnership lately subsisting between Nicholas Tolmie Tresidder and Robert White, both of Falmouth, in the county of Cornwall, heretofore carrying on business as Attorneys, Solicitors, and Notaries Public, under the firm of Tresidder and White, was, on the 15th day of December last, dissolved by mutual consent; all debts owing to the said partnership are to be received by the said Nicholas Tolmie Tresidder : As witness our hands this 29th day of March 1838. *Nichs. T. Tresidder. Rob. White.*

Two of John Tresidder's sons followed their father into the legal profession. **Nicholas Tolmie Tresidder** was articled as a Clerk to his father at the age of twenty-two, for which he paid the princely sum of £100 [14]. It was not simply a matter of entering the practice[xxiii]. Lawyers needed to register, which he did in 1804. They were sworn in, which was done before Lord Chief Justice of the King's Bench at the Old Bailey[xxiv]. Nicholas's formal title was 'one of the Attorneys of his Majesty's Court and of the King's Bench and Common Pleas at Westminster.' Nicholas Tolmie operated out of offices in town, with his partner, Robert White, living over the shop in Church Street and renting out *Tregoneggie*. The partnership lasted until 1838[xxv].

Ann Genn (1783-1861)

There were international connections too. In 1811, Nicholas Tolmie married **Ann Genn**, who came from an American family, although the family were originally from Cornwall. Ann's grandfather, **James Genn**, was county Surveyor of Prince William County Virginia, living near the other Falmouth, in Virginia[15]. In 1748, he took the sixteen year old George Washington out on an extended expedition, to teach him surveying. They climbed the Blue Ridge Mountains; they surveyed the beautiful Shenandoah Valley and canoed across the southern branch of the Potomac River, sleeping under the stars, shooting wild turkeys, watching Redskins dance, eating with jack-knives[xxvi].

---

12. *John Tresidder (1754-1810) married Christiana Thomas Buxton (1758-1825) in 1780.*
13. *Samuel Tresidder (1747-1766) and William Tresidder (1748-1803) were the sons of Samuel Tresidder. (1713-1800) and Jane Lanxon. John's father, Nicholas Tresidder (1718-1781) had died by then.*
14. *Nicholas Tolmie Tresidder (1782-1861) married Anne Genn (1783-1861) in 1811.*
15. *James Genn (1716-1781), the grandfather of Ann Genn, came from Greensboro in Maryland. He was living near Catletts (Catlett) on the 'Falmouth' road.*
16. *George Washington (1732-1799) [NR] first President of the United States 1789–97, went travelling with James Genn in March 1748. Freeman. Vol 1 p202-223.*

four days. On the 3d of Nov. went to tea at the prisoner's again. He recollects the invitation given on the Sunday previous, when his mother expressed her disinclination to go, and said she was taken ill the last time. Witness went to church with his mother on 3d of Nov. and knew her to be in good health. On that day he called at the prisoner's about three o'clock, Donall was at home; on his return a second time to the house, he found preparation made for tea: the table was in the middle of the room, near the window; Mrs Donnall sat at the table, Mrs. Jordan sat next to her, and his mother sat next the fire place on one side; the prisoner sat opposite to her, with Samuel Downing, Edward having by his mother desire removed, and sat between his mother and Mrs. Jordan; the tea was prepared, and they were waiting for the cocoa, which was soon brought in by the servant. The prisoner rose from his seat for the purpose of handing bread and butter to the ladies, and the witness's attention was soon drawn by the prisoner's passing between Mrs. Jordan and his brother from behind, and spilt some of the tea on his mother's gown, when his brother said, "Donnall what are you about?" the prisoner made no reply, but gave his mother some bread and butter.— Prisoner went direct to the table, and returned to his seat; just as he was seated, he was called, and went out. Witness had often drank tea with him; sometimes the servant attended during tea, and at others, Donnall officiated himself. His mother was drinking part of the second cup of cocoa, when she complained of being very sick, gave the residue to the witness, and he placed the cup on the table. She drew off, and requested him to make haste and go in and open the door, that she might go home; he did so, and followed immediately after. He thinks the prisoner came in soon after, with Mrs.

Extract from the court proceedings of the trial of Robert Sawle Donnall, 31 March 1817

As I was going to St Ives I met a man with seven wives,

Each wife had seven sacks, each sack had seven cats,

Each cat had seven kits: kits, cats, sacks and wives,

How many were going to St Ives?

William Edward Walmsley Tresidder (1796-1855)

George Washington learned from him the value of buying up undeveloped land, dividing it into tracts and selling it on as demand for land grew. When he qualified, George was commissioned as a Surveyor in Virginia. Ann's father **William Genn**'s family went into shipbuilding, and came over to Cornwall to invest in the packet ship business[17].

The man in charge of the Packet ships was the 'Packet Agent', Benjamin Pender[18]. His son Francis became chums with Ann's eldest brother, **James Genn**[19]. They formed the law firm of Pender and Genn together, a law firm still going under the name of Nalders[xxvii]. James Genn became Deputy Town Clerk of Falmouth, and his business partner, Francis Pender, became the Mayor and his son became Town Clerk[20]. The Tresidders were thus increasingly well connected. The Genns moved to Wood Lane, a sought-after part of the new town, higher up the hill.

Not all went well though; Ann and her sisters were brought up in Falmouth. She was probably the best matched of the girls in her family. Another sister, **Mary Genn**, married a mercer, a dealer in cloth[21]. The mercer's sister married a doctor, who couldn't pay his way. In 1816, having just married her, he stupidly hatched a plan to pay off his debts (£125) by poisoning his wealthy 64-year-old mother-in-law (worth £14,000). He tried lacing her tea a couple of times but that just gave her stomach cramps and she 'urged and strained' and vomited it all up until she was well again. He achieved the desired result with an arsenic sandwich. Despite tampering with the evidence, trying to get the body buried with undue haste, and evading arrest, the jury at the County Assizes took just 20 minutes to acquit him. Character witnesses, including Mary's husband predominated and science, such as it was, was turned aside. Why? It might have been the onions! You could safely decide 'whodunit' I think and, bluntly, conclude the jury had been nobbled - there's just no evidence[xxviii].

❋ ❋ ❋ ❋

Town Clerk of St Ives

Does the riddle on the left refer to the Cornish St Ives or the ones in Dorset or Cambridgeshire? The Cornish one was a busy fishing port near Land's End. It had many cats, to stop the rats. St Ive's or St Ives? It is the church of St Ive. In my youth, the apostrophe was placed before the 's'. Now everyone spells it St Ives.

Nicholas Tolmie's younger brother **William Edward Walmsley Tresidder** was also a solicitor, articled to his father John in 1815, eleven years after Nicholas Tolmie[22]. In those days, training took five years[xxix]. William found work in St Ives, and married **Fanny Newman Tremearne** in 1829. Her family were fish merchants trading in London as well as St Ives.

Pilchards were big business in Cornwall in the 19th century. Fanny's father would have gone out with the seine – a large net that hauled up quantities of pilchards or mackerel in one go. The

---

17. *William Genn (1754-1835) married Phillis or Philippa Tiddy in 1781. The Genn family house was 28 Wood Lane.*

18. *Benjamin Pinder (1742-1812) [NR] of Budock Vean, now an hotel in the parish of Constantine.*

19. *James Genn (1782-1845) married Peggy (Margarete) Hawke (1785-1845) in 1808. They were next door neighbours to the Tresidder family (Nicholas Tolmie, Ann, William and John Nicholas) in Church Street the 1841 census. Francis Pender (1778-1849) [NR]*

20. *William James Genn JP (1811-1890) was Town Clerk of Falmouth 1851-85.*

21. *Phillis Genn married (1793-1874) married Nicholas Tresidder (1799-1874) in 1836. Samuel Downing married her sister Mary Genn in 1818. Samuel's sister Harriet married Dr Robert Swale Donnelly in 1816.*

22. *William Edward Walmsley Tresidder (1796-1855) married Fanny Newman Tremearne (1809-1873) in 1829.*

fishing season was from August to October. The fishermen worked together; one would stay up in the lookout hut above the bay to spot the shoals of pilchards. The Huer, as he was called, would call out '*Man the Seine*' and the cry would go out around the town. This is the origin of the saying '*Hue and Cry*'. They would jump into their luggers and drag the enormous seine right across the bay, locking their catch inside.

Cornish fish were sold across the continent, as far away as Italy. Mevagissey was unusual, preparing them in oil after the fashion of French sardines. St Ives, like most Cornish ports, packed the fish in salt barrels. When the railway reached as far as Penzance in 1867, and St Ives ten years later, the pilchards were sent up to London. Being an oily fish, the pilchard would supplement the whale oil that lit the streets of London. It was a boon for Sherlock Holmes or Charles Dickens roaming the streets at night – they'd have identified with the distinctly fishy smell in the air.

As a side-line, William became a Lloyd's insurance agent, a Vice-Consul for Sweden and Norway and 'Receiver of Wrecks'[xxx]. William and Fanny settled at 8 Tregenna Terrace, with a nice view out to sea, well above the stench of fish markets by the harbourside[23]. In 1844, he was one of three attorneys (and the only notary) in the town[xxxi].

His nephew, **William Tolmie Tresidder**, joined the family profession[24]. Indentured to his father, Nicholas Tolmie, in March 1836, he carried on working for his father for the next ten years and took over from his uncle when he died[xxxiii].

William Tolmie, a single man, lived with his two widowed aunts Fanny and Christiana on the Terrace. **Christiana Tresidder**, sister to Nicholas Tolmie, had married a naval midshipman, **Robson Cruse**, in 1814 who served on *HMS Tonnant* at the Battle of Trafalgar[25]. Robson Cruse was promoted to Lieutenant and took part in a dramatic rescue of the officers and crew of the *Nightingale* when it ran into trouble off the coast of the Isle of Wight in 1829.

William Tolmie did well enough to become the Town Clerk as well as Commissioner to the Borough Courts and Stannary Courts, Clerk to the Borough Justices and Clerk to the Harbour Commissioners. I remember seeing a newspaper cutting of him at his retirement with the most enormous white fluffy beard to rival any Captain Birdseye. At the age of 57, a few months before Christiana died, he married his aunt Fanny's niece, a girl half his age, Matilda Tremearne. William Tolmie died aged 91 in early 1909 not long after Matilda, who had succumbed the previous autumn. Too distraught or too sick, and with no children, neither had drawn up a proper will.

Manning the seine

Huer's hut at Newquay

Robson Cruse's buttons and dagger

---

23. *8 The Terrace is now a guest house called The Rookery.*
24. *William Tolmie Tresidder (1817-1909) married Matilda Tremearne (1847-1908) in 1875. Her father, John Newman Tremearne (1804-1880), was Fanny's brother.*
25. *Lt Robson Cruse RN (1785-1831) married Christiana Philoena Tresidder (1784-1875) in 1814.*

John Nicholas Tresidder's flowing locks

There was an Old Man with a beard,
Who said, 'It is just as I feared!
Two Owls and a Hen,
Four Larks and a Wren,
Have all built their nests in my beard!'

Edward Lear

John Wallis Barnicoat (1814-1905)

A Doctor in the family

William Tolmie was the only solicitor of his generation. Nicholas Tolmie's second son was **John Nicholas Tresidder**[26]. John Nicholas, as I shall call him, decided on a different path. With the move of the Packet ships to Southampton from 1834, the world was changing. The horizons of its citizens, certainly those of Falmouth, were growing wider.

Not only did he have a grandfather who'd been born in America, and a great grandfather who'd tutored George Washington, but there was a great uncle who'd died in New York, an uncle who'd died in Chile and a brother-in-law, **William Hooton**, who was trading in South America[27]. His uncle **Samuel Tresidder** had been a Lieutenant in the Army, and died in India in 1824[xxxiv]. John Nicholas decided to join up. He'd chosen a profession new to the Tresidders – medicine. His cousin was a chemist[28]. His aunt's brother-in-law was a Surgeon. Maybe the poisoning story had also engaged his interest.

John Nicholas trained in medicine at St Thomas's Hospital in London. Compared with today, the training was basic. He was especially qualified in 'cupping', a practice which few of today's medics would recognise, but which the Chinese still practise – it involved applying suction to bring the blood to the surface of the skin. After St Thomas's he returned to practice for a time at Church Street in Falmouth whilst applying for the job with the East India Company.

Almost all the surgeons in the Indian Medical service sported voluminous beards and John Nicholas proved to be no exception. It is said that Victorian ladies considered that '*Kissing a man without a beard was like eating an egg without any salt.*'[xxxv] Beards were popular in the British Army until its defeat by the Zulus in South Africa at Isandlwana in 1879 when English soldiers' jawbones, complete with the beards, were taken home as trophies and hung up like antlers on the living room walls[xxxvi]. After that, shaving became de rigueur. John Nicholas, retiring a couple of years before, never had to give up his beard, and didn't see the connection between the contents of his beard and disease, unlike Edward Lear in his Book of Nonsense, one of the first books my father bought me[xxxvii].

John Nicholas married twice, one after the other died. Both wives were from Falmouth and both went to India with him. The first marriage, in January 1845 at Falmouth was to **Elizabeth Carlyon Barnicoat**, taking place three months before they set sail. Elizabeth was the daughter of a HM Customs officer, **Humphry Barnicoat**[29]. Humphry's job title was 'First Clerk to the Collector and Warehouse keeper for Bonded Goods', effectively he was in day-to-day charge of Her Majesty's operations in Falmouth. Whilst David Haskins (see Chapter 1) was occupied catching miscreants, Humphry was extracting duty from legal imports.

✳ ✳ ✳ ✳

New Zealand becomes British

Elizabeth must have been excited by the talk of the mysterious East, with its peacocks and elephants, temples and lakes, its veiled begums and jewelled maharajahs – or was it because of her brother? **John Wallis Barnicoat**, at the age of 27, had set sail three and a half years

---

26. *Surgeon-General John Nicholas Tresidder (1819-1889) married Elizabeth Carlyon Barnicoat (1915-1855) in 1845 and Emily Hooton Courtis (1830-1917) in 1857.*

27. *William Tresidder (1762-1782) died in New York; William Genn (1788-1830) died in Chile; William Hooton (1811-1877) married Anne Christiana Tresidder (1812-1900) in 1838; Lt Samuel Tresidder (1791-1824).*

28. *Thomas Corfield (1816-1887) married (1) Catherine Skinner (1813-1853) and (2) Marcia Clarke Burnley (1830-1912) from Boston Spa, Yorkshire.*

29. *Humphry Barnicoat (1778-1850) married Elizabeth Bullocke (1788-1865) in 1810.*

earlier, to go to live in New Zealand, which had been a British Colony for less than a year[30].

Articled as a Civil Engineer in Falmouth, John found a new profession when he stepped foot in New Zealand. As perhaps he'd heard about James Genn measuring out virgin ground in Maryland, here, in New Zealand, John Wallis did the same thing with a friend he'd met on board ship.

Moving to a new land is never straightforward particularly when it has never been occupied by Europeans before. John Wallis and his friend got caught up in a dispute with the Māori Chief of Wairau. The New Zealand Company had ridden roughshod over agreements with the locals so the Chiefs, who had adopted Christianity, felt used and abused as a result. They went into battle, guns were fired, and John was accused of running away but, as he said, "We did run from the fight, for the fight had already ceased."

New Zealand, in keeping with most new colonies, required a pioneering spirit. John Barnicoat married **Rebecca Hodgson**, daughter of an Inspector of Schools, one of the first in the country. Rebecca's grandfather was a Unitarian Minister for a time at Batley, Yorkshire and her uncle was **Sir Henry Tate**, the sugar magnate – leaving Yorkshire, Henry made sufficient fortune to endow an Art Gallery in London that specifically supported British art. The Tate Gallery now has an outpost at St Ives[31].

John Barnicoat entered politics in 1853. He became the Speaker in the Nelson Provincial Council and a member of New Zealand's Legislative Council (1883-1902).

Constance Barnicoat, one of their daughters, became one of the first women journalists and one of the first women mountain climbers[32]. Based in neutral Switzerland in the First World War, she climbed the mountains in the Bernese Oberland in her free time, wearing trousers and alone with men – unheard of at that time. Outspoken, she earned a living countering German propaganda in Berne during the week – Berne was earning a reputation as the 'Plotting Ground and Listening Post of Europe". A mountain in the Southern Alps is named after her and one in New Zealand. Sadly, she contracted cancer during the war – and despite being one of the first to be treated by X-ray, she died aged 50 in 1922[xxxviii].

Sir Henry Tate (1819-1899)

❄ ❄ ❄ ❄

India beckons

The Barnicoats were good friends of the Tresidders. There'd have been daily dealings between the Falmouth Customs and the lawyers sorting out goods going abroad. There'd have been much talk of foreign matters when the ships arrived and when they set sail. John Nicholas Tresidder would have overheard it all as he practised his medicine in Falmouth and studied for extra qualifications.

There were numerous hoops to go through to get to India. John Nicholas's father had to apply on his behalf for an indenture and, in addition, he had to be recommended by someone influential and be nominated by a Director of the East India Company[xxxix]. Once examined by *viva voce*, he was at last commissioned on 1 March 1845. He and new wife Elizabeth duly set sail for Bengal. The story of his time in India is related in Chapter 6[xl].

Johnnie, Annie and Rosie Tresidder, 1862

---

30. *Hon John Wallis Barnicoat MLC JP (1814-1905) married Rebecca Lee Hodgson (1831-1902) in 1849. He emigrated on the Lord Auckland, sailing from Gravesend on 25 Sep 1841, arriving 26 Feb 1842. The Treaty of Waitangi (6 Feb 1840) gave the Crown sovereignty and a Royal Charter declaring New Zealand a colony was signed in November 1840.*

31. *Rev William Tate (1773-1836), father of Sir Henry Tate (1819-1899) 1st Baronet, founder of Tate and Lyle Sugar and of the Tate Gallery.*

32. *Constance Alice Barnicoat (1872-1922)*

Rosie – Mary Rosalind Saunders – née Tresidder (1850-1931)

Lt Robert Power Saunders RA (1839-1871) of HM's 107th Regiment

The Royal Albert Bridge, 1859, joining Cornwall and Devon, designed by Isambard Kingdom Brunel for the Great Western Railway, managed by Charles Saunders. Still in railway use, with the 1970s road suspension bridge behind it.

Of Elizabeth's five children, only three survived into adulthood. All three maintained an adult connection with the armed forces. **Annie**, the oldest, married a young officer in the Indian Army (see Chapter 6)[33].

Rosie married **Robert Power Saunders**, another dashing young lieutenant, in the Royal Artillery[34]. After he died in India, four years later, she first returned to Dulwich, and then to Falmouth after her children grew up. Her in-laws were entrepreneurs: Robert's father, William Septimus Saunders, traded in Ile Maurice (Mauritius), which is where Robert was born[35]. **William Septimus** didn't have much joy: he lost his first wife's family in a shipwreck; he was taken to court over a partnership deal, and ended up himself drowning off Holyhead[xli].

Robert's uncle **Charles Saunders** had had more luck[36]. He was one of the first great men to start the Great Western Railway (GWR, God's Wonderful Railway). From the very start in 1833, he was its Secretary and General Superintendent of the railway, working with the visionary engineer Isambard Kingdom Brunel. The line got to Twyford in 1839 with the widest brick arch (ever) over the Thames at Maidenhead (still extant), and reached Plymouth in 1849. They put the line along the coast at Dawlish to save money[xlii]. Brunel also designed the famous Tamar railway bridge, 'Royal Albert Bridge' which opened in 1859, the year he died. The railway finally reached St Ives in 1877. The St Ives section was the last broad gauge line (7ft 1/4 in) to be built in England. Any dreams Brunel had of delivering a more comfortable ride were buried with him. The cheaper standard gauge (4ft 8 1/2 in) chosen by George Stephenson years before pleased the money-men more and is the one we still travel on today[xliii].

Charles Saunders fought some of Brunel's costly schemes, but was generally overruled; his Directors were a group of Bristol businessmen. Charles, liked by both staff and customers, earned a reputation for the company through its efficient operation, still the case when I travelled on the Westbury line at the start and end of school terms. Re-privatisation messed things up – and it has been near the bottom of the league for efficiency ever since. Charles was awarded a pension, virtually unheard of, on his retirement in 1864 for his services. His eldest son who went to India, another Charles, features in Chapter 6.

John Nicholas and Elizabeth's eldest son, **Tolmie John Tresidder** was known as **Johnnie** in his childhood and **Jack** in adult life[37]. He enjoyed a distinguished career with the Royal Engineers and John Brown's steel. After a spell at Dulwich College, he went for officer training at Woolwich and Engineering training at Chatham. Two years later, after marrying **Amy Buckland**, the Army posted him to Malta. During his time there, from 1875-84, he master-minded a major project: the sewerage system for the fortified town. Both London and Calcutta's better drainage systems had stopped the cholera endemic so new systems were 'must haves' elsewhere. From 1880, he was appointed its Project Manager and he was promoted to Captain in 1884.

In 1887, when Queen Victoria reached her Golden Jubilee and celebrations were held all round Britain – at the time one of the longest reigns of any English monarch – Jack also had much to celebrate. He retired from the Army in the November having been made a Companion of the Order of St Michael and St George (CMG) in the Queen's Jubilee honours, and joined John Brown & Co. That same year he patented an armour plating process for Royal Naval ships.

Jack joined John Brown & Co as a Director moving to Ecclesall to live near their steel works at Sheffield[38]. There, at the Atlas Steel Works, he carried out many experiments. To make the

---

33. *Elizabeth Anne Tresidder (1846-1929) married Horace Moule Evans (1841-1923) in 1866. It seems to be a tradition in their family for everyone to be called by their second name, as almost all their children were.*

34. *Mary Rosamond Tresidder (1847-1923) married Lt Robert Power Saunders (1839-1871) in 1867 at Jhansi, when Rosie was 19. They had three children. One died young. Lt Col William Power Saunders (1869-1938), Arthur Bertram Saunders (1870-1872), Mary Saunders (1871-1956).*

35. *William Septimus Saunders (1803-1850).*

36. *Charles Alexander Saunders (1796-1864).*

37. *Capt Tolmie John Tresidder CMG (1850-1931) married Amy Ada Buckland (1853-1908) in 1874.*

38. *John Brown & Co Ltd.*

steel harder, he chilled the face of the hot metal late on in the process, driving water along the surface by small jets, making sure the pressure was exactly right, preventing the steam from forming globules. A clean even hard edge was the result he achieved.

Jack patented a hollow cap for armour piercing shells, and an attachment to the armour for 'decapping' a shell, protecting ships with steel mats. His slide rule was used to calculate the speed at which a shell struck its target. It was the time of an arms race; the Harvey Company of America, Krupp in Germany and Dolman Long in Middlesbrough were consequently snapping at his heels. There was good money to be made from a British Navy with rather more ships in its fleet than it does today. In 1908, he was awarded the Gold Medal by the Institute of Naval Architects and also the Bessemer Gold Medal – awards for keeping Britain ahead of the field.

John Brown's Atlas Works, Sheffield

When Elizabeth died, John Nicholas came back from India briefly to marry again at St Giles Camberwell to **Emily Hooton Courtis**, and to take her back to India. Both Emily's mother's and her father's families were international traders. Her father was Mayor of Falmouth and John Nicholas's sister was already married into that family[39]. However, the children of the first marriage weren't impressed by their step-mother. They didn't understand how important that marriage was for their father. Annie and Rosie received gold bangles as presents but if these were designed as a bribe, they weren't a success.

1903 Armour plating chilling process first introduced at the Atlas works

❋ ❋ ❋ ❋

Retirement

Emily gave birth to 10 children in the second marriage and all but one survived. All but two were born in India. John Nicholas was a Deputy Inspector of Hospitals by the time my grandfather **Everard** was born in Jabalpur in 1871. When he retired six years later, Dr Tresidder was given the courtesy military title of Surgeon General[xliv]. On return to England, they lived in one of the best parts of Dulwich.

The Tresidders stayed in Palace Road until John Nicholas's death and all but one of the boys had left school. Emily's eldest girls, **Ethel** and **Mabel**, both toured Europe in 1898-9. They visited Everard at his school in Switzerland[40]. The family stayed close to their Hooton cousins in Croydon, whose boys were also at Dulwich College. One of them, a contemporary of Everard, would have joined Everard at Lausanne had John Nicholas not died and Everard returned home to England[41].

John Nicholas Tresidder, my great-grandfather, had those swarthy features of the Syro-Phoenicians, the dark brown curling hair and brownish skin. With the exception of Rosie, his second daughter, he was the last of his line to live in Cornwall – until, that is, I bought my cottage in Pentewan, near Mevagissey. His letters showed that he cared about what his children did – his past was their future. No doubt he was grateful he'd lived out the biblical 'three-score years and ten' for he underlined his past by naming his house after the greatest event of his life, a story which will emerge later on. But now there are some intriguing and mysterious aspects of another – possible – branch of my family, discovered during a visit to Scarborough.

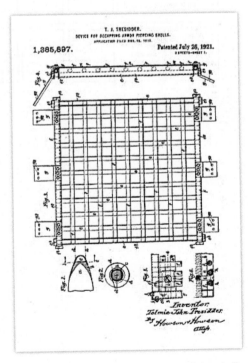

Device for decapping shells

---

39. *Anne Christiana Tresidder (1811-1900) married William Hooton (1810-1877) in 1838.*

40. *Ethel Tresidder (1862-1956) married James Allen (1863-1960) in 1893; Mabel Tresidder (1868-1937) married Campbell (George Campbell) Hathorn (1864-1957) in 1905; Hilda Alice Tresidder (1875-1939) married Douglas William Oliver (1872-1947) in 1896.*

41. *William Hooton (1873-1956).*

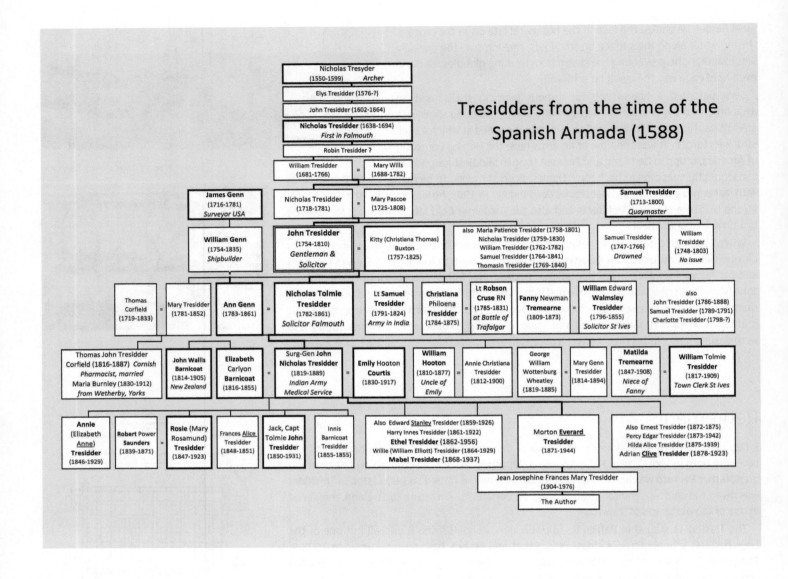

Tresidders from the time of the Spanish Armada (1588)

Other Notes and References

i. *Hydrangea arborescens was brought to England around 1736 from Pennsylvania, so not there in Nycholas's day, but now spectacular.*

ii. *Historia Regum Britanniae by Geoffrey of Monmouth, c1136. The village church is dedicated to Saint Constantine Corneu ap Conomar (Constantine of Cornwall) who ruled Dumnonia (Wessex) c435–c443. He was named after Emperor Constantine the Great (274 or 288-337) [NR] who was proclaimed emperor at York in AD 306 and professed Christianity after the Battle of Pons Milvius in AD 312. A zealous Christian, his mother St Helena was probably born in Asia Minor, though some believe that she was from Colchester, daughter of 'Old King Cole', spelt Coel or Caer-Lyn (Carlyon?)*

iii. *An English-Cornish Dictionary: Archer – saithor, sethar, zethar.'*

iv. *Herodotus BookIII Ch115. Written in 450, he called the British Isles 'Cassiterides' or 'where tin comes from,'... from 'the extreme borders of world.'*

v. *Evidence from Pennant Jones, of St Mark's Salisbury, 15 Sep 2013. It was the year after Emperor Constantine had issued the Edict of Milan (313) proclaiming the absolute and unconditional toleration of Christianity and other religions in the Roman Empire together with the restoration of all church buildings. Ferrar (Eusebius) Book 3, Ch 5 p130: Eusebius (260–340) confirmed that some apostles or missionaries 'have crossed the Ocean and reached the Isles of Britain.' Caerleon, originally the Roman fortress Isca on the banks of the River Usk, is frequently cited as the site of King Arthur's fabled court and castle.*

vi. *John Twynne (c1501-1581) [NR] writing in De Rebus Albinicis Britannicis, 1590.*

vii. *Penhallurick p182.*

viii. *Ibid p187. 2,500 Roman coins dating from the 3rd century AD were found in the silt.*

ix. *A ducat weighed 3.5 grams of gold; gold price on 22 Jan 2018 approx £31/gram – but gold was rarer.*

x. *Yeats p11. "There was a tradition that [the Pollexfens] had been linked with Ireland for generations and once had their share in the old Spanish trade with Galway."*

xi. *Penryn, Truro, and Helston lost their petition to King James I after the plan was supported by the Governor of Pendennis Castle. Sir Nicholas Hals, who was probably in the Killigrew's pay.*

xii. *When Arwenack Manor was about to occupied by Parliamentary troops in 1646, Royalist troops from Pendennis Castle bombarded it and set it on fire.*

xiii. *18 Jan 1652/53 [until 1751, the new year started on Lady Day, 25 March.] The Charter authorised markets once a week and fairs twice a year.*

xiv. *The quay was authorised in 1661; one was built near Arwenack Manor after 1670. The new king's father, Charles I (1600-1649), had been executed outside the Banqueting Hall, Whitehall, London in 1649.*

xv. *Wrigley. Cornwall grew at a faster pace than any other counties apart from the Industrial North, Midlands and Sussex.*

xvi. *Pensacola, St. Augustine, Savannah, and Charlestown, USA.*

xvii. *Gay p80. Samuel Tresidder was Wharfinger in 1774. 'It is a post of great confidence.' He termed Tregoneggie his retirement project.*

xviii. *Abstract of Title of Mr Nicholas Tolmie Tresidder to two thirds parts undivided of the tenement of Tregoneggie in the parish of Budock in the County of Cornwall. Cornwall County Records Office Ref X263/5 and research for Andrew Allen emailed 8 Nov 2013.*

xix. *London Gazette 24 Nov 1858 records Bickland Water as running through the estate.*

xx. *Land Tax Assessment for Cornwall 1799.*

xxi. *Gay p174. UK Articles of Clerkship: John Tresidder took out Articles of Clerkship under Peter Bown Harris in 1790.*

xxii. *Pigot's Directory 1844.*

xxiii. *UK Articles of Clerkship 1756-1874. Dated 5 Oct 1804, registered on 22 Oct 1804 and sworn at The Old Bailey on 4 Nov 1809.*

xxiv. *Nicholas Tolmie Tresidder was sworn in before Edward Law, Baron Ellenborough PC KC (1750-1818) [NR],Lord Chief Justice of the King's Bench, at the end of his 5-year apprenticeship, in 1809.*

xxv. *Evidence from Lottie Raby-Smith e-mail 19 Nov 2013.*

xxvi. *Freeman pp202-223.*

xxvii. *At one stage: Marwick, Nalder, Hocking & Genn.*

xxviii. *https://archive.org/details/b20443559 accessed 22 Jun 2015.*

xxix. *Court of King's Bench: Plea Side: Affidavits of Due Execution of Articles of Clerkship, Series I; Class: KB 105; Piece: 25. The National Archives of the UK. Witnessed by Francis Pinder.*

xxx. *Post Office Directory 1856. The Merchant Shipping Act of 1854 first codified 'Receivers of Wrecks'.*

xxxi. *Pigot's Directory 1844.*

xxxii. *Articles of Clerkship. Court of King's Bench: Plea Side: Affidavits of Due Execution of Articles of Clerkship, Series III; Class: KB 107; Piece: 12. National Archives of the UK, Kew,*

xxxiii. *Oriental Herald June 1825 Vol 5 No 18 p752: Lt Samuel Tresidder (1791-1824) of HM 30th Regt is buried in the East India Company's Old Lunar Lines Cemetery at Secunderbad, the 'twin city' of Hyderabad, Andhra Pradesh, in the former Madras Presidency of India.*

xxxiv. *Daily Telegraph 18 Feb 2013. Letter from Dr Adrian Greaves.*

xxxv. *Lear p5.*

xxxvi. *X-rays were first used for treating cancer (largely unsuccessfully) in 1903. By the 1920s it was becoming more routine.*

xxxvii. *Indian Office Records, British Library L-MIL-9-390. 7 Nov 1844. John Nicholas Tresidder was recommended by Thomas Weeding Esq, had a viva voce on 5 Feb 1845 and was nominated by Director John Shepherd.*

xxxviii. *Indian Office Records, British Library L/MIL/10/76 ff77-78.*

xxxix. *The barque Doncaster.*

xl. *Daily Telegraph 5 Apr 2014. In 2014, a section of railway line washed away in a storm. It cost £35m to put right, using 6,000 tonnes of concrete and 150 tonnes of steel. 8,000 people per day were normally using the line.*

xli. *The "gauge war" led to a Parliamentary 'Gauge Commission'. Its 1846 report favoured standard gauge. The Bristol and Gloucester line was converted to standard gauge in 1854, which brought mixed-gauge track to Bristol Temple Meads station. Passengers changed trains when travelling between the north and south.*

xlii. *London Gazette 29 June 1877. The date of his return to the UK is unclear.*

Cornish Coastline by Elsie Tresidder

Scarborough and the Silver Spoons

The red front door creaked open when the Scarborough Council officer pushed at it. We could just make out the chequered hallway as we walked in; original plasterwork stood out against the cheap partitions. As we strode through the rooms, the dust of ages rose from our feet from the Council carpets. What might *Londesborough Lodge* have looked like in 1853, when Albert Denison bought it? What games had I**da Denison** played on the original carpet with her neighbours, the Sitwell children[1]?

Londesborough Lodge, Scarborough – seaside home of Albert Denison

Through the bay window we saw the majestic vista of gardens stretching down to the Rotunda Museum and the South Bay, a view now masked by the trees that had grown. We'd walked amongst the tiled basement, which had been used as Turkish Baths from 1925-76, and into the butler's quarters. "The BBC used it as a studio until recently," said the official – and now we were standing in the dining room at *Londesborough Lodge*, the former home of the Denisons. My father's middle name was Denison. His grandmother was a Denison[2]. Half his mother's brothers were called Denison. One of his uncles changed his surname to Denison. My father Paul had no escape – they all called him Denison. Then there was the strange case of silver cutlery with a Denison crest on them. Had those spoons once graced the table in this very room? What was this Denison connection? I hoped that this house would give me a clue.

Two doors away in *The Crescent* was the former seaside home of the Sitwell family in what had by my time become an Arts Quarter with the Art Gallery and a Natural History Museum. My work had taken me to Scarborough. The Council officials were hoping to develop an economy which didn't rely simply on the holiday trade. I'd passed by a large portrait of a Denison in the Town Hall without really looking too hard, on the way to a meeting called by the Chief Executive to see how the 'cultural industries' could help the economy. The Council had commissioned a number of studies but each one had ground to a halt. Now, however, with all the Heads of Service in the one room, a solution had been reached. The Natural History Museum in *The Crescent*, which was full of stuffed birds which had started moulting, could be converted into a Centre for the Creative Arts. People would be able to create, display and promote their products, both arts and technology; hopefully the place would pay for itself – Edith Sitwell would have approved of the plan if not Osbert and Sacheverell. The best bits of the building would be restored, thus the house is now used for the things that the Sitwells were famous for – the arts[3].

The Sitwells – Sacheverell, Edith and Osbert

The Sitwells' mother was Ida Denison. The Council told me that the Denison family's seaside home *Londesborough Lodge*, might be up for sale and it was then that the penny dropped. Could this home of holiday romance be a family heirloom, and restored from obscurity and decay?

---

1. *Lady Ida Emily Augusta Denison (1869-1937) married Sir George Reresby Sitwell Bt JP MP (1860-1943) in 1886 and had three children: Dame Edith Louisa Sitwell DBE LittD (1887-1964); Sir Francis Osbert Sacheverell Sitwell CH CBE LLD DLit FRSL FRIBA JP, 5th Baronet (1892-1969); and Sir Sacheverell Reresby Sitwell CH LittD JP, 6th Baronet (1897-1988).*

2. *Arabella Annie Denison (1845-1926).*

3. *With European money on this and other projects, and the energetic direction from the unsung Douglas Kendall and others, the town was granted the title of the most Enterprising Town in Europe in 2009.*

Londesborough Lodge's gardens, now a public park, had all the hall-marks of extravagance, stretching down the valley towards the sea with their own hermit's cave. Built in 1839, the Lodge was bought in 1853 by Ida's father, **Albert Denison, Baron Londesborough**, who spent large sums of money on it[4]. The Denisons had once been the toast of Scarborough; whenever the family came to stay, a mile of red carpet was put out to welcome them[i]. Londesborough Road still runs directly from their Seamer estate into the town. Wouldn't it be good if if I could buy the house and bring it back to life, with or without the red carpet?

✳ ✳ ✳ ✳

Rags to Riches

Albert's grandfather, **Joseph Denison** was the son of a Leeds woollen cloth merchant[ii]. He arrived in London in the late 1700s with just a few shillings in his pocket, unable to read or write. He had a letter from a domestic servant at Dillon & Co, an Irish bank, which gave him a job as an errand boy. He worked hard and learned to read and married the domestic servant[5]. Dillon's promoted him to counting house clerk, where he totted up the money though he never learned to write properly. He was a dissenting Christian all his life. After his first wife died and Dillon's got into financial trouble, he married again. His new wife helped him set up business in Princes Street, near the Bank of England in London, employing his former boss. He linked up with Heywood's, the Liverpool bankers, who steered him towards untold fortune. He formed the firm of Denison, Heywood, and Kennard with offices in Lombard Street, dealing in both domestic and foreign loans, what we'd now call a bank. He bought houses: one in London at Jeffries Square (where the *'Gherkin'* now stands), *Denbies* in Dorking (now a vineyard), and *Seamer* in Yorkshire, which he bought from the Duke of Leeds[6]. He left £50,000 to each of his daughters when he died and most of his possessions to his son, William Joseph.

Joseph's only son, **William Joseph Denison** took the business from strength to strength as well as entering parliament in 1796 as a Whig MP, representing Camelford in Cornwall[7]. He was one of the founders of the Reform Club – I've even seen his picture there on another work-related venture. He actively supported Parliamentary reform at the time of William Wilberforce – they were both MPs for Hull at various times[8].

Akin to Dickens's Scrooge, William Denison was frugal. He kept his finances under lock and key and begrudged spending any of the money he'd inherited. He'd rather entertain a friend by buying his own steak, bringing it home wrapped up in a cabbage leaf, instead of taking the guy to one of the many chophouses[iii]. He refused a peerage, saying that one of his grandfathers had been a hatter and the other one a labourer. He felt his place was more 'at the head of his own ledger than in the pages of the peerage.'

The Denison bank grew and, by the time he died, William headed up the 'Forbes' wealth list of his day, one of the wealthiest men in England. He passed on an inheritance conservatively estimated at the time as £2.3m but he had no direct heirs. It largely went to the owner of *Londesborough Lodge*, **Albert**, who changed his surname to **Denison**[iv]. Money therefore – but where did the influence come from?

✳ ✳ ✳ ✳

---

4. *Albert Denison, Baron Londesborough KCH FSA FRA PBAA VPAA VPAI PMAS PNS (1805-1860).*
5. *Miss Sykes.*
6. *30 St Mary Axe, built for Swiss Re and now London offices of the Standard Chartered Bank. See also East Yorkshire Landed Estates p17.*
7. *William Joseph Denison MP (1769-1849).*
8. *Denison was MP for Hull 1806-7; William Wilberforce had been MP for Hull 1780-84 .*

Climbing into the king's bed

Elizabeth Denison, Joseph's daughter and William's sister, is the source of the Denison influence[9]. She'd married a minor Irish peer, **Henry Conyngham** (pronounced Cunning-um) in 1794. His great aunt had bought Conyngham Hall in Knaresborough, Yorkshire, in 1796, extended it and given it its name. She'd no children, so the title passed to the Burton family (no relation to my wife). They took the name Conyngham in 1781 – there was a whole lot of name changing in this family. Henry Burton was now a Conyngham and, being the elder twin, he inherited the Barony at the age of twenty in 1789. He married Elizabeth five years later but it wasn't Henry who provided the influence – that came from her winning personality[10].

Henry did help her break into court circles but, having got there, Elizabeth – or Betty as she was 'commonly' known – made headway in a 'Page 3 model' sort of way. She was considered 'vulgar', by the ladies of court. With a mother a cockney from Tooley Street, and a blunt broad Yorkshireman for a father, it was *what* she said as much as how she said it, for she didn't beat about the bush[v]. Court etiquette preferred mannered, if waspish, clever phrases which implied more than they said. Whatever was said, it was Betty's wealth and beauty that carried her through; never short of male attention, she took advantage of it in the shadows of the Vauxhall Gardens and the candle light. A social climber if ever there was one, she put herself about. Even the Tsarevitch of Russia, the future Nicholas I, fell for her.

And climb she did. According to the Duke of Wellington, Betty decided as early as 1806, at the age of 37, to become a mistress of the Prince of Wales, who was five years older than she was[11].

Elizabeth Denison, Marchioness of Conyngham (1766-1832)

* * * *

More Cunning than Cautious

Prince George ('Prinny') was to become the future George IV, the fattest, most extravagant king we've ever had. When his father, the 'mad King' George III, was declared 'of unsound mind' in 1811, Prinny was given the title Prince Regent[12]. As Regent, he could now do his own thing without his papa telling him off all the time.

Betty made friends with his mistress of the time, Lady Hertford[13]. The year before the old king died, Lady Hertford was finally put out to grass. 'I never saw anyone in such high spirits as he was at the St Carlos's Ball,' wrote Lady Cowper in 1819[vi]. 'Lady Conyngham has carried the day completely, and they say the other is quite dished.' Betty was 49 and George 57 but I wonder if there wasn't some mutual attraction somewhat earlier. He'd put favours her way long before that.

The Regency period in England was the most profligate in the history of Britain. It invented the National Debt. The wealth of the sugar and tobacco plantations of the West Indies, fuelled by the Slave Trade, was enriching landowners across Britain, the richest in Europe. Their sons were sent on a high-rolling gap year – the 'Grand Tour'. They went round Europe absorbing the high culture and sampling the low life. Beau Nash's Bath and Jane Austin's Pemberley were the height of fashion. Architecture, interior decoration, painting, sculpture, costumes, carriages,

Conyngham Hall, Knaresborough

*Georgie loves good ale
and Georgie loves good brandy
And Georgie loves his C_n_g_m
as sweet as candy!*

---

9. *Elizabeth Denison (1770-1861) married Henry 1st Marquess of Conyngham (1766-1832) in 1794.*
10. *On 5 July 1794 at St Andrew Undershaft, near her childhood home in the City.*
11. *George Augustus Frederick, later Prince Regent and then George IV (1762-1830) [NR] Field Marshal Arthur Wellesley, 1st Duke of Wellington KG GCB GCH PC FRS (1769-1852) [NR].*
12. *George William Frederick, King George III (1738-1820) [NR].*
13. *Isabella Anne Seymour-Conway, Marchioness of Hertford (1759-1834) [NR] inherited Temple Newsam, near Leeds, from her father in 1807. George ate partridge pie there with her in 1806 and presented her with rolls of Chinese wallpaper and tapestries (left over from Brighton?).*

servants' livery, silver, furnishings, fireworks, music, eating – all were hitting new heights. They brought back 'bling'. Each generation has to say something modern. Theirs was bigger and better than ever before.

'Georgie Porgie' was the chief of all the prodigal sons. On coming to the throne, he hired the architect John Nash to rebuild *Buckingham Palace*[14]. Prior to that, he'd indulged in the astonishing, gorgeous, incomparable Brighton Pavilion. Buckingham Palace was a financial disaster. Nash was not known for economy any more than the Prince. Brighton was no better. Nash was in the process of bankrupting the Trevanion family who'd commissioned him to build *Caerhays Castle* on the south coast of Cornwall[vii]. The Parliamentary Commission of the Lords of the Treasury had some very caustic things to say about Nash[viii]. Added to which, most of the roofs leaked.

The Pavilion at Brighthelmstone, what we call Brighton, was an Oriental fantasy – onion domes, minarets, Indian-Gothic windows, fretted stone verandas. The interior defied gravity with its cast iron 'bamboo' columns. There was a dome of plantain leaves, another of scallop shells. There were dragons and gilded birds supporting chandeliers. There were lights shaped like water lilies. Even the kitchen had no expense spared. Dazzling copper pans were arrayed under more faux bamboo. George was twenty-one when he first took mistresses there, copying his wicked uncle, who had set up his own seraglio nearby[15]. Brighton still had a reputation when I was young for 'dirty weekends'. All Prince George's fault, and a certain Mrs Fitzherbert, his first love[16]. Brighton still attracts the unconventional.

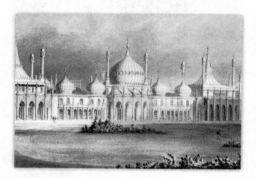

The Royal Pavilion, Brighton

George became king in 1820. He didn't lack for choice of women – he knew what he liked, and was totally besotted with Betty. At his London Palace, *Carlton House*, he spent night after night constantly 'kissing her hand with a look of most devoted submission'. He'd hold her hand at the dining table all the time he was drinking. A Coronation was normally a rather sedate affair, but not this one. He spent the whole time 'nodding and winking' at her. At one point he took a diamond brooch from his chest, and, 'Looking at her, kissed it, on which she took off her glove and kissed a ring she had on[ix].'

The coronation wasn't stress-free either. Beforehand, he'd put his wife, Caroline of Brunswick, on trial for adultery (that was a laugh)[17]. The popular 'Queen' had arrived at Westminster Abbey and was refused admittance. She tried every door. No one let her in and she died within a month of the coronation. On her death bed, she'd asked to be buried in Brunswick, which meant arranging for the coffin to be taken out of the country via Harwich. The authorities tried to slip it away quietly but the population thought otherwise. The way was blocked by the jeering crowds until the soldiers gave up and re-routed it through the City. London gave her a proper send-off.

Queen Caroline's coffin procession, 1821

We often think of the Regency period as one of calm and certainty; it was anything but. There was a revolution taking place on the other side of the channel, and frequent riots in England. There was even a riot about the price of tickets for Covent Garden – things were far from certain [18]. George didn't pause for thought; after the coronation; he shot off to Slane in Ireland to see the Conynghams' Irish estates, wining and dining, carousing and storytelling. He kept company with

---

14. *John Nash (1752-1835) [NR].*
15. *Henry Frederick, Prince and Duke of Cumberland and Strathearn (1745-1790) [NR].*
16. *Maria Anne Smythe (1756-1837) [NR] married Edward Weld [NR], then Thomas Fitzherbert [NR] and, illegally, George, Prince of Wales. They parted when George, who owed £600,000, married Caroline of Brunswick in 1795. Only thus would his father pay off his debts.*
17. *Caroline Amelia Elizabeth of Brunswick-Wolfenbüttel (1768-1821) [NR].*
18. *The Old Price Riots of 1809 were caused by rising prices at the new Theatre at Covent Garden. Perhaps the worst riot was the one which culminated in the 'Peterloo Massacre' at St Peter's Field, Manchester, in 1819. 15 were killed and many injured. There was chronic famine and unemployment after the end of the Napoleonic Wars in 1815. The cavalry charged the crowd of 60-80,000 that had gathered to demand the reform of parliamentary representation.*

the rakish Irish demi-monde whom the estate manager described as more normally occupied in 'thieving and lying'[19].

It didn't take long for Betty to get her hands dirty. One of the first scandals was the way she wangled a church post for her sons' tutor[20]. Church jobs meant an easy income. Despite much opposition, she got her way. The Conynghams and the King then lived as a ménage à trois at Windsor and Brighton[21]. George came to depend on depend on Betty for decisions small and large. For example, one night, when she ordered the Pavilion's Saloon to be lit up, George said, 'Thank you, thank you my dear. You always do what is right; you cannot please me so much as by doing what you please, everything to show you are mistress here.'[x]

The King heaped presents on her, including the crown sapphires given by the Papal Legate. She used the king's horses and carriages and the palace chefs for dinner parties at her home[22].

Betty dabbled in politics to some good effect. She tried to stop some of the more extreme policies of the day. She put pressure on Ministers to ease the criminal code and, against all odds, she sponsored the cause of Catholics.

Betty liked spending money. When one of the King's Private Secretaries kept too tight a rein on her extravagant spending, she engineered his resignation and had him replaced with someone who indulged her.[23] She gave George the moral courage to stand up to his Ministers. They called her 'La Regnante' or the 'Vice Queen', with a certain irony. Betty was probably the one woman he actually loved for her mind as much as for her body – she was growing as plump as he was. She talked to him straight, even if it was considered vulgar. George found he liked 'vulgarity'.

Mocked for it, her husband Henry enjoyed his second-hand status in the Carlton House set. He was raised to a Marquess, sworn into the Privy Council, and given other high offices, including Lord Steward of the Household. He was Captain, Constable and Lieutenant of Windsor Castle. He liked the title 'Baron of Minster Abbey' best. It allowed him to enter the House of Lords without being elected by his Irish peers.

As he grew older, the King's temper got worse – over-indulgence affected his health. He became more and more dependent on Betty. The rest of the court couldn't wait for her come-uppance but it never came. There was the odd little tiff: '*Bécassé* (you silly goose), avaricious etc...' which was blown up by the gossips and evaporated in the wind (his wind)[xi]. A courtesan tried to blackmail her, demanding money to keep her son Francis and one of her former lovers out of her memoirs which made her faint all the time, but she recovered and looked younger for it[24]. However weary she became, George's affections never really strayed, though there was a close shave with a Russian Ambassador's 40-year young wife, Dorothea von Lieven[25]. Fortunately for Betty, she gave the portly king the cold shoulder. In the end, George became so possessive of Betty that she felt smothered (literally probably.) She thought about leaving him when her eldest son died, but she couldn't bring herself to write the letter.

'A voluptuary under the horrors of digestion ' A caricature by James Gilray 1792 of George, as Prince of Wales, ballooning from his over-large appetite, fork still in his mouth and waistcoat holding on by a single button. "He drinks spirits morning noon and night," said the Duke of Wellington. Breakfast on 9 Apr 1830 comprised 3 beefsteaks, 2 pigeons, ¾ bottle of Mosel wine, 1 glass of champagne, one glass of brandy, 2 glasses of port.

'The guard wot looks after the Sovereign'

19. *According to Richard Parkinson, Lord Conyngham's manager of the Slane estates.*

20. *Rt Rev Charles Richard Sumner (1790-1874) [NR], Bishop of Llandaff 1826, and Winchester 1827-69.*

21. *The Royal Lodge.*

22. *at 7 Hamilton Place.*

23. *Lieutenant-General Benjamin Bloomfield, 1st Baron Bloomfield GCB GCH (1768-1846) [NR] was replaced by Sir William Knighton, 1st Baronet GCH (1776-1836) [NR].*

24. *Harriette Wilson (1786-1845) [NR] was casting aspersions about John Brabazon Ponsonby, 1st Viscount Ponsonby GCB (1770-1855) [NR]. The Duke of Wellington who was similarly approached, famously said 'Publish and be damned.'*

25. *Princess Dorothea von Lieven née Benckendorff (1785-1857) [NR].*

Bifrons, Patrixbourne, Kent

The King's death in 1830 was little mourned. It meant the end of all that influence. Henry broke his staff of office at the funeral and died two years later. Betty fled to France with a few keepsakes – well, more like several carriages full, having spent all night packing. She returned to England when all the gossip had died down and lived out her days in Kent at Patrixbourne near Canterbury, dying at the ripe old age of 92[26]. Although the King had bequeathed her all his gold and silver plate and all his jewels, of which there were masses, she refused the lot (well, almost)[xii].

✳ ✳ ✳ ✳

Betty's three sons

The Conynghams had three sons, all before Betty got hitched to George, but was the third one actually his – a royal bastard, as it were? Her eldest son, **Henry**, was educated in Dublin and became an MP for Donegal, but he died at the age of 27 and did not inherit[27].

Betty's second son **Francis** was a Page to the King in his youth[28]. He was made Master of the Robes and First Groom to the Bedchamber when George became King[xiii]. This post was possibly the closest one could ever get to royalty. It meant dressing George in the morning (kings didn't know how), eating with him, and guarding his access. At one stage, the job had meant wiping the king's bottom – they must have been good chums. Francis ended up a full General in 1874, Lord Chamberlain (1835-9) and Under-Secretary at the Foreign Office (1823-26).

Francis's boss, the Foreign Secretary, was Lord Castlereagh. In 1822 Castlereagh committed suicide[29]. When someone suggested that he should be replaced by his foe, the able and ambitious George Canning, Betty screamed in alarm[30]. The King turned to her: "Very well, if you like I will not appoint him; I will change the Government and put in the Whigs."

Betty supported the Whigs who opposed the Tory government but many disagreed. To sort it all out, Francis was given the job as Under-Secretary under Canning. Two monarchs later, Francis had the job of telling Victoria she was to be the next Queen.

The third son was the 'royal bastard'. **Albert** hated the gossip and insinuations about his mother's life and his possible ancestry. But he was the lucky one. With a change of name, he inherited most of his uncle William Denison's wealth and estates.

His uncle's will was clear. He was to keep his wealth in property, buying large tracts of land in Yorkshire and Lincolnshire. He also bought property around Market Weighton, near York, and the village of Londesborough. He was Lord of the Manors of Willerby, Staxton, Spaldington, North Dalton, Elmswell with Little Driffield, Flixton, Fridaythorpe, Goodmanham, Kilham, Market Weighton, Tibthorpe, Londesborough, Middleton on the Wolds, Nunburnholme, Routh, Shipton, Skerne, Speeton, Thwing, Watton and Hutton Cranswick[xiv]. He bought the manor of Selby and other estates from the Petre family, and Grimston Park, Tadcaster, from Lord Howden.

Frances, Lord Conyngham, informing Victoria she was Queen

26. Bifrons, Patrixbourne, Canterbury – in 1837 Elizabeth donated stained glass windows (from Switzerland) to the church and in 1857 paid for its restoration.
27. Henry Joseph Conyngham (1795-1824).
28. Francis Nathaniel Conyngham, 2nd Marquess Conyngham (1797-1876).
29. Robert Stewart, Viscount Castlereagh, 2nd Marquess of Londonderry KG GCH PC (1769-1822) [NR] Foreign Secretary 1812-22, lived at Loring Hall (Woollet Hall), Water Lane, North Cray, Kent. He was MP for Tregony in 1794-6.
30. George Canning FRS MP (1770-1827) [NR]. His son Charles John Canning, 1st Earl Canning KG GCB GCSI PC (1812-1862) [NR] was Governor-General of India at the time of the Indian Mutiny (Chapter 6).

Educated at Eton, briefly, he'd spent a year in the Royal Horse Guards. Thanks to his brother, he had a free 'Grand Tour' as a paid diplomat for the crown, in Berlin, Vienna and Florence. He became the MP for Canterbury, was knighted in 1829 and created Baron Londesborough in 1850[31]. He bought *Londesborough Lodge* in Scarborough 3 years later.

Albert was a keen archaeologist – the world's second oldest purpose-built geology museum lay at the bottom of his garden[32]. Archaeology was a new science in the twenty years leading up to Darwin publishing his 'Origin of the Species'[33]. Albert was elected a Fellow of the Royal Society of Antiquaries in 1840 and of the Royal Society in 1850. He was the first President of the British Archaeological Association in 1843. He was President or Vice-President of countless other archaeological Societies, local and national. He took an interest in old coins: becoming President of the Numismatic Society. When advised to go to Europe for a health cure, he went round Greece and Italy searching for old coins and ancient history.

Albert Denison, Baron Londesborough (1805-1860)

The Denison family had arrived, now an accepted part of London Society. They were members of the London Clubs, Honorary Colonels of Regiments, and Hereditary Vice Admirals of the Yorkshire coast. They married into established families with royal connections like the Dukes of Somerset and Earls of Westmoreland. They were MPs, Freemasons; one even married a Churchill who was a Lady-in-Waiting to Queen Victoria. Their Scarborough holidays put the place on the map and the town became the best-liked seaside spot in the North. The Denisons held 53,000 acres in 1883, giving them an annual income of £68,000, more than most people earned in a lifetime. They owned not only *Londesborough Lodge* but also *Londesborough Park* near Market Weighton, *Blankney Hall* in Lincolnshire and a London house in Grosvenor Square. Both the London house and *Blankney Hall* had over 20 live-in servants. There was a feudal air about it all.

Edward VII ('Dirty Bertie') stayed as his guest in the *Lodge* three consecutive years in 1869, 1870 and 1871. He used *Blankney Hall* for his secret assignations with various mistresses. He relied on people like the Denisons. It kept him out of the way of his mother, Queen Victoria. He liked his food and his women – 8 course breakfasts, 12 course dinners as well as lunch, tea and supper. There were reputedly 10,000 notches on his bedpost[xv]. He often overstayed his welcome – for some families it meant budget cuts afterwards. The Denisons didn't even notice; they were the idle rich.

Shooting party at Londesborough, Yorkshire. Edward VII centre.

This Denison line fizzled out after another three generations. The 4th Earl had only one child, a daughter who married unwisely some five times[34]. They had to sell the land. And after death duties, there wasn't much left.

⁂ ⁂ ⁂ ⁂

A Puzzle

Sadly I did not buy *Londesborough Lodge*, but it is being restored and it has encouraged me to look again at my family tree. Was I related to these Denisons? My great grandmother and her family had boasted about these connections to the point of self-belief. I can find no evidence, nor of another Denison family, which also had its origins in Leeds.

---

31.   *Berlin 1824, Vienna 1825, Florence 1828, Berlin 1829-31. MP for Canterbury 1835-41, 1847-50.*

32.   *The Rotunda Museum built by William Smith, the father of English geology, in 1828.*

33.   *Charles Robert Darwin, FRS (1809-1882) [NR] On the Origin of Species by Means of Natural Selection, or the Preservation of Favoured Races in the Struggle for Life was published in 1859.*

34.   *Hugo William Cecil Denison, 4th Earl of Londesborough (1894-1937)'s daughter was Lady Zinnia Rosemary Denison (1937-1997).*

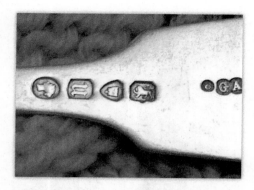

A **William Denison** ran a woollen merchants William Denison & Co, in Kirkgate Leeds. He died in 1782. After his brother Robert died, their wealth went to their nephew, John Wilkinson who, guess what, changed his name to Denison[35]. John (now Denison) ran the Leeds firm with his brother Edward[36]. He moved to Ossington in Nottinghamshire, and married twice. His sons were all high-fliers, including lawyers, a Speaker of the House of Commons, a Judge, a Bishop of Salisbury, an 'extreme High-Church' Archdeacon of Taunton, and a General who became a Governor of the Madras Province of India[37].

Am I related to any of these? I very much doubt it, yet there is a curious connection I have been unable to decipher. My father's grandmother, **Arabella Annie Denison**, kept a box of silver cutlery under her bed. This box had probably belonged to her brother, Willie Denison[38]. She seldom used it. The cutlery is still in the family, handed down via her son, Bernard Wiggins, who then used it on a daily basis[39]. It is now with his granddaughter Susan Kay[40].

The fiddle-pattern spoons and forks are dated London 1875/6, the work of silversmith George Adams, who managed one of the largest producers of top quality silver in Victorian England, the firm of Chawner & Co[41]. The wooden canteen and the silver itself both bear the Denison crest – not the Ossington Denisons, but the Londesborough ones: a hand holding a chalice, pointing to the sun in the sky. And the emblem appears in the fourth quarter of a shield in the photograph of my great uncle Bishop Wand (see Chapter 18). To quote from the College of Arms:

> *Crest: issuant from clouds to sinister, a dexter arm ppr habited gu cuffed erm, the arm charged with a covered cup or and pointing with the forefinger pointing to an estoile radiated or.*

So maybe there is a family connection after all.

---

35.   *John (Wilkinson) Denison MP (1759-1820). His mother was Ann Denison, sister to Robert Denison (1720-1785) and William Denison (1714-1782).*

36.   *Edward Wilkinson (1761-1836).*

37.   *Speaker John Evelyn Denison, 1st Viscount Ossington PC (1800-1873; Ven George Anthony Denison (1805-1896) Archdeacon of Taunton 1851-96 in 1853 preached on 'the Real Presence'. He was deprived of his office after refusing to recant, but won an appeal on a technicality; Lt Gen Sir William Thomas Denison (1804-1871) was Governor of New South Wales, Australia 1854-61 and Governor of Madras Province India 1861-66.*

38.   *Rev William Henry Denison MA (1848-1915) married Mary Sophie Lee French (1851-1920) in 1876.*

39.   *Bernard Henry Wiggins OBE CBSZ (1878-1972).*

40.   *Susan Hester Kay (b1948).*

41.   *George William Adams (1808-1895) [NR], sole proprietor 1852-83.*

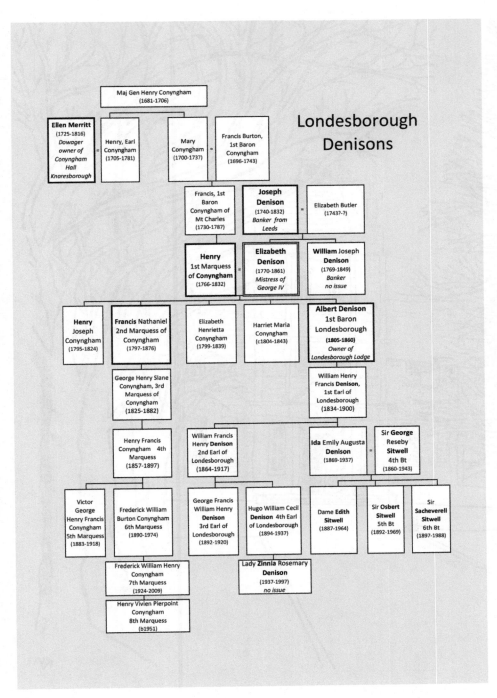

Londesborough Denisons

Maj Gen Henry Conyngham (1681-1706)

Ellen Merritt (1725-1816) *Dowager owner of Conyngham Hall Knaresborough* = **Henry, Earl Conyngham** (1705-1781)

Mary Conyngham (1700-1737) = **Francis Burton, 1st Baron Conyngham** (1696-1743)

Francis, 1st Baron Conyngham of Mt Charles (1730-1787)

Joseph Denison (1740-1832) *Banker from Leeds* = **Elizabeth Butler** (1743?-?)

Henry 1st Marquess of Conyngham (1766-1832) = **Elizabeth Denison** (1770-1861) *Mistress of George IV*

William Joseph Denison (1769-1849) *Banker no issue*

Henry Joseph Conyngham (1795-1824)

Francis Nathaniel 2nd Marquess of Conyngham (1797-1876)

Elizabeth Henrietta Conyngham (1799-1839)

Harriet Maria Conyngham (c1804-1843)

Albert Denison 1st Baron Londesborough (1805-1860) *Owner of Londesborough Lodge*

George Henry Slane Conyngham, 3rd Marquess of Conyngham (1825-1882)

William Henry Francis Denison, 1st Earl of Londesborough (1834-1900)

Henry Francis Conyngham 4th Marquess (1857-1897)

William Francis Henry Denison 2nd Earl of Londesborough (1864-1917)

Ida Emily Augusta Denison (1869-1937) = **Sir George Reseby Sitwell 4th Bt** (1860-1943)

Victor George Henry Francis Conyngham 5th Marquess (1883-1918)

Frederick William Burton Conyngham 6th Marquess (1890-1974)

George Francis William Henry Denison 3rd Earl of Londesborough (1892-1920)

Hugo William Cecil Denison 4th Earl of Londesborough (1894-1937)

Dame Edith Sitwell (1887-1964)

Sir Osbert Sitwell 5th Bt (1892-1969)

Sir Sacheverell Sitwell 6th Bt (1897-1988)

Frederick William Henry Conyngham 7th Marquess (1924-2009)

Lady Zinnia Rosemary Denison (1937-1997) *no issue*

Henry Vivien Pierpoint Conyngham 8th Marquess (b1951)

Other Notes and References

i. *Pleasures and Treasures of Britain p350.*

ii. *http://www.historyofparliamentonline.org/*

iii. *Launceston Examiner 19 Jan 1850.*

iv. *Ward p17.*

v. *Launceston Examiner 19 Jan 1850.*

vi. *Levy p152.*

vii. *Williams p109ff. Caerhays was built in 1808. John Trevanion Purnell Bettesworth-Trevanion MP OW (1780- 1840) [NR] could never repay his debts estimated at £300,000 (the castle cost perhaps £70,000), and fled abroad to escape the consequences, hotly pursued by the Bailiffs. The Williams family purchased Caerhays in 1854.*

viii. *Davis pp94-99.*

ix. *Levy pp159,163.*

x. *Dictionary of National Biography from the Diaries of Charles Greville 21 May 1821.*

xi. *Levy pp174, 175.*

xii. *Susan Rumfitt., jewellery consultant, 12 Feb 2015, estimated them to have been worth £1m at the time.*

xiii. *Office Holders p63. Francis Conyngham was Under-Secretary for Foreign Affairs Jan 1823-Mar 1825.*

xiv. *Ward p17.*

xv. *Winter & Kochman p165. 10,000 notches on the bedpost is considered a conservative guess.*

Dauntsey's School, Wiltshire

Happiest Days of our Lives

Every now and then a book appears which awakens a tide of imagination for a whole generation. *Tom Brown's Schooldays* did that in 1857. It recalls the pranks of every boy – fist-fights, bullying, pea-shooting, friendships, absconding, overlaid by the 'moral thoughtfulness' of Dr Arnold[1]. *Rugby School* produced some of the overlords of the British Empire (including a relation, see Chapter 6). This new breed found that *'life is a whole, made up of actions and thoughts and longings great and small, noble and ignoble'*. Their schooling meant *'Failures slid off them like water off a duck's back feathers.'* The book changed the public mood – schools changed from the 'bad, wicked, filthy' bear-pits to places of moral respectability[i].

My great grandfather, **William Thomas Haskins**, became Headmaster of **Courteenhall Grammar School** in about the same year as that seminal book, 1857[2]. In a smaller way (his school was a sixth of the size) he was a local legend, and today is considered its 'most famous headmaster'.

William Thomas Haskins (1824-1898)

1857 was also the year that *Dulwich College* was reformed by an Act of Parliament and taken to new heights by Dr Carver[3]. My great uncle **Jack** was among the first of the new in-take[4]. Jack and his brothers, and his cousins the Hooton's, boarded at Mrs Field's house, Plasgwyn's. **William Hooton** designed cap colours for Plasgwyn's, later adopted by Orchard House[5]. Sixteen of my mother's family – Tresidders and Hootons – went to Dulwich. Day fees were then £15 and boarding fees were about 55 guineas. Hours were 9am-1pm and 2-4pm with half days on Wednesdays and Saturdays. All went to chapel on Sundays, including day boys if living 'within a convenient distance'.

Dulwich College new buildings 1869

Education came into its own for two main reasons. The first were the efforts of one man, Lord Shaftesbury who'd spent his life trying to make all sorts of human conditions better despite clocking up huge debts (see Chapter 17)[6]. His *Mines and Collieries Act* of 1842 stopped all women, girls, and boys under ten working in the pits[ii]. Shaftesbury introduced many other reforms which, along with the writing of Charles Dickens, captured a mood for reform. The second spur was the 1855 *Northcote-Trevelyan Reforms* of the civil service[iii]. A proper education now became an absolute necessity – to get a job was no longer who your parents knew, but could you pass the entrance exams?

In 1846, the College of Preceptors had been born, to improve standards of teacher training[iv]. By 1861, Ragged Schools, which originally taught children to read the bible, were educating 40,000 in London[v]. The 1870 Education Act meant schooling for all to the age of 13[vi]. Until then, only a few at the upper end of society could afford to send their boys to boarding school, and then only the boys – their daughters often stayed at home.

The National Union for Improving the Education of Women was set up in 1871 to promote

1. *Dr Thomas Arnold (1795-1842) [NR].*
2. *Or possibly 1856. William Thomas Haskins (1824-1898) married Elizabeth Whitehead (1828-1892) in 1850.*
3. *Canon Alfred James Carver (1826-1909) [NR], Master of Dulwich College 1857-83.*
4. *Tolmie John Tresidder (1850-1931).*
5. *William Hooton (1873-1956).*
6. *Anthony Ashley Cooper, 7th Earl of Shaftesbury KG (1801-1885) [NR].*

Sydenham School, as designed by Sir Joseph Paxton (of Crystal Palace fame). It opened for girls, using the first floor, in March 1861. The towers were never built due to lack of funds. Annie and Rosie boarded with 7 other girls at 12 Park Terrace, Albert Road, with Elizabeth Sykes, 'a teacher of a Ladies' School', in charge.

equal education. *Blackheath High School* was the first of twenty-six Girls' Public Day School Trust schools. My great auntie **Bertie** and my mother **Jean Tresidder** went there[vii]. Bertie's elder sister, **Elsie Garden** my grandmother, boarded at Stockport[7]. As a town on the Lancashire coast, Southport was one of a kind. In 1868, it had 60 small private schools for young ladies, daughters of self-made men. Here the girls could live away from the muck and brass where the money was made and practise domesticity. There were five schools alone in Westcliffe Road, the best part of Birkdale where Elsie boarded in the 1890s.

At Elsie's school, *Dagfield School* for young Ladies, the girls weren't aiming for careers but for polite society. This was the world of the social arts – how to give a dinner party, play music, paint, speak French, dress for fashion. *Dagfield* was run in the late 1880s by the Misses Neary, sisters in their thirties, Mary, Katherine and Frances[viii]. The school had some 50-75 girls from 11-18. The Misses Neary would have set them up in a way of living that lasted the rest of their lives. As another Southport headmistress declared, 'My pupils will never need to *do* anything[ix].'

My sister Ann's school for young ladies was founded in Kent in 1878 by a pioneering clergyman[x]. Great aunts **Annie**, and **Rosie**, whose parents were in India in the 1860s, were at a school in Sydenham just after it started, boarding with seven other girls in a house near the re-sited Crystal Palace[8].

1857 was a seminal year. Not only was it the year that *Tom Brown's Schooldays* was published and *Dulwich College* reformed; it was the year of the Mutiny in India (see Chapter 6) and the year my grandfather **Charles Haskins** was born[9]. It was the year that his father, William Thomas Haskins, became Headmaster at Courteenhall and the year Oxford University introduced a new qualification (below degree level) called the Associate of Arts – one which Charles himself achieved. The idea was to encourage the middle classes like my grandfather Charles to aim higher, even if a degree wasn't needed for a decent job.

Few 'thinking' men needed a university education. Barristers might start there before being trained at the bar. Clergymen often found their calling through Oxford and Cambridge, where daily chapel was a routine and the dons were ordained. Surgeons were beginning to be trained more rigorously at hospitals. Solicitors, bankers, accountants and architects learnt on the job through 'articles', for which they had to pay. Commissions in the armed forces were purchased. For the 'doing' occupations, apprenticeships were the means of entry for most trades, starting at 12-14 years of age, at a third of the cost of 'articles'. As the British Empire grew, demand for boarding education increased. The British Armed Forces was then over double its present size and there was an empire to run. With families accompanying the civil servants overseas, children were sent home to boarding school at the age of eight.

Perhaps the earliest Haskins to go to a boarding school was **Joseph John Haskins**[10]. *Reedham's School* near Croydon was an orphanage in all but name. It had been rebuilt on a new site in 1858 in the Surrey Hills by Rev Andrew Reedham, as an 'Asylum for Fatherless Children'. Joseph John joined the school a decade later, his father having died when he was four. There were 260 orphaned children at the place with him in 1871. Subscribers voted for the children they thought worthiest to attend. With annual visits from the Lord Mayor of London,

Reedham School. Purley, Surrey

---

7. *Bertha Louisa Garden (1877-1955); Elsie Annie Garden (1871-1950) boarded at Dagfield School for Ladies in the 1890s.*

8. *Elizabeth Anne Tresidder (1846-1929), Mary Rosamund Tresidder (1847-1923).*

9. *Charles Haskins AA BA (1857-1934).*

10. *Joseph John Haskins (1859-1917) was son of Joseph John Haskins (1826-1863) the author's great great uncle, brother of William Thomas who you will read about in this chapter. Joseph John Senior died when he was four. Joseph John Junior stayed on in London and worked as a Tram Conductor. He married a French servant working in Bedford, Eugenie Alexandre Ligneau (1857-1944) and they had one daughter.*

Reedham's was well regarded but it was still an orphanage, with candle-lighting and meagre heating. It did not give him much in the way of qualifications. Joseph John did not return to Bedfordshire. He became a London tram driver, living in two rooms which in 1890 cost him 6 shillings a week.

Most of my father's Oxford uncles (Wiggins), like their father, went to *Magdalen College School.* Most of my generation of Wiggins cousins went to minor public schools. My own school, *Dauntsey's,* was a 'Direct Grant' school in the 1960s – the government directly sponsored local pupils to learn alongside fee-paying pupils like me. In my youth, these elderly Oxford uncles were fond of telling me that schooldays would be the happiest of my life. I didn't believe them, of course. Indeed, some of my cousins said their schools were still brutal in the early 1960s, but mine was creative and friendly.

Dauntsey's School was built in a village nestling under the northern scarp of Salisbury Plain. It had a generous and gentle ambiance; like its landscape setting it had wide horizons and a pastoral outlook. Quirkily, we wore shorts all the year round, like Prince's Charles's school *Gordonstoun;* in the 1930s, the staff had done the same[11]. The boys had done practical things like making the bed frames and the dining room tables. They'd levelled a field to make a hockey pitch, filling old railway trucks with earth and trundling them along old railway lines, emptying the earth on the other side of the slope[xi]. We picked potatoes in the fields, for *Dauntsey's* had been an agricultural school, primarily for farmers' sons. In the 1960s it still had its own farm producing milk and bacon.

Whilst some schools of my era were Spartan, mine was Athenian. Nowadays the emphasis is on indoor swimming pools and en-suite study rooms, luxuries never considered in the days of dormitories and discipline.

Dauntsey's School, which the author attended, started in this building in 1553. In 1895, with Mercers Company funding, it was moved to a larger site.

Versatility, adaptability, co-operation, service – these were all the elements that had marked [Dauntsey's] out as an individual place, free from the dead hand of privilege and tradition

Hodges p6

The Victorian School

One schoolmaster who seems to have got it right was my great grandfather, **William Thomas Haskins**, seen right with his wife Elizabeth. William Thomas, as he'll be called in this book to differentiate him from other Williams in the family, wanted to be a teacher but got off to a false start. For one reason or another, among them the state of the family's finances, his father arranged an apprenticeship for him to be a tailor, like his younger brother, Joseph John.

William Thomas was apprenticed to a John Dunkley. Dunkley lived at Wootton, near Northampton, a centre of lace-making. Practically all the women in the village, population 750, made lace. Dunkley also had property interests and encouraged William Thomas to take up country pursuits. One day, at the age of 16, when he was out bird-scaring, William Thomas was involved in a shooting accident. The gun exploded when it shouldn't. He had to walk the three miles, holding his injured limb, spouting blood like a fountain, to the Northampton Infirmary, where he watched while the doctor amputated his left hand above the wrist without an anaesthetic. There were few prosthetics in those days so he was given a hook, as per Abu Qatadar, or Captain Hook of the Peter Pan story – all a bit too near the knuckle.

Tailoring was not possible with one hand, so William Thomas asked if there was a chance to follow his chosen profession. Dunkley felt a bit responsible. He sought an opportunity for him to train to teach at the National School in Bedford[xii].

By the age of 25, William Thomas had not only trained as a teacher, he was both married and the Master of a little Church School near his wife's family's home, Overseal, Ashby-de-la-Zouch, where he stayed until 1855. At the age of 32, he was made headmaster of the

Mr & Mrs W T Haskins

11. *Charles Philip Arthur George, Prince of Wales (b1948).*

This sampler, by Elizabeth Whitehead is dated March 1837, and now in Northamptonshire Rcords Office. Stitched when she was 9 years old, it portrays the last verse of a popular 1818 hymn by James Montgomery, with the last line changed:

O Thou, by whom we come to God
The Life, the Truth, the Way;
The path of prayer Thyself hast trod:
Lord, teach us how to pray!

The Old Schoolhouse, Courteenhall – schoolroom on the right, headmaster's house on the left

Courteenhall Grammar School's most famous Headmaster

Grammar School in the grounds of Courteenhall, having previously taught at St Sepulchre's Northampton, which is where Sir Charles Wake knew of him[12].   He became Courteenhall's most famous headmaster

In August 2013, the present owner of Courteenhall, the 14th Baronet Sir Hereward Wake invited me to see where my great grandfather lived and taught[13].   I tingled all over as I was given coffee in the very house where my Grandfather was born. Sir Hereward and Lady Wake handed on the large Georgian seat of the Wakes to their son for tax reasons (and he to his son). They modernised and enlarged the School House and which was to be their home of choice for many years. Sir Hereward was in his nineties when I met him. He took the trouble of scrubbing up my great-grandfather's grave the day before I arrived. They showed me all round their beautiful estate.

William Thomas and Elizabeth Haskins lived a bit like squires themselves in their time. The school and the school house were set in a Repton landscape near the big mansion[14].   They must have been invited to the grand house on more than one occasion and would have taken care to imitate the manners, customs, speech and dress of the gentry. This must have helped succeeding generations of Haskins' gain an entry into a higher class of society, having the confidence to say what you choose to say without offence, to play around with the rules, to command respect and to give orders in some sort of effortless way, employing ever so gentle speech and manners. Their schoolhouse had an imposing front door, a baronial staircase and two floors of bedrooms. The attic, where the junior boarders lived, was only accessible through these bedrooms so, as Lady Wake observed, Elizabeth would have had full command over all the boarders' welfare.

Elizabeth was well liked. "One of the sweetest and most loveable of her kind," said the Rector, Rev Archie Wake[xiii].   "One of the most genial and kind-hearted friends we shall ever meet;" "No word that can be said would be too good for such a woman. A better wife no man ever had and a kinder mother could not be found nor a better friend to everybody," said another[xiv].

Writing after Elizabeth's death, some friends recalled their visits to Courteenhall: "I felt I had lost a relation and one whom I had a great regard for. How often I used to fancy I could hear her pleasant hearty laugh – the laugh we heard frequently at Whitsuntide during the almost annual visit. What agreeable times they were! How I looked forward to that holiday season. She gave me a thoroughly warm welcome and was so cordial in all that she did – nothing seemed a trouble if it could add to her visitors' comfort[xv]."

The Wake family is one of the few families to hold onto their possessions since the Norman Conquest. The first Hereward the Wake ('the Watchful') goes down in history as the first 'Robin Hood'. From a base in the Fens, he led a war of resistance against William the Conqueror for five years until defeated in 1071. His resistance was the most prolonged of any, and not until William had defeated him could he call himself 'Conqueror'. He found refuge in Cornwall[xvi].

It is not clear whether the Wakes were Anglo-Saxons, Danes or even Normans. Some say Hereward the Wake was the son of Earl Leofric, who was married to Lady Godiva, who rode naked through the streets of Coventry to make her husband lower the taxes. Others think that he was the son of Asketil (any relation?) a prominent Anglo-Danish magnate – the Danes had been rulers of the East of England up to Edward the Confessor's reign, i.e. only 30 years before the Norman Conquest. On the other hand, the Wake family might have simply been trying to foster good connections to increase their popularity after being granted land by William the Conqueror.

---

12. *Sir Charles Wake Bt (1791-1864), 10th Baronet [NR].*

13. *Sir Hereward Wake Bt MC (1916-2017),, 14th Baronet [NR] married Julia Rosemary Lees (b1931) [NR] in 1952.*

14. *Humphrey Repton (1752-1818) [NR] – this was one of his first. The stables were by John Carr (1723-1807) [NR] from the part of Yorkshire where I live, architect of Harewood House and Wood Hall, Linton.*

Whatever happened then, their connections are still good now. They have made some impact on British history (the odd General, Admiral and Archbishop). The eldest son is still called Hereward to this day[xvii]. Indeed, the joke is that their Lord's Prayer goes as follows: "Our father, who art in heaven, Hereward be thy name…" The Wakes took on the present estate not long before William Thomas's grammar school was built in 1670s.

Courteenhall Grammar School was a small-scale grammar school for local boys. It was similar to the old *Dulwich College*, or the old *Dauntsey's School* near the West Lavington church in Wiltshire. By the time that I went to *Dauntsey's* in 1962, it had been on a new site for seventy years[xviii]. Like *Dulwich*, it had grown to accommodate over 400 boys. Courteenhall didn't.

Courteenhall School was founded under a 1672 bequest of £500 in the will of Sir Samuel Jones. He was a merchant, MP and Colonel, who had acquired the estate in 1647 in the middle of the Commonwealth period. His great nephew, Samuel Jones, a Wake who had had to change his name to inherit, completed the school building in 1680. It was the charitable thing to do, to give thanks to God for your blessings – even better to do it after your death, when you don't need the money!

Elizabeth Whitehead (1828-1892)

For about 220 years, the Grammar School provided a free education for 30-50 local boys aged 10 to 17 years old, sons of farmers and business people. It covered the twelve nearby parishes, including Blisworth. The older boys walked or came by pony. The boys received a fine education including Latin and Greek. My largely self-taught great-grandfather also offered Scripture and Divinity (two separate subjects), French, pure and applied Maths, Drawing and Design, Book-keeping, Land surveying, Science and Chemistry and something called 'Entropius', which was about character-building, I imagine[xix].

"This home to the Muses" giving free education to young men four miles around the neighbourhood, this Samuel Jones Knight, a munificent patron of letters, has richly endowed. Henry Edmunds and Francis Crane Esq have together faithfully completed his wishes. AD 1680.

There was just one large schoolroom, with a raised seat for the schoolmaster at one end. The assistant master, or usher, sat at the other. This was the norm – *Rugby's* schoolroom was just larger. On each side were benches (or 'forms') for the boys. The little boys sat in the front. We talk of 'forms' today (e.g. 'sixth form'). The word originates from these benches. Boys moved up from the first form to the sixth form as they became more proficient. In 1846, a system of trained pupil teachers was introduced and one such was my grandfather **Charles** who started when he was not yet 14 years old.

Latterly the schoolroom was used as an elementary school. It is preserved in its original mode by a charity and used for community functions. It still has its original furnishings. A photograph of our ancestor, **William Thomas** hangs on the wall. He must have been a well-read person if he knew classics. All three daughters learnt to play the village church organ[xx]. A government commission reported in 1868 that the standard of education was higher than elementary schools[xxi]. All the Haskins have been good at Maths and this comes from William Thomas. He was the church Treasurer and in 1864, he was appointed Treasurer of the General Associated Body of Church Schoolmasters in England and Wales.

He must have cut quite an impressive figure as headmaster, with his red face, long beard, wooden arm and long iron hook[xxii]. Though a man of kindly eye, seeking the best for everyone, it must have been the ultimate terror to misbehave, to be held by the neck with his hook and cuffed with his other hand. Good behaviour was a definite requirement.

William Thomas was a man of many parts, an all-rounder, interested in everything, something they frown on these days. I was marked down in a 1978 fast stream civil service interview for being too much of a 'dilettante'. 'Polymath' I'd call it – isn't that a compliment? (It didn't help me pass). My son Jonathan wonders if Leonardo da Vinci isn't the greatest human of all time for his innovative lateral thinking[15]. His latest hero is Elon Musk, a South African who made his money on Zip2 and PayPal software. Musk now lives in the USA designing zero-emission cars (Teslas) that go faster than Aston Martins, hydrogen batteries to power your home, hovering rockets a tenth of the cost of NASA's, and levitating hyperloop trains which could travel from Birmingham

Schoolroom, Courteenhall Grammar School

15. *Leonardo di ser Piero da Vinci (1452-1519) [NR].*

The School House, c1898

It had long since come to my attention that people of accomplishment rarely sat back and let things happen to them. They went out and happened to things.

Leonardo da Vinci

to London in 8 minutes (eat your heart out HS2)[xxiii]. Like these men, my sons and I like to think 'outside the box'. Not that we'll reach the heights of Leonardo or Elon Musk, but we have the same dreams.

As well as the range of talents that he displayed in the classroom, William Thomas did other things. He carried out land surveys for the parish. He took some of the boys with him in order to give them practical experience. He put his hand to architecture. He had a beautiful cursive script. He looked after the church accounts. He even helped the villagers to draw up their wills [xxiv].

When William Thomas Haskins died, however, the school was in a decrepit condition [xxv]. The Wake finances had suffered severely from the agricultural depression – estate workers were being laid off all over the place and Sir Hereward even gave up his London Club memberships [xxvi]. With the 1870 Education Act giving powers to a local Board of Education, a decision was taken to close it. Hereward[16] Wake wrote to Charles (my grandfather) who was a teacher at Eastbourne at the time, imploring him to take it on, but it was not to be[xxvii]. It would have been a drain on resources to bring it up to standard, the pay would not have been high, and numbers had dwindled.

William Thomas and Elizabeth were highly thought of. Their gravestone was given pride of place, situated directly outside the south porch of St Peter's Church, Courteenhall where the family had worshipped throughout. In 1851, a hundred out of the 127 population in Courteenhall regularly attended church.

✳ ✳ ✳ ✳

St Peter's Courteenhall, with Elizabeth and William's gravestone near the north porch

Outside St Peter's North door

Same grave 100 years later

---

[16]. *Sir Hereward Wake (1876-1963), 13th Baronet [NR]*

Waiting for the Executioner

My father was sketchy about his family. He mentioned an uncle or two, one who took him sailing in the Blackwater estuary off the Essex coast and one who went to Wales. There was an engineering factory, someone in the motor trade and a cousin called **Minnie Louise Haskins**, who wrote the poem, *The Gate of the Year*, which George VI used in his Christmas broadcast in 1939 after the outbreak of the Second World War[xxviii].

Essentially all this is true except for Minnie[17]. She was no relation. I've traced her family back to 1781 in a place called Warmley, near Keynsham, outside Bristol. Her father made a success of manufacturing drainage pipes on an industrial scale, and she was brought up in a comfortable Georgian house, Warmley House, which is now a care home. Minnie had a good education, which enabled her to pursue an academic career in London – the London School of Economics – but she was no relation of mine.

William Thomas and Elizabeth had three girls and four boys. Apart from the two eldest children, George and Lucie, who were born in Overseal, his first school, the rest were born at Courteenhall. The girls' names all end with 'ie' which was the usual style in those days. My grandfather Charlie or Charles was the second son, the first to be born at Courteenhall. He was the third child.

The eldest, **George Haskins** started life as a gardener (see Chapter 9), first at Kensington Gardens and then at Stowe – two prestigious locations, possibly introduced to him by friends of Sir Hereward Wake[18]. Whilst in London, he met and married Elizabeth Ballingall. Elizabeth's father had moved from Scotland to London as a baker and met Elizabeth's mother from Shadwell[19].

George and Elizabeth had three children. The eldest, **Nellie Haskins**, married an ironmonger's son, **Alfred Hartwell**, from Bourton-on-the-Water, whose ambitions outstripped those of his brothers'[20]. Alfred founded Hartwell's Motor Sales after the First World War, in Park End Road Oxford, between Nuffield College and the railway station. Still going today, long after he died in the 1950s, Hartwell plc now has 29 dealerships across 14 sites, from Abingdon to Grimsby. The inter-war years were a good period to make a fortune in the car trade. Oxford grew from strength to strength on the back of Lord Nuffield's Morris plant at Cowley. Maybe this is why I and others in the family have a love of impressive cars. My father owned a large bull-nosed Morris early on.

Once George had secured the position of Head Gardener at Stowe, his brother **Frank Haskins**, eleven years younger, found a job as an Estate Clerk, living with George and Elizabeth until he married in 1893. The two brothers ran Stowe for nearly twenty years. In 1889, when the third Duke died leaving no direct heirs, the house had no real future[21].

George must have decided it was time to move his family to Cardiff and set up a factory making mineral water with whatever gratuity he'd been given[xxix]. He and his son Charles Haskins

'Waiting for the Executioner'. The last time all the siblings were together in the house where they were raised. With William Thomas Haskins's death in 1898, the house was no longer theirs. This photo, shows his children: Frank, Lucie (Mrs Perkins), George, Annie, Arthur, Bessie (Mrs Berry), and Charles, the author's grandfather

I said to a man who stood at the gate of the year, 'Give me a light that I may tread safely into the unknown', and he replied, 'Go out into the darkness and put your hand into the hand of God. That shall be to you better than a light and safer than a known way!'

Christmas card 1940 from the British Consulate in Detroit – from Arthur and Rosemary (neé Tresidder) Bray

William Thomas Haskins with his granddaughter Nellie

---

17. *Minnie Louise Haskins (1885-1957) [NR] left Bristol to become a lecturer at the London School of Economics, dying single, in the place she made her home, Crowborough. Her poem is inscribed on the resting place of George VI and his wife Elizabeth (the Queen Mother) at St George's Chapel, Windsor.*

18. *George Haskins (1851-1915) married Elizabeth Ballingall (1855-1915) in 1879 and had three children: Charles, Nellie and Alice. Charles set sail from Bristol for Montreal on 31 May 1911 on SS Royal Edward (2nd class).*

19. *Alexander Ballingall (1820-1906) married Ellen Freeman (1830-1909) in 1854.*

20. *Nellie Haskins (1880-1951) married Alfred Reginald Hartwell (1876-1955) in 1905.*

21. *Richard Plantagenet Campbell Temple-Nugent-Brydges-Chandos-Grenville, 3rd Duke of Buckingham and Chandos GCSI PC DL (1823-1889) [NR].*

Impressive cars, thanks in part to Hartwell's of Oxford. Paul Haskins 1930 with his bull-nosed Morris, aged 25

Annie Haskins on the stage

made a go of it until Charles emigrated in 1911. By that time, George and Elizabeth were ensconced in a nice house on the embankment of the river Taff with a view down to the river.

Frank stayed on at Stowe, having married a school-teacher, a tailor's daughter from Northampton, and moved to an estate cottage at nearby Dadford where they had three children[22]. He attached himself to a local estate agent and continued to supervise *Stowe Park*[23]. Between 1903 and 1919, he was Secretary of the Oxford & Aylesbury Tramroad Company which had been started in 1870 by the Duke of Buckingham to link up his estate. After the Duke and then his nephew died, the company never succeeded in bringing the railway as far as Oxford[xxx]. Probably just as well, for they planned to knock down buildings at the end of Oxford's attractive High Street and build a terminus; the line would have crossed unspoilt water meadows. The part of the line that had been built was closed in 1935.

Lucie Haskins married **George Perkins,** a master butcher[24]. Like her sisters, Lucie learnt to play the organ and played for Courteenhall church. Her organ playing is what people most remember. For over 35 years she played at Blisworth church, the village near Courteenhall where they had set up their butcher's shop in the 1880s[xxxi]. She played well and sang out loud to her own accompaniment. "Often at a winter service she would spread her handkerchiefs out across the keys of the organ to keep her fingers from direct contact with the cold 'ivories'.[xxxii]"

Bessie played the Courteenhall organ after Lucie married and moved to Blisworth. She in turn wed **Fred Berry,** a 'collector' (hire purchase representative) for Singer sewing machines, and had eight children[25]. From Acton in North London they moved to New Sawley, in Derbyshire. Fred tried his hand at a variety of jobs from cycle finishing to lace-frame fitting but, ultimately, all reverted to the clothing trade – their boys starting in the lace industry.

Annie was the centre of her parents' world in their last years at Courteenhall, helping her father with the school[26]. She had the womanly skills to create a home after her mother died. She knew how to dress and look the part. She took a large part in village life, putting on two plays with her brother Arthur at the Rectory Lecture Room in 1887: *Cut Off with a Shilling*, a farce was 'played uncommonly well and Miss Haskins well merited the plaudits she received from a crowded and thoroughly appreciative 'house'. Arthur, in his double part of the Colonel and Sam, was 'quite inimitable'[xxxiii]. There was a prologue and epilogue, which they'd composed especially, and the whole thing went down a storm with the audience wanting more. In May, *The Blue Coat and Brass Buttons* gave similar pleasure, and they announced that a festive gathering was to take place to celebrate Queen Victoria's Golden Jubilee.

The high point of life in many a villager's memory was the Golden Jubilee celebrations, something happening right round the country in 1887. In the Barley Sheaf in Gorran, Cornwall, there is a large poster advertising a similar event some years later, but the Golden Jubilee was the memorable first. Courteenhall was no exception. Sixteen year old Arthur came third in the Obstacle Race and second in Throwing the Cricket Ball. In the evening, the Rectory Gardens were lit up with Chinese lanterns, the fernery with fairy lights and a candle was lit in every window in the village which made the place truly magical. Refreshed by a good supper,

22. *Frank Haskins (1862-1945) married Turville Edith Watts (1873-1945) in 1893 and had three children Frances Marion Haskins (1894-1959), William Frank Haskins (1900-1986) and Elizabeth Turville Haskins (1906-1989).*

23. *In 1915 Frank is entitled Assistant Overseer.*

24. *Lucie Haskins (1855-1931) married George Frederick Perkins (1856-1934) in 1878.*

25. *Bessie Haskins (1859-1930) married Frederick Berry (1854-1922) in 1881 and had 8 children: Herbert Berry (b1885), Percy C Berry (b1887), Winifred A Berry (b1887), Gladys Berry (1889), Harold Berry (1892) Doris Bessie Berry (b1898) and Eva Ballingall Berry (b1900) [this last middle name was Bessie's brother George's wife's surname].*

26. *Annie Haskins (1866-1947).*

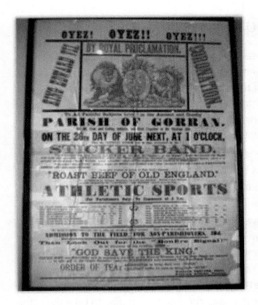

the dancing commenced, which 'kept up till a late hour, owing to the spirited playing of Miss Haskins – one of the happiest days ever spent.'

Arthur was the last boy to leave home[27]. Aged 20, he applied for a number of jobs and eventually got one which took him first to Cambridgeshire and then Essex as a mechanical engineer. He moved to Chelmsford where he joined the Hoffman Manufacturing Company at Chelmsford, starting out as an engineering draughtsman. He found lodgings at St John's Cottage in St John's Road, with a Cornish lady, Ethel Macpherson and her two children. He stayed with her for the rest of his life[28]. He never married. He worked his way up to the top as works manager, no small feat. In its heyday, Hoffman's employed 7,500 staff over a 50 acre site – it was a larger operation than Marconi, the other major employer in the town.

The Hoffman factory became crucial to the war effort. This was the Britain's first ball bearing manufacturer, not a riveting profession you might say but, in its day, it was as ground-breaking for communication, as the internet is today. It achieved world-wide recognition for the precision with which it manufactured its products, which were snapped up all over the world. It could boast an accuracy of 1/10,000th of an inch which was going something in 1900.

The ball bearings were used by most vehicles and machinery coming on to the market. This was especially important in the First World War, which was won largely through its tanks. With that and another member of my family responsible for the armour plating, recalled in Chapter 2, you could say we at least helped to win the war.

As Arthur improved his standard of living, he and Ethel moved out into the country to some fancy houses – *Hammonds* in Little Baddow, *Hillside* in Springfield Road and *Hatchmans Farm* in Woodham Walter near Maldon. His brother **Charles**, my grandfather, moved to Essex to be near him. His sister Annie faded from view. The photograph which she called 'Waiting for the Executioner' (Page 55) was the last record we have of her life.

✳ ✳ ✳ ✳

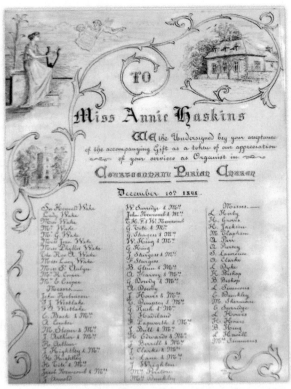

A token of appreciation for Annie Haskins when she ceased to be Organist at Courteenhall, with hand drawings of St Peter's Church, the Schoolhouse and the muse of music

Arthur Haskins (1877-1947)

---

27. *Arthur Haskins MBE (1877-1947).*
28. *Ethel Jane Macpherson née James (1882-1975?) [NR] of Cornish parents was from Madron.*

New College, Eastbourne 1873-1907

Cameron House, Leatherhead c1900

White House in Bridge Street, Witham, is now called Bridge House.

Charles goes into teaching

My grandfather Charles, William Thomas's second son, following his father into teaching was the first Haskins to graduate with a degree, albeit at the age of 27, after studying in his own time. After helping his father as a 'pupil teacher', he studied at *Abington House School* in Northampton, where he secured the Associate of Arts qualification at the age of 18. He matriculated to the University of London at the age of 20, did two years as an intern student and then studied part-time, graduating in 1884[xxxiv].

Charles found a teaching job at New College, Eastbourne[xxxv]. *New College* had been built on land near Compton Place Road, which was being developed by the Davies Gilbert family. They also owned Trelissick, beside the King Harry Ferry on the River Fal in Cornwall, which is now a popular tourist spot run by the National Trust[29].

New College, a public school taking-in over 135 boys, was run by Frederic Schreiner, eldest brother of the sensational author Olive Schreiner[30]. Frederick was seventeen years Charles's senior. Son of a missionary, Schreiner, had studied, like Charles, part-time at London University[31]. He'd married a girl he'd met whilst teaching at Taunton and moved to Northampton to be near her parents, where he taught at Clevedon College[xxxvi]. It was probable that here he met the Haskins family and this may have encouraged Charles to take the same route.

Charles must have been impressive enough for Schreiner to remember him from his Northampton days, once *New College* was established in 1873. He offered Charles a job in about 1879, before the young man had finished his own studies. They worked together for 20 years, Charles being appointed Second Master. Then in 1897/8 three events shook up his life. He married **Dora Wiggins** and within months his father died and Schreiner retired. It was the end of an era and the start of another.

Maybe the stress of the new life was too much for Dora. She took to her bed at regular intervals – including during her father-in-law's funeral; maybe she felt isolated or her clever charm was not working. *New College* wasn't a success under the new Head; Dora couldn't wait to start a new life somewhere else. The masters and pupils clubbed together to buy Charles and Dora a silver tray as a 'token of esteem' when they left. The Haskins's acquired *Cameron House* in Church Street, Leatherhead [32]. *New College* limped along for a few more years, to 1904 (seniors) 1907 (juniors) until *Eastbourne College* bought the site, used the playing fields and leased the buildings to a Prep School[xxxvii].

Dora was good at short-term spending: any money Charles had inherited would have quickly been swallowed up on *Cameron House*, and she soon splashed out on a separate house for the family[xxxviii]. Why Leatherhead? Neither of them knew the place and there was no family nearby. It was not like his father's old school at Courteenhall, with a benevolent patron, where Charles had been so happy[xxxix]. Charles was good with people but I am less certain about his business acumen. Dora was better at spending than saving.

---

29. Carew Davies Gilbert (1852-1913) [NR] was linked to the ancient Cornish Carew family through his mother. He did much to develop what is now a National Trust house and gardens using the money he made from developing Eastbourne into a coastal resort. He also supported the building of a number of schools and colleges in the Eastbourne area.

30. Olive Emilie Albertina Schreiner (1855–1920) [NR] was well before her time with her book The Story of a South African Farm which broke all sorts of conventions; it addressed issues such as faith, race, feminism, premarital sex and transvestitism.

31. Frederic Samuel Schreiner BA (1841-1901) [NR] was twenty-eight when he gained his BA in 1869, matriculating 6 years earlier when at the Wesleyan School Taunton.

32. 33 Church Street, Leatherhead.

By September 1911, Charles was attracted by a business proposition near his brother Arthur, in Essex. He bought a quarter share in the *White House*, a school in Witham, with two others, from a chap who was emigrating to Australia. They didn't check the finances, and legal wrangles dogged them for the next couple of years[xl]. Charles was titular headmaster and drew a salary – or that at least was the idea. The school in Bridge Street had one large school room at the back – the pupils were made to enter by a step ladder. It was not as palatial as Cameron House or his father's school in Courteenhall. By now he was probably regretting rejecting the Wake offer but he stuck it out until his children, my father Paul (see Chapter 16) and Nancy, were grown up.

The schoolroom was entered by a ladder

Charles Haskins sitting on the left, c1919, with Paul Wand (Paul Haskins's cousin – see Chapter 18) bottom left

✳ ✳ ✳ ✳

The Legacy of William Thomas Haskins

William Thomas Haskins had been the first Haskins to teach but he was not the last. As well as his son Charles following in his footsteps, Charles's daughter, my aunt Nancy, trained to teach and found a teaching job in Derbyshire before she married. My sister Ann had inclinations that way but my father wasn't keen. She joined Evans Bros, a publishing house which specialised in children's education and brought home wonderful posters which she put up in my bedroom, a great inspiration to me.

I taught Religious Education (RE) at *Chadwell Comprehensive School* in Essex for two and half years but I gave it up as a bad job and joined the civil service. I ran a church youth club in Petts Wood during the 1970/80s. Called the *Young '70s* (later *'80s*), I had to disillusion some old folk who thought the club was for them! We went on a number of camps, weekends away and outings, all infinitely memorable.

I married into a family which has become involved in education. My mother-in-law taught adults in Barnsley. Her aunt Kitty had trained at Whiteland's College in Chelsea and taught in the Walworth Road near the Elephant and Castle[33].

Youth Club with the Bishop of Rochester, David Say c1980. Author on the left

Young '70s Camp in Fawkham Green, Kent
The author sitting centre and his nephew
Simon Gates 4th from the right

School Bell – from
Charles's schools,
possibly his father's

My brother-in-law Michael Burton has taught psychology and his wife Margaret is currently Deputy Head of a special school in Huddersfield[34]. Their daughter Lois is teaching in north-west London[35].

Education helped my grandfather step up in life. For many in the 20th century, the display of certificates and photographs of someone at a graduation ceremony on the parlour wall was hugely symbolic, an escape from the social backdrop they'd been born into.

For some then, schooldays are the happiest. Pupils of William Thomas Haskins remembered their time at Courteenhall throughout their lives. As one ex-pupil said thirty years later, in a letter to my great aunt Annie:

"Thirty years is a long time… yet it is close upon that time since I left the old grammar school. I shall always, however, have very kindly feelings and remembrances of the days spent there – I feel what success I have met with in after-life is partly due to the excellent training received under your father as a lad. I can well remember not only the excellent book knowledge that all of we boys received but also the truly patriotic moral and upright principles which were instilled in to us, truth, loyalty and duty being strong planks in your father's programme of education. He not only endeavoured to teach us to be clever lads but upright and true also." [xli]

✳ ✳ ✳ ✳

---

34. *Michael Ian Burton BA (b1960) married Margaret Aspinall BEd MEd (b1962) in 1985.*
35. *Lois Margaret Burton BEd (b1993).*

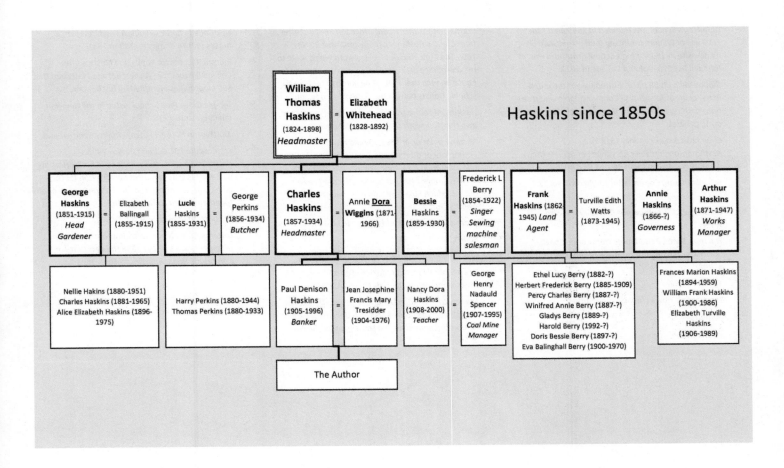

Haskins since 1850s

Family tree:

William Thomas Haskins (1824-1898) *Headmaster* = Elizabeth Whitehead (1828-1892)

Children:
- George Haskins (1851-1915) *Head Gardener* = Elizabeth Ballingall (1855-1915)
- Lucie Haskins (1855-1931) = George Perkins (1856-1934) *Butcher*
- Charles Haskins (1857-1934) *Headmaster* = Annie **Dora** Wiggins (1871-1966)
- Bessie Haskins (1859-1930) = Frederick L Berry (1854-1922) *Singer Sewing machine salesman*
- Frank Haskins (1862-1945) *Land Agent* = Turville Edith Watts (1873-1945)
- Annie Haskins (1866-?) *Governess*
- Arthur Haskins (1871-1947) *Works Manager*

Grandchildren:
- Nellie Hakins (1880-1951), Charles Haskins (1881-1965), Alice Elizabeth Haskins (1896-1975)
- Harry Perkins (1880-1944), Thomas Perkins (1880-1933)
- Paul Denison Haskins (1905-1996) *Banker* = Jean Josephine Francis Mary Tresidder (1904-1976)
- Nancy Dora Haskins (1908-2000) *Teacher* = George Henry Nadauld Spencer (1907-1995) *Coal Mine Manager*
- Ethel Lucy Berry (1882-?), Herbert Frederick Berry (1885-1909), Percy Charles Berry (1887-?), Winifred Annie Berry (1887-?), Gladys Berry (1889-?), Harold Berry (1992-?), Doris Bessie Berry (1897-?), Eva Balinghall Berry (1900-1970)
- Frances Marion Haskins (1894-1959), William Frank Haskins (1900-1986), Elizabeth Turville Haskins (1906-1989)

The Author

Other Notes and References

i. Best p14.

ii. The 1842 Act preventing boys under 10 going down coal mines was raised to 12 years under the Coal Mines Regulation Act of 1860.

iii. Proposed by Sir Stafford Northcote (1818-1887) [NR] and Sir Charles Trevelyan (1807-1886) [NR], an Order in Council 21 May 1855 introduced recruitment by exam, in a hierarchy of grades – administrative, executive and clerical – and promotion on merit.

iv. Originally, the Society of Teachers, in 1849 it was granted a Royal Charter. In 1998 it was renamed the College of Teachers. Kitty Morley neé Grant was an Associate.

v. Picard p27.

vi. Elementary Education Act 1870 established schooling for all children between 5 and 13 years, in England and Wales.

vii. Bertie aged 14 is shown living in Blackheath in April with Bertie's half sister Margaret in 1891; Jean Josephine Frances Mary Tresidder (1904-1976) attended the High School 1913-24. Her half-sister Margaret Jane Garden, who married John Jekyn Cooper, a mining engineer, in 1879 lived at 31 Shooters Hill, on the edge of Blackheath.

viii. In 1876. Unequal Educational Provision in England and Wales p243. In the 1871 census, Netherfield School is at 23 Westcliffe and Dagfield School at 24 Westcliffe Road. By 1891 they appear to have combined. Elsie's received a medal from the Misses Neary of Dagfield School. In 1891 Census the Misses Neary are resident at the Netherfield premises. Dagfield was still going, under different hands, during the Second World War.

ix. Marsden pp241, 233.

x. www.goudhurstlocalhistorysociety.org. Goudhurst Ladies' College started as Mount Villa in 1878, it moved to the Goudhurst site in 1882. In wartime it moved to Charnes House, Eccleshall 1940-46 and then to Doddington Hall, Nantwich, from 1946, closing in 1985. Rebecca Kendon (1862-1957) [NR] was headmistress from 1883-1950. Her father, Rev Joseph Kendon (1830-1903) [NR] had first founded Bethany School for boys and girls in 1866.

xi. Dauntseian. Spring 1965: Manor dining tables: Summer term 1930; Warrington Playing Field: 1938-45.

xii. Bedford Records Office Ref HT 3/7: Minutes of a meeting of the Harpur Trust held on 3 Sep 1840: 'A person of the name of Dunkley attended this meeting and stated that his apprentice William Haskins had met with a serious accident by the explosion of a gun by which the amputation of his hand had become [necessary] and requesting the Trustees allow him attend the National School at Bedford for a year with a view of qualifying for the situation of a Teacher or some other trade for which the loss of his hand would not incapacitate him. Resolved that the apprentice be allowed to attend the National School for the above purpose providing the Mayor should be paid upon inquiry that the statement of the master is correct but the manner of supporting him during the year be left to the master and the father of the boy.'

xiii. Letters of condolence Northamptonshire Records Office Ref X6838. 13 Apr 1892. Rev Archibald James Wake (1856-1925) [NR].

xiv. Letters of condolence Northamptonshire Records Office Ref X6828. Thomas Gardiner [NR], 10 Nov 1892; John Haskins. Leighton Buzzard, 6 Apr 1892.

xv. Letters of condolence Northamptonshire Records Office Ref X6828. I Richardson [NR] of 114 Highbury New Park. 4 June 1892.

xvi. The Children's Encyclopaedia Vol 6 p3831.

xvii. My father used to speak of Joan Wake MA (1884-1974) [NR], the present Baronet's great aunt, who did much to curate 1,000 years of the Wake archives and to provide the basis of the Northamptonshire Records Office.

i. *Dauntsey's School was founded in 1553 under the 1542 will of William Dauntsey (and established on its new site in 1895), King's School Grantham was founded in 1528, Dulwich College in 1613.*

ii. *Gibbon Vol 5 Ch 32 p372. Entropius was a eunuch in the court of Arcadius at Constantinople who rose from nothing to become a Roman magistrate and army general.*

iii. *Churchwarden's accounts 1818-73. Northamptonshire Records Office Ref 86P/79 The daughters between them earned £4 a year.*

iv. *Schools Inquiry Commission 1868 xxxvii, Vol 12 p331.*

v. *Gordon p223. Photographs from Sir Hereward Wake.*

vi. *The High Speed 2 train route from London to the North was in consultation stage at the time of writing.*

vii. *Gordon p222.*

viii. *The estate is now in first class condition.*

ix. *Gordon p213.*

x. *Northamptonshire Record Office Ref X6828. Letter from Charles Haskins to his sister Annie 20 Nov 1898 'Did I tell you that Mr Hereward Wake wrote to me a very nice little note? He evidently seemed to house an idea that I might be going to take on the school. Dora is better now, I am pleased to say.'*

xi. *Haskins, M Louise p9; the opening lines are etched into the stonework of St George's Chapel, Windsor.*

xii. *At some point after 1891, George moved to 34 Taff Embankment Grangetown Cardiff, a newly built bijou Victorian residence overlooking the river. Later he moved 100 yards down the road to 28 Blaenclydach Street with an even better position over the Taff.*

xiii. *Jones p52. Bucks Herald 16 Aug 1911, 14 May 1919.*

xiv. *Kelly's Directory 1890.*

xv. *Freeston, Part II, Issue 111.*

xvi. *Courteenhall Parish Magazine. Feb and Jun 1887. Northamptonshire Records Office ZA3937.*

xvii. *University of London General Register. The author was 31 when he gained his Open University degree. Ken Burton gained his the same year, at the age of 56.*

xviii. *New College had 136 boys, 8 teaching staff, 2 nurses and 14 domestic staff in 1881.*

xix. *Alumni Records for Pupils and Masters - New College Eastbourne   A Short Selected List from the 500 biographies identified by Bill Bowden.*

xx. *Temple Grove Prep School lasted in the New Hall buildings until 1935.*

xxi. *Dartington House, Linden Gardens, Leatherhead.*

xxii. *Letters dated 31 Oct and 20 Nov 1898, Northamptonshire Record Office. Charles Haskins wrote to his sister Annie of his affection for the place and how happy they had all been once again together at their father's funeral.*

xxiii. *Chelmsford Chronicle, 9 May 1913.*

xxiv. *Letter of Condolence Northamptonshire Record Office Ref X6828 27 Oct 1898 from Mr Graty of Cambridge Road, Bromley to Annie Haskins.*

Oxford Life

Watlington lies at the foot of the Chiltern Hills, a chalky ridge that stretches diagonally across Oxfordshire. At the bottom of this scarp lies the small market town, with a Town Hall and church. At the end of Hill Road lies the White Mark, cut into the hillside, where the Wiggins family took their constitutional strolls[i]. The traffic these days clogs up the main street, as it has become a rat-run off the M40. Residents, including the current occupants of *Hill House*, have campaigned to ban the lorries.

There's a tenuous Cornish connection to Watlington – in 1307-12 & 1331-5, the Manor was owned by two successive Earls of Cornwall and Wallingford – one being the notorious favourite and lover of Edward II, Piers Gaveston.   When Henry VIII died he left it to his daughter Elizabeth I but her successor King James sold it off in small lots to raise money. By 1664, the rights and privileges of 'Lord of the Manor' were held by **Thomas Wiggins** of Clare who sold it by public subscription to build a Town Hall[ii].   Thomas was one of my many **Wiggins** ancestors[1].

The Wiggins family goes back in Watlington to 1530 and before. They remained in the place for four centuries. In my father Paul's childhood, his aunts, uncles and cousins used to stay there in the long hot summer holidays. He said the farming life was best portrayed in Flora Thompson's *Lark Rise to Candleford*. Every village household had its own chickens and pig, which they'd fatten up with the potato peelings and left-overs. It was one of self-reliance and cooperation. A simple life, satisfying most. There was no sense of injustice; the better-off helped the needy. They lived near the bone but, they said, "The nearer the bone, the sweeter the meat."[iii]

Thomas Wiggins lived in the hamlet of Clare nearby – one of Paul's uncles was named Clare. By the time of **William Wiggins**, my great grandfather, there were three farms: Watcombe, Dame Alice, and Mill Farms, mostly rented[2].   Together, he held over 600 acres in Watlington and the neighbouring hamlet of Britwell Salome. The Wiggins were yeomen farmers. They'd been there for ten generations, rooted to the land – passing it on from generation to generation. The Wiggins family were middlemen, overseers. These Yeomen were the men who generally got things done.

Land was normally passed to the elder son. Other sons had to make their own way. William's brother **Walter Wiggins** farmed Charville Farm, near Reading, not far from where my sister Barbara and her children now live[3].   William's father **Moses** farmed at nearby Lewknor, inheriting it from his uncle, also **Moses Wiggins**[4].   Probably half of Oxford was covered by relations but our William was the last Wiggins to farm in Watlington. In 1897, the Watcombe Manor estate was put up for sale.

Allusions to the Old Testament don't stop with the name Moses; the Wiggins really were the patriarchs of Watlington. William's father farmed 352 acres by the 1850s, employing 18 men, boys and servants [5].   Those were the heady days of farming.

Proclamation of George V's Accession to the throne outside Watlington Town Hall. William Wiggins is standing to the right of the Town Clerk on the podium

Pyrton Farm, Watlington, home of the Wiggins in 1800

1st Cousins 1924: Denie Wiggins (1905-1971), Nancy Haskins (1908-2000), Phyllis Wiggins (1908-1989), John Denison (1911-2006), Norah Wiggins (1909-2001), Hugh Wiggins (1911-1989), Bobbie Wiggins (1913-1992), Paul Wand (1912-1934), Willie Denison (1913-2010), Margot Wiggins (1914-1993), Kay Wand (1914-2006), Joan Denison (1916-2011)

Charville Farm, home of Walter, William Wiggins's brother c 1910. He had an only daughter and the farm was given up when he died

---

1.   *Thomas Wiggins (1602-1672).*
2.   *William Wiggins JP (1836-1913) married Arabella Annie Denison (1845-1926) in 1868.*
3.   *Walter John Wiggins (1840-1909) married Mary Amelia Belcham (1845-1907) in 1871*
4.   *Moses Wiggins (1771-1807) gifted his nephew Moses Wiggins (1801-1878) '…all and every my messuages or accoutrements lands hereditaments and premises with their appurtenances situate and being in the parish of Lewknor and in Lewknor Mead near Easington in the said County of Oxford." Will of Moses Wiggins the elder. Lewknor is close to the M40 Watlington junction. Moses the elder gifted much of his estate to another nephew William Hester Wiggins (1757-1840), the author's great great great grandfather.*
5.   *Moses Wiggins (1801-1878) married Eliza Stephens (1808-1857) in 1835.*

With the repeal of the Corn Laws in 1846-49, and wheat imported from the expanding plains of America, prices went down and by the end of the nineteenth century William Wiggins had had enough of farming, or perhaps his wife Annie had. They steered their children away from it but some farmed by devious means. **Philip** used his skills in Africa and **Herbert**, a clergyman, farmed his Glebe farms himself – he enjoyed 'getting his hands dirty'[6]. It is difficult for a family to leave farming behind. My father told me he'd wanted to become a farmer but the family saw no financial future in it. Instead, he sent me to a former agricultural school in the hope perhaps of some continuity.

William Wiggins was an Oxford County Councillor – larger than life, with energy and ambition, espousing the Victorian virtues of 'character and perseverance'. A bit of a bully, bossy certainly; judgemental, over-confident, a big fish in a small pond, striding across his world. He had a cleft palette and was difficult to understand but that didn't stop him barking out what he wanted to say. He was a Justice of the Peace – with more power than today[iv]. He gave generously to the community. He chaired the School Board following the Education Act in 1870, helping to found the Lecture Hall – becoming one of its first Directors[v]. He was elected a Waywarden of the Highways Board, and a member of the Parish Council[vi]. He became the Treasurer and Life Trustee of a number of charities when they were overhauled and was elected a County Councillor by a large margin. He was Vice-chairman of the Horticultural Society and served on the Cottage Hospital Committee. In fact, there was hardly anything in which he did not have some say.

Personalities are passed on – William knew that from his pedigree books. He's one of the reasons my sisters and I have a community sense, verging on public duty. Organisation and management are crucial in farming but there's something more: there's a sort of cultural initiation going on at the same time, delegating downwards but keeping everyone, including the animals, happy.

✳ ✳ ✳ ✳

From left, standing: Den, Hugh, Clare, Paul Wand, Nancy Haskins, Charles Haskins, Norah, Herbert Denison, John Denison, Phyllis, Neville. Sitting: Amy, Mary, Ethel (neé Elliott), Dora, Marie (neé Briting), Arabella Annie (neé Denison), Dorothy (neé Taylor). Kneeling: Mervyn, Margot, Willie Denison, Joan Denison, Donnie (the dog), Bobby, Kay Wand. All are Wiggins by birth except where named. 18 Aug 1923

---

6. *Philip Arthur Wiggins (1874-1929) married Amy Beatrice Laws (1877-1935) in 1907; Rev Herbert Bouchier Denison MA (1885-1966), born Wiggins, married Alice Dorothy Taylor (1883-1971) in 1910.*

The Denisons

William married **Arabella Annie Denison** in 1868. Ah! The Denisons – were these the ones from Chapter 3? Annie's father was **Henry George Denison**, someone who seemed to have no impact on life, and few interests except those of Chapter 3, the idle rich – yet he was more idle than rich[7]. He dressed like the landed gentry, went shooting if not hunting and fishing. He name-dropped and hankered for invitations but there's little evidence of him doing anything. He'd depended on the rent of properties which he'd acquired on marriage, in 1843, to **Mary Masters**, a plumber's daughter from Reading.

When Henry and Mary set up home at Walnut Tree Mansion on the Salisbury Road, half a mile out of Andover, their eldest son William met with a fatal accident[8]. He was two years old. Mary's elder brother **Francis Masters** was staying with them[9]. After breakfast, Francis went into the drawing room and the two year-old went with him. He played with the child – perhaps tickling or 'tig': William ran into the corner of the room but someone had left a loaded gun there with a shot belt hanging from its muzzle. The child caught the belt and pulled the weapon towards him – Francis sprang off the sofa to grasp the gun. Fast as he was, it still went off. The whole charge went directly into the head of the child. Poor William struggled three or four times before dying. The doctor only took seven or eight minutes to get there, but he was too late. The jury at the inquest declared a verdict of 'accidental death'[vii]. Needless to say Francis Masters can't have been the most popular member of the family that day.

Henry and Mary quickly moved to be nearer Henry's brother, to Wavendon and Woburn Sands, now part of Milton Keynes, where they had another son whom they also named William[10].

William was the family name. As well as his elder brother, Henry's father was a William. This **William Denison** had been Rector of Cublington, 15 miles nearer Oxford – a typical country parson of the Jane Austin era; well educated in a parish not overly well-endowed[11].

Henry's grandfather and great grandfather were also clergymen called William. They'd little in common with the king's mistress of Chapter 3 and more with a king's chaplain. Rev **John Denison** had been chaplain to James I and, successively, Vicar of all three churches in Reading, a great preacher who advocated Sabbath observance and kneeling at communion – he was buried at St Mary's, where Annie's parents had married[12]. He'd written many learned treatises and bequeathed some 'very special good books' to the Bodleian Library[viii]. John might have had a brother or cousin called 'Bishop Denison' who died in Bishop's Stortford (hence *Bishop's* Stortford?), and whose descendants moved to Boston USA, but the evidence for this is less conclusive[13].

Annie Denison (1845-1926)

❋ ❋ ❋ ❋

---

7. *Henry George Denison (1813-1879) married Mary Masters (1825-1913) in 1843.*
8. *William Henry Robert Denison (1844-1846).*
9. *Francis Masters (1821-?).*
10. *The Villa, Church End. Henry's brother was William Henry Denison (1811-1890) who married Sarah D'Oyly Quelch (1816-1898) in 1837 and farmed 78 acres of Hardwick Farm, Woburn Sands in 1871. Henry's son was Rev William Henry Denison (1848-1915) who married Mary Sophia Lee French (1851-1920) in 1876.*
11. *Rev William Denison MA BD (1763-1834) Rector of Cublington 1805-34 married Caroline Mary Tipping Aveling (1789-1831) in 1808.*
12. *Rev John Denison DD (c1573-1629).*
13. *Bishop Denison (1513-1604).*

The Oxford Dons

The **Denisons** had been in Oxford for two generations at least. **William Denison**, the senior (my great (x5) grandfather) was Principal of Magdalen Hall 1745-55[14]. He didn't have an easy start in the job. The Vice Principal, 'Mr E____s' (Evans?) had expected to be offered the post and when he didn't get it, he plotted to get his own back, and set about pocketing most of the money. As the bursar, he held all the responsibilities for income and expenditure. He charged the students for their Commons and Batels (student fees etc) and ordered and paid for all the work done on the place. *Obsonator*, or *Manciple*, was the name for Bursars in those days. As Principal, William had no say in such matters. The tradesmen, however, complained to him that they weren't being paid. Things were so bad that after three years of trouble, William sacked his Manciple and told the tradesmen to sue the man directly.

Being literary gentlemen, the two of them put out a barrage of pamphlets to broadcast their views about each other – there was no Twitter in the 1740s. The pamphlets went round the town to the amusement of all. Their choice of words was historic in all senses (see box) and the case wound up in court. Something must have come right for William – he stayed in his post for ten years and ended up as Proctor of the University.

His son **William Denison** (the younger) took over as Principal for the next 30 years (1755-86)[15]. It was the age of 'pluralism'.[16] Like Elizabeth Denison of Chapter 3, he angled for church posts to supplement his income. As well as his Oxford job, William was Rector of two livings in Hampshire (Chalton and Clanfield)[17]. He'd have paid the curate a pittance to take the services and would have pocketed the income from the tithes.

Magdalen College and Magdalen Hall were both founded by the same man on the one site [18]. Magdalen Hall was established in 1448. It became known for its adherence to the protestant teachings of John Wycliffe, who printed the bible in the English language. Heresy. Like his disciple, John Huss (see Chapter 1), Wycliffe was burnt at the stake. By the time of the English Civil War, a hundred years later, Magdalen Hall was popular with the parliamentarians and the puritan party which chopped off the King's head and ruled England as a republic for ten years.

A fair representation of
the CASE
Between
The Principal of Magdalen Hall and Mr E____s, late Manciple thereof etc.

It would be somewhat difficult to point out Subjects of more trifling Purport in Themselves, or less worthy the Attention of the Publick, than the several Matters offered in a Series of Half-penny Libels, lately published and dispersed in these Seats of Learning, by a low and unequal Immitator of the ingenious and exalted Literati of Grub Street, who calls himself Mr E.

Now to follow this penetrating, this divining Genius into the Sink of his Futility and Nonsense, is a Province, in which, with great Reluctance, I engage, being well allured that the Labours of a Scavenger must be Curae Dulces compared to mine. But as Reptiles, of the lowest Class, are sometimes furnished with a Degree of Poison, and as some of the Filth, so plentifully scattered by the Pen of this wrong-headed, wretched Writer, may happen so far to adhere as to create a fort of Uneasiness in generous Minds, unacquainted with the Manners of the _____ ____ "Tulci Turba impia Vici" and strangers to the Flowers of Billingsgate Oratory, I find myself inclined to bestow on a dark and prurient Scribbler the same Pains which, for our own Sake, we sometime bestow on a dead Rat behind our wainscot; and to drag him into Day-Light, with no other Intent, than to remove an actual Nuisance arising from the Stench.

Extract from a pamphlet on behalf of William Denison

Rev William Denison DD (1725-1786) Principal of Magdalen Hall, Oxford

---

Magdalen Hall

1448	Founded by Bishop William Waynflete
1745-55	William Denison I, Principal
1755-86	William Denison II, Principal
1815	Act of Parliament to move to Hart Hall
1822	Move completed.
1874	Achieved College status and renamed Hertford College

---

14. William Denison MA BD, (c1696-1755) Principal of Magdalen Hall 1745-55.
15. Rev William Denison DD (1725-1786) Principal of Magdalen Hall 1755-86.
16. The Pluralities Act of 1838 stopped men holding more than one benefice (e.g. being the priest of more than one parish).
17. 6 miles south of Petersfield.
18. William Waynflete (c1398-1486) [NR], Bishop of Winchester 1447-86, Lord Chancellor of England 1456-60. Magdalen Hall was where the Swithun's Buildings now are.

The Hall moved sites in 1822. In Turk Street, Hart Hall, with Catholic leanings, had ceased trading twelve years earlier – the last Principal had lived in luxury with no students. Magdalen College saw a chance to ask the Hall to leave. It offered to repair the Hart buildings and to pay for Magdalen Hall's move. Nothing happened until an 'accidental' fire destroyed half of old Magdalen Hall's buildings, and one of the Hart Hall buildings 'collapsed'. Then, something was done.

Once the move had taken place, Magdalen Hall grew in stature. By 1846, it was the largest 'Hall' in Oxford, being granted 'College' status in 1874. As there couldn't be two Magdalen Colleges, it was renamed Hertford College using an earlier name for Hart Hall — the lodge bears the arms of both Halls and in pride of place above the door of the Great Hall stands the large portrait of my great (x4) grandfather, William Denison, the younger.

Hertford College, Oxford

* * * *

Hill House

When William Wiggins, my great grandfather, retired, he acquired *Hill House* in Watlington. The 1820s house was set in its own grounds on Hill Road, which led to the White Mark scored into the chalk of the Chiltern Hills. It had greenhouses, a vegetable garden, extensive outbuildings, tennis courts and, of course, a croquet lawn. It had two rows of tall round-headed windows and a timber-clad extension, covered in *Japanese Creeper*[ix]. The house is currently home to the Oscar-winning actor Jeremy Irons, who played Charles Ryder in the 1981 TV version of *Brideshead Revisited*, a novel which was based on Evelyn Waugh's student days at Hertford College.

William was churchwarden of St Leonard's church for over 37 years[xi]. He was largely responsible for having the Watlington church rebuilt. In 1874, it was in a pretty deplorable condition, semi-derelict. Like too many churches of that period, incumbents had been draining the church coffers for their own pocket for a hundred years. The perpetual curate in charge, Arthur Lloyd, who later became Bishop of Newcastle, encouraged William to stand as Churchwarden[19]. From that point on, William gave his energies to the church. He raised the £4,000 needed to reorder and repair the fabric, employing architects H J Tolit and Edwin Dolby[xii]. It took more than a year to complete. The north aisle, the vestry, the organ chamber and the South Porch were renovated and the roof was replaced. Inside, the galleries and the old box pews were swept away – along with an ornate eighteenth century mausoleum (which they didn't have permission to move!) New pews, an altar rail, a pulpit, and a lectern were installed – the place was larger, fresher. William didn't let up, joining the Diocesan Synod when it was first formed: constantly on the look-out, encouraging donors for more enhancements; his enthusiasm lasted long after the curate had left. His last Vicar summed it up by saying, "One thing that is written across his life was that he was a worker, a labourer amongst them all. He loved his parish[20]. The clock in the Watlington church tower was in his memory. The gilded altar and reredos (rear panelling), designed by C E Kempe in the manner of Fra Angelo, were donated in memory of his wife Annie[xiii].

William Wiggins
(1836-1913)

St Leonard's Watlington c1900. Later, a clock was installed in memory of William Wiggins.

---

[19]   *The Rt Rev Arthur Thomas Lloyd (1844-1907) [NR] Bishop of Newcastle 1903-7. William was a member of the Diocesan Conference from its inception in 1875.*

[20]   *The Rev Sidney Charles Saunders (1851-1914) [NR] sermon at Matins, Sunday 4 Aug 1913. History of the Wiggins Family p6.*

The Reredos in memory of Annie Wiggins (née Denison)

Tea at Hill House – to the left of William Wiggins is his wife Annie and in the deck-chair her mother Mary (neé Masters, the plumber's daughter). In the foreground Eleanor Agnes Allnutt (1860-1931) [NR], daughter of the Watlington farmer who took over the Watlington farms when William retired.

William and Annie imbued their whole family with a competitive edge. As my cousin Barbara wrote:[21] "All were concerned with 'going up' and 'getting on' in the world. Energetic, practical, dictatorial, down to earth, they organised everything on a fair and mutual basis of give and take which did not inhibit a great deal but empowered them with a mission to improve the lot of those around them. 'Salt of the earth,' they were hardworking, benevolent, much given to good works for the public good, giving of their time and energy to the 'good of the whole'. They received awards of the world in consequence."[xiv]

William and Annie Wiggins had fixed ideas about the career-paths for their sons. They were destined for the professions – two became doctors, one a lawyer, one a clergyman. There was a banker and a schoolmaster and four sons tried their luck in Africa. The daughters were supposed to marry men with prospects.

The children grew up in cast-off clothing from their elders. The boys attended *Cowley* Prep School (which their father had also attended) and *Magdalen College School* which until 1894 was on the corner of the High and Longwall Street[22]. They cycled the 16

Hill House in the 1900s

Hill House today

miles each way. It would be an exaggeration to say they helped the foundation of British Leyland but they put a lot of trade the way of Mr Morris's bike shop in Cowley[23].

William and Annie's second son, **Philip Wiggins** was a Chorister at *Magdalen College School*[24]. Since Tudor times, every May Day morning it has been the practice for the choir to sing *Hymnus Eucharisticus* at the top of the College Tower, beside the Magdalen Bridge[25]. Crowds gather to watch in large numbers these days. The practice of ducking a chorister in the Cherwell has suffered from the 'health and safety' regulations - in the last twenty years it's been more the case of students jumping off the bridge. When Philip was chosen by the Pre-Raphaelite painter, Holman Hunt, as a subject for his painting, it was because of his large head – his school chums teased him endlessly about it afterwards[26].

❇ ❇ ❇ ❇

May Morning on Magdalen Tower by Holman Hunt. Philip Wiggins's head is showing at the back in the centre behind the main choirboy.

21. *Barbara Hester Kay (1923-2011)*
22. *History of the Wiggins Family pp3,5.*
23. *William Richard Morris, 1st Viscount Nuffield GBE, CH, FRS (1877-1963) [NR].*
24. *Philip Arthur Wiggins (1874-1930) married Amy Beatrice Laws (1877-1935) in 1907.*
25. *Since the 7th century.*
26. *William Holman Hunt OM (1827-1910) [NR].*

Croquet

Dr 'Den' Wiggins (1873-1937)

Den Wiggins was the eldest son[27]. When he qualified in 1897 he joined the modest staff of Greenwich Union Infirmary, a Poor Law hospital fronting onto the east of Vanbrugh Hill and Woolwich Road. Junior doctors were paid about £100pa, probably below his mother's expectations, but there were prospects. Life was rough in Greenwich in the 1890s. One case involved a woman who tried drowning the last of her litter of eleven children (the others were already dead) in a butter tub – she'd spent all her money on drink. A crowd of local boys followed her about jeering and hollering, calling her 'Old Mother Gilby' and tearing at her dress. The sickly four-year-old was rescued by a well-wisher and taken to the Infirmary[xv].

Den was to remain there for the whole of his career, taking over in 1913 when Walter Burney, the Medical Superintendent, died[28]. The Workhouse with a medical wing became a fully equipped hospital with over 1,000 beds by the time Den died in 1937, with an out-patients department, pharmacy, antenatal clinic and a nurses' sick bay facility. It was renamed St Alfege's Hospital after the church the other side of Greenwich Park.

Den was a Freemason, belonging to the Frederick Lodge of Unity in Croydon. In 1911, he was its Master and later reached the exalted rank of Provincial Grand Director of Ceremonies for Surrey.

Den Wiggins and my mother's father, **Everard Tresidder**, were in the same profession and knew each other socially. Everard had been schooled on Lake Geneva and employed a Swiss girl, **Marie Briting**, to look after my mother. Den ended up marrying her. To the Wiggins family this was a new experience – they'd go 'Oh Marie' in a mysterious way, as if she was a strange bird of paradise. Marie died in her thirties of tuberculosis (TB) but she brought two children into the world, Bobby and Margot. Though never thought of as part-Swiss, the children had an exotic bloom and wide smiles. Margot's real name was Margaret but always Margot – pronounced with a silent 't', as Margot Astor said to the racy Jean Harlow, *"Like in 'Harlow'"*[29]. They lived in a flat in the institution, overlooking the Thames with high ceilings and tall windows. Beyond the heavy brocade curtains was a magnificent view of ship after ship sailing out on the evening tide with the setting sun shining on their superstructure, highlighting the crimson rust on their hulls.

Marie Briting (1892-1926) was first the author's mother's Swiss governess before her marriage to Den and the author's father's Aunt by marriage afterwards

With no mother around from the age of twelve, **Margot's** girly talk revolved around boys, and whose bed she'd hopped in or out of[30]. She married three husbands before settling down to married life in Rhodesia (Zimbabwe), though when that became difficult after independence she fled to Durban, later returning. One of her three husbands was her first cousin Willie Wiggins.

First cousins, who met often in the holidays at Hill House, my father Paul encouraged **Bobby Wiggins** to start his stamp collection. It ended up with book upon book of 'penny reds', some of the earliest and most valuable of adhesive postage stamps[31]. I once had a 'penny red' but Bobby collected them with military precision. He re-formed original sheets – using the codes in the corners. He researched the order of printing them, and matched them to the printer's

Margot Wiggins (1914-1993) in 1926

---

27. *Dr William Denison Wiggins MRCS LRCP (1873-1937) married Marie Julie Briting (1892-1926) in 1912. The hospital was closed in 2001, demolished in 2006 and in its place housing built as 'Greenwich Square'.*

28. *Walter Charles Skardon Burney (1849-1913) [NR].*

29. *retort to the 'blonde bombshell' film star Jean Harlow (1911-1937) [NR] when the witty Margot Asquith, Countess of Oxford and Asquith (1864-1945) [NR] was correcting the way she spoke her name.*

30. *Margaret Denison Wiggins (1914-1993) married (1) George Symons DSC (1907-?) in 1935 (2) William Blethyn Wiggins (1913-2010) in 1947 (3) George Brooking Gilbart-Smith MC (1908-1978) in 1952.*

31. *William Robert Denison Wiggins (1913-1992) married (1) Pamela C Gill (1919-?) in 1940 (2) Diana V Harris (b1928) in 1949 (3) Susan Grigg (?-1993).*

Bobby Wiggins (1913-1992) holding the author's sisters, Barbara and Ann in July 1939

Audrey Wiggins (b1951) presenting a bouquet to the Queen at Hurlingham 1967

The Wiggins at Hunstanton

The Wiggins came down
like a wolf on the fold,
And the heads of their mallets
were gleaming like gold;
And the aim of their eyes
were like 'steel' on a lea,
While the blue waves rolled lightly
at 'Hunston' on Sea.

Croquet Association Gazette 2 Sep 1933

plates. He deciphered roller-flaws, the positions of the check-letters and other deviations – he could determine which 'die' had been used: he published his results in 1974 and 1982[xvi].

Bobby was keen to follow in his father's footsteps as a doctor. His uncle Neville helped his slow progress through Medical School[xvii] He became a consultant anaesthetist whose gentle bedside manner attracted a private practice sufficient to support four children through private education.

Bobby Wiggins was a prominent member of the croquet scene in the 1950s to 1970s, playing Association Croquet for England (against New Zealand) and helping with administration. He was on the Croquet Federation's Council from 1951 to 1980 and its Vice-President until his death in 1992. In a blazing summer week in June 1961 he won the Compton Cup for the fourth year running[xviii]. His son David Wiggins, a fireman (my generation), played in the 1990s at Woking with Jeff Dawson, who has since acted as Chairman of the Croquet Association and a lot more besides[32].

Croquet – played with mallets, coloured balls (blue, red, black, yellow) and hoops 3¾ inches wide, was introduced by the Irish to England in the 1860s. It briefly went out of fashion when 'Lawn Tennis' was introduced but came back into its own during the Edwardian era – sometimes played with double the number of balls and players. The Wimbledon tennis club renamed itself the 'All England Lawn Tennis and Croquet Club' in 1899 and so it remains to this day. Croquet's golden age was the 1920s and '30s, when international tournaments began and the rules were standardised.

In the 1930s, the Wiggins were known for descending on tournaments and carrying off the prizes. As the Croquet Gazette said in 1934 *"It is perhaps not strictly true to say that 'Wherever there is a Wiggins there is a winner,' but very nearly so."*[xix] At Hunstanton, in 1933, the parody of one of Byron's poems was composed for the Croquet Gazette[xx]. **Den** was the winner of the All-England Handicap in 1929. Den's brother **Bernard Wiggins** was a National Croquet Referee and on the National Federation's Council 1946-1954. Bernard's wife, **Phyllis**, won the honour of Women's Croquet Champion of England. Bernard (at 94) is gazetted as the 8th oldest active player in the world (ever), His brother **Neville** (at 84) the 76th, though their brother **Herbert** was, they said, the better player[xxi].

Den and his brothers learnt on the lawns of *Hill House*, Watlington. In my childhood I played a form of Golf Croquet although my childhood garden, unlike *Hill House*, was full of odd banks and trees. Bobby, a grand master of Association Croquet, sneered at this but, in recent years, Golf Croquet has attracted a large following. My sister Ann plays it regularly at her club and I play both games – there are even a couple of trophies irreverently named the 'Robert Haskins Trophy' at the *Ripon Spa Hotel* Club, which are as much to do with the number of years I have been running these club competitions as the frequency of winning them. I've now learnt to play Gateball introduced by Suzuki Kazunobu in Japan in 1947. This was encouraged by General MacArthur when the country had almost no

The next generation – Josh (b2007) and Ben (b2005) Simpson

---

[32] *David Charles Denison Wiggins (b1954); Jeffrey R Dawson (b1956) [NR].*

viable leisure activity[33]. Based on croquet, you have to keep your wits about you – far faster with more balls, larger teams on smaller courts. It has outstripped croquet with more than 10 million players in 45 countries.

❋ ❋ ❋ ❋

Another Denison name-change

Annie's younger brother was a country parson[34]. The Rev **William Denison** had bought the advowson (patronage) of Carlton with Chellington in Bedfordshire in 1876 for around £7,000[xxii]. In 1909, he took over as Rector of Thrandeston when his father-in-law died (population 282, income a substantial £347 in 1913). His nephew Herbert Wiggins had finished his training as a curate and it made sense for him to be the next Rector of Carlton. Just like the Denisons in Chapter 3, Herbert Wiggins changed his name to **Herbert Denison** in order to inherit the living, with its glebe farm of 406 acres[35].

Rev William Denison (1848-1915)

Herbert married **Dorothy Taylor**, whose father Rev **Samuel Taylor** was on the staff at the Cathedral in Calcutta in 1872-3. A fellow of Calcutta University and in charge of St Thomas's Calcutta 1874-80 and 1883-92, he spent time in Assam and Morar as well[36]. He returned to run a thriving church in Portsmouth: St James, Milton. The Taylor family were all musical.

Herbert and Dorothy had three children. The eldest **John Law Denison** joined the BBC Symphony Orchestra in 1934[37]. Music critics thought him perhaps the best French horn player of his time. When, in 1965, he stepped up as General Manager of the Royal Festival Hall he became a central figure in the musical life of Britain. Once the National Theatre and Hayward Gallery developed into the South Bank Arts complex, he took the role of its Director of Music, retiring in 1976.

In old age the second son, **Willie**, looked the splitting image of my father, who was eight years older. After Willie divorced Margot, Den's daughter, he married Margarita, a Cuban heiress. As a surveyor, he set out to run Margarita's sugar plantations but when Castro took over in 1960 they were all confiscated[38].

The youngest was **Joan**[39]. She married one of her father's curates, Rev **Dick Gutteridge**, the priest who was to officiate at my wedding to Carolyn in Barnsley in 1985. Joan and Dick had a shared interest in music. Dick's father was a Professor of Law, first at London then at Cambridge[40]. Dick's grandfather ran a very successful department store in Naples, which is still going strong. **Michael Gutteridge** had come from Selby in Yorkshire and at one stage

The Rectory, Carlton, Bedfordshire, c1910

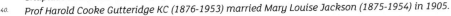

33. *Gen Douglas MacArthur (1880-1964) [NR] oversaw the occupation of Japan 1945-51.*

34. *Rev William Denison (1848-1915).*

35. *Rev Herbert Bouchier Denison MA (1885-1966), born Wiggins, changed his surname. He married Alice Dorothy Taylor (1883-1971) in 1910. After Brasenose Oxford he trained for ordination in Newcastle, was curate in Benwell 1908-11 and Worsley Manchester 1911-13, he was Rector of Charlton with Chellington 1913-23, with service as an Army Chaplain 1915-17. Vicar of Luton 1923-25, Rector of Clayton with Keymer 1925-33, Bexhill 1933-41, Hartfield 1941-46, Hemmingford Abbots 1946-55.*

36. *Rev Samuel Benjamin Taylor MA (1841-1921) married Marianna Georgiana Law (1859-1930) in 1882.*

37. *John Law Denison CBE (1911-2006) married four times.*

38. *William Blethyn Denison (1913-2010) married (1) Margaret Denison Wiggins (1914-1993) (2) Margherita C Walter Y Revas (3) Micheline?*

39. *Dorothy Joan Denison (1916-2011) married Rev Dick (Richard Joseph Cooke) Gutteridge MA (1911-2000). He was curate at Edgbaston 1935-38 and Bexhill 1938-40. Rector of Brampton 1945-52, Chaplain to the RAF 1952-68, Fellow at Oxford 1968-72 and Priest-in-charge at Longstowe 1972-3.*

40. *Prof Harold Cooke Gutteridge KC (1876-1953) married Mary Louise Jackson (1875-1954) in 1905.*

The Denisons - seated Dorothy and Herbert; standing John and Willie; kneeling Joan.

Gutteridges from Naples – this branch in Florence

John Denison (1911-2006) as a boy and in later life'

Neville Wiggins at Cheltenham playing croquet with Harry Murray in the 1930s. Croquet connoisseurs will note the kick boards and yard line for placing balls after they have left the lawn. Others will observe the dress code – the hats, no 'whites' and leather soled shoes.

Arthur Wiggins (1889-1920) in Canada c1918

the family lived in Wetherby – his sister Jane was born there[41]. Michael gave money to found *Wesley House*, the Methodist Theological College in Cambridge. After Cambridge, Dick taught for a time. He became an RAF Chaplain after enjoying his time as Rector of Brampton, on the edge of an RAF base. He ended his days back at Cambridge as a Librarian at Trinity Hall.

✴ ✴ ✴ ✴

The Magician

Neville Wiggins was the second youngest of William and Annie's twelve children[42]. The youngest, **Arthur Wiggins** committed suicide aged 31 just before Christmas in 1920 after he'd been accused of homosexuality as a schoolmaster[xxiii]. Never something Neville had a problem with – he liked girls too much – having an eye for younger women as you'll read in Chapter 14. The age difference between Neville and his wife was 21 years. Neville was 53 when he married the engaging and personable Molly, one of nine attractive sisters, just two months before war broke out in 1939. Molly, his secretary, had a touch of the Blarney stone about her. The husky voice and the floppy blond hair were magnetic, the thing of film-stars. Her father, an Irishman from Cookstown, worked for the Ministry of Agriculture and Fisheries inspectorate, living at Monkbridge in salubrious Headingley, Leeds[43]. Neville and Molly's children, **Elizabeth** and **Christopher**, were younger than my two sisters[44].

Neville retired to Hill Rise, a property with an intriguing octagonal tower and pointy-hat roof, in Peartree Lane near Cooden Beach, just along the south coast from Bexhill. The place had easy access to the golf links and was near enough to his brother Herbert for them to go off playing croquet together. We'd go down to see them pretty often in the summer weekends, using back roads to avoid the queues of tiny box Ford cars clogging the narrow main roads. We'd drive past *Batemans*, Rudyard Kipling's house[45].

Neville also went out with my mother, who was eighteen years younger than he, before she met Paul, his nephew. You could still see the sparkle remain in his eye as Neville and my mother greeted each other. They looked forward to these family get-togethers. I remember two things about those lazy hazy Cooden days – the Beach Hut on the shingle strand, where I learned to swim in the wild waves, and the three-wheeler pedal cars, in which Christopher Wiggins, for those all too fleeting moments the nearest thing to a big brother, raced me round the verges of the vegetable garden. They were unique, those 'Autocars' – hands revolved the pedals and feet steered the wheels[46]. There was a croquet lawn of course – with two central posts[xxiv].

When it was time to return home, the family would line up and we'd hug and say our goodbyes. Neville was a member of the Magic Circle; still mischievous and always young at heart, he'd produce a penny out of my ear – to this day, I don't know how he did it.

---

41. *Michael Gutteridge (1842-1935) married Ada Cooke (1840-1921) in 1872. Jane Staniland Gutteridge (1848-1924) was born in Wetherby, Yorkshire.*

42. *Robert Victor Neville Wiggins (1886-1970) married Molly Crawford (1907-1992) in 1939.*

43. *Walter Ruddell Crawford (1865-1927) married Annie Maud McBride in Lisburn near Belfast in 1892, living first at a farm at Tullaghoge near Tyrone in Northern Ireland, then at Monkbridge House, Headingley.*

44. *Elizabeth Neville Wiggins (b1940) married Victor Oscar Sousa (b1931) in 1969 and Christopher Neville Wiggins (b1942) married Betsy Linda Fumagalli (b1949) in 1978.*

45. *Joseph Rudyard Kipling (1865-1936) [NR].*

46. *They were steered on the front axle and driven by hand-operated levers connected to cranks on the single back wheel.*

The Rivals

Mary Wiggins, the eldest of William and Annie's twelve children, never married – it was her sister's fault[47]. Her sister, **Dora**, had the 'second child' syndrome. Second to Mary in almost everything, Dora developed a devastating charm. She spent her life trying to 'keep up with the Joneses'.

Mary had fallen for a school teacher called Charles Haskins. They were getting on very well when Dora realised that she might be 'left on the shelf'. So Dora put on her charm and snaffled Charles from under Mary's nose. Having lost her first love, Mary never married.

For Dora it was more about the conquest than the consummation. She was quixotic and would take to her bed at the slightest set-back. Having captured Charles, she effectively refused to sleep with him. The family had to be called in to explain the essential facts of life. In the end, she produced two children, one being my father Paul. Having fulfilled her marital obligations, she returned to the life of a semi-invalid, being waited on hand and foot, despite the fact that, like all the other Wiggins, she had the constitution of an ox.

My father Paul was, for Mary, 'the son she'd have liked to have had'. As the eldest, unmarried of her generation, Mary had a Virgin 'Queen Bee' quality. Her siblings deferred to her opinions and judgements – there was some sort of 'rock-like' dependability about her. She was more a mother to Paul than Dora ever was.

Mary Wiggins (1870-1946) in 1938 holding a six-week-old Brigit Addison

Dora Wiggins/Haskins/ Murray (1871-1966) in her Cheltenham garden

In 1934, with her first husband, **Charles Haskins**, dead and with her children both married, Dora decided to move to Cheltenham. Dora planned for her brother Bernard to move there when he retired from Zanzibar at the same time. Cheltenham had an excellent croquet club – I still use the croquet mallet that stood in her hallway[48]. Dora was always out for the conquest, and made the best of her appearance despite her thinning hair. Dora's eyes were blue. She wore dresses to match. Down at the croquet club, she looked very well in her blue summer suit, white hat, gloves and sunshade, white collars and cuffs, her cheeks well rouged and over-powdered, with her best wig just showing a touch of grey among the auburn waves and her wide thin mouth painted with crimson lipstick. Although in her early sixties, she made a pretty enough picture as she wandered on the green grass by the pavilion, among the little tables and chairs set out in the shade for tea. It took her less than a year to ensnare a second husband, 69 year-old Lt Col Harry Murray, whom she took home to her pebble-dashed semi-detached in Mead Road a short walk away[49]. When the rouge was washed off, the teeth put in the nightly glass, and the wig set on its stand in the bedroom, did he have second thoughts? If so, he was too polite to say[xxv].

Dartington House, Linden Gardens, Leatherhead c1909, Paul Haskins at the gate, Charles Haskins holding his daughter Nancy (1908-2000) on the balcony

Harry Murray doted on Dora. He had spent most of his life in India (see Chapter 6.) His first wife had died in 1933. He'd also come to Cheltenham for the croquet – indeed there is an apocryphal story that the government's spy station, GCHQ, moved to Cheltenham because then Director, Sir Edward Travis, liked croquet and this croquet club had the best reputation[50]. Harry would do the housework as Dora got ready to go out. He'd be in the kitchen whilst she entertained the cream of Cheltenham society with a game of bridge. She never learnt to cook much. She bought the most inappropriate fancies instead of the basic commodities. After Harry died in 1948, she lived for another 15 years, the years I knew her. She went deaf (unless she wanted to hear) and gathered an enormous array of hearing aids, few of which functioned properly. She'd impose herself on the family of her nephew Bobby (the croquet player/stamp collector) for a month and with my sister Barbara for a week or two. Her eyes lit up if a man

35 Mead Road, Cheltenham

---

47. *Mary Emmeline Wiggins (1870-1946).*
48. *Charles Haskins died in March 1934 of an enlarged prostate, which they did not know how to treat.*
49. *Lt Col James Harry Stewart Murray (1866-1948) had married Margaret Richardson (1869-1933) in 1895.*
50. *Sir Edward Wilfred Harry Travis KCMG CBE (1888-1956) [NR] was Director of the Government Communications Headquarters (GCHQ) from its formation to 1952.*

came into view. She ended her days in a nursing home aged ninety-five, semi-conscious for several weeks. Strong-willed to the end – she found it hard to die.

Mary remained in Watlington, at Gorwell Corner with her devoted friend Miss A Jones. She enjoyed my father Paul's visits – last seeing him just before she died in the cold winter of 1946, when he was home from Army leave.

✳ ✳ ✳ ✳

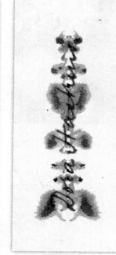

'Ghost' Autographs Christmas 1918

Some not so famous quotations

William Wiggins had two strange mottos[xxvi].   The first was odd for someone who dabbled in every pie. *'Never be helpful.'* 'Helping' resulted in disaster, according to William. If you offer to wash the dishes, you'd inevitably do it wrong or, worse still, break or chip something. If you offer to do the gardening, you'd end up being accused of preserving the weeds and destroying the plants.

The second dictum was *'Neither a borrower or lender be.'* William said it with feeling – he'd lent a friend £1,000 and never saw it again. If you must help someone, it is best to assume you're giving them a gift, he said.

Annie, his wife, lived on after William's death in 1919 for another seven years. She donned 'widow's weeds' like Queen Victoria, black crepe-de-Chine dress with lawn cuffs and widow's cap. She loved to welcome her family of 12 children and 20 grandchildren. They'd return to Watlington most summers, and Christmases too, from wherever they were in the world. She managed with two live-in staff – a cook and a housemaid. When she died in 1926, the heart went out of the place and with Mary's death in 1946 the Wiggins' centuries-old continuity with Watlington and Oxfordshire came to an end.

William Wiggins holding his first grandson Paul Denison Haskins (1905-1996) together with his family. Standing: George, Kathie, parents Charles and Dora Haskins, Herbert; Sitting: Neville, Annie, William, Den, Mary; in front: Arthur, Philip and Amy.

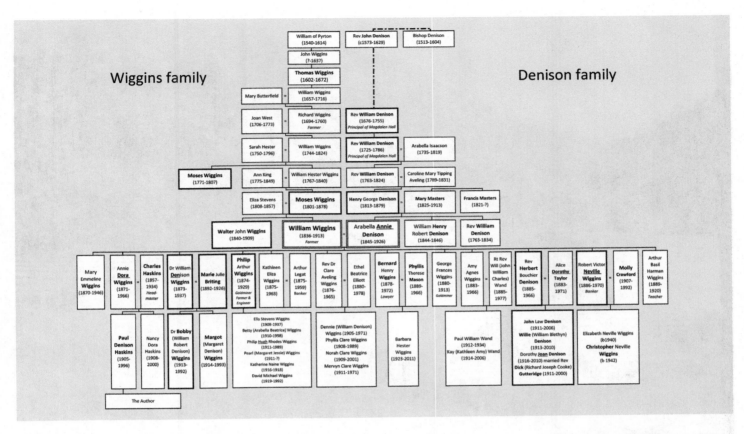

Other Notes and References

i. The White Mark was cut in 1764 by the local Squire, Edward Horne, to make the church look as if it had a spire when he looked out of his window.

ii. Lobel pp. 210-252. In 1664, 55 freemen of Watlington, paying a pound each, purchased the manor, preparatory to the building of the Town Hall on the waste of the manor.

iii. Thompson. pp19, 430.

iv. Obituary quoted in Hatcher p6. William Wiggins JP was a county magistrate for Watlington Petty Sessions Division from 1895.

v. Obituary quoted in Hatcher p5. In 1869, when the Lecture Hall Company was founded, William Wiggins became one of its Directors.

vi. Ferrar pp28, 208. Waywardens were similar to mini-Police Commissioners today - under the 1833/36 Highways Acts they were elected annually to maintain the King's highways – roads and footpaths, and side drains, to clear the snow, fill potholes, impound stray cattle and to raise the income through rates. Before that, the Waywardens had the power to commission all parishioners for 6 days service a year to maintain roads. Under the 1862 Highways Act (25&26 Vic.c.61), District Highway Boards were established made up of JPs together with Waywardens elected by constituent parishes. Waywardens were unpaid, working alongside paid Surveyors appointed by the Board.

vii. Berkshire Chronicle, 26 Sep 1846.

viii. Oxford Convocation 1629; Coates p336f.

ix. Parthenocissus tricuspidata or Boston Ivy.

x. Daily Telegraph 12 Oct 2013. Jeremy Irons (b1948) [NR] had become patron of Watlington Against Pollution, an action group to prevent HGVs using Watlington as a rat run from the M40 to the M4.

xi. From 18 Sep 1875. Like the author, William Wiggins started as a Churchwarden half way through a year. Wiggins served under 5 Bishops.

xii. Lobel pp. 210-252 and Sherwood and Pevsner p829. The builder was Martin of Hereford.

xiii. British Listed Buildings. Grade II* English Heritage Listing 247586. 1963. Sherwood & Pevsner p830.

xiv. Kay p118

xv. http://www.oldbaileyonline.org/images. jsp?doc=189205020106. The case of Mary Ann Gilby, aged 32, inflicting grievous bodily harm on George Gilby 2 May 1892. Sentence: four month's Hard Labour.

xvi. Wiggins W R D: Penny Blacks were printed in 1840. Penny Reds (various shades) from 1841. (Alphabet I: Yellow-brown in 1841; red-brown in 1843; brownish-red in 1845; Alphabet II: red-brown, lake-red, orange brown and bluey red-brown in 1852.) Letters in the top corners were introduced in 1858.

xvii. Neville Wiggins's bank statements held by his son Christopher.

xviii. 18-24 Jun 1961. Neville made it to the semi-final in the 'match of the week'.

xix. Croquet Association Gazette 26 May 1934, p86.

xx. http://butedock.demon.co.uk/cgs1919/ accessed 2014; Croquet Association Gazette 2 Sep 1933: On 14 Aug 1933 the 'A Block' winner was Rev H B W (Herbert) Denison; 'C Block' winner: W R D (Bobbie) Wiggins; 'D Block' winner: Miss J Denison (Joan, later Gutteridge) 'a maiden of sweet seventeen and a very promising player'; 21-26 August 1933: Mrs B H (Phyllis) Wiggins, and Rev H B W (Herbert) Denison made the semi-finals: also playing were Neville and Bernard Wiggins.

xxi. http://butedock.demon.co.uk/cgs1919/ages.php accessed 25 Apr 2017

xxii. Pratt.. Appointment of Parish Priests to the 'freehold' of parishes in the Church of England is made by 'Patrons', in the past individuals who bought and sold the advowson but now more often in the control of the Bishop of the Diocese.

xxiii. PDH letter 9 Jun 1918: Arthur Basil Harman Wiggins MA (1889-1920) was a housemaster at Ashbury College Ottowa.

xxiv. Smith p169ff. Neville's croquet lawn retained two centre posts or 'pegs' – the 'Hale' setting which was replaced by the 'Willis' setting (with one peg) in 1922. (Standing on one ball in Association croquet was banned in 1870.)

xxv. Kay p88. I am indebted to my late cousin Barbara Kay (née Wiggins) for this description.

xxvi. Kay p117f.

Rice paddy fields in Nepal

Indian Empire

An early entry into the visitors' book at *Penquarry*, where we used to stay in Cornwall, just up from Hemmick Beach near the Dodman, was Sir Herbert Baker and his family[1]. How he discovered the Grose's humble bungalow with its outstanding view, I don't know but it was a good choice[i]. On the walls of his home at *Owletts* in Kent, are his designs for the layout of the new Delhi government buildings on *Raisina Hill*, drawn up after Britain announced, at George V's Durbar (Coronation) in Delhi in 1911, that the capital of India was to move from Calcutta (Kolkata) to **Delhi**.

The main Secretariat building, New Delhi, by Sir Henry Baker.

As a student of architectural history, this intrigued me, as Sir Edwin Lutyens is often cited as its architect[2]. Baker was the main man behind what became known as 'New Delhi'. He won agreement for the fifteen square mile site and conceived the overall scheme. He designed the Secretariat buildings, Parliament House and bungalows for Members of Parliament. Lutyens, possibly my favourite arts and crafts architect, was brought in by the Permanent Secretary of the India Office, **Sir Richmond Ritchie**, the first of my many relations in this story of India[3]. Lutyens had opposing views on the site and the size and shape of the buildings but ended up designing the Viceroy's Palace, at the end of the Rajpath, which he did with panache and invention.

Lutyens wasn't very clever at the politics with a small 'p' – his humour bordered on flippancy. It didn't go down well with the Viceroy, a career civil servant – he was 'a thorn in his side' as far as Lord Hardinge was concerned[4]. Lutyens and Baker also fell out, witty Lutyens describing it as his 'Bakerloo'. Meanwhile Baker handled the project with business-like efficiency even if, ironically, Lutyens won most of the lasting credit.

The Viceroy's House, New Delhi, by Sir Edwin Lutyens

The city of **Delhi** was a major casualty of the Indian uprising fifty-five years earlier when in 1857 the Indian soldiers employed by the East India Company rebelled, along with many in the population. In an attempt to regain control, the British almost entirely wiped out the Indian culture there. The Red Fort, the palace of the emperors, was converted into barracks, its audience chamber into an officer's mess, and the Muslim shrines into cattle sheds. Not just the fabric of the buildings was vandalised but the people as well. The carnage on both sides was merciless. Anyone who is squeamish should avoid the sections coming up headed *Terrible Tragedy* and *The final capture of Lucknow* and possibly skip the whole chapter.

During my visit India in 2012, I met Housna-Tara Prakash, whose gracious hospitality enabled me to tour some of Calcutta and Darjeeling. In conversation with her, I remembered that my mother had had a problem with her entry in the 1961 census. We joked at the time that the rather basic census form would infer that she was an immigrant because her father was born in India. This chapter is mainly about *his* father, **John Nicholas Tresidder** who spent the whole of his career in India[5].

It wasn't my first visit to the Asian continent. I had visited Nepal for work; a separate country sandwiched between India and Tibet. I felt strangely at home in Calcutta, the British capital of India for over 300 years.

The Red Fort, Delhi

---

1.   *Sir Herbert Baker KCIE LLD DCL RA FRIBA (1862-1946) [NR].*
2.   *Sir Edwin Landseer Lutyens OM KCIE PRA FRIBA (1869-1944) [NR].*
3.   *Sir Richmond Thackeray Willoughby Ritchie CB KCB ISO (1854-1912) Permanent Secretary of the India Office 1910-12.*
4.   *Charles Hardinge, 1st Baron Hardinge of Penshurst KG GCB GCMG GCSI GCIE GCVO ISO DL LLD PC (1858-1944) [NR].*
5.   *Surgeon-General John Nicholas Tresidder (1819-1889) married Elizabeth Carlyon Barnicoat (1915-1855). in 1845 and Emily Hooton Courtis (1830-1917) in 1857.*

Howrah Railway Station

William Makepeace Thackeray (1811-1863)

William Ritchie (1817-1862)

On my first day, I jumped into a rattling Tata taxi and took a trip to Howrah railway station, perhaps the largest railway terminus in the world, the hooting car horns sounding to me like hoopoe birdsong. The colours, the heat, the bustle and scents all came wafting back. Here were the origins of a British dominion, stretching more than 1,000 miles across northern India and 2,000 miles south to Ceylon (Sri Lanka).

One of my more remote relations was the author **William Makepeace Thackeray** who was born in Calcutta[6]. His father first went out in 1798 with the East India Company[7]. William's mother was 'one of the reigning beauties of the day'. I relished reading Thackeray's 'The Rose and the Ring' when I was young[ii].

Thackeray's son-in-law and cousin, **Richmond Ritchie**, rose to be Permanent Secretary of the India Office. He was the one who recommended Lutyens for the Delhi job. Richmond's father, **William Ritchie**, was a barrister in Calcutta, a member of the Council for India[8]. His impressive 1862 monument, in St Paul's Cathedral Calcutta, says he was Vice Chancellor of the University for 20 years[iii]. It goes on to praise his 'clear intellect,' a 'sweet and generous temper,' his 'highest education', and much more besides.

Working with Richmond in Whitehall, London, was another relative of mine – practically the only true Cornishman on my father's side. **Henry Seccombe**, a First Secretary in the India Office, features briefly in Chapter 12[9]. His father, **Sir Thomas Seccombe**, was an Under-Secretary in the India Office, 1872-81[10]. Sir Thomas was born in a farm outside Grampound, near Truro, in Cornwall. He entered the civil service through 'open competition' (instead of family connections) and worked his way to the top.

Britain's hold over India was unlike any other colony. It started as a 'partnership' and then became a full-blown Empire. The Battle of Plassey in 1757 consolidated British influence under Warren Hastings[11]. In the thirty-odd years 1845-1877 that my great grandfather spent in India, it altered again. The uprising of 1857, the Indian Mutiny or the 'Great Rebellion', depending on which side you were on, ended up with wholesale slaughter of many British families and the British reversing the tide by annihilating perhaps a million Indians[iv]. It could be said that one member of my family started it and another one ended it, with my great-grandfather caught in the middle; but, first, some background.

✷ ✷ ✷ ✷

Early Days

Since 1600, there'd been a British presence in India. Elizabeth I granted a Royal Charter to the Honourable East India Company, which got nicknamed 'John's Company', or *Kampani Jahan*, after the Mogul Emperor Shah Jahan, whose father first granted right of entry[12]. In theory, the East India Company was a vassal of the Moghul (Mughal) Emperor but it increasingly called the shots. Since the 1800s under the Wellesley's (the Duke of Wellington and his brother Richard) Britain had been consolidating its hold[13]. By the 1850s, the Company had a civil service of 'Writers' like Thackeray's father of about 5,000 British, plus an army of over 200,000 native troops[v].

---

6. *William Makepeace Thackeray (1811-1863) Author.*
7. *Raymond Thackeray (1762-1815) married Anne Becher (1792-1864) in 1810.*
8. *William Ritchie (1817-62).*
9. *Henry Lawrence Seccombe (1841-1910) married Emily Ann Wiggins (1846-1930) in 1876.*
10. *Sir Thomas Lawrence Seccombe CB KCSI GCIE (1812-1902) was born at Creed.*
11. *Warren Hastings (1732-1818) [NR] Governor-General of India 1773-85.*
12. *Shahabuddin Muhammad Shah Jahan, Shah Jahan (1594-1666) [NR] Emperor 1628-58.*
13. *Richard Colley Wesley, 1st Marquess Wellesley KG PC PC(Ire) (1760-1842) [NR], Governor-General of the Presidency of Fort William (Bengal) 1798-1805 [NR].*

The British taxpayer paid nothing towards the upkeep because the Company survived on its profit. Many an Englishman, in whatever capacity, came back wealthier than when they went.

The East India Company divided India into three 'Presidencies': *Bengal* or *North West* (at 'Fort William') stretching to Afghanistan; *Madras* (Chennai, at 'Fort George') in the South; and *Bombay* (Mumbai) in the West. Almost the whole of this story is concerned with the North West, the land of the River Ganges, with Calcutta in the east and Delhi in the west.

The East India Company gave the local rulers security. It helped them bring in a steady income and to sort out petty disputes through the application of British justice. The Company's headquarters were in the east – hence the '<u>East</u> India Company'. By the 1800s, **Calcutta** in the east had become a miniature version of Whitehall. Delhi in the west, where the Emperor resided, had seen a flowering of the eastern arts: poetry, architecture, music, dancing, painting and science. Incidentally, our 'Arabic' numerals come from India; the Arabs actually call them 'Hindu numerals'. Islam and Hindu lived in harmony side by side and the emperors intermarried. The Mutiny was to change all that.

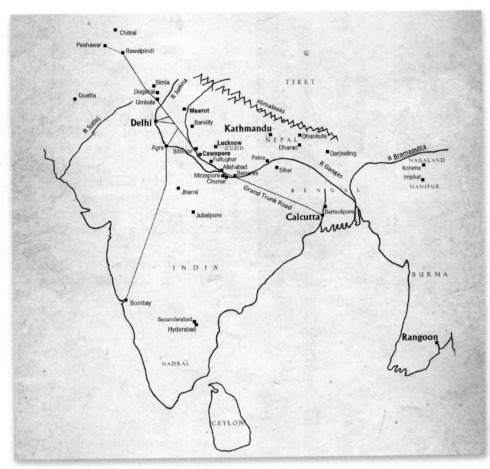

India 1857

One of my relations, **Charles Elliott,** was 'British Resident' in the high days of Delhi culture in 1823-5. He'd come top of his class at Haileybury, the officer cadet school in Hertfordshire. In Calcutta, Charles learnt Persian and Hindi and took exams at Fort William College, which Richard Wellesley, as Governor-General, had set up in 1800[13].

Charles quickly rose up the line, becoming a Judge at the age of 30[14]. In 1822 aged 46, he was posted to **Delhi**, to the court of the Moghul Emperor, Akbar Shah II[15]. Charles was to become the Emperor's British agent in his court, and representative of the East India Company's Board of Revenue. It was an influential position. Some would say it was more than that. The Governor General was 1,000 miles away[16]. Charles was 'remarkable for integrity, decision, and soundness of judgment[vi].'

Emperor Akbar II (1760-1837)

14. *Charles Elliott (1776-1856) was appointed Judge at Futtyghur c1806, Circuit and Appellate Judge at Bareilly a few years later. In 1821, aged 45, he was appointed Judge at the Sudder Court, the chief court of appeal.*

15. *Akbar Shar (1760-1837) reigned 1806-37.*

16. *William Pitt Amherst, Earl Amherst GCH PC (1773-1857) Governor General of India 1823-1828 is chiefly remembered for refusing to kowtow to the Chinese Emperor in 1816 and thereby being refused an audience.*

Hall of Audience, Delhi

In 1823, Charles was promoted to the job of British Resident at Delhi. This post was one of few reporting directly to the British Government. Part diplomat, part adviser, it was the top job in Delhi, administering the civil service there and monitoring the activities of the Emperor. The picture below is probably him riding on an elephant in one of the Emperor's processions[vii]. The Emperor never moved out of his palace without Charles's say so. The British Resident was the instrument of princely rule in India.

Whether Charles was keen to espouse the cause of Christianity, he certainly set an example. He arranged an increase in the 'pension', which the Company gave the Emperor[viii]. The Emperor was so grateful, he wanted to reciprocate in the eastern way but Charles wouldn't take money. To cement their relationship, Akbar asked Charles if he could adopt Alicia, his wife, as one of his 'daughters', whereupon one of Akbar's real daughters placed a ring on Alicia's finger – the largest emerald they'd ever seen[17]. It would be nice to think that this was the same emerald ring my mother wore, which was enormous – but that one was inherited through her Aunt Bertie (Chapter 10).

Charles took the Bishop of Calcutta, Reginald Heber, to see the Emperor[18]. Heber recalled they entered the court in princely fashion, on a procession of elephants, through the myriad of outlying courts, bowing low in obeisance.

"Opposite to us was a beautiful open pavilion of white marble, richly carved, flanked by rose bushes and fountains, and some tapestry and striped curtains hanging in festoons about it, within which was a crowd of people, and the poor old descendant of Tamerlane seated in the midst of them. Mr Elliott here bowed three times very low, in which we followed his example. …. Mr Elliott then stepped forwards, and, with joined hands, in the usual Eastern way, announced, in a low voice, to the Emperor, who I was."

Charles Elliott was the British agent or Resident 1820s around the time of this procession through the streets of Delhi

Bishop Heber on the other hand was full of evangelistic zeal[ix]. Under William Wilberforce and the Clapham Sect (see Chapter 11), evangelical Christianity was taking a hold. Previously, the East India Company had encouraged fraternisation with the local women including intermarriage which had calmed and comforted hot-headed youths from England, softened their 'ferocious manners' and tutored them in the local ways and behaviour[x]. Our current Prince William has a little bit of Indian in him, through his mother Princess Diana. His great-great-great-great-great grandfather[19] was Theodore Forbes who had a 'local wife', Eliza Kewark. By the

17. *Alicia Boileau (1779-1851) married Charles Elliott (1776-1856) in Calcutta in 1802.*
18. *Rt Rev Reginald Heber DD (1783-1826) [NR], second Bishop of Calcutta 1823-26, visited in Delhi 1824.*
19. *Diana, Princess of Wales is descended from Eliza Kewark (c1795-?) who was part Armenian and part Indian. She gave birth to Katherine Scott Forbes (1812-1893) in India. Theodore Forbes (1788-1820) was a Writer for the East India Company. Katherine was brought up in Scotland and married James Crosbie (1810-1878); their daughter was Jane Crosbie (1843-1917). Her daughter was Ruth Littlejohn (1879-1964) and her daughter was Princess Diana's mother, The Hon Frances Burke Roche, Countess Spencer (1936-2004). The rare Indian 'R30b' DNA gene has carried through the female descent to Prince William.*

1820s, however, the wives of the officers were being encouraged to join their husbands out in India, to 'rein in their behaviour'[xi]. Heber, the author of well-known hymns such as 'Holy, Holy, Holy', unconsciously fostered a process of polarisation between the civilisations, which helped to sow the seeds for the Mutiny.

John Nicholas Tresidder (1819-1889) – a painting by Lorna Tresidder (b1938)

Indolent Officers

By the time my great grandfather, John Nicholas Tresidder, arrived in India twenty years later in 1845, the bond of fraternisation had been blown away. Whilst Heber had showed a sniffy superiority towards the 'natives', now there was 'rarely a note of kindness'[xii]. 'Arrogance, insolence and selfishness' were too often the distinguishing trait of the indolent English Officer[xiii]. The instruction book said: *'Your duty as a soldier… is to conciliate the native soldiery, pay attention to their prejudices, and respect their forms of worship, at least as far as not ridiculing or making yourself obnoxious to them by inference.'* All too often, this went unobserved[xiv]. The whip was used on native men without thought. Words were exchanged, hardly Christian. The average officer was only 16 or 17 years old going straight from school – more used to nights with friends on the (champagne) bottle; days of tiger hunting and pig-sticking, if not lying in bed with Thackeray's latest novel and keeping out of the midday sun[xv]. Soldiers' discipline and training were largely left to the Indian Officers and the British Sergeants.

No longer did the nodding rapport occur between the indigenous dweller and the foreign sahib, supping together or sharing a joke. No longer did the officers learn the cultured ways of the local courtesans. Married officers had to listen to moralising and 'put on an extra allowance of manners' in front of their English ladies[xvi]. Lobster salad, sponge cake, bread and marmalade replaced kebabs and biryanis. Cities like Calcutta and Cawnpore (Kanpur) owed more to Harrogate, Eastbourne or Cheltenham – on the surface. But underneath, they smelt, tasted, talked and thought like India ever had.

✳ ✳ ✳ ✳

Day in the life of an 1850s Army Officer

4 am	Parade
7 am	Cup of Tea
9/10 am	**Breakfast** – 'tea or coffee, goats' milk, butter, bread, chapattis, fish, mutton-chops, or grill, and curries.'
2 pm	**Tiffin** – 'more curries and chops, and cold meat and pickles, and pale ale.'
7.30 pm	**Dinner** – soup (hot thick, 'a veritable warm jelly'); fish; joints of mutton, stews, ragouts; sweets; sherry, beer, soda water, champagne; followed by a smoke: the pipe had replaced the hookah.
9.30 pm	Bed

John Nicholas Tresidder (1819-1889)

Dr Tresidder

What did my great grandfather, **Dr John Nicholas Tresidder**, expect when he and his newly-wedded wife sailed for India in 1845? Had he heard of the exotic Maharajahs who were dripping with jewels, or the elephants and dancing girls, and the sycophantic fuss by retinues of servants? Was he ready for the noise, the vibrant colours, the smells, and the heat of the food or the heat of the weather?

Commissioned into the East India Company's Medical Service on 1 March that year, he sailed out the long way – round the Horn of Africa[xvii]. Suez wasn't an option. It took him nearly five months to reach Calcutta. It was never an easy journey – one of his daughters was later to lose her life in 1851 at the Cape of Good Hope[20] ... his future son-in-law's father had lost practically all of his first wife's family there in 1836[21]. Dr Tresidder sailed up the 100-mile Hooghly River and stepped ashore on **28 July 1845**.

Calcutta had been in the hands of the British since the seventeenth century. The Fort William was 'the most regular fortress in India', erected in 1757, and the classical Government

Calcutta from the Esplanade

House built by the Marquess of Wellesley stood on the edge of the grassy Maidan – larger than Hyde Park, the flat open area giving protection from attack[xviii]. It was surrounded by government buildings, St Paul's Cathedral and the Calcutta General Hospital. For the first month, John Nicholas (as I shall call him) was based there. His senior colleagues brought this 'griffin', as they termed new officers, up to scratch on procedures[xix]. He quickly adopted the style of an 'officer and gentleman': dressing for dinner, with white kid gloves, holding a knife and fork correctly, using the correct forms of address, calling on people at the correct hour, showing his visiting card, knowing the precedence in a mess and speaking the military jargon. 130 years later, when I joined the civil service, it was much the same – I filled up three pages of military acronyms in the first few days[22]. My father tutored me about leaving the bottom button of my waistcoat undone and eating peas on the back of the fork[xx]. Not all is lost. Today, displaying a mobile phone at the dinner table is frowned upon and it's still good to know how to shake hands properly[xxi].

Assistant Surgeons were the bottom officer grade in the Indian medical service, and paid 330 Rupees a month[xxii]. The Medical Corps, which stretched back to 1612, was an arm of the military from 1745. Surgeons went straight into service after training at British hospitals. The word 'surgeon' described the duties of battle: to stitch up wounds, to amputate limbs to avoid gangrene. John Nicholas gained early experience with General Wheeler in the first Sikh war in 1846, the 'Army of the Sutlej', named after the river valley in north-west India[23]. In the second Sikh war he was once again near the north-west frontier, at the battles of Chillianwalla (near the Jhelum River) (13 Jan 1849) and Goojerat (Gujrat) (21 Feb 1849), 24,000 British against double the number of Sikhs. Artillery enfilades, with the infantry mopping up after; the cavalry breaking up the Sikh masses, the capturing of most of their cannons; his was a long day[xxiii].

The Sutlej hills looking towards the Himalayas, 100 miles from the 1849 battles

Elizabeth Carlyon Barnicoat (1816-1855) on her wedding day to Dr Tresidder

---

20. *Frances Alice Tresidder (1848-1851) died in Table Bay on the 850 ton sailing vessel Essex.*
21. *Sophie Antoinette neé Wiehe (1807-1836) and Louise (b1827), Emma (b1829), William (b1830), Alfred (b1833) and Sophie (b1835) Saunders drowned on the Doncaster 17 July 1836.*
22. *In Defence Secretariat Overseas, Property Services Agency, Croydon 1973-75.*
23. *Major-General Sir Hugh Massy Wheeler KCB (1789-1857) [NR].*

The Sikhs have given their loyalty to the British crown ever since. As none of them smoke tobacco, they were given the job of guarding the ammunition dumps across the empire. In the First World War 70,000 fought in the Flanders trenches[xxiv]. In Hong Kong, when I was there in the 1980s, they were employed as policemen. John Nicholas earned a medal and clasp for his services in the Punjab.

Chunar Fort

John Nicholas had left Cornwall forever when he'd taken his newly wedded wife **Elizabeth** to India[24]. For the next ten years, they lived an elegant existence as their children grew up in Mirzapore and Chunar in central northern India, the part now called Uttah Pradesh. They produced five children in those ten years. Their first-born **Annie** arrived twelve months after their arrival. Two girls followed[xxv]. **Johnnie**, their eldest son, was born five years after their arrival[25].

Mirzapore (Mirzapur) – city of Princes – was one of the most elegant cities in the centre of Northern India, a beautiful silk town on the Ganges with Chunar 30 miles upstream. When the Tresidders lived there, Chunar Fort, on a rocky bank above the river, housed a prison and was the centre for 'invalid battalions', soldiers laid up on light duties.

To get around this vast country, the John Company had built the Grand Trunk Road from Calcutta up the Ganges river valley as far as Peshawar in the north-west. A railway was being constructed alongside. The principal army supply depots were dotted all along this transport artery – Calcutta, Benares (Varanasi), Chunar, Allahabad, Futtehpore, Cawnpore, Agra, Allyghur, Delhi, Umbala (Ambala), Lahore, Chillianwalla, Peshawar. In 1854, a primitive 'telegraph' had been laid, which greatly speeded communication. Riverboat travel was still the traditional way to get about, however – most freight went by water. **Rosie**, their second child, was born on board a riverboat between Mirzapore and Chunar[26].

The telegraph system in the 1850s

✳ ✳ ✳ ✳

Cawnpore in the 1850s

In 1854, John Nicholas was posted further up the Ganges to **Cawnpore,** as Civil Surgeon. Cawnpore was a plum job in the Indian Army. It had the second largest European population in India[xxvi]. There was a feeling of wealth and status. The garrison town housed some 3,500 troops commanded by 70 British officers plus roughly 200 British soldiers, a fair few of whom ended up in the sick-bay – what with the mosquitoes, sanitation and venereal disease[xxvii]. There were plans to enlarge the hospital.

Cawnpore from Christ Church tower

The officers had huge white rendered homes, surrounded by large gardens, 3 or 4 acres, interspersed with forest trees[xxviii] The vegetable plots grew mangoes, guavas, salads, and beans. They had a legion of servants to cope with the horses, the grounds, the fine dining and the children. There was even ice, stored in icehouses. The gardens were the best in India.

On the high ground, there was a Church, a Free School, Assembly Rooms able to hold 1,000 people, a theatre, library and the Freemasons' Hall. There was a Telegraph Office and a Post Office near the canal. There were band concerts and 'private theatricals every week; balls, and picnics, and dinners every evening[xxx].' The horseracing was famous. You could buy fish, fowl, snipe, duck, partridge or quail. In the boulevards, in the early evening, the band played softly as the wives and their husbands went for a slow evening drive – the promenade[xxxi].

View from the garden of the Tresidder residence in Agra in the 1860s. The Cawnpore home was similar.

24. *Elizabeth Carlyon Barnicoat (1816-1855).*
25. *Capt Tolmie John Tresidder CMG (1850-1931).*
26. *Mary Rosamund Tresidder (1847-1923).*

'My favourite trotting cart.'

John Nicholas Tresidder's establishment of 38 paid servants, probably assembled at Agra in the early 1860s. An example of one of his unique photographic collages

Procession into Lucknow

There was obsessive observance of manners and decorum – the English in India were more English than the English back home. At the weekends, you could take your buggy (horse and trap) down to the water's edge. One picnic of lobster salad would be particularly memorable[xxx]. It was hot. The road surface was watered down each afternoon, like in Paris, to keep the dust in place. Dust storms poured off the plains. Most of the day you'd spend indoors. The rooms had an early form of air-conditioning: windows were covered with *tatties*, made of *khus*, a scented plant. Bearers sprinkled them with water every few minutes – and as the hot winds dried the tatties, the evaporation cooled the room. The ceiling fans wafted back and forth as punkha wallahs slowly tugged the ropes on the verandah – I wonder what the punka wallahs overheard....

Cawnpore garrison was important enough to be commanded by a Major-General. It was Tresidder's old General, Sir Hugh Wheeler. As well as the wives and families, John Nicholas's duties included care of the locally-engaged civilian staff and the prison population. He gave medical assistance to the Commissioner at **Bithoor** (Bithur), fifteen miles up-river, for which he was paid an extra 100 rupees per month (33% extra).

When Britain had conquered the Maratha Empire in 1818, they'd exiled the Peshwa, the titular 'Prime Minister' of India, to Bithoor. A generous pension of 200,000 rupees was delivered every three months to his new palace, in bullock carts piled full of gold coins[xxxii]. Crucially, Dr Tresidder attended the Peshwa as his medical officer.

✳ ✳ ✳ ✳

The condition of Oudh

John Nicholas Tresidder was well thought of. On 4 December 1854, he accompanied Colonel Sir James Outram to **Lucknow** (Lakhani)[27]. Outram had been appointed Resident of Lucknow, with a brief to assume control of the state of Oudh as its first Chief Commissioner. The two of them slept the first night at the King's Palace. The following morning, a newspaper reports:

"About 8 o'clock a magnificent cavalcade of elephants beautifully caparisoned, started from the Residency Gates, where the royal procession headed by the Heir apparent and the Minister fell in, and we all proceeded to meet the Resident.... We went to the Char Munzil Palace where a magnificent breakfast was provided, to which justice was done by the Europeans and Native gentry. The procession was really magnificent, so large a sewaree not having been seen for some time; Rupees were thrown from the elephants and scrambled for in fine style by the unwashed, many of whom were knocked over and tumbled through Chuppers to the great annoyance and terror of the sable beauties therein concealed. The usual tamasha of elephant fights, sword exercise, ram fights, Hyena and Donkey combat (very slow) with a tiger and buffalo fight finished the fun".[xxxiii]

27. *Lt-General Sir James Outram, 1st Baronet GCB KCSI (1803-1863) [NR].*

The state of Oudh (or Awadh) stretched from Cawnpore to Nepal. It had lost its full independence in 1775, when the East India Company had been 'engaged' to 'defend' it – Cawnpore garrison was the result[xxxiv]. The wealthy Nawab Vizier of Oudh crowned himself King in 1819 to the strains of *God save the King* and turned Oudh's capital, **Lucknow**, into one of the most fabulous cities of the world[28]. The limestone stucco, the Corinthian columns, the scented fountains, golden domes and minarets put the Royal Pavilion in Brighton (Chapter 3) into the shade – unlike the Prince Regent, the king of Oudh could afford the cost. However, by the time this man's great-nephew ascended the throne in 1847, the kingdom was in a shambles[29]. Whilst the King indulged in courtesans, the tax collectors wrung the farmers dry, and everyone feuded with everybody else[xxxv]. The British were in despair. Was the answer to rule it directly? Dalhousie had thought so.

Residency at Lucknow

As the youngest Governor-General in history, the impatient and imperious Marquess Dalhousie had arrived in Calcutta in 1848 with a mission to make India truly British[30]. Scrupulously polite, with bright-blue eyes, he could reduce British Generals to jelly[xxxvi]. He ostracised staff who 'croaked' (complained). He pushed ahead with the transformation of the civil service, the judicial system, a postal service, public works department, railways, telegraph system, coinage, afforestation, canals, irrigation, new roads, schools, hospitals, twisting the rules if need be and riding roughshod over local feelings. He overspent – there was a £8m deficit, so he looked around for extra income, and imposed heavier taxes[xxxvii].

Dalhousie brooked no opposition. 'Annexation' was his solution to everything[31]. His first job was to take over the Punjab after the Sikh wars. Burma (Myanmar) was next to be 'annexed' (1852).

It didn't take Dalhousie long to re-interpret the **Doctrine of Lapse** – a Hindu law which allowed a local ruler with no direct heir to 'adopt' a son to take over and rule after he died. Dalhousie was having none of it: 'Where the right to [rule the] territory by lapse is clear, the Government is bound to take which is justly and legally its due,' he wrote, and summarily 'annexed' Satara, Jhansi and Nagpore (Nagpur) and some others[xxxviii]. Colonisation therefore, by another name. He wanted to do the same in Oudh.

The *Oude Blue Book* of 1855 was no different from the 'dodgy dossier' for the 2003 Iraqi invasion. Dalhousie ordered General Wheeler to ride out from Cawnpore and arrest the King in early 1856, and exile him to Calcutta[32]. Many thought it unwise. William Sleeman, a Cornishman, and previous British Resident of Oudh, had the courage to write[xxxix]. But Dalhousie wasn't listening.

Neither Sleeman nor Dalhousie was there when the worst happened. Sleeman retired in 1854 and died on his way home. Dalhousie sailed to England in 1856 worn down by stress. Like too many British civil servants, he'd left the hardest job to last and had someone senior approve his slip-shod solution. He'd moved on before (as the civil servants would say) the 's*** hit the fan'[xl]. The annexation of Oudh had been Dalhousie's ambition from the start but he'd not found the time or the means to address the issue properly. He left the new British Resident of Lucknow, Outram, to recruit and train a native army of 15,000[xli]. Today they call what he did a 'moral hazard'[xlii].

Words from India that have entered the English language

My father-in-law, Ken Burton, regularly talks of doing the dhobi, meaning doing the washing. It comes from his days on the ships where the dhobi wallahs (laundry workers) were often recruited from the colonies. Others from our Indian heritage:

Avatar	Mogul
Bangle	Pariah
Bungalow	Pashmina
Cash	Polo
Catamaran	Punch
Chintz	Pyjamas
Chutney	Sorbet
Cummerbund	Shampoo
Cushy	Shawl
Dinghy	Tank
Ginger	Tattoo
Guru	Taut
Juggernaut	Thug
Jungle	Toddy
Lacquer	Verandah
Mantra	Yoga

28. *Ghazi-ud-Din Haidar Shah (c1769-1827) [NR].*

29. *Wajid Ali Shah (1822-1887) [NR].*

30. *James Andrew Broun-Ramsay, 10th Earl and 1st Marquess of Dalhousie KT PC (1812-1860) [NR], Governor-General of India 1848-56.*

31. *Prior to the British, individual rulers (Rajahs, Nabobs etc) owned and ruled individual states, many originally owing their power to the Emperor in Delhi. Reality was different – there was no clear constitutional relationship and the British played that to its advantage.*

32. *Proclamation 13 Feb 1856.*

The new Governor-General, Lord Canning, was George Canning's son[33]. The military officers breathed a sigh of relief. The native rulers and population thought about revenge. They needed someone – anybody – that they could revere, a monarch not oceans away in a rain-sodden murky Britain, but one in their midst.

✳ ✳ ✳ ✳

Dr Tresidder's important patient

Nana Sahib (1824-c1857) – the ogre in the British eyes – Peshwa of the Mahratta dynasty who led the mutinous soldiers in Cawnpore

John Nicholas's wife, **Elizabeth**, took their children home to England in 1851 to put the eldest ones into school[xliii]. When she returned, they had another child. It was to be their last. Elizabeth died in 1855, a month after giving birth to their second boy – **Innes** lived for only 19 days[34]. John Nicholas buried them both in Cawnpore's cemetery and resumed a bachelor's life. He studied local languages with a view to passing a language test. He considered the causes of cholera, which was rife in the state prison[xliv]. There was a new hospital in the offing. He was beginning to explore the new medium of photography and it is probable he was a Freemason – the Lodge was called Harmony and Nana Sahib was a member.

Nana Sahib, the wealthy Peshwa's adopted heir, was a Freemason and John Nicholas's patient – amongst other things, he'd been treated for an infected toe. The Nana, as Tresidder called him, was to become the chief villain of the Indian Mutiny as far as the British press was concerned[35].

'Baji Rao, the previous Peshwa, had died in 1851[36]. Though one would like to think the Nana would be overjoyed to inherit, he wasn't, as he wasn't his direct heir, and had fallen foul of Dalhousie's policy on the *Doctrine of Lapse*. The cartloads of bullion had stopped arriving and he still had all his retainers to pay – how was he to carry on? The Nana decided to petition Queen Victoria direct. Being a Hindu he didn't care to cross the sea himself, so he sent his elegant young Muslim secretary, Azimullah Khan, to go in his place[xlv].

Azimullah Khan would have died as a boy in the 1833 famine had he not been taken in[37]. The Society for the Propagation of the Gospel (SPG) mission's Free School had rescued him and the Cawnpore Commissioner's family gave him work[xlvi]. From a poor start in life, he'd received much Christian charity and possibly too much male attention. Athletic, exotic, with dark olive colouring, he knew how to ingratiate himself on London society when he got there and he certainly did so, but not as the Nana intended. It was 1854. He spent the summer, and the £50,000 the Nana had given him, taking advantage of society women[xlvii]. Lucie Duff Gordon, the wife of the Prime Minister's cousin, introduced him to Dickens, Thackeray and Macaulay[38]. Dressed like a gentleman, he was feted like a Prince and took every advantage... but it was social advantage: he was not to see the Queen. His mission was a failure. Those women had diverted his attentions. 'Like moths in the candlelight, they will fly and get buried,' he swore[xlviii].

---

33. *Charles John Canning, 1st Earl Canning KG GCB GCSI PC (1812-1862) [NR], Governor General and Viceroy of India 1856-62. The Queen wasn't consulted. Lord Lansdowne wanted to get him away from his mistress. George Canning (1770-1827) [NR], Prime Minister in 1827, briefly appears in Chapter 3.*

34. *Innes Barnicoat Tresidder (6-25 Nov 1855) lived 19 days, buried on 26 Nov. Elizabeth died on 7 Dec 1855 aged 39 years and 11 months and was buried the next day at Cawnpore.*

35. *In the author's family, silly children were told off by saying 'You Nana' meaning 'you idiot'.*

36. *Baji Rao II (1775-1851) [NR] named Nana Govind Dhondu Pant (1824-c1857) [NR] to succeed him. Nana was a nickname: 'few in years'. Nana was one of Baji Rao's wives' sisters' sons, adopted in 1832.*

37. *Azimullah Khan Yusufzai (1830-1859) [NR].*

38. *Lucie, Lady Duff-Gordon neé Austin (1821-1869) [NR].*

He'd been their plaything, not for the first time. He hated himself – and them. He returned home to explain his failure to the Nana as best he could. He didn't hurry back.

In his infuriation and frustration, his hatred deepened for a race of people with their Christian religion. He visited the Crimea to observe the British Army in action, and saw the mud and incompetence for himself. He recalled the fate of his Muslim mother placed into poverty because his father, a mason, had been thrown off a roof and deliberately killed by an army officer[xlix].

On board ship, as he travelled home, Azimullah looked down into the depths of the sea. He had time to think. His mind worked overtime. He'd bide his time and play the nice guy.

⁂ ⁂ ⁂ ⁂

Dr Tresidder diagnoses the condition

From as far back to the beginning of 1857, John Nicholas would have heard about the chapatis. No one knows the origins of this tradition – of the passing of unleavened bread cakes between villages, like wildfire[l]. It was 100 years since the Battle of Plassey. Brahmin soothsayers had predicted the British Empire would last no longer than a hundred years, 1757-1857. Milestones, a symbol of British rule across India were being ripped out of the ground, unnerving the officers' wives. If they'd bothered to learn the language, they'd have overheard their domestic staff muttering. John Nicholas had picked up the gist of what they were saying. A colleague had obviously taken it seriously enough to drink enough medicine to poison himself[li]. A priest had been advised by his butler to send his wife and children to Europe before it was too late[lii]. There'd be serious asides at the Freemasons' Lodge where all faiths and creeds met. They'd be talking about the problem of the cartridges that had to be torn open by teeth.

Under Dalhousie's modernisation – I blame him – the army were introducing the Enfield 'Minie' muzzle-loading rifle. It had been used to good effect in the Crimean War. Unhappily, the English paper tubes containing gunpowder and lead bullet (cartridges) had to be held in the teeth and came with greased wrappers. In England, mutton fat was used. At Dum Dum, the contractor had inexpertly over-greased the paper with bullock fat[liii].

In times of rebellion, it is not what's true but what people believe. The rumour spread, with indecent haste, that pig and cow fat were both being used. As Hindu did not eat cow and Muslim avoided pig, both could be upset at the same time; so it allowed the troublemakers to sow the seeds of dissension. The authorities used every means to dissuade them but the sepoys, the native soldiers, were past listening to reason[39].

Leadership training teaches you that staff like challenges – but don't push them over the cliff-edge. The

---

1840	MRCS
1842	Licentiate of Society of Apothecaries
1844	Certificate in cupping
Mar 1845	Commissioned into the East India Company's Medical Service
July 1845	Calcutta General Hospital
Sep 1845	British Dragoons, Chinsurah
Dec 1845	21st & 60th Native Infantry, Benares
Jan 1846	Army of the Sutlej, First Sikh War
May 1846	49th&62nd NI, Benares, Mirzapore and Mhow
Nov 1846	British Garrison, Chúnar
Aug 1848	Temporary promotion
Nov 1848	Army of the Punjab, Second Sikh War
Jan 1849	Battle of Chillianwalla
Feb 1849	Battle of Goojerat
May 1849	Return to Chunar.
Aug 1851	Civil Surgeon, Mirzapore
Oct 1851	Elizabeth & children return to England
Mar 1853	Shekhawatee Battalion
Jan 1854	Civil Surgeon, Staff Surgeon Cawnpore.
Nov 1855	Innes Tresidder born and dies, Cawnpore
Dec 1855	Elizabeth (née Barnicoat) dies, Cawnpore
Mar 1857	Leave (furlough), Calcutta
Apr 1857	Furlough, 'private affairs' (5 mths 25 days)
May 1857	Mutiny
Aug 1857	Marries Emily Hooton Courtis, Camberwell
Oct 1857	Returns to Calcutta. Special duties.
Nov 1857	Senior Ass Surgeon, Right wing of 42nd Royal Highlanders, Allahabad & Cawnpore
Dec 1857	Action at Cawnpore & Sheorajpore Ghat
Oct 1858	Promoted to rank of Surgeon. In the civil charge of Cawnpore 'for special Public reasons' by order of Governor-General
Dec 1860	In charge of European Depot Hospital, Cawnpore, which he closed.
Mar 1861	42nd Native Infantry, Agra; got ill after epidemic and moved to Calcutta to apply for sick leave
Feb 1862	To England on sick leave (1yr 8mths)
Nov 1863	Returned
Dec 1863	Native Infantry & Civil, Banda
Apr 1864	104th Fusiliers
Jul 1865	4th Regt Native Infantry and Civil, Jhansie
Mar 1865	Surgeon-Major 4th&8th Native Infantry and Civil Surgeon, Jhansie
1868	4th Native Infantry, Allahabad
1869-70	Sick Leave England
1871	Deputy Inspector-General of Hospitals Saugor Circle, based in Jubbulpore (Jabalpur)
1873	Deputy Inspector-General of Hospitals, Umbala (Ambala) Circle
1874-7	Deputy Surgeon-General
Mar 1877	Retired. Hon Surgeon-General of India

---

39. *Sepoy: regular soldiers armed, trained and largely dressed in European style. Derived from the Persian sipahi.*

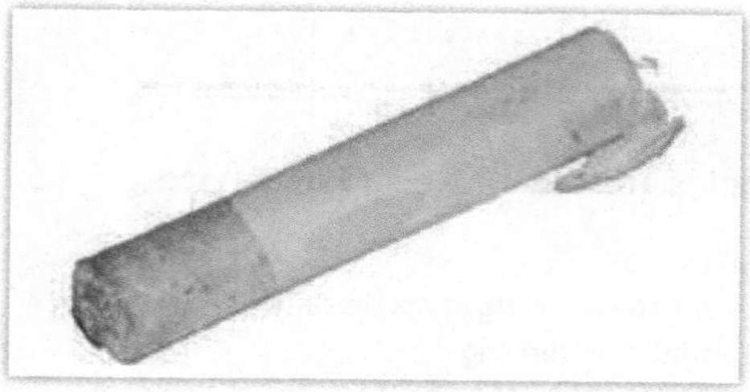

A greased cartridge

sepoys, the backbone infantry, were standing on that cliff. Promotion prospects had reduced[liv]. Pay was not keeping pace with prices, in some cases reduced. Cost-cutting measures were being introduced. Perks, like free postage and elephants for the Indian officers, were being withdrawn[lv]. British officers, many without language skills, were being moved between the native regiments far too frequently for them to win the respect of their troops[lvi]. Lack of continuity took its toll. "Year by year the separation of the officers and their men seems to increase."[lvii]

Somebody was deliberately whipping up dissent. The secret visit of Nana and Azimullah Khan to the native soldiers of military stations up and down the Grand Trunk Road, on the pretext of a pilgrimage, could have had something to do with it[lviii]. Rumours that flour was being defiled with bone-meal had no basis of fact. A theory that the Brits would require Hindu men to marry English war widows from the Crimea was pure fantasy. That soldiers were to give up their religion for Christianity, though, had an element of truth – Colonel Steven Wheler commanding the 34th Bengal Infantry at Barrackpore, for instance, 'was terribly given to preach' and read out the gospels to his sepoy soldiers on parade[lix]. The main reason was a breakdown of understanding between the two cultures.

Barrackpore, 15 miles north of Calcutta where Col Wheler was based, reported trouble on **29 March 1857**. A soldier, Mangal Pandee, 'ran amuk' calling on his fellow sepoys to rise up[41]. He shot and wounded a sergeant, an officer and a horse, and aimed his gun at a General[lx]. He wounded himself, was court-martialled a week later, and hanged the next day. He was not alone. He'd been put up to it[lxi].

Eleven days before the incident, Dr John Nicholas Tresidder had arranged to start leave in England ('furlough') 'on private affairs', handing over his responsibilities to Assistant Surgeon Horatio Harris[42]. It was impeccable timing. The day of the Pandee hanging, Tresidder's ship set sail for Europe[lxii].

* * * *

High blood pressure at Meerut

The Pandee incident was not an isolated one. On the jungle borders of Nepal, a bandit called Fuzil Ali shot and decapitated another relative, **Charles Elliott Boileau** who was the Deputy Commissioner of **Oudh**[lxiii]. Sepoys (soldiers) at **Umbala** (Ambala) who'd agreed to use the greased cartridges had had their huts burned down[lxiv]. The same happened at **Meerut**. There was passive resistance in **Behar** (Bihar Sharif). A fakir in **Agra** was preaching holy war, like the fanatical Mullahs do today[43]. There was mad talk at **Patna**, and wide circulation of provocative pamphlets everywhere[lxv].

John Nicholas's personal reasons for leaving India were unarguable. It was his first leave from duty for over 10 years. He was in search of a second wife and was to marry **Emily Courtis** on 26 August. Before he stepped onto English soil at the end of **May**, India was in ferment.

Wars are often triggered by a single incident. One of my relations could be said to have triggered the Indian Mutiny. [43]Brevet Lt Col **George Carmichael Smyth**, the step-uncle of William Makepeace Thackeray, had been put in command of the 3rd Calvary at **Meerut**, the Artillery HQ, 50 miles from Delhi under the command of General Hewitt[44]. 'The youngest

---

40. *Mangal Pande(e) (1827-1857) [NR]; Today, he's celebrated as a freedom fighter.*
41. *Dr Horatio P Harris (1824-1857) [NR].*
42. *Ahmed Ahmadullah Shak, 'the Maulvi of Faizabad', was imprisoned for sedition.*
43. *Brevet is a courtesy title indicating temporary promotion without the pay.*

of eight competitive boys, the product of a tough public school, querulous, irritable and uncharitable, this unpopular officer decided to bring the matter of the greased cartridge paper to a head[lxvi]. Ignoring the advice of his junior officers, he announced a firing parade, to test *tearing* versus *biting* and to prove, once and for all, there was no issue. The 90 men selected, however, took a solemn oath to refuse. Smyth had no empathy with their way of thinking. They said they'd lose their caste and be unable to return to their families[lxvii]. He pushed on.

It was a stand-off. 'Authority' without 'respect' doesn't work. The Colonel was seeking to impose his will over men in an impossible situation. Apart from five, they all refused, so what would you do then? George escalated the problem, calling in the Deputy Judge-Advocate-General[lxviii]. Each soldier was sentenced to 10 years hard labour – a few younger boys to 5 years. A plea for leniency to General Hewitt failed – indeed Hewitt thought they should have been hanged.

Worse, George arranged a special parade of the whole Garrison on **Saturday 9 May** 1857 – the whole of Meerut was aghast, including the British. The eighty-five troopers, some of whom had spent 30 years fighting for the British, were stripped of their uniform in front of their fellow men. As they were led away in ankle irons, some threw their boots at Carmichael Smyth – the ultimate insult.

It was insufferably hot. The following day, the Meerut bazaars were fermenting because they'd heard the Indian troops were going to be disarmed. Sometime before the evening church parade, all hell broke loose[lxix]. The native troopers, sowars, broke open the magazine, took out the guns, galloped off to the jail, bashed open the doors and released their comrades plus a thousand other criminals. The sun was setting. When another Colonel tried reasoning with them, he was riddled with bullets[lxx]. Fired up with the excitement of killing an English officer, there was no going back. In the pitch dark, the petty criminals raged through the lines massacring men, women and children at random, setting fire to the houses with 'remorseless barbarity'[lxxi]. Carmichael Smyth did everything but visit the lines of his own regiment. Not a single senior officer in Meerut knew how to respond. None had seen this coming. Some had been taking a siesta. It was a Sunday.

Stripping the troops on parade at Meerut – May 1857

Death of an officer at Meerut

✳ ✳ ✳ ✳

Coronary attack at Delhi

In **Delhi**, 19-year-old **Lt Edward Vibart** had just come back from visiting his family in Cawnpore, where he'd attended his father's Regimental Ball. His father, Major Edward Vibart, was a close friend of Dr Tresidder, and commanding officer of the 2nd Native Cavalry[45]. Edward junior wasn't expecting what happened next in Delhi. It was the start of the summer, and the quiet time when it was the custom for the British regiments to decamp into the hill stations to escape the heat, leaving just Edward and a few British officers in charge of the Native regiments. General Anson, Commander-in-Chief, had decamped even sooner than normal.

In the cool of the evening, as the moon rose over Meerut, around nine o'clock that night, the rebel soldiers left the Meerut mayhem and galloped off to Delhi, having cut the telegraph line before they left, so no one knew they were coming[lxxii]. The following morning, they

Major Edward Vibart (senior) (1807-1857) c 1850

---

44. *Maj (later he was to self-style himself Maj-Gen) George Munroe Carmichael Smyth (1803-1890) (the regimental rank of Lt Col was never confirmed). Fortunately, he is not a blood relative. Three marriages separate him and the author.*

45. *Maj Edward Vibart (1807-1857), father of Lt later Col Edward Daniel Hamilton 'Butcher' Vibart MC (1837-1923). EDH Vibart's second marriage was to Isabella Louisa Horn (1867-1946) in 1893.*

Lt later Col Edward D H Vibart (junior)
(1837-1923)

William Stephen Raikes Hodson
(1821-1858)

Simla from Jakho Hill

entered the Red Fort, the royal palace, much to the surprise of the eighty-year-old Moghul Emperor, Bahadur Shah Zafar[46]. Uninvited guests, they swigged back his bhang and ate his choicest sweetmeats without a by-your-leave, and asked the Emperor to lead a revolution against the British[lxxiii]. The last thing old Zafar wanted was to unbalance a carefully controlled relationship between Hindu, Muslim and the British administration. He didn't want to be the figurehead for a revolt, but couldn't deny that *he* was rightly the paramount leader of the Indian continent, the monarch in their midst.

The rebel numbers, increasing hourly, made short work of anyone who got in their way. 'They murdered ladies in a brutal manner, burning them half, and then cutting them up, and stripping them naked.'[lxxiv] Edward was sent to the rescue. It was a miracle he got out alive. They killed the tollhouse keeper, the manager of the telegraph office, the bank manager, the British Resident, a Chief Magistrate, the commandant of palace guards, the priest of St James Church, his lovely daughter and many more. The British fled to a camp on the Ridge, the hills above Delhi, and waited for orders from the Commander-in-Chief, General Anson. It was a long wait. There was no telegraph to the hill stations. Anson didn't read the gravity of the situation; reinforcements weren't sent and the advantage of surprise was lost. More and more rebels poured in through the gates of the Emperor's palace.

Lieutenant **Willie Hodson**, another distant relation, was in the cool hills at Dugshai[lxxv]. His Commander-in-Chief was at Simla, 40 miles north, even further out of contact. Hodson had long complained about the army's promotion system. Generals Anson, Wilson and Hewitt were all out of their depth[47]. Not only them: there were cavalry commanders who couldn't mount horses, and Brigadiers so blind they didn't know which way their soldiers were facing[lxxvi]. George Anson, brother of the Earl of Litchfield was 'the best whist player in Europe' but hadn't seen action since Waterloo, forty years earlier.[lxxvii] Neither did he act when advised. [lxxviii] "I will never give in to their beastly prejudices," he said[lxxix]. The quarter-masters couldn't get together transport, tents or supplies. When he was finally ordered to return to Delhi by the new Governor-General, the stress proved too much. Anson conked out half-way home[lxxx].

General Wilson, who took over, was more organised and had strategic ingenuity but became anxious and indecisive under pressure[lxxxi]. The more he delayed, the worse he became. 'He cannot stand on his legs,' complained Hodson[lxxxii]. General Hewitt had no redeeming qualities in Hodson's view – he was 'in a state of helpless imbecility.'[lxxxiii] Hewitt's poor decisions at Meerut and subsequent inaction had failed to stop the mutiny in the first place[lxxxiv].

Willie Hodson was not your normal officer; usually their only qualification would be their parents purchasing a commission for them[48]. After Rugby (under Dr Arnold), Hodson had studied at Cambridge for a degree. He'd then slipped into the East India Company's Army via the Guernsey Militia, with a flattering reference[lxxxv]. He distinguished himself in the first and second Sikh wars. Grazed by bullets in his cheek and finger, was he patched up by my great-grandfather? After the first war he'd been befriended by Sir Henry Lawrence, the local Political Agent[49]. Hodson lived with him at Simla, sleeping in his office and learning the mysteries of politics[lxxxvi]. For two years, he acted as Assistant to the 'very able' Commissioner **Charlie Saunders**, another of my relations. Charlie was the son of the Charles Saunders, who was building the railway to Cornwall (Chapter 2)[50].

There were few who didn't know Hodson. Willie was brazen and self-confident but he often overstepped the mark. He charmed women 'combining all the gentle playfulness of the boy, the deep tenderness of the woman and the vigorous decision of the soldier.'[lxxxvii] His blond good looks,

46. *Mirza Abu Zafar Sirajuddin Muhammad Bahadur Shah Zafar (c1776-1862) [NR].*
47. *General George Anson CB (1797-1857) [NR], Lt-Gen Sir Archdale Wilson Bt (1803–1874) [NR], Maj-Gen William Hewitt [NR].*
48. *Brevet-Major William Stephen Raikes Hodson (1821-1858).*
49. *Sir Henry Montgomery Lawrence KCB (1806-1857) [NR].*
50. *Charles Burslem Saunders (1821-1888) married Matilda Harriott (1819-1877) in 1845.*

his restless roaming unforgiving eyes and his impetuous temper polarised people. Colleagues plotted behind his back to bring him down[lxxxviii]. Yet in war, he was the man to have on your side. He had invincible swordplay. He could control the fight, like a cat with a mouse, playing with the victim before cutting him down. In peace, he was in trouble for embezzlement, and for his treatment of natives, but those who valued his soldierly skills, particularly the Sikhs, remained in awe of him. In the heat of battle, he could be counted on – he didn't as much as flinch. He'd raise his soldiers' spirits with his panache and, yes, even humour.

Hodson was to be the man of the hour. Anson appointed him quartermaster and gave him carte blanche to form his own regiment of 1-2,000 Sikh cavalrymen, nicknamed 'Hodson's Horse'. They'd follow him anywhere. "I never let my men take prisoners," he said[lxxxix]. The star of the moment, his exploits were soon to fill the London papers.

The first thing Hodson did was ride to **Meerut** and re-establish communications. He rode relentlessly in those first five days, getting next to no sleep, to pass messages and to persuade someone, anyone, into action. 250 miles in two days, fighting some of the way. Unbelievable energy and resolve.

Hodson's Horse

✳ ✳ ✳ ✳

Massacre Ghat at Cawnpore

Chapatis were exchanged, and insurrection broke out in cities across northern India. Jihadists, Mujahedeen, fanatical and untrained, came from nowhere. In **Calcutta**, the new Governor-General Lord Canning carried on as normal. However nervous underneath, he reeked impenetrable calmness and expected everyone to attend the Coronation Ball[51].

Men from Hodson's Horse

In **Cawnpore**, General Wheeler attempted to keep a cap on things. His half-Indian wife helped him know the native mind[52]. He kept in regular contact with Sir Henry Lawrence who'd succeeded Outram as Chief Commissioner at **Lucknow**. Wheeler decided to prepare for the worst and constructed a makeshift fortress out of some half-built barracks and a thatched building used as an hospital. Crucially, there was a large patch of open ground all around. He dug ditches and threw up a 4ft embankment. He ordered his officers to sleep with the men, and went round the ranks himself reminding them of the campaigns they had all fought together. He tried to keep it all secret but he'd not reckoned with the officers' wives.

Throughout May, it had been getting hotter and hotter[53].

Tempers frayed. The wives gossiped. Inevitably, around **21 May**, the jittery women moved their children into 'Wheeler's Entrenchment'[xc]. They soon missed their creature comforts. The dust blew through the open windows. Everything was hot – plates, cutlery and chairs. The wind acted like a blast furnace, blowing the hot air hotter. The shutters blew off their hinges. The furniture blew across the room. Yellow dust smothered everything, including the view. Washing facilities and toilets were next to non-existent. Water came from a distant well. Rations were tight. Fine wardrobes and pale complexions were a thing of the past.

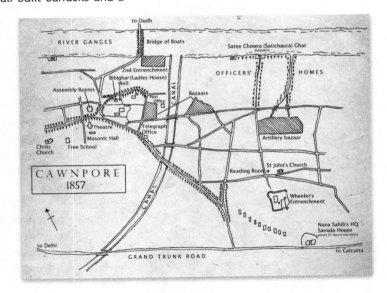

---

51. *The anniversary of the Coronation was 28 June. 650 attended.*
52. *Frances Matilda Marsden (c1795-1857) [NR] had first married Wheeler's friend, Thomas Oliver (1784-1841) [NR] in 1810. He went to Java in 1813, leaving her for Wheeler; she married Wheeler in 1842, after Oliver's death in Afghanistan.*
53. *Up to 35ºC (95ºF), sometimes 45ºC (113ºF)*

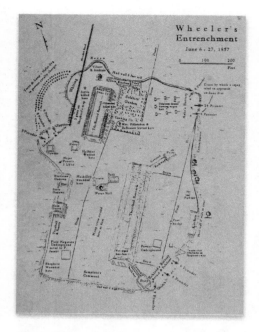

Remains of Wheeler's entrenchment

The Massacre Ghat

It was Major Vibart's 2nd Native Cavalry who broke the peace, along with the 1st Native Infantry. Unlike the Meerut story, they respected their commanding officer but any side is let down by its weakest link. On the night of **2 June**, a British ex-officer (who'd a General for a father) was rolling around drunk in the dark when a picket guard challenged him. Not only did the ex-officer ignore the order 'advance and be recognised', he produced a pistol and took pot shots at them[xci]. When put on trial he was excused on the grounds he was drunk – that was enough to tip the balance: everyone knew he should have gone to prison – one rule for the Meerut soldiers and another for the English officers was 'not on'. The mutineers broke into the treasury, let the prisoners out of the jail and made for the magazine. Over breakfast, they persuaded the rest to join in and then they all rode off to Delhi.

That would have suited Wheeler – he could hold out if they left but Nana Sahib (or more likely his agent Azimullah) realised he had better leverage locally if they stayed: 'Whoever controls the Ganges valley controls India,' went the saying. Could he, the Nana Sahib, be the ruler of India? Egged on by Azimullah Khan, the Nana caught up with the rebels and persuaded them to mutiny locally[xcii].

For three weeks in **June,** the British troops and families at Cawnpore holed up themselves in Wheeler's Entrenchment – 900 British with only 300 in uniform, the rest civilians. With Nana Sahib's cavalry charging at the buildings – bullets puncturing the flimsy walls, random people fell where they stood. Claustrophobic, sweltering hot, little sanitation, revolting smells, scanty bedding, starvation rations, and restricted medical care. They were dealing daily with death. Pock-marked walls. People were shot collecting water from the well.

The British soldiers worked robustly and imaginatively to counter these attacks – on no occasion were their defences breached. Underfed, with uniforms rotting on their skin, coated with grime, they were continually under fire. Staying alive was a lottery. They buried their dead down one of the 60-foot wells – about 300[xciii]. The rebels lost over 700 men[xciv].

Eventually a truce was agreed. The gunfire ceased on 24 June when a lone English woman walked across the parade ground with a message from the rebels. General Wheeler was tired and worn out. His son's head had been blown off by a cannon ball – he didn't trust the Nana but his officers urged him to negotiate. They were eating dog and had only three more days of rations. The rains, arriving any day, would wash them out and rust their guns. Nana Sahib promised to transport them down river to Allahabad. Early on 27 June they were escorted to the water's edge, jeered at by the crowd. Major Vibart was the last to leave. It was 9am when they reached the landing place on the dried up Ganges, the *Satee Chowra* (Satichaura) *Ghat*, one of the loveliest of watering places, the haunt of rhesus monkeys.

The monkeys. The whole thing was a trick. Once they had climbed onto the 30-foot boats, the boatmen jumped ashore, setting the boats' thatched roofs on fire. Thousands crept out of the bushes and opened fire. Within ten minutes the river was running red[xcv]. Smoke shrouded the horror. By 10am, it was all over. The men who remained were finished off. The women were taken to a house in town. Some men including Maj Vibart and Dr Harris managed to get their boat out of the mud, put out the fires, duck the bullets and steal away but were caught 18 miles down-river. Only four of the whole contingent escaped.[xcvi]

There are two stories about how 32-year-old Horatio Harris, Dr Tresidder's stand-in, met his death. In one version, he was captured near a village called Pewundee on **28 June**[xcvii]. The local chief sent him to Nana Sahib, who pronounced, 'Cut off his head' but the Hindu soldier on duty refused, going so far as to offer Dr Harris his own sword. 'Am I a butcher?' argued the soldier, from a caste of warriors. Harris was taken away and murdered by Muslims, soldiers with no such qualms.

In the other version, he was rounded up on **29 June** with the officer party who'd been caught downstream[xcviii]. They were bound and taken to Cawnpore in a cart. Before they reached Nana

Sahib's HQ, Major Vibart had bled to death. The Nana ordered the women to be taken away and the men executed but Mrs Harris refused, saying, "If he must die, I will die with him." When the other wives tried to follow her example, they were dragged away – only Mrs Harris remained clutching a child in her arms. One of the men asked if they could pray. They knelt down and as they tried to shake each other's hands through the ropes, the Oudh Irregulars opened fire, finishing them off with their swords. The bodies were eaten clean by the vultures and the skeletons left to bleach in the sun.

✳ ✳ ✳ ✳

The king of Oudh was a Shia Muslim as were most of the new soldiers. The volatile Muslim mind thought differently from Hindus or Sikh soldiers. A strong belief in the after-life was not unique, but the strong sense of righteousness put others on their guard. Was it arrogance or an inferiority complex? Separation by choice? Resistance to integration can lead to alienation, marginalisation, and degrees of suspicion, which in turn can bring on feelings of victimisation. At the very least it leads to problems of communication.

Some contend that the current 'Holy War' began with Hassan-al Banna and the Muslim Brotherhood 100 years ago, after the actions of the British in this insurrection. The Deobandi sect, for instance, was set up some ten years after the Mutiny against the British, based on fixed teachings of the eighteenth century[54]. It seeks totalitarian control over people's lives and as such is political – the Taliban is just one arm of that movement. Similar in so many ways to Arab Wahhabism, it is punitive in instinct; it is isolationist – it does not advertise on or encourage the use of social media[xcix]. 600 mosques in Britain follow this path; it has Chaplains radicalising Muslims in prison[c]. Its UK headquarters, the 'Oxbridge of the traditional Madrasa world', is in Dewsbury, Yorkshire[ci].

Brutal barbarism and unequal respect of human dignity by Muslims goes back before the crusades. Enslavement of others was and still is a way of life for some (Chapter 11) and pain and grief and lack of mercy considered part of life and death. Not all Muslim regimes have been uncompromising, I am glad to say. The Emirate of Cordoba in Spain (756-1031), under Amir Abd al-Rahman, developed an open society but it later went wrong[55]. Under al-Rahman it was one of generosity, learning, tolerance and inter-faith harmony. The Delhi of 1850 was similar... but there is a tipping point, beyond which relationships implode overnight. Bosnia in the 1990s for example – good neighbours one moment; no love lost the next. The blood heats up, emotions lose control and religious rhetoric takes over.

God wants peace, in my book. There is too little peer-regulation of mullahs/imams or their interpretations of the holy book. Like Constantine and attempts by other English kings, Henry VIII made Christianity an 'established' religion in order to control it. Perhaps Prince Charles will write a 'black spider' memo suggesting the same for Islam in the UK: rules, honours, a place in parliament and prayers for the Sovereign; and clarity about the practice of religion for the good of this island people.

✳ ✳ ✳ ✳

---

54. *Shah Waliullah Dehalwi (1703-1762) [NR]*
55. *Abd al-Rahman ibn Mu'awiya ibn Hisham ibn Abd al-Malik ibn Marwan (731–788) [NR].*

'The most Terrible Tragedy of our age' [56]

Nautch girls – dancing courtesans

The Highlanders go into battle before Cawnpore

It was three weeks since the massacre at the water's edge. The surviving 200 women and children had been locked up in a villa in the city, first to the *Sevadah Kothi*, and thence to the 'Courtesans' House,' the *Bibighar*[cii]. In charge was a twenty-eight year-old retired nautch (dancing) girl from the court of the Nana's father, Baji Rao[57]. It was as if she had succeeded to the throne. She bossed everyone about, she and her bodyguard lover, Sarvur Khan. The women laughingly called her the 'Begum'. There wasn't much to laugh about. She limited their rations and put them to work, grinding the gram[cvi]. They sheltered under the dripping washing up against the midday sun[ciii]. There were no chairs, no shoes either. They cut their hair to the scalp to avoid the lice.

Azimullah Khan advised the Nana and his generals: "Leave one 'Phirangee' (foreigner) alive and he will destroy you."[civ] But the Nana wanted to keep them as hostages – he could hear the rumblings of General Havelock's approaching army[cv]. His brother had returned from a skirmish at a bridge over the Pandu River, nursing a shoulder wound and demanding a summit meeting[58]. Havelock's Highlanders, the Black Watch, were like "mad horses, or mad dogs," he said, "Caring for neither cannon nor musketry."[cvi]

The women had been incarcerated for eighteen days in the Bibighar. On **15 July**, they heard the townspeople moving out of town. The British guns were louder; they prayed.

At 4pm the death shots of three British commanders from Futtehpore (Fatehpur), rang out. At 5.30pm, their doctor and servants were taken away. The women were to be next – the uncompromising Azimullah had persuaded the vacillating Nana once again. The Begum ordered soldiers to bring the women out. The men had conferred, however. The best way to save their own skins, they reckoned, was to have nothing to do with it, but one of Nana's Generals said he'd shoot them dead if they didn't[59]. Reluctantly, they trooped after the Begum. As the sepoys pushed and prodded, the British women pressed themselves against the walls. Their sons, copies of their courageous fathers, did their best to protect their mothers. Each clung to the other, to the pillars, to anything, hanging on for grim death. The soldiers found it impossible.

The Begum and the General agreed to shoot them where they were. The first rank poked their muskets through the venetian blinds and opened fire at point blank range. A second squad moved forward. The sight and sound of what they saw was so appalling that they couldn't go on. They emptied their muskets in the air and staggered back in disgust. They'd all had enough.

Frustrated, the Begum took over. Her lover brought in an execution gang; two were Muslim butchers, one a swordsman. Methodically, the five men cut their way from pillar to post, five against 200 defenceless women and children. Stabbing proved inefficient. Slicing off the necks was the speediest. If the women protected their necks with their arms, they'd slice those off too. A child was hung by his neck on a hook – the blood dripped down the wall[cvii]. The pool of blood grew wider as the slaughter continued, oozing across the floor as they cut their way across the room. Sarvur Khan was clumsy and broke swords as the women ducked and dodged[cviii]. A crowd outside prevented escape. In less than an hour the place was silent. By candlelight, the five men searched for signs of life until the Begum locked the doors and took her lover home for his reward.

Next morning, a party arrived to dispose of the bodies – scavengers who made their living from the remaining valuables, cutting off the fingers to snatch the rings. Bodies were

---

56. *said George Trevelyan in Cawnpore.*
57. *The dancer and courtesan, Hussainee Khanum [NR].*
58. *Bala Rao Pant [NR] was brother to Nana Sahib.*
59. *Ramachandra Pandurang (1814-1859) [NR] nicknamed Tatya Tope after the hats the British wore.*

everywhere, heaped along the wall. They chose to fill a nine-foot wide irrigation well near the house. After a while, they found a group alive, saturated in the blood of their companions. Before the swords could make an end of them, two of the women ran to the well and jumped straight in, dropping fifty feet to their death. Whilst the children ran rings round them, they dragged out the other bodies. Stripping them clean, they chopped them up to make enough room in the well. Eventually the children were rounded up; some say they were flung in alive.

That evening the Nana suffered a further defeat against the approaching Havelock's army. Sweating profusely and 'looking greatly alarmed' he made his escape, taking his shattered men the fifteen miles to his palace at Bithoor. An empty city greeted Havelock's troops the following morning – startled pigs feeding on human excrement amongst broken bottles scuttled amongst the rain-soaked papers stuck against 'torn and scored' tree-stumps. The stench from the Bibighar was overpowering; three officers prised open the creaking doors. A swarm of flies rose 'like swirling cinders' from the floor. They gasped at the handprints on the hacked walls, the straw hats and children's shoes among the gore, inches thick, which stuck to their boots like glue. They looked down the well: underneath, the putrefying body parts, going green; on top, the white corpses of the three last children.

They clutched loose strands of women's hair lying on the ground. They vowed that for each hair they held they would kill a 'Pandee'[60]. The image of that room haunted the British for the next half century. From then on, British soldiers, as they went into battle, repeated to themselves: *'Remember Cawnpore'*.

Attack by General Havelock's troops on the mutineers

❋ ❋ ❋ ❋

No surrender at Lucknow

Fifty miles away at **Lucknow,** Hodson's friend, Sir Henry Lawrence, Commissioner of Oudh, kept things calm until Cawnpore collapsed. On **30 June**, though, he rode out to meet the rebel troops. It didn't work. Cutting his losses at 200 dead, he decided to blow up his arsenal and retreat indoors. That was no better. He found himself surrounded on three sides by high rebel buildings. Sooner or later it was bound to happen. A sniper aimed, a shot rang out and it shattered his thigh – over the next two days they could not stop the bleeding. As he lay there dying, surrounded by his senior officers, he continued to think strategically: "No surrender," he commanded. "Let every man die at his post; but *never* make terms. God help the women and children."[cix]

Gungoo Mehtir, one of the slaughter-house slayers, sentenced to be hung 8 Sep 1859 (note the chains in his left hand.) Dr Tresidder's captioned his photograph:

'Tried at Cawnpore for hacking to death with swords the Futtehguah Fugitives taken by the Nana – also for hacking the women and children at the Slaughter House Cawnpore on 15 July 1857 and for throwing the living wounded with the dying and the dead together into the Well – also for cutting off the arms, noses and ears of 9 of Havelock's spies – seven of whom died in consequence. The two living mutilated men were part of the evidence against him – convicted and hanged at Cawnpore 8 Sep 1859.'

The siege was terrible. 850 British soldiers, aided by 150 civilians and 700 loyal sepoys (plus 1,300 other mouths to feed), against 10,000 troops trained in discipline by the very British they were now attacking. Bombardment was from close quarters but at least they had better defences than at Cawnpore. Better food, more privacy and a church to bury the dead. The siege just went on and on. By **July**, things were desperate. When would Lucknow be relieved?

Lucknow lookout from the Battery

What the soldiers found in the Bibighar, the 'Ladies' House'

60. *Mutineers nicknamed after Mangal Pande (1827-1857) [NR] (see page 88).*

Storming Delhi

The ex-King of Delhi

Tresidder's friends, the Vibarts, and their three youngest children had met their fate at Cawnpore. Their eldest son was on his own in **Delhi.**[cx]

Delhi was a huge challenge. There were far larger numbers on either side than Cawnpore or Lucknow. On **14 Sept**, the British captured the city of Delhi and meted out their vengeance. Edward Vibart was put on standby. "The order went out to shoot every soul," wrote Edward, recording one incident. "It was literally murder… I have seen many bloody and awful sights lately but such a one as I witnessed yesterday I pray I never see again. The women were all spared but their screams… Heaven knows I feel no pity, but when some old grey bearded man perhaps is brought and shot before your very eyes…."[cxi] Edward was ironically nicknamed 'Butcher' after that. By the afternoon, there were 1,170 British dead with only a quarter of the city taken. Soldiers, rebels and innocent citizens lying stiff and prone together along the streets. The English field hospital on the Ridge was a hell-hole. As well as the thousands dying of cholera, there were the amputations[cxii]. Legs, arms and fingers were discarded with no time to clean up. Hodson was horrified by the speed with which discipline and morale fell. "For the first time in my life I have had to see English soldiers refuse repeatedly to follow their officers."[cxiii]

Two days later, the Emperor Zafar slipped out of the city by water, making for the Sufi shrine of the 300-year-old tomb of Hoomayoon (Humayun), the second Moghul Emperor. The white marble dome glistened in the early morning sun. Other city dwellers took it as a signal to leave. As they squeezed through the gates, the British shot unarmed men and boys, stripping them of their possessions, just as their comrades had done – no human rights on either side. On **20 Sept**, the British stormed the Red Fort. Hodson and his men circled the city walls to flush out the rebel camps but found them abandoned[cxiv]. Vibart took part in the 'clearance' between the Delhi and Turkaman Gates – no life was spared: in Kucha Chelan, poets and artists, representing high culture of the Moghul dynasty, were indiscriminately cut down. Muslims were *persona non grata*.

By sunrise on **21 Sept**, the city was deserted.

One of Willie Hodson's spies informed him where the Emperor was. General Wilson grudgingly gave him permission to capture Zafar saying, if he 'wanted to go, he could do so at his own risk, but he would have to manage the whole thing himself.'[cxv] With 50 men, Hodson rode the seven miles to the tomb. He sent in two of his staff to negotiate surrender, and waited. Hodson had already made a 'deal' with the Emperor's favourite wife Zinat Mahal, to preserve her life and those of her son and father.[cxvi] He was promising to do the same for the Emperor. After a nerve-wracking two hours, a messenger came out to say the Emperor wanted to speak to him directly.

"I rode to the spot… dismounted for a moment and reassured the King and the Begum (both of whom were evidently much agitated and frightened) by the promise that his life would be spared, provided no attempt was made at a rescue."

The scene was tense. Fifty men against several thousand. Hodson said the journey back to Delhi was the longest ride he'd ever ridden, surrounded by seething crowds. He saluted and handed the Emperor over to the new Commissioner, his old colleague, Charlie Saunders. "By Jove, Hodson! They ought to make you commander-in-chief for this."[cxvii]

General Wilson was amazed, but he'd a problem – the Governor-General, Lord Canning, insisted on unconditional surrender.

The following morning Hodson, by now a Brevet-Major, returned to bring in the three Princes, two sons and a grandson of the Emperor, who'd masterminded the opposing forces[61]. Believing they would be given the same terms, the princes were told they must surrender unconditionally[cxviii].

---

[61]. *Mirzas Mughal (1828-1857) [NR], Khirzr Sultan (1834-1857) [NR] and Abu Bakr (?-1857) [NR].*

Willie Hodson looked around at the thousands of onlookers. Audaciously he demanded they lay down their arms. Amazingly, they did. It took two hours, giving the others time to escort the Princes the seven miles back to the city walls. Then he caught up with them. He ordered the Princes out of their cart, stripped them naked, took out his Colt revolver and shot them dead[62].

This was war; his world was on a knife-edge. He'd just seen six or seven thousand rebels laying down their arms but already they were plotting their revenge[cxix]. It was either them regaining the initiative, or his to keep. He decided. Timing was everything. In subsequent enquiries Willie was criticised – not for this crime of humanity but for his leniency in granting the Emperor his life. The envy from his colleagues was enormous. He was nearly court-marshalled but Charlie Saunders, the new Commissioner, came to the rescue. "The responsibility was that of my predecessor," he said, knowing full well that his predecessor was dead.

It was Charlie's job to tell the Emperor, now called the 'ex-king of Delhi', about the three princes. He took along his 'exceedingly pretty and nice wife' Matilda[cxx]. The 80-year-old sat, she said, like a beast in a cage, cross-legged on a cushion, dressed in white on a courtyard verandah. Two attendants feebly wafted their peacock fans: the last pretence of royalty. Zafar sat in silence. He trained his eyes on the ground. Behind a curtain sat his favourite wife, Zinat Mahal. Her only interest was to promote her son. When Charles told Zafar about what had happened, he became depressed, but Zinat Mahal beamed from ear to ear: her son would now be the official heir. It was a hollow victory. All were to die in captivity.

Zafar, commanding his most poetic language, asked Matilda to be 'an ambassador' between him and Charlie.

"I answered '*Kubeen Nai*' which means 'No never' … I spoke to the guard …and said I hope you will keep the king safe. Don't let him run away. 'Oh no Ma'am', there's no fear of that; we are a great deal too fond of him.'" [cxxi]

The Saunders were civil; many weren't[cxxii]. William Hodson's wife felt pity mixed with disgust that the most magnificent king in the world had been reduced to a dirty muslin tunic in 'a low, close, dirty room which the lowest slave in his household would scarcely have occupied.'[cxxiii]

Tomb of the second Moghul Emperor Humayun (1508-1556), seven miles from Delhi: the hiding place of Emperor Shah Zafar in Sept 1857

✳ ✳ ✳ ✳

Relief of Lucknow

Capture of the 'King of Delhi'

Lucknow was still holding on. They had to. Lawrence's last words (before he died of his wounds) were 'No surrender'. On **20 July** Havelock ('Old Phlos' they called him) started out from Cawnpore[cxxiv]. It took six days to ferry his 1,500 men across the Ganges. He had a fight on his hands as soon as he entered Oudh, and made little progress. Cawnpore itself was tense. It wasn't until September that Sir James Outram returned to Cawnpore having gathered sufficient reinforcements from Britain and Ceylon. He crossed the Ganges with 3,000 men and 17 guns. By **25 September**, the two of them had crossed the wooded plains of mango and neem grass and 'hewed' their way into the Lucknow Residency with a loss of 500 men. The relief of Lucknow.

It was a false dawn. Outram and Havelock dug in, thinking it would demoralise the rebels but they were outmanoeuvred, locked in and trapped[cxxv]. There were now some 50,000 rebels sitting outside, nearly the same number as at Delhi. The Nana was seen, but not heard[cxxvi]. It took two more goes to relieve Lucknow properly.

---

62. *Hervey Harris Greathed (1817-1857) [NR] died of cholera.*

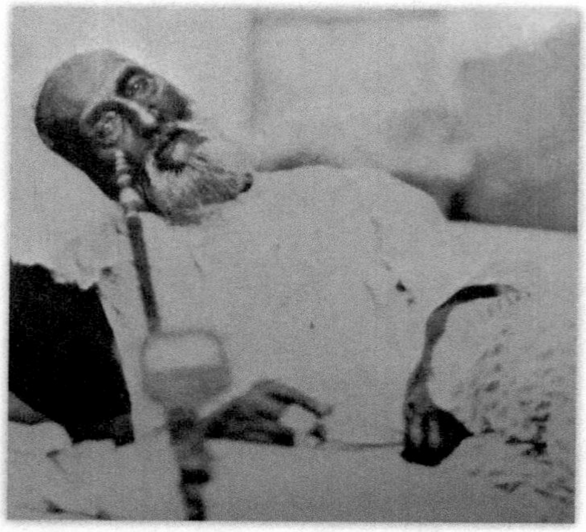

Only known photograph of the Emperor Shah Zafar (1776-1862) 'The most magnificent king in the world had been reduced to a dirty muslin tunic.'

It must have been something of a relief to see 5,000 men and 3,000 camels approaching across the plain. Sir Colin Campbell, who'd been appointed Commander in Chief, reached **Cawnpore** on **3 November**[cxxvii]. Lord Clyde, as he later became, had fought in some stunning victories in his time: Corunna in Spain, the decisive victory in China that won Britain Hong Kong, and at Balaclava in the Crimean War[63]. He set off over the newly constructed bridge of boats across the Ganges[cxxviii]. Reaching the outskirts of Lucknow, he deviously hugged the Goomtee (Gomti) River, attacking from the east, ensuring supplies, the telegraph and ammunition kept pace. The fighting was heavy. It took him three days to annihilate the enemy. **The second relief of Lucknow**.

There wasn't much left of the city by the time he'd finished, on **17 November.** Campbell ordered its immediate evacuation and returned to Cawnpore with the British civilians. At Cawnpore, the rebels were still at large. His next job was to sort that out.

* * * *

John Nicholas returns

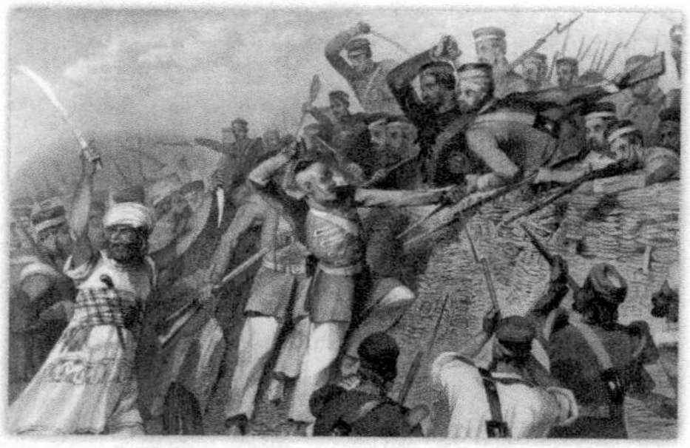

Assault on Lucknow

Dr John Nicholas Tresidder joined Campbell's army after he had arrived back in Calcutta with his new wife **Emily**, Emmie as he called her, on **6 October 1857**. He'd been recalled along with other officers on leave[cxxix]. He took his bride back to India the slow way, round Cape Horn[cxxx]. At the end of the month, he had set out with the Black Watch, the 42nd Highlanders as they pushed their way up to Cawnpore via Allahabad. And whilst Campbell went on to Lucknow, he remained in Cawnpore, one of only a handful British government people who knew anything about how the place operated. He was put on 'special duties' and in charge of the civilian hospital. Hospital arrangements at Cawnpore were next to non-existent. There was a lack of officers and few local staff[cxxxi]. Cholera had been rife since August[cxxxii].

When Campbell returned from Lucknow he found that 25,000 rebels had overwhelmed the town three days before. One wag remarked, "Here we are with upwards of 2,000 European [British] soldiers in almost as bad a predicament as that unfortunate General [Wheeler] was with but 210 men." Wheeler had lasted three weeks but now 2,000 had lost it in three days[cxxxiii]. Fortunately, John Nicholas was safe. His fellow officers had constructed a better entrenchment near the river. Flames lit up the night sky as Campbell arrived at dusk. On the banks of the Ganges, he planned his attack.

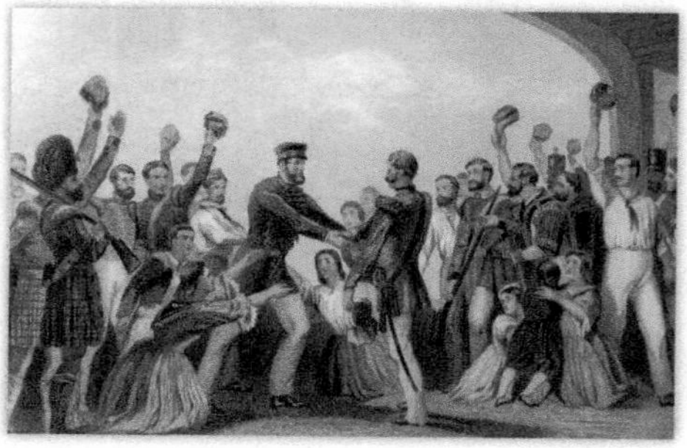

Relief of Lucknow under General Havelock

On **6 December**, 5,600 more British troops and 35 more guns arrived, and he was ready for the counter attack. John Nicholas saw action that day with his Highlanders. His sword, which I still have, certainly looks as if it saw blood. With them was a naval contingent of 24-pounders. One of them wrote: *"I can't tell you how jolly it was seeing the brutes run. I could hardly believe my eyes. I felt perfectly mad, and our men got on top of the guns, waving their hats and yelling... It was most awfully exciting."*[cxxxiv] The rebels were chased for another ten miles.

John Nicholas took part in another skirmish at Sheorajpore Ghat three days later, chasing rebels who'd escaped. He won two Medals and two Clasps for his services in those two encounters. The Black Watch (without Tresidder) went on to clear up the remaining rebels in Oudh, chasing them up into Nepal. Subsequently, its Rana Prime Minister was to ask for British assistance to rid his country of them[cxxxv].

Azimullah Khan died on the way to Nepal. No one quite knows what happened to Nana Sahib. Some say he escaped to Nepal too, leaving look-alikes behind. Once they thought they'd caught him. As late as 1874, John Nicholas was directed to Gwalior by the Viceroy (as Lord Canning was now called) to identify an emaciated well-spoken fakir, who had convinced

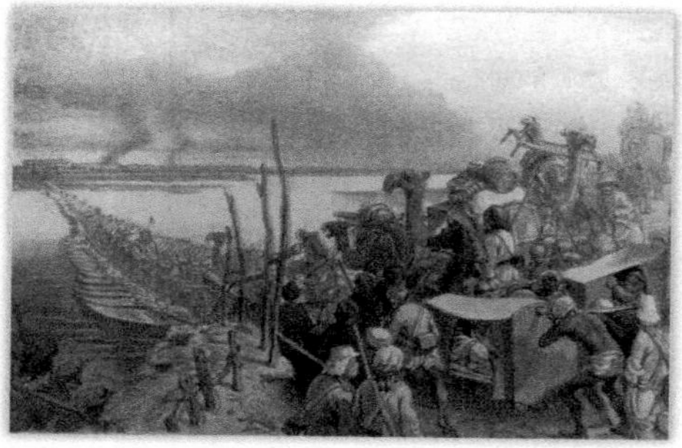

The Bridge of Boats across the Ganges

63. *Field Marshal Campbell, 1st Baron Clyde GCB KCSI (1792-1863) [NR] was born Colin Macliver, and took the nom de guerre Campbell.*

the Maharaja of Scindia that he was the culprit[cxxxvi]. John Nicholas shrugged his shoulders. The Nana was younger. 'Not more than 38 years of age....' This was 'not the round face of the Nana and not the Nana's eyes or expression," he said[cxxxvii]. Though others noticed a scar on his forehead, there were no signs of marks from the earrings he wore. The handwriting was different. But it was difficult: the real Nana was, in his opinion, "An excessively uninteresting person," who, "might have passed for the ordinary shopkeeper of the bazaar had it not been for the Mahratta contour of his turban."[cxxxviii]

The English public were baying for blood. John Nicholas stuck it out. He had undertaken surgery on the Nana's foot and this person had no such scar. But a lingering doubt remains: one wonders whether each had done the other a good turn – Nana tipping him off and saving his doctor's life and, in return, the doctor saving his. It is unlikely our Cornish family trait was up for such subterfuge, if the *Times* journalist William Howard Russell, in the next story, can be trusted.

Highlanders of the 93rd Regiment, dressed more smartly than in battle

✳ ✳ ✳ ✳

The Officers' Mess

It wasn't until Christmas that the rebels were no longer a problem in Cawnpore and civilian life reached some sort of normality. The Civil Administration was set up in Duncan's Hotel in **December**, a rambling place, riven with shot, windows broken, some with frames gone altogether and only rickety chairs left in a small garden[cxxxix]. Dr Tresidder shared the mess with John Sherer, who'd come from Agra and was now the Chief Magistrate and Collector (of taxes)[64]. Lt Mowbray Thomson, one of only two officers to survive the massacre, was acting as Chief of Police[cxl]. Sherer recalled Tresidder's care for his friends:

"The day was actually fixed for Parsons to have his arm amputated; but Tresidder declared that if the case were entrusted to his individual care, he thought he could save the limb. Arrangements were accordingly made, and permission obtained; and Parsons and Clark – the latter, though better, was still in a ticklish condition – were removed to Duncan's Hotel, where, with better air, specially prepared food, and the constant attendance of Tresidder in the house, they both got quite well. Parsons retained his arm, and Clark gave up trying to recover his watch chain [which had become embedded in his flesh]. They both lived for some thirty-eight years after these events, and died within a month or two of each other. Clark was wounded dangerously in the stomach, the bullet carrying in part of the chain of his watch, links of which came away one by one, leading to the mild pleasantry that he was delaying recovery in search of his lost property.'"

John Nicholas Tresidder

In **February 1858**, an altercation at Calpee caused Mowbray Thomson to suffer 'extensive damage' to his thigh, which was repaired by the same 'skilful surgeon'[cxlii]. In 1859 John Nicholas took care of Sherer for three weeks in his home, ill with jungle fever[cxliii]. Tresidder received formal thanks of the Government three times for what he did over these thirty months[65].

They saw some interesting people pass through. One was the now legendary **William Hodson**. John Sherer had been Willie's fag at Rugby, making his coffee, boiling his eggs and sweeping his study. When Hodson arrived, Sherer ushered him into his room and shut the door. The two of them talked of the biggest sensation of the last year – Hodson's shooting the three Delhi Princes in cold blood – here was the man who'd done the deed. There was 'no harshness or bravado' in Willie's voice, said Sherer. 'In a calm, argumentative tone … he had convinced himself that a stern political necessity existed,' which gave him the unique chance 'to pause a sudden and lasting terror,' and effectively end the Mutiny[cxliv]. Hodson had drawn a line in the sand.

When he left, Hodson left a coat for Sherer to have mended, for old times' sake, as it were. He was never to collect it.

Felix Beato, who had taken photographs in the Crimea, came by. He and John Nicholas joined forces. John Nicholas must have taken some trouble to show him round for his photographic techniques improved thereafter and copies of photographs attributed to Beato appear in Tresidder's contemporary photograph album[cxlv].

Another visitor from the Crimea was William Russell, the celebrated Times reporter who had unflinchingly exposed the frightful conditions in the Crimea: disease, starvation and lack of boots[66]. His reports had been the chief motivation for Florence Nightingale (the 'Lady with the Lamp') to go out and improve conditions for wounded soldiers[67]. Russell had even met Azimullah Khan in Europe[cxlvi].

Over the Cawnpore dining room table of the Officers' Mess, Billy Russell's roving eye lighted on one man. Was this my great grandfather?

John Sherer and Dr Tresidder

Hodson's visiting card

"Figure, lean and angular, narrow round shoulders, big splay feet; hair fiery-red, dishevelled , and matted in snaky masses; beard and whiskers, if possible, more red and fierce than the hair; forehead low and receding, but broad and bumpy over the brows, which are two elongated white knobs, from which spring a few red hairs; eyes feline; nose large, coarse, aquiline; mouth huge and coarse, covered as to the upper lip with red hairs, growing wildly in carrot-coloured spikes and garnished with a few massive fangs, the intervals between which had once been fixed by dentristic art."

'But this queer outside [physique] belonged to a man of ability…. He had read a good deal and had mastered the outward works of Aristotelian logic. He always commenced at first principle, and set argument on a right basis, by questioning every statement made, in the most general and uncontroversial spirit. Of course this failing was

---

65. The Bengal Presidency was now the North West Province;it included Bengal, Calcutta and Darjeeling in the east
66. Sir William Howard Russell CVO (1820-1907) [NR].
67. Florence Nightingale OM RRC (1820-1910) [NR].

a source of much quiet amusement to us. Suppose one said at table, "I think the Zemanders are against us," there was one voice heard at once, "Why do you think so? I think the contrary, I call on you for proofs:" – or that it was remarked, "Jones nearly rode over a boy this morning close to the church;" our friend would remark, "Nearly is a relative term in reference to time and space; and, from what I heard Jones say, I believe it was several hundred yards from the church; nor was it established that it was a boy."' [cxlvii]

A camel train

My grandfather had a similar pedantic style, picking something apart[cxlviii]. I fell into the same habit at college in Canterbury. None of us had shocking red hair but Dr John Nicholas Tresidder did have masses of auburn hair, as described, sprouting from all parts of the face. Maybe this eminent journalist was entitled to employ a little professional licence.

A siege train of elephants, similar to the one that entered Oudh

✳ ✳ ✳ ✳

The final capture of Lucknow

Throughout **February 1858**, Campbell's immense army occupied Oudh. It was an awesome sight. Mile after mile of bayonets glinting in the sun, followed by an enormous procession of bearers and camp followers with all the supplies. It was 'like a huge boa constrictor, coiled and ready for its spring'[cxlix]. 'Never less than five hundred carts stuck in ditches or inextricably jammed'. Mutinous camels kicking portmanteaux and elephants lumbering off for a nearby drink[cl]. This time, Campbell brought Lucknow properly back into British possession[cli]. They used a pincer movement: Outram from the north and Campbell from the east. By **9 March**, they were in position[clii].

Hodson died in the assault. He died as he had lived, rashly storming the main palace, the *Begum Kothi*, before his troops had properly secured a way into the building[cliii]. As the sun was setting, his body was lowered into a grave at the foot of a clump of bamboo, in the garden of the Martiniere, the school that had been called the 'Eton of the East', to the dirge of bagpipes. The Commander in Chief, Colin Campbell, that rough Glaswegian who'd been through countless wars, broke down into grief-stricken sobs[cliv].

The capture of Lucknow under Sir Colin Campbell, later Lord Clyde

✳ ✳ ✳ ✳

The Aftermath

There were scenes I have not dwelt on throughout this story – of captured sepoys being stripped, tied to the ground and 'branded all over every part of their bodies with red-hot' irons, or of the cruel British Commander who made the culprits lick a square foot of the floor clean of the blood in the Bibighar before they were hanged[clv]. Or the Muslims who had pork stuffed down their throats or were sewn into pig-skins. I have not mentioned the old men, women and children who were burnt in their houses by the British; of torture, impaling and burnings alive[clvi]. Almost every tree on the Grand Trunk Road was strung up with bodies. I haven't spoken of the men who were tied to the front of cannon before being blown into smithereens, like the Moghuls did of old[clvii]; or of the summary trials that Sherer and his colleagues had to perform. John Nicholas photographed some of the insurgents after they had been tried and before they were hanged (see page 95).

Picket of the Highland Brigade – this brutal scene was to be found all along the Grand Trunk Road

A man is tied in front and the cannon fired, blowing him sky high, as the Moguls did. Tresidder's friend Dr Murray who witnessed this said, "The pieces of flesh and bone are scattered all round & the head goes bounding in front."

All Soul's Cawnpore, built built by the Memorial Committee. Dr Tresidder was its Secretary

The angel placed over the massacre well – by Carlo Marochetti 1860 – the most visited tourist destination in India for years after

Taj Mahal, Agra, painted by Lady Canning

The sepoys would rather be shot than bayonetted. Over 860 were bayonetted in the courtyard of the palace where Hodson lost his life[clviii]. In Delhi, wildcat officers had been laying into anyone who upset them. English soldiers were raping Indian women – revenge, they said[clix]. 'Clemency' Canning sought to stop the butchery[clx]. Saunders strived to stay their hand. Attitudes had to change.

The mutiny affected other parts of India – the 6,000 held hostage in Agra, the uprisings at Bareilly, Gwailor, and Allahabad where wholesale slaughter took place. Or Dinapore, Arrah, Jhansi, Azimghur, Futtehpore, Bermpore, Allyghur, Najafgarh, Nimach, Nasirabad, Nowgong. Or Julipigoore, Jullunder, Rajpootana, Malwa, Benares, Sattara, Ahmednuggur and so on, but none was as dramatic as those my relations experienced.

Promotion to the rank of Surgeon followed quickly for Dr John Nicholas Tresidder – on 30 October 1858. He remained in medical charge of the civilians at Cawnpore until 18 December 1860. He received a special grant for his services following his promotion. He kept on a private practice, and looked after the railwaymen as well[clxi] The British Government took over direct rule from the East India Company and the Medical Service was reorganised. 1857 was the watershed year. The British Empire ruled India for the next 90 years.

Cawnpore became a magnet for visitors; more went here than to see the Taj Mahal – tantalized tourists wanted to examine the scenes of carnage. The place was so unsightly that in August 1859, a Cawnpore memorial committee was set up with Dr John Nicholas Tresidder as its Secretary and his friend John Sherer as a member[clxii]. They decided to build a memorial park around the well. They commissioned a memorial church, All Souls', near Wheeler's Entrenchment.

The Viceroy's wife, Lady Canning, sponsored the statue of a downcast angel clutching palm leaves[clxiii]. Pre-1947, people dismounted from their horses and carriages and walked past the entrance as a sign of respect[clxiv]. Since Independence, the park has been renamed Nana Rao Park, after the 'Nana', and the angel moved to All Soul's churchyard.

✳ ✳ ✳ ✳

The exile

Emperor Zafar's **Delhi** trial began haphazardly in **January 1858**. Commissioner Charlie and Matilda Saunders had ring-side seats. It lasted two months, with the Deputy Judge Advocate General (Matilda's half-brother) prosecuting[68]. Predictably, the 'ex-king' was found guilty. Hodson's solemn promise to preserve his life, his wife and his senior son was honoured. They were to be exiled to Rangoon (Yangon) in Burma but it wasn't until the following October that anyone deemed it safe enough to move them. The 89-year-old Zafar and his family were transported across India on bullock carts.

"He was removed as quickly as possible," recorded Matilda[clxv]. "Everything was kept quite secret, though of course [Charlie] knew it long before ... No one crowded to see them go. It was completely still and quiet at that early hour."

✳ ✳ ✳ ✳

[68] *Major Frederick Joseph Harriot (1810-1859).*

Photography at Agra

In March 1861, John Nicholas Tresidder changed jobs[clxvi]. He was posted to a native infantry regiment at Agra, 160 miles north-west of Cawnpore. It was his friend Sherer's previous station. Beside the Jumna River was the Taj Mahal, the beautiful tomb of the beloved wife of the Moghul Emperor Shah Jahan, recalled in the East India Company's nickname – *Kampani Jahan*[69].

Doctors at Agra. Dr Murray left of the table; Dr Tresidder extreme right.

At Agra, the Tresidders made friends with Deputy-Inspector of Hospitals, Dr John Murray and his wife[70]. Murray had been there since 1848 and took up photography a year later[clxvii]. They may have met in London as they were both on leave there at the same time[clxviii]. Before he returned in November 1857, Murray arranged for photos he'd taken in 1855 to be displayed in a London exhibition, and be published. Two years later he teamed up with Agra's ex-head of the Public Works Department, who'd just retired. This was another distant relative of mine, Major-General **John Boileau**[71] Boileau coordinated the London end with the publishers Hogarth[clxix].

There was a keen photographic society. As well as taking each other's photographs, the group 'put the world to rights' and made firm friendships[clxx]. John Boileau was somewhat Falstaffian: 'His sayings and doings were the subject of many widely current anecdotes.' A man of 'infinite jest, of most excellent fancy', he built the church at Agra and paid for its cost overrun[clxxi]. Murray went on war work to Delhi in February 1858 and met the half a dozen photographers active there[clxxii].

John Boileau (1805-1886) helped the Agra photographers publish in London

Like learning to fly today, photography was out of reach for most[clxxiii]. You needed a technical mind and perseverance. You needed time to record what you'd done last time, so you could do something different on your next attempt. It was expensive. Many of the surgeons who'd trained at Edinburgh, like John Murray, experimented before they came out. An older contemporary of theirs, Dr John McCosh, recommended the hobby in his book *Advice to Officers in India* (1856)[clxxiv].

William Fox Talbot's calotype process (which Murray used) was taken up by enthusiasts in the early 1840s. Like Murray, John Nicholas printed albumen or using mainly salt-paper. 'French paper, Canson frères, is the best, and does not get damaged by damp.'[clxxv] He'd arrange the dark room beside the studio, and light it with a red or yellow lamp. The camera was made of 'good substantial mahogany, clamped with brass, made to stand extremes of heat.'

Expeditionary photography

For his negatives, Tresidder would have used the wet collodion glass plate process introduced in 1851, pouring iodine on collodion, the staple cure for war wounds[clxxvi]. The glass 'plates' – whole plates 6½ x 8½ inches in size, half or quarter, depending on the camera – were coated with the syrupy mixture. He'd wait a few seconds and the mixture began to set. Before it dried, he'd 'dunk' it into a solution of silver salts, tilting it to and fro and, hey presto, here was a light-sensitive film of silver iodide. It was like alchemy. He'd put the plate in the camera and 'take' the photo (exposing the plate from about 10-30 seconds) and then 'develop' and fix the plate whilst it was still moist[clxxvii]. He'd wash the plate and coat it in a special varnish[clxxviii]. Whoever it was had to keep stock still during the exposure.

The result (when done well) had pinpoint clarity. Crisp, detailed negatives could be produced quickly – less time in the Indian heat. Unlike the French daguerreotype method, many prints could be obtained from one negative. John Nicholas developed a technique for creating 'combination prints', many subjects combined into a single print, which his family called 'collages' (see the one of his staff at Agra on page 84). He may have got the idea when

A darkroom

---

69. *Shahabuddin Muhammad Shah Jahan, Shah Jahan (1592-1666) [NR] married Arjumand Banu Begum, Mumtaz Mahal (1593-1631) [NR] in 1612 after a long engagement. She was his second and last wife, dying in childbirth.*

70. *Dr John Murray (1809-1898) [NR].*

71. *Maj General John Theophilus Boileau (1805-1886) retired in Feb 1857 with the honorary rank.*

Instantaneous! If this is Tresidder's son Johnny, the photo was taken c 1853

he was in London in 1857; Tresidder appears to have been the only person doing this in India[72].

Tresidder's photographs of the people of the North-Western Provinces were displayed in the Indian section of the International Exhibition, called the 'Great London Exposition' of 1862, in South Kensington – the site where the Natural History Museum and the Science Museum now stand. The Viceroy, Lord Canning, and his wife encouraged some of the first attempts to capture the varied scenes and people of India. Officers, particularly surgeons, were asked to send in 'interesting subjects'[clxix]. It was the start of an association between photography and ethnography, helping officials to identify the type of people they were governing. Tresidder's amateur studio was extraordinarily egalitarian. His was one of the first annotated private albums in India's history[clxx]. It covered such a large range of people. As well as family and friends, his photographs honoured the colonial rulers, anointed the new professional Indians, and recorded for posterity some of the villains of the uprising. Whoever they were, his subjects often sat in the same chair, carved JNT[clxxi]. In some small way he helped balance Anglo-Indian relations[clxxii].

Elizabeth Anne Tresidder (1841-1923), the eldest daughter in c1862

⁎ ⁎ ⁎ ⁎

Annie and Rosie

After schooling in England, John Nicholas's two eldest daughters joined him in India. Young girls coming out to India were on the look-out for husbands and nicknamed the 'fishing fleet'. They had the pick of a host of young officers. There was a lively social round. By July 1865 John Nicholas had been promoted to Surgeon-Major and was living at **Jhansie**, having served at Bareilly and Banda.

Elizabeth Anne Tresidder, to use her full name, had been eleven at the time of the Mutiny. In 1866, aged 20, Annie married the 25-year-old Lieutenant, **Horace Moule Evans**.

A year later, her sister, **Mary Rosamund Tresidder**, married Lt **Robert Saunders**, first cousin of Charlie Saunders, the Delhi Commissioner. Robert sadly died four years later but Rosie managed to bring three children into the world in that short space of time. Rosie moved to Dulwich when her father retired and was the only one of his fifteen children to return to Cornwall.

Horace Moule Evans served most of his career in the east of India, in the Assam tea-growing border country near Burma. As a Wing Officer, he took part in an expeditionary force against the tribes in the Daffla Hills, east of Butan (1874-75)[73]. The Dafflas used to raid Assam in the 1830s and demand their dues – cloth, salt and goats. By the 1850s, it was money they were after. In 1870, they'd taken the law into their hands – a runaway slave and a dowry dispute – and Evans joined a 1,000 strong force (plus 1,200 coolies and 40 elephants transporting supplies) to keep the peace[clxxiii]. The precipitous paths worried Horace – his troops sometimes formed cordons round the edge of the narrow tracks that cut their way into the sides of the sheer cliffs; enabling Horace to pass by on the inside[clxxiv]. By the time he'd been promoted to Major, it was the neighbouring Nagas (1879-80) who were the problem. Slowly these primitive tribes on the edge of the Brahmaputra Valley were being subdued, and the local chiefs were persuaded to rule in the British way. Thirty years earlier, the Governor-General had thought it pointless: it "would be as costly as it would be unproductive;" but, following the Mutiny, full-scale colonisation was the order of the day – it protected the profitable tea plantations[clxxv]. At Khonoma on 24 November 1879, Evans's 43rd regiment, together with the 44th, stormed what was considered an impregnable Naga hill stronghold[clxxvi]. Horace won the India medal

The Lushai expedition – finding the gun of a murdered officer in the grave of the chieftain

---

72. *Oscar Gustav Rejlander (c1813-1875) [NR] exhibited 'The Two Ways of Life' at the Manchester Art Treasures exhibition in 1857, with its 32 separate negative images. Prince Albert kept a copy on his wall until his death.*

73. *Captain. 41st Bengal Infantry.*

and clasp and was awarded Brevet promotion to Lieutenant Colonel. He was quickly made up to a full Colonel in 1885.

In 1888, tribal chiefs were demanding the heads of Englishmen as dowries for their daughters. In 1891, Evans led a force of 400 of 43rd Gurkha Light Infantry to 'promenade' through the area.

Just south of this, the Manipur valley connects India with Burma. The Kamhow, Lushai and Sooktie hill tribes were continually causing trouble, taking slaves and feuding[clxxxvii]. The capable Maharaja of Manipur, assisted by the British Political Agent, did his best to keep the peace – Tresidder's friend Mowbray Thomson had been Political Agent there in 1872[clxxxviii].

Twenty years later, in 1891, it was the scene of a minor Indian Mutiny of its own. The Maharaja died leaving numerous warring sons. The 'Senapati' was the strongest but the British followed protocol and his eldest brother was crowned king. The Senapati disagreed and turfed him out – leaving the British government in a quandary – what to do next? The decision it made was a failure in human relations.

The British plan was to arrest the Senapati and install the next son in line. A fine solution, if you are miles away at Government House, and you ignore what the Commissioner and his political agent had advised, yet it was the Commissioner and his political agent who had to make it happen. When they arrived, the Senapati separated them from their troops and killed them both, along with the army colonel and several others. The incident was astonishing enough to be the topic of a London parliamentary debate. Horace was appointed to lead the military enquiry, which resulted in the court-marshalling of the two senior officers who had run away with the wounded; he recommended Victoria Crosses for the two officers (one a Gurkha) who'd rescued the situation. The palace was razed to the ground, the perpetrators hanged or transported for life and the state of Manipur, whilst not quite 'annexed', was placed firmly under British control with a child king. The decisive action brought the matter to an end and for Horace the award of another clasp to his Indian medal and Commander of the Order of the Bath (CB). His next command was Cawnpore itself (1893).

Horace was promoted to Brigadier-General in 1895, Major-General a year later and drew full pay as a Lieutenant-General[74] in 1899, though he effectively retired in Dec 1898. He and Annie retired near where Annie had been at school. When their children's schooling was over, they moved to Steyning in Sussex[75].

Emily Hooton Courtis (1830-1917), accompanied Dr Tresidder to Cawnpore directly after her wedding. After he died she moved to Devon and was wheeled about in a Bath chair.

✳ ✳ ✳ ✳

When Annie's father John Nicholas Tresidder retired in March 1877 (with the honorary rank of Surgeon-General)[74], he and Emmie went to live in Dulwich, in Palace Road; in order that Annie's smaller half-brothers could attend Dulwich College as day-boys. John Nicholas named his home *Cawnpore House* – 'remembering Cawnpore', as his Highland soldiers had said. The Tresidders kept bees and enjoyed London, travelling in the open trucks of the new-fangled steam underground railway, choking on the smoke and blackened by the soot, but 'well worth it.'[clxxxix] John Nicholas died in 1889 of Bright's disease. Emily finished raising her last child, **Clive Tresidder**, in Croydon and then moved to Paignton in Devon, where she sat out in the fresh air and was carried upstairs to bed, outliving her husband by nearly thirty years[76].

---

74. *From 1859, all officers of over 25 years' service were given a step up with an honorary rank on retirement, if recommended by their Head of Department.*
75. *Edgcombe, Crescent Road, Steyning.*
76. *Adrian* <u>Clive</u> *Tresidder (1878-1923).*

Brigadier William Harry Evans
(1876-1956)

Lt Col James Harry Stewart Murray
(1866-1948)

The Two Harrys

Horace and Anne's third son was **Harry Evans**[77]. After King's School Canterbury, he joined the Royal Engineers, training at Chatham. In 1894, he was posted to Chitral on India's North West Frontier and took part in the Somaliland Expedition (1902-04). During the First World War, he won a DSO on the Western Front, suffering permanently from a gas attack.

In 1896, another Harry, **Harry Murray**, was commissioned into the same Royal Engineers[78]. His father had been a Colonel in the Indian Army and his grandfather an Assistant Under-Secretary at the Foreign Office[79]. His great grandfather, John Ravenshaw, had been Chairman of the mighty East India Company in 1832[80]. After 2 years training, Harry was posted to Quetta. He joined the Military Works Service, and remained there for most of his career. He learnt Pushtu, Hindustani and Persian and rose to the rank of Lieutenant Colonel. Harry Murray was my step-grandfather on my father's side.

Though ten years younger, Harry Evans became Harry Murray's boss. As Brigadier, Evans was the Army's Chief Engineer in India. He was based at Quetta from 1919-39. The two Harrys both worked in Quetta, the military station that coordinated all of the logistics for the wars in Afghanistan. Their job was much like the District Works Offices in Nepal that I knew in the 1980s.

Painstaking accuracy sets the Tresidders apart – Harry Evans was no exception. He also had a dry sense of humour: once, when commanding the Royal Engineers in Peshawar, an irate Chief Commissioner couldn't get his bath tap to work. A message summoned him personally to the house. Evans checked – the reservoir had been undergoing some cleansing; wickedly, he arranged for the flow to resume *just* as he arrived at the Commissioner's house.

"Now, what did you say the problem was?" Harry asked his irate client.

"My bath water doesn't run, dammit!" said the high-blown Commissioner, with a few choice words about the efficiency of Evans's organisation.

"Well, let's go see," suggested Evans. So they went to the bathroom and he turned on the tap. The tap gulped, and water gushed forth freely....

"Seems to be all right to me," opined Harry looking at him quizzically.

The story is close to my heart. I was to work in similar situations – for some nine years my job involved buildings for the armed forces. Humour helped to prick balloons and deflate a situation.

Harry Murray retired to Reigate in 1921, having first moved to Rawalpindi, near Islamabad, as *Assistant Commanding Royal Engineer* and to Dehra Dun as *Deputy Assistant Director of Military Works*[81]. Soon after his wife died in 1933, my widowed grandmother snapped him up on the croquet lawns of Cheltenham (see Chapter 5). They married in 1935.

Harry Evans retired ten years later than the other Harry. In his retirement, he devoted most

77. Brig William <u>Harry</u> Evans CSI CIE DSO FZS (1876-1956) Chief Engineer, Western Command, India, and Secretary, Public Works Department, to the Agent to the Governor General, Baluchistan married Winifred Elizabeth Young Harvey (1866-1945) in 1902. They had one son, Dr John William Evans MA DSc ScD (1906-1985).

78. Lt Col James <u>Harry</u> Stewart Murray (1866-1948) married (1) Margaret Richardson (1869-1933) in 1895 and had four children (Winifred (b1898), Marion Doris (b1899), Edward Harvey (b1901) and Bruce Hayden Richardson (b1905) and (2) Annie Dora Haskins (neé Wiggins) (1871-1966) in 1935. Neither Harry was a shortened version of 'Henry'.

79. Col Harvey Young Murray (1841-1897) son of James Murray (1807-1878) who married Charlotte Ravenshaw (1817-1878) in 1838.

80. John Goldsborough Ravenshaw (1777-1840) Director of East India Company 1819-40, Deputy Chairman 1829-31, Chairman 1832.

81. April 1918 Rawalpindi; May 1920 Dehra Dun; Sep 1921 retired. Lt Cols are addressed as 'Colonel'. Contrary to family opinion, he was promoted well before retirement.

of his spare time to his butterflies. Like my great uncle Clare in Africa (Chapter 12), was his way of relaxing after a day at the office. Harry had 'caught the bug' on the chalk downs above Canterbury as a schoolboy. In Chitral he saw outstanding examples – he was spellbound. Darjeeling, Ceylon and Burma didn't escape his attentions; he became an expert on distribution patterns. From 1923, he published keys that allowed identification of this Indian species. In retirement, he lived close to the Natural History Museum, cataloguing over half a million specimens. He calmly carried on throughout the Second World War despite a shortness of breath and bombs dropping all around; his wife sensibly moved to Bournemouth. A bomb actually did explode a hundred yards away from his desk and he practically lost his hearing – he'd been working by a museum window overlooking the Cromwell Road.

Harry's only son, **John Evans**, took up Entomology as a career, rising to be Deputy Chief Scientific Officer in the UK. In 1954, he was made Director of the Australian Museum in Sydney, moving it forward to become the respected scientific institution it is today.

Harry Murray, on the other hand, enjoyed my grandmother's company, spending most of his days cooking, playing croquet and knitting Fairisle jumpers. He died the year I was born.

✳ ✳ ✳ ✳

Postscript

In the 1970s and 80s I worked for the Property Services Agency (PSA), that had taken over the job of building and maintaining the military estate from the likes of the two Harry's. For three years in the 1980s, I managed the accounts and personnel in the Far East – a job that included Nepal, where the British army recruited Gurkha soldiers. Nepal's relationship with Britain stems back two hundred years to the Treaty of Sergauli (1816). For a hundred years (1846-1951), Rana Prime Ministers ruled the country under a titular king. Jang Bahadur Rana spent a year in Britain in 1850 and got on so well with Queen Victoria that she saw him six times[82]. As a result, he brought British architecture to Nepal. The Rana Palaces are completely at odds with anything else in the rest of Nepal. Sadly, the catastrophic earthquake of 2015, flattened not only these but much else besides.

entrance to a Rana Palace 1987

Gurkhas have been part of the British Army since the time of Waterloo. Two hundred years later (2015), some 4,500 competed for 126 places. At the time of my visits, the PSA maintained three Gurkha recruiting stations: one at Kathmandu, Nepal's capital, and one at each end of the country – Pokhara and Dharan[83].

Kathmandu is 1,400 metres (4,600ft) above sea level – much higher and the air becomes rarefied. A mixture of exotic, religious (like old Tibet), and a princely past (Rana Palaces), and spread out over three separate areas. The old centre has the bustle of an age-old trading place: street sellers, pedlars, musicians, beggars (not many) – average income £10 per annum. Mixed in the crowd were back-packing Europeans – some who'd arrived on old London buses arranged by Paul Sykes from Barnsley – psychedelic hippies 'finding themselves'[84]. The European girls were mostly wearing flimsy cheesecloth tops that left little to the imagination. In the stinking market there were over-ripe bananas, rubbish heaps and men urinating in the gutter. Carpets hung outside the shops (four now live in our house), brass and silverware, bamboo flutes, macramé, silk from Tibet – the streets were a series of Aladdin's caves.

Carpet shop in Kathmandu 1990

In the Durbar Square, the carved wooden buildings, three to five storeys high, rose out

Durbar Square, Kathmandu 1990 – the sacred Royal Kumari's window is on the third floor

82.   *Maharaja Junga Bahadur Rana GCB GCSI (1817-1877) [NR]*
83.   *Neville Wiggins's daughter Elizabeth (b1940) accompanied her husband Dr Victor Sousa (b1931) to Pokhara for two years in the 1970s.*
84.   *Paul Sykes (b1943) [NR]"*

The 'unwashed' – children at Biratnagar airport 1987

The Officers' Mess Dharan 1987

Up in the clouds

Tamur Valley

of this world. From one, a Kumari child goddess would appear for seconds by her latticed window. Chosen for her dark hair and dainty hands, 'her neck like a conch shell, her body like a banyan tree, her eyelashes like a cow, her thighs like a deer, her chest like a lion and her voice soft and clear', her feet were never allowed to touch the ground. Crowds of people waited below, hoping that she will glance down at them. When she did, the palace courtyard was filled with devotion and awe. Sadly, my patience ran out waiting for her to appear.

Getting to Nepal was an experience in itself. The plane on which I was to make my first trip to Kathmandu in August 1987 was cancelled, as the King had decided to use the only Jumbo 737 belonging to Nepal Airlines to send his son to Eton[85]. This son later shot up his family over a domestic spat, which effectively ended the monarchy and handed control to Maoists.

The internal flight from Kathmandu to the eastern area of Nepal nearly came off the end of the runway. The small plane I was due to join on the way back actually did. It was a bumpy 25-mile Landrover ride from Biratnagar airport across the flat Terai to Dharan, our eastern depot. Constant hooting helped to move most of the sacred cows and the less sacred chickens plus the myriads of people off the dusty road.

Once I was asked to take my dinner jacket for a mess dinner in Dharan – all the way from Hong Kong to the second poorest country in the world. I remembered the dress shirt and black tie but forgot the black shoes – oh horror! As we dined in state, I kept my feet well under the polished mahogany table as we were served lobster mousse, cold Greek summer soup, lamb and strawberry meringue. The regimental silver obstructed conversation with the people opposite so I spoke mainly to a well-decorated Gurkha Captain sitting next to me, wearing a Victoria Cross. One of many Gurungs in the regiment, the Gurungs had soldiering in their blood.

This bygone era of values is as much admired today by the Indian military as by my earlier ancestors[cxci]. On the walls in the corridor were photos of heroes from past ages – my great uncle Sir Horace Moule Evans had been Honorary Colonel of 2nd Battalion 8th Gurkha Rifles[86].

True to tradition, Gurkha Royal Engineer officers ran our PSA District Works Office – they presented me with a special tie decorated with the Gurkha kukris, which I wear on Remembrance Sunday; a brass water ewer, which has found a place in our garden; and a game of tigers and goats, which we play when children visit.

One of the local staff took me up into the foggy foothills of the Himalayas, surmounting staggering heights, across the raging Tamur River, up breath-taking hair-pin bends, with no crash barriers to hold your fall – he told me a bus had fallen over the edge the week before – a not uncommon tragedy[87]. The road had been built by the PSA about 15 years earlier – at the time, soon after I joined PSA, I'd applied for a job there but had been turned down through inexperience. The sappers had built many roads like this a hundred years earlier – the two Harry's were part of that.

At the far end of the road, 3,000 feet further up, was a small clean village that might have been out of Tudor times, apart from the stunning Himalayan backdrop. No glass in the windows, top floors overhanging to prevent the rain entering the open-doored ground floor, no lavatories – merely a patch of earth at the end of the village. I was ushered into the one and only 'café' and given warmed goat's milk under an advert for Nestlé's baby powdered milk! Powdered baby's milk was certainly the one product the people of Dhankuta did not need.

On the way back, through the dark and mist, Deoman our driver navigated the twists and

---

85. *King Birendra Bir Bikram Shah (1945-2001) [NR]; Prince Dipendra Bir Bikram Shah Dev (1971-2001) [NR]. Some think it was a conspiracy by the King's unpopular brother Prince Gyanendra Bir Bikram Shah Dev GCMG (b1947)*

86. *Lt Col Walter James Evans DSO JP (1878-1959) said his photograph was hanging in the Gurkha Mess at Dharumsala, Himachal Pradesh, in 1921.*

87. *'KK'(Karmal Kumar) Pradhan.*

turns with consummate skill. It was a long slow drive and the mist was dense. It was a relief to stop before the steepest incline. No more than an unlit clearing, Beheri Tar was nicknamed 'Charlie's Point' after a visit from the Prince of Wales a year or two before. Mine host, Krishna Limbo, ushered me through his door flaps to meet his friends sat on rugs round a central fire. As I stared through the flickering flames at half a dozen bearded men, I remember asking myself: was it so hard to see them because of the mist or because of the smoke? They gave me a small glass of raksi, aniseed flavoured spirit, and we enjoyed an hour's humour as you might find anywhere else in the world. Then it was down the spiralling hill into the dense night.

Stopping for a drink. Deoman the driver, the author in his topi and KK Pradhan.

Twenty-five years later, in the summer of 2012, I was just 100 miles from Dharan, returning from Darjeeling in a 4x4, past an Indian Army base in the Jorpokhri wildlife reserve. Not a lot had changed from the two Harrys' days – single storey whitewashed barrack blocks, shaded lawns, tennis courts, inside the barbed wire; calm forests beyond. Authority; tranquillity. People confident at a leisurely pace, the quiet punctured by the occasional military vehicle, the vibrant bustling bazaar banished half a mile down the road. The ambience was more confident than the state of Oudh in the 1850s, but over lunch the day before with a Government Minister, he was able to retain the easy confidence of a person with 17.5% of the world's problems on his shoulders. The challenge was as big now as it had been in Dalhousie's or Canning's day.

Dankuta 1987

You can't expunge 400 years of British influence overnight, nor want to. English is still the official Indian language. The roads, railways, administration and postal service carry on in much the same way. Many still hold fast to the continuity, security, productivity, ingenuity, purpose and justice that the British brought. The Indian Medical Service won a worldwide reputation. Many of the best doctors who've looked after me in hospitals in Hull, Harrogate and Leeds have come from that continent. The English academic education introduced by **Lord Macaulay** (another far-flung relation) helped India meet the world[88]. Contrariwise, the English officer classes acquired a sense of decorum, manners, karma, generosity and poetry as well as numeracy and a better sense of order.

Britain wasn't all good for India. Despite Sir Herbert Baker and Sir Edwin Lutyens' best efforts at sympathetic new architecture, much of the vernacular legacy failed to survive the hostilities. The 1857 extermination of artists and 'Macaulayism' contributed to high caste Indians losing interest in their heritage. The Mutiny also fostered tension between Muslims and Hindus that spilt over in the 1947 'Partition', when Britain gave up the Empire. It's still causing problems today. Yet the number of contented 'Asians' wanting to live in England is testimony to Britain having done something right. Can we in Britain live up to their expectations? Cultural crossover contributes to creative energy – will we avoid the communication failures and lack of empathy that led to the wholesale destruction of 1857?

Charlie's Point

✷ ✷ ✷ ✷

---

88. *Thomas Babington Macaulay, 1st Baron Macaulay, PC (1800-1859).*

Indian lingo

Words of the same sound have many spellings. 'ee' in 1850s is written 'i' today.

Ayah = Maid, nanny

Beebee (Bibi) = mistress, dedicated courtesan

Begum = Noblewoman

Bhang = cannabis (marijuana) drink

Brevet = courtesy rank awarded in the field, without the higher pay (Regimental ranks were usually purchased)

Buggy = 2-wheeled carriage with sprung suspension and hood

Caste = ethnic group or occupational class

Chupper or Chupra = straw hut

Chuprasee = office servant

Durbar = royal pageant, meeting

Fakir = religious ascetic wanderer

Furlough = Leave/holiday entitlement

Ghar = House

Ghat = River steps, landing stage

Ghee = Clarified butter

Gram = chickpea flour, grain

Gurkhas = soldiers from Nepal

Jihadist = Muslim fighter on a holy mission

Kothi = Palace or large town house

Khus tatti = screen made of vetiver grass

Mahratta = Maratha caste from an Empire (1674-1820) originally from central west India

Maulvi = qualified religious leader; Sufi mystic

Moghul (Mughal) = Emperor

Mullah = Muslim religious leader – often unqualified, political rabble-rouser

Nautch = seductive dance

Newab = semi-autonomous Muslim ruler

Peshwa = Chief or Prime Minister (Mahratta)

Phirangee or firangi = foreigner

Punkha = Framed cloth ceiling fan

Rana = noble family who ruled in Nepal

Raksi = spirit made with millet (Nepal)

Resident = British head in an Indian state, part-diplomat, part Chief Executive

Rupee = Indian currency

Sahib = Master or 'Sir', as used in civil service

Satee (Sati) = wife joins body of dead husband on his funeral pyre

Sepoy = Native infantryman (foot soldier)

Sowar = Native cavalryman (horseman)

Sewaree = Elephants in procession

Tamasha = Great show, performance or fuss

Terai = marshy jungle

Tiffin = Light meal, luncheon

Topi = soft cloth cap shaped like a fez

Unwashed or untouchables = Dalits with no caste – the lowest class of society

Vizier = High Minister (Muslim)

Writer = East India Company desk officer

Zemindar = Local landowner or ruler

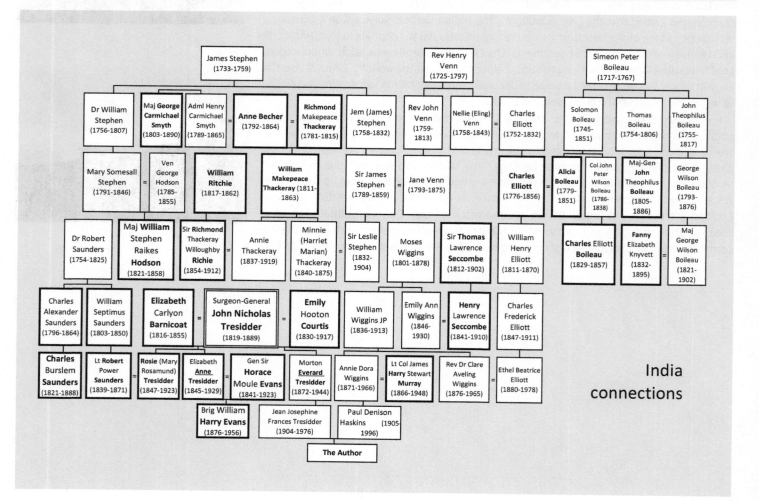

India connections

Other Notes and References

i. National Trust Properties 1961. Mr & Mrs Henry Baker with an anonymous donor are recorded as donating 12 acres of Hemmick to the National Trust in 1957. In a lette (Aug 1974), his son Henry confirmed that when they stayed at Penare and Penquarry each September, his parents bathed at Hemmick 4 times a day.

ii. Thackeray, Rose and the Ring.

iii. http://www.higherednwb.net/universityeducation.htm. Despite the contemporary tombstone stating an earlier date, the Indian Department for Higher Education records its formal establishment as five years before his death, in 1857.

iv. The number of British killed is thousands. Most commentators put the figure for Indian deaths in the hundreds of thousands. However, In War of Civilisations: India AD 1857 p1897, Amaresh Misra puts the figure at 10 million, although at one point he confuses lacs (Indian for 100,000) and millions. With few records to go on except the contemporary descriptions and the 2 million returned letters 'not now at this address' in the Lucknow Post Office, 1 million across the whole country is more probable.

v. Royal Commission on the Sanitary State of the Army 1863 Vol 1. In 1856: Officers 8,324; Non-Commissioned Officers (NCOs) & men 39,108; Native 235,221; Total 280,325. By 1861, the native numbers were down to 137,804.

vi. Gravestone at St Mary's Tattingstone, Suffolk

vii. The Moghul Emperor Akbar Shah II in procession with his sons and the British Resident, Delhi c1811-1819 [BL]

viii. From £20,000 to £25,000 per annum. Mason p280: by 1857, the Emperor was receiving £10,000/month.

ix. Kaye, Christianity in India p330. From one protestant mission church in 1813, by 1824 there were 8 in Calcutta; and at least 5 other cities; more in construction. Heber became Bishop thanks to his friend Charles Watkin Williams-Wynn (1775-1850) [NR], President of the Board of Control overseeing the East India Company.

x. Quote from Rudyard Kipling, source unknown.

xi. Misra A, War of Civilisations p4.

xii. Russell, Vol 1 p190.

xiii. Forbes-Mitchell, Relief of Lucknow p107. 'British' as a term was seldom used. 'European' was the normal description. 'English' was used to include the Scots etc. as from the 1745 Rebellion the Scots were forbidden to call themselves such.

xiv. Ward p10

xv. Johnson pp88, 89, 97; '...the angry gentleman who has been disturbed in his Pendennis'. Russell, p189.

xvi. Johnson p92.

xvii. L/MIL/10/76 ff77-78 Indian Office Records, British Library

xviii. Bradshaw's Continental Railway Guide, p304, describes Calcutta of 1863 well.

xix. Roberts F. Letters p108.

xx. Diary of Henry Silver quoted by Ray p362. Thackeray once quarrelled with a fellow Punch contributor, Douglas Jerrold, because he 'ate peas with a knife and therefore was not fit company for him.'

xxi. Daily Telegraph 7 Sep 2013 p31: 'Squeeze but not too hard; dip, not vibrate, the hand; kiss on each cheek, not an air smack, never pulling the person to you; maintain eye contact, keep the back straight, head up and chin in.' The Times 7 Nov 2013 'Don't grunt, don't turn your back on people.'

xxii. Bengal Regulations 1851 Ch V p49, quoted in Crawford p377. 1851 figure for the Bengal Presidency. This included R100 house-rent and R30 conveyance allowance. Private income was on top. About £1/10 Rupees =£33 or £400 a year. A sepoy received about 7 Rupees a month Sepoy and the Raj p54.

xxiii. Hunter p78 40,000 Sikhs; 53 of their 60 cannon.

xxiv. www.bl.uk/world-war-one/articles/the-indian-sepoy-in-the-first-world-war#sthash.XvIJIgWX.dpuf accessed 15 Nov 2014; Heathcote in Sunday Times 23 Nov 2014 and The Sepoy and the Raj p39: Perhaps half the 140,000 Indians (90,000 soldiers, 50,000 others) who went to France were from the Punjab, serving at Ypres, Givenchy, Neuve Chapelle, Festubert and Loos, suffering 9,000 losses and winning Victoria Crosses.

xxv. N-1-70, folio 7, British Library. British India Office Ecclesiastical Returns, Parish register transcripts from the Presidency of Bengal, Baptism Register records Elizabeth Anne Tresidder (1846-1929) was born 5 July 1846 and baptised at Benares on 28 July 1846.

xxvi. Ward p50; Trevelyan p15. Over 40,000.

xxvii. Ward p111: Parliamentary return. Royal Commission on the Sanitary State of the Army in India 1863 Vol 1: Venereal Disease affected 34.5% of soldiers in the Bengal Presidency.

xxviii. Trevelyan p5.

xxix. Misra A, War of Civilisations p94.

xxx. Russell, Vol 1 p194. Johnson p96: Maj Johnson wrote home about the most delicious lobster salad that he had ever tasted on a picnic by the river in Oct 1856 with Fanny Boileau (1832-1895), a relation. Fanny (née Knyvett) and her children were in Lucknow during the siege. One child, Ina, died there. See also Russell, Vol 1 p182: 'Who comes next in that very smart buggy, with the bay mare' 'That is the doctor of the station.'

xxxi. Collier p171.

xxxii. Ward p35 The exchange rate was about £1/10 Rupees

xxxiii. Bombay Times, 19 Dec 1854 p4948.

xxxiv. Under the Treaty of Fyzabad 1775.

xxxv. Bombay Times, 5 Mar 1855. 'Who can wonder that under such a government, man in Oudh should be an incarnation of evil? Rack-rented by tax collectors and farmers; plundered and outraged by the soldiery; oppressed on all sides by those whose vice or accident has raised to power and elevated to the commission of crime, the tenantry and peasantry are everywhere reckless, lawless, and in the arms against all regal authority.'

xxxvi. Hunter p32, Napier p198. Gen Charles Napier's (1782-1853) [NR] resignation in 1850 amounted to constructive dismissal.

xxxvii. Napier p75.

xxxviii. Ward p59.

xxxix. Kaye, History of the Sepoy War in India. Vol 1 p136: Letter to Lord Dalhousie April 1852; Ward p58, 61. 'In September 1848 I took the liberty to mention to your Lordship my fears that the system of annexing and

absorbing Native States ... might some day render us too visibly dependent on our Native Army; ... accidents might occur to unite them ... in some desperate act.' Major General Sir William Henry Sleeman KCB (1788-1856) [NR] was son of an Exciseman in the same area of North Cornwall as David Haskins, but 100 years earlier.

xl. King & Crewe p357: 'Moral Hazard' they call it these days. The Governor-General had obtained agreement from the Company's Court of Directors in London without telling them the whole story. This was a situation in which "one party to a transaction is prepared to take dangerous risks because the individual or firm in question knows that, if the worst happens, the other parties to the transaction will be the ones to suffer."

xli. Johnson pp83, 84; Rees p33.

xlii. King & Crewe p357: A situation in which "one party to a transaction is prepared to take dangerous risks because the individual or firm in question knows that, if the worst happens, the other parties to the transaction will be the ones to suffer."

xliii. Allen's Indian Mail, 18 Oct 1851 p618 – departed Calcutta for London on the Essex 26 Aug 1851

xliv. British Library India collection 2/4/830 of 1855 and E/4/841 pp965-8, 14 Jan 1857.

xlv. Heathcote, The Military in British India pp60-61.

xlvi. Ward p22; Chaudhuri Volume 8 Part 2 p255: an observer in 1834 said that the 1833 famine brought Cawnpore 'to the brink of ruin.' Charles George Hillersdon (1822-1857) [NR] was Magistrate and Collector of Cawnpore, the chief civil officer, in 1857. He, Lydia and their children died in the massacres. The Society for the Propagation of the Gospel was run by Revs Carshore and Perkins [NRs].

xlvii. Roberts, Letters pp111, 120: Letter from Lt (later Field-Marshal, Earl) Roberts to his sister 31 Dec 1857; Bombay Times 15 Aug 1857: '5 lacs of Rupees' = R500,000 or £50,000.

xlviii. Russell, Vol 1 p166.

xlix. Misra A, War of Civilisations p14.

l. Palmer, J A B, p1. George Harvey, Commissioner in Agra, calculated a rate somewhere between 160 and 200 miles a night. The chapatis were passed by the village watchmen.

li. Ward p110. His bungalow was then burnt down.

lii. Story of the Cawnpore Mission p46. Rev Haycock of the SPG Mission died in the entrenchment.

liii. Kaye Vol 1 p524; Bombay Times 11 May 1857 p84.

liv. Napier p11; Allen's Indian Mail, 15 Apr 1857: Fort William 27 Feb 1857: "The Rt Hon the Governor-General is pleased to direct that the staff salary of the pay master and superintendent of native pensioners of the Barrackpore circle shall be reduced to Rupees 250."

lv. Kaye A History of the Sepoy War p221.

lvi. Napier Part 2 Ch III see p239.

lvii. Allen's Indian Mail, 15 Apr 1857: "...1st Regt of Native Infantry under marching orders from Viziangram to Kurnool mutinied on 28 [Mar] ... not a single Captain, be it remarked! Need we wonder that the Government are now reaping as they have sown – Spectator." Also, Allen's Indian Mail, 29 Apr 1857 p269.

lviii. Russell, Vol 1 p168.

lix. Canning p53; Copland etc p177; Allen's Indian Mail, 2

Jun 1857: "A dim hazy conviction that Christianity is winning the game, that conversion is only a question of time, is undoubtedly a sign of the hour in all ranks of native society." Kaye, Christianity in India p484: John Kaye, in the Governor-General's office, wrote two years later: "If it had not been disastrously interrupted by the Sepoy rebellion," there would have been "State patronage of Christian education" by the mid-1870s.

lx.   *Palmer, J A B, p30-1. The 19th Native Infantry (NI) were to be disbanded over previous insubordination over the cartridge issue. Pandee, of 34th Native Infantry, shot at British officers from the 19th NI, shouting 'It's for our religion. From biting these cartridges we will become infidels.'*

lxi.   *Misra A, Mangal Pandey p94ff. His boyhood friend Nakki Khan was in touch with insurgents in Patna, Cawnpore, Gwailor, Behrampore and Meerut. Mangal was also in a difficult love triangle and high on bhang.*

lxii.   *Allen's Indian Mail, 19 May 1857 pp 299, 304 & 305; 2 Jun 1857 p353: Dr Tresidder departed for Marseilles on 8 April on paddle-steamer Bentinck, arriving in England 20-26 May 1857, taking about 6 weeks. He went via Suez overland to Alexandria and then by rail across France – the French railway had opened in 1855. The Suez Canal wasn't to open until 1869.*

lxiii.   *Allen's Indian Mail, 29 Apr 1857: on 8 March 1857. Low p15: Ali was working for the Maulvie of Faizabad. Charles Elliott Boileau (1829-1857) was a cousin of the author's great aunt Ethel Wiggins (née Elliott)*

lxiv.   *Hibbert p74.*

lxv.   *Allen's Indian Mai,l 29 Apr 1857 p268.*

lxvi.   *http://www.dnw.co.uk/auction-archive/special-collections/lot.php?specialcollection_id=118&lot_id=42119 accessed 13 Nov 2014; IOL L/MIL/9/227; IOL. Dalhousie had moved the Artillery HQ from Dum Dum, Calcutta, to Meerut, 50 miles from Delhi*

lxvii.   *Palmer, J A B, p6.*

lxviii.   *Allen's Indian Mail, 9 Jun 1857 p368: Maj J F Harriott (possibly a relation of Charles Saunders' wife and prosecutor at the Emperor's trial) reported 'All the men stated they could see no objection to the cartridges.... All is very quiet.' How did he get it so wrong?*

lxix.   *Palmer, J A B, p57, 72ff. As the service was delayed to 7pm, the parade would have been 6.30pm. The sun set at 6.40pm and the moon rose at 8.55pm.*

lxx.   *Hibbert p82: Commandant of the 11th Native Infantry.*

lxxi.   *Allen's Indian Mail, 30 Jun 1857 p393.*

lxxii.   *Dalrymple p141; Mason pp276-280: The cable was cut sometime between 9am and 4pm.*

lxxiii.   *Dalrymple p214. In Napier p272, General Napier had warned four years earlier:: 'The Delhi king is a mere effigy, yet he forms a moral rallying point round which gather the dreams of discontented princes, feeding on prophecies.'*

lxxiv.   *Allen's Indian Mail, 30 Jun 1857 p396.*

lxxv.   *Hodson was with the 1st Fusiliers*

lxxvi.   *Trotter p109.*

lxxvii.   *Hibbert p72.*

lxxviii.   *Young 1857 p19 quoted in Dalrymple p194. Roberts, in 'Forty-One Years in India' Vol 1 p96, refutes this.*

lxxix.   *Yadav p41, quoted in Dalrymple p139.*

lxxx.   *Allen's Indian Mail, 15 Jul 1857 p427: General Anson died of cholera at Karnal on 27 May along with many others who contracted it at Umbala.*

lxxxi.   *Roberts, Forty-one Years in India p213.*

lxxxii.   *Hodson p294.*

lxxxiii.   *Hodson p190.*

lxxxiv.   *Johnson p123. "If a little grape[-shot] had been scientifically administered in the first instance in Meerut, it would have put a stop to all further proceedings," said one contemporary.*

lxxxv.   *Hodson's reference was from Sir William Napier KCB (1785-1860)*

lxxxvi.   *Trotter pp44-6.*

lxxxvii.   *Trotter p350.*

lxxxviii.   *Arnold Life p36. Thomas Arnold wrote, "His expansive and impulsive temper won him many friends, and for my own part I always liked him greatly. His faults were arrogance, rashness, and a domineering temper; if one bears this in mind, it is easy to understand the errors into which he fell in India."*

lxxxix.   *Dalrymple p102.*

xc.   *Ward pp118, 384.*

xci.   *Kaye, A History of the Sepoy War Vol 2 p307; Ward p149: Lt William Edward Cox [NR]*

xcii.   *Gupta p66-70 Kaye, A History of the Sepoy War. Vol 2 p311.*

xciii.   *Thomson p89.*

xciv.   *Ward p312; Thomson p164.*

xcv.   *Hibbert p192; however, Ward p340: Wheeler may have been slaughtered at the Ghat or with the party rounded up with Maj Vibart.*

xcvi.   *Ward pp541, 551. Lts Delafosse, and Thomson; plus Privates Murphy and Sullivan who died soon afterwards. Subsequently: Private Murphy was guardian of the memorial gardens built round the well, which for a decade had more visitors than the Taj Mahal. The officers returned to their army careers. Maj-Gen Henry George Delafosse CB (1835-1905) [NR] took part in the Relief of Lucknow, recuperated in Calcutta (My Diary Vol 1 p117) and later joined the Sikkim and Frontier War. He retired to Jersey; Gen Mowbray Thomson (1832-1917) [NR] wrote an account whilst recovering from his wounds, and was later Political Agent in Manipur.*

xcvii.   *Shepherd p146.*

xcviii.   *Hibbert p195.*

xcix.   *Daily Telegraph 29 March 2016 What is Wahhabism? The reactionary branch of Islam said to be 'the main source of global terrorism'.*

c.   *Times 19 Apr 2016, BBC Radio 4 PM 2 Jun 2016.*

ci.   *https://hamidmahmood.co.uk/2012/11/01/the-dars-e-ni%E1%BA%93ami-and-the-transnational-traditionalist-madaris-in-britain/ accessed 9 May 2016*

cii.   *Gupta p139; Ward p408, Hibbert p194. Numbers vary.*

ciii.   *Gram is flour made from chick-peas.*

civ.   *Ward p406.*

cv.   *Johnson p126ff. Major General Sir Henry Havelock KCB (1795-1857) [NR] would have arrived earlier except he and Outram were shipwrecked on the way there. They set out from Bombay on 1 June and made it to Calcutta 17 June instead of a week earlier.*

cvi.   *Shepherd p116.*

cvii.   *Forbes-Mitchell, Reminiscences p19; Forbes-Mitchell, The Relief of Lucknow p25. "The wall all around the hook on a level with it was covered with the hand-prints, and below the hook with the footprints, in blood, of a little child."*

cviii   cviii *Collier p171-2.*

cix   cix *Ward p449.*

cx.   *JJFMT's diary 29 July 1922 and address book: the Tresidder and Vibart families were still seeing each other in the 1920s and 30s. The Vibarts gave the author's parents a Minty fireside chair for a wedding present – it had long use. Maj Edward Vibart (1807-1857), his wife Emily and their 3 youngest children (two older daughters were in England) all died. His son in Delhi, Lt later Col Edward Vibart, married into the Horn/Saunders/Barnicoat/Tresidder family.*

cxi.   *Letter from Lt Vibart to his Uncle Gordon 22 Sep 1857 British Library Indian collection Eur135/19.*

cxii.   *Letter from Lt Vibart to his Uncle Gordon 22 Sep 1857 British Library Indian collection Eur135/19.*

cxiii.   *Hodson p296.*

cxiv.   *Dalrymple p387; Trotter p261.*

cxv.   *Dalrymple p390; Letter from Hodson to Charles B Saunders 29 Nov 1857 para 5, DCO Archive Mutiny Papers File No14.*

cxvi.   *Dalrymple p343; Hodson's letter to Saunders 29 Nov 1857, Delhi Commissioner's Office Mutiny Papers File 14: H.M. Malika-i-Zamani Nawab Zinat Mahal Begum Sahiba (1821-1882) [NR], her son Mirza Jamma Bakht (1841-1884) [NR], her father Amir ul-Mulk, Samsam ud-Daula, Nawab Ahmad Quli Khan Bahadur, Muzaffar Jang [NR].*

cxvii.   *Trotter p266.*

cxviii.   *Dalrymple p396: "Imagining that sooner or later they must be taken, the princes resolved to give themselves up unconditionally, fancying, I suppose, that as we had spared the King, we would spare them." Lt MacDowell.*

cxix.   *Dictionary of National Biography*

cxx.   *Trotter p107.*

cxxi.   *Dalrymple p400*

cxxii.   *Dalrymple p407.*

cxxiii.   *Kaye, The History of the India Mutiny Vol 2 p169. Susan Annette Hodson (neé Henry) (1820-1884) was later given a grace and favour apartment at Hampton Court Palace.*

cxxiv.   *Old Phlos' was Havelock's nickname at Charterhouse, where he was happier 'philosophising' than on a sports pitch. Allen's Indian Mail, 29 Oct 1859 p759.*

cxxv.   *Misra A, War of Civilisations p1281.*

cxxvi.   *Allen's Indian Mail, 16 Nov 1857 p770; Misra A, War of Civilisations p1300.*

cxxvii.   *Campbell had arrived in India 14 August 1857 Allen's Indian Mail, 1 Oct 1857*

cxxviii.   *Sherer p217. Campbelll's conduct of the Battle of Chinkiang, in the Opium Wars, July 1842, had brought the defeat of Nanking and the Treaty that handed Hong Kong to Britain in perpetuity.*

cxxix.   *British Library IOR/E/4/846, p126. Order No 137 of 1857, 5 Aug: 'With reference to our letter dated 8 July No 116 we have to inform you that the undermentioned officers have returned, or are about to return, to their* duty: Asst Surgn J N Tresidder MD'

cxxx. Allen's Indian Mail, 30 Jun 1857 p407: Order at the Court of Directors 29 Jun 1857 directed all military officers on furlough to return. Allen's Indian Mail, 15 July 1857 p447: House of Lords 29 Jun 1857: 10,000 extra troops were sent to India.

cxxxi. Allen's Indian Mail, 1 Oct 1857 p641.

cxxxii. Ward p468.

cxxxiii. Shepherd p153.; Russell, Vol 1 p206: According to William Russell: of the 5,536 infantry and 946 horses at his disposal in Nov, Sir Colin left 2,402 troops in Cawnpore, 1,000 men in reserve at Dilkoossha (Dilkusha), and advanced on Lucknow Residency with the remainder. Outram and Havelock had had 2,683 men and 527 horses in July.

cxxxiv. Verney p98.

cxxxv. Hibbert p373. Jang Badhur Rana, real name Bir Narsingh Kunwar (1816-1877) [NR] was ruler of Nepal; the king had little power. He consolidated good relations with Britain through a visit to London in 1850-1.

cxxxvi. Thames Advertiser, Vol VIII Issue 1935, 6 Jan 1875 p3. The impersonator was arrested on 21 Oct 1874.

cxxxvii. Gupta p196, 198.

cxxxviii. Sherer p165. Tresidder describes the Nana as 'Between thirty and forty years of age, of middle height, stolid features and increasing stoutness.'

cxxxix. Russell, Vol 1 p169.

cxl. Ward p461

cxli. Sherer, p275.

cxlii. 4 Feb 1858 The Story of the Cawnpore Mission p252, 256.

cxliii. Ibid p321.

cxliv. Sherer, 1857 p288.

cxlv. Willcock p135: Felice Beato (1832-1909) [NR] – identical to known Beato prints though not attributed as such in the Tresidder album. It could have been a joint enterprise.

cxlvi. Ward p48.

cxlvii. Russell, Vol 1 p186-7

cxlviii. His 'love letters' to his future wife, Elsie, were in this style from the start. See Chapter 13.

cxlix. Forbes-Mitchell, The Relief of Lucknow p103.

cl. Hibbert p358.

cli. Willcock p72.

clii. Outram and Campbell started out from Chakar Kothi on 9 March 1858

cliii. Forbes-Mitchell, Reminiscences pp211-2. Hodson died at the Begum Kothi on 12 March 1858 on Campbell's second assault on Lucknow.

cliv. Forbes-Mitchell, Reminiscences p218. 'The whole army, which admired his talents, his bravery, and his military skill, deplores his loss .... I attended his funeral yesterday evening, in order to show what respect I could to the memory of one of the most brilliant officers under my command.' signed C Campbell, C-in-C East Indies. I have assumed there was music: the bagpipes played Flowers of the Forest earlier for another funeral.

clv. Shepherd p228; Forbes-Mitchell, The Relief of Lucknow p25

clvi. Dalrymple p314

clvii. Dr John Murray's Diary 18 Jan 1858, quoted in Willcock p119. "Saw a mutineer blown away from a Gun – Took a view No. 18 – when they were reading the sentence to him; then got out of the way; the pieces of flesh and bone are scattered all round & the head goes bounding in front– the body appears to swell and burst – like a shell – death must be instantaneous."

clviii. Hibbert p360.

clix. Saunders initiated an official enquiry which found no evidence of rape by Indians of English women.

clx. Allen's Indian Mail, 29 Oct 1857 p722. Changing British sentiment was not easy. When his Deputy, Mr J P Grant had liberated 150 of Col Neil's prisoners there was a 'bitter outcry'.

clxi. Notes from Kanpur Graveyard quoting the Maxwell letters

clxii. Bombay Times and Journal of Commerce 17 Sep 1859 p599; Maj-General Sir John Eardley Wilmot Inglis (1814-1862) [NR] in the chair, C R Thornhill, Commissioner, and Rev W Key, Principal of Bishop's College, with John Sherer and others.

clxiii. clxiii Ward p550. The angel statue was by Baron Carlo Marochetti (1805-1867) [NR], a childhood friend of Lady Canning.

clxiv. Willcock p148

clxv. Dalrymple p444.

clxvi. British Library, Indian Office Records, L/MIL/10/76 ff77-78

clxvii. Willcock p62.

clxviii. Encyclopaedia of Nineteenth Photography p964. Murray left Agra on 27 Apr 1857.

clxix. Willcock p61, Encyclopaedia of Nineteenth-Century Photography p965: Picturesque views in the NW Provinces of India: 26 selected from 600 negatives. Boileau wrote the words and Murray took the photos, most of which had been exhibited at Hogarth's Art Rooms, 5 Haymarket, London in 1857. These photos contributed to later efforts to preserve the Taj Mahal for posterity.

clxx. Source Sean Willcock 7 Dec 2012

clxxi. Low Foreword, p37. John Boileau retired in Feb 1857 and was given the honorary rank of Maj-General.

clxxii. Willcock p71.

clxxiii. Bingham. Silver Nitrates cost 5/- (5 shillings), Paper 2/6 a quire, Iodine 1/-, Nitric Acid 3d.

clxxiv. McCosh p7. Dr John McCosh (1816-1894) [NR] was from Edinburgh University. "I would strongly recommend every assistant-surgeon to make himself master of photography in all its branches, on paper, on plate glass, and on metallic plates...especially the new process by Collodion for the stereoscope.."

clxxv. McCosh p7. Albumen was mixed with ammonia chloride, and gave a glossy appearance (though sometimes it crackled). The sepia effect of early photos resulted from sulphur in the atmosphere or the 'Hypo' fixing agent not being thoroughly washed out.

clxxvi. A solution of pyroxylin, dissolved in ether; iodine and gun cotton were available in his surgery Frederick Scott Archer (1814-1857) [NR] made details freely available, unlike Fox Talbot.

clxxvii. Developed with pyrogallic acid mixed 24:2 with galacial acetic acid and fixed with 'Hypo' (sodium thiosulfate) or potassium

clxxviii. Gum sandarac and oil of lavender

clxxix. British Library, India Office Records IOR/P/15/21: Bengal Proceedings 17 Jun 1861, 3311.: A circular by the officiating Foreign Secretary, Sir Edward Bayley, Jun 1861, addressed to provincial administrations lists tribes and requests photograph likenesses. With a brief description of origin, physical characteristics and general habits. A hundred copies of People of India were produced costing more than £1,400, plus the time taken to take the photos. Falconer p65: It could been one of the reasons for John Nicholas Tresidder's posting to Agra – the Inspector of Mails had proposed charges so preposterous that he had been told to stop.

clxxx. Viswanathan

clxxxi. Willcock p138.

clxxxii. Willcock p141.

clxxxiii. British Library, Indian Office Records IOR L/MIL/17/18/24; http://himalaya.socanth.cam.ac.uk/collections/naga/record/r87694.html accessed 11 Dec 2014

clxxxiv. Source: Lottie Raby-Smith 29 April 2015

clxxxv. Misra S, The Nature of Colonial Intervention in the Naga Hills, 1840-80. p3274, quoting Lord Dalhousie's Minutes, 1848, edited by Verrier Elwin, 1969. www.chinworld.info/category/article/ accessed 16 Dec 2014. Dr Lian H Sakhong. Correction of Dr L H Sakhong claims on Lt Steward's death.

clxxxvi. Mackenzie p137. 51 British were killed or wounded that day, 24 Nov 1879.

clxxxvii. Mackenzie p157.

clxxxviii. Mackenzie p172. Maharaja Sir ChandraKirti Singh KCSI (1831-1886) Maharaja of Manipur 1834-44 and 1851-86; succeeded by SuraChandra Singh (c1855-1891) Maharaja of Manipur 1886-90.

clxxxix. (GA) Gwendoline Allen's notes 21 Apr 1980

cxc. Dharan was a Gurkha recruiting station from 1953-93

cxci. See also Misra A, Mangal Pandey p31.

Doctor. "YOU WOULD PROBABLY FEEL MUCH BETTER IF YOU HAD ALL YOUR TEETH OUT."
Patient. "YES, I SHOULD, DOCTOR. THIS LOT NEVER FITTED FROM THE DAY THEY WERE PUT IN."

Spoonful of Sugar

Houses of Parliament completed 1852, six years before the 'Great Stink' 1858. In the foreground, the new St Thomas's Hospital rebuilt 1860 as the 'Nightingale Training Hospital'. John Nicholas Tresidder trained at St Thomas's 20 years earlier, and married his second wife in 1857 at St Giles' church nearby.

The Stygian Pool

In London, the 'Great Stink' of 1858 hit rich and poor alike. People were dying of cholera in their thousands. It had been a long hot English summer. The Thames was an open sewer. Luckily, in some ways, the newly constructed Houses of Parliament, built on reclaimed land, was beside the stinking river.[i] The legislators felt the full effects of the fermenting effluent as it floated past their windows.

It was like something out of Dante's Inferno. Closing off the front rooms didn't help, nor holding handkerchiefs over their noses. They talked about moving the seat of parliament – London had come to a standstill. Everybody demanded action.

In a record eighteen days, a bill was passed to revamp the Thames – sewers and embankments. The system, designed by Sir Joseph Bazalgette, had the desired effect[1]. Similar systems were introduced later in Calcutta (still functioning) and in Malta, the latter overseen by my great uncle **Jack Tresidder**[2]. That one, for a population of 60,000, cost £100,000 which at today's currency might now be valued at half a billion. Each has performed well for over a hundred years. Drawings have been lost – the former Mayor of Calcutta told me they didn't know where the pipes now ran. London is starting afresh. It is costing over £4 billion.

Tolmie John (Jack) Tresidder (1850-1931) as a schoolboy

Cholera had found its way from India by 1831. The first cholera pandemic was in India in 1816/7, decimating Calcutta[ii]. It killed more British troops than any battle had. It reached Russia in 1830, Britain in 1831, and Germany and America in 1832. There were cholera outbreaks in London throughout the 1840s. The Brontë sisters in Yorkshire died of it[iii]. Two in every 1,000 people died of cholera-related diseases. It was far worse in India, where 58 in every thousand soldiers died[iv]. Jack's father, **Dr John Nicholas Tresidder** was off on long-term sick leave himself in 1862. He'd picked it up in Agra, treating others of the disease. He had another period of illness in 1869-70.

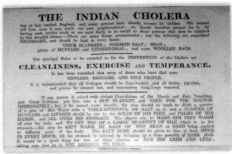

Like others of his generation, John Nicholas had been taught that the cause was a consequence of bad air – 'Miasma', gasses from the 'filth'. His colleague described cholera as follows: *"Engorgement of the arterial system, suppression of all glandular secretion, of bile, of urine, of saliva; hence congestion of the lungs and asphyxia, imperfect oxidation of the blood, and lividity of countenance, cramps and spasms, clammy coldness and death."*[v] Dr Tresidder thought the cure had something to do with diet and wrote to the authorities to ask that prisoners, some of the worst casualties, be better fed[vi]. He and his colleagues were inching towards an answer when they moved soldiers and prisoners after an outbreak. *Allen's Indian Mail* got nearer to the truth in 1857 when it concluded that a Police Magistrate's death had something to do with his drinking bad water[vii].

Punch holding his nose

---

1. *Sir Joseph William Bazalgette CB (1819-1891) [NR]. His grandfather founded the Bazalgette family fortune as a tailor to George IV.*

2. *Tolmie John Tresidder CMG (1850-1931).*

Rev Henry Moule's 'green' Earth Composting Closet. There was a hopper at the back and a handle to pull.

A barber's pole outside a hairdresser's in Leeds. The red and white recalls the blood from the time when barbers were experts with sharp blades.

Up to 1865 no one could agree if it was contagious or not. Tresidder thought it was. In 1856 and 1861, his friend and mentor Dr John Murray reported in detail on the situation in Agra and, on his retirement, Murray gave a lecture in London on the causes[viii]. About the same time, the **Rev Henry Moule**, uncle of John Nicholas's son-in-law, a parson in Dorset, started investigating the link between the disease and sanitation. He was not the only parson to be concerned about his community. The Rev Patrick Brontë was rebuilding the drains at Haworth following the early deaths of his literary daughters[3]. Henry Moule patented the dry earth closet in 1860[4]. The Army & Navy Stores sold it for 30/- (£1.50) – he believed in returning soil to the land, not dumping it in the water. The patent was widely taken up by the Indian government in hospitals, 'lunatic asylums' and gaols. Following trials in Bengal, the Punjab and North Western Provinces, Henry was awarded £500 in recognition.

Health care has come a long way since Dr Tresidder left Cornwall to train to be a Surgeon at St Thomas's Hospital in Camberwell. In 1840, surgeons were no more than one step on from barbers, as gentleman's hairdressers were known. My hairdresser still has a red and white striped pole outside his premises recalling the blood and bandages of blood-letting, amputations and dentistry. In the early 20th century men went to the barbers for a shave. Shaving was done with sharp open-bladed knives – 'cut-throat' razors. One slip and deadly consequences. Three of the Haskins family were barbers – though no Sweeny Todd's in the family have come to light so far.

In the 1840s, Victorian medicine was still struggling to emerge from the hocus pocus of the Middle Ages. As late as the 1920s my father experienced 'quacks' plying 'cure-alls' in Lincolnshire markets. Midwifery was the provenance of the 'Mother Gamps' – women with experience but no education. John Nicholas was trained to keep records and write treaties on serious cases. Surgeons were originally lower in status to physicians who had been university trained. Capability with the cutting blade has reversed that status, with their title 'Doctor' reverting to 'Mr'.

After the Crimean War (1853-55), where Florence Nightingale had reorganised the field hospitals to improve hygiene and patient care, she returned to London and largely took to her bed for the rest of her life. From there, she conducted voluminous correspondence. I wonder whether she ever met John Nicholas who'd returned to London the same year as she had. I can find no correspondence but the following year, 1858, she lobbied hard for a Royal Commission to look into the Indian situation. Two years later, she made a detailed submission to the Commission, which reported to parliament in 1863.

Dr Snow had sound evidence of a link between water and the disease at the Broad Street pump as early as 1854. Nearly twenty years later though, ten years after the reforms, his discovery was still not accepted by authorities in Calcutta[ix]. Nightingale was one of the reasons – she had perpetuated the 'miasma' theory. However, she was able to report that mortality amongst the soldiers in India had declined from 69 deaths per 1,000 at its height, to 18 per 1,000, thanks to improvements that the likes of Dr Tresidder and his colleagues had implemented following the Royal Commission report.

John Nicholas Tresidder was respected for his concern for people. He was often put in charge of civilians, families and VIPs. Young Lt Vibart, who had lost his parents and half his siblings in the Cawnpore Massacre, writing in his private notebook from the other side of India, described 'Dr T' as, "A charming man, generous, affectionate and affable. Richly deserves all the gods send him. A downright good sort. An estimable character. He is a long way off. I worship him from afar.[x]" Tresidder's confident, no nonsense, approach (as advocated by Florence Nightingale and practiced by Indian Medics ever since) was one that people trusted.

---

3. *Rev Henry Moule MA (1801-1880); Rev Patrick Brontë MA (1777-1861) [NR].*
4. *Dry earth system. Patent No.1316. 28th May 1860.*

Tresidder had had no training in tropical medicine before being posted to India. They learnt on the job and conducted experiments to test out theories. At some stage, he invested in a microscope. Before my father's uncle, **Clare Wiggins,** went out to Africa in 1901, thirty years after John Nicholas had retired, he sought out his own tropical medicine training. He planned ahead, and bought a microscope and a centrifuge so he could detect parasites – it cost him three months' wages. His was to be the only microscope in the Protectorate. The Customs made him pay 30% tax on it. Typically, when the Principal Medical Officer wanted to borrow the microscope, this Wiggins wired back to say, "Will send microscope on refund of customs duty!" He won, but then the Wiggins's generally did, even if it meant dying in a ditch over it.

Microscope owned by my great grandfather Surgeon-General John Nicholas Tresidder

✳ ✳ ✳ ✳

Sleeping Sickness

Clare Wiggins arrived in Africa in 1901 at the same time as Sleeping Sickness, *Trypanosomiasis*. Around Lake Victoria it became the biggest hazard of the African continent – worse than the 2014 Ebola crisis.

A doctor at the Church Missionary Society hospital in Kampala first noticed it. First there were eight cases; 6 months later 200. Thousands more were infected with this mysterious disease. It swept right round the lake shore. Once again, no one could work out the cause. It resisted every kind of treatment and no one who caught it seemed to escape death. By 1902, 30,000 had died. Like the 2014 Ebola crisis, there were heavy predictions that the entire population was doomed. In 1903, a Colonel Bruce was called in by the Royal Society. He concluded it was caused by a kind of *trypanosome* caught by the bite of a species of tsetse fly called *glossina palpalis*. The areas infected were low lying; the flies lived in the marshes.

Kavirondo fishermen on the shores of Lake Victoria

By 1905, perhaps two thirds of the population had indeed died. It was like the Black Death in Europe – whole villages were exterminated. Europeans were not immune. A whole series of investigations into the treatment were begun into the origin of the disease. The life history of the fly was studied, and special measures introduced to manage the population.

A 'Sleeping Sickness Commission' was launched, and Clare volunteered to join a team doing extended investigations in 1906-07 though it meant sending Ethel and their child home for 18 months whilst he camped out around the shores of the Lake. He found the culprit tsetse on the banks of every stream right up to the foothills of Mount Elgon. He trespassed into areas where the tribes had never seen a white man and would flee before him. The witch doctors would 'make medicine', placing curses outside his tent to drive him away – usually the head of a cock inside a circle of beads or pebbles. At Jinja, he examined the salivary glands of individual flies, expressing the contents on a slide. It took 751 flies before he found one with hundreds of *trypanosomes*.

Dr Tresidder and Florence Nightingale may have met in London in 1857

Just one fly in every 750 was enough. He concluded that all it needed was water, bushes, trees, a fly and one infected person. Remove any one and the curse was lifted. Planting of citronella grass was one solution. If he cleared the lake shores, within two days the fly was free of the poison. A benefactor of my school, Lord Edmond Fitzmaurice, headed up the International Conference in London on the subject 1907-8[5].

✳ ✳ ✳ ✳

---

[5]. *Edmond George Petty-Fitzmaurice, 1st Baron Fitzmaurice PC (1846-1935) [NR] as a Foreign Office minister held the title of First British Plenipotentiary at the London Conference on African Sleeping Sickness 1907-8.*

*Dr Morton Everard Tresidder (1871-1944)
aged 45 years, the author's grandfather*

Dr Stanley Tresidder (1859-1926), Milly (1859-1938) with their daughter Beryl (1899-1939). Stan was born in Cawnpore two years after the massacre.

Doctors in the house

Dr John Nicholas Tresidder had seven sons including my grandfather **Morton Everard Tresidder** – like many Tresidders, Everard was called by his second name[6]. Five of the seven sons became doctors, training at Guy's Hospital, near London Bridge – a rum lot. They were General Practitioners of the *Dr Finlay's Casebook* era, practising surgery on kitchen tables if they had to. Remedies were basic, though some of their medicines work just as well today, if it's possible to get hold of them. I still use Whitfield's Ointment to stop uncomfortable fungal itches in awkward places – Colin, our chemist in Wetherby, recalled an old-fashioned cure that no doctor had prescribed. Tincture of iodine, for cuts and wounds, milk of magnesia, for sleeplessness and teething as well as stomach complaints, are remedies now found more in the USA than under the NHS, but they function as well as they ever did. The Nepalese still wash their raw vegetables in a solution of iodine before eating.

There was a fifteen year gap between the eldest and the youngest of these five doctors. **Stan Tresidder** was the eldest[7]. He emigrated to Australia after qualifying in 1883, met and married Millie McDouall and set up a surgery in Glenn Innes, halfway between Brisbane and Sydney in New South Wales. Both their first two sons died in 1901, so they decided to return to England with their youngest, Beryl. Stan first set up shop as a General Practitioner (GP) in Nottingham and then moved to Askern near Doncaster. His sister remembered Beryl as 'an awful flirt' – she married a sales rep, had two children but died suddenly one night at their home in Bickley, aged just forty.

Stan's tallest brother **Harry Tresidder** followed Stan to Australia. Some called him the 'black sheep' of the family[8]. Why, I'm not sure – the others were pretty bad. He married Mary Hathorn (pronounced Hawthorn) in 1895 and established himself in a place called Dubbo, in '*the Bush.*' As my great uncle Will explained, '*Bush* is a most intriguing term. It does not refer to a dwarf kind of tree but to the country as opposed to the town. The interesting thing is that you never seem quite to catch up with it: it is always a little further on. You never actually yourself live in the bush, although you speak quite readily of your friends doing so. It is always a little remoter and wilder than your immediate vicinity. And of course if you 'go bush' altogether, you return to the state of nature,' in a Bear Grylls sort of way[xi]. In 1910, Harry and Mary moved to New Zealand, creating a large extended family of their own.

Stan's brother **Willie Tresidder** was the first to go to Nottingham. He married **Gertie** and set up home at 12 Shakespeare Street[9]. The youngest doctor, **Percy Tresidder**, qualified in 1895 and joined Willie and Gertie in their big house in Nottingham in 1901, large enough for three adults, four children, and four servants as well as the surgery[10].

I'm not sure Percy was a good influence[11]. Willie got to know (in the biblical sense) an underage solicitor's daughter, Annie Clayton. They'd been carrying on for some eighteen

6.   *Dr Morton Everard Tresidder (1872-1944).*

7.   *Dr Edward Stanley Tresidder MRCS LRCP (1859-1926) married Millie (Laura Amelia) McDouall (1859-1938) in 1887. One child reached adulthood, Beryl Fergus Tresidder (1899-1939) marrying John Randolph (Jock) Kerr (1896-1971) in 1934. Millie was great great niece of 6th Earl of Dumfries, Patrick McDouall-Crichton (1726-1803), whose Adam house, 40 miles south of Glasgow, was rescued by Prince Charles in 2007.*

8.   *Dr Harry Innes Tresidder MRCS LRCP (1861-1922) married Mary Hathorn (1860-1953) in Sydney in 1885 and moved to New Zealand, living in Queen Street, Onchunga, Auckland 1913-22. They had 10 children, Clive, Hal, Hilda, Madeline, Sibyl, Percy Hugh, Alan Leslie (father of Jack and grandfather of Megan), Harry and Doris May.*

9.   *Dr William Elliott Tresidder MRCS LRCP (1864-1929) married Gertrude Jane James (1864-1953) in 1894 and divorced her in 1903.*

10.   *12 Shakespeare Street had thirteen living rooms, a bathroom and an office.*

11.   *Dr Percy Edgar Tresidder MRCS LRCP (1873-1942) married Mary Clayton (1891-1947) in Nottingham in 1916. Mary married George Watts (1895-1975) 4 months after Percy died.*

months and he'd taken her to Bexhill for a holiday. In 1903, they were enjoying the delights of adultery in a first class railway carriage steaming out of Birmingham when Gertie found them out. She swiftly divorced him and Willie went to live at the other end of the country with his mother Emily in Paignton, whilst Percy kept the practice on. Emily, for all her straight-laced religion and 'widow's weeds', loved to have her boys around her, whatever their faults, and there were plenty[xii].

Willie's son, **Gordon Tresidder,** was not much wiser than his father. At the age of 42, also practising as a Doctor in Nottingham, he was taken to court for getting too frisky with a girl after a dance in Llandudno, Wales[12]. The 20 year-old bank clerk had got as far as climbing into his car[xiii]. Gordon had his arm in a sling, he said, which didn't allow him to do too much, but it didn't stop her accusing him of 'assault'.

Percy didn't stop seeing the Claytons once his brother had left Nottingham. At 42, in 1916, he married naughty Annie's sister, **Mary Clayton**. She was seventeen years younger than he was but, hey, there'd been an even bigger gap between Willie and Annie.

The handsome, feisty, naughty Percy was my grandfather Everard's closest brother and closest 'friend'. He was Godfather to my mother and on her marriage in 1932 he gave her his dining room furniture, for which he had no further use for in England[xiv]. He was well-liked by his straight-laced sisters who seemed to make an exception for him. He was just very naughty. In about 1930 he moved to the Côte d'Azur. A year later he made a will; he'd broken up with his wife Mary having taken up with his receptionist, Kathleen Pitman[13]. He moved to Juan les Pins on the French Riviera, known for its dubious hedonism and wealthy social milieu[xv].

It didn't take Percy long to attract an 'Instructress in the French Language'. Marie Anne Therese de Fermery and he grew fond of her as the years went on. By 1941, his wife Mary had been entirely cut out of his will and the erstwhile mistress Kathleen excised too. Now Marie-Anne was the chief beneficiary but there were two other female friends on board. He died in 1942, in the middle of the Second World War, when the south of France was under Vichy rule. By then he was extremely wealthy. How did he create this wealth? The answer may be in Chapter 13, which describes his closest brother, **Everard Tresidder**, my grandfather – born into the same mould as all the others.

✳ ✳ ✳ ✳

Dr Percy Tresidder (1874-1942), the lovable rogue

Emily Hooton Tresidder (née Courtis) (1830-1917), mother of 5 doctors

Dr Tolmie Gordon Tresidder (1898-1963), Dr Willie's son

Percy's home in the South of France – Palais Rhodanier, Avenue l'Estérel, Juan les Pins.

---

12.   *Dr Tolmie Gordon Tresidder MRCS LRCP (1898-1963).*
13.   *Probably Kathleen Vera Pitman (1901-1997).*

Barbara Haskins (b1937) as a student at Addenbrooke's Hospital Cambridge 1956

The District Midwife

As a family, we seem to have continued John Nicholas Tresidder's interest in health care. We step between the great and the good and the poor and wanting, lifting people up when they are down and mediating with those in charge.

My sister **Barbara's** path towards nursing began at the age of nine when she took her First Aid box to school with her[14]. Girls at *Stratford House*, near Bickley Station, used to come to her to be patched up rather than seeing 'Matron'. They saw sympathy and healing, the two requisites of a good medic. She also communicated a good understanding of how babies were made, what with me coming along when she was 11 years old.

Barbara thought long and deep about where to train and plumped for Addenbrooke's, Cambridge, in Jan 1956 after her sister Ann talked of meeting some nice Cambridge boys on her holiday in Minehead. The hospital was (then) in the centre of town, with her student hostel only a short walk away. Added to which, her cousins the Gutteridges lived nearby. She enjoyed Cambridge and the escapades with the male undergraduates. In those days, college gates were locked at night, and you needed to be physically fit. To get in after the gates were locked, Barbara climbed over the mortuary gate, scaled the fire escape and tapped on one of the girl's bedroom windows, having arranged with her beforehand. The following year she shared a flat in Trumpington Street. She had her own room (and a front-door key) which came in handy. Barbara was the only student of her year to be retained as a staff nurse – they trusted her because they said she'd always been honest about admitting her mistakes.

Barbara set out to become a Queen's Nurse. This meant training in Bermondsey, in similar conditions to *Call the Midwife*, bicycle and all. There was even a religious connection – St Olave's. Londoners might have been poor but they understood the place of the church in their lives. District nurses and midwives were on a par with doctors and priests and were 'looked up to'. She was cycling along one day when someone called her over:

"Would you come and see my mum?"

"Why?"

"She's just died."

Barbara obviously had won their trust, albeit her ambition was to care for the other end of life. Barbara was sponsored by Berkshire's health authority to become a midwife. She had six-month stints at Bromley and Cheltenham and bought a scooter to reach her widely spread-out patients faster than by bike. Health Visitor training at Brighton followed, after which she took a job as District Midwife and Health Visitor at Watchfield, where she was given a Mini to speed around in. Watchfield was next door to the Royal Military College of Science at Shrivenham, near enough to see me on Exeat Sundays at my boarding school in Wiltshire. When I reached the sixth form, she moved to the other end of the county, to the village of Twyford, east of Reading. It had a population of 2,000 people in 1966; fifty years later it is three times the size, big enough to have a Crossrail station..

Barbara gave up District Nursing to concentrate on midwifery as soon as she could. She found midwives were fat and jolly (not thin and judgemental like the Health Visitors). And there was a product at the end of it. In a six week temporary placement at Maidenhead, she delivered 16 babies. In all, she delivered about 500 babies in their homes before settling down to raise her own family.

Nurse Haskins with her scooter 1960

[14]   *Barbara Pauline Margaret Haskins SRN SCM QN HVCert (b1937).*

Barbara is not the last of my close family to enter the profession. My other sister Ann's daughter, **Bridget** Gates, is an Occupational Therapist[15]. **Louise Bradshaw,** Bridget's daughter, is a Doctor in Glasgow. Bridget's husband, Jeremy Bradshaw, started out with a smidgeon of an idea to follow his parents into medicine – both his parents, **David** and **Elsa Bradshaw**, were in General Practice in Sheffield. He's ended up doing something more esoteric[16].

Jeremy's family, the Bradshaws, moved less than a dozen miles in 200 years until his father David's Grammar School education qualified him for University. The Bradshaws had been small farmers or farm labourers in the area called Garstang, north of Blackpool. Some of David's ancestors are buried in Pilling churchyard – Jeremy's great (x6) grandfather was born there in 1718.

Jeremy Bradshaw is now Pro-Vice Chancellor (International and Doctoral) at the University of Bath. Bridget met him when he was studying zoology and molecular bio-physics at Oxford. He went on to teach at the College of Medicine and Veterinary Medicine in Edinburgh, where he became its Dean. Perhaps he caught our family's 'wandering' habit: his research has meant him spending part of every year across the globe. For example, he led a project which resulted in the Zhejiang-Edinburgh Institute in China and is now a visiting professor at the University. Zhejiang University was founded in 1897 by the Mayor of Hangchow (Hangzhou) - Lin Qi, who would have been inspired by my two missionary relations in Chapter 10.

✳ ✳ ✳ ✳

Like John Nicholas Tresidder who was concerned about the cause of cholera and with not much more than a spoonful of sugar to make the medicine go down, each generation has to face up to a new medical challenge. Forty years ago, one my school friends became a doctor and helped to find a cure for Aids; this generation is looking for a cure for the Zika virus. Tomorrow: who knows? Breakthroughs in molecular bio-physics are happening all the time. The average age of a sample 420 relatives is just over seventy – the biblical 'three-score years and ten'. With new cures and healthy living, people are surviving longer these days[xvi]. Will our descendants eventually outstrip Methuselah, who lived, according to the bible, for a phenomenal 969 years?[xvii]

Bradshaw Pedigree

Thomas Bradshaw (1719-1781)
|
Matthew Bradshaw (1746-1795)
|
James Bradshaw (1770-1840)
|
John Bradshaw (1814-1890)
|
James Bradshaw (1872-1949)
|
James Norman Chadwick Bradshaw (1899-1969)
|
Dr James David Bradshaw (b1927)
|
Dr Jeremy Peter Bradshaw (b1959)
|
Dr Louise Fiona Bradshaw (b1991)

---

15.   *Bridget Mary Gates DipCOT (b1962) married Prof Jeremy Peter Bradshaw DPhil CIBiol FIBiol FHEA FSB (b1959) in 1984. Their second daughter: Dr Louise Fiona Bradshaw MBChB (b1991).*
16.   *Dr James David Bradshaw MB ChB DMRT FFR FRCR (b1927) married Dr Elsa Mary Mellor MB ChB (1926-2016) in 1952.*

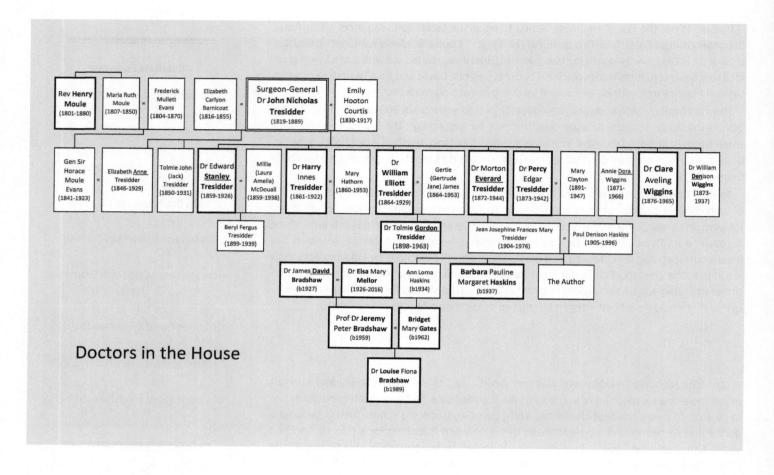

Doctors in the House

Other Notes and References

i.   The Lords chamber was completed in 1847, the Commons chamber in 1852. The architect was Sir Charles Barry FRS (1790-1860) [NR] with Augustus Welby Northmore Pugin (1812-1852) [NR] as his acolyte. 'Stygian pool' refers in Greek mythology to the River Styx, which people had to cross to reach the next world – or drown for eternity.

ii.   Murray p3 points to accounts of the disease before 1817.

iii. Emily and Anne Brontë died in 1848-9 and Charlotte in 1855, authors of Wuthering Heights, Tenant of Wildfell Hall and Jane Eyre. Dr John Snow, one of the first to prove that cholera was waterborne, died in June 1858 at the height of 'The Great Stink.'

iv.   Royal Commission on the Sanitary State of the Army in India 1863 Vol 1 – zymotic disease as at 31 May 1859.

v.   McCosh p217.

vi.   British Library, Indian Office Records, IOR/Z/E/4/26/ T347; IRO/E/4/830p1479-1482, 841 p965-8; IOR/ Z/E/4/28/T392; IOR/Z/E/4/29/E394; /C520; /M530; /844, p1405; /T393. Dr Tresidder. Opinion of respecting causes of illness of prisoners in Mirzapore jail. c1855.

vii. Allen's Indian Mail, 9 Jun 1857 p375: 'It served to illustrate our position as to water being the cause.'

viii. Murray, On the channels through which cholera is communicable.

ix.   The Hindu Patriot, 13 Jan 1873, p63. The Epidemic Fever in Bengal 1873. quotes Lt Col F T Haig, author of Notes on the drainage and water supply of the Hooghly District.

x.   British Library Ref F135/69. His descriptions of others in this private pocket book were less flattering: 'A meddlesome coward. Quarrelsome and grasping.' 'Harum scarum.' 'Bumptious, selfish, arrogant.' 'Double dealing.' 'Fickle. Selfish to an abominable degree. I despise his cleverness.

xi.   Mitre p3.

xii. Widow's weeds were black clothes worn by a widow in mourning, emulating Queen Victoria.

xiii. Daily Mirror 14 Oct 1941. Dr Tolmie Gordon Tresidder MRCS LRCP (1898-1963) was 42.

xiv. Percy gave the oak gate-legged dining table and the money to purchase the dining room chairs currently in the author's dining room; the carved bureau and sideboard were sold soon after Paul Haskins's death.

xv.   Juan le Pins was one of the first summer resorts on the Riviera, in 1882. In 1924, it was developed by a Nice restauranteur who wanted to create Miami on the Côte d'Azur. He teamed up with a wealthy American, and opened the legendary Art Deco hotel La Provençal. The hedonistic life-style of the wealthy socialites was pictured by F Scott Fitzgerald in Tender is the Night (1934) – Juan le Pins was where women shed their reserve and first donned one-piece swimsuits. Percy lived at Palais Rhodania, Avenue de l'Esterel.

xvi. Psalm 90v10: 'Our days may come to seventy years, or eighty, if our strength endures; yet the best of them are but trouble and sorrow, for they quickly pass, and we fly away.' NIV.

xvii. Genesis 5 v 27: 969 years. King James version.

Vanity

The Leviathan of Literature

'It is vain,' said Dickens, 'to recall the past, unless it works some influence upon the present.' I am working on that one. You could call this chapter a bit of vanity. It boasts unforgivably about my literary connections, of which I have none, in reality.

"Writing a book?" you ask, "You're dyslexic!"

"If Agatha Christie, Leonardo da Vinci, Jamie Oliver and W B Yeats can do it," I cry, "so can I."

Ask my father, sister and nephews. We are prone to simple written errors – like *were* and *where* – and putting letters in a *wrod* the wrong way round. My sister Barbara as a student nurse, writing home about washing-up *bowls*, would write *bowels*. My Principal Lecturer, when I was training to teach, said,

"If you can't spell, how do you expect your pupils to do so?"

She was right and I learnt – then I joined the Civil Service where everything was checked and double-checked. I couldn't go wrong. I did, of course – a draft letter for John Prescott, a leading word-mangler, was returned for re-drafting[1].

Bleak House, Broadstairs, Kent

Dickens used to creep away to Europe and Broadstairs to wring another novel from out of nowhere. He'd tramp the streets of London at night, seeking new insights. Writing is a lonely business. This book's been written in two stages. First stage: find out who your family are; second stage: write it down. The first stage became addictive. The second stage has required many revisions – I now know some of what Dickens went through.

At least I knew who Charles Dickens was. My father had the complete works on the top shelf of his bookcase. I'd even read one or two of them. They were good reads, once you had got past the first two hundred pages. When I was a young adult instructor with the Army Cadets in Canterbury and Whitstable, one of my chums, who worked on the Kentish Times, lived at Bleak House in Broadstairs. It was named after the book of the same name, some of which Dickens wrote there[i]. Broadstairs was his summer residence for 22 years. My friend had a little museum in the study near the front door.

I'm related to **Charles Dickens**, through my great aunt **Annie**[2]. She married **Horace Moule Evans**[3] (Chapter 6). Horace's father, **Frederick Evans**, was Dickens's printer and publisher[4]. Thereby hangs a tale.

Horace's great grandfather made paper in Bristol[5]. In the late 1780s or early 1790s, he moved to London and set up shop with his son-in-law **Joseph Evans**[6]. Joseph, who was Horace's grandfather, ran a successful stationery business. **Frederick**, Horace's father, went into the same line of business. After a spell in Southampton, Fred formed a partnership with the more experienced William Bradbury[7].

Charles Dickens (1812-1870)

1. *John Leslie Prescott PC, Baron Prescott, (b1938) [NR] Deputy Prime Minister 1997-2007.*
2. *Charles John Huffam Dickens (1812-1870) married Catherine Thomson Hogarth (1815-1879) in 1836.*
3. *Elizabeth Anne Tresidder (1846-1929) married General Sir Horace Moule Evans KCB (1841-1923) in 1866.*
4. *Frederick Mullett Evans (1804-1870) married Maria Ruth Moule (1807-1850) in 1830*
5. *Thomas Mullett (1745-1814).*
6. *Joseph Jeffries Evans (1768-1812) married Mary Anne Mullett (1776-1845?) in 1796. He was the son and she the niece of Rev Caleb Evans DD (1737-1791) of Broadmead Baptist Church, Bristol (see also Chapter 11).*
7. *William Bradbury (1800–1869) [NR] begun as a printer in Oxford Arms Passage St Paul's, London.*

'Pater' Evans (1804-1870)

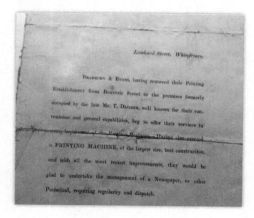

Bradley & Evans move to Lombard Lane in 1833

Punch weekly dinner menu in the 1890s

Bradbury and Evans set up in premises in Bouverie Street, London, in 1830 and moved to Lombard Lane in Whitefriars in 1833[ii]. They bought the latest thing in printing, a massive steam-driven cylinder machine. They kept this and twenty other smaller ones running round the clock, six days a week. They were known as the most efficient printing press in England. At one stage, they employed 800 men, paying high wages for good work.

One of their main successes was printing monthly publications (a shilling (5p) a go) which Dickens had conceived as a way to serialise his hugely successful stories. In 1843, the story *A Christmas Carol* sold out in 6 days[iii]. It was phenomenal. It catered for a new readership of the emergent middle classes. It contrasted all the sorts of occurrences that my forebears would have known. Shabby-gentility mixed with finery, wash-houses, inn-keepers, artisans, attorneys, apothecaries, actresses and hard-nosed widows with their 'own means' – the world of some of my relations. His tortured souls, and waifs and strays scandalised polite society. This was a radical departure from normal story-telling. It gave a voice to the voiceless. Some of the newly educated middle class readers identified with the life they'd left behind, others with what they newly encountered. Prison life or the poor-house contrasted with the sleepy sloppy snobbish civil service. The squalid back streets of London mixed with the cant of commerce and counting houses. They were the 'tales of two cities'. Reformers like Florence Nightingale, Quakers like Titus Salt (Saltaire), and Ebenezer Howard of the Garden City movement, were influenced by his writing.

Bradbury & Evans took over the *Punch* magazine in 1842, a year after its launch. It started their *publishing* career. Like most start-ups, they weren't particularly expert but they'd struck lucky. **Frederick Evans**, the 'father' of the enterprise, was nicknamed 'Pater'. Within a few years, *Punch* was a national institution. It earned them £10,000 a year from the 40,000 copies each week[iv]. Dickens never wrote for *Punch*. It was their world, the world of Tenniel, du Maurier, Kean and Thackeray[8]. Punch was fun from the very start – weekly dinners, Bacchanalian binges, theatricals[v]. The team of funny men was egged on by the jovial 'Pater' Evans. One of his party tricks was bowling pineapples down the weekly dinner table without a single breakage on the way[vi]. With his rotund figure and shining spectacles, his good-humoured countenance, which always saw the best of a situation, he endeared himself to almost everyone. The friendships that he made there, he said, gave him the happiest moments of his life. 'A round, ruddy, genial, cheery, busy little man,' said one author[vii]. He might have been the model for Pickwick in Charles Dickens's *Pickwick Papers* if Dickens had been familiar with his printer in 1836. Evans was the hearty one[9].

Merry and cheerful; we have Bradbury and Evans to thank for some of the fun of Christmas – party games and a slap-up feast. Up until then people viewed it like the Puritans, as a Pagan feast, and not the done thing[viii]. By 1839, Bradbury and Evans were presenting the Dickens household with an enormous Christmas turkey. Perhaps in honour of that, Dickens wrote *A Christmas Carol* in 1843, the year the first Christmas card was printed. Crackers and Christmas trees came later, in 1848, after the royal family had been pictured with one in the *Illustrated London News*, which Bradbury & Evans also printed. From 1843, every year they published a Christmas book, written by either Dickens or Thackeray.

A Christmas Carol was the turning point for the firm. In 1844, Dickens turned to Bradbury & Evans for help. Dickens always feared the debtor's jail. He'd spent part of his childhood there, with his dad[ix]. When he heard how little he'd earned from *A Christmas Carol*, he felt short-changed by his old publishers, Chapman & Hall.

8.   *Sir John Tenniel (1820-1914) [NR] also illustrated Alice in Wonderland. George Louis Palmella Busson du Maurier (1834-1896) [NR] was grandfather of the author, Daphne du Maurier (1907-1989) {NR}. Charles John Kean (1811-1868) [NR]. William Makepeace Thackeray (1811-1863).*

9.   *The Posthumous papers of the Pickwick Club.*

It wasn't all their fault. Dickens had a large family and an extravagant wife. He liked to go abroad. He'd been living on tick, treating Chapman & Hall as his personal bankers. He'd taken large advances and refused to own up to the consequences. He demanded colour plates, mass publicity and low prices for his novels. Chapman & Hall's old fashioned ways didn't sit well with Dickens' desire for order and exactitude. Dickens was a 'control freak'[ix]. He decided to let them go and to ask his friends Bradbury & Evans to act as publishers as well as printers.

Bradbury & Evans published the sequel to *A Christmas Carol* in 1844, called *The Chimes*[10]. Close behind came *Dombey and Son*, in the traditional monthly serialised format. Whilst *The Chimes* ("a little dismal") outstripped *CA Christmas Carol* in profit, *Dombey* made even more[xi]. It was an enormous success. The first printing of Part 1 (25,000 copies) sold out within hours. Dickens was incredibly pleased. "The *Dombey* sale is BRILLIANT!"[xii] "I have got, by some few thousand pounds (I could count the thousands on one hand), ahead of the world. *Dombey* has been the greatest success I have ever had."[xiii] Practically for the first time in his life, thanks to his new publishers, Dickens had spare money in the bank.

Not everything went well. Together they started a paper called *Daily News*, to rival the *Morning Chronicle*. It lasted less than a year. Bradbury & Evans lost their investment of £22,500 and more. Not a cheap mistake, but Pater Evans calmed everyone down and normal life resumed. They made up for it with a quarter-share in Dickens's new weekly, *Household Words* (1850-59)[11]. Most authors of the day wrote for it, including that Cornish parson we met in Chapter 1, Rev Hawker of Morwenstow.

William Makepeace Thackeray, a distant relation on my father's side, had his first major success with Bradbury & Evans[12]. No other publisher would touch his first full-length novel, *Vanity Fair*. It took the world by storm. *Pendennis* followed. Bradbury & Evans had a party and gave him an engraved silver punch bowl in celebration[xiv]. For their honest dealings with Thackeray, they never lost his loyalty.

David Copperfield (1849-50), *Bleak House* (1852-3), and *Little Dorrit* (1855-7) gave Dickens similar success. The semi-autobiographical Copperfield earned Dickens high critical praise. The easy, gentle style reflected Dickens at his most comfortable. His children were growing up. The money was rolling in. Bradbury was making sure everything was as it should be. Evans was keeping everything cheerful and light[xv]. What could possibly go wrong?

'Pater' Evans and Charles Dickens and their wives had become close friends. They took holidays together in Boulogne, where three of the Dickens' sons were at school[xvi]. They conducted business in a Pickwickian manner. But every rise has a fall ... Dickens' love life got complicated.

By 1858, the rumour mill was in full flow. Scandal was just round the corner. It could be that Charles was secretly sharing more than just his house with his wife's younger sister Georgie, **Georgina Hogarth**, but the gossips were elaborating another story, about his infatuation with Nelly Ternan or was one the foil for the other?[xvii] Was he weaving a trail of deception, whereby his friends gossiped about Nelly when his real secret was Georgina?[13] Georgina had been living in his house since she was fifteen[xviii]. Earlier, another sister who'd lived with them had died, aged seventeen[14]. He became obsessively distraught. Was Evans the one who saw through Dickens's gauze of deceit? Their 'Bohemian' friends 'were far from faultless but this was incest, and incest was an anathema[15].

William Makepeace Thackeray (1811-1863)

Charles Dickens, his wife Catherine and her sister Georgina Hogarth (1827-1917)

10.   *The chimes: a goblin story of some bells that rang an old year out and a new year in.*
11.   *It contained 24 pages, cost two old pence, and came out every Wednesday.*
12.   *William Makepeace Thackeray (1811-1863).*
13.   *Ellen Lawless Ternan (1839-1914) [NR] was the same age as Dickens' eldest daughters.*
14.   *Mary Scott Hogarth (1819-1837)*
15.   *George Cruickshank, William Frith and Wilkie Collins, for example.*

Cast of the Frozen Deep (family players). Fred Evans junior is standing fifth from the right. Charles Dickens is lying in the front. Charley his son to his left. Bessie Evans (his future daughter-in-law) seated on chair behind.

Catherine Hogarth (1815-1879)

The principled son, Charley Dickens (1837-1896)

Had Evans family's Baptist values (see Chapter 11) come into play?[xix] Dickens' reputation as a family man, full of fireside cheer, meant there was too much to lose. He and Georgina attempted to remove every trace of scandal, burning diaries and letters, and for about 100 years they were successful[16].

Amateur dramatics started Dickens's infatuation with Nelly. Taking his cue from *Punch*, he'd converted his children's schoolroom into a mini-theatre. In 1857, he put on The *Frozen Deep*, a play written by his friend Wilkie Collins[17]. Evans's eldest son played a member of the ship's crew and Evans's daughter one of the heroines[xx]. Dickens played the hero, the Captain of the *Sea Mew* – Queen Victoria heard about it and asked to see the play, so he arranged a private viewing in Regent Street[xxi].

In August, they were asked to put it on again, this time in Manchester. To protect their reputations (legs on show), his daughters were replaced by professional actresses. The Ternan family, a mother and three girls, were ready and available and offered their services. Nelly, probably the least accomplished, was given the part of an ingénue courted by a rascal played by Dickens in *Uncle John,* a risqué farce that followed the serious drama. Dickens played the rascal on and off-stage. He gave Nelly a bracelet but it fell into the wrong hands – the shop delivered it to his wife, **Catherine**.

His eldest son, **Charley Dickens**, spotted the two together on Hampstead Heath and told Annie Thackeray. The news was soon out[18]. In the autumn of 1857, Charles started sleeping in a separate bedroom[xxii]. Catherine wasn't the adorable thing he'd married. After eleven children she'd put on weight[xxiii]. In May 1858, he sought a formal break. As his publisher and close friend of the family, Fred Evans was concerned about the course that things were taking. Dickens's nature was changing; he was becoming secretive and self-serving – it was like as if he was on cocaine: "Thinks himself God now," said one of his friends[xxiv]. In June 1858, Catherine decided she would sign a deed of separation. To help sort the mess out, *Punch* editor Mark Lemon offered with Evans to act as Trustees on Catherine's side.

If that wasn't bad enough, against all advice, Dickens published a rebuttal, dressing it up as if nothing had happened. Evans and Lemon had counselled silence. He wrote the piece for *Household Words*. The *Times* and provincial papers published it but *Punch* didn't[xxv]. It wasn't that sort of paper, they said – too serious for a comic journal and, anyway, they hadn't been asked to do it[xxvi]. They had hit a nerve. Whatever it was, it hurt hard. Dickens vowed never to speak to Evans or Lemon again.

It didn't help him that Dickens's eldest son took his mother Catherine's cause; his sister Kate would've done so too if she'd been old enough[19]. The Evans's had been one of the closest families to the Dickens's and the children had been brought up in each other's homes. Indeed, Charley had been tacitly 'engaged' to **Bessie Evans** since the age of seven[xxvii]. Sadly, Evans's wife **Maria** had died

> *"... I most solemnly declare, then – and this I do, both in my own name and in my wife's – that all the lately whispered rumours touching the trouble at which I have glanced are abominably false, and that whosoever repeats them after this denial will lie as wilfully and as foully as it is possible for any false witness to lie before Heaven and earth.*
> *CHARLES DICKENS"*

extract from Dickens' rebuttal: Times 7 June 1858

16. *Georgina Hogarth (1827-1917).*
17. *William Wilkie Collins (1824-1889).*
18. *Ann Isabella Ritchie (neé Thackeray) (1837-1919) was the author Thackeray's daughter.*
19. *Kate (Catherine Elizabeth Macready) Dickens (1839-1929). The age of independence was 21.*

in 1850; she'd been close to Catherine and would have probably kept the balance better than Fred. Whilst the eldest daughter, **Margaret Evans**, consoled Catherine, the youngest daughter Bessie tied the knot with Charley[20].

For Dickens, this was all too much. "Charley will probably marry the daughter of Mr Evans, the very last person on earth whom I could desire so to honour me." Catherine went to the wedding, but not he.

Perhaps it was his upbringing. Dickens never did allow himself to be wrong. Impatient in the sense that 'he was the type of man who would break a window if it would not open.'[xxviii] Decisive, direct – many thought him arrogant[xxix]. He twice refused Queen Victoria an audience after he staged his drama for her because he thought it wrong to appear before her in costume[xxx]. Appearances were everything to him – sheer vanity.

For the last twelve years of his life, Dickens, now separated, waged war on anyone who stayed close to either Catherine or Evans. Thackeray found himself in the middle. Dickens suspected him of letting slip gossip about his relationship with Nelly – and with his sister-in-law Georgina[xxxi]. The two men quarrelled in the Garrick Club in front of others and Dickens stalked out. Thackeray decided to stay friends with Catherine; the men didn't speak again until near the end of Thackeray's life[xxxii]. It had shortened it probably – he died of a stroke in 1863. Charles, with a change of heart, appointed himself Chief Mourner[xxxiii]. 2,000 attended Thackeray's funeral one cold winter's day in Kensal Green[xxxiv].

"The first thing that tempts a woman is vanity," said Lady Godolphin[xxxv]. Georgina had the man and Nelly his flattery. In 1860, four years after he bought it, Charles moved his children (and Georgina) to his new Rochester home, Gad's Hill[xxxvi]. Georgina had now replaced Catherine – in every way?[xxxvii] Behind Georgina's back, he was still wooing Nelly, who was no push-over. Nelly admitted later that she loathed the very thought of his intimacy[xxxviii]. Dickens led a double life as 'Charles Tringham' when he went to see her[xxxix]. He bought her a house in London[xl]. He rented homes in Slough and Peckham for her to stay in. He published her sister's stories. He packed his sons off to all quarters of the empire so they weren't too close to their mother or his double-life.

Charley, the eldest, tried to stay above it all. He lived with his mother from July 1858 until he married in 1861. His godmother had paid for him to go to Eton and, in 1853 at age of 16, she'd sent him to Leipzig to learn German[21]. After two years there, he'd joined Barings Bank and worked there for four years[xli]. He'd travelled to India, China and Japan in 1860 in the hope of trading in tea. Perhaps he visited Bessie's brother, the 18-year-old Horace Moule Evans, who'd joined the Indian Army two years before (see Chapter 6). In 1861, Fred set up his eldest son, Frederick Moule Evans, in the papermaking business[xlii]. Charley returned to England in the January and became a partner in the new firm in the October, marking his marriage to Bessie.

Charles wouldn't have much to do with Charley and Bessie to start with. When their children came along, soon after the marriage, he softened his attitude and the whole family were to spend Christmas together at Gad's Hill[xliii]. Charles found the children a consolation for the loss of his old companions[xliv]. He made this Christmas-time extra special. When Charles died in 1870, Charley bought Gad's Hill at auction, under the noses of Georgina and the executors, and settled Bessie and his family there. Charlie and Bessie's children never made much of their lives, at one point accepting charity.

With Charles Dickens's withdrawal of patronage, funds at Bradbury & Evans got tighter. In 1859, when Charles sold *Household Words* for £3,550, they were given a paltry £500, despite owning quarter share and taking Charles to court to get it[xlv]. They set up *Once a Week* to rival Dickens's new journal *All the Year Round*. It had stories by Tennyson and drawings by Millais

Gad's Hill, near Rochester, Kent – scene of a Christmas reconciliation

---

20. *Margaret Moule Evans (1837-1909) married Robert Orridge (1825-1865) in 1860.*
21. *Angela Georgina Burdett-Coutts, 1st Baroness Burdett-Coutts (1814-1906) [NR].*

and Tenniel but it didn't lure the public as Dickens could. It folded. Bradbury & Evans held rights to publish Dickens in America but lacked the cash to make it work. They sold out. In 1861, they had to sell their share of Dickens' copyright on the books they'd published and then, in 1865, they gave up control of the firm to their sons. A year later, art dealers from Manchester, Agnews, took over the partnership[22]. The paper-making business also failed.

By December 1868, Evans was in the bankruptcy court and ousted from the Garrick Club[xlvi]. He died in the home of Frederick, his eldest son, less than two years later. It was within a month of the death of his *Punch* editor, Mark Lemon, and less than a fortnight after the death of the less-than-perfect people's-favourite Charles Dickens. Like in his *Tales of Two Cities*, written when he first met Nelly, this flawed man, Dickens, died masquerading as a good one. Evans never did make sense of how he had so deeply offended this erstwhile friend, his son-in-law's father, England's celebrated author. To the end, he hoped for reconciliation. It never came.

John Yeats (1839-1922)

❊ ❊ ❊ ❊

The Irish Poet

Not one famous author but two. The Tresidders are related to another by marriage through my grandfather's brother Clive who married a Pollexfen. The cream of the Irish authors, **William Butler Yeats**, was her first cousin[23]. Yeats won the Nobel Prize for literature in 1923.

W B Yeats ('Willie' they called him) came from a Dublin family. His father **John Yeats** was an accomplished artist, who'd spent time in London[24]. He was one of a *fin de siècle* group centred round Bedford Park in 1887-99, with its De Morgan tiles and Morris wallpapers. His mother, **Susan Pollexfen**, thought she was marrying a barrister but soon after they married, John gave up law and took up art. Susan harboured a grudge for the rest of her life – never once stepping foot in his studio[xlvii]. She constantly worried about money; silent and reserved, she hated both London and her husband's effervescent Pre-Raphaelite friends. She was frightened of affection yet deeply needed it – she felt out of place in the metropolis and craved for her familiar countryside. After a stroke in 1887, she withdrew even more into herself.

William Butler Yeats (1865-1939)

The Yeats came from a line of faded gentility. Two generations of Church of Ireland parsons hadn't made them rich. The Pollexfens were from a darker past. They'd used the Western fringes of Ireland as their secret staging post for the business of piracy. The Pollexfens, trading off their illicit trade (see Chapter 2), had interests in the Americas and the West Indies – some say they'd plantations there. William's parents-in-law's family, the Middleton's, were no different – they had smuggling interests in South America and the Channel Islands[xlviii].

Susan's father, **William Pollexfen**, was the wealthiest man in Sligo. With a roll in his gait and animal magnetism, he dominated business, property, council, church and sea[25]. He had few friends[xlix]. He used the Freemasons and the Middleton's to get his way – with a scar on his hand and a violent temper, he'd horse-whip a man if he had to[l]. He'd a hatchet by his bed in case of intruders – his saintly wife could hardly turn over in bed without his say-so[li].

Silent and smouldering, William Pollexfen had run away to sea from Brixham at the age of 12. "Gone to sea through the hawse hole," was the way he put it[lii]. But there were Pollexfens in Ireland before him. William went to Sligo and cared for one of his aunts who'd lost her husband and gained a fortune. Money was the motto. He'd no time for education [liii]. By his forties, he'd ships plying forth between the American continent,

Susan Pollexfen (1841-1900)

---

22. *Sir William Agnew (1825–1910) [NR] and Thomas Agnew (1827–1883) [NR] of Thomas Agnew & Sons.*
23. *William Butler Yeats (1865-1939) lived at 8 Woodstock Road, Bedford Park, London 1887-99.*
24. *John Butler Yeats (1839-1922) married Susan Mary Pollexfen (1841-1900) in 1863.*
25. *William Pollexfen (1811-1892).*

Portugal, Spain and Liverpool. After he married, his wife Elizabeth gave birth to a child every year between 1839 and 1858 – a vast family. He expected his sons to get rich as quickly as possible and his daughters to marry well. Dominating in every way, the Pollexfens were a bossy and bad tempered lot[liv]. The Yeats couldn't stand them any more than the Tresidders could. Yet the Yeats family relied on them over-much to sort out their wobbly finances which just made the Pollexfens even more sneering and snivelling.

William sent two of Susan's brothers to Liverpool. **Charles Pollexfen** was particularly sour and unpleasant[26]. He set himself up as a corn merchant and shipping agent for the family business. 'He could endure nobody except abject slaves or flatterers'[lv].

William Pollexfen (1811-1892)

The other, John Pollexfen, became a master mariner[27]. He was a true Pollexfen, a sailor through and through. He was trusted by his fellows, despite his natural reserve. When a ship's captain was at death's door, the captain dismissed all his officers, sons of Liverpool merchants, and called for John, the young bo'sun – they said John had the salt sea water in his blood. He'd married a Liverpool girl with Irish ancestry at St Asaph in 1871 and based his family at Liverpool. He was seldom there, though; sometimes she neither. Life at sea made John amiable and he'd seek out the Bohemian Yeats household when he docked at London – they intrigued him[lvi]. His children brought themselves up, in the suburbs of Liverpool – Bootle and Formby. **Muriel Alice**, one of these daughters, married my great uncle **Clive Tresidder**[28]. The Tresidders thought her a cross-patch and had little time for her.

Alice Pollexfen (1876-1923)

Did my grandfather, with famous writers at both ends – his eldest half-sister with her connection to Dickens and his youngest brother with his connection with Yeats – learn anything to improve his life? Not much, judging from his story in Chapter 13, though it may have made him vain.

For there are other writers too. On my mother's side, there's the influential twentieth century journalist **Constance Barnicoat**, and the novelist **Jack Tresidder** as well his step-daughter **Megan**[29]. All three were born in New Zealand; Jack now lives in France. There's also the Chief Executive of the company that made 'Big Brother', **Tom Barnicoat**[30].

'He never found his rest ashore, moping for one voyage more'.

W B Yeats on John Pollexfen
'In Memory of Alfred Pollexfen

Clive Tresidder (1878-1923) married a Pollexfen. He was a property auctioneer in London, here outside his cottage at Paignton, Devon c1914

John Pollexfen

---

26. *Charles William Pollexfen (1838-1923).*
27. *John Anthony Pollexfen (1840-1900) Second mate in 1868 and Master in 1871, married Mary Jane Gorman (1845-1917) in 1871.*
28. *Adrian <u>Clive</u> Tresidder (1878-1923) married Muriel Alice Pollexfen (1876-1923) in 1907.*
29. *Constance Alice Barnicoat (1872-1922); Megan Sarah Tresidder (1958-2001).*
30. *Thomas Humphry Barnicoat (b1952), a 3rd cousin, was at Endemol 1990-2004, now Chairman of Somethin' Else Productions.*

Virginia Woolf (1882-1941) with her father Sir Leslie Stephen (1832-1904) at Talland House, St Ives

Antonie Boileau de Castelnau de la Garde de Ste Croix de Boiriac (1381-1459)

On my father's side, through my great aunt Ethel, there's **Virginia Woolf**, whose maiden name was Stephen[31]. Virginia Woolf wrote *To the Lighthouse* (1929) inspired by her holidays at St Ives. Her father, Sir **Leslie Stephen,** had a house which looked out over Godrevy Bay[32]. He'd married the author Thackeray's youngest daughter, Minnie. His lasting contribution was the invention of the Dictionary of National Biography, which is now a national institution.

Virginia's modernist open-ended unconventional stream-of-consciousness reminds me of some of my mother's more flamboyant women friends – whose letters I enjoyed reading[lvii]. Virginia was a snob, socially and intellectually, but she has now become an icon of feminism. "A woman must have money and a room of her own if she is to write fiction."[lviii] She certainly explored those possibilities in some depth in bed with Vita Sackville-West. Vita's home, *Knole Park* in Sevenoaks, had 365 rooms, one for every day of the year[33].

Ginny (or Ginnum or Ginia), as the family called Virginia, took her place in a wide literary circle[lix]. There were her mother's Pre-Raphaelite friends. There were her brother's Cambridge friends, such as Lytton Strachey and E M Foster[34]. She married another Cambridge friend, Leonard Woolf[35]. Together, they were the fulcrum of the 'Bloomsbury Group'. They bought a small printing press: the Hogarth Press and published the books of their friends, T S Eliot and Katherine Mansfield[36].

The list goes on. Christopher, my son, says we must all be related to everyone if we go back far enough. There's some truth in that. My great aunt Ethel (Wiggins née Elliott) had a direct connection with William the Conqueror[lx]. A research study by Stanford University has tracked the relationships between authors[lxi]. Consequently, there is a tenuous family connection to all of those listed below:

W H Auden, Robert Bridges, John Buchan, Winston Churchill, Willkie Collins, Charles Darwin, Charles Dickens, Daphne du Maurier, T S Elliot, E M Forster, Graham Greene, Aldous Huxley, Christopher Isherwood, C Day Lewis, Thomas Babington Macaulay, Laurence Olivier, George Orwell, Vita Sackville-West, Lytton Strachey, William Makepeace Thackeray, Virginia Woolf, Evelyn Waugh and W B Yeats.

'Vanity, vanity,' said the preacherman[37]. I am not sure how helpful it is to know about all this when writing this book. It puts the pressure on a bit.

[31.] *Adeline Virginia Stephen (1882-1911).*

[32.] *Talland House, which Sir Leslie Stephen KCB (1832-1904) stayed 1882-94 until the Porthminster Hotel was built in front of it. He married (1) the daughter of the author William Makepeace Thackeray, Minnie (Harriet Marian) Thackeray (1840-1875) in 1867 (2) Julia Prinsep Jackson (1846-1895) in 1878. Julia had previously had four children by Herbert Duckworth (1833-1870). Virginia was a product of the second marriage. Leslie taught maths and moral sciences at Cambridge.*

[33.] *The Hon Victoria Mary Sackville-West, Lady Nicolson CH (1892-1962).*

[34.] *Julian Thoby Stephen (1880-1906); Giles Lytton Strachey (1880-1932); Edward Morgan Forster OM CH (1879-1970).*

[35.] *Leonard Sidney Woolf (1880-1969).*

[36.] *Thomas Stearns Eliot OM (1888-1965); Katherine Mansfield Beauchamp Murry (1888-1923) [NR].*

[37.] *'Meaningless! Meaningless!' says the Teacher. 'Utterly meaningless! Everything is meaningless. What do people gain from all their labours at which they toil under the sun? Generations come and generations go, but the earth remains forever.' Ecclesiastes 1v2 in the New International Version.*

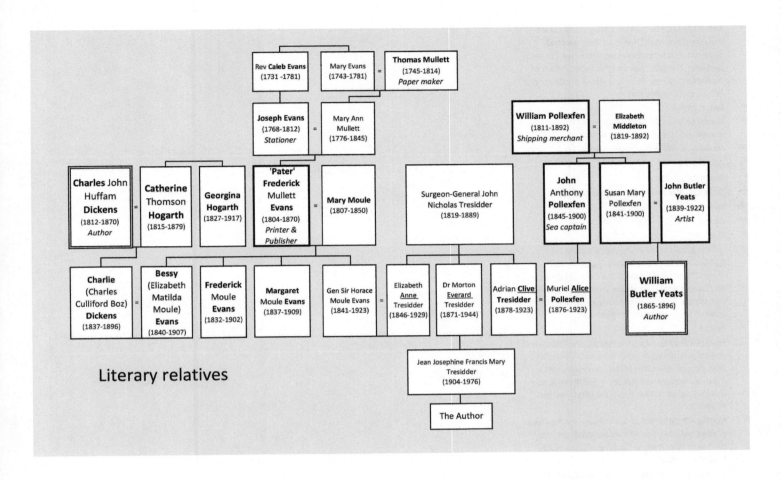

Literary relatives

Other Notes and References

i. Patten p216. The novel *Bleak House* was conceived in Feb 1851. The first part was published on 28 Feb 1852. Dickens stayed in Broadstairs for long periods – May to November – from 1837-59. He latterly rented Fort House (its original name) where he had a study overlooking the English Channel. When writing *Bleak House*, he was buying Tavistock House in London and needed the money.

ii. Bodleian Library Mss.Eng.Lett.398/2 f177.

iii. Picard p24. The first run was 6,000 copies.

iv. Oxford Dictionary of National Biography

v. Ray p361; Patten p163.

vi. Adrian p62.

vii. OxfordDictionary of National Biography

viii. Standiford p104.

ix. Patten p17. Charles's father, John Dickens (1785-1851) was arrested for debt in Nov 1834.

x. Knight Vol 3 p117: Once a stage curtain caught fire. The audience jumped up and were rushing to the exit. Dickens, who was acting at the time, immediately rushed to the footlights. "Sit still, every one of you." 500 terrified spectators did sit still. He carried on as if nothing had happened.

xi. Letter 20 Jan 1869 from Dickens, quoted in Frith Vol 3 p234.

xii. Patten p185.

xiii. Ibid p197.

xiv. Thackeray's Letters Vol 2 p530. A few years later Thackeray was making over £600 a month. Patten p230.

xv. Letter 14 March 1850 from Dickens Pilgrim Vol 6 p64.

xvi. http://spartacus-educational.com/DICbradleyEvans.htm accessed 4 Oct 2014; Oxford Dictionary of National Biography. Page N. Vol 1 p639.

xvii. Tomalin, p8.

xviii. Hawksley, p28.

xix. Patten p261: Angela Burdett-Coutts charitably felt it was simply a case of 'incompatibitie de'humeur'

xx. Page, Vol 5 p254.

xxi. Page, Vol 5 p250. Gallery of Illustration, Regent Street. The performance was also watched by Prince Albert, Prince Leopold of Belgium, Prince Frederick of Prussia and Hans Christian Anderson (1805-1875) [NR].

xxii. Patten p255.

xxiii. Francis Jeffrey Dickens (1833-1839) and Dora Annie Dickens (1850-1851) died young. Catherine put on weight between 1849 and 1852, during the writing of David Copperfield – did her husband's attentions 'stray' during that time?

xxiv. Adrian p134. "Thinks himself God now," said Shirley Brooks.

xxv. The Times 7 June 1858

xxvi. Adrian p133. Once a Week 1 1859 p3. Bradbury &

Evans never considered inserting 'statements on a domestic and painful subject in the inappropriate columns of a comic miscellany.'

xxvii. Hawksley p185.

xxviii. Bowen Vol 3 p30.

xxix. Nayder p290. The topic of many Punch weekly dinners; quoting the Diary of Henry Silver.

xxx. Tomalin p72.

xxxi. Dickens, Interviews and Recollections p68f: Letter to his mother, May 1858. Thackeray discussed Georgina as well as Nelly at the Garrick Club.

xxxii. Tomalin p120.

xxxiii. Page, Vol 1 p637.

xxxiv. http://exhibits.lib.byu.edu/literaryworlds/thackeray/ accessed 19 May 2015: 30 Dec 1863.

xxxv. Page, Vol 1 p281.

xxxvi. Page, Vol 1 p639; Vol 5, p239. Gad's Hill, at Higham, 3 miles outside Rochester, was purchased by Dickens on 14 Mar 1856.

xxxvii. Pilgrim Vol 8 footnote p608: 'CD may well have felt that Evans had too openly, at some stage, espoused Catherine's cause against his own. CD may also have believed Evans had re-told or at any rate believed in the scandal about Georgina and himself. This would explain Georgina's continuing animosity against the Evans family. He never met Evans socially again.'

xxxviii. Page, Vol 5 p356.

xxxix. Nayder p283.

xl. Tomalin pp121, 156-7. In 1859, Nelly's sisters Maria and Fanny 'acquired' 2 Houghton Place, Ampthill Square near Dickens's home and transferred it to her a year later. The subterfuge and cost suggests Dickens supplied the money. In 1865, it was let to a tenant and not occupied by her again.

xli. Bowen, p170.

xlii. Nayder p277. Frederick Moule Evans (1832-1902) married Amy Lloyd (1838-1926) in 1859.

xliii. Hawksley, pp227-9. December 1869.

xliv. Patten p311

xlv. Bowen Vol 5 p288.

xlvi. Dictionary of nineteenth century journalism.

xlvii. Murphy Sligo, p50.

xlviii. Ibid p6.

xlix. Pyle p19.

l. Jeffares p102. The Pollexfens dominated the sea harbour; they had the only steam tug in the port. The Middletons had a depot in the Channel Islands and brought goods to and from South America. 'His smuggling eventually turned into general cargo traffic between Sligo and the Iberian peninsula'.

li. Pyle p5.

lii. Yeats p10; Murphy, Sligo, p10; Pyle p3. The Pollexfens go back in Devon seven generations before William. They thought themselves of Cornish ancestry. "As in a dream, I remembered that Uncle Fred Pollexfen said that the original Pollexfens were flying tin men from Phoenicia."

liii. Murphy, Family Secrets, p13. The Pollexfens, 'regarded intellect and education with unconcealed contempt because to them it seemed to bring only poverty and failure.' John Butler Yeats.

liv. Murphy, Family Secrets, p12. 'The crossest people I have ever met' said Ellen Yeats. J B Yeats described his first visit: 'The family gathered in force, mostly in one room, all disliking each other. At any rate alien mutually, all in gloomy silence.' Lily Yeats: 'There was no merry talk there. People walked soberly about. There were no pet names or caresses. Life was serious and silent. No merry talk at meals or running to and fro.' 'The whole family were brought up as if they did not belong to each other'.

lv. Murphy, Family Secrets, p16.

lvi. Murphy, Sligo, p33.

lvii. I am thinking of Joan Dolton and Norah Redmore – repetition, parody, whimsy, and lack of syntax.

lviii. Woolf, A Room of One's Own, p3. She was uncomfortable with the working class James Joyce (1882-1941) [NR], author of Ulysses

lix. Lee p104.

lx. The line to William the Conqueror is through the Boileaus. Alice Boileau (1779-1851) was Ethel's great grandmother.

lxi. http://kindred.stanford.edu/# accessed 4 Oct 2014.

1.

Garden Gates

Of the four natural elements, earth, air, fire and water, our family is fairly earthy. Recently, we have been known to fly round the world and there was plenty of fire and water whilst I was researching this Chapter. The hotel in the Lake District burned down[i]. Carolyn and I had gone to the Lakes for the weekend after I had spent some days at the Records Office at Barrow-in-Furness The firemen retrieved some old papers but although the laptop melted the boys had taught me well. The manuscript was stored on the internet, in 'the cloud'. They'd probably have said "I told you so" otherwise.

More specifically, the family is associated with wood. **Charles Elliott** was a cabinet maker in the Regency period. He made a large fortune (see Chapter 11). My great aunt **Fanny Garden** made furniture. My father **Paul Haskins** built a caravan out of wood. His best friend, Jack Dolton, owned a timber firm (see Chapter 14). They were friends with Bill Redmore, who also owned a timber yard[1]. Paul's garden was full of trees. He was good at pruning silver birches to make them stay elegant. He chopped the logs into kindling for the drawing room fire, which he laid before breakfast. Paul always had plenty of wood if he wanted anything.

Not just on my side... my wife Carolyn's great grandfather, **Willie Machen**, trained as a cabinet maker, a lucrative trade, and taught his sons, **Frank** and **Harry Machen**. **Frank Machen** ran a cork merchant's in Barnsley, buying and selling cork mats to the London shops. Harry passed on his skills to his nephew **Ken Burton**[2]. Ken has made tables, benches, news racks and bathroom fittings, still in use today.

Queen's Head, Troutbeck, in flames 6 June 2014

❉ ❉ ❉ ❉

Garden Studios

Jonathan Haskins my son is making his fortune from wood. In his student days, Jonathan lived in Leicester[ii]. He let his garage to a friend of his, Jean Lombard, for £60 a month[3]. Six months later, sawing away, the council inspectors arrived to explain that a residential garage wasn't the place to do business. The neighbours had complained. Jean moved but they kept talking and Jonathan came up with the idea of garden studios – high spec living space, carpeted, insulated, with electricity and everything you might expect, but in the garden. Had they been around 150 years earlier, Parson Hawker of Morwenstow (see Chapter 1) might have bought one.

Grand Designs Exhibition Birmingham October 2009

Jon and Jean each invested about £500 for an advert in the Grand Designs magazine. They named their enterprise 'in.it.studios' and were soon offered a prime position near the front stage of the Grand Designs Exhibition auditorium in Birmingham. It was a novel idea in 2009. A TV episode followed and their webpages attracted serious buyers: footballers and tennis stars. Jon and Jean made enough to cover the costs of the exhibition and more and were soon the largest customer of their wood supplier – a customer with the smallest of premises.

Barn 8, Tiger's Close, Leicester

---

1.   *Arthur Martin Dolton (1862-1946) [NR] who married Caroline Turner Glanville (1872-1944) [NR] lived at 24 Kidbrooke Park Road. He owned Dolton, Bournes and Dolton Ltd, Archangel Wharf, New Cross. Their son, Paul's best man, was Jack (Arthur Henry St John) Dolton (1905-1981) [NR]. Bill (Alfred Askham) Redmore (1894-1963) [NR] owned Howard & Wilton Ltd, Canada Wharf, Trundleys Road, London SE8.*

2.   *William Joseph Machen (1853-1940); Harry Machen (1881-1943); Kenneth Burton (b1924); Frank Machen (1893-1950).*

3.   *Jean Lombard (b1982) [NR] is male and from South Africa.*

Jonathan Haskins at Get Laid Beds

George Haskins (1851-1915) with his wife Elizabeth and children Charles and Nellie

Stowe, once home of the Temple-Nugent-Brydges-Chandos-Grenville family, now a public school and National Trust landscaped estate. [Palladian Bridge]

Quickly growing out of that move to Duncan Road, they were offered a modern unit near Glen Parva, a Young Offenders' Institution – not that they employed any of its residents. I'd had something to do with building Glen Parva in the early 1980s, so I was interested to see it – from the outside. Since that time, when Willie Whitelaw was 'getting tough on crime', the prison population has grown from 45,000 to 86,000. It was 10,000 in 1918. I thought 45,000 was too high and now it is double[i].

The bed-making business – ***Get Laid Beds*** – overtook the Garden Studios business and they have since moved again. All this is history in the making – unfinished. The rest of this chapter is about some other people. Two were gardeners. A third bore the surname 'Gates' and the fourth the surname 'Garden'.

❋ ❋ ❋ ❋

The Royal Gardener

Stowe House and Gardens, in Buckinghamshire, occupies acres of countryside not far from the Silverstone racetrack. At one time Stowe was the most prestigious garden in England. 'Capability' Brown had laid out the grounds 100 years earlier – with William Kent he started a revolution in garden design – wide sweeping landscapes flowing up to the door of our country's great houses[4]. The resultant park was complemented by something even more astounding. As far as the eye could see, it was peppered with follies – temples and obelisks and arches – holding golden statues that shimmered in the sunlight. The wealth invested outstripped almost every other landed estate of its day.

My great uncle **George Haskins**[5] was employed as Head Gardener by the 3rd Duke, Richard Plantagenet Campbell Temple-Nugent-Brydges-Chandos-Grenville. The Duke had royal connections and had managed to persuade George to leave the Royal Gardens at Kensington, where he was living near Hyde Park Gate, and move to Stowe. George was head gardener at Stowe for about 20 years from his marriage in 1879 to at least the time when his daughter Alice was born, in 1896.

In its heyday, Stowe was the place to be invited – a sort of cross between Alton Towers and Buckingham Palace, with fabulous gardens visited by European royalty. There was an 'endless variety of culture' and the flower borders were 'the perfection of a gardener's art.'[iii] Ostentation was the thing. The Dukes of Buckingham & Chandos competed to have the most outstanding display of finery and frippery anywhere in Europe. Their overindulgence unseated them. By 1847, their debts were so large that their connections, their titles, their positions, and their great offices of state could not save them from the wrong sort of headlines.

The Duke went bankrupt owing over £1million[6]. His only option was to auction the contents of the house in the sale of the century. His son soldiered on. He was a politician and Governor of the Madras Presidency in India 1875-80. The monumental park remained. By the 1880s, when George and his brother Frank were administering the place, it had lost much of its dignity. In 1889, the third Duke died, leaving no direct heirs, so the family tried to sell the house for £200,000 but no one wanted to buy it. The place was let to the Comte de Paris, who died there in 1894; after which it remained unoccupied until 1901. Since 1923, Stowe House has been a Public School and the National Trust has been restoring the grounds to their former glory at considerable expense.

---

4.   *Lancelot Brown (1715/6-1783) [NR] and Samuel Wyatt (1707-1807) [NR].*
5.   *George Haskins (1851-1915), son of William Thomas Haskins of Courteenhall – see Chapter 4.*
6.   *Richard Plantagenet Temple-Nugent-Brydges-Chandos-Grenville, 2nd Duke of Buckingham and Chandos KG GCH PC FSA (1797-1861) [NR].*

George moved to Cardiff, opening a bottling plant with his son until the son upped and emigrated to America[7].   His brother **Frank Haskins** stayed at Stowe as its Agent[8].

Frank Haskins (1862-1945)

✳ ✳ ✳ ✳

Gates

It didn't matter if the fruit tree fell over when my father brought in a marquee for my sister Ann's wedding, in 1959. She was my father's first-born and this her big day – he was immensely proud. The garden was otherwise at its best. The exciting summery event heralded the end of the austere 1950s and the start of my adolescence in the Beatles era. I was almost eleven years old, had taken my first sip of Pimms and was pleasantly content.

Ann was never unoccupied after she left school in 1951, often the centre of attention – if it wasn't the plays, the parties, the evening classes or dressmaking, there was her talk of them all. She gravitated to a group that met in the Pavilion of the local Recreational Ground, principally to play Hockey, but there were social events too. She went on trips to Minehead and the Broads with them. One of the group was the hockey goal-keeper, who later played for Kent and Lancashire, husband-to-be, **Michael John Gates**[9].

Michael's father Reggie, full name **Reginald Victor Gates,** was the youngest of seven[10]. He moved to Orpington as an accountant with the electricity company. He'd come from Dover, from a family of three generations of sea mariners, operating 'Home Trade Passenger ships' across the English Channel. **Wilson Gates**, Reggie's great (x3) grandfather had originally come from Canterbury in about 1795[11].   He'd been apprenticed as a bricklayer and was probably drawn to Dover as a result of the demands of the Napoleonic Wars. Dover Castle was being fortified – did he help built those underground vaults which were used as barracks in that and subsequent wars?[iv]

It was Wilson's grandson, **John Thomas Gates**, who first went to sea[12]. He married Jane Rosina Austin. Her mother had been born in Plymouth and her grandfather was a fisherman who began life in Exeter. They'd come to live together on the sea front in Dover in a row of houses called Fishermen's Row which changed its name to Seven Star Street at some stage. The story goes that a group of Channel Pilots lived at one end and wanted to name it 'Pleiades' after the star constellation they used to steer by night but, being rather a mouthful, people preferred its English name. The 'Middle Row' of Seven Star Street was the home of several generations of the Gates family, snuck behind a non-conformist chapel. The road was demolished in two stages to make way for the new railway system in 1843 and 1910, and was completely cleared in the 1930s when the whole area became a marshalling yard. On his retirement, Reggie and his wife Nan moved to Whitfield, near Dover.

Nan (Nancy) May, Michael's mother, was one of four girls and two boys. Her father, **George May**, had come from Manningtree, on the River Stour, on the Essex/Suffolk border[13]. His grandfather **William May** had made much money as a miller in Brantham[14]. George had joined the army at fifteen (and probably lied about his age) and rose to the rank of Staff Sergeant Major 1st Class in the Army Service Corps. He'd seen service in Dover, where

Hawthorns hockey team. Goalkeeper, Michael Gates (1932-2009), in the dark shirt

On the Norfolk Broads – Micky (Michael) Gates on left

Middle Row, Seven Star Street, Dover with original fisherman's cottages, which were cleared away for the railway

---

7.   *Charles Haskins (1881-?).*

8.   *Frank Haskins (1862-1945).*

9.   *Michael John Gates (1932-2009) married Ann Lorna Haskins (b1934) in 1959.*

10.   *Reginald Victor Gates (1900-1979) married Nancy May (1906-1984) in 1929.*

11.   *Wilson Gates (1758-1844) married Thomasin Bubbers (1761-1837) in 1777.*

12.   *John Thomas Gates (1832-1904) married Jane Rosina Austin (1838-1923) in 1857.*

13.   *SSM George Henry May (1868-1908) married Marion ? (1868-?) in 1889.*

14.   *William May (1797-1864) married Elizabeth Girling (1801-?) in 1819 and left some £40,000 in his will.*

The retirement of William Gates, captain of Channel steamers (1866-1930?)

Celebrating the start of a new generation in 1960: Reggie Gates (1900-1979), the author, Michael, Simon Gates & Ann (née Haskins), Paul Haskins and Nancy Gates (née May) (1906-1984)

With some of Barbara's 500 babies

he met Marion, an Army clerk from Woolwich. After the first two children were born, it was off to Dublin (1893), Hound Barracks in Southampton (1905), and the Transvaal in South Africa (1906). They returned to Dover where their youngest, Nan, was born. George died when she was only a year old, in 1908, aged 40, leaving Marion to raise the six children on a small army pension.

When they married, Ann and Michael bought a brand new starter home in Meopham, Kent[v]. A year later, the first of the next generation appeared on the scene, **Simon Gates**. By the time his sister **Bridget** came along, the new tree in the Petts Wood garden was well on the way to becoming the prolific bearer of juicy Victoria plums[15].

✳ ✳ ✳ ✳

Seed Salesmen and altered accents

According to a survey by a jeweller, the thing brides most regret about their wedding day are the inappropriate remarks made by the Best Man in his speech. Hair and make-up come next; then the weather[vi].

As Best Man at my other sister, **Barbara Haskins**' wedding to **Ian Simpson** in September 1968, I cracked a joke about Barbara (a district midwife) looking after children in one sort of nursery whilst her new husband looked after plants in another[16]. Ian was managing Waterers' Garden Centre near Twyford, outside Reading on the A4, the Great Bath Road. A length of the road was full of flowers – the Floral Mile.

Ian started his career apprenticed to the Parks department of Liverpool Council. Garden Centres were in their infancy and Waterers' dominated the Reading scene. I spent a couple of weeks watering plants as one of my first summer jobs. Ian had a strong Liverpool accent.

Though he didn't know it, gardening was in Ian's genes. His great great great grandfather **Thomas** was a working gardener as well as Parish Clerk in Fairford, Gloucester[17]. Fairford is still a delightful market town, though now mostly known for its long runway used by British Aerospace. There used to be a Simpson's garage there until quite recently and there is still a Simpson's field – the field where the family grew seeds[vii].

The Simpsons had some get-up-and-go. When the movement of goods by train was possible, Thomas's son **James** set out for London to trade in seeds[18]. At the age of 24, he married **Charlotte Smith**, a London girl. As business improved they moved home from Stockwell to an up and coming bijou area – Leytonstone.

The Gloucestershire/London connection continued into the 1870s. Their eldest son, **James William**, fell in love with a girl from Fairford, a gamekeeper's daughter, **Esther Crabb**[19]. However, they went to live in Liverpool – did they elope? There's no evidence they ever made their partnership legal[viii]. The trade in seeds had changed – it now looked west. Liverpool in the 1870s had moved on from the slave trade of the 1820s and the Irish emigration of the 1840s to grain imports[ix]. The repeal of the Corn Laws (1846-49) changed everything[x].

Ian's grandfather **Christopher Simpson** grew up in a crowded household, for James died at the age of 50, leaving Esther to raise five daughters under 20, not to mention three more over 20[20].

---

15. *Ven Simon Philip Gates (b1960) Bridget Mary Gates (b1962).*
16. *Barbara Pauline Margaret Haskins (b1937) married Ian Simpson (b1944) in 1968. They have since divorced.*
17. *Thomas Simpson (1777-1864) married Elizabeth Bowle (1782-1865) in 1806.*
18. *James Simpson (1820-1894) married Charlotte Smith (1820-1899) at St John Hoxton in 1844.*
19. *James William Simpson (1846-1896) got together with Esther Anne Crabb (1848-1905) in 1869.*

Christopher and his brother **Harry** worked first as office boys and when they were 25 as railway porters[21]. When Christopher married **Lillie Hingley** in 1907, aged 31, he'd gone to sea as a ship's steward.

Their son, **Ronald Simpson**, was Ian's father. He'd married **Eileen Ridgeway** just after the war broke out, two days before Christmas 1939[22]. Eileen had a grandfather, **Henry Boase**, son of a Master Mariner from St Ives, who'd come to Liverpool to earn his fortune as a shipwright. Thus her grandchildren Luke, Hugh and Naomi Simpson have Cornish blood on both sides of their family[23].

Ronald Simpson (1911-1980) and wife Eileen Ridgeway (1913-1986)

As far as Ian was concerned, he was a Liverpudlian through and through, but accents are transient, as the Liverpool comedian John Bishop discovered on *'Who do you think you are?'* Bishop's family also came from London. The Simpsons' accents have changed as each generation found new places to live. Over the six generations they've altered from a rolling rural West Country burr, via Cockney and the Liverpudlian 'Scouse', to today's 'Estuary English' of the Reading area[xi].

The Haskins's find it harder to change their accents. I found Barnsley difficult. When I ordered a sherry at the Royal Hotel, it must have been years since anyone had asked for one. I pointed to the large casks set in the back wall which must have been put there when the hotel was built – the liquor was sheer nectar, to quote Bertie Wooster. After first asking if I wanted a half or a pint, an enormous glass 'schooner' eventually arrived at my table with a cherry floating on top. My sister Barbara has the vestiges of the cockney accent of at least 4 generations earlier – just little things, like 'orf' for 'off'. My wife Carolyn, whose family has lived in Yorkshire for generations, can adapt better than me though she's not lost the Northern short 'a's. She laughs at Barbara saying 'orf', and Barbara laughs at Carolyn for saying 'garriidge' (I say 'gararrrge'). Carolyn wins the argument by saying that if that's correct, that place in South London should be pronounced as the 'Eleph-aren't and Carstle' instead of Elephant and Castle.

✻ ✻ ✻ ✻

James Garden

The remainder of this chapter concerns **James Garden**[24]. The story in our family was that as a Scotsman with the surname Gordon entering England, 'What's your name?' they asked. With his best rolling r's he replied 'Gaurrrrdon.' "Ah, Mr Garden,' they said, 'Come this way…'

Cockney rhyming slang
Adam & Eve = believe
Dicky bird = word
Jimmy riddle = piddle = toilet visit
Mother's ruin = gin
Plates of meat = feet
Titfer = tit for tat = hat

Cornish dialect
Directly = soon but not very soon
Emmett = Tourist; ant
Pisky layd'n = absent-minded
Stank = walk heavily
Put t' Bodmin = committed to the asylum
Turk = naughty, mischievous, disobedient
Wozza Madder Withee? = what's wrong?

Liverpudlian 'scouse'
Bevvy = drink
Bizzies = Fuzz = the police
Gobshite = boaster, liar or worse
Jigger = alley
Kecks = underwear
Kidda = friend
Rellie = relative

Yorkshire dialect
'Appen = Possibly
Chuckies = Eggs
Given back word = let you down
Four times = 4x fish & chips
Sithee = I'll be seeing you
Snap = packed lunch
Tyke = Yorkshireman

James Garden

---

20. *11 Ridgeway Street. (No connection with Ian's mother, Eileen Ridgeway.)*

21. *Christopher Frederick Simpson (1875-1937) and Harry Simpson (1871-1897). Harry died at the age of 26. Christopher married Lillian Annie Hingley (1877-1939) at St Clement Toxteth in 1907. Lillie, from Peckham, joined her uncle in his West Derby confectionery business.*

22. *Ronald Simpson (1911-80) married Eileen Ridgeway (1913-86) at Dovedale Road Baptist Church in 1939.*

23. *Henry Boase (1844-1894).*

24. *James Garden (1822-1896) married (1) Fanny Baynes (1820-1866) in 1850 and (2) Frances Ellen Garratt (1845–1930) in 1868. His gravestone in the Dalton civic cemetery, which is behind the Cemetery Chapel, states his birth two years later. His baptism was in 20 July 1822.*

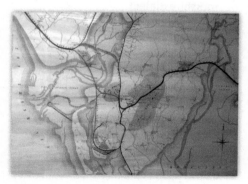

James Garden

Map of Furness.

Map of Furness. Barrow harbour bottom left; Dalton half-way between Barrow and Ulverston.

Railway proposals

Furness

North of Morecambe Bay is the Lake District. To its west, there is an area few know about, called the Furness peninsular. If you are going to Lake Windermere's southern end, you might head for The Swan Hotel at Newby Bridge. If you travel on a train, you might reach Ulverston, a little market town a few miles further. However, it is doubtful you'll want to go further west – to Dalton-in-Furness or to Barrow-in-Furness unless you are visiting one of the major employers such as BAE systems or Vickers shipyard. Currently, there are 4,000 in the shipyard, building a new generation of nuclear-powered submarines. At its height, there were many more.

Barrow-in-Furness and Falmouth are similar in one respect. 200 years apart, they started from nothing and grew at a staggering rate under the direction of motivated men. Both have natural deep water harbours, protected from the west winds. Cornwall had its tin mines – the Furness peninsular had high quality iron deposits. First they exported the ore, and then they learnt to process it into steel. Later still, they used the steel to build ships[xii]. There was a demand for armoured plated ships in the years leading up to the First World War (see Chapter 2).

The railway helped the place grow[xiii]. From 150 people in the late 1841, Barrow grew to 60,000 by 1890[xiv]. In 1866, there were 22 builders in Barrow itself. During the expansion, the place was like coastal Spain in the late twentieth century, one large building site. Someone likened it to the unlikely combination of Birkenhead and the Wild West[xv]. Three thousand navvies camped in wooden huts under a foot of stagnant water – with one privy for 80 people. The Barrow Harbour Act of 1848 enabled a stone pier in place of the wooden one. The docks grew between 1867 and 1881. James Garden helped build Ramsden Dock in 1876-8.

The chief players in the growth of Barrow were Henry Schneider and his partner Robert Hannay, both mining magnates and James Ramsden, who arrived in 1846 as the railway engineer and ended up running the whole place[25]. The landowners were the glue that held it together[xvi]. They were the Duke of Devonshire and the Duke of Buccleuch, who operated through his agent, Edward Wadham[26]. They charged a levy on each ton of ore that was mined. Iron ore production rose from 1,200 tons in 1800 to 1.4 million tons by 1882[xvii]. All of these people came to depend on my great grandfather. Like Falmouth, one or two men of vision were helped by energetic achievers such as James Garden.

Most of the workers at Barrow came from outside, labelled 'off comers'. They included Cornish miners. Cornish miners and their engines were straddling the world, sharing their skills with speculators. The Schneiders owned tin mines in Cornwall and even shipped Cornish engines to Mexico[xviii]. They brought up 500 Cornish miners and their families to their Park mine, near Dalton – later bringing two more tranches of 2-300 miners. Cornish miners also came to Mouzell Mines (the Cornish way of saying Mousehole) near Dalton along with miners from elsewhere[xix]. They lived an almost self-contained life for thirty years at Roose (Rouse?), with their own school and chapels[xx]. The Cornish worked at 'Stank' mine – stank being a derivation of *Stannick/Stannary*; named after tin, they were looking for coal and found iron ore.

25. *Henry William Schneider (1817-1887) [NR]; Robert Hannay (1807-1874) [NR]; Sir James Ramsden (1822-1896) [NR].*

26. *William Cavendish, 7th Duke of Devonshire and Earl of Burlington KG PC (1808-1891); William Henry Walter Montagu Douglas Scott, 6th Duke of Buccleuch & 8th Duke of Queensberry KG KT PC JP DL (1831-1914) [NR]; Edward Wadham (1828-1913) [NR].*

James Garden had come down from Scotland in the 1840s, along with many others suffering from the highland potato famine. Some 1.7 million people left Scotland during the period 1846–52[xxi]. His family came from Banffshire. His father was a mason. Cullen is an ancient Burgh or administrative area on the North coast of Moray, above Aberdeen [27]. Its church was founded by Robert the Bruce, the Scottish hero after whom my mother said I was named. Later, the family lived at Rathven, a few miles west.

James had 3 brothers and 3 sisters – all called Garden but sometimes mistaken for Gordon. James may have come down as early as 1840 with his brother **John**. John found work as an apprentice boot maker in Broughton-in-Furness[xxii]. John married at Broughton-in-Furness the same year as James, 1850 and emigrated to Australia a couple of years later [28]. John called their house at Barr Creek, Victoria, on the other side of the world, 'Cullen House' after their childhood home[xxiii].

James was probably apprenticed to the largest builder in Barrow, William Gradwell, who built the rows of the brick tenement houses in the early days[29]. The brusque straightforward Gradwell, the 'syndicate man', who always found a way of joining the winning cartel, never probing anyone's motives, was stand-offish; not everyone could cope with him but James could – Gradwell never lost the rough edge of the Victorian self-made man. When he became mayor after all the others, it turned out to be a good choice for he was a man of the people. Sadly, he lost his fortune through over-speculation.

James was probably apprenticed at the same time as **Thomas Baynes** – they were the same sort of age except Thomas had come from Lancaster where his father was a merchant's clerk[30]. James fell in love with Thomas's sister, **Fanny Baynes** and, still in his 20s, married her at Dalton-in-Furness in 1850 and set up home in this older town. He was ambitious and by 1855, he'd built Fell Croft for himself and had four cottages for his quarry-workers. Fanny was not the strongest of women, often ill, but she had three children by him – **Elizabeth, Margaret** and **William James Garden**. Elizabeth died aged eight.

Holker Hall – the large West wing extension was built by James Garden in 1871. The rounded first-floor corner window lit the Duke's favourite room.

✳ ✳ ✳ ✳

Odd fellows

James acquired the Hamilton House site in 1857 and bought the site adjoining in 1869. He designed a special window for the sickly Fanny to look over the hills stretching to the horizon, but she passed away in 1866. For two years he was a widower, bringing up his young family with the help of a few staff.

It didn't take long for James to become established. He was introduced to the Oddfellows Society, by Gradwell and others. My uncle and godfather, **George Spencer**, wanted me to join the same organisation but I didn't find it had a strong profile in the South of England[31]. In any case, I was odd enough. Of course, James may have belonged before he came down from Scotland. The Society gave travel warrants to enable people free movement to seek work. In any case, he moved straight to the top. That same year he became a Trustee of

Millwood built by James Garden for Edward Wadham in about 1857

27. *James's father John Garden (1793-1865) married his mother Elspet Gaudie (1797-1876) in 1819. They lived in Castle Street, Cullen, in 1851 with Bathia (1831-1907), Isabella (1834-1908) and William (1837-1890).*

28. *John Garden (1826-1910) married Jane Hannah William Margaret Douglas (1827-1907) at Broughton-in-Furness in 1850.*

29. *William Gradwell (1820-1882) [NR]*

30. *Thomas Carter Baynes (1823-1900).*

31. *George Henry Nadauld Spencer (1907-1995) was the son of a Derbyshire coal mine owner. When the mine was nationalised he remained its manager. He married the author's aunt Nancy Dora Haskins (1908-2000) in 1933.*

Ulverston Station

Gasometer at Askam, James Garden second left

Abbotswood, built by James Garden for Sir James Ramsden in 1857

St George's Barrow-in-Furness. The North Aisle and the Church Hall to its left are in the same style of stripped, almost dry-set, high quality dressed slate from the Burlington slate quarry near Kirkby-in-Furness and sandstone from St Bees. Architect E Paley.

the organisation. This was an organisation of masters of their trades – it had influence. For example, in 1856 and again in 1867-71, he was an overseer or guardian of the poor in the parish[xxiv].

James was also a Freemason along with most of the movers and shakers of the area[xxv]. When Myles Kennedy, the son of the influential Ulverston mining family and fellow mason, married in 1860, James headed up one of the wedding tables[xxvi]. From 1875-81 he was on the Committee planning to install gas to the neighbourhood.

James Garden was a good worker, a stone mason like his father. He was a decent man, caring, considerate, likable and not self-serving; unostentatious in his generosity and an eye for people. He had high standards and an attention to detail. Gradwell and James kept their respect for each other throughout their working careers. The two teamed up for Ulverston Station (1874-8). Garden did the stone work, Gradwell the brick. They did the same at St Peter's parish church at Lindal-in-Furness (1884)[xxvii]. Thomas Baynes worked with them as plumber, glazier, blacksmith and gas fitter.

By 1861 James was a 'master builder'. He knew the properties of stone and wood and could calculate structural capacity. He employed 350 men and 15 boys at the height of his business when in his forties[xxviii]. He worked in granite, sandstone and limestone. He used a number of quarries, mostly the Duke of Devonshire's[xxix].

James gained a reputation with his top clients, all wanting his stone-built craftsmanship, coming back for more, despite Dalton's Vicar remarking that when Garden charged £70 for an additional item, "it would cost £17 if it had been done by anyone else."[xxx] The gulf between the wealthy and the workers is still noticeable in Barrow today.

James built many a magnificent house for those who could afford them. *Abbotswood* in Abbey Road was the home of James Ramsden (1857). James built a secret room which you could climb in through the mirror above the fireplace, just like in *Alice through the Looking Glass*[xxxi]. *Millwood* was built for the Duke of Buccleuch's agent, Edward Wadham (c1857). James built an extension to *Leighton Hall* for the Gillow family (1870), the furniture people – my dining room chairs were bought from Waring & Gillow the year the two firms combined. The Duke of Devonshire's place, *Holker Hall* (pronounced *Howker* by the locals and *Hooker* by the family) burnt down and James built its replacement in 1871 in mock Elizabethan style. This was one of the largest houses that James built and the loveliest[xxxii]. With its billiard room, it reminds me of *Lanhydrock*, near Bodmin, also rebuilt after a fire.

Houses built by James Garden

- Abbotswood, Barrow
- Bellsfield, Windermere
- Crosslands, Barrow
- Harecroft, Gosforth
- Holker Hall, Grange-over-sands
- Leighton Hall, Carnforth
- Millwood, Barrow
- Oaklea, Barrow
- Prior's Lea, Barrow
- Stone Cross, Ulverston

Alice through the Looking Glass was the 1871 sequel to Alice in Wonderland

James worked with good architects, recommended by Ramsden and Schneider. The Lancaster practice of Paley and Austin, one of the best in the North of England, often used James Garden – their preferred builder[xxxiii]. The architectural critic, Nicolas Pevsner, considered Hubert Austin, a pupil of the architect Sir Gilbert Scott, the 'genius' of the partnership[xxxiv]. Up until then most had been castellated confections similar to those of John Nash such as *Childwall Hall* in Liverpool and *Caerhays Castle* in Cornwall[xxxv].

Pevsner, who surveyed Britain and much of Europe, thought 'the highest European standard of their years' came from the Paley & Austin churches[xxxvi]. James built two churches in Lonsdale, near Ingleton Falls, Yorkshire, in 1868-70. St Oswald at Thornton-in-Lonsdale, with its beautiful sandstone mullions set in limestone, received a grant of £5,000 in the will of Felix Slade[32]. Slade often resided at nearby *Halsteads*. When he died, he left money in his will to a number of Universities. The University of London decided to set up the Slade School of Fine Art – Slade died before my grandmother was born, but was her love of painting in any way associated with this connection?[xxxvii]

Altogether, local historian Walter Johnston (who gives lectures on James Garden) has tracked down 108 properties James Garden built, not including the houses. After the 1870s Education Act, James set about building schools at Dalton, Ulverston, Grizebeck, Kirkby-in-Furness and Newton. He won the paid job of 'Surveyor of the Highways in Dalton' in 1866/67.

James was churchwarden of Dalton Parish Church for one year in 1858. In 1883, Sir James Ramsden, Edward Wadham and James Garden sat down together and planned the rebuilding of Dalton church. Dalton was a popular church with ancient connections to Furness Abbey. Judging from the engraving of the old church, there was nothing very much wrong with it but this was the heady age of church building, with large congregations and wealthy donors prepared to stump up sizeable sums of money. The Vicar, Rev Paddy Morgan, had been there some 45 years and his church was full to overflowing[33]. At the vestry meeting in April he handed over the chair to Edward Wadham, who promptly reconvened the meeting across the way in the Cavendish Arms[xxxiii]. The contract was let to James Garden. It was contracted to cost £8,404 but by the time he had finished, it had cost £11,553, much to the chagrin of the church officials[xxxix].

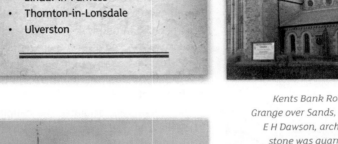

Churches built by James Garden

- Blawith
- Bootle
- Burton-in-Lonsdale
- Dalton (Anglican, Catholic, Wesleyan, Primitive Methodist & Baptist Churches)
- Grange-over-Sands United Reformed Church
- Kirksanton
- Lindal-in-Furness
- Thornton-in-Lonsdale
- Ulverston

The old St Mary's Dalton

St Oswald, Thornton in Lonsdale, built by James Garden for Paley and Austin in 1870. Arthur Conan Doyle, author of Sherlock Holmes, married here.

Kents Bank Road United Reform Church, Grange over Sands, built by James Garden for E H Dawson, architect, costing £2,400. The stone was quarried in Haworth, Yorkshire.

Public buildings built by James Garden

- Abbey Hotel extension
- Barrow Cemeteries
- Conishead Priory 'hydro'
- Coniston Station extension
- Dalton Council offices
- Gasworks and pipes
- Haematite Iron Works, masonry work
- Naval buildings
- Railway tunnels
- Roads
- Schools, Kirkby
- Stations on Furness railway
- Whitehaven station

---

32. *Felix Slade (1790-1868).[NR] Thornton-in-Lonsdale church was largely rebuilt, apart from the tower.*

33. *Rev James Morrison Morgan (1820-1898) [NR].*

The new St Mary's Dalton built by James Garden in 1885

Bookcases in the Surveyors' Department of the new Town Hall made by James Garden

Hamilton House, 80 Market Street, Dalton-in-Furness, home of James Garden (1822-1896). The front of the house, onto the street (left), was built first, out of Limestone. The entrance porches have changed since then, more than once. The large Italianate window would have lit the original grand staircase. There were windows top and bottom on the left-hand side. It was extended several times. There were 2 stables backing onto Station Road and a yard. There were auction rooms at the back of the property.

The church was still not out of debt in 1890 five years after it was finished. The final amount, £247 10s 5d was put up by Edward Wadham, a close friend of the Vicar and a beacon of good sense throughout[xl]. Whatever else you could say it was good value for money. The church has had almost no repairs to it in its recent 130-year history[xli].

❋ ❋ ❋ ❋

Home at Hamilton House

If you step behind the main thoroughfare in Dalton-in-Furness and walk 50 metres down towards the station, you'll come across Garden Terrace. Back where you started, at 80 Market Street according to the Post Office, and 78 according to the present owner, you will find Hamilton House, my grandmother's childhood home.

Since our family left, in 1906, the place had been a shop, first a draper's, then a Home and Colonial Store. The current owner bought the 7,500 sq ft property in the 1990s. He's been energetically putting it back into a house, making something of the warren of bedrooms, rearranging the staircases, working with the different building materials. Like many, he assumed the family was Hamilton and the Terraces were built in the garden. Not so. The Terrace was named after my great grandfather **James Garden** who built the houses on the meadow. The fine houses in Garden Lea (1901) also perpetuate his name. It is not clear why it was called Hamilton House, except that the Duke of Hamilton is considered the premier noble of Scotland.

The Gardens accumulated the trappings of wealth – Sevres vases; Dresden, Crown Derby, Wedgwood and Worcester china; Chippendale, Sheraton, Spanish and Gillow furniture; 2 pianos, Brussels carpets, tea caddies, numerous clocks, over 30 oil paintings, 200 books, and a magic lantern with slides – very modish. They subscribed to *Punch* and *All the Year Round*. The girls were educated in art, the boys in boxing, cricket and fencing[xlii].

James had his own personal valet, two horses and carriages[xliii]. His offices in Market Street near the railway station were fitted with both band and circular saws for sawing wood and stone. He rang a bell to summon his workers. His carpenters' and joiners' shops made window frames, hand-rails, balusters and cupboards. Some of the first furnishings of *Barrow Town Hall* would have been made there[xliv].

His second wife, my great grandmother was an orphan – we will call her Frances to distinguish her from his first wife. **Frances Ellen Garratt** was brought up with her step brother in Salford Manchester by her step-mother Ann. Frances's mother died when she was 6 years old and her father had died when she was 10. Her father **Thomas Garratt** made money in wholesale merchandise and married his second wife, Ann Woodhead, just two years before he died, so Frances was lucky not to have been completely destitute[34]. How she met James Garden is conjecture. Did she work in James's office? Or look after his children? She was some twenty-three years younger than James yet she seems to have had the upper hand – a liberated lady before her time. She had flowing, confident handwriting and was well able to master the intricacies of the law of contract – she signed leases for quarries in her own name in James's lifetime. The wedding was in Manchester Cathedral, in 1868, just as her father's own marriages had been[xlv].

Frances had five children, 3 girls and 2 boys. The eldest, **Fannie**[35], did not marry. She interested herself in the arts and crafts movement, lived in Kensington and Forest Hill and

---

34. *Thomas Garratt married Frances Fantine (or Fentem) (1819-1851) in 1844 and Ann Woodhead (1826-1893) in 1853.*

35. *Frances Isobel Garden (1869-1949).*

had her own studio where she made furniture. She was the epitome of all Aunt Fannies, an inveterate collector, and a shambolic organiser like her sister Elsie, my grandmother.

After she left school, **Elsie** lived at home and occupied herself in maidenly pursuits[36]. She married in 1900, after a period of approximately thirteen years. How did she *really* occupy *all* that time? Did she undertake further education? Travelling? Painting?

Fannie and **Elsie** were 2 years apart. Bertie came along six years later. In between were the boys, Charlie and Gordon[37]. **Charlie** trained to be a mining engineer and took his skills round the world[38]. He fought in the first war in the Special Company of the Royal Engineers, rising to the rank of Major, settling in Devon with his wife, Ethel. **Gordon** went to sea at the age of seventeen[39]. He met a grizzly death, as you will find out by reading on. **Bertie** was the last daughter to marry, in 1903[xlvi].

For the last fifteen years of his life, James suffered from Bright's disease, the degeneration of the kidneys, like another of my great grandfathers, John Nicholas Tresidder. James's death, in **May 1896**, marked the end of an era. James Ramsden was to die 5 months later, Henry Schneider the following year. William Gradwell had met his end in 1882 and the Duke of Buccleuch two years after that. The Duke of Devonshire had died in 1891. Only Edward Wadham was to outlive them all.

After James died, Frances had to handle all James's affairs for herself. She had an enormous amount to do. He left a going concern with a large workforce, yards and contracts for the supply of stone and other building materials. There were 30 cottages with rents to collect and leases to control. Of course there was a foreman and head clerk to help her as she took care of her daughters[xlvii]. Fannie and Elsie were still at home together with eighteen-year old Bertie. All three sons were abroad by the time James died.

James left two wills, one dated 1890 and a later one in 1895. Neither could be found – they had been 'accidentally destroyed'. Some skulduggery was suspected and there was an expensive court case. In the event, the details which had been held at the solicitor's office were used. Frances persuaded William James Garden, her step-son from the first marriage now in Australia, to renounce his right to all the real estate[xlviii]. She got the other executors to resign and took over all the executive decisions herself[40]. The money was held in trust for her children, during her lifetime, but when she made some rash decisions at the time of the Wall Street crash, there was no one to stop her. Gordon and his sisters talked about it in 1900. They consulted lawyers in London but at 23 years old and still at home under her mother's influence, Bertie was reluctant to be part of another expensive legal action and nothing went through.

By 1906, with Bertie, married, Frances spread her wings. The business went into free-fall. She found someone to rent Hamilton House on a seven year lease, subsequently renewed twice. She went to live near her daughters in London, choosing Waldemar Mansions opposite Fulham Palace. Hers was a carefree time of travel and frittering her fortune. During the First World War, rents halved and Frances's living costs rose. She gave her tenant an option to buy. He was running Hamilton House as a clothes shop ('drapery, outfitters, millinery') but in 1918 he was called up on active service and met his death the month before the war ended[xlix]. His widow bought the house for £2,700, borrowing the money to do so.

Frances Ellen Garden (1845-1930)

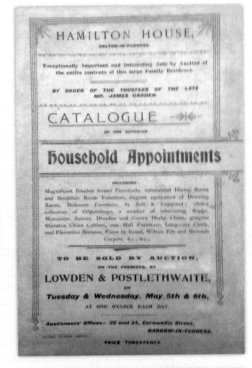

Fannie Garden (1869-1949) making a desk

---

36. *Elsie Annie Garden (1871-1950).*
37. *Bertha Louise Garden (1877-1955).*
38. *Charles Arthur Garden (1873-1931) married Ethel Normanton (1884-1958) in 1913.*
39. *Henry Gordon Garden (1875-1919).*
40. *The executors were John Jekyn Cooper, his son-in-law; George Paterson, a Surgeon in Dalton; and John Young McIlraith, an accountant, late of Barrow, who had moved to Manchester.*

Elsie Garden (1871-1950)

A Lake District painting by Elsie

Frances ended her days in Crowborough in Sussex. **Bertie** had married a bank manager living in Shanghai and on his retirement they'd bought a large mansion called Ingleside. **Fannie** never married, dying in a home for poor gentlefolk in Chislehurst not far from us (but leaving more money than anyone realised). **Charles** had retired to Exmouth and **Gordon**, as the next chapter reveals, met his end in unusual circumstances. **Elsie**, my grandmother, married a doctor in Blackheath and spent many holidays painting in Cornwall (Chapter 13). However, it was Bertie who first fascinated me with her stories of the Far East.

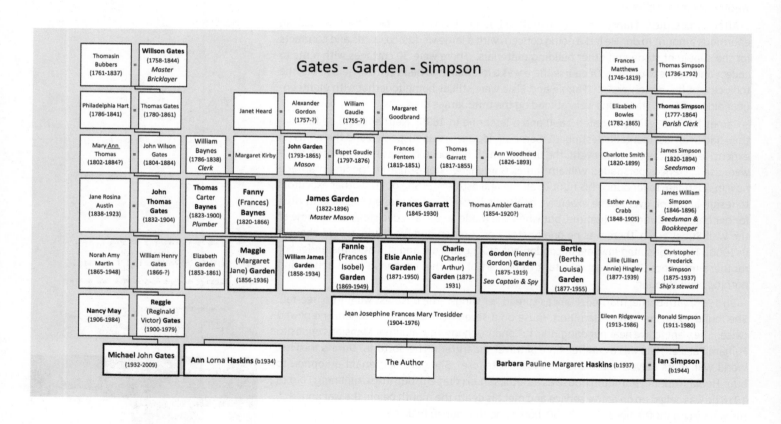

Other Notes and References

i. The Queens Head, Troutbeck, burnt down on the 70th anniversary of D Day, 6 Jun 2014.

ii. 11 Castle Street. Leicester must have something going for it. Winners are pouring out of the city. In 2013-14: winners of the Snooker Championships, Rugby Premiership, 1st Division Football Championship, The X Factor, the Great British Bake-off and the Great British Sewing Bee. In 2016, winning the Premier Football League and World Snooker Championships on the same day. Mark Selby won the snooker again in 2017.

iii. Kelly's Directory 1915.

iv. see www.doversociety.org.uk accessed 11 Aug 2015.

v. 11 Bracondale Avenue, Meopham.

vi. The Times 12 Jun 2014. 52% regret the best man's jokes.; 38% regretted their Hair and make-up, 34% felt they should have spent more on the day; weather upset 33%, the wedding dress 32%, Honeymoon (31%), photographer (30%) – oh dear. Survey by jeweller Vashi Dominguez.

vii. Ref Jules Gibson, Apr 2014.

viii. No registration of a marriage between James and Esher has been found.

ix. Farrar & Brownhill; Belchem: The Liverpool population in 1851 was 376,000. 200,000 more were living on the Wirral. 1,750 ships, 503,000 tonnage, were registered to Liverpool. In 1799, ships sailing from Liverpool transported 45,000 slaves from Africa.

x. Importation Act of 1846

xi. Thomas Simpson (1751-1751), the Parish Clerk's grandfather, came from Lincolnshire, so yet another accent.

xii. The Bessemer process was introduced to Barrow Steelworks in 1866. In 1869, 10,000 tons of steel railway lines were exported to America.

xiii. Kellett pp6-8. The engines arrived in 1846, the year James Ramsden, aged 23, arrived to manage the Engineering Department. The line opened for passengers in 1847, who travelled in a sheep-van, Sundays only. It linked with the Whitehaven and Furness Junction Railway in 1847 and to Lancaster by 1857.

xiv. Kellett p24; 1841 Census: In addition, there were 5 other small communities that are now part of Barrow.

xv. Mannex 1866: Barrow has the 'combination of appearance of Birkenhead and a gold-finder's city on the edge of one the Western prairies in America.'

xvi. Banks pp4,45; Kellett p45ff quoting from the Barrow Herald 1890:. Henry Schneider first visited the Lake District for a holiday in 1839. He already had experience in the mines in Mexico. He was secretary of the Mexican and South American Company at the age of eighteen. Robert Hannay came from Anwoth, near Gatehouse of the Fleet in Kirkcudbrightshire, and lived at Springfield House, Ulverston. He entered into a partnership with Henry Schneider, forming the Schneider, Hannay & Co in 1853. Sir James Ramsden was Managing Director of the Furness Railway Company 1866-95, Mayor of Barrow-in-Furness 1867-72 and also produced the design for the steam yacht Gondola on Coniston Water, built in 1859 for £1,100 and now run by the National Trust.

xvii. Barnes p94.

xviii. Ibid p38; Banks pp3-20. John Schneider & Co were mining at the Great Wheel Vor mine near Helston (tin), South Wales (coal), Mexico and Australia (copper). Engines from Harvey's of Hayle had gone to the Fresnillo mines in Mexico in 1835, 1838 and 1844, being landed at Vera Cruz and hauled overland. The Schneider family was of Swiss origin. The firm initially invested £50,000 in Furness. After a number of false starts, they discovered the richest deposits of ore in the Duke of Devonshire's land at Park, near Dalton.

xix. Miners also came from Staffordshire and the Isle of Man.

xx. Trescatheric p28. Letter from Walter M Johnston 1 Jul 2014. There were also Cornish miners at Mouzell Mines near Dalton. Others came from Staffordshire and the Isle of Man.

xxi. http://www.bbc.co.uk/scotland/history/land_and_votes/scottish_potato_blight/ accessed 2014

xxii. John Gordon (19) is listed in the 1841 Broughton census. Ten years later he is a master boot maker employing 2 apprentice bootmakers in The Square, Broughton.

xxiii. Daughter's wedding invitation 1877.

xxiv. Soulby's Ulverston Advertiser and General Intelligencer 25 Dec 1856; Obituary Barrow News 9 May 1896.

xxv. Walter Johnston 23 Mar 2016 and the 1865 certificate of membership signed by the Earl of Zetland Grand Master of the United Grand Lodge : having been a member of Scottish Grand Lodge, James Garden joined the Lodge of Furness in 1864 and moved to the Baldwin Lodge when it was founded in Dalton in 1872. With others (and E G Paley) he made the building alterations for the first meeting place, the old Manor near (and owned by) the railway which became the Abbey Hotel (partly demolished in 1953-4 and now called the Abbey Tavern;; he built the Masonic Hall in Slater Street Dalton which later became the meeting place of the Baldwin Lodge after they moved from the Castle.

xxvi. Soulby's Ulverston Advertiser and General Intelligencer 25 Oct 1860. Myles Burton Kennedy (1862–1928) [NR] was the first chairman of North Lonsdale Iron & Steel Co.

xxvii. An iron church, dedicated to St Peter ... will shortly be replaced by a stone structure, erected by the Duke of Buccleuch and Messrs. Harrison, Ainslie & Co.' Harrison & Ainslie, an iron mining company, paid for the building. The builders were Gradwell and Garden.

xxviii. Census 1871.

xxix. Soulby's Ulverston Advertiser and General Intelligencer 1 Oct 1857: Quarries included: Stainton, Skelgate and Yarlside (limestone) at Dalton; Greenscow (granite) at Askam; Hawcoat (sandstone) at Barrow, as well as Crossgates (8,141 tons of limestone in 1867) and Maiden Lands – which was leased in Frances Garden's name.

xxx. A History of St Mary's p38.

xxxi. North West Evening Mail. 15 June 2014. It was the secret entrance to the Ramsden treasure trove. The house had dry rot and was demolished when there were no direct heirs. Through the Looking-Glass, and What Alice Found There was the Christmas 1871 sequel to Alice's Adventures in Wonderland by Lewis Carroll.

xxxii. Brandwood pp90, 125–126. A disastrous fire had necessitated the rebuild. The West wing was new. The Duke thought it the 'best loved house in England'.

xxxiii. Started by Edmund Sharpe (1809-1877) [NR] who retired in 1851, Austin joined the firm in 1868. It was renamed Austin & Paley when Paley Senior died in 1895. Edward Graham Paley (1823-95) [NR], Hubert James Austin (1841-1915) [NR], and Henry Anderson Paley (1859-1946) [NR] were expert at Victorian gothic invested Elizabethan, prevalent in the area.

xxxiv. Pevsner p44. Sir George Gilbert Scott (1811-1878) [NR] was architect of Victorian gothic of St Pancras Station and Brighton College, He 'restored' and altered many of the cathedrals in England and Wales.

xxxv. Childwall Hall was built by John Nash for Isaac Greene whose daughter Mary married Bamber Gascoyne (1724-1791) [NR]; their sons Bamber (1757-1824) [NR] and Isaac (1763-1841) [NR] were MPs for Liverpool. A great-grandson, Robert Arthur Talbot Gascoyne-Cecil, 3rd Marquess of Salisbury KG GCVO PC FRS (1830-1903) [NR] was Prime Minister (1885-6, 1886-92, 1895-1902). Another, Maj-Gen Sir William Julius Gascoigne (1844-1926) commanded British troops in China and Hong Kong (1895-8) and is remembered by Gascoigne Road in Kowloon.

xxxvi. Pevsner p45.

xxxvii. The Slade School of Art was Alma Mater of Ben Nicholson OM (1894-1982) [NR].

xxxviii. Barrow Records Office BPR/1/C/5/12/9

xxxix. Barrow Records Office Ref BPR/1/C/5/12/36. 25 May 1883 under the supervision and design of Paley & Austin Architects, Lancaster. Signed by Edward Wadham and James Ramsden and witnessed by Thomas Butler.

xl. Barrow Records Office BPR/1/V/7/1.

xli. Rev Allan Mitchell, Vicar, says quinquennial inspections seldom require work on the structure. The belfry has been enhanced and now has 10 bells provided by a £110,000 English Heritage grant.

xlii. An 'Old English' cut-glass water jug in Frances's will is still in the author's possession and a tortoise-shell tea caddy is in his sister Ann's possession.

xliii. Barrow Records Office Ref BDB 17/SP3/12: Sale catalogue May 1920, and (JG) the will of James Garden: His 'attendant' Joseph Raiper was left £1 in James's will.

xliv. Barrow Record Office Ref BA/S/D/3/5. Advert in Barrow-in-Furness, Ulverston and District Illustrated 1895; 1896.

xlv. Manchester Diocese was carved out of Chester Diocese in 1847 and the collegiate church of St Mary, St Denys and St George became a cathedral.

xlvi. Ethel's father, Charles Henry Normanton (1843-1906) was born illegitimately in Ashton under Lyne in Derbyshire. He moved around in search of work. He settled not far from the Garratt family, who may have known him. Charles and Ethel had two boys, Mowbray (1914-1978) and Quentin (1917-1944). Mowbray, an RAF pilot, was 'shot to pieces more times than I can remember by vast numbers of Jap aircraft which were very much superior jobs to the antique things (Hurricanes) we were coping with which must have been 'wished' onto the Air Purchasing section by some pretty astute second hand dealers.' He escaped from Java. Quentin, a Flying Officer in the RAF, died at the hands of the Japanese after the fall of Singapore. Letter from Mowbray Garden. March 1943.

xlvii. Mark Carven and Mark Rickhall received £50 and £30 respectively in James's will.

xlviii. The real estate (30 houses plus Hamilton House and some land) was worth £4,365. William accepted £3,000, his sister Maggie £2,000.

xlix. Barrow Record Office Ref BSUD/D/14/4 and BDHJ/431/3/1/1-BDHJ/431/3/5/2.

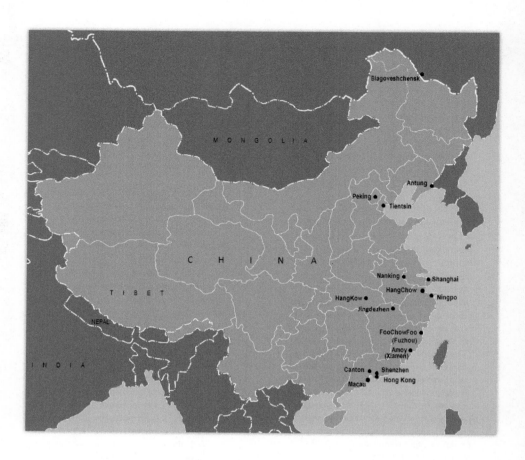

China

Our family has had an exotic fascination for the Orient for 150 years – its people, their dress, its buildings. In my dressing up box are tattered costumes from the time when Shanghai was the dazzling dancing world of glamour[1]. If there's ever an occasion (pantomimes), I'll grab the part of an Eastern potentiate. My great aunt **Bertie**, whose sense of dress was historic, brought home more than fine clothes and exotica from China[2]. As well as pagoda match-boxes and ivory fans, there was that air of mystery, pizzazz. Her voice rang with light confidence, humour and irony.

Bertie was 14 years younger than her husband, **Jack Smart.** After Jack died in 1939, she lived out her last years in Crowborough. Although I was only seven when she died, I remember her vividly. She was larger-than-life, amused at everything, relaxed and fun to be with, with her outrageous dress sense and the wealth to indulge it. Jack was the manager of the Shanghai Branch of the Hongkong and Shanghai Bank when Shanghai was in its heyday. It was the jazz age with carefree morals such as practised by the doubtful Duchess of Windsor, the dubious Wallis Simpson, who sought out the sinful side of Shanghai long before she educated Edward VIII in its ways [3]. Jack and Bertie's only son, **Douglas Smart**, was my Godfather. He spent his working life in Hong Kong. China enchanted me for all sorts of reasons.

Bertie Smart (née Garden) (1877-1955) in her garden with her niece Jean Haskins (née Tresidder) (1904-1976).

✳ ✳ ✳ ✳

The Opium Wars

Before the Opium Wars, China was closed to Europe. Traders were allowed into the one port, Canton (Guangzhou) for about six months of the year.

Britain couldn't get enough silk, porcelain and tea during the early 1800s – all unique to China. China had the secret of their production. It would only accept silver in payment. Despite the fact the East India Company had the exclusive trading rights, it found it was losing money. Eventually it discovered something which went down well with the Chinese: opium[4].

The East India Company grew the opium in Bengal and made the short crossing to Canton across the South China Sea. Because it was addictive, opium sales took off with avengeance. A Chinese Emperor had forbidden its trade a hundred years before, but his mandarins ignored this edict[5]. They were 1,400 miles away in the south of his vast empire, growing very rich. It did not take long for silver to start to flow out of China instead of into it.

Dressing up, in 1959, with our noses in the air. The author, second left, with his cousins David (b1954), Audrey (b1951), Geoffrey (b1950) and Bernard (b1953) are trying to look like Chinese mandarins.

---

1. *1920s.*
2. *Bertha Louisa Garden (1877-1955) married John Douglas Smart (1863-1939) in 1903.*
3. *Edward VIII (1894-1972) abdicated in 1936 to marry Wallis, Duchess of Windsor (born Bessie Wallis Warfield; also known by her married names of Wallis Spencer and Wallis Simpson) (1896-1986) [NR]*
4. *Foreign traders were excluded from April to September, depending on winds and cargos. Whampoa Island was the landing place for their Factories.*
5. *1729 by Emperor Yung Cheng (1678-1735) [NR].*

Ingleside, Crowborough, 1924, home of the Smarts after Jack's retirement in 1922.

Wild Shanghai party in Fancy Dress c 1905. Bertie seated to the right, Jack, the sweep, bottom left.

When in 1833 the British Government ended the East India Company's monopoly, trade increased. The new Emperor was in a right strop – a reclaimed drug addict himself, he launched a campaign to stop it[6]. He sent his top mandarin, Imperial High Commissioner Lin, to sort it out[7]. Lin's hard line, ordering that all stores of opium in the Canton docks to be burnt, literally inflamed the situation.

As far as the two top traders, James Matheson and William Jardine, the *Tai Pans* of British business, were concerned, that meant war. They went back to London and lobbied parliament[8]. In 1840, Lord Palmerston, as Foreign Secretary, mobilised 3 battleships, 14 frigates and sloops, and 4 armed steamers carrying 4,000 troops[i]. The Royal Navy bombarded town after town halfway up the coast to Peking.

Imagine then the Emperor's officials' surprise when the only land demanded in settlement was what Palmerston later complained was a 'barren rock, with hardly a house upon it.'[9] Hong Kong harbour was the prize they wanted. The **Treaty of Nanking** 1842 also opened the 'Treaty Ports' – Amoy (Xiamen), Foochowfoo (Fuzhou), Ningpo and Shanghai.

The opium now poured into China fivefold and by 1856, when the Chinese tried again to stop it, seizing a British vessel, another war began. The British stormed Canton. They moved northwards and occupied Tientsin (Tianjin). A new treaty was concluded in June 1858.

But the following year, when the British envoy, Sir Frederick Bruce, was repulsed on his way to Peking (Beijing) to ratify the treaty, war resumed – the Emperor's Summer Palaces were notoriously ransacked and Peking fell[10]. A **Convention of Peking** was added to the **Treaty of Tientsin** which let Britain gain a further patch of land, this time **Kowloon** peninsula south of Boundary Street on the mainland side of Hong Kong harbour. The biggest changes were freedom of religion. Foreigners were able to travel freely. Opium was legalised and China was crushed.

The New Territories, the size of Cornwall, came later, in 1898, after another dispute – this time on a 99-year lease. Ninety years later, when I was there, the Island and Kowloon had grown so much that the people couldn't survive without water or food from China. Negotiation was inevitable. Sir David Wilson and Sir Percy Craddock were busy negotiating in complete secrecy, much to the disgust of many local Chinese[11]. The sinologists were stumbling, however – Margaret Thatcher literally[12]. In her head, she thought it would be as easy as winning the Falklands War but she was poorly briefed and had little concept of the culture. The Chinese mind-set was totally foreign to a Grantham shopkeeper's daughter. During her meeting with Deng XiaoPing, he spat into a large spittoon every time she tried to make a point – deliberately[13]. Unnerved, Thatcher tripped down the steps on the way out. Terribly inauspicious, said everybody, on both sides. Bad ji. Like Lord Napier 150 years before, she'd been outwitted. Unlike Palmerston, she chose not to send her troops in. Hong Kong has been returned to China under an agreement allowing British-style government for a further 50 years – 'one country, two systems,' said Deng XiaoPing.

6. *The Daoguang Emperor (MinNing) (1782-1850) [NR] reigned 1820-50.*
7. *Lin Tse Hsu (Zexu) (1785-1850) [NR].*
8. *Sir James Nicolas Sutherland Matheson, 1st Baronet (1796-1878) [NR]; William Jardine (1784-1843) [NR].*
9. *Henry John Temple, 3rd Viscount Palmerston KG GCB PC (1784-1865) [NR] Foreign Secretary for most of the 1830s-1851, Prime Minister 1855-58, 1859-65.*
10. *Sir Frederick (William Adolphus) Wright-Bruce, GCB (1814-1867) [NR].*
11. *David Clive Wilson, Baron Wilson of Tillyorn KT GCMG PRSE (b1935) [NR]; Sir Percy Cradock GCMG (1923-2010) [NR]; Wilson chose a Chinese name with unfortunate connotations. One translation was 'two ghosts knocking at the door'. Another was 'hypocrisy to the extent of danger'. He changed it.*
12. *Baroness Margaret Hilda Thatcher LG OM PC FRS (née Roberts), (1925-2013).*
13. *Deng Xiaoping (1903-1997) [NR] Paramount Leader of the People's Republic of China 1978-92.*

The Taiping Rebellion

It was soon after the Convention of Peking, which allowed in foreign missionaries, that **Arthur Moule** arrived in China[14]. The first cousin of my great aunt Annie's husband, Horace Moule Evans (Chapter 6), set foot on Chinese soil in 1861. Prior to that, missionary effort had been cloaked in secrecy since Robert Morrison first established a foothold in 1807[15]. Hudson Taylor, a missionary from Barnsley, had arrived in 1856, and a year later **George Moule**, who was Arthur's brother[16]. Hudson Taylor started a mission, translating the New Testament into colloquial Chinese, wearing oriental clothes and a pigtail like the Chinese. He learnt the local dialects. The approach worked. Taylor was the most influential missionary of the nineteenth century, founding the China Inland Mission in 1865. The number of Christians soared during the 50 years of his activity.

Arthur was 26 when he stepped off the ship at Ningpo. After training at the Church Missionary Society's (CMS) College in Islington, he married Eliza Bernau, a missionary's daughter, and set off to join his brother George, who'd arrived four years before[ii]. The brothers stayed in Ningpo for the next fifteen years. Soon after they arrived, the two of them found themselves in the middle of a revolution.

One thinks of China as a peaceful place until the British turned up. It was anything but. The Chinese Emperor had little grasp on his provinces, a problem to this day: 'Commanding an empty fortress,' was how they put it. The ethnic population, the Han Chinese, resented their rulers from Manchuria[17]. During the long reign of the Qing Dynasty (since 1644) there had been plenty of rebellions.

When Arthur and George arrived in China, the leader of the T'ai P'ing (or Taiping) rebellion, Hung Siu-ts'uan (Hong Xiquan), had been stirring things up[18]. In 1850 he'd spotted how defenceless the Emperor's forces were. He'd discovered a smattering of Christianity and altered it to his advantage. Using portions of the tracts he'd been given, he formed a 'Society of Worshippers of God', the Shang-ti Hwei. Ten years' later, the Taipings controlled 13 of the Chinese Provinces, holding sway over an area the size of Europe[19]. Starting with noble aims, it ended up like ISIS/Daesh with motley crowds of sensation seekers 'lacking character, education or morals.'[iii] 20 million lives were lost by the time Hung Siu-ts'uan had enthroned himself as 'heavenly king' in Nanking in 1853[iv].

Hung Siu-ts'uan enforced a corrupt version of morality. Opium smoking, adultery, gambling, tobacco, alcohol, prostitution, foot-binding and slavery were all prohibited. The Taipings executed anyone who pillaged. They were the first to end the imperial edict for all Chinese men to wear pigtails or 'queues'; but it was very much 'off with your head' if you refused to pay your Taiping taxes[v].

Arthur's stories of the rebellion make interesting reading. Ningpo was a walled city. When it closed its gates against the Taipings, he and George escaped to the north bank of the river and watched the Taiping invade the city. It was like medieval warfare: the defenders using spiked pieces of timber, dropping them on the invaders. The Taipings found tables and mattresses, put them over their heads and the beams bounced off. They scaled the walls 'like wild cats'. The Manchu soldiers fled, shedding their uniforms and merging in with the crowded population.

Bishop George Moule (1828-1912)

Archdeacon Arthur Moule (1836-1913) and Eliza's Golden Wedding in 1911.

The Taiping sign of Blessedness and the beatitudes

14. *Ven Arthur Evans Moule BD (1836-1918) married Eliza Agnes Bernau (1842-1925) in 1861.*
15. *Rev Robert Morrison DD FRS (1782-1834) [NR] married (1) Mary Morton (1792-1821) [NR] in 1809, (2) Eliza Armstrong (1795-1874) [NR] in 1824.*
16. *James Hudson Taylor MRCS FRGS (1832-1905) [NR]; Rt Rev George Evans Moule DD (1828-1912) married Adelaide Sarah Griffiths (née Moule) (1828-1909) in 1847.*
17. *The Qing Dynasty (1644-1912).*
18. *Hong XiuQuan (1814-64) [NR].*
19. *1,200 miles long by 600 miles wide – 26,000 square miles in 1861.*

George and Arthur did their best to save refugees, Christian and non-Christian. The Taiping chiefs eventually gave them passes to allow them through the gates. The first time through, a burly guard seized Arthur by the shoulder, broke a stick over the backs of the Chinese men and ordered them all to go back. Arthur's terrified companions were scared stiff. They beseeched Arthur to obey the guards but, as only a self-confident Englishman of the nineteenth century could, Arthur looked indignant, told the guard off, and marched the party off to the waiting ferry.

By now, the British had a foothold in China. The Royal Navy ousted the Taipings but when Arthur's first son was to be born, in September 1862, a mighty army of up to 100,000 Taipings was about to retake the city for a second time. The remaining British naval captain had only 70 men but he ordered them to march round the city walls giving the impression of a strong English Army defending them. It did the trick. The townsfolk spread the word and the danger went away. It wasn't until 1864, three years after Arthur arrived, that the British succeeded in putting down the Taiping revolution for good[20]. General Gordon was one of the British commanders who cleaned things up, earning the Emperor's untold praise[21].

I mention General Gordon because I've heard it told that my great grandfather, Dr John Nicholas Tresidder, tended to his medical needs. Exactly how or when I am uncertain. Gordon was Military Secretary to the Viceroy of India for a short time in 1879, two years after John Nicholas Tresidder had retired. Had they met in London? 'Chinese' Gordon was a bit of a loner, and an evangelical Christian. After some years lying fallow, he was asked by the Egyptian government to take over the job of Governor of Sudan. He was cut down in Khartoum, provoking grief in England on a scale similar to that which followed Princess Diana's death[vi].

Gordon was seen as a martyr and a hero. Gordon songs and Gordon poems poured from the printing presses. Gordon memorials were unveiled and Gordon Boys' Clubs opened all over the country. Over twenty-five books were written about this hero, plus a far greater number of pamphlets and articles. In 1898, General Kitchener reaped his revenge on Sudan[22]. His troops defeated most of the Mahdi army at the Battle of Omdurman.

George and Arthur were masters of all their trades: evangelism, pastoral work, education, writing and speaking in Chinese, composing hymns and journalism for the North China News. George published a classical Chinese version of the Book of Common Prayer[vii]. Arthur preferred preaching, not only inside church, but also in schools, on board boats and along the roadside, working from village by village. The brothers set up a mission at Hangchow and another at Chuki.

Arthur returned to Shanghai in 1882 after a break in England and was appointed Archdeacon of mid-China, two years after his brother George had been consecrated Bishop of Mid-China. Arthur stayed for 12 years more until 1894 when ill-health forced him to resign. He left behind a congregation of 180 members, 5 schools and 7 Chinese teachers. After eight years back in England, he couldn't keep away and returned to serve in Chekiang and Kiangsu until the age of 76. In retirement, he was appointed Vice President of the CMS.

George, who stayed on, was mixed up in another rebellion – the Boxer Rebellion (1899-1901) – appalling for both Chinese and Western Christians. The British Consul persuaded him to leave Hangchow for the relative safety of Shanghai. When he returned, he found that his friends, the Chinese officials, had made sure his house and its contents were intact. His wife, Adelaide, died at Hangchow in 1909 – she'd been by his side for 52 years. When he died three years later, at his brother Bishop Handley Moule's home at Auckland Castle, Durham, *The Times* commented: 'When George had originally gone to China, protestant converts numbered

1908 Episcopal Conference, Hangzhou. George is sitting second right with his wife Adelaide

20. *When the British entered Nanking the heavenly leader, Hung Siu-ts'ian (1813-1864) [NR], committed suicide.*

21. *Maj-Gen Charles George Gordon CB (1833-1885) [NR] nicknamed 'Chinese Gordon'.*

22. *Field-Marshal Horatio Herbert Kitchener, 1st Earl Kitchener, KG KP GCB OM GCSI GCMG GCIE PC (1850-1916) [NR]*

a few thousand at most. By 1900, very many thousands suffered death with calm courage and since then Chinese Christendom has rapidly increased.'[viii]

George and Arthur Moules' pioneering work lived on to the next generation – five of their sons were missionaries. George's eldest son, **Henry** served in Hangchow and Ningpo for 18 years and Henry's brother in-law, **Norman Pope**, died in St Andrew's Vicarage, Kowloon where my nephew, **Simon Gates**, was to minister 75 years later[23].

※ ※ ※ ※

A Study in Oxford

In 2006-7, I spent an academic year in Oxford with the Centre for the Study of Christianity in China. It was largely funded by supportive church members in America. I slept and worked in the small bungalow in Polstead Road, which had once belonged to 'Lawrence of Arabia'[24]. His parents had built it at the bottom of their garden for him. His portrait was in a stained glass window. The garden was full of juicy fig trees brought home from his travels. I had a bed in one room and an office in the other with a small kitchen and bathroom in between.

My Oxford year opened up a moving legacy of commitment over conflict. I learnt not only of early Chinese missionaries but also of what is currently happening today. I met people who were active behind the bamboo curtain – ethnic Chinese Americans, Singaporean publishers, Malaysian-born politicians, Hong Kong educationalists, as well as Chinese academics and business people. I met Hudson Taylor's great grandson and the brother of the Last Emperor of China, himself a Christian. I met the Chinese Ambassador at Lambeth Palace and some of those diplomats that had lost us Hong Kong. It showed me the sacrifices that English, American and Chinese Christians have made to spread the gospel – martyrs.

The aim of the Oxford Centre in the short time I was there was to bring Western and Eastern Theology closer together – mutual study and understanding. Essential: in the West we talk of Christianity but in China there is Catholicism and Protestantism, two of five 'official' religions. Then there are the unspecified underground churches.

Western thought does not translate directly in the East and vice versa, as a Tokyo student once explained to me – she had two parallel thought processes going on inside her brain, hence the importance of the Christian creeds being fully understood. Christianity is not a Western religion imposed on China – it has been there since the 7th century but universal dialogue helps. For example, in 1860, the weird Taiping cult got going from a misreading of tracts put out by one of Robert Morrison's Chinese helpers. As recently as 2014, members of the 'Third Redemption of Christ' or the 'Apostolic Congregation' battered a woman to death in a McDonalds Restaurant in Zhaoyuan because she wouldn't give them her contact details[ix].

The Centre's plan was to network with the twenty Theological schools dotted around the Universities in China. We invited some of their Professors over to Oxford for a three-month sabbatical. We set up a Chinese theology library. We organised academic conferences, one in the Library of Congress at Washington and another at the British Library in London. These inspired new research and scholarship during the 200th anniversary year of Robert Morrison's first footstep onto Chinese soil. Sadly, the Oxford Centre was all too short-lived but its good work carries on.

Lawrence of Arabia's bungalow in Polstead Road, Oxford. Two Chinese Professors on sabbatical in 2007

A bridge between cultures: academics from around the world in front of the Library of Congress in Washington commemorating the two-hundredth anniversary of Robert Morrison's arrival in China

---

23. *Rev Henry William Moule BA (1871-1953) CMS Missionary in Hangkow 1896-1900; Shaohing 1900-02; Hangkow 1902-13; Ningpo 1913-15. Examining Chaplain to the Bishops of Mid China and Chekiang; Rev Norman Christopher Pope BA (1882-1918) was 36 when he died; Ven Simon Philip Gates MA (b1960).*

24. *Thomas Edward Lawrence CB DSO (1888-1935) [NR].*

East window of the Morrison Chapel Macau, with the opening words of St John's Gospel 'In the beginning was the word'

The Morrison Chapel in Macau

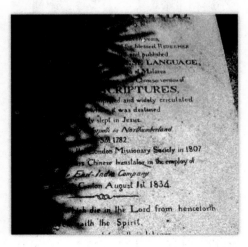

Robert Morrison's grave

The Morrison Chapel, Macau

Robert Morrison features in our family history in another way. For two years after his first degree, my nephew **Simon Gates** helped to run the chapel in the cemetery which Robert Morrison had bought to bury his first wife[25]. Macau (Macao) had been a Portuguese colony since 1557. Situated on the west bank of the Pearl River about 40 miles west of Hong Kong, Macau was the haven for European traders lying over from Canton, before Hong Kong was established by the British.

Robert Morrison published the first Chinese bible (completed 1819), and a Chinese-English dictionary (1823) and printed many pamphlets. He was paid by the East India Company to help in its negotiations with the Chinese authorities. He accompanied Lord Amherst in his (failed) attempt to parley with the Emperor of China in 1816[26]. John Morrison, his son, picked up a fluent knowledge of written and spoken Chinese and played a crucial part in the ceding of Hong Kong to the British in 1843[27].

Both John and his father were buried at the East India Company's Protestant graveyard in Macau[x]. What started as a cemetery chapel became a place of regular worship. Under the trusteeship of the British Government and later the Hongkong and Shanghai Bank, it has been run as an Anglican Church.

Simon went to Macau in 1982 with the Church Missionary Society (CMS) to teach English in an Anglican School despite the fact that few of the teaching staff spoke English and Simon spoke no Chinese or even Portuguese, the official language. CMS had complained that the previous volunteer had been allocated unsuitable accommodation – a partitioned-off corner of one room, used as Kindergarten by day and a music room at night – so Simon was invited to share the vicarage of St Mark's church. He found the air-conditioning a God-send.

Simon's fertile mind was soon finding ways to cure the boredom of too few lessons to teach and he found the Vicar, Paul Lau, more than happy for him to preach occasionally at the Morrison Chapel. The current church building dates from 1921, after an Archdeacon had discovered it being used as a firecracker factory and had had it restored[xi]. The congregation was small when Simon arrived. There was a borrowed organ and 15 tatty hymn books[xii]. The 200th anniversary of Robert Morrison's birth had been forgotten, so they celebrated his 201st[xiii]. By Lent 1983, they'd started all sorts of improvements – Evening Services, Businessmen's monthly lunches and a Gideon's group – 40 attended the October Harvest Festival.

The Rev Joyce Bennett, one of the first women to be ordained in the Anglican Church, came over to preach. She had the care of CMS missionaries in the Far East including Simon[28].

Of course not all goes well. The inscrutable Chinese tend to put up the bamboo curtain when they want to express their displeasure. In his first year, Simon decided to fail half his students as they weren't pulling their weight. Much loss of face all round and Simon found that his planned trip to China failed to materialise: 'No visas possible.'[xiv] Nevertheless, his message had hit home and next year the standards were higher. The Vicar, Paul Lau, seemed to be criticised for stirring his people up with the gospel. He'd appointed Simon Vice-Chairman of Vestry, the Finance and the Development Committees. Then the church authorities demoted Paul Lau and chucked Simon out of the Vicarage. Simon found himself back in that partitioned classroom, with a 30% cut in pay. As the partitions were only 6-foot tall, the sleeping quarters were very noisy, quite apart from privacy issues, cooking and washing. Nothing else was

25. *Ven Simon Philip Gates (b1960) married Helen Rosalind Shepherd (b1967) in 1996.*
26. *William Pitt Amherst, 1st Earl Amherst GCH PC (1773-1857) [NR], later the weak Governor-General of India 1823-8. He was shipwrecked on the way home from Peking having failed to meet the Emperor.*
27. *John Robert Morrison (1814-1843) [NR].*
28. *Rev Joyce Bennett OBE BA DipTheol CertEd PhD (b1923) [NR] ordained in 1971, was an unofficial member of LegCo. She headed up St Catherine's, a high-rise school for girls in Kwun Tong and remained in Hong Kong from 1949 until she retired in 1983.*

provided but a cold-water tap in the garden and the use of an incredibly dirty kitchen. All hugely demoralising.

A Sixth-former's family gave Simon a meal and a shower each evening and the congregation of the Morrison Chapel came to the rescue. Thanks to some stalwarts, notably Brenda and Richard Histed, a flat was found for him. The gospel began to flourish again. The Chapel was repainted, the curtains and hangings replaced. Carpets and heaters were installed. He was invited to join the Rotary Club, which sponsored an Interest Club. At this stage, Simon was still considering his role 'as a future minister.'[xv] It is a huge testament to his conviction that these machinations did little to dissuade him. The church is made up of sinners (including me); I have seen more than my fair share of church politics as a Churchwarden who had to handle a nasty pastoral breakdown between Vicar and Congregation in Wetherby. If you hold onto something higher in life, miracles often happen. Simon saw a miracle over his two years and the English church in Macau has born testimony to that ever since.

Bay of Macau, drawn by George Chinnery in the 1850s, is now filled in and full of skyscrapers

❋ ❋ ❋ ❋

Stimulating Shenzhen

Twenty something years later, in 2007-2008, my son **Jonny Haskins** spent a year in Shenzhen[29]. Shenzhen is just over the border from Hong Kong and hardly existed when Simon was in Macau. It was established as a Special Economic Zone by Deng Xiaoping in 1980. It aimed to ride on the coat-tails of the capitalist Hong Kong, retaining Chinese control by the one-party socialist state. In 1989, when Deng effectively orchestrated the mowing down of students in Tiananmen Square to squash democracy, China was in a parlous state – economically poor and undergoing political change. *'Gate of Heavenly Peace'* it was not. But as I write, China has amassed mountains of money[xvi]. High speed trains run to the top of the world in Tibet. A diaspora of students sucks up knowledge across the world. One of my bosses, in his previous job, had advised China on the building of its first nuclear power station; now China is advising Britain[xvii].

Brenda and Richard Histed with Simon Gates, Sep 2013

Shenzhen literally means 'Deep Drains' – it was built on paddy fields. In 1988 I could stand at Mai Po, a peaceful place, and look over to the lush verdant landscape on the Chinese side. Coolies with conical straw hats, balancing sticks with loads on either end, tended the farmland – it was a place where the Chinese tried to escape to Hong Kong. Now the roles are reversed. Thousands go from Hong Kong to work in Shenzhen, almost a Province in its own right. Enlarged to 790 square miles, the sub-province is covering itself in concrete – there are over 200 buildings over 200 metres high and millions of dollars of foreign investment pours in. I expect that one day it will have cars that stop at the traffic lights, drive on the correct side of the road and stop at pedestrian crossings. Shenzhen is more like modern China than either Macau or Hong Kong and the open sewers inhabited by rats which Jonny saw daily are almost a thing of the past. Jonny went there to do his year out in architecture, between degrees, at a similar age to Simon.

Shenzhen looking towards the Hong Kong border

29. *Jonathan Neil Haskins (b1986).*

Marks and Spencer's traded in the Ocean Terminal, Hong Kong, in 1973. M&S subsequently retrenched, opening again in 1988.

Jon's Slinky – showroom project – put into construction, which led to many more showroom commissions after he left China

Douglas Smart (1904-1977) with his wife Alice Mead in 1951

After Macau, Simon went back to Durham University to train for the ministry, returning to Hong Kong as an Associate Minister for four years 1991-5 at St Andrew's in Nathan Road. There he met his future wife, Helen Shepherd, who was on a posting with Marks & Spencer[31]. So here we have history repeating itself: Simon, Helen and their three children regularly return to China, visiting an orphanage in mainland China.

"Nowhere is success so successful as in the East," said my great grandfather's friend, John Sherer, 100 years ago[xviii]. Both Simon and Jonny found the heady scent of the Far East intoxicating. Exhilaration and dejection come in heady doses. Westerners in the Far East are handed a lot more rope to hang themselves. Used wisely, the rope could haul them up to great heights. Here, it enabled them both to reach potential they didn't know they had so early in their career. "I ... make all the decisions and then expect to be told off but at least it gets things done," wrote Simon in 1983[xix].

Decisiveness: I found many Cantonese reluctant to err but eager to fulfil. In the imperial past, the Chinese practice was to wipe out a whole family if the Emperor's displeasure fell on one member of the family, which rather adjusted people's thinking, if not the gene pool[xx]. Some of the jobs I have seen others do in the British Civil Service would have dashed all originality from my brain but I was lucky. Right or wrong, the Far East has proved to be a good learning experience for all of us.

Jonny's experience was not so extreme as Simon's in one respect but a shock to the system, nevertheless. Shenzhen was more Chinese in custom and practice than even Macau was. He arrived in Shenzhen with similar hope and euphoria – 'I love it here' – soon to be challenged by the sparse living, the sparse diet, the sparse medical provision and the strange oriental logic. Yet he shone at work and his architectural designs were speedily converted into reality in front of his eyes, by people who assisted him in ways that would never happen in Britain. He made good friends.

❊ ❊ ❊ ❊

The Hong Kong Architect

It was my architect Godfather who helped to acquaint me with China. Jack and Bertie's son, **Douglas Smart**, was my mother Jean's first cousin[31]. The same age as each other, Douglas and Jean were close, as close as people could be on the opposite side of the world. They'd spent time together when Douglas was training to be an architect. Both of them were single children, from the creative side of my family[xxi]. Douglas was born in 1904 in the penthouse of the Hongkong and Shanghai Bank on the Bund in Shanghai – his father, the Bank Manager, lived 'over the shop'. HSBC (as it now is) had been founded in 1865[xxii].

Apart from the Second World War, Douglas spent most of his working life from 1931 as an architect with the Hong Kong firm Palmer & Turner[xxiii]. Both the Hongkong Bank's HQ at 1 Queen's Road Hong Kong and its principal branch in Shanghai had been designed by Palmer & Turner[xxiv]. When it came to rebuilding the one in Shanghai, Douglas's father Jack was just about to retire and he spent his last days briefing the chief architect 'Tug' Wilson on a daily basis[32].

Jack returned to England (via New York) in 1922 just about the time the old Victorian baroque building was being knocked down. Ten years' later, when the bank wanted to show off with a *Moderne* stunner in Hong Kong, Wilson was commissioned again. Douglas, newly qualified as

---

30. *Helen Rosalind Shepherd (b1967) married Ven Simon Gates in 1996. Their children are Charis Ruth Gates (b1999), Anna Rosemary Gates (b2001) and Samuel Nathan Gates (b2004).*

31. *George Douglas Smart (1904-1971) married Alice Louise Mead (poss 1917-2001) in 1950. They had no children. She had been married before and had a daughter, Yelena Beaugrand.*

32. *George Leopold Wilson FRIBA (1880-1967) [NR].*

an architect and still in his twenties, was taken on. Having come back with his father via New York in 1922 he had seen the shape and style of modern architecture there, of which there was almost nothing in London[xxv]. Douglas sat down to work with Wilson on the design of the white 12-storey *Art Deco* Hongkong bank structure so unlike anything built there before, and unlike anything Wilson had touched previously. By the time it was finished, 4 years later in 1935, the new structure dominated the central harbour-front. It set a new standard. Hong Kong's first skyscraper, the first with air conditioning, was the tallest building anywhere from Cairo to San Francisco. It had a helicopter landing pad on the roof and 12 lifts that sped to the top at 500 feet per minute. Breath-taking.

In the noise of war, work was drying up in Shanghai and Hong Kong. Douglas opened a branch office in Rangoon. He escaped the Japanese invasion as a result and helped re-establish the Hong Kong office after the war , becoming senior partner after Wilson retired in 1950. As the mainstay from the 'Old Guard', 'gruff, bluff and often brusque,' he was incredibly 'well-liked by both the staff and clients.'[xxvi] I guess I was the son he never had. He sent me amazing presents – £25 at Christmas at a time when my grandmother sent me two half-crowns (25p) – a tricycle that I was never parted from and a bicycle he won in a raffle at a London Club[xxvii].

In 1950 at the age of 46, Douglas married **Alice Mead**. They lived on the Hong Kong Peak, latterly in a luxurious flat he fashioned at Ho Tung Gardens, 500 metres above sea level, with its wonderful views of sea so blue, with the misty mountains floating in the sky[33]. It was one of the former homes – all sumptuous – of Sir Robert Ho Tung, the first Chinaman to live on the Peak[xxviii].

In 1962, Douglas retired to Piltdown in Sussex where he'd designed his own state-of-the-art house on a plot of land that his mother had acquired, with under-floor heating, a circular staircase, bar, curved sofas, a macerator in the double-sink, an American-sized fridge, bidets in the bathrooms, a sun-patio with a view to die for and a golf course beyond – all taken for granted now but awesome in its time[xxix]. He died in Stoke Mandeville Hospital after falling down the stairs in a Calais hotel on Christmas night 1970[xxx].

⁂ ⁂ ⁂ ⁂

Hong Kong Bank, Palmer and Turner architects 1935

Jahore State Building 1939 at Johore Bahru, near Singapore, was commissioned by the Sultan to help streamline British colonial rule. This model was made for the Golden Gate International Exposition – San Francisco's 1939-40 World Fair. Douglas Smart second left. It was the tallest building in the town until the 1970s

The Falls, on the Peak, Hong Kong – built by Palmer & Turner for Sir Robert Ho Tung in 1928 – Douglas Smart lived in a flat there in the 1950s

The author on his tricycle October. 1952

Central Hong Kong when Douglas retired in the 1960s – much of it built by Palmer & Turner

Douglas and Alice Smart on the staircase at Parkwood House, Piltdown – with decanter and soda syphon on the bar, 1962

33. *Victoria Peak is 552 m (1,811 ft) high*

Missie Lee

As well as Douglas and the dressing-up Chinese-style, I relished an Arthur Ransome book which I had won as a school prize in 1958. I was nine and couldn't put *Missie Lee* down. It tells of Captain Flint and the children shipwrecked off the coast of China and rescued by a Mandarin's daughter whose only wish was to attend Cambridge University. On the way to a conference in Kuala Lumpur, fifty years after reading that book, I found myself penning a pantomime loosely based on the story[xxxi]. The attitudes of those fictional Chinese and the antics of those fictional children had sustained me throughout those fifty years.

The Chinese still use the teaching techniques pioneered by missionaries such as George and Arthur Moule, yet their methods are now being studied by English educators because they are getting superior results. The British education model thought up by Lord Macaulay (another distant relative) in the 19th century went right round the world[34]. A tour guide in St Lucia told me, 'We use the education system you taught us and we do it better;' yet English public schools and universities are full of aspiring middle-class Chinese who have some of the same ideals as Missie Lee[xxxii]. The pupils may prefer the flexible exploration of ideas, but their tiger mothers' lust after straw boaters, the old boy network and the consequential work opportunities that the kudos of English education attracts. Carolyn and I acted as guardians for the son of Carolyn's boss at *Sara Beattie Secretarial College* when we returned from Hong Kong. Whilst at *Bootham School* in York, Colin Fan was the third generation to use the tuck box depicted in Chapter 16.

Tuck Box – with the third generation's name painted on the top

Gordon Garden (1875-1919)

Shanghai Cup 1919

✳ ✳ ✳ ✳

The Spy who came in from the cold

From the days of Drake, Rashleigh and Hawkins, there was adventure in discovery, the Far East included. Auntie Bertie's youngest brother, **Gordon Garden** born in 1875, liked adventure too[35]. He qualified as a Master Mariner of foreign-going ships in March 1905 at the age of thirty, having first signed up for the sea, aged seventeen, on square-rigged sailing vessels[xxxiii].

In February 1896, Gordon travelled across the snow-covered United States of America, with packing cases, and even an incubator, planning to settle in San Francisco[xxxiv]. His travels took him from Southampton via New York, Detroit, to Chicago. He took the Union Pacific railway the 3,000 mile journey through Council Buffs, Cheyenne, Green River and met cowboys and Indians at Winnemucca (where the women gambled all day) before arriving in San Francisco dusty and unshaven.

By 1911, Gordon had decided California was not for him, and had found service in China as an Imperial Customs Officer at Hangkow (Wuhan)[xxxv]. He was living with his wife Minnie, 500 miles up the Yangtze River whilst his younger sister Bertie looked out from the security of the bank's penthouse over the Bund in Shanghai, near its river mouth. Gordon was expecting to be posted to Antung (Dandong), a town on the border between Manchuria and (North) Korea – the Japanese were infiltrating and it needed someone with diplomatic skills to sort things out.

Apart from a couple of well-composed letters and some engraved silver, there's little of his life of risk and adventure for us to cling on to. It was a period of international insecurity, with the 'Last Emperor' of China overthrown and the Russian Revolution in its infancy. Nothing was settled in Siberia two thousand miles to the north of where he lived. I have

---

34. *Thomas Babington Macaulay, 1st Baron Macaulay PC (1800-1859).*
35. *Henry Gordon Garden (1875-1919).*

a silver cup that Gordon won in March 1919, when he played in the Shanghai Golf Club's monthly tournament. Six months later, his body was dumped outside the British Embassy in Shanghai.[xxxvi] He'd been murdered in the Siberian border town of Blagoveshchensk. Is it just my imagination, or was Gordon Garden a spy? Who'd bothered to transport his body 1,350 miles across bleak terrain to the city of Shanghai? Who was the someone who was making this significant statement?

❋ ❋ ❋ ❋

A twenty-five year old in Hong Kong

If Hong Kong meant 'fragrant harbour' in 1830, it stunk to high heaven when I stepped off the plane at Kai Tak in November 1973.

I was twenty-five. I'd been in the Civil Service for seven months. I was amazingly privileged to be asked to go alone on a short-duty visit. The flight on an RAF VC10 took 24 hours from Brize Norton, stopping at Cyprus and the Maldives[36]. It flew over the war in Vietnam, which I could see below me. From a stuffy over-heated classroom of eight months earlier, I was sitting in the sun on the old Admiral's barge, in the eastern extremities of British waters. I was served with a Gurkha curry just the way my mother had been brought up to do it, with all the extras on the side – bananas, raisins, coconut – a totally foreign experience compared to my former East End of London teaching job.

The place was full of American servicemen on R&R. 'Suzie Wong' was going great guns in Wanchai. My hotel in Hysan Road, Causeway Bay, opposite the office, seemed

Hong Kong Harbour from the Peak, Dec 1973. Connaught Tower/Jardine Matheson House stood alone on the left. The other tall building is the Furama Hotel with its revolving restaurant at the top. To its right is HMS Tamar Royal Naval Base, and land reclamation is happening apace in front of Wanchai. Beyond that is Causeway Bay. Across the harbour on the left is the Star Ferry Terminal at Tsim Sha Sui on the Kowloon peninsula and at the back is the long strip of Kai Tak airport runway into the sea. Behind that, the Lion Rock hills divide Kowloon from the New Territories (new in 1898)

HMS Tamar Admiral's barge 1973

to be entirely staffed by boys in their early teens – secondary schooling wasn't compulsory in those days. Causeway Bay came alive at night, incense mixed with the smell of *ho sin* sauce, the naked light bulbs of the orange stall lit up the *Mama-Sans* touting outside the Fook King Joy massage parlour; a metal forge puthered out acrid flames between the snake restaurant and the quail stall; the birds, still alive, already plucked.[xxxvii]

One night, I walked alone up a path on Caroline Hill, one of many places then covered in tin huts. No one threatened me but the dogs growled, and then roared in chorus. I can still hear in my head the echoes that rang round the valley as I scarpered back down the ill-lit path – hounded out. Another night after dinner at the Jumbo Restaurant, I walked on the rat-infested boardwalks between the junks of Aberdeen Harbour. The harbour was a lot fuller. At that time Hong Kong had a floating population of 80,000. Murray MacLehose, the Governor, was set to change all that, constructing high-rise building after high-rise,

Wanchai Market 1973

Junks in Aberdeen Harbour 1973

Stanley Bay

View from Repulse Bay, Hong Kong Island

The Lily by Norman Foster (centre) replaced the apartments where the author resided at Repulse Bay

Surrounded by nothing in 1973, Connaught Tower was later renamed the Jardine Matheson building. Widely known as the tower of the 1,000 ***holes

all commanding magnificent views of the harbour, transforming the expectations of the local population[37]. There were two huge 'accidental' fires, perversely destroying humans as well as dwellings, in the ten days that I was there.

I had 1950s photos from Douglas in my pocket. By the 1970s, the buildings were double in height. The heavy Empire stone mansion blocks with their pillared verandas were being replaced by skyscrapers soaring up to the sky. The tallest was on reclaimed land, the 50 storey Connaught Centre, just completed, another building by my godfather's firm, Palmer & Turner.[xxxviii] The Centre was Jardine Matheson's signature statement in the heart of the commercial district. With its round windows it was occupied by their be-suited executives. The local Cantonese in their notoriously foul-mouthed way got it subtly right; they called it the Tower of the 1,000 ****holes.

✳ ✳ ✳ ✳

Three years in Hong Kong

The buildings had doubled in height again by 1987, when I and my young family went to live there for three years. The 1935 Hongkong Bank building had been torn down and Norman Foster's put in its place.[xxxix] Doubling the height: the *La Ronda* revolving restaurant in the Furama Hotel, where I had entertained my MOD counterpart in 1973 was still there at 33 storeys high[38]. However, there was a new one – the 1980 Hopewell Centre's *Revolving '66'* [floors] *Restaurant* now had the commanding view.[xl]

We led a privileged life in Hong Kong. By then, the locals liked being governed by the British. There were no bakers trying to poison the 'Gweilos' as there had been in 1857, no riots as in 1919 or 1967.[xli] There were no executions of Chinese criminals on the beach as there had been in the 1890s. Crime happened between the Triads but not generally with us expats. One American visitor saw the Rolls, Bentleys and BMWs and remarked, "Wow. These people must be rich" – it was only the billionaires who owned big cars. Few else could afford them. One Chinese lady had a pink Rolls Royce. We had a three-cylinder Suzuki, the smallest hatchback in the East, but it went up hills faster than her Rolls. The hills were steep. We lived on the south side of the Island in Repulse Bay[39]. Coming home from Causeway Bay on the

---

37. Crawford Murray MacLehose, Baron MacLehose of Beoch KT GBE KCMG KCVO DL (1917-2000) [NR] Governor of Hong Kong 1971-82; as well as the 10-year Housing Programme, he introduced 9-year compulsory education, and began the Mass Transit Railway (MTR). He set up the Independent Commission Against Corruption (ICAC) in 1974.

38. Lt Col Denis James Patrickson (1917-2001) [NR].

39. 129 Repulse Bay Road (Yat Ye Sam, Chin Sui Wan Do) was rebuilt after the British left by Chinachem. Designed by Sir Norman Foster, and called The Lily, it stood empty whilst Nina Wang (Kung Yu Sum) (1937-2007) [NR] disputed her husband's will.

No 6 bus was a roller-coaster ride; the top floor leaned alarmingly round each corner. For some of my time I worked in the military HQ building, appropriately (for a quarter Cornishman) called HMS Tamar.[xlii]

We belonged to two 'clubs' of the colonial type, one for Officers in the Services and the other for staff of the out-posted GCHQ[40]. We went to the Anglican St Stephen's Chapel in Stanley. At our first service, there were just a faithful few. We helped raise funds to build a meeting hall. Partly because of the fast turn-over of people on short-term contracts and the lack of any other obvious candidate and partly because of our energies in fundraising, I was elected Church warden early on during my tour. We had a change of Priests half way through. The new priest-in-charge used to the best advantage the hall that the first had had built. I struggled to reach the front to read the lesson at our last Easter service, with 250 people squashed into the restricted space and more in the adjacent hall.

Fundraising for the hall extension afforded lots of opportunities to get together. Junk trips to Lamma Island, Tram parties along Des Voeux Road, Skittles evenings at Chung Hom Kok, and Barn Dances in the China Fleet Club. There was a memorable Italian evening in our joint apartments with our friends and neighbours, the Kirkwood's, which involved ordering several items from a menu written in Italian, resulting in people eating ice-cream and gravy with a fork[41]. One member of the congregation was Ivy Fung, wife of the owner of the McDonald's franchise[42]. They lived in a big house below us in Repulse Bay with plenty of Filipina maids. When we began a kneeler project, she'd be bringing in a completed one each week – she'd set her whole household on the job.

In 1988, I helped organise the St Stephen's fete. There were parachutists from the nearby army base. Our saluting officer was amused by the wide-eyed winks he received from the pretty majorettes from the women's prison, as they processed past. A Jaguar car could be won if you threw a six on all six dice. We managed to make $150,000 (£12,500), a great deal more than any fete I've been part of in England.

The Gordon Hard Junk c1988

clowning at St Stephen's Fete, 1987

✳ ✳ ✳ ✳

The Japanese occupation of Hong Kong 1941-45

The chapel was set in St Stephen's College. It had been built in 1950 in memory of those British civilians who were interned on the Stanley peninsular during the Second World War. The Japanese captured Hong Kong on Christmas Day in 1941. When the Japanese arrived, the school was being used as a field hospital. They bayoneted the 60 helpless patients in their beds, shot the doctors and raped the nurses.[xliii] They interned some 3,000 individuals behind the barbed wire in Stanley Prison and the College grounds.

Another member of our congregation was May Ride, the wife of a heroic geneticist[43]. Nicknamed the 'Smiling Tiger', her husband had escaped from Shamshuipo camp under the Japanese occupation and set up the British Army Aid Group, which smuggled food drugs and money in and people out.[xliv] Over 1,000 escaped from one or other of the various camps across Hong Kong during those years of imprisonment.[xlv]

At the fete – Carolyn in white with friends, the Walkers. The boys (in blue) with Conchita and her friend on left.

Robert and Carolyn Haskins at the top of Tai Mo Shan

---

40. *United Services Recreation Club (USRC).*

41. *Lt Col David Kirkwood was Command Paymaster for the British Armed Forces in Hong Kong 1988-9.*

42. *Lady Ivy Fung née Kan (c1913-2000), wife of Sir Kenneth Fung Ping-fan (1911-2002).*

43. *Col Dr Sir Lindsay Tasman Ride CBE ED MA DM LLD RCS LRCP RAM (1898-1977) [NR] married his second wife, Violet May Witchell, (1915-1999) [NR] after the war. She had also been his secretary and had been interned at Stanley.*

Christmas Eve nativity 1989

Christopher Haskins, star of the show, at his christening, is being held by his Filipino amah, Conchita del Gala. His mother Carolyn is standing on the right between Raymond Tang from his father's office and Tessa Walker, a 'proxy' Godmother. The author is holding up son Jonathan by the (heavenly) blue doors. Simon Gates is sporting a beard and dog collar.

Hong Kong staff: the author second left with the Accounts team: Teresa Tam, John Lee, Suila Wong, Raymond Tang, David Wong and YK Lee. 1987

One of my godfather Douglas's fellow architects, Godfrey Bird, was interned at Stanley and audaciously helped the Army Aid Group from the inside[44]. When the Japs discovered what he was up to, he was tortured for three weeks. He was tied to an open coffin, with a cloth over his face; hung upside down under a running tap until he became unconscious; and had his arms tied behind his back with flex and raised until his full weight rested on his shoulder joints.[xlvi] He admitted nothing.

He survived but others who broke down were not so lucky. The beach where we sat on our first Sunday after church had 40 years earlier run with the blood of seven internees. They'd been executed after public torture for admitting operating a short-wave radio set in the rafters of one of the accommodation blocks – the Geneva Convention did not seem to apply.[xlvii] Wanton acts of cruelty, moods hard to fathom, face slapping, *binta*. Killing by machine gun or bayonet might follow with only the occasional flicker of pity.[xlviii]

One of my accounts staff, John Lee, was about fifteen years old in Kowloon when the Japs invaded. With his brother 'Jock' (these were their Western names), they started what was to become a successful laundry serving the Japanese, and, after the war, the expats and hotel trade. All was to be extinguished in the stock market crashes of the 1960s. I first met John when he paid me my expenses in 1973. The Chinese staff all used abacuses in those days. They gave me the last one, found in one of the cupboards when I went to work there full-time in the 1980s.

The Tiananmen Square crack-down on democracy by Deng XiaoPing occurred less than two months after our son Christopher was born – tanks rolling over students. Yes, Christopher has a Chinese birth certificate. Not long before that, my nephew Simon had rung to ask us to take in his Vicar's daughter, who'd been hitch-hiking round the Far East and had landed up in Hong Kong without much money[45]. She was back-packing in a gap year. After working in the bars in Lan Kwai Fong, she took off through China, ending up in Pakistan. Not a good time, we thought. Since then she's spent 3 years as the British Ambassador to Zimbabwe. It's difficult to say which was the most awesome.

After three years, our time was up. We went to Hong Kong with a boy under a year old and came back with an extra one of much the same age. Carolyn wanted to stay – another member of the family intoxicated with the Far East – but I hankered after Cornwall, even if the ragged coastline of Shek O or Big Wave Bay had the calmer seas and warmer water.

Sunset over the South China Sea

---

44. *Godfrey Vernon Bird RIBA GM (1907-1979) [NR], was the third generation of his family in Hong Kong. His father Herbert William Bird RIBA (1872-1945) [NR] was a partner in the firm when it was called Palmer and Bird. Godfrey was awarded the George Medal.*
45. *Deborah Jane Bronnert CMG (b1967) [NR] Ambassador to Zimbabwe 2011-14. Currently Director General, Foreign and Commonwealth Office.*

China Clay

The Minton china, which Bertie used, still graces our table on Christmas Day[46].   Ironically, she bought it from a British pottery.   Yet you'd not be wrong in thinking that fine china was actually invented in China – until the 1760s, it was the only country with the basic material and know-how to make hard-paste porcelain – translucent dinner plates that rung like a bell when you tapped them.   A Plymouth chemist discovered the secret component in Cornwall, kaolin – a name that comes from the Chinese mountain near Jingdezhen[47].   Kaolin, or 'China Clay' as it's called in Cornwall, transformed the Cornish economy.   In my youth, there were white China Clay 'pyramid' spoil heaps all behind St Austell.   Now the waste is processed, the quarries are hidden, but a million tonnes of kaolin are still extracted from central Cornwall each year and lithium for batteries may be the next commercial venture.[xlix]   In 2015 the residents of Treverbyn were seeking to declare one of the 'pyramids' as a World Heritage Site.   At least the clay workers of Cornwall didn't have to contend with slavery, the subject of the next chapter.

Bertie's Christmas party Shanghai 1903 – Bertie seated at the head of the table with Jack Smart standing on the right. High ceiling, flock wallpaper, oil lamps, pictures from home, Chinese pots on the dresser and the Minton china

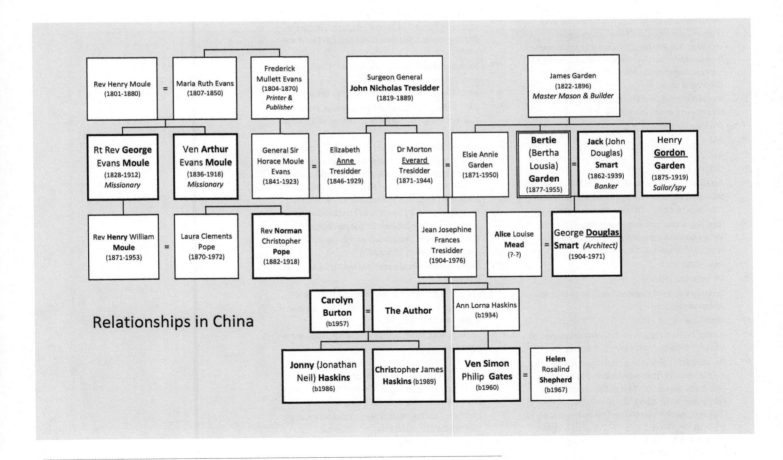

Relationships in China

---

46.   *The Haskins family have only half the set - 12 of most things.*
47.   *William Cookworthy (1705-1780) [NR].*

Other Notes and References

i.   *Ride p24*

ii.   *Eliza's father Rev John Henry Bernau (1805-1890) was a missionary, originally from Prussian stock, who spent 20 years at Bartica Grove in British Guiana. After Eliza's mother (Anna Maria Pasche (1776-1845)) died, he married again (Maria Stephen (1808-1891) at Chelsea) and became the first Vicar of All Saint's Belvedere, Erith. 19 years old, Eliza had a taste for the missionary life.*

iii.   *IS or ISIS (Islamic State in Iraq and Syria); Daesh or Da'ish is an acronym for al-Dawla al-Islamiya al-Iraq al-Sham, meaning Islamic State of Iraq and the Levant, but it sounds like Daes meaning 'one who crushes something underfoot' or Dahes, 'one who sows discord'.*

iv.   *Moule, Half a century in China. p33.*

v.   *Ibid p58.*

vi.   *email Dik Lukman 9 Apr 2014: Lt Cmdr James Weber RN (1854-1927), a distant relation, was in the Naval party which was sent to relieve General Gordon at Khartoum in 1884/5. He fought at the Battle of Abu Klea and subsequent engagements on the expedition, He was probably the first rating to be promoted to an officer, as a result of outstanding leadership.*

vii.   *The Times 8 Mar 1912.*

viii.   *Ibid*

ix.   *www.chinesechurchvoices.com accessed July 2014.*

x.   *Originally purchased as a place to bury Robert Morrison's first wife Mary, the chapel began to conduct Protestant baptisms, weddings as well as funerals and has been known as the British, English or Morrison Chapel ever since.*

xi.   *Ride p63. Lindsay and May Ride did much to restore the cemetery as well as write about it.*

xii.   *SPG letter Jan 1983.*

xiii.   *Ibid.*

xiv.   *Ibid.*

xv.   *SPG Letter Oct 1982.*

xvi.   *The South China Morning Post 27 Oct 2016, records 400 billionaires in China. The Wall Street Journal 12 Oct 2017, says that this is 100 more than in the US*

xvii.   *Daya Bay nuclear power reactor opened in 1991. Sir Andrew Gordon Manzie KCB BSc CBIM FCIOB (b1930) was Chief Executive of PSA 1984-90.*

xviii.   *Sherer p187.*

xix.   *SPG letter Dec 1982.*

xx.   *'Death by 9 degrees' meant all family up to 9th cousins were exterminated.*

xxi.   *JJFMT letter 16 Jan 1971.*

xxii.   *Lambot & Chambers, p95. In 1956, the Hongkong and Shanghai Bank had only 4 branches in Hong Kong.*

xxiii.   *The architect's firm was first established in Hong Kong in 1868, and from 1880 called Wilson and Bird. In 1891 it was named after its then Directors, Clement Palmer and Arthur Turner. It is now P&T Architects and Engineers Ltd, with over 600 professional staff. It has offices in Hong Kong, Singapore, Shanghai, Bangkok, Taipei, Kuala Lumpur and Jakarta. Its Directors are principally Chinese.*

xxiv.   *King F, plate 1: The Hongkong Bank's HQ 1886 building at 1 Queen's Road Hong Kong was nicknamed 'Jackson's Folly' after its manager; its principal branch in Shanghai that Jack and Bertie lived in was built in 1883.*

xxv.   *Douglas had sailed with his parents from New York to Southampton in the SS Majestic in Dec 1922. Perhaps the nearest comparison in London is the University's Senate building, competed two years later in 1937 and Broadcasting House, 1932. Barnsley's Town Hall of 1932 captures something of the excitement of Moderne, being stark white and cubist although of classical motif.*

xxvi.   *Purvis p77.*

xxvii.   *RJH Diary 20 June 1958: "I found my bicycle awaiting me."*

xxviii.   *JJFMT Letter from Bertie Smart 2 Feb 1955; Purvis p41; Architectural Appraisal of Ho Tung Gardens. p29. Palmer & Turner built The Falls on the Peak for Sir Robert Ho Tung Bosman KBE (1862-1956) [NR] in 1927. It was intended for his second wife, Clara Cheung (1875-1938) [NR]. In 1953 it was converted into six flats. Prior to that Douglas lived on the Peak at 26a Lugard Road, part of the 1889 Bishop's Lodge.*

xxix.   *RJH letter 23 Dec 1962. Parkwood House.*

xxx.   *JJFMT Letter from Alice Smart 15 Jan 1971 "We went up to our hotel room when on the last step he had a dizzy fit and fell down backwards. He had the hangman's knock and dislodged a cervical vertebra...."*

xxxi.   *Haskins RJ, Pirates of the Far East 2007.*

xxxii.   *HEFCE, April 2014 & May 2015: The Chinese account for 23% of the total UK Master's degree population in 2013/14, maths being their favourite subject (as it was Missie Lee's).*

xxxiii.   *Masters and Mates certificates held in the National Maritime Museum. 033902.*

xxxiv.   *(HGG) A Voyage from England to San Francisco, 1896.*

xxxv.   *(HGG) letter dated 9 Jun 1911 to his mother, headed I M Customs, Hangkow. Hangkow is now part of Wuhan in Hubei Province.*

xxxvi.   *Letter 21 Jun 1996 to the author from Shirley and Allen Garden, Narromine, Australia: "James's youngest son Henry Gordon was apparently in the diplomatic staff in Shanghai in 1909 [sic] when he took a little trip across the border into Siberia and his body was returned to the Embassy about 2 weeks later, I don't know what he was doing there but I don't think the Ruskys liked it whatever it was." His probate records his death at Blagoveshchensk on 10 Sep 1919.*

xxxvii.   *Mama-San is the local name for a brothel manager or a procurer.*

xxxviii.   *The Connaught Centre is now called Jardine House.*

xxxix.   *The Hongkong and Shanghai Banking Corporation was redefined as HSBC in 1991.*

xl.   *The Hopewell Centre's Revolving 66 was actually on the 62nd floor.*

xli.   *Gweilo is Cantonese slang for hated foreigners. Popular during the Opium wars. Literally 'ghost' or 'white' men. On 15 Jan 1857, a bakery tried to poison all the bread, which was only being eaten by Westerners.*

xlii.   *HMS Tamar military HQ had been named after a supply ship that used to be stationed in the harbour.*

xliii.   *Birch & Cole pp13, 23, 29.*

xliv.   *Ibid p90.*

xlv.   *Ibid p100.*

xlvi.   *Purvis p70.*

xlvii.   *Birch & Cole p59. They were captured 7 Jul and executed 29 Oct 1943.*

xlviii.   *Ibid p68.*

xlix.   *Cornwall Council's Technical Paper M1 China Clay.*

Eyelids of the Morning

Cornwall is the first land that British sailors see when returning from the Atlantic. It has also seen its share of invaders. The North African Corsairs snatched men, women and children from the Cornish coastal villages with impunity. The Barbary pirates burnt whole settlements such as Newlyn, and seized fishing vessels out at sea. In 1636, St Keverne was attacked several times in the same year. One who got away, said, "If the hands be smooth, they was ransomed, but if the hands be rough, they was sold as slaves." A rough-handed slave would fetch £40, a smooth-handed £80 and a 'fair maiden' up to £300. Male captives would be made to row galleys, shackled naked to their seats. They were whipped constantly, with a 'bull's pizzle', usually on their backs or bellies and soles of their feet. For up to 19 years they could be found sleeping, eating, defecating and urinating in the place where they sat.

Ottoman rulers thought Christian slaves the best. The Caliph in Baghdad in the 10th century had had 4,000 white slaves – male and female palace slaves were circumcised to make them seven times more valuable. Church towers in Cornwall were often hidden from the coast to avoid being seen from the sea. Just as well – the whole congregation of a church in Mount's Bay was taken at one time[1]. Collections for 'poor slaves' were a firm feature in 1700s at Falmouth's church. The white slave markets flourished all along the Barbary Coast – Libya, Tunisia, Morocco.

In 1816, Admiral Pellew struck back in Algiers[1]. He used 5 ships of the line, 4 frigates and more besides. He spent 50,000 rounds of ammunition and 118 tons of gunpowder and managed to release 3,000 slaves but many lives were lost in the process. If, as some thought, there were 20,000 slaves there, 17,000 didn't get away and it was about the only English effort of its kind. Not until France invaded Algiers in 1830 did the white slave trade decrease. Only then could the British truly sing 'Rule Britannia ... Britons never, never shall be slaves.'

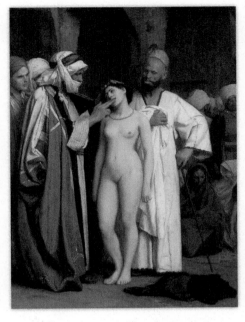

Slave Market, by Gerome

The Bombardment of Algiers, 27 August 1816 Chambers

✳ ✳ ✳ ✳

Wilber

The blackbird came for the breakfast scraps, a memory from the past. It had a white feather in its wing. We used to cut up the bacon rind to beak-size portions. The bird table was outside the kitchen window in the rose bed. The tame blackbird of my childhood was grateful for the regular supply of food that we gave it in the nesting season. My mother named the bird Wilberforce. We called it 'Wilber' for short. She knew something that failed to register with us at the time – our distant family tie with William Wilberforce (see chart at end of chapter).

William Wilberforce is chiefly known for his anti-slavery campaign but it was his Christianity that drove him to pursue this quest[2]. He was born in Hull, a seaport that dealt in the profits of slavery. He lived three years of his childhood in Westminster so knew where the country was governed. At the age of 21, straight out of Cambridge, Billy (as his grandfather called him) became Hull's Member of Parliament (MP) and later was MP for Yorkshire. He formed a close relationship with a fellow student from his university, William Pitt, who became the youngest

---

1. *Admiral Edward Pellew, 1st Viscount Exmouth GCB (1757-1833) was Cornish with connections with Flushing and Penzance*
2. *William Wilberforce (1759-1833), MP for Hull 1780-84, MP for Yorkshire 1784-1812.*

Slavery Abolitionist, William Wilberforce MP (1759-1833). His epitaph in Hull reads:

'England owes to him the Reformation of Manners. The world owes to him the abolition of slavery.'

Holwood, Keston, Kent, as designed by Decimus Burton

Holy Trinity Clapham

Prime Minister at the age of twenty-four[3]. Indeed, Billy had an immense capacity for making friends. In 1784, on a train to join his family, on tour in Italy and Switzerland, he leant over the shoulder of a passenger to see what he was reading and not only made friends but turned around his life[ii].

After that, 'Billy' wanted to go into the Church full time but another friend, John Newton, persuaded him to enter the House of Commons[4]. Newton had been a seaman on a slave ship. At sea from the age of eleven, he'd been press-ganged into the Navy. At eighteen he'd been flogged for desertion, and ended up a slave himself under the control of an African princess. After escaping, he nearly drowned off the coast of Ireland and, when he called out to God and was rescued, he vowed to live a Christian life. His best known hymn, *Amazing Grace*, summed up his reason for living.

Newton reasoned that Wilberforce could do more good in the nation's parliament than in a small parish church, and so it was to be. William Pitt invited him down to his new home at Keston in Kent[iii]. Sitting under a large oak tree after some garden work in 1787, they looked out over the Weald of Kent and Pitt turned to Wilberforce:

'Wilberforce, why don't you give notice of a motion on the subject of the Slave Trade? You have already taken great pains to collect evidence.... Do not lose time."

Pitt set up an inquiry into the slave trade in 1788, and had it report to the Commons in April 1789. Petitions had been piling in and Wilberforce made sure they were looked at. He made a three and a half-hour speech, describing the facts in gruesome detail but he got nowhere. Slavery was a fact of life, everybody said. "If it's good enough for the Muslim Corsairs, it's good enough for us Christians."[iv] A Select Committee met, a bill was passed, but vested interests won out. It took another twenty years for the trade to end, in 1807. Twenty years – and that was only the *trade* in slaves. It took another twenty-six years to do away with slavery itself.

Wilberforce settled at Clapham ten years after that meeting with Pitt under the oak tree. He attended the same church – Holy Trinity on the Common – as I did when I was first married. The rector in his time was **John Venn**[5]. Wilberforce published a book that year: *Practical View of the Prevailing Religious System of Professed Christians in the higher and middle classes in this country contrasted with real Christianity.* It doesn't sound very sexy, but it became a best seller. It called on people to practise Christianity seriously. Wilberforce found himself leader of a pressure group, which had been started by John Venn's father, **Henry Venn**, who'd been a curate at the same church[6]. The nation was simmering with revolt. The rich toffs – the aristocracy – were out of step with the common man. This new 'evangelical' movement caught the public's curiosity. It saw 'immorality' as the chief cause for the other wrongs of the time. If there was proper family life, with religion the central guiding force, society would come right. It did.

The pressure group was nicknamed the 'Clapham Sect'. They didn't stop with slavery. They helped found the Church Missionary Society (CMS) in 1799, funding some of the first missionaries to India[v]. The same group helped start the British and Foreign Bible Society (1804). It also started Sunday Schools which trail-blazed the education system we have today. Many of the association football clubs that now form the Premier League came out some of these crusading efforts[vi].

---

3. *William Pitt MP 'the Younger' (1759-1806) [NR] was Prime Minister 1783-1800, 1804-6 during the Napoleonic wars and the Regency period.*

4. *Rev John Henry Newton (1725-1807) [NR] wrote Amazing Grace, Glorious things of thee are spoken and How sweet the name of Jesus sounds.*

5. *Rev John Venn MA (1759-1813). (John Venn FRS (1834-1923) of 'Venn's diagram' was his grandson.)*

6. *Rev Henry Venn MA (1725-1797) Curate of West Horsley 1750-4 where he increased the communicants from twelve to sixty; curate of Holy Trinity Clapham 1754; Vicar of Huddersfield 1754-59.*

William Wilberforce saw the end of slavery just before he died, in 1833. A year later, 800,000 slaves, chiefly in the British West Indies (the Caribbean), were set free. Sierra Leone, with its capital 'Freetown', resettled some of these and still has a township named 'Wilberforce'. His efforts haven't stopped modern slavery – rife in North Korea or North Africa, forty million worldwide; 100,000 girls a year go into prostitution in India alone[vii]. Official estimates suggest there are 13,000 slaves in the UK[viii].

Members of the Clapham Sect crop up on both sides of my family. Sarah, Wilberforce's sister, spent all her income, some £300 or £400 a year, on charity, keeping £10 to buy clothes. Often she'd be seen walking along the Clapham streets in tatters. One member of the Clapham Sect was so outraged that he tore her skirt from top to bottom, saying,

'Now, Mrs. Stephen, you _must_ buy a new dress.' She calmly stitched it together and wore it again the following day.

Sarah married the second generation **James Stephen**, nicknamed **Jem**[7]. There were three generations of Stephens all with the same Christian name, all involved in righting the wrongs inflicted by their fellow men. The first James was a poor farmer's son who left Scotland to make his way in the world[8]. He ended up in a debtors' jail, where he fought for the rights of prisoners under *Habeas Corpus* and trained his son 'Jem' there[ix]. Jem followed his uncle and brother out to the island of St Christopher's (St Kitts) in the West Indies (Caribbean) where he saw such terrible abuse that he came back and wrote about it. He made friends with William Wilberforce and gave him most of the low-down for his speeches[9].

Jem's gifted son, **Sir James Stephen**, worked on the cause from inside the civil service, drafting the sixty sections of the 1833 Slavery Bill in record time[10]. As Permanent Secretary of the Colonial Office, his hold over the Colonies was so tight that he was nicknamed 'King Stephen', 'Mr Over-Secretary' and 'Mr Mother Country'. He considered the 'mother country' had an absolute duty to guard the seemingly worthless natives in the colonies. His legacy has helped Britain's standing and authority in the world, head and shoulders above other European powers whose reputations amongst their local populations were not so noble.

The Stephen family's notorious hedonistic lifestyle – the Bloomsbury Group – came a generation or so later. One wag summed it up by saying they 'lived in squares, painted in circles and loved in triangles.'[x] **Virginia Woolf** (née Stephen) and her elder brothers, sisters and half-brothers had indulged in tainted love during a liberal childhood – their father, **Leslie Stephen**, had lost his Christian faith[xi]. Nevertheless, Virginia could never fully reconcile herself to this way of life, and, when it came to writing about it in her autobiography in 1941, she committed suicide[11].

But that was later. In the Wilberforce and Pitt's period (see Chapter 3), morals were so low it was difficult to act as a God-fearing Christian and not look out of place – the Clapham Sect was ostracised. Our modern-day parliamentary laws, mostly based on their Christian moral code, we now take for granted. We admire racial equality, concern for the poor, education for all, yet such principles have been hard won. Wilberforce and the Clapham Sect succeeded because they did more than live out their own lives[xii]. More than the Liberty and Fraternity of France and America – they looked to a third dimension and found 'respectability'.

'Let true Christians...boldly assert the cause of Christ, in an age when so many who bear the name of Christians are ashamed of him... restoring the influence of religion and of raising the standard of morality.... Let them be active, useful, generous towards others, manifestly moderate and self-denying in themselves.... a manifest moderation in all temporal things.... Let them cultivate a catholic spirit of universal good-will, and of amicable friendship towards all those, of whatever sect or denomination.'

Practical View of Prevailing Religions
William Wilberforce

Jem' James Stephen
MP (1758-1832)

"No free man shall be seized or imprisoned, or stripped of his rights or possessions, or outlawed or exiled, or deprived of his standing in any other way, nor will we proceed with force against him, or send others to do so, except by the lawful judgement of his equals or by the law of the land.

To no one will we sell, to no one deny or delay right or justice."

Magna Carta 1215 British Library translation from the Latin.

---

7.   *James Stephen MP (1758-1832) married Ann Stent (1758-1796) in 1783 .*

8.   *James Stephen (1733-1779).*

9.   *James Stephen MP (1758-1832) married Ann Stent (1758-1796) in 1783 and Sarah Wilberforce (1758-1816) in 1800.*

10. *Sir James Stephen PC (1789-1859) married Jane Catherine Venn (1793-1875) in 1814 and became Permanent Secretary in 1836.*

11. *Adeline Virginia Stephen (1882-1941).*

One family connection with the Clapham Sect is Cornish one. Through my mother's great uncle, the **Rev Humphry Barnicoat**, we are related to the Freshfields[12]. **James Freshfield** founded the firm of solicitors that still advises the Bank of England. As well as being an active member of the Clapham Sect, James Freshfield became a Trustee of the Church Missionary Society. He helped it into funds in the same way as my next subject, **Charles Elliott**[13].

✳ ✳ ✳ ✳

The Cabinet Maker, Charles Elliott (1752-1832)

The furniture man

Charles Elliott, my great (x5) uncle by marriage on my father's side, came to know Wilberforce through his second wife, **Nellie (Elling) Venn**. Nellie's father, the driving force in the Clapham Sect, the outstanding cricketer, at one time a curate at Clapham, was now Vicar of Huddersfield. His son was now Rector at Clapham. Charles and Nellie married in 1785 and in the 1790s they moved to Clapham Old Town, close to her brother's church, Holy Trinity[14]. With Wilberforce nearby, Charles aided the Venn's to nudge the Church Missionary Society into existence; in 1799 he was voted on to its first committee and by 1808 he was chairing the AGM[xiii].

Charles came up from Burnham or Maldon in Essex in about 1768 to seek his fortune. Like Joseph Denison (Chapter 3), the teenager arrived with little more than the proverbial shilling in his pocket and found a job as an apprentice cabinet maker. It was the time when the gentry were reaping fortunes from sugar and tobacco, planted by slave labour. Their sons came back from their 'Grand Tour' of Europe with stacks of Italian paintings and statues and wanted somewhere to display them. They'd seen the villas of Palladio and wanted one similar on English soil[15]. This was the rise of 'architects' such as William Chambers, Robert Adam, John Carr, and cabinet makers such as Hepplewhite, Sheraton, and Chippendale[16].

By the age of 22, Charles had a thriving upholstery business. He kept the name 'Davis & Elliott' despite becoming its sole owner three years after formation. His firm's fame came to the notice of those profligate royals of Chapter 3 and, by 1784, Davis & Elliott was furnishing Buckingham Palace and cleaning the Houses of Parliament[xiv]. His satinwood and mahogany furniture was of the highest quality and Charles prospered – during the Napoleonic wars he, like the Freshfields, was able to lend William Pitt's government large amounts of money at high rates of interest. One of Davis & Elliott's schemes was to import furnishings and panelling from the houses of the French nobles who'd been guillotined in the French Revolution. They bought it cheap and sold it dear. Admiral Nelson appears to have stayed in his lodgings in New Bond Street – at least that's where the bill for the amputation of his arm was sent after the Battle of St Vincent[xv]. One of Elliott's subsequent commissions was arranging Nelson's funeral, one of the largest and grandest occasions ever. It took five days, ending with the coffin being lowered through the floor into the crypt of St Paul's during a 5-hour Evensong[xvi].

Drawing room of Davis & Elliott furniture at Langley's, Essex

'Nelsons funeral carriage designed by Davis & Elliott

---

12. *Rev Humphry Lowry Barnicoat (1820-1893) was brother in law to John Nicholas Tresidder's second wife, and brother of his first wife.*

13. *Maj James William Freshfield HAC MP JP (1774-1864).*

14. *Charles Elliott (1752-1832) married (1) the daughter of the Rector of St James Piccadilly, Sarah Ann Sherman (1754-1784) in 1775 and (2) Nellie Eling Venn (1758-1843) in 1785. They moved to Grove House in Clapham.*

15. *Andrea Palladio (1508-1580) [NR].*

16. *George Hepplewhite (1727-1786) [NR]; Thomas Sheraton (1751-1806) {NR}. Thomas Chippendale (1718-1779) [NR] was born in Otley and provided furniture for many Yorkshire houses such as Nostell Priory, Harewood, Newby Hall, and Temple Newsam. Davis & Elliott's business was situated at 95 (now 104) New Bond Street, London.*

When he retired, aged 64, in 1816, Charles and Nellie moved to Brighton[xvii]. By then it had become a classy watering hole. The Prince Regent and his latest mistress were half a mile up the road. Charles's seafront house, on the West Cliff site of the current Metropole hotel, had the better position – overlooking the beach. It was full of people coming and going. Between his two wives, Charles had sired 14 children, so there were countless grandchildren to entertain[xviii].

The children did a variety of good things. His son **Charles Elliott** went to India (Chapter 6)[17]. His daughter **Charlotte Elliott** wrote 150 hymns including '*Just as I am....*' Another married **Hugh Pearson**, Dean of Salisbury, whose son was, for 41 years, Rector of Sonning, where my nephew Luke now lives[18]. Then there was **Henry Venn Elliott**, a thunderous preacher at the church that his father had had built[19]. People came from far and wide to hear him. His wealthy congregation topped the list of donors for the Church Missionary Society. By his death in 1865, the number of CMS men sent to foreign parts stood at over 450, from a standing start of five. Much of what we call the Anglican Communion worldwide can trace its origins to the work of CMS.

Charlotte Elliott (1789-1871)

Elliott's ethos carried on. Another of Charles's grandsons, **Charles Boileau Elliott**, followed his father Charles to India but after a short spell came back to study at Cambridge, becoming Rector of Tattingstone in Suffolk[20]. One of *his* daughters, **Mary**, married **Handley Moule**, a leading evangelical theologian who was the first Principal of Ridley Hall, Cambridge (1881), and later Bishop of Durham[21]. And so here we have another connection between my father and mother's sides of the family. Handley Moule was one of a group of talented sons of Rev Henry Moule, the Vicar of Fordington in Dorset, whose sons George and Arthur we met in China (Chapter 10)[22]. Henry married **Mary Mullett Evans**. Through her, I am related to some of the leading lights of the Baptist Church.

Bishop Handley Moule (1841-1920)

* * * *

The Baptists of Bristol

Frederick Evans, the friend who fell out with Dickens (see Chapter 8), was Mary's brother. They were both born in London but their family originally came from Wales. There were six generations of Baptist ministers beginning with one who, like John Bunyan, had become a rebel priest in 1660. Perhaps the most celebrated of them all was their grandfather, the Rev **Caleb Evans**[23]. He and his father, Rev **Hugh Evans**, led the Baptist church in Bristol for 61 years[xlix]. Living in one of England's chief slave ports, they supported the ending of slavery. As early as 1788, Caleb was sending petitions to London. Caleb never saw the abolition: the year he died, 1791, the Abolition of Slave Trade Bill was lost, followed by a national boycott of 'slave sugar'.

---

17. *Charles Elliott (1776-1856) and Charlotte Elliott (1789-1871).*
18. *Sarah Maria Elliott (1751-1858) married Very Rev Hugh Nicholas Pearson DD (1776-1856) in 1803. Pearson wrote some popular books on the history of Christianity in Asia and India, one of which he dedicated to William Wilberforce, Their son, Canon Hugh Pearson (1817-1882) had the 'cure of souls' of Sonning (originally pronounced Sunning) 1841-82. There is a village hall, a set of alms-houses and a road in Sonning named after him.*
19. *Rev Henry Venn Elliott (1792-1865); St Mary's, Brighton was a 'Proprietary Chapel' built in 1827. It was rebuilt after the roof and walls collapsed in 1877.*
20. *Charles Boileau Elliott (1803-1875).*
21. *Harriet Mary Elliott (1844-1915) married The Rt Rev Handley Carr Glyn Moule (1841-1920) in 1881.*
22. *Rev Henry Moule (1801-1880) married Mary Mullet Evans (1801-1877) in Melksham, Wiltshire, in 1824.*
23. *Rev Caleb Evans DD (1737-1791) and Rev Hugh Evans (1712-1781).*

Hugh Evans had come to Bristol because he needed treatment on his foot and he never went back. He stayed with family who took him to Broadmead Baptist Church where Bernard Foskett was the driving force[24]. Foskett had started a Baptist College. Hugh began to study there and was baptised, in 1730 when he was 18 years old.

When Bernard Foskett died in 1758, Hugh took over. He and his son Caleb formed a good team. Theirs was an open and inclusive church in the Bunyan tradition. They welcomed outsiders. They weren't given to disputes about doctrine. Hugh and Caleb were gifted preachers. They could take a large subject, lend it authority and hold an audience until it was a 'blaze of devotion.' 'The influence of his father was apostolic, the popularity of the son proverbial,' wrote one[xx].

The Baptists wanted well-read ministers, just like other churches. As dissenters, they weren't permitted to join an Oxbridge college, so Caleb was sent to London to learn Hebrew and Greek at a Dissenting Academy in the Mile End Road[xxi]. After ministering there for a few years he re-joined his father in Bristol. The traditions of the Evans's are still alive through the Bristol Baptist College – its students have had a big impact on the way the church developed in the United States.

Religious practices take various forms, some of them more exaggerated than others. The next two stories are fairly challenging.

✳ ✳ ✳ ✳

The Actress

Fred Evans's son **Horace** married my great aunt Annie (Chapter 6)[25]. Aunt Annie's parents, my great grandparents, **John Nicholas and Emily Tresidder** were Plymouth Brethren – termed 'Exclusive Brethren' today. They practised this style of Christian faith towards the end of their life after their children had become adults, so none was brought up with it, though **Ethel**, one of the grown-up daughters, used to go with her mother to the meetings after John Nicholas died. Ethel married into the Brethren[26].

Begun in the 1830s, under the leadership of John Nelson Darby, the Brethren were not extreme[27]. My great grandparents would have been Christians in the tradition of Wesley's 'Great Awakening'. Non-conformist chapels sprung up all over Cornwall. Pentewan, a village of 234 souls in 1891, had three places of worship. They would have believed in the Trinity, the Resurrection of the body and the Athanasian Creed. They would have trusted in the authority of the scriptures. They held to the doctrines of justification by faith and predestination. Their preachers would have condemned the Catholics who thought that bread turned into Christ's flesh at the Eucharist – to them it was just a symbol. They keenly awaited the 'rapture' of the second coming of Christ as told in the Book of Revelation.

Their faith guided their lives. They said prayers at both ends of the day and grace before meals and that was about it. Today, however, the 'Exclusive' Brethren are effectively cut off from the evils of the world. Though strong in numbers, the Brethren don't seek out new souls to join their number. Numbers increase by having children. Few leave. In a way, it is a happy existence but if there is a family split, it doesn't turn out well.

Pentewan Chapels. The 1880 Wesleyan Chapel on the hill is now two holiday homes. The Bible Christians built the big one in North Road in 1889. It was demolished by a German bomb in 1942

The young actress, Fanny Stirling, whose real name was Mary Ann Hehl (1813-1895)

---

24. *Rev Bernard Foskett (1685–1758) [NR].*
25. *Frederick Mullett Evans (1804-1870)'s son Gen Sir Horace Moule Evans KCB (1841-1923) married Elizabeth Anne Tresidder (1846-1929) in 1866.*
26. *Ethel Tresidder (1862-1956) married James A Allen (1863-1960) in 1893.*
27. *John Nelson Darby (1800-1882) [NR].*

One such was the story of Fanny Stirling[28]. **Fanny Stirling** was probably the best known comedy actress on the London stage in her day. That day began in the 1829 and lasted for fifty-seven years[xxii]. Her real name was Mary Ann Hehl. Having returned at the age of sixteen from a traditional Catholic convent education abroad, she found her father, an Assistant Quarter-Master-General of the Horse Guards, in prison having lost everything on the gambling tables[xxiii].

With good looks, brains and breeding, she decided to turn to a line of work that did not, shall we say, have too much decorum. At least one of George IV's lovers (see Chapter 3) had been on the stage[xxiv]. The upright William Gladstone, the Prime Minister, (well, there were rumours of prostitutes) said Fanny had been his 'first love'[xxv]. It wasn't long before she got hitched to a fellow actor, who took her up to the North, out of harm's way. His name was Lambert, but he called himself Stirling on the stage. Eventually he became Director of the Drury Lane Theatre, but that was after they'd gone their separate ways.

The marriage didn't last much beyond 1838. She picked up where she left off and moved back to London. Her reputation as a fine actress only increased. People believed in her. The proscenium arch and footlights vanished as they soaked up the plot. As Ellen Terry said, "She swept onto the stage and, in that magical way never never to learned, filled it. She had a breadth of style; such a lovely voice, such a beautiful expressive eye! ... Her smile was the most fascinating, irresistible thing imaginable."[xxvi]

Fanny retired to have Fan, her daughter, in 1842[29]. She went in and out of retirement umpteen times. She upstaged most of the great actors of her time including the great Henry Irving and Charles Kean. She and Kean became inseparable and Kean wrote the part of Peg Woffington in *Masks and Faces* especially for her. It made her into a star[30]. In one of her most striking roles, as the Nurse to Ellen Terry's Juliet, she 'had the play *[Romeo and Juliet]* all to nothing', making a small part the dominating feature of this Shakespeare play, one of Sir Henry Irving's great achievements[xxvii]. 'One of the most amusing, natural, and irresistible old women ever imagined, lives before you, treads the stage, and asserts a phenomenal importance in the action of the play,' wrote one critic[xxviii].

Fanny broke the glass ceiling – she was the first female to address an all-male actors' dinner, in 1862[xxix]. It is quite possible it was her name in lights that made the name 'Fanny' so popular in Victorian times. Quite a few of my relations had that name. She made speeches and acted in charity concerts to the end of her life. She ended her days married to a long-standing admirer, a past president of the Society for Civil Engineers who'd made his money on the railways[31].

Fanny's personal life was not as comfortable as it seemed on the surface. She hoped that Fan, her daughter, would follow her onto the stage but Fan had seen enough of her mother's lifestyle. Instead she eloped with James Allen on her 21st birthday, in 1863[32]. James was a Plymouth brother and Fan broke off all contact with her mother. Was it Fanny's Catholic faith, her riotous lifestyle, or Fan's anonymous father leaving her money ... or was it a simple love-match which turned Fan towards James and the Plymouth Brethren? Fanny never saw her nine grandchildren, let alone found the chance to welcome them into her home in Portland Place, or into her (substantial) bosom[xxx]. Fanny sought refuge in her Catholic confessors and faux respectability but that did not make up for her loss.

...We hope to indulge the audience with a roar;
Not that of lions, which a dread imparts,
But roars of laughter coming from your hearts;
We trust you'll find our English flag unfurling,
Our pieces current, and our actors sterling.

Recital by Fanny Stirling at the Lyceum 1 April 1839 ahead of a play with her husband Edward Stirling, called *Lady Mary Montague, or Courtship and Matrimony*

(Allen p55)

Fanny Stirling as Juliet's Nurse with her 'adopted daughter' Mary Anderson

---

28. *Mary Ann Hehl (1813-1895) married Edward Lambert (1809-1894) in 1832 at St Olave, Hart Street, London. When they separated, they did not divorce.*
29. *Frances Mary Lambert (1842-1929).*
30. *Dame Ellen Terry GBE (1847-1928) [NR]; Sir Henry Irving (1838-1905) [NR]; Charles John Kean (1811-1868) [NR]. Charles Kean and Fanny were almost certainly lovers. Peg Woffington (1720-1760) [NR] was popular on stage (and in many lovers' arms) a century earlier.*
31. *Sir Charles Hutton Gregory KCMG PPSCE (1817-1898) married Fanny Stirling in 1894*
32. *Frances Mary Lambert (1842-1929) married James Allen (1832-1936) in 1863.*

Andrew Allen (b1945)

The Brethren

Sitting on a picnic bench overlooking Pentewan Valley, I spent an enlightened afternoon with Fanny's great great grandson, **Andrew Allen**[33]. His great grandparents had been the ones to separate from Fanny. For three generations the Allens had been true to their faith. Andrew told me of the reasons for his choice to break from the Plymouth Brethren in the 1970s. Second cousins, we had met once before, when I was 3½ years old and he was 6¾, at his Grandmother Ethel's 90th birthday. Ethel and my mother wrote to each other. Ethel used to tell her how her family were getting on, with phrases like 'I am so thankful that all our children have been brought to know the Lord and to follow Him. It is the greatest of all blessings.'[xxxi] Ethel's house in South Croydon was Victorian in character, with green paint and wallpaper (full of lead and arsenic) and heavy curtains[xxxii]. There was a surprising notice in the lavatory (as we called it) "God is watching your EVERY move" which quite alarmed my sister Barbara as she wiped her bottom.

From the humble start of our joint great-grandparents, Brethren life became more and more intense. This went back to 1910 under James Taylor Senior's leadership in New York[34]. Ethel's generation was not too affected but things went haywire when James Taylor Junior took over in the mid-1950s[35]. These were Andrew's childhood years; he was four years older than me. Taylor Junior made much of the biblical teachings on separation from the world. He decreed that members should not eat or associate in any way with non-members. Ethel's tea party in 1952 was the last to which we were invited. It suited me, a freer spirit, even at that age. Didn't Christ release us from the law? Give us free will?

Andrew's childhood was full of incidents about whom he could or could not play with, and which people in the street his family could or could not assist, because they were or were not 'one of us'. He 'stood out' of school assemblies. No scouts or football. No celebration of Christmas, 'as men speak'. A number of the Brethren, not least Andrew's aunts, were pretty fed up with Taylor's erratic leadership. When Taylor swore at a meeting, it didn't enamour himself to his followers. Then Taylor was caught in bed with a woman – more dissent, more desertion, but Andrew's family in North London stayed with it. There was a calm pattern to their life; they had all their friends. It was a loving place to be, and Brethren folk were well off, having none of the worldly pleasures to spend their money on,

James and Ethel surrounded by their family two days before her 90th birthday in April 1952. That's the author, aged 3½ sucking his teeth. Top row: Peter, Daphne, Priscilla, Elliott, Desmond & Daisy Allen, Jean, Ann, Paul and Barbara Haskins. Sitting: Frances Haughton neé Allen, James and Ethel Allen, George and Sybil Hathorn (pronounced Hawthorn). Below: the author with Andrew Allen.

with jobs in trade and commerce.

At nineteen years old, Andrew went to Sydney. When he came back, he was full of the way Bruce and John Hales were leading the Brethren there[xxxiii]. He was feted on his return – his Brethren friends were interested in this new approach. Andrew had supped at the table with the current leader of the Exclusive Brethren, John's son, Bruce David Hales[xxxiv].

It was not to last. The 'Exclusive' door closed on him once more. New rules: women to hang their hair loose, drums in the meetings. He couldn't attend university or join a profession. Eucharist services were to begin at 6am in the morning. In my time in the 1970s, during my ecumenical activity, I knew a family of Plymouth Brethren but they were not so extreme, even if the pretty teenage girls looked odd wearing their straw hats to church.

Andrew married Erica, from within the close circle of his parent's friends, and had two children. It prayed on his mind, however – this approach to living, worship and the future. He

---

33.   Andrew Nigel Allen (b1945) married Erica M Evershed (b1950) and had two children Lucy Allen (b1969) and Zoe Amanda Allen (b1971).
34.   James Taylor Sr (1870–1953) [NR].
35.   James Taylor, Jr (1899–1970) [NR].

discussed it at work. It was the 1970s: pop culture, free love, safe sex, more money, smarter clothes. The world was changing. The more he thought, the more he decided he could live as a normal citizen. Walking along the Embankment near the Tower of London and listening to a busker playing *New Jerusalem*, he made up his mind.

Erica, Andrew's wife, and their children all left the Brethren at the same time. The effect was cataclysmic, terminal. The whole of their life with their extended family was now denied to them. All that they had been taught about the evil in the world was turned on its head. They were cut off from their main support system. Did they continue to pray? What did they do on Sundays? Andrew had a few work colleagues to turn to. Erica was at home, dependent on him. All association with their extended families had ceased. Heartache. Andrew did not see his mother again[36]. Imagine that poor woman, not unlike her grandmother-in-law Fanny Stirling on the other side of the divide, silently searching her soul as she bore the grief. It was like a death. She wrote letters to Andrew that were never posted. Her family had to carry on as before, without him. It was almost more difficult for Erica's family – two sisters who could not now help each other when illness took over.

The sun shone on our salads as we chewed over all those years between our meeting in 1952 and now. Andrew, with a new wife and a houseful of grandchildren, is happily settled and able to search for some of the more significant stories in his eminent family history.

✳ ✳ ✳ ✳

Letters to a great-nephew

You are probably wondering why I called this chapter 'Eyelids of the Morning'. My great Uncle Will (see Chapter 18) wrote a book, one of many, in his nineties when I was in my twenties. This one was never published, as he died before it was quite finished. He called it *Letters on the Ministry*, addressed to me with the idea that I would follow him into the ordained ministry. He captured this phrase from the Old Testament book of Job, to make a point[xxxv].

The eyelids both protect and reveal. Similarly, that is the job of priests. To protect and reveal. Without the eyelids' protection, our eyes wouldn't last long. Without them opening, we wouldn't know what went on. 'Who has not experienced the supreme tenderness of the moment when the sleeper, child or wife, has first opened the lids and looked up with a smile of recognition at the face bending down and watching the dawn of consciousness?'[xxxvi] Doesn't this say more about creation and the meaning of life than science, religion, history or politics? *Res ipsa loquitur*, to borrow my father-in-law, Ken Burton's favourite phrase[37].

All too often of course, the human race mucks things up. The eyelids flutter beguilingly, and 'seduce foolish men'[xxxvii]. Eyes can also become an agent of hate. 'It is well to look at [our] life ... and to see it whole. We should try to see it objectively from the outset. We need to know its opportunities and its dangers, its advantages and its drawbacks, its helps and hindrances, its place in our hopes of our own salvation as well as its service to others.'[xxxviii] It's easy for an old man to look back. It's harder for a young one to look forward. I suppose that's why the young study history, the bible and other words of wisdom. I'm only just starting to grasp what it is all about. Best to make sense of things as soon as you can.

Church as a child for me wasn't too hard. I was rescued from the dreary bits – my family seldom went to church. Cornwall was different. We went to St Goran (Gorran) church[xxxix]. At Easter-time, the primroses hung round the light-white Pentewan-stone pillars. There was a faithful choir of three – one croaky bass and two warbling women who were so old they used sticks to hobble up the aisle. The church is in good heart, even if there's now no choir

The eyelids both protect and reveal. Without the eyelids' protection, our eyes wouldn't last long.

---

36. *Daisy (Margaret Isobel) Carter (1900-1980) married James Elliot Allen (1894-1978) in 1922.*
37. *'The thing speaks for itself'.*

'There is a vile principle abroad to-day among the semi-pagan people who are so often met with in modern life – that the great thing is to 'fulfil yourself'; to 'do as you please irrespective of parents, teachers, spiritual pastors and masters.' It is the rebel-devil's parody of liberty – liberty, which without the noble balance of loyalty to right is licence, the straight path to basest slavery. But the vile principle is a travesty of the true principle; 'let the Lord fulfil you on the lines on which He made you, as to individual cast of character.'

Handley C G Moule 2 Oct 1913

and most weren't born in the village. Gorran church has just undertaken a massive building project, setting the pace for tomorrow. Churches like Gorran have had a community role for a more than a thousand years. They're a place of contemplation, a respite from the weary world. They're a moral compass for a village or town – each age feeds from them anew. That is important and it matters to me.

They say religion is 'caught not taught'. I had a good Scripture teacher at my prep school, who gave me a passion for the exciting stories in Old Testament[38]. I was Secretary of the Christian Union at *Dauntsey's* as a result. *Dauntsey's* was a school that allowed free thought, so yes, we did explore our freedom in more ways than one. A chaplain from a nearby school, speaking at one meeting, was outraged by my refusal to accept the bible at face-value. But then I had no right to consider ordination (I didn't take Holy Orders in the end) any more than sons of landed gentry 200 years before. Yet there was an inner urge to do something more with my life. In a bus garage in Bristol, I entered into a contract with God. It was a Billy Graham Crusade. The bus garage was the only place big enough to hold the crowd. It was there I put my life in God's hands.

Handley Moule, 'Holy Mouley', the Bishop of Durham, wrote in 1913 that 'freedom' did not mean doing as you pleased[39]. Unlike the Girl Guides' latest version of the 'Promise' – ask a Girl Guide what 'Being true to yourself' actually means. It is more complex. We are part of a bigger picture.

My religion has made me think over the years – about jobs, girls, drugs, etc. It's kept me on an even keel. I've gone too near the edge more than once but I haven't fallen over (yet). Miraculously. The church has helped. It has allowed me to be concerned for others and to be positive. I've learnt the value of saying sorry. I haven't got too concerned about the reasons why I am not the Prime Minister. I'm not resentful because I'm not luxuriating on a tropical island with vast wealth.

Okay, you may say, but can't family, friends and humanism do all that instead? Isn't religion about punishment, fear and retribution? Sorry, but I don't find any of that in Christ's teaching. How do you think I learnt to love one's neighbour, and to be positive? It didn't come naturally. Regretfully, I am feeble and foolish but I still see daily the warmth in other people's eyes, the real gates of heavenly peace.

Where's the proof that God exists? Jesus living, dying and living again was a well-known fact at the time, even to his doubting friend Thomas. Scientists continue to try to piece together how the world began. All the data is against any of us being here. There are so many layers of particle physics which suggest we shouldn't exist. After the Big Bang, equal amounts of matter and anti-matter should have cancelled each other out, leaving an empty universe. String theory has concluded there are a vast number (roughly 10^{500}) of possible universes out there, each with its own laws of physics. So hands up those who say that life is ended when we 'die'? That we still have to work it all out is obvious, isn't it? So we are back to those eyelids of the morning.

And then what? Most potter along and hope they get through. Or do we just stay 'true to ourselves'? Or do we seek out something better? Do we go hell for leather and follow the moralists who ascribe pure reason to themselves and emotionalism to everybody else? Or do we adopt eugenics to improve the world?[xl] Ethnic cleansing? Communism? A Caliphate? To me, it's all about that child waking up in the morning, and scraping the bacon and crumbs onto the bird table. It's about someone higher and better than me who loves me and forgives me – unconditionally – and me trying to emulate him (her).

38. *Elizabeth Mary Waddy (1917-2001)*
39. *Rt Rev Handley Carr Glyn Moule DD (1841-1920)*

According to *www.houseofnames.com*, the Haskins family motto is *Finem respice*, 'Consider the end.' Where will it all end? I don't feel particularly blessed, unlike my great aunt Ethel. Yet, walking along the Gruda, edged by the indigo sea, with Cornish foxgloves sighing in the hedges, and Lamledra commanding the view; with skylarks serenading the heavens; and the rural silence only broken by the bullocks' breathing, I begin to understand what my small role in God's kingdom could be – call Him what you like. I'm a confirmed Christian, not someone who's signed up to a set of propositions. I believe in something more. I'm committed to the trinity of God (Father, Son and Holy Spirit) in mind, body and soul, rooted with others who shape and refresh me. I don't have a secret formula. There are no guarantees. It's faith. I've lived and worked with Buddhists, Sikhs, Taoists, Hindus, Jews and Muslims and we all share a wonder of a wider world. We testify to our ancestors of a life in an age to come.

Buddha and Confucius both advise you not to believe simply because parents or society say so. Seek out for yourself the mandate of heaven. I have, through frosted glass. I am hoping one day it's all going to become crystal clear to you, even if I won't be around to rewrite this chapter[xli].

The Gruda looking to Lamledra with St Austell Bay beyond

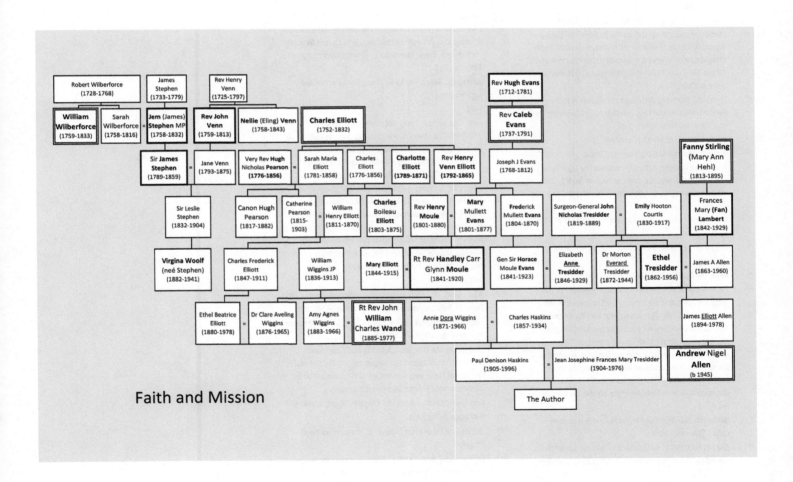

Faith and Mission

Other Notes and References

i.   Milton p12.

ii.   The book was either William Law's A Serious Call to a Devout and Holy Life or Philip Doddridge's The Rise and Progress of Religion in the Soul. The reader was Rev Isaac Milner FRS (1750-1820) [NR].

iii. William Pitt the Younger was born at Hayes Place, near Bromley, Kent. He later owned Holwood House, Keston, nearby. Its 'Wilberforce Oak' survived until World War 2. He also owned Pitt's Cottage, Westerham, Kent. His great-grandfather Thomas 'Diamond' Pitt MP (1653-1726) [NR] bought Boconnoc near Lostwithiel in Cornwall with wealth he'd accumulated as Governor of the Madras Presidency in India. Before parliamentary constituencies were reformed, Boconnoc which owned land at Old Sarum. Old Sarum had no population and two seats in parliament – a 'Rotten Borough'. It started the Pitt political dynasty.

iv.   Hernon p94.

v.   Kaye, Christianity in India p275. Having failed to introduce an amendment to the India Bill of 1793, he succeeded in 1813 when the Charter of the East India Company was renewed, following debate in parliament 22 Jun 1813. Lord Castlereagh proposed a Bishop and three Archdeacons.

vi.   Including Barnsley, Birmingham, Bolton Wanderers, Everton, Manchester City, Southampton, Swindon Town and Tottenham Hotspur.

vii. International Labour Organisation, 2017.

viii. Kemp R. Modern Slavery Strategy, BBC2, 17 Jan 2014.

ix.   The Habeas Corpus Act 1679 codified the legality of imprisonment, which extended back at least to John or his father Henry II. It was written into the 1215 Magna Carta.

x.   The witticism is ascribed to Dorothy Parker (1893-1967) [NR].

xi.   Lee p126 quotes an incident at Talland House in Cornwall.

xii. Matthew 28v19, Mark 13v10, Mark 16v15.

xiii. Charles Elliott was also a committee member of the British & Foreign Bible Society, and belonged to the Prayer Book & Homily Society, the Society for Bettering the Poor, the Society for the Suppression of Vice, the Philanthropic Society, which put penniless boys out as apprentices and girls into service, and the Marine Society which trained poor boys to serve at sea. He kept a low profile in the Clapham Sect' by virtue of his Royal commissions and having a brother-in-law who led it.

xiv. Barton pp293, 360. Buckingham Palace was then called 'Queen's House'.

xv.   The bill for £135.1s.0d was sent to 96 New Bond Street, owned by Elliott, who worked and first lived next door at No 97.

xvi. Spragg p53. http://www.nationalarchives.gov.uk/nelson/gallery8/ There were four coffins, inside each other like Russian dolls: the inner made from wood salvaged from the French flagship at the Battle of the Nile, L'Orient; then lead, wood and finally gilt, which is what they mourners saw. On 9 January 1806 thousands lined the streets, along with 30,000 troops, to watch the march from Whitehall to St Paul's Cathedral. The procession included at least 10,000 soldiers. The five-hour funeral service was attended by 7,000 people including seven royal dukes, 16 earls, 32 admirals and over 100 captains together with 48 seamen and 12 marines from HMS Victory. The carriage remained at Greenwich until 1826.

xvii. Westfield Lodge, Brighthelmstone.

xviii. Twelve children survived infancy.

xix. McKibbens p34.

xx.   McKibbens p35.

xxi. The Clarendon Code was named after Edward Hyde, 1st Earl of Clarendon (1609-1674) [NR]. It was a series of laws passed 1661-1665. These laws re-established the Anglican Church after the Commonwealth period. The Corporation Act (1661) required all municipal officials to take Anglican Communion. Nonconformists were thus excluded from public office. The Act of Uniformity (1662) made the Book of Common Prayer compulsory for worship. The Conventicle Act (1664) forbade unauthorised worship of more than 5 people. And the Five-Mile Act (1665) forbade a Nonconformist ministers coming within 5 miles of places where he had formerly ministered. These laws were only rescinded 150 years later, in 1812.

xxii. Allen p25. According to Sir Henry Irving at her last performance.

xxiii. Ibid.

xxiv. HRH George p52. Mary Robinson (neé Darby) (1758-1800) [NR] had been two seasons on the stage of Drury Lane, when he met her. Frances Villiers, Countess of Jersey (1753-1821) [NR] also took part in amateur dramatics of one sort and another.

xxv. Allen p48. William Ewart Gladstone MP (1809-1898) [NR] Prime Minister 1868-74, 1880-85, 1886 and 1892-94. When lunching with Mary Anderson (Mme de Navarro as she became) at the Lyceum during the Romeo and Juliet season said, 'You will be seeing Fanny Stirling tonight. Please tell her from me that she was my first love. No harm to tell her now."

xxvi. Terry p164.

xxvii. Allen p206. In 1882 Fanny Stirling appeared with Ellen Terry as Juliet, reprised in 1884 with Mary Anderson.

xxviii. Edward R Russell is quoted from Macmillan's Magazine in The Stage Life of Mrs Stirling p205.

xxix. Ibid p174. The Dramatic, Musical and Equestrian Sick Fund Association. Its senior cousin, the General Theatrical Fund, was still not admitting women to its dinners when Dickens addressed it in 1863.

xxx. Fanny and Charles lived at 3 Duchess Street, London.

xxxi. [EA] letter 3 Dec 1954.

xxxii. James and Ethel Allen lived at 31 Normanton Road, Croydon.

xxxiii. W Bruce and John S Hales. The current leader, Bruce David Hales, is John's son. The numbers of Brethren in the UK are estimated by one source to be about 16,000.

xxxiv. In 2012 the Brethren incorporated under the name Plymouth Brethren (Exclusive Brethren) Christian Church Limited.

xxxv. Job 3 v 9 and 41 v 18.

xxxvi. Wand, Letters on the Ministry p4.

xxxvii. Proverbs 6 v 24, 25ff.

xxxviii. Wand, Letters on the Ministry p5.

xxxix. St Goran church has a 13th century porch, a 14th century south aisle and 15th century tower built over an original Norman cruciform church. The tower was rebuilt in the 17th century.

xl.   For example, Permitting the Destruction of Unworthy Life. Karl Binding. 1920.

xli. 1 Corinthians 13, the first passage the author read in public, is a good place to begin.

African Adventures

If the Tresidders were known for India, then the Wiggins settled for Africa. Dr Livingstone had opened up the continent in the 1850s[1]. Britain had won the Boer War in the 1880s. There was a rush for Kimberly diamonds and a subsequent land grab by Cecil Rhodes in the 1890s[2]. England was caught up in the 'romance' of the Africa. Fathers imagined rich pickings for their sons. William Wiggins, my great grandfather, saw possibilities for his children[3]. Five of them went to live and work in Africa. Three died there, whilst two returned after years of government service. One dabbled in police work, mining, transport and engineering. Kathie married a banker there but this chapter is mainly about my great uncle Clare Wiggins, a doctor in British East Africa (Kenya) and Uganda. First, something about his brothers and their sister.

Clare Aveling Wiggins (1876-1965)

George Francis Wiggins (1880-1913).

✳ ✳ ✳ ✳

The Wiggins in Africa

Philip was the first of the brothers to think about Africa. He saw an advert to join the British South Africa Police (BSAP)[4]. Cecil Rhodes, as Prime Minister of the Cape Colony had sent a Pioneer Column to expand British rule from Matabeleland into Mashonaland, in the north of what became Rhodesia (now Zimbabwe). By the time Philip arrived in 1896, the Matabele were in revolt and a force including Philip was sent to sort it out. During the fighting in the Matopo Hills, Philip rose to the rank of Sergeant Major. His Colonel was Robert Baden-Powell, who learnt most of his Scouting skills there[5].

Philip Arthur Wiggins (1874-1930)

The age of steam reached Africa with George Wiggins and Arthur Laws (1872-1927)

When land was later handed out, Philip picked up some mining claims. Many dreamt of fortunes, but easy pickings were few and far between.

Philip was running the Dalny mine when he met **Arthur Laws**[6]. Arthur had been trained as an Engineer and Philip persuaded his father to send out some second-hand steam tractors. They set up a flourishing transport business, and made enough money to visit England[i]. Arthur and Philip were business partners on and off for the rest of their lives. In England, Philip met Arthur's sister **Amy Laws** and married her in 1907 in Salisbury Cathedral (the Rhodesian one). Sadly, in 1927 Arthur committed suicide over the love of a girl thirty years younger[ii].

It was a precarious existence, living in frame houses with 'malthoid' roofs and walls, or thatched huts with scorpions and creepy-crawlies. Water was carried in buckets on a wheelbarrow from a windmill over a well. There were bouts of malaria and Blackwater Fever. Yet there were governesses, schooling, church on Sundays, Sunday School and picnics. There was even a Model T Ford.

Philip's projects

1840	MRCS
1896	British South African Police
1898-?	Dalny Mine
?-1906	Steam Engines
1907	Lion Pools Mine, Gatooma
1908-13	Dalny Syndicate
1913	Firewood supply for Cam & Motor Mine, Gatooma
1916	Railway work, Hartley
1918	Odzi River bridge foundations
1919	Salvaging sunken warships
1925-30	Odzi River Road Bridge Umtali River Road Bridge Mefort River Bridge QueQue River Bridge Sombrela-Shabam Railway Bridge Marabala Sawmills and wagon construction

---

1. *David Livingstone (1813-1873) [NR].*
2. *Rt Hon Cecil John Rhodes DCL (1853-1902) [NR].*
3. *William Wiggins JP (1836-1913).*
4. *Philip Arthur Wiggins (1874-1930) married Amy Beatrice Laws (1877-1935) in 1907.*
5. *Lt Gen Robert Stephenson Smyth Baden-Powell, 1st Baron Baden-Powell Bt OM GCMG GCVO KCB (1857-1941) [NR] founded the Boy Scouting movement in 1907-10.*
6. *Arthur Moore Laws (1872-1927).*

RHODES

Mighty dreamer of dreams, with the will that makes them true;
Rhodes! He who worked till his lifelong vision grew
From a noble heart's desire
To the work of a noble man;
Who gave himself to his country to work
And his mind to think and plan.

Noble mind and high ambition,
True to England's own tradition
That her sons work for her good.
Into the Matopos, hills of uncarved stone,
The champion of justice and of natives' right
To see us make them free, nor rashly smite:
That all should freely live, and only bow
From love, to conquerors, who fair rights allow.

High in the Matopos, in a place he knew
That, for its beauteous grandeur, he called "The World's View":
"There," said he, "Let me lie and rest
Thou who art beside me, do thou my behest.
When I am gone, let me be laid to sleep
Far from the city's noise, in silence deep;
Here where I dreamed my dreams, by the grand scene inspired,
Here let me rest, for I am very tired."

There now our Founder sleeps, in quiet and peace;
And there he'll sleep until the world shall cease.
But when the end of all things comes, he shall tear the rocks asunder
And he'll rise from out the grave with wild lightning and thunder
And he'll dream and work in heaven, as he did below on earth
And he shall be held in heaven, as a jewel of priceless worth.

Ella Stevens Wiggins (1908-1937)
1919 Aged 12 years

Rhodesia (North and South – Zambia and Zimbabwe) was named after Cecil Rhodes (1853-1902) [NR]. He was admired then (by black and white) as Nelson Mandela has been. His Rhodes Scholarships at Oxford (he directed they be granted irrespective of race or religion) are still educating potential world leaders. His company, De Beers, is still the top diamond company in the world. Some have accused him of colonialism, racism or slavery, the common mediocrity of his time, but the evidence is contradictory. Colonialism, he thought, helped impose European cultural values on one of savage and brutal regimes worse than the Middle East today. Before taking over land, he obtained signed concessions, introduced employment contracts; encouraged education, civility and mutual respect; he brought prosperity in place of brutal warring overlords, one of whom features in this chapter. [Prof Nigel Biggar. Times 22 Dec 2015 p29] When the removal of his remains from the Matopos Hills was suggested in 2012, Godfrey Mahachi, Zimbabwe's director of monuments said, "The call for the removal of the grave is not new but our view is that it is part of national history and heritage." [Times 22 & 24 Dec 2015]

Philip and Amy had six children, one dying young. The eldest, **Ella Wiggins**, was a precocious child, whom my father rather fancied[7]. She was a free spirit and liked older men. On graduating from Cape Town University, she married one of her lecturers. They came to London where she worked in the library of the London School of Economics. When her marriage didn't work out, she moved in with a civil servant. She died of cancer of the neck aged 29 – who knows what she would have accomplished.

Life in the African veldt was always unpredictable. Ella's brother, **David Wiggins**, who in his adult life established a farm in **Rhodesia**, was to die a grizzly death, hacked to death by President Mugabe's 'War Vets' after returning home one evening[8]. It was 1992, the year of the Zimbabwe Land Acquisition Act. The government published a list of farmlands for redistribution. It gave landowners 30 days to object. Strong-arm tactics of the War Vets overrode ex-British law.

Like his elder brother Philip, **George** avoided studying for a profession by following Philip to Africa.[9] Around 1908 they formed the Dalny Mining Syndicate but the clash of two Wiggins' hot-heads tired them both out and George struck out on his own. He died of pneumonia at the age of 32 at the Eldorado Mine in 1913. Some said he had lost the will to live over his unrequited love for a married woman.

David Wiggins (1919-1992) with his sisters, Betty and 'Pearl', May 1930

A magnificent African in a loin cloth arrived at Philip's home one day. He'd a large trunk on his head, a spear in one hand and led a Great Dane called 'Gelert' with the other. The trunk contained all George's possessions, including six pairs of kid gloves, each with one finger missing, as George had lost a finger in an accident[iii].

Kathie, George and Philip's sister, was both good-looking and a good socialiser[10]. She went to stay with her brother Clare (more of him later) and met **Arthur Legat**, son of an Edinburgh lawyer who was an inspector of the National Bank of India in Uganda[11]. After marrying in Entebbe, they settled in **Nairobi**, Kenya, Arthur taking the job of

---

7. *Ella Stevens Wiggins (1908-1937) Philip had six children. The others were Betty (Arabella Beatrice) Wiggins (1910-1998), Philip Hugh Rhodes Wiggins (1911-1989), Pearl (Margaret Jessie) Wiggins (1914-?), Katherine Naine Wiggins (1916-1918) and David Michael Wiggins (1919-1992). Ella married David Martin Goodfellow (1901-?) on graduating in 1929 and then lived with Teddy (George Edwin) Fussell (1889-1990) 6 Tavistock Place (1936), in Bloomsbury. Her death was registered in her former married name.*

8. *David Michael Wiggins (c1942-1992).*

9. *George Francis Wiggins (1880-1913).*

10. *Kathleen Eliza Wiggins (1875-1963) married Arthur Alexander Legat OBE (1875-1959) in 1910 at St John's, Entebbe.*

11. *Arthur's father, Robert Legat (1831-1877), was a 'Writer to the Signet'.*

Manager of its branch there. On retirement, they resided in a beautiful house (with 100 acres) at Limuru and bred race-horses[iv].

The other brother in Africa, **Bernard** trained as a lawyer. He joined the colonial service in Uganda and was posted to **Zanzibar**[12]. Zanzibar was an island off the eastern coast of Africa with a world monopoly on cloves – Christmas wouldn't be the same in our house without bread sauce made with an onion pierced with cloves. The island had become prosperous from the trade in slaves under its Muslim rulers but, in 1890, the Sultan made it a British protectorate and the British abolished its slave trade[v]. Bernard began by pleading cases on behalf of the native population. He was popular with the judiciary because he brought cases to court quickly. 'I can't see any point in hanging about,' he used to say. He was fluent in the native Swahili and could solve most squabbles before they came to court.

Bernard liked entertaining. Single until the age of 44, he had ten servants and a cook and a Spode white china dinner service with a pink and gold rim which had come from the Sultan of Zanzibar's palace[13]. The Sultan

Arthur Legat (1875-1959) & his wife Kathie (née Wiggins) (1875-1963)

Gardine, Limuru, Kenya

Bernard Wiggins (1878-1972) entertaining well

was a friend who made him a Commander of the Order of the Brilliant Star of Zanzibar[vi]. They met again when the Sultan came to London for Queen Elizabeth II's coronation.

Bernard retired in about 1935[vii]. His Indian clerk stayed in contact until his death. In wartime, back in Britain, Bernard received regular supplies of dried fruit, figs, dates, crystalized apricots and cloves with a note saying, "I look on you as a father and your daughter as a sister."

Bernard on the right and his wife Phyllis (née Mason) (1889-1966) on the left handing out prizes for croquet

✳ ✳ ✳ ✳

Clare Aveling Wiggins

However, this chapter is mainly about their brother **Clare**, because Clare wrote down his life story[14]. Clare took to me in some mysterious way. Perhaps I showed promise, or a peaceful personality or my interest in ordination. He sent me some amazing Christmas presents. The finest was an enormous Times Atlas of the World, quite different from the one we had at school. It had fabulous detail on every country, not just the red coloured ones. I kept it in my bookcase until it fell to pieces and my wife Carolyn bought me a replacement.

Clare is usually a girl's name but he was named after a village where his family had farmed.

Bernard Camping in Zanzibar 28 Oct 1916

---

12. *Bernard Henry Wiggins OBE CBSZ (1878-1972) married Phyllis Therese Mason (1889-1966) in 1922.*
13. *Sayyid Sir Khalifa II bin Harub Al-Said GCB GCMG GBE (1879-1960) [NR].*
14. *Rev Dr Clare Aveling Wiggins CMG MRCS LRCP (1876-1965) married Ethel Beatrice Elliott (1880-1978) in 1904.*

Brilliant Star of Zanzibar

Born at *Watcombe Manor* in Watlington and schooled at Oxford, he received six years of medical training at St Mary's London, followed by a year at Fulham Infirmary.

Clare didn't know what to do after he qualified. He thought of applying for the Indian Medical Service (IMS) which had the highest reputation. His uncle, **Henry Seccombe**, was Senior Clerk at the India Office and arranged for Clare to meet the chairman of the Indian Medical Board[15]. Clare was short-sighted and wore spectacles – rimless in the hope that people didn't notice. Because of his eyesight, the Chairman suggested Uganda instead of India – and as he was to dine with the Foreign Secretary, Lord Lansdowne, that night, he promised to mention the matter to him[16]. It wasn't just what you knew but who you knew.

Three or four days later, a telegram arrived, appointing him Medical Officer, subject to fitness test. Clare had to see the Foreign Secretary's Principal Private Secretary, The Hon Eric Barrington[17]. It was 1901 and the British Empire was at its zenith. Barrington had an enormous office – Clare made the long walk up to the far end and stood before his desk. Barrington looked up:

"Ah, there must be some mistake," he said, "I rang for Dr Wiggins."

"I am Dr Wiggins," Clare replied.

"I meant the Dr Wiggins who is going to Uganda."

"I'm going to Uganda," Clare said. There was a long pause whilst Barrington eyed him up and down.

"I suggest you go away and come back in ten years' time."

Clare had had the same problem with patients on the Fulham wards. They'd ask him to fetch the Doctor, with a frequent "there's a good boy."

After several questions about his education and parents, questions not permitted today, Barrington ended the interview in the traditional manner.

"Do you have any questions?"

"Yes sir; what pension do I get when I retire?"

"Pension? PENSION? Good heavens boy; no one lives to draw a pension."

Uncle Clare lived until he was 89, drawing his civil service pension for over 40 years.

✳ ✳ ✳ ✳

Africa as it was

Mombasa is on the east African coast with a natural deep-water harbour. In 1901, it had only been in formal British possession for 3 years. Prior to that it had been a possession of the Sultan of Zanzibar; and before that, of the Sultan of Oman. In the 16th century, when the Jesus Fort was built, it was Portuguese. In Uncle Clare's time, Jesus Fort was British officers' quarters; the native housing had spread north from the pier and the European's houses to the south. The offices and shops stretched along a narrow street leading to the landing place. The 660-mile railway to Lake Victoria started here[viii]. At that time, the island was mostly covered in low scrub and baobab trees. Now the town has spread to the mainland. With a million people it is the second largest city in Kenya.

Mombasa quay c 1901

15. *Henry Lawrence Seccombe (1841-1910) was a First Secretary in the India Office. He married Emily Ann Wiggins (1846-1930) in 1876.*

16. *Henry Petty-Fitzmaurice KG GCSL GCMG GCIE PC, 5th Marquess of Lansdowne (1845-1927) [NR], was Foreign Secretary 1900-05, India Minister in 1880 and Viceroy of India 1888-94.*

17. *Hon Sir Eric (Bernard Eric Edward) Barrington KCB (1847-1918) [NR] Principal Private Secretary to the Secretaries of State for Foreign Affairs (Foreign Secretaries) 1886-92 and 1895-1905. Assistant Under-Secretary of State (Under Secretary) for Foreign Affairs 1906.*

To reach Mombasa, Clare had sailed through the Suez Canal, down the Red Sea and changed ships at Aden. The new ship hugged the coast, sailing 'against the monsoon'. Swimming with seasickness, Clare swayed off the ship and onto the jetty to be informed he would be taking over from his predecessor the following day. He booked into the Mombasa Club, founded just 5 years previously with its 60-odd members, all men, mostly government officials. Still a private club, and still in existence, today it has 2,500 members. After the meal, on that first evening, they elected him Club Secretary – his predecessor having fulfilled that role. Being his first evening, it was probably best to accept.

Ex-pat (or 'Colonial') life has its ups and downs. There were some heavy drinkers. Drinks started at 11am with 'elevenses'. At the St Andrew's dinner, which Clare had to organise, a bottle of whisky stood proudly in front of each place-setting. As the meal progressed, his colleagues remarked how well young Clare was keeping up with the old soaks – he didn't let on that he'd filled his bottle with lemonade.

Clare quickly sought to change the uncooperative relationship between the government and the Church Missionary Society (CMS) – "Don't employ a 'Mission boy'; they steal things," he'd been told. The CMS hadn't made a good fist of things either, added to which Mombasa was Muslim and Christians were being persecuted. In 1895, up country, the evangelical first Anglican Bishop of Mombasa, Bishop Hannington had been killed by the King of Buganda[18]. The explorer Ernest Gedge was critical of the way the CMS was run: "Everyone claiming the right to hold individual opinions," in glaring contrast with the Roman Catholic Church's mission. "Book learning and theoretical knowledge are undoubtedly very excellent things in their way, but unless such knowledge is applied to the task of turning out not only religious, but at the same time practically useful individuals, its value is considerably lessened."[ix] Bishop Hannington had had more zeal than sense[x].

A few days after arrival, Clare walked the mile north through the native town to visit the CMS Hospital at Mzizima. It was well-planned with separate wards, all thatched. Clare promptly offered to help once a week on operation days. When he told his boss, he was threatened with suspension. "Government officials are to have no dealings with the missionaries," he was told. Independent to the last, Clare announced he would be operating the following Wednesday in any case. Nothing further happened. Later, in 1909, in Uganda, Clare was to sit on the governing body of the country's CMS, the first non-missionary to do so. Things had improved.

During his time as Mombasa Club Secretary, he entertained Winston Churchill and the Aga Khan[19]. When someone put the Aga Khan up for membership, members objected – the Aga Khan was not 'one of us'. In the end, the vote was passed by a majority of one, Clare's. The Aga Khan, head of the Nizari Ismaili Shia Muslims in the provinces of the west of India, with god-like status, was the toast of European society. In his twenties, he'd already been knighted by the Queen. Clare remarked about the champagne he was drinking – didn't his religion forbid alcohol?

"That's true," he smiled, "but in my case, the moment the champagne touches my lips, it changes into pure water."

View from the Jesus Fort, Mombasa, c1901

Vasco de Gama Street, Mombasa c1901

Mombasa Anglican Cathedral. Clare was present at its 1905 consecration.

18.   *The Rt Rev James Hannington (1847-1885) [NR].*
19.   *Sir Winston L Spencer-Churchill KG OM CH (1874-1965) was Correspondent for the Morning Post in Africa from 1899, making his maiden speech in parliament 1901. Under-Secretary of State for the Colonies 1905-08. Sultan Sir Muhammed Shah, Aga Khan III, GCSI GCMG HCIE GCVO PC (1877– 1957) [NR], was the 48th Imam of the Nizari Ismaili community. First President of the All India Muslim League, he pushed for the establishment of the Muslim state of Pakistan. He was President of the League of Nations 1937-8.*

179

Clare met Winston Churchill again in 1907 when he was Under-Secretary of the Colonies. Churchill had chosen to travel the whole of Africa from South to North and later published a book about his travels[20]. Clare, on the other hand, was on a visit to one of his outlying 'hospitals'. The train had stopped because of a 'washout' – everyone had to change. On the platform, Churchill spotted Clare and for the rest of the journey they shared a railway carriage, exchanging views, some of which filtered into the book. Churchill concluded that Uganda had the brightest future of all the countries in Africa – a future that Clare was to help create.

Things here weren't quite like England. On Clare's desk, on his first day, there was a note from the Superintendent of Police. One of his men had been bewitched by a witch-doctor and was convinced he'd die at midnight. Clare found nothing wrong and sent him back for duty. Later in the day he was back, asking to be admitted. Clare asked his Indian orderly to keep a watch and promised to return at midnight. He joined a dinner party at the Jesus Fort and forgot about the time – when the Fort's gong struck the first of twelve strokes, he jumped up and dashed back to be told the man was dead. His hospital assistant was laying out the body – the man had never moved until the first stroke of twelve, at which point he had fallen back on the bed, dead.

Life was full of hazards. On Christmas Day 1902, the Provincial Commissioner invited him and all the local Europeans to a party at Kisumu. Clare had been camping on the west side of Kavirondo Bay (Winam Gulf) on a scientific investigation. He walked into Kisumu during the afternoon, accompanied by his 'boy'. In Africa, 'boy' meant a male domestic servant but in this case it *was* a boy. They walked round a small bay, hollowed out during the rainy season. After the Christmas evening's entertainment, including a 'ping pong' match which Clare won, it was time to go home. Clare gave the boy the choice of going home round the bay or going through the water. The boy chose the quick way. Clare had a change of clothes but the boy took off his kanzu, his ankle length robe, folded it up, put it on his head, and put their paraffin lamp (to see by) on top of that. It was a **very** dark night and the water was deeper than expected – up to Clare's waist and up to the boy's armpits. Suddenly there was a terrific snort from a hippopotamus just three yards ahead. The boy and the lamp disappeared. Clare called out again and again but there was no reply. It was pitch dark, and he'd no idea which way to go. All he could do was stand still until daybreak, up to his waist in the water.

It was a long night – very long. A Christmas night like no other. Clare wondered why he had ever left the shores of England to come out to this confounded country. The following day the boy's kanzu was found floating in the water. Some months later, when the lake dried up, they found the lamp but the boy's body was never discovered.

Distances covered on foot were huge. Three or four months into the job, Clare was sent to tend a District Commissioner at Malindi, 80 miles up the coast. It was a quiet place, with a long sandy beach. An Indian Bazaar and a few houses for the government officials dotted the shoreline. John Milton mentioned Malindi in Paradise Lost[xi]. A magnificent Chinese fleet had visited it in 1414; and Vasco da Gama called in 1498[21]. It was a centre for the slave trade until the 1800s. The only way for Clare to get there was to walk along the coast – it took him two days. The Commissioner was 'run down'; he'd been saving to get married and had not been eating. Clare prescribed a generous diet, and gave him a 'tonic'.

---

[20] *My African Journey.*

[21] *Admiral Zheng He (1371–1433) [NR], a castrated Muslim eunuch of the Ming Emperor YongLe (1360-1424) [NR] conducted 7 voyages with up to 63 huge ships and 28,000 crew. Vasco da Gama, 1st Count of Vidigueira (c1460-1524) [NR],*

Clare had to be fit. When a plague broke out at Mbale, he walked the 85 miles to sort it out. Starting at daybreak, it took him two days. Overseeing the building of an isolation hospital fifteen miles outside Kampala in 1907, he walked there, coming home for the weekend. It took him three hours each way – 5mph wearing his pith helmet (topi) – the sun's rays were 'dangerous'[xii].

Perhaps the most amazing walk was on leave to and from Britain in 1919 at the end of the war. There was no transport, so he walked to Egypt up the Nile. He returned with his wife Ethel, who'd spent the war in England and his brother Bernard. They took a boat to Alexandria and a train to Khartoum. They sailed to Gondokoro near Juba, and walked the next 100 miles to Nimule in Sudan. They waded the rivers up to their armpits, Clare carrying Ethel on his shoulders. From Nimule they caught a steamer down the Mountain Nile to Butiaba on Lake Albert. They walked 35 miles to Hoima, and then set out for Entebbe, another 145 mile trek.

Clare had many opportunities to explore on his own. He must have been the first European to climb the 1,751 metre high Mount Homa, on the shores of Lake Victoria, and the 4,865 metre high Tororo Rock, which was 40 miles from the lakeside[xiii]. Because he was the first, there was no path and no guide – no local man would venture up there – there was a local taboo. Fearless, he went on his own. In their missionary years, years later, Clare and Ethel both climbed Mount Elgon twice, leaving their names in the bottle on Jackson Summit (4,165 m).

Uncle Clare was a keen entomologist. He sent butterflies back to Prof Edward Poulton, at Oxford University's Natural History Museum – Poulton knew him well and visited him in Africa in 1905[22]. Clare sent not only butterflies but also dragonflies, beetles and other insects. They came from Toro, Nyanza, Mombasa, Taveta, and Kisumu. There was a set of 153 male *Pierines* which he'd captured in a single sweep of the net in Jinja by the Ripon Falls in 1906.

Being Oxford, the Museum pressed for more research specimens. They asked Clare to ship back a rare whale-headed stork. It is still on display today. The next request was the skeleton of a hippopotamus. This was shot on the same excursion on Easter Monday 1916. He buried the hippo in his garden so it would rot. A year later, when he dug it up, Clare cleaned it and packed the bones in a zinc-lined packing case. However, by the time it arrived in Oxford, four small foot bones went missing – the customs had opened it up and had not sealed it again properly. The next request, for a pregnant giraffe, he ignored[xiv].

Primitive living

Kisumu on the equator, or Port Florence as it was called, was the western terminus of the Uganda railway. It was the principal port on Lake Victoria – 27,000 square miles of water – the highest dockyard in the world. All the steamers on the lake were built there. There were smart houses with shady trees and a backcloth of hills overlooking the wide expanse of Kavirondo Bay. Magnificent ships waited in harbour with all mod cons – spacious decks, baths and electricity. Immaculate staff in smart blue jackets; officers parading in white on the bridge. The air was cool and fresh. It was like a Swiss lake in the summer, the heart of a continent, a thousand metres above sea level.

Tororo Rock, Uganda

The bird shot by Clare Wiggins on Easter Day 1916 is still on display in the Oxford Museum of Natural History. The Balaeniceps Rex – Whale-headed stork or Shoebill – is the rarest of Ugandan birds, 5 foot tall which lives for up to 50 years.

Kisumu market

Kisumu tribeswomen

"Amekwisha kwenda."
- He is gone

Clare moved to Kisumu after six months at Mombasa. He had no notice about his move. The telegram said the Medical Officer (MO) had been struck down with Black Water Fever, Smallpox and Dysentery and they needed him fast. There was a train the following morning, so Clare packed his belongings – taking provisions for 6 months. The Club gave him a farewell dinner and waved him off at the station. 650 miles later, the train stopped at Kibos. He only had to walk the last six miles.

Clare's dispensary at Kisumu was built of wattle, daub and thatch amongst the nettles, brambles, thistle, and evergreen[xv]. There was 'no money' for a hospital, just two or three grass huts for emergency cases. There were two outlying surgeries, one at Mumias and the other at Nandi. At Nandi, the Kavirondo (Luo) tribe were stark naked, except for the married women who wore a tail of maize fibre, ornamented with beads, kept in place by a belt of beads round the waist. The beads covered nothing yet they were faithful to their partners, unlike the more attractive Masai[xvi].

Kisumu was the capital of the Nyanza Province[xvii]. The Province transferred to British East Africa in 1902 so the railway could be all in one country. Named the 'Uganda Railway', it has ended up in what's now Kenya – the Uganda railway goes to Uganda. 32,000 Indians with railway knowledge had been brought in to build it. 6,000 chose to remain. By the 1970s, 90% of the Ugandan economy depended on them. In 1972, Idi Amin arbitrarily threw them out, using African leaders' dubious logic, which decimated the economy along with everything else. Britain arranged for them to settle in the UK and many ended up in Leicester. This crumbling Midlands mill town found a new lease of life.

At Kisumu, he found the Medical Officer's house deserted. It wasn't much of a house. Two circular huts under one roof with a narrow veranda; doors but no windows, just spaces in the wall. A house boy shambled up.

"Where is the 'dokitali (doctor)?" asked Clare.

"Amekwisha kwenda." He is gone, was the reply.

"Gone? Is he dead?"

The boy limply pointed at the hills. He'd gone birds-nesting. He wouldn't be back before nightfall.

The Dokitali couldn't be that ill. Clare looked around for the District Commissioner (DC)'s office and tried the building with the Union Jack.

"I've come to relieve the MO. I hear he's sick."

The DC laughed and gave him lunch. He introduced him to the Provincial Commissioner (PC). They explained. The MO had become so depressed they just had to find a replacement. At one point the MO had decided he was dying, summoned the four other Europeans to his bedside and distributed all his worldly possessions to them – gun, camera, ring etc. Next morning, he felt better and wanted them back. They were all returned except for the ring, which had been given to an African woman living with the Engineer – she only agreed to return it when the guy bought it back from her. Clare stayed with the PC until the MO at last vacated his quarters. They never saw him again.

The colonies were run with few staff. At Kisumu, there were only three other British. The District Commissioner spent most of his time 'on safari'. The other two were often laid up with fever and Clare found himself in charge. He'd found the best way to escape malaria was to wear boots, as in the Sudan, made of thin red leather right up to his hips. He used a mosquito net at night. Despite all the Malaria Commission reports, he didn't take quinine unless he actually *had* malaria – those who took 5 grains a day ended up with Black Water Fever as well.

These few civil servants had to make things up as they went along. One day a consignment of money arrived in timber boxes too heavy to carry. One bright spark hit upon a scheme of sawing the boxes in two and nailing new sides to each half. Sound in theory, it turned into a nightmare in practice. As they sawed, a fountain of cents and half cents spilled out all over the floor. They had to count several thousand pounds of half-cent coins before they could confirm that everything was present and correct.

Governing an embryonic country was rife with danger. Before Christmas 1903, Clare was sent to map the tsetse fly population on the shores of Lake Victoria. He was accompanied by nine local Askari police, 2 dug-out canoes, eighteen paddlers and a steersman. Whilst the others rowed, he sat on a camp chair in the middle, the empire displayed in its full pomp and circumstance, even in the back-woods of Africa. It must have been a formidable sight. Then the bad news. He found the natives didn't like the Askaris. So here he was, in a strange land, all on his own, with an enemy tribe. In these circumstances, most would have retained their security force but not Clare. He sent them home. After that, Clare was surrounded: he was one of the few white men they'd ever seen. Perhaps it was because he was a doctor or because he was a Wiggins but Clare had less anxiety than his colleagues, who were relieved they hadn't been asked to go.

One of the oldest missionaries in Africa 1903, sitting in style in a dug-out canoe, made from a solid tree trunk

On another occasion, at the Nozia River, Clare pitched his tent in a place where the grass was short and decided to bathe. The last thing he took off was his spectacles – Clare was very short sighted. He laid them on his towel on the bank so he could find them easily when he got out. After the swim, it took him some time to clamber back onto dry land, which he did with some difficulty. He found the towel and put his glasses on. He could see again. He looked around, only to find a couple of hundred men, women and children staring at him as he rubbed himself dry. The next day, after a hot day's butterflying, he rashly followed the same procedure only, this time, there were a couple of thousand looking at him, on both sides of the river. Quite a spectator sport – none of the Kavirondo people had seen a naked white man before.

Africa can be cruel. For those of you with delicate constitutions, I suggest you 'look away now' for the next five paragraphs. We often hear stories, but Clare saw the full effects of such cruelty at close hand.

On a Sleeping Sickness Extended Investigation in 1905, Clare camped at Jinja under a tree called Mutesa's tree. The following morning, he found out how the tree got its name. 'Mutesa the First' was the Kabaka of Buganda, the local king of Uganda[23]. A few years earlier, he'd decided to do some medical research, African style. He wanted to know what the most important organ in the body was. So he captured 3,000 of the Basoga tribe and had them cut up piecemeal – he sat under the tree while the slaughter went on. Before him were entrails, innards, organs – all extracted whilst the victims were alive. At the end of the second day, the Kabaka pronounced that the heart was the organ he was looking for.

Kabaka Mutesa I (1856-1884) [NR]

In 1907, Clare supervised the building of an isolation hospital at Buwanuka. On his first day, as he approached the site – a gentle slope of coarse grass – something darted across his path, about the size of a large dog.

"I stopped and asked my interpreter what it was, and he said 'A man', and ran and brought him back to me. He was a ghastly sight and I felt really sick."

The man had no hands, no feet, no lips, no nose, no ears, no eyelids, and no private parts. A basket under his chin caught his saliva. He grinned and told Clare his story. The Kabaka, Mutesa I, kept a herd of cattle and his herdsmen found there were three short, so they exacted punishment on the nearest village. Thirteen of its inhabitants – women and children – were mutilated in this way. He was the only survivor. Clare expressed his disgust and the man simply laughed. The interpreter said, "He says you don't see the joke" for afterwards, when they counted the herd again, they found them all there.

On another occasion, in 1909, Clare met an old woman who had been one of the Kabaka's cooks. One day Mutesa had found a hair in his soup. He ordered both her eyes to be gouged out and both her hands chopped off. When Uncle Clare expressed his deepest sympathy, the woman replied "But there *was* a hair in the soup." How anyone could find laughter or logic in such adversity is almost unique to Africa. This Kabaka was known as Mukabya, 'He who causes weeping'.

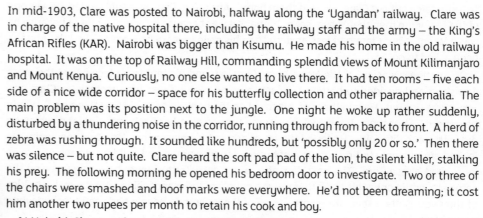

❋ ❋ ❋ ❋

The start of civilisation as we know it

Nairobi in 1900, one year after its start

In mid-1903, Clare was posted to Nairobi, halfway along the 'Ugandan' railway. Clare was in charge of the native hospital there, including the railway staff and the army – the King's African Rifles (KAR). Nairobi was bigger than Kisumu. He made his home in the old railway hospital. It was on the top of Railway Hill, commanding splendid views of Mount Kilimanjaro and Mount Kenya. Curiously, no one else wanted to live there. It had ten rooms – five each side of a nice wide corridor – space for his butterfly collection and other paraphernalia. The main problem was its position next to the jungle. One night he woke up rather suddenly, disturbed by a thundering noise in the corridor, running through from back to front. A herd of zebra was rushing through. It sounded like hundreds, but 'possibly only 20 or so.' Then there was silence – but not quite. Clare heard the soft pad pad of the lion, the silent killer, stalking his prey. The following morning he opened his bedroom door to investigate. Two or three of the chairs were smashed and hoof marks were everywhere. He'd not been dreaming; it cost him another two rupees per month to retain his cook and boy.

At Nairobi, Clare was busier, with a medical staff of eight, none of them European. Because Nairobi was on the railway line, it had become the centre of civilisation. Settlers and traders were pouring in with little infrastructure to support them. Many sought help from Clare, the Government Medical Officer. He was supposed to charge for his services but, like the NHS, few paid up.

One patient was Lady Plowden. Her husband, Sir William, was a Justice of the Peace on the same Bench as Clare's father. She had 'jiggers' (burrowing fleas) in her feet and refused to permit her boy to remove them[xviii]. Clare's response was also to refuse – the native African was far more of an expert that he was. On another occasion, two Italian Counts were staying at the best hotel in town, the Norfolk. One day after breakfast, they thought they had food poisoning. The hotel manager phoned him in some distress and Clare gave each of them an emetic. They coughed up seven rolled slices of ham between them. They'd swallowed them whole – holus-bolus. The hotel manager was so pleased he doubled the 15 Rupee fee that Clare had charged.

Perhaps it was his churchgoing or perhaps his genes but Clare was a good volunteer and organiser. He was the first ever Secretary of the Nairobi Golf Club. Later he was Secretary of the Entebbe Club and its Tennis Club. As Secretary of the Nairobi Club, he met the Elliott family, Charles and Alice and their six daughters[24]. An apocryphal story says that the girls were so attracted to him that their mother threatened to end his medical career unless he married one of them. He chose the prettiest, Ethel. At least three of her sisters remained spinsters all their lives – perhaps they were as fierce as their mother.

---

[24] *Charles Frederick Elliott (1847-1911) married Alice Mary Johnstone (1852-1942) in 1877 in Tamil Nadu, India.*

In one respect, 1908 Nairobi was not much different to 2018 when a meeting to form a church was called, "There were not many of us there.... Very few were keen churchgoers, but those of us who used it were very proud of it." The church started off small, built of corrugated iron. Later they built a stone cathedral, with a catholic-dark nave – the lighter chancel was added later.

Clare and Ethel's marriage in 1904 was the first marriage of white people in Nairobi. Because there was no church, they married in the Railway Institute[xix]. Two years later, when they discovered it wasn't licensed for the 'solemnization of matrimony' one jester suggested they could 'get out of it' if they wanted. The marriage lasted sixty-one years.

Ethel was never someone with whom I found much in common. Clare seemed to do the talking and have the ideas but Ethel didn't have to say much to be heard – he'd listen to her carefully. She had a crisp and imperious way of speaking. Hers was an Anglo-Indian family, used to issuing orders, a trait she passed down to her eldest son **Denie** (pronounced Dennie) and her eldest daughter **Phyllis**[25].

In 1909, Clare moved his family to **Entebbe**, the capital of Uganda on the shores of Lake Victoria. The exchange swap with an MO from Uganda allowed him to escape another stint at Kisumu. Their house was on the 'front row' facing the tennis club. It had five rooms with mosquito nets all round. They had 11 staff to look after his family. Not as comprehensive as in Indian postings, but extensive. The cow boy looked after a herd of fifteen cows, which Clare kept until 1911. The yield was 'absurdly' low – half a pint per cow per day; did some of it maybe end up elsewhere?

Denie was Clare and Ethel's firstborn, arriving two weeks after my father[xx]. My father Paul (Denison Haskins) held the dubious title of eldest of 20 first cousins, but Denie had the better education. After school in Oxford and University at London, he went to work at the Colonial Office. He trained to become a surveyor and worked for what became the Ministry of Overseas Development. He spent his twenties in Nigeria, marrying **Masie MacNair** in 1933[26]. There is (or 'was' – if climate warming continues) a Wiggins glacier in the Antarctic named after him.

In 1910, at the age of 33, Clare became Deputy to the Principal Medical Officer for Uganda. It came with a handsome salary of £600 per year. His boss went on leave almost at once. Clare took over and pretty much carried on when his boss came back, his boss being as indecisive as he was sickly. Eventually, eight years later when his boss retired, Clare drew the senior pay.

As the senior Government Medical position in Uganda, Clare was one of a small coterie of

Marriage of Clare and Ethel in 1904. Behind, Ethel's parents, Charles and Alice Elliott with two of her five sisters.

Government House Entebbe c1909

Denison and Denie

Clare and Ethel's staff in Entebbe

- Head boy
- boy's toto
- Cook
- cook's toto
- Dhobi (washing) boy
- Water boy
- Fish boy
- Wood boy
- Cow boy
- Garden boy
- Ayah (children's maid).

This was reduced later by three:
- one toto for cook and boy
- A large water tank replaced the water boy
- The Dhobi boy, Zakayo, became Head boy.

The Wiggins Glacier, Antarctica

---

25. *Lt Col William Denison Clare Wiggins OBE CMG (1905-1971) and Phyllis Clare Wiggins (1908-1989).*
26. *Denie (William Denison Clare) Wiggins OBE CMG (1905-1971) married Mary Isabel MacNair (1907-1991) in 1933. Her father was a manufacturer in North London – horsehair and methylated spirits. On retirement in 1968, Denie was Director of Overseas (Geodetic and Topographic) Surveys.*

officials who ruled the country. Britain's rule of law there started in 1888 with much the same genesis as in India. The Imperial British East African Company, authorised itself, *'To undertake the duties of general administration, imposition and collection of taxes and administration of justice in areas under its control'*. It wasn't until 1920 that a formal Legislative Council was established. The LEGCO was chaired by the Governor with seven members. The Ugandan LEGCO first met in March 1921 and Clare was a member until he retired aged 45, in June 1922.

✳ ✳ ✳ ✳

Clare Wiggins (seated centre) Principal Medical Officer of Uganda, with his staff 1914

Africa revisited

Clare left Uganda under a bit of a cloud. His family and friends nicknamed him 'Dreyfus' – after an officer in the French army who'd been wrongly convicted of treason, protesting his innocence, dividing opinion, and was eventually proved right[27]. When Clare grew a moustache he even looked the part – he'd fallen out with the acting Governor whose son desired to be a doctor. The boy was smoking fifty to sixty cigarettes a day and had *mitral stenosis*: Clare didn't think he'd make the grade and advised him to get fit. Stung by this, the boy's father did everything in his power to obstruct Clare. Behind his back, he tried to cancel Clare's honour (a CMG). Wiggins's don't take things lying down – it was the talk of the Colonial Service from the Cape to Cairo. Everyone (almost) was on Clare's side.

It only took 4 years of retirement for Clare to become restless. He'd read about a 'World Call for Missionaries'. The Mission to Lepers had asked him for advice and he offered to go to Ngoro in the north west of Uganda to try out a new treatment – *hydrocarpus esters*. He took his family, at some risk to their lives, and lived on his pension. The British Empire Leprosy Relief Association paid for a house, the drugs and gave him £2,000. Daughters

27. *Lt Col Alfred Dreyfus (1859-1935) [NR]. The miscarriage of justice haunted France from 1894 to 1906.*

Norah and Phyllis left Abingdon School and received 6 months training – Phyllis in nursing and Norah secretarial. They set off in August 1927, stopping off in South Africa on the way, where they were shown round Robben Island, then closing down as a leper hospital[xxi]. Later, Nelson Mandela got to know it only too well, spending eighteen of his twenty-seven prison years there[28].

As they stepped off the boat at Mombasa, the Wiggins family were greeted by Zakayo, their head houseboy whom they'd last seen in 1922. How did he know? He resumed duties in Ngora as if there'd been no break.

Clare selected five sites for the clinics, taking advice from the Ngora tribal Chiefs. He was worried his earlier spat would have put him out of sorts with the government people but they needed him more than he them. A drought worked to his advantage – the government asked Clare to distribute aid.

The first clinic, at Soroti, was ready within the year. It seemed natural enough to arrange a grand inauguration and Clare recruited the Bishop to bless it[29]. The Saza Chief encouraged all lepers to come. Thousands turned up but to their relief, not all were potential patients – Africans like a blast and had brought their friends and relations.

It was a 70-hour week. The record was 625 injections in one day. The head man, Onesimus, would say a prayer, then lead everyone in the Lord's Prayer and a hymn[xxii]. Onesimus stayed on when Clare and Ethel returned to England and helped run the Kumi hospital for over 25 years.

Leprosy had a high social stigma. It was a deforming disease with no hope of a cure. The Leprosy Centres at Kapiri (150 adults) and Kumi (150 children) were the only places where lepers could live in dignity but, as cures were found, the need for the centres disappeared. Kapiri became a general hospital, moving to Ongino in 1934, and the other became the 'Wiggins School'. Both suffered total collapse during the 1985-92 civil war, but both have been restored. Leprosy is still prevalent in the world. India has discriminatory laws prejudicing the rights of lepers. Only in 1996 did Japan rescind a law which forced segregation, abortions and sterilisation of lepers. Attitudes have still to change[xxiii].

Clare did a lot of hands-on work, impressing the locals who'd seldom seen a senior educated white person doing DIY. He helped build two schools and a wing at the Frieda Carr Hospital that became known as the 'Wiggins Ward'. He built a dormitory at the girls' school and reroofed the chapel of the boy's school. Ethel equipped it – blankets, cutlery and other supplies.

The whole family returned to Oxford in 1931 where Clare worked as an Examiner, living in Leckford Road, North Oxford, a couple of streets away from where I was to live in 2006-7. Clare was ordained a deacon in 1942 and as a priest a year later at the age of 66, becoming the Vicar of Pyrton with Shirburn near his old family home[xxiv].

The Manor, Upton Grey with its garden designed by Gertrude Jekyll, 1950s

In 1950, Clare and Ethel moved to Upton Grey in Hampshire. They occupied one half of the *Manor House* with a colleague who'd served in Africa occupying the other. It was there that I knew them. The Arts and Crafts architect Ernest Newton had given the house a makeover in the tile-hung vernacular style and Gertrude Jekyll had designed the garden[xxv]. It had a croquet lawn and a long drive, which he planted with cowslips. Clare tended the large vegetable patch, read theology, sewed tapestries and wrote up the story of his life.

The quiet and humble daughter Norah retrained as a missionary and as a teacher with the CMS. She became Principal of the girls' school in Ngora. In her spare time, she translated the Bible into Ateso for the British and Foreign Bible Society – a mammoth task. By the time of Ugandan Independence in 1962, she'd taken on the role as Secretary for the Bishop of Soroti[30].

Upton Grey Manor from the drive

---

28. *Nelson Rolihlahla Mandela (1918-2013) [NR].*

29. *Rt Rev Arthur Leonard Kitching (1875-1960) [NR], Bishop of the Upper Nile 1926-1936.*

30. *Rt Rev S Tomusange [NR] in 1962. Ateso is spoken today by 2 million Iteso tribes on the borders of northern Uganda and Kenya.*

Clare Wiggins's family: Mervyn, Phyllis, Judith, Clare, Ethel, Norah, Masie, Mona, and Dennie in 1947

Independence Day Celebrations

Mulago Hospital, Kampala

The loud and forceful Phyllis took up domestic science and held a post at *Cheltenham Ladies College*. This must have suited her clipped speech and brusque nature. Bossiness and clever put downs, absolute certainty and unequivocal assertion were the product of Oxford society. Her shy younger brother Mervyn must have felt swamped[31]. At Cheltenham, Phyllis met her life-long companion, the 'delightful Miss Gem' who was a Housemistress there[32].

In 1954 and 1964, Clare and Ethel celebrated their Golden and Diamond Weddings. They invited the extended family – I was 6 and 16 at those parties. Being Easter-time, we went on the way back from Cornwall.

Clare and Ethel went back to Uganda to visit Norah at Ngora in 1938, 1950 and 1962. In 1962, when Uganda became an independent country, they were official guests at the Celebrations, seated behind the Duke of Kent[33]. For a couple in their 80s, it was a fast-paced ten days[xxvi]. There were receptions, a State Ball, state banquet, a garden party, tattoo and fireworks. One event was at the Governor's church, St John the Evangelist, where Clare had been its first Churchwarden and his sister Kathie had married[xxvii].

At the Tattoo, Sir John Hathorn Hall, a previous Governor, captured the feelings of many in the 60,000 audience when he spoke of the Wiggins as 'the Grandfather and Grandmother' of the immense crowds there[34]. Indeed, Ugandans often adopted surnames of people they respected. 'Wiggins' was one of the most popular.

The Duke of Kent made the hand-over speech and Milton Obote responded[35]. Obote, the new Prime Minister, subsequently went the way of many independent African rulers; in his case, it only took him four years. In 1966 he suspended the constitution and declared himself President. Matters got so bad that, by 1971, his chief General, Idi Amin, ousted him. Uganda then entered an even worse reign of terror – Amin became 'the Butcher of Uganda.'[xxviii] When Obote regained power in 1979, matters didn't improve – even more died during Obote's second term of office than they had under Idi Amin. Yoweri Museveni finally ousted Obote in 1985 following a civil war. With all this bloodshed, there was no peace until about 1992 but, like most African leaders, Museveni clings onto power beyond his natural term.

During this 1962 stay, Clare had built up a good relationship with the new Minister of Health, Dr Lumu[36]. Within three years Obote had dashed Lumu's plans. Frustrated, Lumu talked to his fellow ministers about how best to thrash things out. The conversation reached Obote's ears and Lumu, along with four others, was put in prison. The shock clouded Clare's last days before he died in July 1965[xxix].

Clare's story covers almost the whole sixty year span of British rule in this part of Africa. From a surgery of mud huts in 1902, with no glass in the window, Clare saw the opening in 1962 of the £2.5m state of-the-art 876-bed Mulago hospital. As Churchill had predicted, Uganda's promise had been fulfilled, thanks to the mighty dreams of noble men – at least during the British rule.

Clare lived a frugal life in many ways. He died leaving almost nothing in his will. He'd lived in rented homes, gave much of his earnings to charity and some to his children, whom he described as the 'great consolation of his life'[xxx]. You may consider that Clare Wiggins led a godly life. That's not the case with our next medical man.

31. *Mervyn Clare Wiggins (1911-1971).*
32. *Grace Harvey Gem (1890-1982) [NR].*
33. *Prince Edward George Nicholas Paul Patrick, Duke of Kent KG GCMG GCVO ADC(P) (b1935)*
34. *Sir John Hathorn Hall GCMG, DSO, OBE, MC (1894–1979) [NR], a previous Governor of Uganda.*
35. *Apolo Milton Obote (1925-2005) [NR] President of Uganda 1966-71 & 1980-85, was of the Lango tribe. Ethel was the first European woman to visit the Lango tribe.*
36. *Dr Emmanuel Bijjugo Sajjalyabebe Lumu (b1916) [NR].*

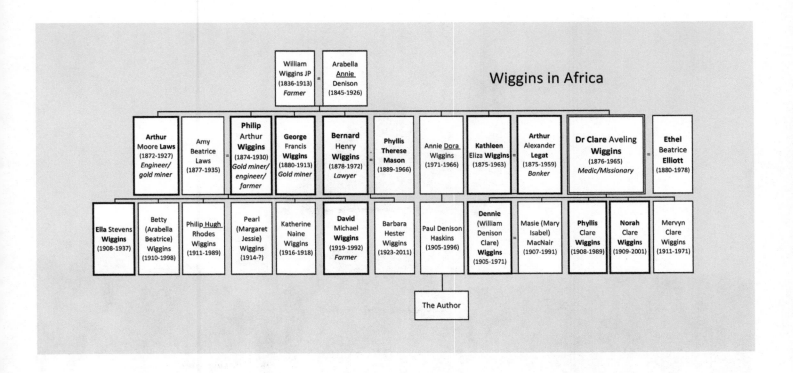

Other Notes and References

i.   Hatcher p7.

ii. Ibid p13.

iii. Ibid p15.

iv. PDH letter from Kathie Legat 25 Feb 1936: Gardyne, Limuru.

v.   Zanzibar was declared a British Protectorate in Nov 1890. The Sultan declared slavery illegal in 1897, some 64 years after Britain, and 34 years after it was abolished in the USA.

vi. London Gazette 11 Dec 1923: "The King has been pleased to give and grant unto Bernard Henry Wiggins, Esquire, His Majesty's Royal Licence and authority to wear the Insignia of the Third Class of the Order of the Brilliant Star of Zanzibar."

vii. Kay p98.

viii. Churchill p219. The early Victorian explorers, and the Buganda people now, refer to Lake Victoria as Lake Nalubale. It is the size of Ireland, with a shoreline 2,000 miles long. Uncle Clare would have deemed the lake to have been the source of the Nile.

ix. The Times 7 July 1893.

x.   (EG) Mss. Brit.Emp.s.290 4/10

xi. Paradise Lost was published in 1667 by John Milton (1608-1674) [NR].

xii. Between 8am and 5pm Europeans would cover their heads. The pith helmet more than anything symbolises the colonial past. It was still in use in World War 2.

xiii. Climbed in 1906.

xiv. Davies and Hull. Clare Wiggins' donations are recorded in the Annual Reviews of the Linacre Professor of Zoology and Comparative Anatomy for 1912, 1917,

1918 and the Presentation Book of the Department of Zoology and Comparative Anatomy for 1934.

xv. (EG) Mss.Brit.Emp.s.290 4/10.

xvi. (EG) Mss.Brit.Emp.s.290 4/3.

xvii. The 'East Africa Protectorate', also known as 'British East Africa', now Kenya, grew out of British commercial interests from the 1880s. It was proclaimed a Protectorate in 1895, transferred from the Foreign Office to the Colonial Office in 1902, and became the Colony of Kenya in 1920. The Capital moved from Mombasa to Nairobi in 1905, halfway along the new railway line, which had started life as a rail depot. The Provinces of Nyanza and Naivasha were transferred in 1902.

xviii. Chigoe flea (Tunga penetrans): sand fleas that burrow below the skin and lay eggs.

xix. Clare and Ethel were married by Rt Rev William George Peel DD (1854-1916), 3rd Bishop of Mombasa 1899-1916.

xx. Paul was born 25 Jan 1905; Denie on 7 Feb 1905.

xxi. Departure from London 25 Aug 1927 on the 'Llandovery Castle', 1st class, via Tenerife and South African ports.

xxii. Iliffe: The 'saintly' Onesimo Busimo [NR] was trained at Mengo Medical School.

xxiii. Michiko Taki 25 Aug 2016, a member of the Nippon Foundation, working with the World Health Organisation. In 2010 a UN resolution resolved to eliminate discrimination. In 2012, there were 232,857 new cases of leprosy, 95% in 16 countries, Brazil being the highest incidence.

xxiv. Clare Wiggins was Vicar of Pyrton with Shirburn 1944-50.

xxv. Ernest Newton, PRIBA, ARA (1856–1922) [NR] winner of the RIBA Gold Medal, was consulting architect to William Willett, author of Daylight Saving, who is remembered by the National Trust woodlands at

Petts Wood, Kent. Newton designed many Edwardian houses near the author's Prep School and the spire of St George's, in Bickley, where Newton lived. Gertrude Jekyll (1843-1932) [NR] created over 400 gardens, many in partnership with Sir Edwin Lutyens. A full set of her 1908 plans for Upton Grey is in the Reef Point Collection at the University of California. Charles Holme (1848-1923), editor of the Studio magazine, was her client.

xxvi. Clare Wiggins was 86 and Ethel his wife 82 in 1962.

xxvii. Clare Wiggins was Churchwarden at St John's 1909-22.

xxviii. The Guardian 12 Oct 2005. As head of the military, Idi Amin ousted Obote while he was at a Commonwealth Conference in 1971 but was overthrown by troops from Tanzania in 1979.

xxix. Although Lumu was later released by Idi Amin in 1971, he had had enough of politics by then and retired quietly – another loss to the country. He was still alive in 2018.

xxx. Kay p12.

Clive's cottage, Paignton, by Elsie Tresidder

Disaster

My grandfather, **Everard Tresidder**, was a bit of a scoundrel[1]. He was a late developer and a rebel to boot. He was born into privilege and a thoroughly Christian household but like most of his brothers, he thought he could do without[i].

Everard associated with the best and worst of society, getting close to the royal family and yet, I suspect, crossing the boundaries into criminal activity. His sexual ethics were wayward and his business affairs doubtful; when he died his finances did not add up. He and his wife separated after my mother Jean married. He died 4 years before I was born – of a heart attack brought on by fright. Nevertheless, he loved my mother, his darling 'Bam' (bambino). He was softly spoken – but scary.

Dr Morton Everard Tresidder (1872-1944)

Everard died before I came on the scene. Not a lot was said about him. There was a portrait at the top of the stairs, the picture on the right. Now I can see the Cornish in him (100%) but he looks weighed down with worldly worries – was it the mass German bombing every night down the street where he lived, his money worries or something else? I became conscious of what the bible said about 'the sins of the fathers being passed onto the third and fourth generations'[ii]. I have often considered my own life in that context – like St Paul, we 'kick against the pricks'[iii].

Everard was born on the New Year's Eve of 1872/3 in Jubalpur (pronounced Jubblepore). Jubalpur was a small town in the middle of India, where his father, the Army surgeon of Chapter 6, had been based. When Everard was five or six, his parents returned to England and made their home in Alleyn Park, Dulwich. He attended Dulwich College as a day pupil in September 1883 but after four years things weren't doing too well. His mind was on anything but his academic tasks – at fifteen he was still in the third year of school (Year 9).

Lausanne, seen here in c1850, progressively developed to the north of the railway

Nevertheless, he made some life-long friends – one was Edward Mountain, 'Uncle Bob' as my mother called him[2]. 'Sir Edward' as the world later knew him, trained as an Insurance underwriter. He famously refused to insure the Titanic. He founded the Eagle Star Insurance Company and went on to make a fortune. Bob and Everard played with pigeons during those early years. It was an interest that was to be more than a passing fancy – they ended up running the national racing scene when pigeon racing was at its height.

Everard was contrary from an early age. When he didn't concentrate on his studies, his parents decided to part him from his pigeons and send him to Switzerland. In 1887, he made the journey through Paris to Jacard's School in Lausanne[iv]. On one trip, he saw the Eiffel Tower half-erected as he crossed Paris. The school was a few minutes' walk above Lake Geneva in a leafy residential quarter. He grew to like his new environment. He adored the gorgeous scenery, the warmth in the summer, the sledging in the winter and the cycling. Cycling was the latest craze – there was a huge variety of cycles, mostly fixed wheels, of all sizes, including one or two 'penny farthings'. Cycling became one of his lifelong passions – long rides right round the lake and up into the hills. He named the bicycle, 'with wheels the same size', that his father bought him: 'Physio'[v]. The fresh air, the new physical and mental challenges all helped him grow in leaps and bounds; he was always growing out of his clothes. Monsieur Jacard's methods of instruction and his new friendships seemed to have done the trick. He wrote home in 1888 to say "I think it was for my own good I came out here as I don't think I should ever have worked at College."[vi]

---

1. *Dr Morton Everard Tresidder MRCS LRCP (1872-1944) married Elsie Annie Garden (1871-1950) in 1900.*
2. *Sir Edward Mortimer Mountain, 1st Bt (1872-1948) [NR] married Evelyn Ellen Regina Seigle (1873-1950) [NR] in 1897.*

Guy's Hospital Boxing Cup 1892, won by Everard Tresidder

Champion Jugo

Mulago Hospital, Kampala

Engraving on a large silver tea-tray, 'As a 'token of esteem from a few North Road Pigeon Fanciers'

His elder brothers were training to be doctors and his father encouraged him to follow. Contrary as ever, he didn't want to be the same. He discussed the idea of being an engineer or a pharmacist instead, but then his father died. It shook him up so much that he vowed to fulfil his father's wishes. He followed his brothers to Guy's where he distinguished himself at boxing. He fought for the hospital in 1893 and he won the United Hospitals Middleweights Cup in 1896. I still have an 1892 Guy's Boxing Cup that he won, sitting on my dressing table.

Everard had not lost his love of pigeons. His friends looked after his birds whilst he was away[vii]. As well as pigeons and cycling, he took to breeding Irish Terriers, large and wiry dogs with handsome intelligent square moustachioed jaws. He entered competitions round the country and ended up at Crufts carrying off the Challenge Certificate for his Champion 'Jugo'. He kept a pedigree book. Many of his dogs started with the letter 'J' – some were biblical – Jehosophat, Jephunneh, Johanna, Jujube, Jay, Jamboree, Jubilate, Juggins to name a few. Even my second name starts with a J as did my mother's first two names[3]. The tradition unconsciously lingers on: both my sons have names starting with a 'J'.

✳ ✳ ✳ ✳

Pigeons

Everard became an expert geneticist long before his time, breeding birds to heights of perfection. By 1899, he was well known in the pigeon world, winning at least 5 first prizes and 3 seconds that year. He wrote to his future wife, "They seem to know me everywhere. Two years ago I was at a dirty little village in Somerset and the man knew more about me than I did myself. Another time I was at Margate and I entered into conversation with a man, who I discovered kept pigeons. We did not introduce ourselves to each other, and to my astonishment he quoted to me what 'Tresidder' says on the subject. I ran away after that, as I found I was contradicting what I had once written about."[viii]

That same year, 1899, he began a life-long friendship with Walter Jones[4]. Jones was the keeper of the Royal pigeons and invited Everard to Sandringham, where they were kept. Mr Jones, as my mother called him (Jones was fifteen years older than Everard) had a day-job as headmaster of the West Newton village school near Sandringham, Norfolk on the border of the royal estate where King George V and his family spent their holidays. My mother's photograph album shows Jones skating with the young princes and of Princess Mary, who was to end up marrying Lord Harewood[5]. The king was a keen pigeon racer, as had been his father, and he gave his sons, the future kings Edward VIII and George VI, specific pigeons to look after, under Walter's supervision. My mother, in her youth, was similarly given jobs feeding her father's pigeons and cleaning out their lofts, and waiting for the bells to ring as they made their way home and 'rang in'.

One of the funniest books I have read, when it is not supposed to be, is my grandfather's book published in the year the Titanic sank, named simply: 'Disasters.'[6] Priced sixpence, this 50 page pamphlet examines the frailties of pigeon racing in a somewhat hectoring tone. Apart from the one success of Barnsley winning the FA Cup that year, there were many disasters. The 'Last' Emperor of China was deposed. Both boats in the Oxford Cambridge

---

3.   *Jean Josephine Frances Mary Tresidder (1904-1976).*
4.   *Joseph Walter Jones (1857-1938) [NR] The Royals raced under the name of J W Jones.*
5.   *HRH Victoria Alexandra Alice Mary, Princess Royal (1897-1965), third child of George V, married Henry George Charles Lascelles, 6th Earl of Harewood KG GCVO DSO TD (1882-1947) in 1922.*
6.   *1912 Disasters A Conscientious Enquiry.*

Boat Race sunk; at the Stockholm Olympic Games, a delirious marathon runner collapsed and died from exhaustion during the race. And there was worse. In May, out of 1,750 pigeons competing in the Swindon race, only 238 finished. In a Rugby race only 5.5% of the birds reached home. Birds were set loose to fly across the sea without much weather intelligence.

In June, they flew 51 birds from the Faeroe Islands some 600-800 miles. It was Everard's decision when to release them. Only 2 reached home. "Result: disastrous." It hurt. "I hoped for the best, and I did my best. I did not do the best," he wrote. It started out all right. Everard persuaded the Danish meteorologists at Torshavn to stay open after personally meeting the London representative. Then he learnt that telegrams from Torshavn came to England via the Shetland Isles, so there had to be someone on duty in Stornoway. He arranged to meet the Director of the Meteorological Office but, 'caught up in medical affairs' (or he forgot), he failed to turn up for the appointment. The result was that nobody was on duty at Stornoway. When the weather blew up the birds, flying against a strong south-west wind, were drenched. They couldn't go forward and they couldn't go back, even if they had the strength to do so.

France was no better. Out of 5,500 birds released in Dieppe, 3% made it home. More disaster. Race after race is listed with these dreadful statistics. The reasons? The main culprit: Meteorological conditions; "No one has ever heard of hunting taking place in a dense fog." Then there was the way the races were organised: Convoyors, Controllers and Conductors needed new standing instructions, with hourly telegrams adopting a 'Convoyors' Telegraph Code' imparting details about Temperature, Sky, Wind direction, etc.

It may not be well known but the Queen still maintains active lofts at Sandringham. They've been there since King Leopold presented the royal family with their first pigeons in 1886.

West Newton and Sandringham Elementary School – c1910

George V and Queen Mary with Walter Jones and a pigeon basket at York Cottage c1910

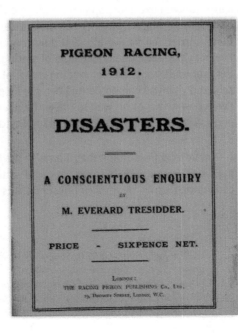

PIGEON RACING, 1912.

DISASTERS.

A CONSCIENTIOUS ENQUIRY
BY
M. EVERARD TRESIDDER.

PRICE - SIXPENCE NET.

LONDON:
THE RACING PIGEON PUBLISHING CO., LTD,
19, Doughty Street, London, W.C.

Princess Mary (later Princess Royal) in her private quarters.

Edward Prince of Wales on the pond at York Cottage

Queen Alexander skating, with Mr Jones on right.

Princess Mary, Queen Alexandra and her sister Marie, Dowager Empress of 'All the Russias', at Loch Muick on the Balmoral estate, 1910

The Royal family outside the pigeon lofts at Sandringham. Walter Jones on the left.

Dr Everard Tresidder with his Aberdeen 400 mile 'YB' candidates August 1936. That year he started breeding with a cross from M Long-Miller in America. It proved even more successful than his own pure strain. 'I am quite certain racing ability is just an inherent a quality as any other.'

33 & 35 Shooters Hill Road, Blackheath

The Royal Pigeon Racing Association (RPRA) is still known for its long races. I have this picture of the royal family: George VI, Queen Elizabeth the Queen Mother, and their two princesses, the present Queen and Princess Elizabeth, with Walter Jones on the left. Even then, our present Queen was clutching a corgi. Currently there are 43,000 pigeon fanciers in Britain[ix]. The sport is declining but debates about lost birds still go on[x]. Pigeons were used in both world wars, carrying messages from the front. In the First World War, the police visited Everard's home suspecting he was a German spy – he narrowly averted another disaster[xi].

After Everard died, my parents kept a clock on their mantelpiece which had sentimental value – the art deco wooden housing contained his favourite pigeon-racing clock, with its very accurate complex brass mechanism. After my mother died, my father took it to the local shop for repair. When he went to collect it two days later, they'd taken out all the brass inner workings and replaced them with an electric motor costing less than £1. What can you say – but another disaster?

✳ ✳ ✳ ✳

Spanish Civil War

After Guys Hospital, Everard found work with a General Practice in Charlton Road Greenwich, lodging at Glenville Villa, Westcombe Park[7]. As well as pigeons, he joined in the social scene of golf and cycling, even chairing an Arts Club Smoking concert – a heavily male affair with an excess of booze and bad behaviour.

Everard got on well with the Practice's junior partner, **Peter Cooper** – and his wife took a shine to him[8]. He was invited to their home in Shooters Hill Road to meet Peter's brother **John Jekyn Cooper**, living in the large and imposing house next door – Stainton Lodge which was big enough to hold parties and dances[9]. A throw-back to the balls in Vienna, in the 1890s girls carried dance cards attached to their dresses on a cord, with a little pencil to write with. Men would ask the girl to dance and, if accepted, would write their name on the card against the programme of pre-arranged dances. One of the men asking one of the girls was my grandfather, Everard.

John was an engineer. He'd met and married **Maggie Garden** whilst in the Furness mining area of northern Lancashire (see Chapter 9). Touring the world in his mining capacity, it made sense to live next door to Peter so Maggie could join in the social whirl of her brother-in-law's family. She'd invite her half-sisters, Fannie, Elsie and Bertie to stay. The middle one, **Elsie Garden** fell for Everard, and they conducted a heavy correspondence from a distance. Everard's pedantic analytical style of writing did not set out to flatter a girl. He'd criticise her grammar, her choice of reading material and her gushing style, but he meant what he said and when he complimented her, she lapped it up. She was 28, and keen to settle down. Everard went out of his way to make the journey north in 1899, via various pigeon and dog engagements. In 1900 they married in Dalton-in-Furness, in the church built by her father (Chapter 9).

Everard and Elsie made their home at the bottom end of Mycenae Road near Greenwich Park with Everard establishing his own Practice, using one of the ground floor rooms as a consulting room[xii]. Jean, their only child, was born in July 1904.

---

7. *Dr Clarke Kelly Morris MRCS (1856-1913) [NR] was senior partner of the practice, ran from his home, Gordon Lodge, 1 Charlton Road, Greenwich.*
8. *Dr Peter Cooper MRCS (1854-1926) married Clarissa Brockbank (1855-1930) in July 1879. They lived at Stainton Lodge, 35 Shooters Hill Road, Blackheath.*
9. *John Jekyn Cooper (1848-1905) married Margaret Jane Garden (1856-c1936) in May 1879. They lived at the semi-detached Regency style house, 33 Shooters Hill Road, Blackheath.*

John and Maggie Cooper moved to Malaga in Spain. John died in 1905 but Maggie stayed on. In 1931 Elsie sailed out there for a holiday[xiii]. Then another disaster struck – in 1936 Maggie was caught up in the Spanish Civil War. All contact was lost and she was never heard of again. Yet one more tragedy.

Maggie Cooper (née Garden) (1856-1936)

✳ ✳ ✳ ✳

The racy biker

In 1923 a further tragedy took place – Everard's youngest brother, Clive, and his wife, Muriel Pollexfen, both died in the same year, he of appendicitis. Clive was the youngest of Everard's brothers, a bit of a madcap. He was only eleven when his father died. Clive was thus a bit of a mother's boy – spoilt, arrogant, and perhaps dependent on women. Regularly visiting Paignton in Devon to care for his mother, he seems to have been making a detour to see his mistress[xiv]. Unlike his Doctor brothers, Clive went into property. He operated out of the West End near Bond Street and acquired an ancient thatched cottage on the water's edge in Paignton[xv]. Paignton was a 'suburb' of Torquay in his day and it was near his mother's home in *Eastleigh Park*[xvi]. My mother Jean spent holidays there when visiting her Granny.

Lynhurst, 36 Mycenae Road, Westcombe Park, Greenwich

Muriel and Clive were only in their mid-forties when they died. Their two children were Rosemary, twelve, and Anthony ten: six and eight years younger than my mother[10]. Everard and Elsie decided the only thing to do was to raise the children themselves. Anthony was found a place at *Felstead School*. The pretty cottage in Paignton was sold and Clive's successful estate agency and his auctioneering business near Bond Street were closed down.

Rosemary travelled with the money that had been left her. In June 1934, at the age of 23, she set sail on the White Star Line for Boston as 'a student intending to make the USA her permanent residence'. She married John Bray in Boston a year later[11]. Born in the Deep South, in Missouri, John was the British Vice-Consul in Detroit. They lived in some 'swell' Foreign Office apartments, overlooking Belle Isle[xvii]. After they divorced in 1973, Rosemary stayed on, living by Saranac Lake in New York State.

Clive's thatched cottage overlooking the sea in Roundham Road at Paignton in 1907. Some say it is the oldest house in the town. It now is one of three standing together but then was on its own. Clive's mother's house was in a terrace a few streets away.

Anthony at St Ives, 1929

Anthony (or Tony as everyone called him apart from our family) turned out to be the biggest scoundrel of them all[12]. All seemed to go well until he discovered girls. At first, he had no interest but in the summer of 1929 in Cornwall, with his debonair good looks, the girls began to chat him up[xviii]. He didn't look back after that. Everard was partly to blame. He's reputed to have said to him, on his coming-of-age,

"Right, time you were a man – let's go to the whorehouse!"[xix]

Anthony's caravan in Pembrokeshire. The site, half a mile south of Newport, was originally bought by Muriel, Anthony's mother, for £20 and was sold and bought a couple of times before one of Anthony's daughters established a home there.

---

10. *Rosemary Muriel Pollexfen Tresidder (1910-1998) and John Anthony Clive Pollexfen Tresidder (1912-2001).*

11. *John Graham Bray (1912-1983) married Rosemary Muriel Pollexfen Tresidder (1910-1992) in 1935. They divorced in their 60s in 1973.*

12. *John Anthony Clive Pollexfen Tresidder (1912-2001) married Ruth Mary Pell (1908-1999) in 1933 and had daughters Lorna N Tresidder (b1938) and Gillian G Pell (b1945).*

Anthony's crane at the gravel pits
Chipstead, Kent. 1955

Marconi masts at Poldhu, Cornwall

Anthony married too young, people said. There's a story that he joined a circus in Lincolnshire. Certainly it was Lincolnshire where he married a timber-feller's daughter, as soon as he was 21. **Ruth Pell** was four years his senior. After the arrival of their first daughter and having conceived a second, he decided he couldn't live up to her aspirations for a conventional suburban (Sidcup) existence, and pushed off.

Anthony spent the rest of his life escaping. Every attempt to chase him for maintenance failed to find him. Not surprising: he'd wiped himself off the face of the earth. He changed his surname to Bardell, kept himself off the electoral register and never lived in a house or flat again.

This peripatetic existence was none the less exciting. He lived in caravans so he could move at a moment's notice. He'd had 49 motor cycles during his life; all bought new, which he took to the TT races on the Isle of Man. From time to time he'd bob up to see my mother in Petts Wood or my sister Barbara near Reading – usually escaping from his last wife or showing off the next. We were the closest thing he had to a family. He picked us up, or dumped us, as the spirit took him.

Anthony was a great romancer. He could tell a good story. He collected five wives in all – I went to one of the weddings. In his eighties, he married a 23-year-old Moroccan girl called Hyatt[xx]. Another Moroccan partner he supposedly 'bought' for £20 dowry and then sold her back because she stole things – a good story but you never knew exactly what to believe. He earned large sums working in the construction industry, operating cranes and diggers – highly skilled employment at that time – and acting as a caretaker for gravel pits. I visited a couple of his caravans too, one right underneath the wireless masts at Crystal Palace:

"I climbed that one last night," he said, pointing to the highest one.

Most of what he said was probable, even if it was invented. He said he'd helped Marconi build the famous radio masts at Poldhu in Cornwall, until someone fell off[13]. And ... was it true he drove Winston Churchill during the war? He lived for the day.

❋ ❋ ❋ ❋

Post Mortem

Meanwhile my grandfather Everard is the subject of speculation. Was he performing illegal abortions? Was there a Spanish Harley Street doctor involved? Had they been discovered and were they expecting a court appearance? When Everard died, did the other doctor go to prison? Was his doctor brother Percy who was in the South of France involved? Such services were in great demand during the war with all the irregular carryings on – particularly with the society ladies who had access to funds. The newspapers regularly reported court appearances of such doctors, but I find no reference to Everard.

A few days before he died Everard wrote from the Royal Hotel at Ascot to my mother. He'd shot off to Ascot principally to get away from the bomb raids. He thought he ought to return and not be scared. Two weeks later he was found dead, from a heart attack, most likely brought on from the fright of those nearby bombs. An hour later, we think, a bomb did indeed drop on the Brigstock Nursing Home with all his books lost or too damaged to be of use[xxi].

13. *Guglielmo Marconi, 1st Marquis of Marconi (1874–1937) [NR]*

Everard left little money compared to his brother Percy. Had something happened? Jean had his solicitor confirm that as an executor she wouldn't be liable for his debts. Had he hidden his money? Was it lost in the bombing? Did he pass his possessions to his 'Matron' or to Elsie, his by now separated wife?[xxii] After his death, his pigeons fetched £50 and his pigeon houses £20 but he owed The *Racing Pigeon* magazine over £30 for advertising[xxiii].

Two years before, his younger brother **Percy Tresidder** had died in France[14]. Percy had been living in Juan le Pins, Antibes, near Cannes since 1930. His long-term mistress was Marie Therese de Fremery and he was not short of other lady bosom friends. When the Second World War began in 1939, he stayed there under the Vichy regime.

Surveying the glittering sea, leisurely languid Juan le Pins must have been an idyllic place in peacetime – hot in summer, balmy in winter laying alongside the crème de la crème. Another resident of the Riviera, the writer Somerset Maugham, described it as a 'sunny place for shady people', but he got out once the war began[xxiv].

Percy didn't. Somehow, Percy accumulated a fortune. He died with £35,000 to his name, forty-four times the wealth of Everard. In his will, Percy had bequeathed a legacy to his favourite brother, but the will couldn't be sorted out. The Germans were progressively occupying the south of France after the Allied successes in Northern Africa, and then Everard died before Germany was ultimately defeated. Ten years later, in 1952, details were still being contested, with the Inland Revenue arguing about the duty payable.

Not even death could prevent another disaster.

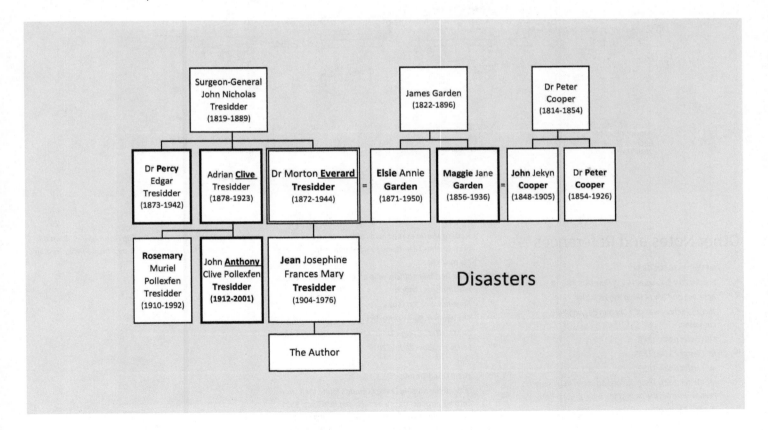

WOTHRICH CAFE
CHEMIN DE LONGERAIE
LAUSANNE

Other Notes and References

i.   MET letter 16 Dec 1888.

ii.   Exodus 20 v 5; Exodus 34 v 7; Numbers 14 v 18.

iii.   Acts 9v5 and 26v14 (King James Bible).

iv.   Jacard's School was at 3 Chemin de Longeraie, Lausanne.

v.   MET letter 6 Nov 1887.

vi.   MET letter 23 Dec 1888.

vii.   MET letter 6 Nov 1889.

viii.   MET letter 3 Sep 1899. Judged by speed in yards per minute – some flew at 30 mph.

ix.   Times 27 May 2013.

x.   Daily Telegraph 28 March 2013.

xi.   MET letter 13 Sep 1914.

xii.   Lyndhurst, 36 Mycenae Road, Westcombe Park, Greenwich. 'Hours of Consultaion: Morning 9-11 (except Tuesday), Evening 7-8.'

xiii.   Elsie and Rosemary Tresidder sailed on the Ranpura, P&O line.

xiv.   Rosetta Martin worked in his office. No written evidence has been found to substantiate that she was his mistress.

xv.   Clive Tresidder's offices were at 37 Albemarle Street, Westminster, London.

xvi.   Bradshaw Section II p31.

xvii.   The Whittier, Burns Drive, Detroit.

xviii. JJFMT letter 26 Aug 1929.

xix.   Lorna Tresidder 22 July 2013.

xx.   Ibid.

xxi.   email Lorna Tresidder 28 Jul 2013.

xxii.   None of the Nursing Home accounts found their way onto his personal balance sheet, and he'd leant £300 some of which was still owed two years later. In all he left just £800, of which duty the debt and the solicitor's fees reduced the sole legatee Jean Haskins (neé Tresidder)'s share to some £540.

xxiii. JJFMT Solicitor's correspondence. £50 was about 2 month's wages.

xxiv.   Maugham p156. William Somerset Maugham CH (1874-1965) [NR] lived in Cap Ferrat further down the coast. He chose to leave France unlike Percy Tresidder.

Twirling Twenties

Dr Everard's only child **Jean** was my mother. Born 8¼lb with light blond hair, the doctor's daughter was hardly ever ill during my childhood[1]. She was sensible about exercise; her only complaint being backache, most pronounced in pregnancy. She wore a corset, not to squeeze her waist like her 14-inch mother's but to support her back – the horsehair mattresses can't have helped. By the time she was expecting me, aged 44, my sisters were pushing her up the steep Cornish hills.

Mind you, she'd be prone to spending the odd day in bed at school with tummy pains – she called them 'the butterflies'. Real enough, but anxiety related. 'Poor attendance' was something I suffered from, but my headmaster found the cure. I was promised a huge chocolate bar if I went through a whole term at *Bickley Hall* without being ill. Amazingly, I won that bar of chocolate first time round and never looked back.

Jean had a professional middle class upbringing, with servants and governesses including Nellie Baker, and Marie Briting from Switzerland. She was not able to cook so much as a boiled egg before she married, and no one told her about the facts of life, which unnecessarily caused her worry.

Jean Tresidder (1904-1976)

❈ ❈ ❈ ❈

Schooling

Jean spent 11 years at Blackheath High School, ending in April 1924 at the age of 19. She studied the usual subjects, including French. She was good at Maths but erratic. Her wandering mind was not much different from mine.

Jean's PE teacher emphasised the need for young ladies to exhibit 'good deportment'. They needed to put their shoulders back and stand straight – it was the sign of women who didn't bear heavy loads. Clean finger-nails and ears were for the same sort of reasons.

Jean's weekly pocket money (1922) was 2/6 (12.5p) – equivalent of half a labourer's daily wage[i]. She spent it on sweets or biscuits costing less than a shilling (5p), biscuits for the dog, film for the camera, pencils, shampoo or the odd item of clothing. A major investment was a bicycle (£1). Some of it went into a Post Office Savings account.

The pencils she used for 'Drawing' – Jean gained a distinction and a certificate from the Art Advisory Board. She had originality and imagination, good powers of observation and 'taste'. Perhaps over-shadowed by her artistic mother, she didn't take it seriously. Like her father and her son, she possessed that counter-intuitive self-deterministic streak. When Jean did put pen to paper, she was good – though she herself under-rated her

Jean's home in Mycenae Road, Greenwich

Jean couldn't cook an egg hardly when she married, and her friend Joan Dolton (whom everybody called Peter) sent her the start of a dusty file of recipes to use, typed mainly. Here's one which starts:

My dear Jean.

In a frantic hurry. Has Barbara got a doll's house, would she like a doll's house or is she too old for a doll's house, please answer by return. I bless you every week for the receipt [sic] for the digestive biscuits. In return have you tried these?

It's for **Ginger Nuts**. The recipe ends,

...and really like shop bought ones, the highest compliment one can have here.

---

1. *Jean Josephine Frances Mary Tresidder (1904-1976) married Paul Denison Haskins (1905-1996) in 1932. She was baptised on 6 Oct 1904 at St George's, Westcombe Park; godparents were Fanny Garden, A Foster, and Percy Tresidder; and confirmed there on 18 May 1920.*

Jean's drawing for her daughter Ann

Hemmick from Penquarry by Jean Haskins

accomplishments. Three of us sat down, for example, in the mid-1960s, to paint the same view of Hemmick Beach in Cornwall. Jean's water-colour attempt was by far the best. My father Paul's, 'painting-by-numbers' attempt was abysmal and my attempt went unfinished – I was reluctant to open the paint box, being colour-blind. The male colour-blindness gene, her father's, jumps a generation and is passed on through the female line. Her father, an early geneticist, predicted I would be like him. I have no daughters so the condition should die out with me.

Education wasn't dumbed down in her day. Her 'General School Examination', the School Cert as it became known, was in its first year. It was exam-based. The English exam comprised a one and half hour essay. Topics to choose from were: *'Fun in literature', 'Lessons of geology', 'Governesses and schoolmistresses in fiction', 'How history has been affected by the characters of eminent personages', 'Exploration', 'Newspapers'* or *'Fashion'*. There was also a précis and questions on grammar.

The subjects rather presupposed a general familiarity with a particular way of life that involved geology and governesses. Fine for her background; not the norm for all. English Literature ('Set Books') covered four Shakespeare plays, four books of poetry, plus Bunyan, Lamb, Stephenson, Austen, Virgil and Chaucer. *'State, with brief quotations, what you gather from the Merchant of Venice to have been Shakespeare's views of filial duty,'* for example.

The algebra text-book used by Blackheath High School in the 1920s was the same one that I used in the 1950s. Very good: they should bring it back. She also took Botany, Arithmetic, French and 'Modern European History' which included an essay on the *'Schleswig-Holstein question'*, the *'unrest' in Russia* or *Greek independence*.

One teacher, a Miss Petherbridge, was her favourite. It was a surprise for Jean to find the same Miss Petherbridge teaching her daughter, Barbara. Barbara was at *Bullers Wood*, the Bromley Girls Technical School after moving from *Stratford House*[ii]. *Bullers Wood* was opposite my own Prep School in Chislehurst – an Ernest Newton designed house like Uncle Clare's in Chapter 12. Sir Sydney Nicholson had established the first School of Church Music at his home there[2]. However, it had closed at the start of the war and became a state school occupied by one that had been bombed out of its own premises in 1941[iii]. *Bullers Wood* was all girls; David Bowie, aka Ziggy Stardust, attended the *Boys* equivalent, **Ravenswood**, four miles away[3]. Barbara, more unorthodox than most, asked Miss Petherbridge why she'd been appointed a prefect. Her answer was pithy: "It takes a thief to catch a thief."

❈ ❈ ❈ ❈

Growing up

As well as acting as her father's receptionist, Jean joined the newly-formed 3rd Lewisham Girl Guides, camping at Shere, near Guildford. A couple of times a year, she'd stay with Everard's friend Bob Mountain and his wife Evie, at their home at *Hill House* Epsom and from 1922 at *Norbury Park*, near Reigate[iv].

Occasionally they'd visit the Mountain's second home at *Oare Manor* on Exmoor, the romantic setting of R D Blackmore's novel *Lorna Doone*[4]. The Doone story is one of the great romantic tales in British literature with its climax a shooting in the church on her wedding day. The villain, Carver Doone, wanted to stop the wedding and marry Lorna himself. After

---

2. *Sir Sydney Hugo Nicholson MVO (1875-1947) [NR] founded the School of English Church Music there 1929-1939.*
3. *David Robert Jones (1947-2016) [NR].*
4. *Richard Doddridge Blackmore (1825-1900) [NR].*

taking a pot shot he fled, chased by her intended, John (pronounced Jan) Ridd. In the ensuing fight, Carver lost his grip and was sucked into a bog. Thus, Lorna and John lived happily ever after. It is no coincidence that Jean and her cousin Anthony's eldest daughters were both given the name Lorna, as was my sister Barbara's eldest daughter, who sadly only lived for 4½ months[5].

After she left school in 1924, Jean spent time in Belgium at the home of the Anderson family in Calmpthout (Kalmthout)[v]. The family lived in an 'Arts and Crafts' house called *Heuvelhof* in a cobbled boulevard of a provincial town set in pleasant parkland on the Belgium/Dutch border.

On return, she studied at the Secretarial School 'for Gentlewomen', run by Constance Hoster in Grosvenor Place, qualifying a year later in December 1925[vi]. Hoster's later moved to South Kensington where it was truly on the map for young and aspiring debs and the like. My elder sister Ann (Lorna) attended in her turn between Oct 1951 and June 1952. In March 1926, Jean went for her only interview and won her only job, as a legal secretary at Le Brasseur and Oakley, Lincoln's Inn[vii].

Jean the Girl Guide, c1920

✳ ✳ ✳ ✳

Dancing the night away

Jean's social life was hotting up. The strictures of many straight-laced households didn't greatly apply to her. Her first cousin, **Douglas Smart** was paying her close attention[6]. There was much ribbing when they went out together whilst he was training to be an architect in Kensington in 1925 and there's an assumption the family would have liked them to get together. Douglas accompanied her to the Savoy for her 21st birthday dance.

Neville (the Chapter 5 Magician), with his persuasive charm, got in on the act[7]. He'd travel up to London making sure he shared her carriage, catching the same train one stop up from hers, at Maze Hill. Eighteen years older than either Jean or Douglas, the second youngest of twelve children with dozens of nephews and nieces not so very different in age, he was more accomplished than Douglas at the chat-up lines. They'd have met at the Infirmary, where Jean's French-Swiss au pair, **Marie,** was now married to Neville's brother[8]. Marie arranged a couple of dance evenings: Marie was a romantic by nature[viii].

Norbury Park, Surrey

Heuvelhof, Calmpthout

Jean's was the generation known as '*The Bright Young Things*' after a dance that she attended, the Chelsea Arts Ball, '*Brighter London, One Hundred Years Hence*', at the Albert Hall in 1922 (ending 4.30am). What would they make of London now? More light, more hype, more forthright perhaps but this was the optimistic 1920s, of opulence and 'gay' abandon, of Scott Fitzgerald and *Orlando*[ix].

Throughout 1925, Neville often took Jean to the Waldorf Hotel, in the Aldwych. The Waldorf with its American connections was a serious player on the social scene. The band, Howard Godfrey and the Waldorfians, was the 'Best Show in Town'.

Dancing was all the rage, fast paced and energetic – the roaring twenties. No more tight corsets, no more long skirts or puffed sleeves; instead, it was the androgynous look and long naked legs[x]. This generation was swaying, hugging, and grinding to new rhythms; decadent, close coupling of bodies. They added their own variations to the traditional dance styles – toddling to the Foxtrot. The seductive Tango was first taught at the Waldorf. The 'Camel Walk' and the 'Lindy Hop' were borrowed from watching the 'Movies'.

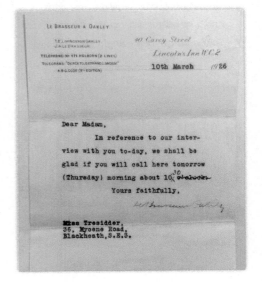

5. *Ann Lorna Haskins (b1934), Lorna N Tresidder (b1938), Lorna Diane Simpson (1976-1976)*
6. *George Douglas Smart (1904-1971)*
7. *Robert Victor Neville Wiggins (1886-1970) married Molly Crawford (1907-1992) in 1939.*
8. *Marie Julie Briting (1892-1926) married William Denison Wiggins (1873-1937) in 1912.*

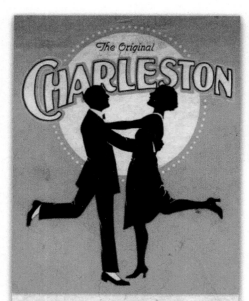

The Ballroom at the Waldorf Hotel

Jean the flapper

The Bright Young Things, as young people in this 'set' were known

In greedy haste, on pleasure bent,
We have no time to think or feel;
What need is there for sentiment
Now we've invented sex-appeal?
We've silken legs and scarlet lips,
We're young and hungry, wild and free,
Our waists are down about the hips,
Our skirts are well above the knee.

We've boyish busts and Eton crops,
We quiver to the saxophone
Come dance, before the music stops
And who can bear to be alone?
Come drink your gin, or sniff your snow,
Since Youth is brief, and Love has wings,
And time will tarnish, before we know
The brightness of the Bright Young Things.

The Chelsea set introduced their own fashion styles: the 'flapper' and the 'sheik' look. The Egyptian craze aped the discovery of Tutankhamun's tomb. Short bobbed hairstyles, close fitting hats or bandanas, short skirts, long bead necklaces and even smoking. Jean was allowed to smoke and go out on her own, unlike many of her age.

No dance epitomised the 1920s as much as the Charleston. It was introduced to New York in 1923. No other dance in this jazz age created such a furore. Who now remembers the 'Bunny Hug' or the 'Turkey Trot'? The Charleston outlasted them all. Outward heel kicks, knocking the knees in time to the music, crossing the hands, and letting the beads fly as they danced the 'Black Bottom'. Neville and Jean joined the Blackheath Concert Hall for the 1925-6 season and went to the Waldorf as well. Dancing at Blackheath cost £2.50 with food extra[xi]. Jean gave Neville a furry animal (rabbit?) for a Christmas present[xii]. He gave her 4 gramophone records[xiii]. Neville would take her out in his racy open-topped car, possibly to Farningham, which had a reputation for courting couples, rather like Maidenhead or Brighton.

Jean was still Neville's regular squeeze in February 1926, dancing most Saturdays during the winter dance season but then their dancing stops[xiv]. Neville's nephew, 'Denison' (my father, Paul Haskins) had come on the scene. A Christmas dance at the Haskins's consolidated things[xv]. After three dances at the Dolton's next door, which had more space, with Jack's sister Biddy and her 'Beau', they formed a close-knit group called 'the Six'[xvi].

Courting ('seeing someone') was a slow process. The notion played on the chivalric 'courtly love' of Arthurian legend or Walter Scott's Waverley novels. In 1928, Paul wrote to her, expressing how good it was to be in love: "It seems too good to be true for me to have a girl like you that will bother to write to me and love me as you do."[xvii] In 1929, he told her, "You really are rather a marvel, really, you know. In fact several fellows have said lately that I am not nearly good enough for you so you must be something out of the ordinary."[xviii] In 1930, Paul was still at work at 1.45am in the morning. He covered a page of the Bank's headed notepaper with over 100 kisses to her[xix].

❊ ❊ ❊ ❊

Young love

Neville's car

The Shack

The Six became four, and Paul, Jean, Jack Dolton and Joan Hole (who was nicknamed 'Peter') managed to get away most 'weekends' after finishing work at lunchtime on the Saturday.

Jack's father was in the timber trade[9]. By 1928, they'd obtained a caravan design from an American magazine. At that stage, caravanning by the middle classes was virtually unheard of in England. Built over the winter, they camped in the grounds of *Norbury Park* countless times. Jean learnt to drive – no driving test needed. She drove Anthony, Rosie and her mother to Tenby in 1928 and Cornwall in August 1929 for their annual holiday – they spent most of the journey talking about caravans. Whilst the girls were away, Paul and Jack invited

Paul & Jean in Cathcart Road Fulham Jun 1927

their friends and together they managed to visit every pub between Norbury Park and the other side of Dorking[xx].

'The Four' – Jean, Jack, Joan and Paul

So successful was the caravan that Jack and Paul extended their ambition. They bought land, *'The Spinney'* at *Walliswood* in Surrey, between Dorking and Horsham[10]. A permanent wooden 'shack' took shape with rather better sanitary arrangements. Each year the facilities improved and the building became more substantial.

It didn't stop Jean going out with other admirers, though Paul remaining sublimely confident. Theirs was a wild social round, motoring up to the glittering Café de Paris perhaps with friends Norah, Tonu or Rex, home at 5am in the morning[xxi]. One Old Etonian friend, Leslie, whom she first met in Torquay, was still doting on her as late as 1943[11]. ('I have had you in mind a lot lately ... What happy carefree days those were, and yet inevitably transitory, to be superseded by the 'realities' of life.")[xxii]. When Paul was off at Army camp with the 23rd Armoured Car Company, which he'd done from 1924, she 'nearly died of laughing' seeing a play called 'The Love Race' with another one of her men friends.

Camping in Norbury Park

Paul, in 'laid-back' Haskins position, liked his big mug of tea.

By January 1930, Jean was engaged to Paul. Jack and 'Peter' were married that year and it was time to put down roots. In 1931, Paul and Jean went on holiday together to Dartmoor and Exmoor. Their marriage took place on 15 June 1932 at St James Kidbrooke, down the road from Paul's home.

Paul's wilful mother, **Dora**, someone you could rely on to cause a fuss if she wasn't the centre of attention, declined to attend[12]. Dora wanted Paul's sister Nancy to be a bridesmaid but Jean was having none of it. So Dora, by this stage living in Duffield, Derbyshire, where Nancy was teaching, decided she couldn't travel and if she wasn't going, neither could the others. Paul's father, **Charles** was mortified[xxiii]. The rest of the Wiggins rallied round, knowing what Dora was like. They wrote reproving letters.

Dora's sister **Mary** arranged for her brother **Clare** to bring her; Dora's brother **Herbert** assisted the Vicar in the conduct of the marriage[13]. Dora's niece **Margot** was Jean's chosen

The completed Shack, Walliswood, Surrey

---

9. *Dolton, Bournes and Dolton Ltd, Archangel Wharf, New Cross. Arthur Henry St John Dolton (1905-1981) [NR] married Joan Alston Hole (1906-1998) [NR] in 1930.*

10. *The Spinney. It is unlikely they ever sought planning permission to build on the land.*

11. *Leslie Parkin Fraser Mackintosh (1887-1946) [NR] Torquay 1926, and Newquay 1927*

12. *Annie Dora Wiggins (1871-1966) married Charles Haskins (1857-1934) in 1898.*

13. *Rev Herbert Bouchier Wiggins Denison MA (1885-1966).*

Paul and Jack off to Paul and Jean's wedding

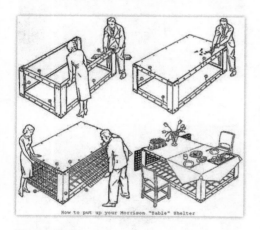

Morrison Shelter

Charnes Hall, Staffordshire, Ann's school to 1946

bridesmaid[14]. In the end Dora gave in[xxiv]. The show went on but Dora was never a favourite of my mother after that. There were no photographs. Jack acted as best man. Jean wore a 'charming' gown of 'Phosphora' ivory satin and sported a sheaf of yellow roses and the reception was at the Tresidders' home, *Lyndhurst*.

They honeymooned at Hartland Quay, near the wild cliffs of Morwenstow, the stamping ground of Paul's great-great uncle David Haskins, ten miles as the seagull flies. They motored down slowly after a night at the Charing Cross Hotel, spending two nights in Lorna Doone Country – Jean was at her most romantic there. On the way home, they stopped at Leatherhead, Paul's birthplace.

✳ ✳ ✳ ✳

Petts Wood

By March 1934, their first-born, **Ann Lorna Haskins**, arrived on the scene, delivered at Uncle Den's Infirmary – he had written a seminal text book for Midwives in 1904[xxv]. Like the majority of well-born women, Jean didn't work after she married. She brought in her old nanny to care for Ann[15]. Others followed.

The rumbling talk of war started soon after **Barbara** was born in 1937 – on St Paul's Day, also the birthday of her father. Churchill's unpopular view, 'no appeasement', held sway in the Haskins household and they started preparing for war. Paul and Jean received an offer to send the girls to America, but Paul had a dream and Jean didn't want to be parted either, so they decided against it. Just as well: the boat sunk. Jean went on various First Aid courses and even learnt to drive an Ambulance[xxvi].

In August 1938, they sold the shack and its grounds for £250. They couldn't see themselves ever getting over there with the petrol rationing and maintenance and other outgoings. No one knew what was going happen. Jack and Paul feared land prices would fall and inflation would rise. However, it's gone the other way and must now be worth more than 2,000 times as much. That thought has encouraged me to invest in property. But then I haven't had to contend with a war.

At the start of the war, Jean took the girls down to Weymouth but that wasn't a success[16]. Paul remained in Petts Wood working in the City. They missed each other[xxvii]. In 1940, having left France, Charles de Gaulle lived in the next road to ours for a few months but found "the nights are too noisily (sic) and my little Anne is frightened."[xxviii] Jean preferred Petts Wood and wasn't going to be split up from her husband, like de Gaulle's family were to be. In 1942, when bombing raids were threatened, the girls sheltered under the staircase. Nanny would usher them under with the remark, 'Mr Hitler is calling for tea again'. Later they had a Morrison shelter in the dining room to sleep under, with a steel top and wire mesh sides.

When Paul was called up to join the army, Ann went off to boarding school. Goudhurst College in Kent had been recommended by the Wrights, who lived opposite but, by Ann's time, the school had moved out of 'bomb alley' to Staffordshire[xxix]. It moved again for Ann's last five years, 1946-51, to Doddington Hall near Nantwich, Cheshire, a stately home by Samuel Wyatt, set in a Capability Brown landscape[17]. I visited her there once, aged two, trundling around its marble hall on a little tricycle, when Ann was Head Girl.

"Ann is very happy, loves every moment at school, enjoys her responsibilities and hates

---

14. *Margaret Denison Wiggins (1914-1993).*
15. *Nellie Baker (1888-1961).*
16. *Mrs Symonds Cranleigh Longfield Road Rodwell Weymouth.*
17. *Samuel Wyatt (1737-1837) [NR]; Lancelot Brown, (1715/16-1783) [NR].*

the idea of leaving."ˣˣˣ Goudhurst was a good influence on her character, but here she was, at seventeen, struggling with 'O' levels. 1951 was the year GCEs were introducedˣˣˣⁱ. The standard of education at that school was debatable. Girls were not heading for careers but destined to be ladies of leisure. Games, deportment and the arts were more important than economics or science. Barbara was perhaps three years ahead of Ann in English. History before 1750 had not been studied.

Jean's parents, Everard and Elsie, separated soon after Jean married. There was still much shame attached to such a situation so little was said. **Elsie** was always called 'Ma'. Ma lived a couple of miles away at St Mary Cray when **Everard** moved to Thornton Heathˣˣˣⁱⁱ. Ma died when I was two, "very inconveniently" in my father's opinion, of hypothermia. The death certificate said it was a heart condition but the two are often associated – it was the day after Boxing Dayˣˣˣⁱⁱⁱ. Her coal bucket was empty and no one was around.

Doddington Hall, Cheshire

Ma was a great hoarder, visiting the Portobello Road and Caledonian Road markets, picking up rare but cracked pots and other impedimenta. She filled her house with knick-knacks. Ann remembers the ostentatious clothes, which didn't quite have the panache of her rich sister Bertie. Barbara remembers the flat irons, from the days before electric steam irons, which you warmed on the stove. The heavy ones kept the heat for longer.

Elsie Tresidder
(1871-1950)

Once, when Ann was sixteen, she dressed in her best, applied full make-up and cycled over to St Mary Cray to see Ma. She knocked on Ma's door and waited. Silence. Then she heard rustling. Ann waited. It took ages for the door to open, because of all the junk in the way. Eventually a crack appeared and a head squinted through:

"Who are you?"

The lack of instant recognition shocked them both. Attractive Ann needed no make-up to look stunning at the best of times.

Ann Haskins - aged 15

My predominant memory (at the age of two) was when my father ushered me into the front room, after Ma's death, when they were clearing the house. The dining room table was stacked with china and he encouraged me to smash it. My little conscience reacted against this. It didn't seem right. I was an unusual boy.

I probably was unusual. Jean took me with her that year to the polling station in the February 1950 General Election. Her friend observed, "We met your mother and Robert going to vote. He seemed to be taking it all very seriously. For once we could not get him to smile."ˣˣˣⁱᵛ Well, it was a cliff-hanger election and these people were being flippant. Father had opined at length at the breakfast table. After 5 years of a Labour Government, which had introduced the Welfare State, National Health System, nationalised railways etc, at much sacrifice in terms of food on the table, the population was growing tired of rationing and penury. I didn't quite follow all the political views as I was only two years old but I was relieved by the outcome.

Old head on young
shoulders – the author
aged two.

I had time to think about most things. I spent long summer hours in the sand-pit at the bottom of our garden, or behind the sofa listening to my mother's friends' chatter. They totally ignored me over tea and I overheard much indiscretion. Mrs Tickner, the 'daily', came over most mornings to do a bit of dusting and to look after me – her attitude to life was more straightforward[18].

Jean took a nap in the afternoon. I'd be placed beside the 'wireless' and told to 'Listen with Mother' on the Radio. Incongruous, I felt, when 'Mother' was upstairs on the bed! I was logical, as well as unusual.

---

18. *Dorothy Gladys Tickner (née Denman) (1912-2005) [NR].*

Jean Haskins (neé Tresidder) (1904-1976) stitching a church kneeler in her Minty chair, a 1932 wedding present from the Vibarts (see Chapter 6)

Lorna Mountain bathing in Exmoor

The Misses Case

Jean died in November 1976 at the age of 72 – that's about par for the course in our family. She had angina … today there are pills and 'procedures'. A collection at her funeral went to buy a patch of land on Nare Head on the south Cornish coast for the National Trust's Enterprise Neptune appeal. By the end of 1976, there were 193 miles of coastline preserved by the Trust – now there are over 775 miles[xxxv].

✳ ✳ ✳ ✳

Holidays in the 1920s

Holidays were important for Jean. They featured throughout the twenties. Her mother would often take her to Cornwall, a detour from seeing granny Emily in Paignton. It was the excitement of the year. She'd prepare lists of what to take, weeks in advance. My sister Ann still does the same.

In the 1920s, Jean wrote a list of things *not* useful to take: white flannel costume, and lots of thin summer dresses (three were quite enough) or straw hats that blew off in the wind. She advised herself not to take holidays in September 'as it gets cold and the evenings short'. It was best, she thought, to travel on a Saturday – something that seems obvious to us but the concept of a 'weekend' was still embryonic. Banks only gave up Saturday working hours when automation was introduced in the 1960s.

Clothes to take on holiday in the 1920s included plenty of silk and crêpe-de-Chine blouses, skirts (tweed or knitted) and Donegal tweed 'suits'. Knitted wool swimming costumes could be very revealing as this photo of her friend Lorna Mountain shows.

Jean would take her camera, a block of writing paper, her tennis racket (in a press), a pack of cards, her prayer book and diary. As a doctor's daughter, her sponge bag would carry all manner of medicines. Hers included glycerine, for her hands, Phenalgin powders for headaches or painful menstruation, zinc ointment and 'camphor ice' cream (not ice cream as we know it!) to soothe the feet.

✳ ✳ ✳ ✳

Westgate-on-Sea

Until I was thirteen, my summer holidays were spent at Westgate-on-sea at the tip of the Isle of Thanet in Kent[xxxvi]. The 1870s houses were of a similar date to Jean's childhood home – we stayed in a four-storeyed terraced house opposite the station. It was run by Kate and Marion Case[19]. These elderly spinsters were set in their ways after a truly Victorian up-bringing. It showed in the dark polished furniture, the red tasselled velveteen table cover and the starched antimacassars on the chairs[xxxvii]. Instead of hot and cold running water, there was a marble wash-stand in the bedroom with a large porcelain bowl and jug. There were 'jerries' (as my father pejoratively called the chamber pots) for when you got caught short in the night, and an enormous brass geyser contraption to heat the bath water (which we never used). We rented a beach hut at West Bay and bathed in the sea.

It was an odd sort of bed and board, not like now. We shopped for the food, which the Misses Case would cook – runner beans, and plums and custard, always burnt. The cooking was so gruesome that in the end we used the one-ring gas stove in the beach chalet. We ate pork pies and cooked sausages in the evening light that once had inspired Turner and, if we were lucky, had proper ice cream with the tin of peaches[20].

---

19. *Kate Elizabeth Case (1877-1968) [NR] and Marion Beatrice Case (1879-1965) [NR], daughters of a London Saltpetre refiner, lived at 'Marion', 30 Harold Avenue, Westgate-on-sea.*
20. *Joseph Mallord William Turner RA (1775-1851) [NR]*

Our car, a Standard (FYM 159), had a 'dickey' boot (or 'trunk'), which opened out at the back[xxxviii]. We rested our trunks and suitcases on the open lid and tied them up with string. With all Jean's saucepans, kettles and other odds and ends, it ended up laden like someone 'newly married'.

It was the days before fast roads. Unlike in modern TV shows portraying the 1950s, few cars then had starter motors. You cranked a handle in the front. The driver's windscreen wiper was motorised but the passenger side was not. It had to be worked by hand. The indicators were amber coloured 'flippers' which (sometimes) stuck out from the pillar between the front and back doors – you mainly relied on hand signals. The doors were hinged the wrong way, so if you opened them while the car was still moving, they swung back and you fell out. It nearly happened to me in Petts Wood Square: I never did it again. The car never went out once we got there. It was not the 'done thing' to leave the car on an open street – it was stored in an old coaching stable by the shops in Station Road.

The shops had fixed awnings for rain protection. I later saw them by the Aare River in Thun (pronounced Tune) in Switzerland, where my wife Carolyn's penfriend lived[21]. I was always comparing things with Westgate when Carolyn first knew me. Thun reminding me of Westgate – 'How could it?' she said, 'This is Switzerland.'

Bank clerks only had three weeks' holiday. Two weeks were used for our Cornwall holiday at Easter. The family spent two weeks at Westgate, so Paul commuted to work for one of the weeks. He got up early, shaved, using the boiling water brought to the room in an enamel jug. Then he set out for the city on the 7.11 from the station opposite the house[xxxix]. From my bedroom window, beside the screaming swifts that nested in the eaves, I'd watch the train leaving – puff puff puff with enveloping black smoke and steam and the noise and stench that sent the train to London.

The promenade, where the beach huts were, was seething with people. The aroma of seaweed (and worse) mixed with the scent of salt and salad cream. A Mr Hobbs hired out deck chairs at one end and, at the other, a constant stream of women queuing for the 'Ladies' next to a constant queue of children buying ice creams. Ice cream and Smith's crisps were the holiday novelties of the 1950s. One of my sisters still liked war-time 'Spam' for lunch. I preferred corned beef.

We spent most of our days digging huge mounds of sand to jump on from the prom, until the tide came up and we were able to go swimming in the deeper water. Sewage went untreated straight out to sea – the jellyfish liked it. Sometimes we'd hunt for shrimps down by the groin or play French cricket with the Cavell family on the crinkly sand.

Out to sea was the 'Shivering Sands' war-time army fort that became the home to one of the nation's best-known pirate radio stations, this one run briefly by the original Screaming Lord Such[22]. When Radio Caroline took it over there was an almighty rumpus over the equipment. The manager ended up dead on the wrong side of a shot-gun.

We came to know the occupants of the other chalets – the Parkers, and their grandchildren the Bolers, and the immensely rich Mary Home (pronounced 'Hume') who lived in Phillimore Gardens in Kensington but had a holiday home in the town[23]. It got to the point that the whole beach knew about Barbara's 'O Level' results before she did – when phoned through to Mr Hobbs, he broadcast the results to anyone who wanted to know. To her chagrin, Barbara only found out later. She passed.

FYM 159

Thun Castle, Bernese Oberland, Switzerland

The author with Mickey Mouse in the 1950s

Mountains of sand

Bill Redmore playing cards with Melanie Mott, Barbara Haskins, the author, Josephine Boler and Andrew Cavell (with his back to the camera) 1960

---

21.   *Brigitte Gsteiger (b1957) [NR].*
22.   *David Edward Sutch (1940-1999) [NR]*
23.   *Mary J Home (1887-1967) [NR] of 26 Phillimore Gardens (third most expensive street in UK 2017) and had a house at 14 Roxburgh Road, Westgate-on-Sea.*

Constant companions, 1959

All aboard

St David's Cathedral

John Stops's Y Bwthyn Gallery at Vachelich, off the St David's-Solva road. The right half was a holiday cottage.

I seemed to be the main attraction for the old ladies. On my account, Mrs Scarborough invited the whole family to lunch at the Grand Hotel at Eastbourne[24]. It was another world for our family who never went out to eat[xl].

The hot weather heated our passions, my adolescent sisters more than me, I suspect, or at least the boys for them. Bikinis had just been invented; Shirley Boler sported a red polka-dot bikini to great effect. The Niekirk boys hovered round the flame[25]. I was not immune; at only ten or eleven, my constant companion for two or three years was Melanie Mott[26]. She shadowed me everywhere, whether I wanted her to or not. The fun fair, Dreamland, was a high point; and the slot machines at the end of Margate pier. Only once a holiday – Paul saw it as a foolish expense; and he abhorred the riff-raff.

One of my parent's friends took me to Calais and Boulogne on the SS Royal Sovereign a couple of times[27]. It was my first experience of having to talk French for a purpose, to buy a tambre-poste. I bought home Swiss chocolates – "Whatever for?" asked my father.

⁂ ⁂ ⁂ ⁂

St David's

When Paul gained a full 4 weeks holiday, we went to St David's in Pembrokeshire[xli]. With a coastline like Cornwall it was still a holy place – the Christian saints from Ireland had worked out their mystery among these folk who fished and farmed just as they had in Cornwall. The sainted people who lived there made us feel most welcome – their conversation coloured by their living past. St David was the patron saint of Wales, St Non his mother. The ancient Britons peopled its landscape; the Syro-Phoenicians had buried their chieftains there looking out to sea. The ancient blue stones of Stonehenge were quarried in the Preseli Hills behind. We went on walks midst scenery untouched by the span of time. Sea pink and campion, samphire and stitchwort coloured the coastal path above the sparkling sea. We took our picnics to the most unlikely of spots, walking great distances with all sorts of paraphernalia, heating our kettle on a primus stove.

The author's niece Bridget Gates at Marlowe Sands in c1970, with a model of a 13th century Welsh castle.

Nowadays, my family has learnt the skills of arranging exotic holidays for themselves. Their horizons are larger than mine. Jonathan owns a part-share of a large house in Orlando whilst my other son Christopher visits friends in far flung places[28]. Perhaps it is because they both flew round the world before the age of two and were brought up on Chinese rice; or is it because there's the blood of the Sea Peoples in our veins?

---

24. *Possibly Alice Scarborough (her married name) (1903-1985).*
25. *Alan F Niekirk (b1929) [NR] Paul H Niekirk (b1932) {NR].*
26. *Melanie A Mott (b1950) [NR].*
27. *Norah Ethel H Redmore, neé Dyer (1906-1985) [NR].*
28. *Jonathan Neil Haskins (b1986); Christopher James Haskins (b1989).*

Reunion, Orlando, Florida

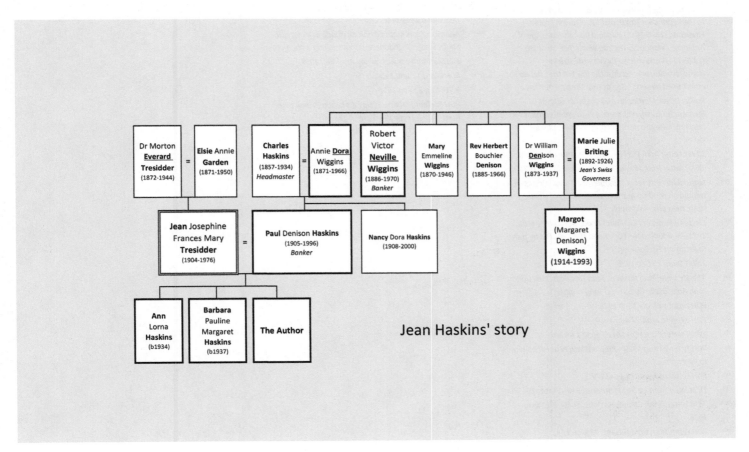

Jean Haskins' story

Other Notes and References

i. www.wirksworth.org.uk/A04VALUE.htm accessed 6 March 2015.

ii. RJH Diary 20 Jun 1958. "Miss Petherbridge gave me some chocolates."

iii. Kent County Council first acquired Bullers Wood for Fire Service training. The bombed Commercial School for Girls was in formerly Wharton Road, Bromley.

iv. The Mountains lived first at Fairlawn, College Road; then West Hill House, Epsom; finally Norbury Park. They owned Oare Manor, Devon. Jean stayed at Norbury Park 15-18 Dec 1922; 16-19 Mar 1923; 21-24 Mar, 21-23 Jun 1924; 23-16 Jan, 27-20 Mar, 20-22 Jun 1925; 1-4 Jan 1925.

v. JJFMT Passport 21 Aug- 4 Sep 1923, again Nov-Dec 1924.

vi. Jean qualified in Gregg shorthand (80 wpm) and typing (46 wpm), Ann learnt Pitman's shorthand. Pitman shorthand is actually the older of the two systems. Gregg's was invented in America in 1888. Pitman's system uses thick and thin strokes to distinguish related sounds, while Gregg's uses only thin strokes and alters the length of the stroke.

vii. Le Brasseur and Oakley's offices were at 40 Carey Street. Jean worked for Mr Ruffle. Law was in Jean's blood – the Tresidders had been lawyers in Falmouth for three generations.

viii. 19 Sep 1924, 14 Jan 1925.

ix. Though Jean wasn't an intellectual, she solved the Telegraph cryptic crossword most days and belonged to the Reprint Society Book Club. Francis Scott Key Fitzgerald (1896-1940) [NR] laid bare the Jazz Age of America. Orlando by Virginia Woolf (née Stephen) (1882-1941) was written for her lesbian lover. Homosexuality was against the law but the Chelsea set entertained all sorts. Gay at that time meant fun.

x. Ruffle, Driver, Martineau and the other men at Le Brasseur & Oakley nicknamed Jean 'John' perhaps for her French-Belgium connections or her androgenous looks.

xi. JJFMT Letter from PDH 29 Jan 1929 (date uncertain).

xii. JJFMT letter from Neville Tuesday possibly Jan 1924.

xiii. Musical flat-disc records played at 78 revolutions per minute on wind-up gramophones. Made of shellac resin, they preceded vinyl.

xiv. Electoral Registers 27 Ulundi Road, Westcombe Park, 1921-26. 1 Kidbrooke Park Road 1928-29. Did he move to Richmond in between?

xv. JJFMT Diary 23 Dec 1926.

xvi. 'The Six' were: Paul Haskins, Jean Tresidder, Jack Dolton, Joan Hole, Biddy Dolton and Tony Bright.

xvii. PDH Letter to Jean 3 Sep 1928.

xviii. PDH letter to Jean 27 Aug 1929.

xix. JJFMT letter from PDH 14 Feb 1930 1.45 am.

xx. PDH letter 27 Aug 1929 – King William IV at Mickleham to Beechams.

xxi. PDH Letter to Jean c29 Jan 1929.

xxii. JJFM letter from Leslie Mackintosh 3 November 1943.

xxiii. PDH Letters from Charles Haskins 29 Apr & 10 May 1932.

xxiv. PDH Letter from Dora Haskins 28 May 1932.

xxv. W Denison Wiggins wrote Midwifery for Midwives in 1904, the year of Jean's birth.

xxvi. Air Raid Precautions, July 1938; First Aid Dec 1938; Home Nursing Mar 1939; Ambulance Drivers Car Knowledge, May 1939.

xxvii. PDH Letter to JJFMT 14 Sep 1939.

xxviii. Waymark p47. Charles André Joseph Marie de Gaulle (1890-1970) [NR] lived briefly at 41 Birchwood Road in 1940.

xxix. Charnes Hall near Eccleshall.

xxx. PDH letter 18 Jan 1951.

xxxi. http://www.oua.ox.ac.uk/holdings/Local%20 Examinations%20Delegacy%20LE.pdf accessed 4 Feb 2016: The General School Certificate (School Cert) was introduced in 1923 and replaced by the General Certificate of Education (GCE) in 1951 which is still current in many former colonies. It was replaced in the UK by General Certificate in Education (GSE) in 1988 and by the General Certificate of Secondary Education (GCSE) in 2015.

xxxii. Elsie Annie Garden (1871-1950) lived at 'Shamrock', 2 Cockmannings Road, St Mary Cray; Everard at 138 Brigstock Road, Thornton Heath.

xxxiii. Letter to JJFMT from Ma dated 26 Dec 1950 and posted on 27th saying it is so cold and to see about the coal.

xxxiv. Letter from Edie Cook to Ann Haskins 28 Feb 1950.

xxxv. National Trust membership was 725 in 1914, 6,800 in 1939 (about the time Paul Haskins joined), 35,900 in 1953 (membership 10 shillings (50p), 500,000 in 1975 and 1 million in 1981. It is now over 5 million.

xxxvi. PDH Postcard Album: Westgate 1950-64, the latter 3 years for a week or less.

xxxvii. Antimacassars stopped hair oil (made in Makassar, South Sulawesi, Indonesia) from spoiling a chair cover.

xxxviii. The Standard car was owned until July 1957.

xxxix. PDH Diary 12 July 1964.

xl. RJH Diary 23 Aug 1958.

xli. PDH Postcard Album: St David's holidays took place from 1962 (except 1964) until 1973.

The Minotaur

I was sitting above Porthcurnick Beach in Cornwall recently, under the canopy of the 'Hidden Hut', the café which serves succulent lunches, on the joint benches we all use, and overhearing a conversation of the adjoining family. "We are going to Crete next week," announced Mum (it was a sophisticated family) "What do you know about Crete?" asked the aunt. "Oh, it's where the Minotaur comes from," said the ten year old boy. My father would have smiled. Sir Arthur Evans was the eminent archaeologist who discovered the lair of the Minotaur at the Palace of Knossos on the island of Crete, and made it part of history that is retold to children to this day.

Sir Arthur Evans was a surrogate uncle to my father Paul. The two formed a bond in Paul's childhood. Evans entertained Paul at his Boar's Hill home south of Oxford throughout his life. On his death he left Paul a bronze replica of Dante's death-mask and a tenth of his residuary estate.

Sir Arthur's life fell into three main phases: before he became Director of the Ashmolean Museum, Oxford; during his discoveries in Crete, and when he was widowed, well-known and a friend of my father Paul.

Arthur Evans was son of the 'great' Jack Evans, the amateur archaeologist and paper manufacturer (John Dickenson Stationery)[1]. Jack was one of the few early geologists and archaeologists who knew more than most Oxford dons about the Stone Age. He'd surveyed many more millstreams, spotted more axe stones and found more evidence of this ancient civilisation than they had. He was one of the first to realise that the Bronze Age came before the Iron Age[i]. It was the new science which had been supported, if amateurishly, by Albert Denison (Chapter 3) when the British Archaeological Association was founded in 1843.

Sir Arthur Evans (1851-1941)

Jack sent Arthur to Oxford. The establishment was ready to entertain the son of someone with so much enthusiasm for his subject. Like father like son, they would say. At Brasenose College, 'Little Arthur' distinguished himself in a rather dubious manner. His examiner recommended him for a first class honours degree but the senior dons were less impressed. He was not your normal student but he was studious. Being the son of the famous Jack Evans was what settled the matter but Arthur's impressive field trips also made a big impression[ii]. Arthur had already travelled across Scandinavia with Frank Balfour, brother of the Prime Minister, looking for seal stones and other artefacts. On a similar mission, he'd traipsed into the nervous Balkans (on the brink of insurrection) dressed in full Turkish costume and fez, and armed with a pistol[iii].

Jean, and Paul Haskins with his sister Nancy on the lake at Youlbury 1933

 ✳ ✳ ✳ ✳

Paul Haskins and Sir Arthur Evans 1920

---

1.   *Sir Arthur John Evans MA DLitt PhD Kt FRS (1851-1941) [NR] was son of Sir John Evans KBE DCL LLD FRS FSA FGS (1823-1908) who was President of the following: Society of Antiquaries 1885-92, Numismatic Society 1874-1908, Geographical Society 1874-76, Anthropological Society 1877-9, British Advancement of Science 1897-8; Treasurer of the Royal Society.*

Margaret Evans née Freeman (1848-1893)

Romance

Arthur fell in love with the Balkans. After graduation, Arthur went back and made it his home. He based himself in the captivating Adriatic city of Ragusa (Dubrovnik). There, he met up with the very same Oxford examiner who'd won him that First, now British Chargé d'Affaires at Sarajevo[2]. One of his daughters, Margaret Freeman, articulate, well-schooled in languages ancient and modern, and with a genuine interest in his work, laid her eyes on this short-sighted quirky intelligent young man with a big stick called 'Prodger'[3]. The Ragusan wind caught in the curls of his hair as it fluttered against his face. His mouth warmed at the sight of her. It wasn't long before the two of them were married.

They remained in Ragusa, at 'Cassa San Lazzaro', from their marriage in 1878 up to 1882. Arthur's exploits found a ready readership in the **Manchester Guardian**, which was interested in the political situation of this smouldering southern extremity of the Austro-Hungarian Empire.

But Arthur and Margaret's time in Croatia ended abruptly. Arthur was hinting too obviously about the prospect of insurrection against this dictatorial regime. Never holding back, the 'pen-viper', as he was later called, would clinically analyse the situation and, as only the English could, delight his readers with 'the truth'[iv]. This time he went too far. His arrogant intervention fuelled activity that would ultimately trigger the onset of the First World War: the heir to the throne, Archduke Franz Ferdinand, was assassinated in Sarajevo by the self-same Slav dissidents that he'd tacitly encouraged[4].

Those southern Slav leaders felt forever in his debt and kept up their connections. He smuggled out young Slavs to live in England so they could avoid being called up to fight for the wrong side in the First World War. My father remembered them turning up for secret meetings at Evans's Oxford home[v]. One of them was Thomas Masaryk, the future president of Czechoslovakia. Evans attended some of the Peace Conferences, including Versailles, going to Paris to support their negotiations[vi]. He visited Ragusa again in 1932[vii]. As late as 1941, the year of Evans' death, the British government consulted him about forming Yugoslavia under Tito[5]. Later that year, the Slav leaders trekked across Europe to attend Arthur's funeral.

✳ ✳ ✳ ✳

Discovery at Knossos

Oxford was where the second phase of Arthur's life began in 1883/4. He'd learnt enough language to become the 'Ilchester Lecturer on Slavonic languages'.

He was soon asked to help find some letters for an enthusiastic collector related to the Fortnum and Mason dynasty, Charles Drury Fortnum[6]. In the process, Evans went into action over the decrepit state of the Ashmoleum Museum, which had been founded by John Tradescant and Elias Ashmole two hundred years earlier[7]. The Keeper and the Vice Chancellor had, between them, managed to lose half the contents; they'd sold the display cases and were using the space for examinations.

My Dear Denis [his name for my father]

I have been thinking about your plans for constructing a caravan and want to help towards the wheels for which I enclose a contribution. I do hope it will be a success but it will take a great deal of carpentering.

The letter goes on to describe his plans to visit Paris and then to fly home – unusual in 1927

---

2. *Edward Augustus Freeman(1823-1892) [NR].*
3. *Margaret Freeman (1848-1893) [NR].*
4. *Prince Franz Ferdinand (1863-1914) [NR] Archduke of Austria-Este.*
5. *Marshal Josip Broz Tito (1892-1980) [NR]. Yugo = Southern.*
6. *Charles Drury Edward Fortnum DCL JP FSA (1820-1899) [NR].*
7. *John Tradescant, the Younger, (1608-1662) [NR]; Elias Ashmole (1617-1692) [NR].*

Despite some opposition the Visitors, as the trustees were called, voted Evans as its Keeper in 1884[8]. A long fight started against vested interests, inertia, procrastination and obstruction. Fortunately, Evans had Fortnum on his side, whose collection of sculpture, bronzes, majolica and rings was promised on the proviso the University would put this 'Museum of Art and Archaeology' on a sound footing. That meant money. Evans eventually persuaded everybody to fund a new building behind the University Galleries and merge the two institutions into one, under his direction. A huge accomplishment, and he did it all within eight years[viii].

Shambling committees bored Evans but he found other things to divert his attention. In 1886, he conducted a survey of Iron Age ruins in Aylesford, Kent. His report proved a connection with the European continent, in an analysis considered 'masterly' to this day[ix].

With his father's money, £3,500 bought him 60 acres on Boars Hill south of Oxford, to build a house for his ailing wife. Margaret was never to live there – in 1893, she died in Alassio, an Italian coastal town, 50 miles from the French border. Distraught, he used black-edged writing paper for the rest of his long life. He went ahead with the house, nevertheless: *Youlbury*, a 22-bedroom mansion with an artificial woodland lake and its own 'Silbury Hill', the Jarn Mound. With an unheard of number of bathrooms and a lookout tower on the roof, *Youlbury* was to be his residence for the next fifty years.

Silbury Hill and Jarn Mound: Silbury Hill in Wiltshire is Neolithic. It has no known purpose. The Jarn Mound was commissioned in 1929 to employ labourers during the depression. It provides a view over the dreaming spires of Oxford.

Youlbury house, Boars Hill, Oxford

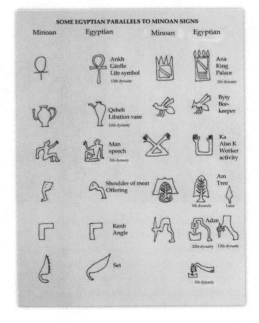

Like that boy on the Cornish beach, I'd read the Greek legend of the Minotaur when I was about ten years old, in *Tanglewood Tales* by Nathaniel Hawthorne. To my father, brought up in the early 1900s with a classical education, the story was second nature. It was a time when archaeologists were beginning to prove the truth of the ancient myths of Homer's Aeneid and Iliad. Schliemann's discoveries at Troy and Mycenae from 1871 had ignited huge interest[9]. Later, much later, Carter discovered Tutankhamen's tomb in Egypt[10].

After Margaret's death, Arthur lost much of his motivation and energy. Mooching about in Italy for a year, rudderless, he bought some seal stones which bore some engravings. He thought about the Cretan jewellery he'd handled in Oxford: he saw what he thought was the same script. Was this Cretan? Was this an undiscovered hieroglyphic script? There were roughly 80 separate characters. Were they Greek or Egyptian or somewhere in between?

Arthur took the next boat to Crete. Arriving in Heraklion, he examined the sporadic excavations going on at Knossos. He saw the iconic carvings of a 'double axe' almost

---

8.   *Prof Benjamin Jowett (1817-1893) [NR], Regius Professor of Greek 1855-93, Master of Balliol 1870-93, Vice Chancellor of Oxford 1882-6 was the chief opponent.*
9.   *Heinrich Schliemann PhD (1822-1890) [NR].*
10.   *Howard Carter ScD (1874-1939) [NR] discovered Tut-ankh-Amen's tomb in 1923.*

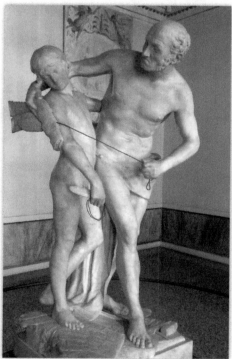

Daedalus had built the Labyrinth and the Palace on Crete but after the Minotaur was slain, Daedalus had to escape. He made wings for himself and his son, attaching them with wax. Icarus flew too near the sun and the wax melted – he fell in the sea. In this sculpture by Canova, Daedalus is adjusting Icarus's wings (Canova, Venice).

Theseus and the Minotaur
– the Greek myth

Once upon a time in the great Greek city of Athens there was much weeping. They'd lost a war against the island of Crete. King Minos, the king of Crete, now ruled all the Mediterranean between Greece and Egypt. He was so powerful that they said that anything he touched turned to gold. He worshipped bulls and his wife had given birth to a monster, half-bull, half-human, which he kept in a Labyrinth, a walled maze in the palace grounds. Now King Minos demanded that Athens send him seven young lads and seven young girls, as human sacrifices to his God-Monster, the Minotaur, as punishment for losing the war. The youths would be thrown into the Labyrinth and devoured by the Minotaur.

The time came for Athens to select the young people. Theseus, the king of Athens' son, was so sickened by this that he volunteered to go himself. The King of Athens was distraught – 'My only son. You are too precious,' he said but, like most sons, he knew better, ignored his father and joined the ship.

On arrival in Crete, the captives were ushered into the throne room and inspected by King Minos. Standing behind the throne was his daughter, Ariadne, who set her eye on Prince Theseus. The blood rose to her cheeks. She saw something there. Nobility? Good looks? Something coloured her passion and urged her on. At midnight, she crept out of her apartment, past the guards. She managed to open Theseus's dungeon door and hand him a sword.

Theseus was determined to slay the Minotaur, so Ariadne gave him a silken string. As he tiptoed into the maze, he unwound the string behind him. He could hear the roar of Minotaur. It frightened him but, determined, he hid behind a pillar until he could catch the beast off guard. He shoved the sword straight through the beast's heart and with a mighty roar the Minotaur breathed his last. Theseus, still clutching the string, found his way back into Ariadne's arms. They kissed and hurried to release his fellow captives. They sailed away before the king discovered what had happened.

Some say Ariadne refused to go with Theseus. Was she torn between filial duty and fear of a foreign land? Or was she just a good girl? Who knows?

Others say that one more tragedy occurred. On the way home, the fourteen young Athenians couldn't help but celebrate in the way young people do. Fuelled by too much Greek wine, they forgot to change the colour of the sails symbolising their victory. Theseus's father, Aegeus, standing on the cliffs as the sun set over the water, looked down on the approaching ship and saw instead the signs of tragedy. There's nothing worse than losing your son. He didn't wait to see the ship unload its inebriated good news. In his grief at Cape Sounion, he jumped into the incarnadine sea.

immediately, and these convinced him he'd most probably found the source of the script. How to buy the site? Others had failed. The Cretan owner of the land wouldn't sell to individuals, reasoning that one scholar on his own could never afford to excavate the site. However, he agreed he would sell to an organisation. Evans promptly conceived the 'Cretan Exploration Fund', not bothering to explain that he was its only contributor. He managed to buy a quarter of the site for £235 with an 'option' on the rest. Six years later, he got the lot[x].

Arthur Evans returned to England to make sure the Ashmolean had suitable direction during his prolonged absence – even if the pay was poor, the leave of absence was generous, he said[xi]. He returned to Crete to find it in the middle of a war between Christians and Muslims, which was to involve the massacre of 700 Cretan Christians, 17 British soldiers and the British Consul in one incident. So, instead of starting, he planned what to do. When relative peace was restored, in 1900, he took on Dr Duncan Mackenzie, who was to work with him for the next thirty years, and an army of labourers[11].

It took only a few months to discover the 'Palace of Minos' at Knossos, a series of over 1,000 interlocking rooms. Based on the ceramic evidence and soil stratigraphy, Evans concluded that the settlement on Crete had preceded that of Mycenae and Troy. He called it the 'Minoan civilisation' after King Minos of the legend. The windowless rooms of the Knossos ruins possessed a maze-like quality.

By 1903, Evans had exposed an advanced city full of artwork and writing, aqueducts, polished floors, baths and even a flushing toilet. The Bronze Age walls of the palace had numerous scenes depicting bare-breasted female priestesses with tiny waists and sacral knots and double-axes, sporting with bulls – centuries older than Solomon's temple in Jerusalem. Arthur was convinced that this great Minoan civilisation had worshipped the bull, even if he couldn't prove the full detail of the Minotaur story.

By 1905, the year that my father was born, his excavations had revealed the full extent of this Palace. Arthur's editorial skills and his personal wealth enabled him to self-publish with lavish illustrations. The large exhibition at the Royal Academy in 1903-4 convinced an adoring public that this was the source of the romantic fable from classical literature. Even the Suffragettes approved of those nubile priestesses – in Knossos he'd shown that the women were in charge. He tidied the place up for tourists, using full-scale architectural reconstruction – his Swiss artists did more than just a 'touch up' job[12].   100 years later, with the highly interactive museums of today, some archaeologists have come round to this way of thinking. Despite him having no architectural training, the Royal Institute of British Architects (RIBA) awarded Evans their Gold Medal[13].

✳ ✳ ✳ ✳

Knossos double axe

Bare-breasted priestess

---

11.   *Dr Duncan Mackenzie PhD (1861-1934) [NR].*
12.   *Émile Gilliérons Junior and Senior [NR].*
13.   *Royal Institute of British Architects Gold Medal 1909.*

Family group at Youlbury in 1933. Sir Arthur Evans, left, with Jean centre with the bob haircut and Paul Haskins (1905-1996) on the right next to his Aunt, Mary Wiggins.

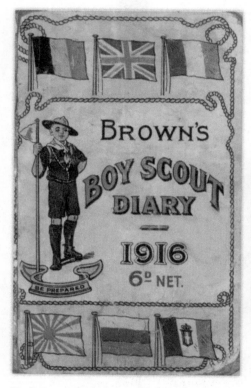

Paul's Scout Diary – in its eighth year.

Training Camp, Youlbury. Sir Robert Baden Powell attended the ground-breaking ceremony in Feb 1926

Youlbury

We come now to the third phase of Arthur Evans' life, a time when he got to know my father. In 1908 he gave up leading the Ashmolean[xii]. He was 57 and decided to devote himself to writing. In the end, he wrote more than 60 articles and books, but he found some enjoyment: Paul and his little friends took his mind off the serious work of chronology and decipherment of the scripts on the 1,800 tablets which he'd found at Knossos. He let his imagination engage in the planning of the extensive grounds he had on Boars Hill. He invited one of the earliest troops of Scouts to use the grounds. On Crete, which he visited once a year, he built the *Villa Ariadne* – making it earthquake-proof so it could store his precious ornaments.

At *Youlbury*, Arthur devised ways of filling his enormous house with people[xiii]. Mackenzie, who was in charge of excavations on the island, used to stay with Evans when he was in England. Arthur invited Fortnum and his friends, Lord Carnarvon who financed the discovery of Tutankhamun's tomb, Sir Leonard Woolley, who'd excavated the tombs at Ur, Sir Edward Poulton and other academics to stay[14]. He went for long walks with the poet Robert Bridges who lived up the road[15]. Margaret's brother Edgar's son, Lance Freeman, came to stay when his parents settled in Virginia[xiv]. He adopted a ten-year old boy, Jimmie Candy, from the village, funding his cure for a loss of hearing from mastoids[xv]. He employed my great aunt Mary as governess, inviting her nephew, Paul my father, to join them as a playmate[16]. They did all the things that certain little boys did to fill their time in those days: tennis, croquet, cricket and playing in the woods.

The boys kept him youthful if eccentric. He could relax with them[xvi]. He'd charge down the

Paul Haskins and Lance Freeman in 1919

Jimmie Candy in Argentina, after leaving school. He returned to start a dairy at Northcourt Farm, Abingdon. He described Evans as 'the kindest man I've ever known.'

14.   George Herbert 5th Earl of Carnarvon (1866-1923) [NR]; Sir Leonard Woolley (1880-1960) [NR]; Sir Edward Bagnall Poulton FRS (1856-1943) [NR]. Hope Professor of Zoology (1893-1933) [NR] (see also Chapter 12).

15.   Robert Seymour Bridges OM MA MB DLit (1844-1930), Poet Laureate.

16.   James Stuart Candy (1902-1999) [NR]; Capt John Lancelot Freeman (1897-1925) [NR] died of wounds incurred at Abbeville. He was five and eight years older than Jimmy and Paul who were too young to join the war.

Youlbury grounds and lake

Luke Simpson (b1970) and Victoria (b1973) in 1991

Sir Arthur and Jack Evans, Jimmie behind, Paul in front, Wales 1919

garden path without warning as if he was in a motor car. He'd throw letters over his head at the breakfast table when he'd finished reading them. He liked order and everyone was summoned to meals by the gong – you were expected to be prompt and dressed in your best. When it was time to go back to work he'd break off a conversation in mid-flow and walk off to his study.

He gave the Scouts some bicycles; he built them a tree house, and bequeathed land to the Scouting Association when he died[xvii]. It is still in use today, as my nephew Luke, a Queen's Scout, can vouch[17]. Evans' interest in boys must surely have raised a few eyebrows even then. With Aunt Mary and his reputation always to think of, I suppose it was safe. What I didn't know until recently was that, at the age of 73, the police apprehended Evans in Hyde Park for consorting with a seventeen-year-old boy of no fixed address[xviii]. My father never talked of any problems of that sort. He and Jimmy remained friends with Evans their entire lives and had only good things to say about their hero.

Scientists are beginning to realise that elderly brains do not decline with age – they only appear to slow down because, like a computer's hard drive when it fills up, there's more information to process[xix]. Arthur didn't let up in his efforts to crack the code of his 1,800 clay tablets. Unlocking their secret was intended to be his personal challenge, his crowning discovery. Sadly, he never accomplished it. This was not to be the Rosetta Stone of the late Bronze Age, proving the connection between the 'sea peoples', Egypt and Greece, as he had hoped. It wasn't until 12 years after his death that Michael Ventris, a young architect, finally cracked the Linear B script in 1953[18].

Instead, Evans enjoyed trips all over the country in his Chevrolet motorcar. Evans took Paul, his Aunt Mary and his friends on some monumental journeys round Britain as well as to Ireland, Paris and the Ypres War cemeteries. Few boys at that time had experienced the full gamut of the killing fields of the First World War, crashing breakers on the Cornish cliffs of King

The Chevrolet

The Giant's Chair, Cader Idris, mid Wales – one of many awe-inspiring natural phenomena that Arthur took the boys to see.

17.   *Luke David Simpson (b1970) married Victoria Louise Graves (b1973) and has two children Lucy Florence Simpson (b2005) and Chloe Louise Simpson (b2008).*

18.   *Michael George Francis Ventris, OBE (1922-1956) [NR].*

Sir Arthur at Corfe Castle, Dorset

Perranporth, Cornwall 1928 – standing: Paul, Arthur and Jimmy; sitting: Margot & Bobby Wiggins with Nancy Haskins

Bull statue discovered at St Just-in-Penwith, Cornwall in 1832

The marble hall at Youlbury. The two wooden 'thrones' are wooden copies of the one found in the Palace at Knossos, Crete

Arthur's birthplace, the windswept austerity of Stonehenge, or the glacial gravitas of the Welsh mountains[xx]. They visited many castle ruins. Most of those ruins, now neatly tended by English Heritage, were ivy-strewn danger-traps in the 1920s. Land's End was covered in litter[xxi]. The side panel shows the extent of his travels with my father. Paul kept the evidence in the form of postcards, carefully preserved in albums. Arthur and Paul were still taking holidays together when Paul was in his twenties.

Arthur died 3 days after his 90th birthday in 1941. A few days earlier, he'd had news of a discovery in Pylos on mainland Greece of King Nestor's Palace, conclusively proving he was wrong – Nestor, King Minos's grandfather, had had a palace at Mycenae which was destroyed by the Dorians of Sparta. Soft clay tablets, baked hard by the fires of destruction, similar to the ones that Evans had brought home from Crete, had been discovered there. It wasn't just the writing but what they showed: the same rationing system, the same supervision of slaves, identical armour. The later Cretans were not Egyptian. They'd come from Greece. Evans's precious tablets were of Greek origin. The shock was too much.

The earlier Linear A tablets have yet to be deciphered. They have more similarities with the Jewish and Phoenician civilisations of the Eastern Mediterranean. There's little consensus, however, on who the 'sea peoples' were, how far they sailed, and their tribal origins. One scholar considers the Jews and the Phoenicians were one and the same[xxii]. Another noted that the monkeys in the Knossos frescos could only have come from northern Nigeria or Ethiopia[xxiii]. A bull statue with a human face was discovered in Cornwall[xxiv]. Its date and origin has been variously described as Egyptian, Phoenician, Grecian or Mithraean but just maybe this Cornish artefact originated from the Minoan civilisation of Crete.

Evans left Jimmie Candy a similar bequest to Paul in his will, and £80 for Mary. Paul kept a bookshelf of Evans' heavy tomes about Crete. Two of my nephews studied Ancient Classics on the back of that inheritance. When Paul inherited the bust of Dante, though, it was reconciled to our loft …. It was a little out of place in our semi-detached suburban home.

✳ ✳ ✳ ✳

Places visited by Sir Arthur Evans with Paul Haskins in his youth

Belgium
Brussels
Menim Gate
Passchendaele
Waterloo
Ypres
Zillebeke
France
Mont Kemmel, Osuaire
Ireland
Glanleam
Killarney
Valentia
Mellifont
Monasterboice
Bedfordshire
Carlton
Chelington
Harrold Green
Berkshire
Windsor
Cambridgeshire
St Neots
Cheshire
Chester
Prestbury
Cornwall
Bodmin
Boscastle
Cape Cornwall
Carn Glooose
Cawsand
Falmouth
Gurnard's Head
Holywell Bay
Lands End
Mullion
Newquay
Pendine
Penzance
Perranporth
Perranzabuloe
Rame Head

St Austell
St Ives
St Just
St Piran
The Lizard
Tintagel
Truro
Derbyshire
Buxton
Castleton
Dovedale
Haddon Hall
Lathkil
Mam Tor
Devon
Branscombe
Brendon
Clovelly
Culbone
Dareford
Dartmeet
Dartmoor
Dartmouth
Doone Valley
Dulverton
Dunster
Hartland
Hay Tor
Lydford
Lynmouth
Lynton
Oare
Plymouth
Pomeroy Castle
Porlock
Seaton
Sidmouth
Stoke Hartland
Swincombe House
The Horner Valley and woods
Torquay
Widdecombe

Dorset
Abbotsbury
Beer
Bournemouth
Cerne Abbas
Charlton
Corfe Castle
Dorchester
Lulworth Cove
Lyme Regis
Selsey
Wimbourne Minster
Durham
Durham
Essex
Chelmsford
Chelmsford
Hatfield Peverill
Witham
Gloucestershire
Chedworth
Cirencester
Gloucester
Stow
Tewksbury
Hampshire
Beaulieu
Christchurch
Hayling Island
New Forest
Porchester
Whitchurch
Winchester
Herefordshire
Hereford
Hertfordshire
Bushey
Isle of Wight
Alum Bay
Freshwater
Needles
Totland Bay
Yarmouth

Kent
Birchington
Dover
Lancashire
Lancaster
Liverpool
Manchester
Lincolnshire
Lincoln
Stamford
Norfolk
Beeleigh Abbey
Boston
Castle Acre
Castle Rising
Great Yarmouth
Kings Lynn
Norwich
Ranworth
Sandringham
Wells on Sea
West Newton
Northamptonshire
Blisworth
Pottersbury
Northumberland
Hexham
Oxfordshire
Abingdon
Bourton on the Water
Chalgrove
Chipping Norton
Great Coxwell
Great Milton
Kingston Lisle
Northleach
Wallingford
Wantage
Watlington
Shropshire
Ludlow
Somerset
Bath

Cheddar Gorge
Glastonbury
Wells
Surrey
Leatherhead
Wallis Wood
Bexhill-on-Sea
Brighton
Chichester
Winchelsea
Warwickshire
Warwick
Wiltshire
Avebury
Bradford-on-Avon
Limpley Stoke
Malmesbury
Salisbury
Stonehenge
Wilton
Worcestershire
Evesham
Worcester
Yorkshire
Scarborough
York
Wales
Barmouth
Bettws-y-Coed
Cader Idris
Capel Curig
Cardiff
Carnarvon
Fairbourne
Harlech
Penarth
St David's

Other Notes and References

i.   *Evans, Sir John, p9.*

ii.   *Arthur Evans was given an annual allowance of £250 by his father – you needed money to study at Oxford. £250 compared with an agricultural labourer's annual wage of about £30 a year.*

iii.   *Evans, Joan p163. Prof Francis Maitland Balfour MA LLD VPBAAS FRS (1851-1882) [NR] was a Harrow school friend. The Prime Minister Arthur Balfour's brother was interested in botany, embryology and animal morphology. He met an early death climbing Mont Blanc.*

iv.   *Evans, Joan, p241 Arthur Evans wrote "I have not 'agitated' or encouraged insurgents in any way but have only pointed out the truth in my correspondence." Nevertheless, he made sure every act of insurgency was reported widely.*

v.   *PDH diary entry 23 Aug 1917.*

vi.   *Harden p15. Horwitz p194.*

vii.   *Horwitz p230.*

viii. *Davies & Hull p17. The designation 'Ashmolean Museum' was given to the extension in 1899 and ultimately the whole building. The old museum was reopened by Statute in 1935 as the Museum of the History of Science.*

ix.   *Cunliffe p6. 'The report was an outstanding contribution to Iron Age studies. In it Evans characterised the Aylesford people as Belgia, showing their differences from the inhabitants of the rest of Britain, and tracing the immediate origins to Northern France, and ultimately back through the Marian culture to the Illyro-Italic cultures of the fifth century' (BC).*

x.   *Macgillivray p150.*

xi.   *Evans, Joan p305. The keeper must be personally at the Museum at least 150 days a year.*

xii.   *Howitz p177. Evans was appointed 'Honorary Keeper' with a permanent seat on the governing body.*

xiii. *Horwitz p130. 3 staircases, 28 bedrooms and 9 baths including a Roman Bath large enough for a swim 2 breast-strokes in any direction.*

xiv.   *Horwitz pp167, 191, 208.*

xv.   *Horwitz p168.*

xvi.   *PDH letter to Sylvia Horwitz 6 Jun 1979: "I have sat at lunches or teas at Youlbury when people like Lord Carnarvon, Bridges, Masefield and even Joan Evans have been present and he never seemed to relax in the same way as he did when he was with young people. He loved a game of Bridge in the evenings but being no mathematician he was not very good"*

xvii. *Clause 22 (a) of Evans's will.*

xviii. *Times 6 Feb 1924. George Cook [NR] 'An act of violation of public decency.'*

xix.   *Ramscar, M etc (2014).*

xx.   *Tintagel was cited as the fabled 5th century King Arthur's birthplace in c1136. by Geoffrey of Monmouth in Regum Britanniae.*

xxi.   *JJFMT letter 31 Aug 1929.*

xxii. *Ganor p270.*

xxiii. *Penhallurick p12.*

xxiv. *Ibid p129.*

The Banker

My father Paul was the first banker in our family with Haskins for a surname. Banking was a step up in the world. It wasn't 'trade'. His mother was very snooty about people in 'trade' – despite *her* mother being a plumber's daughter.

Few were bankers in my wider family. Of course there was Joseph Denison (see Chapter 3), if you can count him. The nearest next thing was the Grylls family. My great aunt Rosie Tresidder's daughter married **Thomas Grylls**, a Director of the **West Cornwall Bank**[1]. His grandfather had been manager of the Cornish bank part-owned by John Williams of *Caerhays Castle*[i]. Williams broke away from his partners and made three generations of the Grylls family co-Directors. The East Penwith Savings Bank, which Grylls had also founded, eventually merged with this new West Cornwall Bank. By 1911 the West Cornwall Bank, with branches at Penzance and Falmouth, had been taken over by Barclays, which appointed Thomas Grylls as its local Director.

Like the Scots banker Arthur Legat (Chapter 12), **Jack Smart**, was also from Edinburgh, that great capital of money[ii]. Son of an Estate Agent, or 'House Factor' as they called them, he married my great aunt Bertie (Chapters 9 & 10)[2]. Banks tended to recruit from Scotland or from the English public schools but the Scottish bankers were better. Whilst foreign banks preferred games players (rugby, cricket, polo) who'd fit in with the British Empire's leisure activities: with a team spirit and a winning temperament, the Scottish bankers took the Scottish Institute of Bankers' qualification from 1875 and had more competence than, say, P G Wodehouse after he left Dulwich[3]. Those in the Hongkong and Shanghai Bank with Bankers' qualifications secured the overseas postings. Some did time at Hamburg or Lyons. In Jack's case it was New York before he was posted to the Far East[iii]. Jack had the plum job of Manager of the Shanghai Branch by the time he married Bertie in 1903. He was 40, she was 25.

Then there was the magician, Paul's rival for Jean's attentions, **Neville Wiggins**. Neville's rise to the higher echelons of the Bank of England – Assistant Secretary at the age of 40 – was in part down to the huge loss of life the Bank had suffered in the First World War[4]. Neville himself had been an officer in those trenches but he never spoke about it. In 1929 he was appointed sub-Agent in the Bank's branch in Manchester before moving to Leeds as Regional Agent in 1934. Somewhat autocratic, he was regarded with awe and reverence by the staff. He'd play cards in the Leeds Club at lunchtime and drove an open-topped Lagonda, eventually marrying a junior member of his staff, the glamourous **Molly Crawford**, moments before the outbreak of war[iv].

Ten years into the marriage, 1949, when he retired, they moved to the South Coast so he could play croquet with his brother Herbert. Earlier in his career, he'd worked in the City of London at the Bank of England – when it was being sensationally remodelled by Sir Herbert Baker, the architect of New Delhi (Chapter 6). Banks closed their doors at about 3pm. Many

Yes, it's a boy! Paul Denison Haskins – voted Woman magazine's 'Finest Baby Boy' in July 1907

Jack Smart (1863-1939)

Neville Wiggins married Molly in St Chad's Headingley just before the outbreak of the Second World War in June 1939

---

1. *Mary Saunders (1871-1956) married Thomas Reginald Grylls (1862-1953) in 1898. His father William Mitchell Grylls (1828-1911) married Elizabeth Farran Penrose (1827-1911) in 1852. His grandfather Henry Grylls (1800-1886) was the first to team up with John Michael Williams (1813-1880) [NR]. Williams and Grylls (West Cornwall Bank) Falmouth and Redruth 1863-1890 merged to form Bolitho, Williams, Foster, Coode and Grylls Bank 1889-1905, which then was then taken over by Barclays Bank.*

2. *Jack's father was William Sanderson Smart (1828-1903?).*

3. *Sir Peregrine Grenville Wodehouse KBE (1881-1975) [NR], author of the Bertie Wooster stories and an exact contemporary of Percy Tresidder (Chapters 7 & 13), worked for the Hongkong & Shanghai Bank 1900-2.*

4. *Robert Victor Neville Wiggins (1886-1970) married Molly Crawford (1907-1992) in 1939 at St Chad's, Headingley.*

Bank of England's former building in the Headrow, Leeds

Schoolwork by Paul's sister Nancy in Witham. Growing your own was a necessary pastime in 1918. (Note the Denison crest (Chapter 3) as her 'Trade Mark')

'River Stour and Dedham Church by John Constable RA'

The author and his sister Barbara on punt in River Wey Navigation, July 1961

a time he'd walk home to Richmond or Blackheath. As a member of the Blackheath Golf Club he teamed up with Doctors Den Wiggins (his brother) and Everard Tresidder. But this chapter is mainly about his nephew, **Paul Denison Haskins**, who eventually ended up winning one of his girl-friends[5].

❋ ❋ ❋ ❋

An Edwardian Childhood

My father Paul was a child of the Edwardian era. Little boys wore dresses (smocks), then sailor suits (Japanese children still do), and then Eton collars[v]. Tradesmen called you 'Master'. The practice of upper classes keeping their children in the nursery had filtered down to the aspiring classes like my grandmother. In the Haskins household, children were seen (but not heard) by their parents before dinner. At boarding school, there were cold showers every morning before breakfast, if not fagging – my father never mentioned fagging[vi].

Though Paul and his sister Nancy were born in Leatherhead in 1905 and 1908 respectively, they grew up in rural Essex; the family had moved there when Paul was six years old. When I was young, he took me to the Tate Gallery and made a bee-line for the Constable paintings of Essex and the River Stour – not far from where he cycled, butterflied, birds-nested and fished[vii]. His uncle Arthur had taken him sailing[6]. He was allowed to roam on his own and got to know the boatmen as they made their way up and down the canal. He liked canals. He later took us punting on the River Wey Navigation near Godalming.

Paul and Nancy attended their father's school at the White House at Witham. Whilst Nancy remained at the White House, Paul was sent on to Brighton College, at the age of 13, just as the First World War was ending. Brighton, where he boarded for four years, was the premier school in Sussex for some 300 boys, with imposing flint-stone gothic buildings designed by Sir Gilbert Scott, the pre-eminent architect of Victorian cathedral restorations[viii]. Paul's Uncle Will had recommended it, as he did for another of his nephews, Hugh Wiggins[7]. It was run by Will's old Headmaster from Grantham[8]. Canon Dawson had greatly inspired Will, a boy of working class roots. Dawson was the one to whom he "owed more than to anyone else…. He was, I suppose, the most notable schoolmaster of his period, not simply because of his uncanny power of persuading parents to entrust their boys to him but because of his extraordinary qualities of leadership. He was a dynamo of energy and could infuse that energy into others…. All in all, he was one of the best men I have ever met."[ix] Paul was placed in the School House.

---

5.   *Paul Denison Haskins (1905-1996) married Jean Josephine Frances Mary Tresidder (1904-1976) in 1932.*
6.   *Arthur Haskins (1855-1940).*
7.   *Rt Rev John William Charles Wand KCVO DD DLit PC (1885-1977) (see Chapter 18). Philip Hugh Rhodes Wiggins (1911-1989).*
8.   *Prebendary Rev William Rodgers Dawson (1871-1936) [NR] Assistant Master 1896-97 and then Headmaster of Grantham School 1898-1906, Headmaster of Brighton College 1906-33. His time at Grantham coincided with William Wand's time there 1897-1904.*

In the school holidays Dora, his mother, would take the family to Watlington, to be close to her parents. There, Paul would spend time with his grandmother, with his aunt Mary and at *Youlbury*, Sir Arthur Evans's home outside Oxford. Evans stimulated an interest in history and in his idle moments Paul would read books like Macaulay's *Lays of Ancient Rome, The Last Days of Pompeii* by Bulwer-Lytton and Gibbon's *Decline and Fall of the Roman Empire*[x]. Later, he collected history books – everything from Arthur Mee's Children's Encyclopaedia to books portraying people of the Empire, many wearing little clothing.

ROLL
OF
Brighton College.
———
FIRST TERM, 1922
———
Brighton:
H. & C. TREACHER, LTD., NORTH STREET

Paul's last term at Brighton was in 1922. He was seventeen and didn't much want to leave school. The summer before, 1921, in an account entitled, *'Written for the future references of what he expects to be but hopes not to be his last Summer Holidays as a School Boy at Brighton College,'* he described his life in detail. The holiday was split into segments: a visit to a school friend Jack Highsted in Lincolnshire, a stay with his grandmother at Watlington, a period at *Youlbury* with Sir Arthur Evans, and just four days at home[9].

The countryside round Sleaford, where his school-friend Jack lived, was still full of those time-honoured sail windmills grinding corn for flour. There was full-on sport most days: swimming, tennis (a ball broke his glasses), croquet, cricket and his first game of golf. The two boys went rowing on the river in Boston and, at Paul's instance, toured every historical building they could find in Lincoln. They were taken round the elegant Mental Asylum by Jack's father, its 'Steward'. The sixteen-year old Jack drove a new motorcycle and sidecar. No age restrictions, no driving test either[xi]. His one 'lesson' consisted of Jack's mother (who probably couldn't drive) sitting in the sidecar. They went to Cranwell, which had just opened as the RAF Officer's College. They toured the airship hangar in the picture overleaf and another full of captured German planes. They went to an auction – where Jack bought an aircraft prop for 5 shillings. They went to the Sleaford market where they observed a number of 'quacks' selling their cure-alls – anybody could describe themselves as a doctor. 'If people tried all the medicines that there were there, there would be no more illness according to them.'

Jack and Paul saw eight films over 18 days at the 'Picturedrome' – silent movies in those days, using carbon arc projectors. There was a comic who made Paul laugh so much that he 'turned the other way for a bit' just to calm himself down. The biggest attraction, however, was walking home arm in arm with Laura Marsden[10]. He was so distracted he couldn't remember anything about the film.

At Watlington there was more croquet and tennis. On the Vicarage lawn there was 'a sort of putting game with obstacles such as a bridge to putt over' – crazy golf we'd call it. There was a game of bridge most evenings or chess with his cousin Denie[11]. His parents were nowhere to be seen. His mother had taken 'rooms' in the village whilst his father slipped off to stay with his niece Nellie and the Hartwell's, in Oxford. Paul (Denison or 'Denis', as they called him) didn't seem to miss them much. He had his Aunt Mary. After 5 days at *Hill House*, he cycled the 16 miles to *Youlbury*, where Aunt Mary and Sir Arthur Evans had him to stay for the next two weeks.

Brighton College study 1921 – boys supplied their own furniture. The table on the right is still used by the author – for plants and parties. The tuck box is still around. The boys rose at 7am to have cold showers.

Market Place, Boston, Lincolnshire 1920s

9.   Jack (John Norman) Highsted (1904-1978) [NR].
10. Laura Peplow Marsden (1904-1994) [NR].
11. William Denison Clare Wiggins OBE CMG (1905-1971).

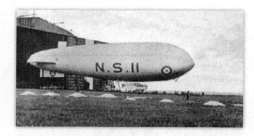

RAF Cranwell 1920s

Freshwater Isle of Wight

St Andrew's Hatfield Peveril.

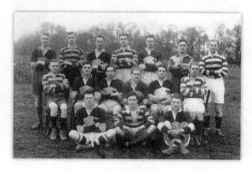

Barclays Rugby XV 1924-25. Paul 2rd left top row

In the big house at *Youlbury*, with its marbled hall portraying the labyrinth of the Minotaur in the floor tiles, he was treated to ice cream, peaches, nectarines and grapes, unseen wonders for most English households. Sir Arthur and Aunt Mary arranged an outing to the Isle of Wight with Jimmie Candy, no small excursion at 25 mph, with the Wolseley breaking down twice. They toured *Marlborough College* 'not half as nice as Brighton except for the chapel' and Stonehenge which they couldn't find, even though Sir Arthur had lectured on it in 1888[xii]. They stayed at the County Hotel at Salisbury and after dinner met up with Paul's aunt Amy and his uncle Will. Will, who'd recommended him for Brighton College, was a Salisbury Vicar (see Chapter 18). The following day there was 'a nice person to take us round the cathedral, a dean or somebody'. After Yarmouth, Alum Bay and then Freshwater, on the Isle of Wight where they stayed a couple of nights, they returned via Winchester, *Romsey Abbey* and *Beaulieu*. Winchester College 'must be the best public school in England'. After the Cathedral's Sunday service, they toured the crypt 'where Druid sacrifices were supposed to have taken place'.

Back at Boar's Hill, Paul was 'elected' Captain of the Youlbury cricket team against the Scouts. His team won by an innings and 26 runs, thanks to his cousin Denie coming over for the match with Paul behind the wicket. Scoring was meticulous – Paul, the budding banker, made sure of that.

After several days at Watlington, where Paul developed and printed photographs of the trip, one of which you see here, he returned to Witham, to prepare the house for his schoolmaster father's new school term, and to pick apples to take back to school.

✳ ✳ ✳ ✳

Paul goes to work

Paul's mother Dora, always the social climber, thought it important to impress. As soon as she could, Paul was to start earning; then they wouldn't have to pay for school fees and she could rent a large detached four-bedroomed house[xiii]. She chose a house near the station in Hatfield Peverel, near Witham, and changed the German-sounding name *'Hiemat'* to the completely random *'St Andrew's'*. The dining room, the smallest room in the house, Dora declared to be the room where Paul's father was to teach: social standing and its relationship with money seemed to elude her; Charles had little say in the matter. The schoolroom was no bigger than"a kitchen, really," said his sister Nancy.

Nancy's letter ended in their mother's handwriting, "It is quite settled that we go to the house at Hatfield." Hmmph. Maybe the new house would give her sufficient social influence for Paul to obtain a banking job. They didn't stay there for more than four years. Paul failed an interview for the Bank of India and one with the Bank of England[xiv]. Paul's earnest, gangling appearance with a receding chin-line disguised a phlegmatic high-brow hard-worker. He decided to have all of his sticky-out teeth removed and used false teeth for the rest of his life[xv]. Most likely his Uncle Neville exerted some influence and Paul found a job in the City Branch of Barclays Bank. He soon wished he lived nearer London[xvi].

The train journey from Essex was slow – it was still notorious in the 1970s[xvii]. Charles Haskins was nearing 70, had lost most of his pupils in the move and Nancy was due to study for a degree in Mathematics at King's London. In 1925-6, he decided to give up teaching and move to Blackheath[xviii]. Paul soon made friends with Jack Dolton next door in Kidbrooke Park Road and it wasn't long before Jean Tresidder came on the scene[12].

---

[12]   *Arthur H St John Dolton (1905-1981) [NR] married Joan Alston Hole (1907-1998) [NR] in 1930.*

Rus in Urbe

Paul married Jean in 1932 (see Chapter 14.) They bought a house in one of the leafier examples of the mock-Tudor London suburbs upstream[xix].

The estate had been laid out by a developer, Basil Scruby, with the help of an enlightened architect, Leonard Culliford[13]. Scruby, from Essex, bought the Kent farmland from speculators (one the son of a farmer at Portloe, in Cornwall)[14]. He persuaded the Southern Railway to build a new station on its newly electrified line – Petts Wood – and this opened in 1928[xx]. The quarterly season ticket, costing £4, attracted bank and insurance clerks and newspapermen working in Fleet Street. The two hundred trains a day took '22 minutes' to reach the city. In exchange for the land and the station, Scruby reaped colossal dividends[xxi]. He could afford high standards. Gardens were long. Culliford laid down wide streets and crucial guidelines. The roads were gently curving, a generous 26ft wide. Houses were a sizeable 14-20,000 sq ft (1,300-1,850m2) with 45-degree roofs and metal Crittall windows; no bungalows, no trees chopped down, and no caravans.

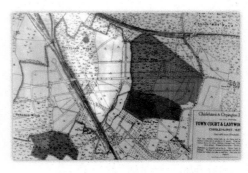

Plan of Petts Wood c 1928. The dot half-way between the railway lines marks 34 Manor Way. The station was built on the left line.

Development of a garden 1932, 2934, 1938

Paul paid £1,000 plus £50 extra for oak on the ground floor. He was the first Haskins to own his own home. Semi-detached, the house in Manor Way had an integral garage (very modern) and rudimentary gravity-fed central heating, also a first. The wide-bore pipework was still functional fifty years later. Being a banker, he was able to acquire a favourable mortgage. His current (cheque) account earned him interest – Barclays management insisted that all transactions went through the one account so they could inspect it, a curb against banking fraud and dissolute living. Paul named their home '*Widdicombe*' (his dyslexia kicking in) after the village on Dartmoor they'd visited in 1931[15]. When it featured in a 1983 BBC film on the making of this garden suburb, his unchanged kitchen ("unnecessarily large," declared his mother) still had its larder, butler sink and an Ascot gas water heater. The garden was a blaze of colour[xxii].

Azaleas 1981

✳ ✳ ✳ ✳

---

13. *Basil Scruby (1875-1946) [NR]; Leonard Arthur Culliford MC Croix de Guerre FRIBA FRICS (1888-1960) [NR].*

14. *Adolphus Orchard Chudleigh (1865-1930) [NR] who was from the East End (his grandfather came from Devon) and his son-in-law James Langdon (1884-1967) [NR] from Treviskey, Veryan, Cornwall.. They had bought the 272 acre Towncourt Farm for £7,474 in 1920 (the year Langdon married). They bought the 120 acre 'unfarmable' Ladywood Estate in 1926 and sold the whole estate to Basil Scruby over a 5-year period.*

15. *The village of Widecombe is pronounced 'Widdicombe'.*

War time

Paul joined the Territorial Army based at St John's Wood between the wars. He knew the army way of life since his schooldays with the Officers' Training Corps[xxiii]. When he was called up in June 1942 for the Second World War, he chose to sign on at Newport, Shropshire, to the Denbighshire Yeomanry, reasoning that a Territorial Regiment would know best how to scrounge good food[xxiv]. An added advantage was that the big field guns, a mile or two behind the front line, put some distance between him and the enemy. He wore a leather waistcoat next to his vest and smoked a pipe to keep the cold away from his bronchial chest. He went to some cold places – training for a re-invasion of Norway that never happened. Whilst Yorkshire winters were bad, at Huntly in the north of Scotland he ended up in hospital.

Army postings 1942-46	
Jun 1942	Newtown, Wales
Jul 1942	Hunmanby
Sep 1942	Leicester, Hunmanby
Jan 1943	Avoch and Huntley, Aberdeenshire
Jun 1943	Ripon, Yorks
Sep 1943	Beverley, Yorks
Oct 1943	Tickhill, Yorks
May 1944	Aldershot, Surrey
11 Jul 1944	left Crookham
12 Jul 1944	sailed
17 Jul 1944	**landed in France**
28 Jul 1944	**Caen**
2 Aug 1944	**Dampierre, Calvados**
3 Aug 1944	**St Owen des Bosaces**
5 Aug 1944	**Le Bény-Bocage**
10 Aug 1944	**Vire, Normandy**
21 Aug 1944	**Tinchebray**
16 Sep 1944	**Belgium**
22 Sep 1944	**Achel**
24 Sep 1944	**Netherlands**
10 Oct 1944	**Oploo, Netherlands**
17 Oct 1944	**Overloon**
20 Oct 1944	**Oedenrode**
23 Oct 1944	**Schnindel**
25 Oct 1944	**Oirschott**
26 Oct 1944	**Moergestel, Nethds**
29 Oct 1944	**Omnel, nr Asten**
1 Nov 1944	**Brussels, Belgium**
1 Dec 1944	**Sevenum, Nethds**
22 Dec 1944	**Heythuysen, Neths**
14 Mar 1945	**Germany**
29 Mar 1945	**Lembeck**
3 Apr 1945	**Osnabrück**
5 Apr 1945	**Minden**
12 Apr 1945	**Celle**
24 Apr 1945	**Lüneburg**
5 Jul 1945	**Bergdorf**
11 Jul 1945	**Bochum**
Nov 1945	Nordhorn
Feb 1946	Gottingen
Mar 1946	Peine
Bold – in action	

Paul never sought promotion. He saw no point in taking formal responsibility if the Bank was continuing to pay him better than an officer's salary. In the First World War, the young officers had led their men out of the trenches 'over the top', to attack enemy lines. They had been the first to be targeted by the enemy. He was happy driving the Commanding Officer and using his signalling training until one young officer insisted he join the Pay Corps. Paul had no desire to leave, so he deliberately failed all the exams, much to the officer's annoyance. With his driver's training in the Territorial Army Tank Corps, his comrades preferred him to be the one to drive the 'passion waggon' home after a heavy night of boozing, for Paul could hold his drink. He was older than most, fitter, more literate and more numerate. They nicknamed him 'the padre' because he was the one to help the less advantaged to write their letters home. Many struggled to read and write.

Cartoon in 'The Howitzer Herald', the weekly Soldier's magazine, which Paul helped to edit.

The K was his truck sign.

Paul spent 1942-44 training. It wasn't until after D-Day that he crossed the English Channel. The wait was long and tedious.

When it came to the real thing, luck had a part to play. Around D-Day our home in Petts Wood suffered war damage[xxv]. Blast from a bomb in the Recreation Ground blew a hole through the roof. No one was in. Jean was returning from a secret assignation with Paul at Crookham, Hampshire. She wasn't supposed to know where he was and no one was supposed to know about D-Day, but she did. Of her two daughters, Ann was away at school and seven year-old Barbara had been deposited two doors away, happily racing snails on the garden wall and sheltering under the dining room table when the bombs landed[16]. Barbara was first on the scene. She headed for our kitchen and was distressed to find the saucepans lying on the floor. "I think the shattered glass is more important, dear," was the reaction. Jean came home to disarray. She even knew what number to ring – no e-mails in those days. "How did you know your husband's here?" exclaimed the operator, dumbfounded.

---

16.   *The friend playing snails was Clare M Goffin (b1938) [NR].*

It took another week before Paul was granted a week's compassionate leave[xxvi]. It helped Paul survive. His unit were preparing to leave for France to back up the initial onslaught but between the time he arrived home on 29 June and returned 6 July, BSM Walsh, who'd taken Paul's seat in the convoy, was killed[xxvii]. Paul eventually set out from Crookham at dawn on 11 July 1944, leaving port the following evening. Six days later he stepped foot on French soil, whereupon he drove through France, Belgium and Holland, entering Germany on 14 March 1945.

Paul said the crowds in Brussels were out of this world, fêting the soldiers wherever they went[xxviii]. On one occasion, a Sergeant ordered him to drive the wrong way. 'If you take that route, Sergeant, we'll be behind enemy lines.' 'I order you.' Paul had more sense, disobeyed orders and went the right way. You could do that sort of thing in a Territorial Army regiment. Our family has impressive spatial skills. At two, our son **Christopher** was solving mazes designed for nine year olds[xxix]. At nine he was winning orienteering exercises designed for eighteen year olds[xxx]. If you ever get lost, do not rely on technology or those who think they know – give Christopher the map.

Once Germany had been conquered, demobilisation took time. The slow release of soldiers was to make sure they didn't make the mistakes of the first war. As Monty said, 'We've won the war, now let's win the peace'[17]. Despite severe rationing at home, Paul never saw any Germans short of food.

Paul spent his last six months in the Army of Occupation as a full time instructor and newspaper editor in the education section[xxxi]. He relished doing something different. A lot of soldiers had little to do in those last few months. On the contrary, he said. It was his most fulfilling time. When his regiment was disbanding, he took a course at the College of the Rhine[xxxii]. Economics, Banking and Music Appreciation. At Gottingen, Paul indulged in nightly Operas and concert performances staged by German orchestras eager to earn a wage.

A generation of men came home with far higher educational standards and knowledge than they had had before the war started. Before they received their 'demob' suit, every soldier was expected to take some sort of examination, including Maths (or Latin) and English[xxxiii].

The month before he was demobbed, Paul ended up doing a senior censorship job, in a posh office, with a couple of staff – the Army wanted to keep him on, offering him a Warrant Officer post. He gained much respect when he interviewed German soldiers. They stared in amazement at his ribbons. The black, white and red stripes of his long service police medal tricked them into thinking he'd won some English equivalent of the Iron Cross.

Paul had, you might say, a 'good war'.

✳ ✳ ✳ ✳

Paul in Brussels July 1945

VJ Day near the Mohne Dam: Privates Atkinson, Wellington, Haskins and Parker

17. *Field Marshal Bernard Law Montgomery, 1st Viscount Montgomery of Alamein KG GCB DSO PC (1887-1976) [NR].*

On the Stage

PETTS WOOD
AMATEUR DRAMATIC
AND
OPERATIC SOCIETY.

Hon. *Secretary* :

P. D. HASKINS,
"Widdicombe," Manor Way, Petts Wood.

Hon. *Treasurer* :

E. T. HEMSLEY,
Lloyds Bank House,
Station Square, Petts Wood.

Phone: Orpington 886.

Paul was Secretary of Petts Wood Amateur Dramatic and Operatic Society. It was soon so popular it split into Operatic and Plays

Find the girl. Daylight Inn, Petts Wood 1951. Ann Haskins, with Hilda Parr and Ann Milner

Crackerjack

Paul had acted as the secretary of the Petts Wood Amateur Dramatic and Operatic Society before the war[xxxiv]. He'd been Stage Manager for the amateur dramatics on the stage in the Daylight Inn. He'd persuaded the architect, Sidney Clarke, to install dressing rooms underneath the stage there, including a hatch door as well as stage lighting[18]. Still going to this day, the 'Operatic' is now performing twice a year in a larger location[xxxv]. I was taken along to its performances at the Orpington Civic Hall as quite a small boy. Depriving me of attendance was used as an incentive when I failed to pass my Common Entrance the first time round.

Paul honed his stage skills during his time in Yorkshire waiting for the real action. *'While Parents Sleep'* was performed in October 1942 at Hunmanby Hall by the Ubique Players[xxxvi]. After the war was over, he stage managed a Christmas show for the troops in Germany in 1945[xxxvii].

My sister Ann featured in several school plays, including *Madame Wang* in *Lady Precious Stream*, a play adapted from the Chinese[xxxviii]. She played Helen of Troy in the 'highly boring' *Trojan Women* by Euripides[xxxix]. After she left Goudhurst, James and Edie Cook, friends of our parents, persuaded Ann, together with a fellow Goudhurst school leaver, the local doctor's daughter, to take part in a Townswomen's Guild play at the Daylight Inn[xl]. The setting of *Find the Girl* was like the school they'd just left. The doctor's daughter had blonde hair and an innocent face, so she acted as goody-two-shoes whilst Ann played the scheming miscreant[19]. Ann performed so well that most of the audience thought she was like that in real life. It wasn't the best way to encourage Ann back onto the stage and she refused further stage roles – she didn't care for that sort of limelight....

On the other hand, I've taken part in 'am-dram' most of my life. My first stage performance was at the age of nine at the Westgate Pavilion at an afternoon shows for kiddies[xli]. The ventriloquist Rod Hull was the compere[120]. All the way from the Isle of Sheppey, he hadn't yet met his Emu or made the big time; he got me up there to recite *The Owl and the Pussy Cat*, which I knew by heart[xlii].

My next stage performance was in a house competition at *Bickley Hall*, where I imitated David Jacobs of Juke Box Jury[21]. The prize was an outing to see the children's BBC programme *Crackerjack* live, and go backstage to meet Eamonn Andrews – to be surprised to find that my sister Ann's friend was one of the hostesses, performing under her stage name Jillian Comber[22]. Suddenly I had to reconcile make-believe with reality. It was a similar shock when, in my twenties in my civil service job, I bumped into the French teacher who had arranged that competition, who was then working as a translator for the Ministry of Defence ("Pays better," he said.)

I was cast as Third Witch in that unlucky play by Shakespeare – so unlucky that my Prep School received notice to quit from some greedy developers. The Headmaster had to call off the production. Instead, we put on three one-act plays. Mine was a comedy set in the First World War trenches. I was cast as 'Captain Crispin Dawes of the Intelligence'. "Intelligence? Impossible!" said the Second Master, knowing my exam results. "He's been miscast."

---

18. *Sidney Charles Clarke FRIBA (poss1893-1959). Head of Charringtons' architects' department. Other inns by him include the Pied Bull at 1 Liverpool Road at the Angel Islington, now a branch of the Halifax, and the Olde Red Lion in Kennington Park Road.*
19. *Ann P Milner (b1934) [NR].*
20. *Rodney Stephen Hull (1935-1999) [NR] spent 1961-71 in Australia.*
21. *David Lewis Jacobs CBE (1926-2013) [NR].*
22. *Jill E Tuck (b1936) [NR]. Eamonn Andrews CBE (1922-1987) [NR] presented Crackerjack from 1955-1964.*

The following year, having passed the exam and now at *Dauntsey's* aged 14, I produced the same play for my new school's Half Term Entertainment. It was called *'Over the Top'*: I have been 'over the top' ever since. I wrote my own material after that, often in collaboration with others and for several years did the link spots between sketches. I was cast as Oswald in *King Lear* with the dubious privilege of being slapped nightly by a future founder of Friends of the Earth[xliii]. My subsequent productions of Entertainments, Pantomimes and Murder Mysteries at Petts Wood and Wetherby have not scaled the heights of Jim Hodges, the English master who pulled off stunning productions at Dauntsey's[23]. It was the only school I've ever come across where a cast of boys performed full scale Opera – Don Giovanni, Cosi fan Tutte, and the Marriage of Figaro to name but three.

King Lear, 1964. . The author, Oswald, front right, between Robert Cook, Lear and Jeremy James Taylor, the Fool.

※ ※ ※ ※

Post war

I was a post-war baby, unlike my sisters. I must have pleased Paul as he wanted a boy. Paul was similarly delighted when Carolyn produced a grandson within a year of our wedding, to carry on the Haskins family name. As soon as he could, he visited Jonathan in Westminster Hospital. He looked into the baby's grey-blue eyes, which shone right back at him, sparkling bright and clear with intelligence and certainty. With a big beam on his face, he declared that **Jonathan Neil Haskins** was 'all right'. Sometime around then he ordered some mugs decorated with so-called Haskins coat of arms and a book of Haskins, purporting to list all the known Haskins's in the world. It was a slim volume[xliv].

Merchant of Venice, May 1966. Robin Barson, Shylock; the author as Salarino and Neil Mitchell, Salanio

Paul worked his entire banking career at the City branch of Barclays in Lombard Street. Like Fleet Street for journalists, Lombard Street was the street for banks, from the time when Joseph Denison was making his fortune. Symbols of each bank, their 'Corporate Image', hung from brackets along the street. Martin's Bank had its Grasshopper sign, and Barclays the Spread Eagle.

After work each evening, wheelbarrow beside him, Paul spent time in his garden, which improved each year. As an eleven year-old, he'd gardened in Essex – peas, lupins, parsley, sweet peas, early potatoes, beans, peppers and lettuce[xlv]. He'd seen rhododendrons and flowering shrubs on the snaking paths in Arthur Evans's extensive grounds. He planted his azaleas in his Petts Wood garden after seeing how they flowered at Longleat on a day out from Dauntsey's. Gardening was his way of winding down at the end of a day at the office. The lawn was big enough for unconventional croquet, with obstacles such as an oak tree in the centre of the line of fire.

The author aged three in 1951

Both Paul and Jean lived in the one home all their married lives. The bequest from Sir Arthur Evans was enough to pay off the mortgage. Jean didn't care to move. She'd seen the effects of break-up with her parents. Paul turned down branch jobs and spent the last twenty years of his career in the overseas section of the City branch. Early in his career he had applied for jobs overseas, but had been considered 'Too thin' – fat men would survive better in the tropics, they said – a fallacy, they later found out[xlvi].

The author's son Jonathan in the same garden 39 years later, aged four

---

23. *Henry James Hodges (b1930) [NR].*

NUBE Executive. Paul Haskins on the right with moustache

My mother put family first and didn't like my father to sleep away from home. She suffered in silence the first time he went to a Blackpool conference in 1957. After saying goodbye to the coach at Danson Park, I recall sobbing uncontrollably all the way home in the back of the car, an outward expression of my mother's inner feelings going on in the driver's seat.

The City was full of small bustling Dickensian lanes and courts, not too different from the Haskins experience of the 1800s. As fathers should, he took me to a spit and sawdust pub, with *gor'blimey* chatter, in Leadenhall Market where the steaks were cooked over an open range. The city types and market men supped together. 'Top of the mornin' guv', they'd go – luverly. My dad would do most of his work in the morning, retire to the pub for a late lunch (just beer) and go home early. All banking work was done the same day. On August Bank Holiday 1939, a week before war was declared, he left work at 7pm and the following night even later, at 9pm[xlvii]. It was all done without the assistance of calculators – electronic or mechanical. He could add up a set of figures in a flash, useful for card games, such as Bridge, where he won every cup at the Orpington Bridge Club – except, as he was keen to point out, the Ladies' Cup![xlviii]

Paul retired from Lombard Street, aged 60, at the same age as his good friend Polly Parrott[24]. They invited 150 of their colleagues to a joint party at *Deacons* tavern in Walbrook. 'As was expected, the party was a great success, and needed the persuasion of the licensing laws to bring it to a close.'[xlix] Paul's major contribution to national life was through the trades union, the National Union of Bank Employees (NUBE), where he was voted onto the National Executive. He set out to neuter the communist employees who wanted to disrupt the complete banking system and convert the country to socialism. Their trick was to call the meetings with the minimum of notice, pack it with their own people, and rely on sluggish non-attendance from ordinary members. Stalinist socialism was the currency of communism at that time. The effect could have been disastrous. Having experienced the 1926 General Strike, when he had volunteered to become a Special Constable, Paul realised better than the Bank of England that any attempt to shake the banking system would have brought Britain down[l]. The Bank fumbled badly after the 1929 Wall Street crash. The ten-year depression that followed was far less well-managed than our 21st century recession has been. Paul put his NUBE agenda ahead of a soaring career.

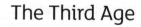

The Third Age

Paul shaved his moustache off on retirement. He'd grown it in the war. After leaving the bank, Paul spent the five years using his overseas banking skills to export paint[li]. His boss was a Tremayne – who talked about his relationship with the Cornish family that had built the mansion at Heligan, now famous for its 'Lost Gardens' (which at that time were very lost) and of the surrounding land, which included the beach at Pentewan[25].

In his retirement, Paul did many things including helping distribute Meals on Wheels – dishing out food to 'old people' who were younger than him. From the time that my youth club had straightened out the churchyard he tended the grounds at St Francis Church. It was the year after Jean (his wife) died. Every Monday, as he gathered up the leaves with a paid helper, he looked at the flowering cherry that he'd planted in memory of Jean, and recollected happy memories. "The wonderful display of daffodils ... delighted our eyes, gladdened our

24.   Joseph Philip Parrott (1905-1973) [NR].
25.   Possibly or possibly not George William Tremayne (1911-1989). If so, his father, William Alfred Tremayne (1874-1957) was a mariner born in Deptford, Kent who was educated at an orphanage in Carshalton, Surrey – no real connection with the Cornish family.

hearts and raised our spirits," wrote a friend in the Parish magazine[lii]. Paul gave up when he was 90, in 1995. Since then, the work has been done by new volunteers, who still recall his time there.

Paul reached the age of 90, like his surrogate uncle Sir Arthur Evans. Like Sir Arthur, he had a ninetieth birthday party. It might be a Cornish superstition, or one from the medical profession, or harking back to the Wars of the Roses, but our family would never have white and red flowers together in one room, for it spelt death. Yet red and white tulips were the only flowers in his garden in the weeks after he died in January 1996. Without telling anyone, he had arranged for his treasured garden to affirm his death in the way it had his life.

90th birthday party, 1995: top Simon Gates, Hugh Simpson, Michael Gates, the author, Ian Simpson, Luke Simpson, Victoria Simpson; middle: Jeremy and Bridget Bradshaw, Ann Gates (née Haskins), Paul Haskins, Barbara Simpson (née Haskins), Carolyn Haskins (née Burton), Naomi Simpson; bottom: Louise and Alison Bradshaw, Jonathan and Christopher Haskins.

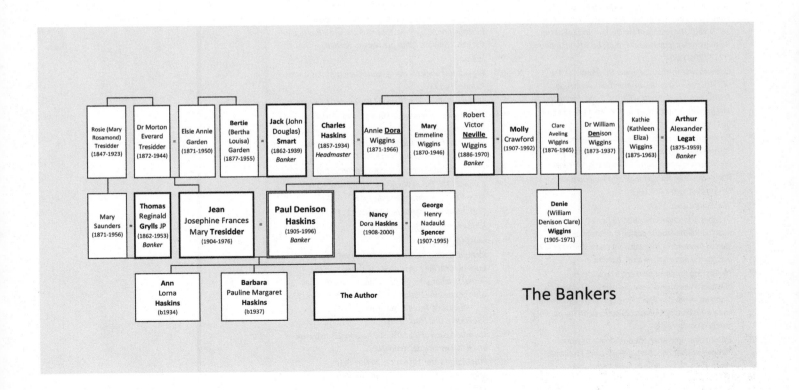

The Bankers

Other Notes and References

i. Williams p124. John Michael Williams JP DL (1813-1880) [NR] was considered 'the richest man in Cornwall'. His family, originally from Wales, had made its fortune in mining around Redruth. His father had bought Caerhays in 1854 and his son developed the garden in the early 1900s with seeds brought back from China. He had broken away from his partners, the Tweedy's.

ii. Scotland banks covered the risk of issuing bank notes until 1844 when they got into difficulty. Since the 1845 Banknote (Scotland) Act they have been required to work under the aegis of the Bank of England, which pulled them out of the mire. Would an independent Scotland want to carry its own risk today?

iii. King p200.

iv. Neville Wiggins lived at 18 Allerton Park, Leeds. The open-topped Morris had been stolen in 1929.

v. Eton collars were large wide starched collars worn outside the other clothes.

vi. Junior boys cleaning senior boys' studies. See Hughes' Tom Brown's Schooldays.

vii. PDH Diary 12 Apr, 24 Jun, 4 Aug 1916, 16 & 19 May, 18 Aug 1917. John Constable RA (1776-1837) [NR].

viii. Sir George Gilbert Scott RA (1811-1878). Hatcher p20. Association of Old Brightonians. Hugh Wiggins was at Brighton about 1924-28; Paul Sep 1918 - Mar 1922.

ix. Wand, Changeful Page p19.

x. Lays of Ancient Rome (published 1888) by Thomas Babington Macaulay, 1st Baron Macaulay, PC (1800-1859), Last Days of Pompeii (1834) by Edward George Earle Lytton Bulwer-Lytton, 1st Baron Lytton PC (1803-1873) [NR], The History of the Decline and Fall of the Roman Empire (published 1776-89) by Edward Gibbon (1737-1794) [NR].

xi. Licences were introduced under the Motor Car Act of 1903, covering both cars and motorbikes; age restrictions were introduced in 1930; the driving test was introduced in 1934 – the first person passing the test was a Mr Beene.

xii. Evans, Arthur J. Stonehenge. Evans postured that Stonehenge was based on the tiliths of Syria, which encircled a sacred or 'family' tree of the All-Father.

xiii. PDH Letter from Nancy Haskins to Paul Denison Haskins Witham 2 Apr 1922.

xiv. PDH Diary 12 Sep 1921.

xv. QI Series K 'Kitchen Sink'. BBC 13 Dec 2013 says it wasn't until the Stuarts copied the Europeans and started to use forks that top front teeth started to stick out, having nothing now to do but smile.

xvi. The Barclay family of bankers, who at the time of William Wilberforce were Quakers and living in Clapham, resided in Paul's time at Leyton, Essex. Paul knew a T B Barclay but no connection with the banking family is confirmed.

xvii. This was the time when the author was at Warren Comprehensive School, Whalebone Lane, Chadwell Heath 1970-73, teaching Religious Education.

xviii. 26 Kidbrooke Park Road. Nancy Haskins attended King's College London 1926-9, emerging with a 3rd class Honours, and an ACA (Divinity). She then undertook teacher training in Roehampton.

xix. The builder was J C Witcombe.

xx. Haskins, Robert, The Stamp of Personality.

xxi. Scruby paid £6,000 plus taking out £1,000 5% preference stock.

xxii. Britain in the Thirties. BBC Film.

xxiii. Royal Tank Corps 1924-31. Discharge certificate.

xxiv. 61st Medium Regiment Royal Artillery (Denbighshire Yeomanry), Territorial Army. War service from 11 Jun 1942 to 24 Jul 1946 Record of Service, Soldier's Service Book and Soldier's Release Book. Army No 1150602.

xxv. D Day was 6 June; Diary entry suggests the bomb damage occurred 19 June 1944.

xxvi. PDH Diary entry 29 June - 6 July 1944 'Leave (compassionate)'.

xxvii. PDH Diary entry 3 July 'BSM Walsh killed'. Diary entry 12 Jul 1944 'Boat left at 2030 hrs'; 17 Jul 1944 'Landed'.

xxviii. PDH Diary 16 Sep 1944 'Moved into Belgium' 24 Sep 1944 'Crossed into Holland' 1 Nov 1944 'went to Brussels'.

xxix. Valentine p51.

xxx. District Scout Camp, Stokesley North Yorks, 27/28 June 1998.

xxxi. It took 10,000 words to fill a weekly edition of the Howitzer Herald, circulated with a readership of 3,000. 61st Medium Regiment, Nordhorn.

xxxii. 7th Formation College of the Rhine Army, Gottingen (Feb-Mar 1946) PDH letter 6 Mar 1946: 'It has certainly been far and away the most comfortable [experience] I have had in the army, probably in my life, from the sheer comfort of living conditions (no work except use of the brain). You will remember that at the beginning of the war I always felt that my brain would not function normally. I feel that after the use it has had in the last 5 months, it has got back to normal.'

xxxiii. Horrocks.

xxxiv. Pre-war rule book for the Operatic Society states it was founded in 1935.

xxxv. Haskins, Robert, The Stamp of Personality p13.

xxxvi. Anthony Kimmins's While Parents Sleep. Performed 27/28 Oct 1942.

xxxvii. PDH Letter from his friend Gill (whose surname was pronounced with a hard 'g') 12 Jan 1946.

xxxviii. S I Hsiung Lady Precious Stream. Performed July 1950.

xxxix. Euripides The Trojan Women was translated by Prof Gilbert Murray, performed July 1951.

xl. Find the Girl was performed 2/3 Nov 1951.

xli. RJH's An Anything Book (aged 9).

xlii. Lear p61.

xliii. Richard Sandbrook OBE (1946-2005) [NR] played the Duke of Kent. King Lear 1964. To the right of the author is Jeremy James Taylor (b1949) (as the Fool) who founded the National Youth Music Theatre in 1976. Alumni include Jessie J, Jude Law, Eddie Redmayne, Sue Perkins and Matt Lucas.

xliv. The World Book of Haskins. 500 households in the UK and 6,000 worldwide, mainly USA.

xlv. PDH Diary 19 Mar 1916, 17 & 24 Mar 1917.

xlvi. At the age of 16, Paul had weighed 9st 4 lbs, was 5ft 11¾ high with a chest of 32 inches.

xlvii. PDH Letter to Jean 6 Sep 1939.

xlviii. Individual cup 1962, Petts Wood War Memorial cup 1964; Ann Kerr cup (duplicate pairs) 1990; Mixed Pairs 1963,1981,1989; Gents Pairs 1968,1972,1981,1984; Betina Cohen-Carr cup 1991.

xlix. Spread Eagle (Barclays' house magazine) March 1965. Held 21 Jan 1965, at Bucklersbury House.

l. PDH Letter from Stanley Baldwin May 1926.

li. Paul worked at Cray Valley Products Ltd in Cray Avenue, St Mary Cray 1965-70.

lii. Dorothy Hutton St Francis Petts Wood Parish Magazine July 1987

Northern Lights

Tadpoles

Soon after I bought my cottage in Cornwall in 1980, I invited my Tadpoles Society friends to a 'Thirties' Week[i]. Tadpoles, I should explain, has nothing to do with frogs, or even Princes, but Cornwall comes into the story. During my Open University studies I studied an esoteric course called *Art and the Environment*. All courses had codes. This one was coded 'TAD 292'. Hence the Tad name for anyone who had been on the course. The course had been conceived by Simon Nicholson, triplet son of Ben Nicholson and Barbara Hepworth, artists who had based themselves in St Ives during the 1930-40s[1].

Carolyn Haskins (née Burton) (b1957)

The St Ives artists' community is still celebrated today. Bernard Leach the potter sent his son David to my school in Wiltshire. Not long ago I spent an Old Boy's day watching cricket, reminiscing with his grandson Jeremy, now in Devon. Three generations of inspired potters: Jeremy vividly remembers playing table tennis with the Nicholson triplets.

Simon Nicholson designed what was probably the wildest course ever invented by any university. It aimed to marry art and the environment when climate-change and global warming meant not much more than a hot day at the seaside; when sculpture parks were storage yards. The course did more than that. It cleared out conventional thinking. Just up my street, except I didn't have much clearing out to do. One student summed it up thus: "TAD certainly turned my life around – and I've never looked back. I may not have become a great and famous artist or writer but the 'creative fire' unleashed by the experience burns brighter with the passing of the years."[ii] The Summer Schools were especially memorable – I met some people there that I shall never forget.

'The Old Inn' cottage interior

The Tadpoles Society was founded by one of its students, a Church Army Officer from Barnsley, in order to perpetuate that experience[2]. I am still a member of that Society all these years later. It enabled people to meet up for weekends – in my case, for a week. My terraced stone cottage has six beds but one night there were twenty-six staying. We held a concert in the Ship Inn ("Can you perform in our pub next," asked one of our audience.) We went skinny dipping on Hemmick Beach, held massage therapy and much more and went away full of memories. One guest, an antique dealer, presented me with my first horse brass in the shape of a spade in a deck of cards. At Newquay I bought a second. Now I have a collection of over 35 – one for every year I've owned The Old Inn in Pentewan.

✳ ✳ ✳ ✳

Around year four, I bought a horse brass portraying the White Rose of Yorkshire. It was the year I met **Carolyn Burton**[3]. I was in the Chief Executive's office with a new section formed to restructure the Property Services Agency (PSA) a government body with 25,000 employees and a £2 billion/year spend capacity, previously called the Office of Works. Its Chief Executive was one of the first private sector appointments to the senior civil service made by Margaret Thatcher. Thatcher's aim was to shake up an organisation founded by Edward III in the 14th century.

---

1. *Simon Hepworth Nicholson (1934-1990) [NR] son of Benjamin Lauder Nicholson OM (1894-1982) [NR] and Dame Barbara Hepworth DBE (1903-1975) [NR], who was born in Yorkshire and resided at St Ives until her death.*
2. *Percy Shaw (1938-1994) [NR] – not the inventor of road cats-eyes of the same name.*
3. *Carolyn Burton (b1957) – no relation of the Burtons in Chapter 3 – married the author in 1985.*

Mount Pleasant, Falklands – RAF Camp and hangars in construction. Stone quarry on hills left of the water tower.

One day, in walked our new recruit, a stunning girl who set the office alight with her flirty talk and charismatic nonsenses. The office realised our mutual interest the day the two of us failed to return from lunch. We'd been flat hunting but she'd tripped over the 'safety' belt of an estate agent's Mini, cracked her elbow and ended up in Westminster hospital. A little explaining to do...

The PSA reorganisation worked for us better than for our Chief Executive. It wasn't long before he was given the sack following a disastrous appearance before the Public Accounts Committee (PAC) where he was viewed as arrogant and complacent over fraud and corruption. Carolyn went on to be an Assistant Private Secretary to the then Minister of Transport, Sir David Mitchell MP (father of Andrew, the short-lived Chief Whip of the 'Pleb-gate' scandal.)[4]

I went back to a job I'd done before. This time, as well as the day job, I was put in charge (not entirely on my own) of the finances of the £400 million project to build a modern-day fortress at Mount Pleasant on the Falkland Islands. It was the largest project ever undertaken by PSA; and had been the subject of another PAC hearing – it was heavily overspending.

Two years later, the project was back on track and on time, and was underspending. It had two runways, hardened aircraft shelters, a naval landing stage, accommodation for some 3,000 troops and 130km of road[iii]. Stone and water were the only local commodities. 900,000 cubic metres of rock was quarried locally. Sand was made from crushed stone. There were 30,000 architect's drawings[iv]. I was on the second plane that landed on the new runway, travelling with my boss in seats A1 and A2. As my family know only too well, I almost always travel in jacket and tie. My boss Jeff Jacobs was more relaxed than me, if that's possible[5]. He wore his usual mufti – open-necked shirt and cuffs undone. Greeted by the commanding officer as we stepped off the plane, the General saluted me rather than Jeff. We hastily corrected the situation.

I was quietly reprimanded by the customs officer, who looked the other way, for bringing two oak tree saplings with me in the cabin without the necessary paperwork. I was honorary Treasurer of the local National Trust Committee for Petts Wood and had dug them up in the woods. Petts Wood had been planted by William Pett to supply oak for Elizabeth I's navy[6]. Oak trees take a long time to grow. I reasoned that a woodland planted 400 years earlier, specifically to supply the Royal Navy, wouldn't miss a couple of self-seeded saplings to supply this British military establishment. The Falklands had few if any indigenous trees. Hong Kong had been similarly afforested after British occupation 100 years earlier[iv]. There was a purpose. It created a more comfortable micro-climate and there were plans to do the same at Mount Pleasant. Thousands of pine cones were placed in plastic beakers on shelves in the greenhouses. When we went to see the Governor, his wife wanted the oaks for her garden. I should have said yes but I was on a mission. As I have never returned to the Falklands, I don't know where they ended up.

I was sounded out about doing a tour of duty on the Falklands as head of PSA Administration. I explained I'd only just got married. I was even offered one of only 6 married quarters on the island for British serving personnel, armed and unarmed. But, as Carolyn threatened to divorce me straightaway, that didn't happen. Nor did I get to see our British military base in Canada – just as I was due to go there, our son Jonathan was born[7].

Family came first, as my mother would say. Instead, I was selected for a three-year posting to Hong Kong; somewhere PSA had flown me in 1973. It was 1987. Most of my passports seem to have been financed by work rather than for recreation.

---

4. *Sir David Bower Mitchell MP (1928-2014) [NR]. His son is Andrew John Bower Mitchell MP (b1956) [NR].*
5. *Jeffrey Jacobs (b1953) [NR].*
6. *William Pett (1552-1587) [NR] was one of a family of Royal shipbuilders from Peter Pett (1530-1589), his father, to Sir Phineas Pett 1635-1694). William's will of 1577 mentions Pett's Wood.*
7. *Jonathan Neil Haskins (b1986).*

Burtons of Barnsley

The horse brass helped me to get serious with Carolyn. I spent Christmas 1983 at the Warrington home of its donor, along with some other Tadpoles. It was my excuse to visit Barnsley. I drove across the Pennines and phoned Carolyn from a working men's club in Rotherham to offer her a lift back to London. I was 'just passing', I told her. It must have been the following year that I asked her father, **Ken Burton**, for permission to marry her, kneeling on the loft hatch as he was showing me his model railway[8].

Ken lost his father when he was one year old. **Thomas Burton** died of consumption as a result of the First World War. He was a printer before the war and a lorry driver during the Italian campaign. He was forced off the road into a ditch and caught pneumonia waiting for someone to rescue him. It developed into TB a few years later and, after Thomas died, Ken's mother **Annie** (Machen) was granted a war widow's pension.

One of the oldest parts of Barnsley was Monk Bretton, where Ken's family came from. The Cluniac monks had erected a chapel-of-ease for the hamlet of Barnsley, St Mary's, in the Middle Ages. Barnsley became the centre with Monk Bretton on the outskirts. Thomas had been brought up there, like his father. When they married, Thomas and Annie, his wife, lived in Barnsley town[9]. When Thomas died in 1925, Annie moved in with her unmarried brother, **Harry Machen**, together with baby Ken and his fifteen-year old sister **Nancy**[10].

Harry Machen (1881-1943)

Ken has fond memories of Uncle Harry, as he became a substitute for his dead father. Harry had been a dispatch rider in the First World War and liked to take Ken on his motorbike, hurtling through the country lanes around Barnsley. Harry began work in the office at Redfearn's Bottling Factory as a shorthand clerk and rose to become its works manager. He was considered a good 'boss'. The factory was near the canal at Smithies before it moved to Monk Bretton. It produced glass bottles with a marble stopper – to open them you had to use a tin opener. As the marble went down the contents began 'fizz'. Harry funded Ken into wireless school and soon thereafter settled down to a married life.

From Honeywell Lane, Ken attended Sunday School at St Mary's. He'd asked to go because his two friends did – mother attended Chapel. Ken also sung in the choir at St John's Staincross. On one occasion, he was selected to sing in Wakefield Cathedral. High church, they wore black cassocks and cottas.

When Ken's sister Nancy married in 1935, he and his mother moved out of Harry's home[11]. That same year, Ken won a Barnsley Borough scholarship to the Boy's Grammar School, named after Robert Holgate, Archbishop of York[12]. Holgate was a contemporary of Henry VIII and heavily involved in the Reformation, the dissolution of the monasteries and the wobbles of religious policy that followed – he was one of the first priests to marry.

It took some skill to escape the same fate as the other Archbishop, Cranmer of Canterbury who was burnt at the stake in Oxford under 'Bloody Mary' Tudor. Holgate got away with imprisonment and a fine, but the stress left its toll. Dying in 1555, he left money to endow three Grammar Schools (mostly with the loot from the monasteries) with Ken's school being one. First based in Hemsworth it moved to Barnsley in 1888. It has had some well-known alumni, not all at the same time as Ken, but impressive nevertheless; as well as Professors and industrialists they include Michael Parkinson the broadcaster and Martyn Moxon[13], the

Martyrs' Memorial Oxford

---

8. *Kenneth Burton (b1924) married Renée Faith Morley (1926-2017) in 1952.*
9. *5 Leopold Street, Barnsley, and in Harry Road.*
10. *Harry Machen (1881-1943) married Amy Ellen Dunningham (1900-1982) in 1938. Edith Annie Burton (Nancy) (1910-1977) married Joseph Rickson (1909-1983) in 1935.*
11. *17 Westbourne Grove, Barnsley*
12. *Most Rev Robert Holgate (c1481-1555) [NR] Bishop of Llandaff 1537-45, Archbishop of York 1545-54*
13. *Sir Michael Parkinson CBE (b1935) [NR]; Martyn Moxon (b1960) [NR]*

cricketer. In 2012 it was pulled down, amalgamated into a super-sized 'Community College' — the name Holgate presumably dumped at the bottom of some ignorant council officer's drawer[vi].

Ken enjoyed his time at school and made friends for life. The French master even took a party to Paris just before war broke out – they stayed at Pension Andre Santé in Rue de l'Estrapade. Ken was turning fifteen when the Second World War began. When he was old enough, Ken left Barnsley for the duration. One of the lucky ones, he returned to his home town and stayed put.

✳ ✳ ✳ ✳

Linen, Coal and Christian Mission

Barnsley is mentioned in the Doomsday Book. It was hardly a town. It only had 200 residents in 1086. A Royal Charter permitted a weekly Wednesday market from 1249. By 1550, there were still only 600 inhabitants.

The weaving trade changed Barnsley. The town straddled the River Dearne. It became a refuge of the linen workers such as **James Burton**, who moved from Lancashire in about 1850[14]. Cotton was supplanting linen. Jane Austen's heroines dressed in fine cotton muslin, mostly made in India. The Lancashire Mills were cashing in on cotton and driving the linen industry to Barnsley.

The linen weavers became the precursors to Arthur Scargill[15]. Conscious of playing on a losing wicket, they militantly held out for better pay. Luddites[vii]. They saw their wages go down and their living conditions go the same way[viii]. **Matthew Bulmer**, Carolyn's great great grandfather, was a hand-loom linen weaver before machines had taken over[16]. He would have kept the loom in one room of his house – 30 Union Street. His daughters would have taken turns to bring in the money, on piece rates. By Ken's mother's time in the early 1900s, things were mechanised. Redbook's was still producing English linen in 1911.

Barnsley also earned a reputation for making glass for bottles, when French Huguenots found plentiful coal and the right clay for crucibles. Harry Machen's firm became a leader. Before the railways, a waterway system went right up to the factory. Water was better for transporting fragile goods and a canal connected Barnsley to the Humber in one direction and Liverpool in the other. One winter, when it froze over, Ken's grandfather skated all the way to Wakefield. Only in the 1850s did mining take over in a big way … the coal mines of Arthur Scargill. fame[ix].

Apart from Arthur and the Luddites, Barnsley has nurtured a surprising number of positive people who've enriched the world: broadcasters, actors, Olympic medallists, entrepreneurs, and even a Secretary of State for Defence and Northern Ireland[x]. Is it the warm lilt of the voice? The high altitude and fresh air? Or the schooling? The most successful Christian missionary of all time came from Barnsley. James Hudson Taylor, founder of the China Inland Mission[17]. Chinese pilgrims turn up to have their picture taken outside Boots, where a wall-plaque records his birthplace. If they all came at once, it would be quite a crowd. There are now up to 100 million Chinese Christians.

✳ ✳ ✳ ✳

The Luddite sign

You must raise your right hand over your right eye if there be another Luddite in company. He will raise his left hand over his left eye – then you must raise the forefinger of your right hand to the right side of your mouth – the other will raise the little finger of his left hand to the left side of his mouth and will say 'What are you?' The answer, 'Determined.' He will say, 'What for?' Your answer, 'Free Liberty.'

Then he will converse with you and tell you anything he knows....

Barnsley Civic Trust
2012

James Hudson Taylor
(1832-1905)

Founder of the
China Inland Mission
was born on this site

---

14.   *James Burton (1806-1868) married Elisabeth Guest (1816-1883) in 1836..*
15.   *Arthur Scargill (b1938) [NR] led the 1984-5 miners' strike.*
16.   *Matthew Bulmer (1818-1879) was father of Harriet Bulmer (1858-1916) who married Willie Machin (1853-1940), Annie and Harry Machen's parents. Annie was Ken's mother.*
17.   *James Hudson Taylor (1832-1905) [NR].*

Don't panic, Mr Mainwaring!

Ken Burton can boast of serving in all three Services. He first joined the Home Guard in the Longcar Centre (behind Della Avenue, where he's lived most of his married life). He was sixteen. Recruitment age was seventeen. The officer in charge turned out to be that self-same French teacher who'd taken him to Paris. He looked Ken up and down, knowing full well what age he was. He wearily noted down the assumed age 17 with a sigh. "What's the world coming to?" he opined. No wonder Ken has liked watching the TV series, Dad's Army. He was in it. There was even the same comedy: one night on sentry duty in the dark of the black-out precautions, a figure appeared through the mist.

"Halt who goes there? Friend or foe?"

"Friend with chips," says the other.

"Pass friend, halt chips."

At the Merchant Navy's North Eastern School of Wireless Technology, *Ashfield House* in Otley, Ken learned Morse code day after day. It was a slow process but eventually it clicked. Ken ended up so proficient that he could take notation whilst reading a novel at the same time.

It wasn't all work and no play – there were hikes to the Otley Chevin and walks to the cinema in town. Ken began to learn the ribald sea songs for which he has since become notorious – always late at night in front of a chosen few on certain inebriated occasions. The lads went to the City Varieties in Leeds, famous for its Music Hall. It included some, shall we say, titillating acts; one involving a lady with not a lot of clothes on, swathed in turtle doves. The lads sat in the front row and chucked breadcrumbs on the stage, resulting in the birds flying away from the task in hand and revealing more than the management intended. On another occasion, Ken and his pals dressed up in white sheets, hid behind the trees down the long drive and scared the living daylights out of the fellows returning from the movies. Was it pink elephants or ghosts they saw?

Ken joined the merchant navy. He was commissioned by Marconi to work on various ships (see inset column). The cargo ships were all painted in the grey of war, with guns sprouting fore and aft. As well as drawing his Marconi salary, he received ship's pay – pay which would stop if the ship was sunk or it arrived in port. Two of his friends from Wireless School met their end the first time out. All pay stopped for them.

Ken sailed the Atlantic a dozen times. The North Atlantic convoys were the most dangerous. He did four runs the whole way there and back. With his ship, the *Queen Adelaide*, there were over 100 ships in the convoy, guarded by naval vessels – corvettes, destroyers and in one case an aircraft carrier. He never knew when German U boats would attack. The first thing he would hear would be a thud as a torpedo hit a ship.

Aircraft carriers were crucial to the success of the war. Ordinary ships were converted to take light aircraft – 'Woolworth Carriers'. One pilot, a cousin of my mother, described it thus: "I am engaged in a comic form of warfare which consists in going to sea with a merchant ship equipped with a catapult, taking with me a Hurricane and a requisite number of bodies. On the approach of the enemy I get shot off the end of the catapult by a few rockets at a prodigious speed. I then (wearing my old school tie) valiantly shoot down the enemy after which there is usually a bit of an anti-climax because there probably isn't anywhere to land the Hurricane, so I throw it away and bale out into the sea, when the Navy pick me up. All good ripe fun."[xi] One has to admire the camaraderie of those days, in the face of battle. It voiced a way of living, speaking and dying that sounded flippant and courageous but disguised their basic feelings.

This was no Dad's Army. Three ships were lost on Ken's second trip in November 1942, including the *Grange Park*, the ship he'd just left. His ship, the *Fort Chill Coating* was carrying ammunition and explosives and was nearly hit. A torpedo passed within inches of the stern

Otley Chevin, from Ashfield House

Ships sailed by Ken Burton 1942-1945

Ship	Route
SS Grange Park	UK – West Africa – UK
SS Fort Chill Coting	UK – Algiers – UK (Operation Torch)
SS Empire Opossum	UK – Newfoundland/ Canada – UK
MV Port Chalmers	UK – New Zealand via Panama – UK (with Governor General's wife Lady Newell and son Francis)
RMS Orduna	UK – South Africa – UK Troops (RAF pilot training)
SS Glenpark	UK – Italy – West Africa – UK
MV Queen Adelaide	Combined Operations to Normandy – UK – North America – New York – Trinidad – Cape Town – South Africa – East Africa – Egypt – Palestine – UK (7 months)
SS Empire Shearwater	UK – New York – Dominican Republic – UK
SS City of Hong Kong	Hull – Glasgow (resigned)

MV Port Chalmers. All ships were painted battleship grey

SS City of Hong Kong

but Ken only learnt about that later. He never re-joined the same ship for a second tour after that. In his next convoy, in March 1943 on the *Empire Opossum*, 16 ships were lost.

After 1943, when the Navy had developed radio detection on high frequency (ASDIC) and could lay depth charges to blow up the enemy submarines, things got safer.

As a Radio Officer ('Sparks'), Ken was a junior member of the wardroom, or saloon, dining with the guests. On the return trip from New Zealand on the *Port Chalmers* there were about two dozen passengers including Olive Newall, the wife of the Governor-General, with her son Francis on his way to Eton. Cyril Newall had been Chief of Air Staff during the Battle of Britain[18]. He'd done much to make sure there'd been sufficient strength in the fighting command. However, he'd been diplomatically shuttled off to the other side of the world when he opposed blanket bombing of German towns. He was not alone. Others who opposed mass civilian casualties included Air Marshall Sir Arthur (later Lord) Tedder. Despite conceiving saturation bombing over enemy lines in the first place (the 'Tedder Carpet) he drew the line at killing civilians[19]. Whereas Tedder kept his head down, Newall had made a fuss. One night on deck, groping in the dark of the blackout order after dinner, Ken bumped into another person on that deck. Lady Newall reached out and embraced Ken rather dramatically, thinking (or so she said) that he was her son!

Though the seas were safer, Ken still wouldn't sail on the same boat twice. Ken had tottered up the coast from Hull to Glasgow in the *City of Hong Kong* and was asked to go on a new assignment to India. Rather than do that, he resigned from the Merchant Navy. It was September 1945, soon after VJ Day. It was probably just as well he didn't go. The *Hong Kong* was wrecked in the Suez Canal.

Ken's third armed Service was the RAF Police, looking after prisoners of war. He joined in December 1945 but never saw a plane in the whole of his year with the RAF. He comforted himself with the one and only flight he'd taken – while still at his junior school. Uncle Harry had taken him for a short trip at a fair at Staincross – it had cost 2/6. For the one year in the RAF, he was stationed at Thetford. His service career had thus turned the full circle. The Service establishment at Thetford – Stanford Battle Ground – was where the TV series Dad's Army was filmed.

✳ ✳ ✳ ✳

Civvy Street

When Ken was 'demobbed' at the end of 1946, he went to work at David Brown's engineering firm in Penistone. After a couple of years, he joined Qualters & Smith Bros Ltd in Summer Lane, Barnsley. The firm had begun life supplying machinery for coal mines but was diversifying, equipping schools and firms with devices for small workshops – machines now valued highly as collectors' items.

Sadly, quality was not enough to save the firm from receivership in October 1979. Redundancy is never good, particularly when the workforce is looking to you for inspiration, but Ken enjoyed his next job, as Senior Office Manager in the Probation Service. He was there for three years, travelling by train to Sheffield.

Ken's final year of paid work was spent in teaching. He spent his time imparting the tricks and tribulations of business studies at Worsborough High School. One year was "Quite

---

18. *Baron Cyril Louis Norton Newall GCB OM GCMG CBE AM (1886-1963) [NR] Governor-General of New Zealand 1941-1946 married Olive Tennyson Foster (1891-1988) [NR] in 1925.*
19. *Marshal of the Royal Air Force Arthur William Tedder, 1st Baron Tedder GCB (1890-1967) [NR].*

enough," he said. There's the business of business and there's learning about it. Ken found that too often the two didn't connect.

After that, like my sister Ann, Ken spent many years as an advisor at the local Citizens Advice Bureau, specialising in employment law. Ann was invited to a Garden Party at Buckingham Palace as recognition for her services. Ken was invited to run the Prince of Wales Trust in Yorkshire but turned the opportunity down. He didn't drive and wasn't about to start. He's stayed a lot fitter than most car owners, walking daily into town.

Like something from 'Last of the Summer Wine' – centre: Arthur Morley dressed in drag. All the Morleys were fun loving.

∗ ∗ ∗ ∗

Denby Dale Pie

Ken married **Renée Morley** in August 1952. Renée was born in Denby Dale, a village towards Huddersfield, featuring a large railway viaduct. There were three mills in Denby Dale – one silk and two worsted, one weaving the finest quality wool fabric, the other spinning the wool.

Denby Dale was known as Denby Dikeside in the 18th century. Even then, it was famous for its pies, not any old pies, Guinness-Record-breaking-gargantuan pies. The 1964 one was 18ft long[20]. Insane, you say, until you realise that they made the first pie to celebrate mad King George III's *recovery* of sanity.

The pie procession passed by the house in *Dalton Row* (later promoted to '*Terrace*') [xii]. Renée's father, **Arthur Morley** took it over from his father, **Wallace McGregor Morley**[21]. Wallace, a coal miner, died when Renée was a year old. He used to rock the cradle to send her to sleep. After he married, Arthur became a greengrocer with a van that toured the outlying countryside. Her family was one of the few in Denby Dale with a motor. Arthur and his wife Edith attended the Methodist chapel, near the cenotaph, Arthur singing in the choir.

Arthur had one brother and two sisters: Harold, Sarah and Laura[22]. **Sarah** married **George Dawson** who wheezed away at the euphonium in the Salvation Army band and **Laura** married **George Lockwood**, a railwayman[23]. The Lockwoods lived in the house they bought next door. Brother **Harold's** family would come up to stay from

Denby Dale Pies

1788	George III recovers sanity
1815	Waterloo Pie
1846	Corn Laws Repeal Pie
1887	Jubilee Pie
1887	Resurrection Pie
1896	50th Anniversary of Corn Laws repeal Pie
1928	Infirmary Pie
1964	Royal births Pie
1988	Bicentenary Pie
2000	Millennium Pie

Denby Dale Band – Arthur sitting left

The 1964 Denby Dale Pie

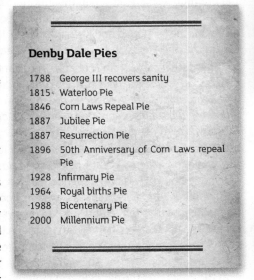

Wallace McGregor Morley (1856-1927) and Faith née Noble (1853-1920)

---

20. *1964 18 foot long, 6 ft wide and 18 inch deep. The Millennium Pie weighed 12 tonnes.*

21. *Arthur Morley (1888-1961) married Edith Helen Lee (1895-1959) in 1921. His father, Wallace McGregor Morley (1856-1927) married Faith Noble (1853-1920) in 1885.*

22. *Sarah Morley (1886-1965) married George Bernard Dawson (1888-1963) in 1918. A Salvation Army Brigadier conducted his funeral service.*

23. *Laura Morley (1890-1955) married George Tom Lockwood (1891-1956) in 1910.*

George & Laura Lockwood; Sarah & George Dawson

Surrey and Arthur would take them all bilberry picking up on the moors around Penistone[24]. Whilst Arthur didn't serve in the First War – he had lost part of his index finger and couldn't fire a gun – Harold did. They said Harold signed for a Scottish regiment so he could sport a kilt[xiii]. Sadly, he found out he'd joined the only Scottish regiment that didn't wear kilts. He wore the green of the elite rifle regiments, with Douglas tartan trews for best. Harold lost both legs in the war – amputated above the knee. He convalesced in Brighton. The Brighton Pavilion of Chapter 3 had had such bad associations for Queen Victoria that she had sold it to the town council who converted it into the 'Pavilion and Dome' Recuperation Hospital.

✳ ✳ ✳ ✳

Craig Ellachie

Arthur's daughter, Renée with Harold's sons Andrew and Kenny in c 1937

Harold's wife, **Kitty** taught in the East End, 'darn ver Wallwerf Rowd' as the Cockneys would say. She'd sometimes take the kids for a treat out into the Surrey countryside. She and her old student friends from Whitelands College would also take wounded soldiers for walks on the Brighton esplanade. They thought Harold must be a Scot on account of his Glengarry bonnet. Scottish soldiers were nicknamed 'Jocks', so she carried on calling him 'Jock' for the rest of his life[xiv]. Harold and Kitty married in 1929, after a chance reunion on the steps of St Martin's-in-the-Fields, in Trafalgar Square, years later.

Kitty's father came from Scotland. The Grant clan came from *'one of the loneliest districts of Scotland, where the peat cottages are darkest, just at the western foot of that great mass of the Grampians which encircles the sources of the Spey and the Dee.'* The main road *'winds round the foot of a broken rock called Crag, or Craig Ellachie,'* to quote Ruskin[25]. **Thomas Grant** was born the other side of Inverness[xv].

'Jock' Morley (1893-1961) recuperating from WW1 c1918 with the young teacher Kitty Grant (1895-1982)

Like my great-grandfather *James Garden* (Chapter 9), Thomas had to leave Scotland to find work and, like my great uncle *George Haskins* (Chapter 9), he became Head Gardener of a grand house[26]. Thomas spent about ten years on the St Giles estate at Wimborne. He had 12 gardeners under him and wore a frock coat to work. He married the Head Cook, Emma Reynolds. Thomas and Emma conceived four children whilst they were there – happy times. The new Earl of Shaftesbury had been in charge for less than a year when he took on Thomas. His grandfather, the great reformer of the Victorian age, had died and his heir had shot himself soon after[27]. The opinion in the Servants' Hall was that the heir couldn't cope with the debts that the old man had built up.

Thomas set about restoring the gardens and having done a magnificent job, the Earl wanted him to make in-roads on his castle grounds in Belfast. However, Emma wasn't willing to go, so Thomas found a new job at *Heatherwood*, opposite Ascot racecourse, working for Sir Thomas Lucas of the Lucas Brothers partnership[28]. The Lucas Brothers were the greatest builders of the 19th century. They'd built the *Albert Hall, Covent Garden, Alexandra Palace, Cliveden*, on the banks of the Thames, and the *Oxford Museum of Natural History*. There were railways including several London terminuses, *York railway station* and its *Great Eastern Hotel*, the *Barnsley to Hull railway* (now closed) and the *Padstow to Wadebridge railway*

Recovery for the wounded in Brighton Pavilion

---

24. *Harold Morley (1893-1961) married Kitty (Kathleen May) Grant (1895-1982) at West Horsley in 1929*
25. *Craig Ellechie is now one word but, for ease of reading, is spelt throughout as Ruskin did,*
26. *Thomas Grant (1858-1946) was born and brought up in Jamestown, near Contin and married Emma Reynolds (1862-1933) in 1889. He did much to restore the neglected estate at Wimborne St Giles.*
27. *Anthony Ashley-Cooper, 9th Earl of Shaftesbury KP PC GCVO CBE (1869-1961) [NR]. He helped found Bryanston School in 1928 at nearby Blandford Forum, with the conversion of the 1894 Norman Shaw house built for the Duke of Portland.*
28. *Sir Thomas Lucas Bt (1822-1902) [NR] was survived by his second wife Mary Amelia Chamberlin (1832-1905) [NR] after which the house was put up for sale - there were no takers.*

(now a cycle track). There may have been a horse racing connection through the Duke of Portland, the Queen's racing manager who owned a stud in Yorkshire and the adjoining estate in Dorset[29].

Heatherwood House was put up for sale after Lady Lucas's death in 1905 and the Grants moved to Winkfield and, later, *Dene Place* in West Horsley.

Thomas Grant was a likeable chap, or was it just luck?[30] Whilst the two eldest children went into service, the younger two, Kitty and **Kenneth**, enjoyed a private education at *Ranelagh School*[xvi]. Who paid for it we don't know. Was it social conscience, where a working class child is plucked from his family situation into something better, like Jimmie Candy had been in Chapter 15? It could have been a grant from the Shaftesbury foundation, The Rector of All Saints' Ascot, who had a soft spot for them both, may have had something to do with it[31].

Young Kenneth was proud of his Scottish ancestry. When his school chums teased him about it, he'd look around. He'd recall the cry of the Seaforth Highlanders who pictured that rugged cliff above the River Spey as they went into battle, summing up all that was Scottish[xvii]. Kenneth would hold his imaginary sword up in the air and repeat the fervent cry of the battle-charge, "Stand fast, Craig Ellachie."

Kenneth was seventeen when the war broke out. He'd secured a place at Reading but instead he opted to enlist as a Second Lieutenant in that same heroic Scottish regiment that he remembered from his schooldays[xviii].   He joined the front at the end of May 1916 but 3 months later he was killed during the Somme Offensive on 26 Aug 1916. Just nineteen years old. The day before, there'd been heavy fighting at Ginchy and aerial bombardment. The British took a short length of the German trench north of Bazentin-le-Petit, one of the most audacious captures of the offensive, one which went the furthest into the German lines. Kenneth would have led his men to a point near Delville Wood. There were high casualties that day; wounded, he'd have been taken to a make-shift camp hospital near Flatiron Copse, where he died[xix].

After the war, Thomas bought a plot of land for £100 in Silkmore Lane and built a house for £500. The house was a memorial to his only son. They called it 'Craig Ellachie'.

Head Gardener's Cottage, Wimborne St Giles c1898. Mag, Kenneth, Kitty and 'Bell' Grant

Head Gardener's cottage in 1978.

Thomas & Emma Grant and their children (l. to r.) Kitty, Bell, Kenny and Mag, in 1898

Flatiron Copse, near Ginchy

---

29. *William John Arthur Charles James Cavendish-Bentinck, 6th Duke of Portland KG GCVO TD PC DL (1857-1943) [NR] Master of the Queen's Horse 1886-92 and 1895-1905.*

30. *Bell (Isabella Elizabeth) Grant (1890-1939) married Alfred G C Blandford (1888-1970) in 1913. She worked as a kitchen maid at Greenlands Henley (now Henley School of Management), he as a gardener. Owned by William Frederick Danvers Smith, 2nd Viscount Hambledon (1868-1928) [NR] son of W H Smith – who built Bovey Castle in Devon. Mag (Margaret Jessie) Grant (1893-1973) did not marry. She started out in Winkfield working for Sydney Christie-Miller (1874-1931) [NR] of the hat company Christy & Co. Kenneth Henry Grant (1897-1916); Kathleen May Grant (1895-1982) married Harold Morley (1893-1961) in 1929.*

31. *Rev William Fairbairn La Trobe-Bateman (1845-1926) [NR] Rector of Ascot Heath 1900-17.*

Reg Morley (1922-1998) in wartime Eygpt

Eric (1935-2002) and Bram (b1932) Morley c1945

Penistone Grammar School, founded 1392.
Tennis in front of the Fulford building, which was
erected in 1910/11, soon after girls were first
admitted and demolished in 2014.

Grammar School

The Morleys, Renée's family, were generally occupied in the wool trade one way or another. Arthur's father was **John Morley**[32]. John was a spinner, more specifically a mule spinner. Three of his brothers were 'fancy waistcoat weavers'. Arthur's grandfather, Thomas Morley from Duffield, was a cordwainer and shoemaker[33].

Renée was surrounded by family, in the Yorkshire way. There were the Morleys, the Lees, the Roebucks and the Nobles all too numerous to mention. Most worked in the mills in one way or the other. One of Arthur's cousins who stands out was **Helah Stephenson**, who married **Henry Haigh**[34]. Henry's father had been manager at the Brownhills Mill and a local Wesleyan preacher. Henry stepped into his shoes as the Company Secretary and Sunday School Superintendent. His wife Helah was nicknamed 'Mrs Blessing' after her habit of handing out little cards/tracts with blessings on them.

Renée was brought up with three big brothers – if not in stature or age, then in playground importance. **Reg** the eldest went to Egypt in the RAF during World War 2[35]. He and **Eric** worked in the worsted weaving mill, Kenyon's[36]. Reg moved to another mill and was offered a job in Workington. **Bram**, with his winning smile and warm handshake, was a representative for industrial diamonds[37].

Denby Dale's nearest Grammar School was at Penistone, higher up into the Pennines. Renée like Ken had won a scholarship, this one from the West Riding. She rode there on the bus but when it snowed and the buses weren't working, they walked the mile from the station. She had three close friends, Barbara, Hazel and Margaret who made up a four for tennis. One holiday she went with some friends to the Isle of Man where they met up with boys they knew from home.

When she left school, Renée found employment close to home at Hinchliffe's mill, which did the spinning. Coming from the grammar school, they gave her a job in the office where she was secretary to 'Mr Harold', the Managing Director, doing all manner of things including his farm accounts and the wages.

Ken and Renée met at a dance in Penistone. They were able to enjoy the relative freedom of movement which post-war Europe allowed and so, when they married, Ken and Renée were able to honeymoon in Le Treport, near the D Day landings of eight years earlier. The Normandy coast was still littered with the Mulberry harbours, the gun emplacements and the detritus of war that I found in Cornwall as a child. They didn't remove the concrete stanchions away from my Cornish beach until the late 1950s.

Ken's mother died the same year as they married; otherwise they might have all shared a home together. Instead, Ken and Renée rented a flat for 18 months in Denby Dale while they saved up for a mortgage[xx]. They bought their house in Barnsley in 1954 and never moved. Ken could walk to work in Summer Lane and Renée joined William Freeman Ltd, making Suba seal hot water bottles. Secretary to the General Sales Manager, she had all the piquancy of blooming health and wore her clothes and intellect accordingly. Parading through the workforce on the shop floor with the tray of tea-cups, she ignored the wolf-whistles.

Then Carolyn came along and their world changed. Carolyn was never one to sit still, bouncing energetically in her pram; there's a film of her playing junior family cricket

---

32. *John Morley (1833-1894) married Martha Lockwood (1832-1921) at Clayton West in 1853.*

33. *Thomas Morley (1801-1876) married Harriet Tyas (1801-?) at Emley in 1824. In 1841 a John Morley aged 13 is on his own in an inn in Denby Dale, looked after by Anne Lockwood (b1796) along with her three children. It could be he was orphaned and came to live with the Lockwoods? Later a George Lockwood married his granddaughter Laura.*

34. *Henry Bowman Haigh (1879-1947) married Helah Stephenson (1883-1957) in 1907.*

35. *Reginald McGregor Morley (1922-1998) married Olive May Dickinson (1925-2017) in 1949.*

36. *Eric Alfred Morley (1935-2002) married Brenda Webster (b1932) in 1957.*

37. *Wallace Bramwell Morley (b1932) married Christine Matthewman (b1936) in 1960.*

at Canon Hall where she appears to be bowling, batting and running for the ball all at the same time. Carolyn went to a Catholic Convent School for infants, where she dutifully learnt her 'Hail Marys'. After St Mary's Church of England Junior School, she became the first of a new generation to attend grammar school[xxi].

Broadway Grammar was mixed – boys and girls – quite an experiment in Barnsley. She attended Pitt Street Guides, enjoying a trip to Switzerland, and found a Swiss pen-friend[38]. She performed ballet at the Civic Hall and featured in a storming school production of *Fiddler on the Roof* in 1975. Geography at Newcastle University came next. Michael her younger brother followed, studying psychology, which he ended up teaching at a Further Education College in Durham.

Renée Morley (1926-2017) on Blackpool Beach 1946

Ballet

✳ ✳ ✳ ✳

West Horsley

The whole of Barnsley took the same summer holiday. Feast Week, as it was called, was the last complete week of August. The workshop closed. Ken manned the office on his own and took other weeks off for his own family holiday. Carolyn, his daughter, while still at Junior School, enjoyed playing receptionist. There were phones to put through via various plugs and wires. There was the post to sort. Early work experience.

Fiddler on the Roof - December 1975 - Carolyn on right

Many holidays were spent with their cousins in West Horsley, where Renée had spent her childhood summers. Uncle Harold, after recovering from the war wounds, had joined the civil service. In 1940/1 **Kenny**, his eldest, won a choral scholarship to *Magdalen College School*, where he sang on May Day, as had my great uncle Philip Wiggins 50 years earlier and where the novelist C S Lewis was a tutorial Fellow[39]. His brother, **Andrew**, attended Christ Church Cathedral Choir School 1945-7 and then won a scholarship to Dulwich where he boarded for 4 years[40]. He finished his education in Auckland, at King's College, and at the University there.

Kenny Morley at Oxford

When I first met Carolyn, she talked a lot about her cousin Andrew – twelve years older than me. Both Kenny and Andrew have ended up in New Zealand, Andrew in the last decade. Kenny emigrated at the age of twenty staying with his father's cousins – brothers of Helah Haigh, based in Wellington[xxii]. Harold and Kitty thought New Zealand sounded tempting and took Andrew out with them where he completed his eduation but they came back after a few years[xxiii]. Kenny stayed, married Doreen and they now have a large family spread out around Auckland.

✳ ✳ ✳ ✳

38. Brigitte Gsteiger (b1957) [NR].
39. Kenneth Henry Grant Morley (b1930) married Doreen Letitia Salter (b1927) in 1954. Clive Staples Lewis (1898-1963) [NR], author of the Screwtape Letters (1942) and the Chronicles of Narnia (1949-54), was a don at Magdalen 1925–54.
40. Andrew Grant Morley (b1936).

Night before the wedding

Piran's Oratory, Perranzabuloe, 6th or 7th century, was under 25 feet of sand in 1835.* Shown here excavated in 1910, and reburied in 1980. Thought to be St Piran's burial place, a number of artefacts including his skull, paraded round Cornwall in the Middle Ages, are now lost. A Norman church nearby was also lost in the sand dunes and was excavated in 2004.

A Cornish Connection

Carolyn and I were married in Barnsley in 1985 , the year of the miners' strike. It was the first time many of my friends and relatives had stepped foot in the county. My father had spent more than a year in Yorkshire during the war but that was about it. The night before the wedding, drunk on a glass of Greek wine and half a pint of beer, I had the typical Yorkshire treatment of being tied to a park bench in my underpants and left for some merry ladies on their way home from the pub to release me.

Carolyn's brother, **Michael**, married **Margaret** four weeks earlier[41]. They'd told no one. Michael rang us in London and I answered the phone:

'We've got married'

'Oh yes, ha-ha. Very funny'

'No, we have.'

'Where?'

'Gretna Green' …

All very romantic and both sets of parents were surprised but delighted.

Margaret has a Cornish connection despite coming from Newton Aycliffe in County Durham, where her family had been mining for at least two generations. Margaret's mother's grandparents, **Samuel and Emily James**, came from Cornwall in the early 1870s, having met and married at Perranzabuloe, near Perranporth[42].

Perranporth on the north Cornwall coastline is named after St Peran (Piran), the patron saint of Cornwall[43]. This is where he landed after crossing the Irish Sea. One story has the Irish tying him to a mill-stone and throwing him over a cliff, hoping to rid Ireland of his uncomfortable truths. The mill-stone washed him up on the Cornish coast – by some miracle, it had floated. It is said that Peran revived the tin smelting industry – white tin oozed out of the black ore in the shape of a cross, the symbol of his calling, and hence the colour of the Cornish flag.

Margaret's great grandfather, Samuel James, was a 'blende' miner – finding all manner of the high-quality ores on the bedraggled wind-blown heath. The mine-workings still poke out from the scraggy bushes. Emily's father had done the same job but by the 1870s the valuable seams were running dry. Miners were emigrating to the four corners of the world. Samuel sought a livelihood in the Durham coalfields, and found work in the Gurney Valley at Coundon Grange, Bishop Auckland. The Black Boy Coal Company had been running a mine since the 1860s and were recruiting[44]. Mining there continued until 1932. Samuel and Emily's children all stayed around the area and three generations further on, Margaret met Michael at Newcastle while studying for her teaching degree. Of their two children, **Lois** has followed in her footsteps. **Rowan** studied stage management at *Liverpool Institute of Performing Arts (LIPA)* and has launched himself into a career in stagecraft, having had the experience of operating the spot-lights at the 2012 Olympic opening and closing ceremonies.

Many of the Northern folk in this Chapter lit up their communities in one way or another. One of our sons, Christopher, is doing more than that. Living in Leeds and working in the home

---

41. *Michael Ian Burton (b1960) married Margaret Aspinall (b1962) in 1984. Their children are Rowan Michael Burton (b1991) and Lois Margaret Burton (b1993).*

42. *Samuel James (1846-1930) married Emily Roberts (1846-1920) at Perranzabuloe Cornwall in 1867. Their eldest children Samuel John James (1868-1941) and Emily Ann James (1870-1922) were born there.*

43. *St Piran 6th Century AD [NR].*

44. *The two youngest children, Joseph Henry James (1879-1945) and Albert Ernest James (1881-1976) were born when their parents were living in the Blackboys Brickyard. William Thomas James (1877-1955) was born in William Street, Bishop Auckland.*

town of Barbara Hepworth's college friend Henry Moore, he works as a trader in electricity for an international brokerage firm – literally, you could say, lighting up the North.

✳ ✳ ✳ ✳

Rowan, Michael, Lois and Margaret Burton

We honeymooned in France and Switzerland, at Berne and at Thun in the Bernese Oberland – staying with Carolyn's erstwhile penfriend. Switzerland was a happy place for us, but did not hold such good memories for the subject of the next chapter.

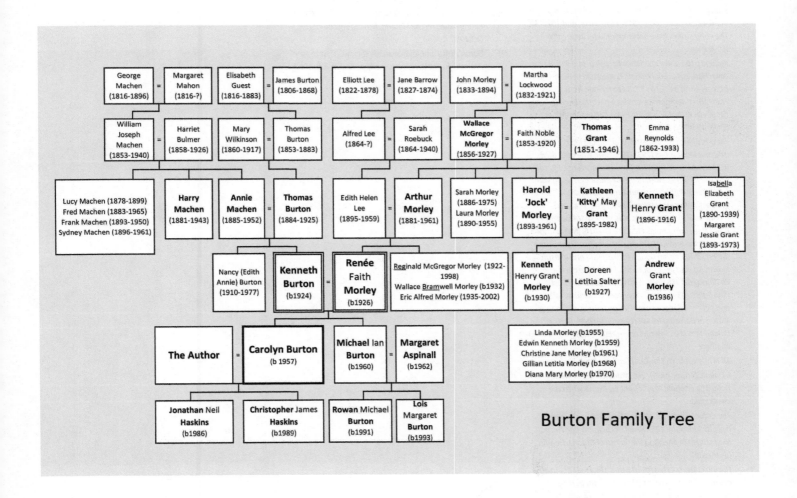

Burton Family Tree

George Machen (1816-1896) = Margaret Mahon (1816-?)

Elisabeth Guest (1816-1883) = James Burton (1806-1868)

Elliott Lee (1822-1878) = Jane Barrow (1827-1874)

John Morley (1833-1894) = Martha Lockwood (1832-1921)

William Joseph Machen (1853-1940) = Harriet Bulmer (1858-1926)

Mary Wilkinson (1860-1917) = Thomas Burton (1853-1883)

Alfred Lee (1864-?) = Sarah Roebuck (1864-1940)

Wallace McGregor Morley (1856-1927) = Faith Noble (1853-1920)

Thomas Grant (1851-1946) = Emma Reynolds (1862-1933)

Lucy Machen (1878-1899)
Fred Machen (1883-1965)
Frank Machen (1893-1950)
Sydney Machen (1896-1961)

Harry Machen (1881-1943)

Annie Machen (1885-1952) = Thomas Burton (1884-1925)

Edith Helen Lee (1895-1959) = Arthur Morley (1881-1961)

Sarah Morley (1886-1975)
Laura Morley (1890-1955)

Harold 'Jock' Morley (1893-1961)

Kathleen 'Kitty' May Grant (1895-1982) = Kenneth Henry Grant (1896-1916)

Isabella Elizabeth Grant (1890-1939)
Margaret Jessie Grant (1893-1973)

Nancy (Edith Annie) Burton (1910-1977)

Kenneth Burton (b1924) = Renée Faith Morley (b1926)

Reginald McGregor Morley (1922-1998)
Wallace Bramwell Morley (b1932)
Eric Alfred Morley (1935-2002)

Kenneth Henry Grant Morley (b1930) = Doreen Letitia Salter (b1927)

Andrew Grant Morley (b1936)

The Author = Carolyn Burton (b 1957)

Michael Ian Burton (b1960) = Margaret Aspinall (b1962)

Linda Morley (b1955)
Edwin Kenneth Morley (b1959)
Christine Jane Morley (b1961)
Gillian Letitia Morley (b1968)
Diana Mary Morley (b1970)

Jonathan Neil Haskins (b1986)

Christopher James Haskins (b1989)

Rowan Michael Burton (b1991)

Lois Margaret Burton (b1993)

Other Notes and References

i.   Autumn 1982

ii.   Mel du Botting. www.open.ac.uk/blogs/History-of-the-OU/?p=2250 accessed 25 Sep 2015.

iii.   Construction News: The Falklands Achievement p17.

iv.   Ibid p29

v.   Afforestation in Hong Kong began in the early 1870s. In the following years, more than 100,000 trees were planted, mostly Chinese Red Pines.

vi.   Horizon Community College, Barnsley, opened in 2012.

vii.   Aspinall and Smith pp. 533-35. Fitzwilliam MSS; www.marxists.org/history/england/combination-laws/luddites-1812.htm accessed 25 Feb 2016

viii.   Kaijage. Linen industry strikes occurred in 1818, 1823, 1825, 1829, 1836, 1843, 1852, 1854, 1855, and 1872-3. The early strikes were accompanied by large rallies of 2,000 men.

ix.   Kaijage p162 and 'Experience Barnsley' at Barnsley Town Hall, 2014. Coal mining is recorded in Barnsley from as early as 1216. It sold to London from 1820s. From 1850, demand increased, whilst the linen industry declined. Arthur Scargill (b1938) [NR] led the Miner's Strike 1984-85.

x.   For example, footballers Tommy Taylor (1932-1958) [NR] and Mark Jones (1933-1958) [NR] who both died in the Munich air disaster; Dame Susan 'Jenni' Murray DBE (b1950) [NR], Woman's Hour presenter; Harry Worth (1917-1989) [NR], comedian; Brian Glover (1934-1997) [NR], actor; Ian MacMillan (b1956) [NR], poet and broadcaster; Joanne Harris MBE (b1964) [NR], author (Chocolat); Barry Hines FRSL (1939-2016) [NR], author (Kes); Dickie Bird (b1933), cricket umpire; Azeem Rafiq (b1991) [NR], Darren Gough (b1970) [NR] and Martyn Moxon (b1960) [NR], Captains of Yorkshire cricket; Ed Clancy (b1985) [NR], cyclist and gold medallist; Paul Sykes (b1943) [NR], developer of Meadowhall and political donor of anti-Europe parties; Baron Roy Mason of Barnsley PC MP (1924-2015) [NR], Northern Ireland Minister; Joseph Locke (1805-1860) [NR], railway engineer.

xi.   JJFMT Letter from Mowbray Garden March 1943.

xii.   6 Dalton Terrace (Row), 346 Wakefield Road, Denby Dale. The freehold was bought by Arthur when the owner died.

xiii.   The Cameronians' (Scottish Rifles) other accolades have included the 1857 Relief of Lucknow and the part they played in enabling the Sultan of Oman to regain his throne.

xiv.   Having corresponded for 10 years, they met again by chance in 1928 on the steps of St Martin-in-the-Fields and were married the following year. They lived in Merton until they bought Symroyde next to Craig Ellachie in 1933 for £835.

xv.   Ruskin p12. The Grants Whisky distillery is at Craig Ellachie or Craigellachie, but there is no close family connection.

xvi.   Ranelagh School started at Winkfield where Thomas and Emma were living in 1911; it moved to Bracknell in 1908. In 1911, Thomas was gardener and Emma cook at Chavey Lawn, Lockes Ride, owned by Lady Florence Elizabeth Alderson (1843-1915) [NR].

xvii.   2nd Battalion of the Seaforth Highlanders.

xviii.   Kenneth Grant joined the 10th battalion of the Seaforth Highlanders (Ross-shire Buffs, the Duke of Albany's. Reading University was formerly an extension college of Oxford University.

xix.   Kenneth Grant is buried in Plot IV J2 at Flatiron Copse, near Ginchy

xx.   Oakfield, Barnsley Road, Denby Dale

xxi.   St Mary's Church of England Primary School; Broadway Grammar School, Barnsley. The Broadway school is now combined with Holgate Grammar as Horizon Community College, and the site has become Kingstone Grange housing estate.

xxii.   Ike (Isaac) Stephenson (1879-1964) emigrated to Wellington on the Ionie in 1906. Luther Stephenson (1892-1975) went to Wellington in 1914 on the Osterley. Kenny sailed on the Materia, leaving Southampton Oct 1950.

xxiii.   Harold, Kitty and Andrew made their way out to New Zealand on the Rangitoto, leaving London July 1952.

The Grocer's Son

Grantham is a small market town in middle England. It is famous for nothing in particular. It is a stop on the East Coast main railway line. From the station, you can see a tall church surrounded by old houses. The nearby Melton Mowbray pork pies are nice but not historic. Nevertheless, it has produced one or two interesting people. One was the scientist, Isaac Newton, who went to Grantham Grammar School[1]. Another was Margaret Thatcher, a grocer's daughter, who spent her school years living above a corner shop in North Parade, and who became the first woman and longest serving Prime Minister of the 20th century[2].

Less well known is the son of another grocer who had also traded as a butcher in Grantham. Like Thomas Wolsey, the butcher's son from Ipswich who became a Cardinal Archbishop and Lord Chancellor under Henry VIII, this one, my great uncle, rose from a similar humble beginning to become one of the great clerics of the Church in England[3]. **William Wand**, as Bishop of London, led the restoration of church life in London after the Second World War[4].

William Wand (1885-1977). The Bishop's crosier is now in a Grantham Church. In the bottom right-hand corner of the shield is the Denison crest of Chapter 3 - a hand pointing to a star

Bishop Wand was my father's 'Uncle Will' by marriage to his Aunt Amy. Uncle Will left a deep impression on me in my childhood, possibly because my father talked about him a lot, and because I knew him quite well. The photo albums go right back. I was christened by Uncle Will at *Fulham Palace* and he dedicated two books to me – he took a strong interest in me when I was considering ordination. The family laugh when I say that I remember my christening. For me, a baptism at any age is more than a ceremony. It's something extra-terrestrial. I certainly remember my father saying to me at five years old, as I sat in the back of his car on the way to my cousin Bernard Wiggins's baptism, "Do you remember?"[5] I did[i].

We didn't have a TV in our house until after I went to boarding school in 1961 – they thought it might distract me from my studies. They were right – as it didn't take much, of course. My first experience of television was at the age of four. We watched the Coronation of Elizabeth II at a friend's house[6]. Suddenly, across the room, I spotted Uncle Will, reading the lesson, in the full glory of Westminster Abbey[ii]. I strode over and stabbed my jammy fingers at the small screen in excitement. "There's Uncle Will," I cried, as if the others didn't know.

Bernard Wiggins's christening at Fulham Palace. 13 Sep 1953

In retirement (he retired at the age of 84 and lived to 92), Uncle Will wrote two books addressed to me – one published (*Letters on Preaching*: each Chapter begun, 'Dear Robert…') and the other (*Letters on the Ministry*) unpublished at his death in September 1977. Perhaps because of him, I was the only pupil in my school allowed to take Religious Education at O level – A level was a non-starter[iii]. A boy who ran the school's Christian Union before me wasn't permitted to take 'O level' RE. Cleverer than me, he went on to become the Dean of Winchester Cathedral[7].

---

1. *Sir Isaac Newton PRS MP (1642-1727) [NR] attended King's School Grantham 1665-60; studying in the same buildings as William Wand 1897-1904.*

2. *Margaret Hilda Thatcher, Baroness Thatcher LG OM PC FRS (née Roberts) (1925-2013) [NR] lived at 1 North Parade, Grantham.*

3. *Cardinal Archbishop Thomas Wolsey PC (1473-1530) [NR] was Lord Chancellor for Henry VIII (1491-1547), who ruled England 1509-47.*

4. *Rt Rev John William Charles Wand KCVO DD DLit PC (1885-1977) married Amy Agnes Wiggins (1883-1966) in 1911 .*

5. *Bernard Robert Denison Wiggins (b1953) married (1) Rosamund Mary Gripp (1954-2012) in 1980 (2) Gail Patricia French (neé Townsend) (b1960) in 2015.*

6. *Norah Ethel H Redmore (née Dyer) (1906-1985) [NR], 38 Kingsway, was partly responsible for developing the author's eccentric side; she toured the world on banana boats; fell in love with a priest from British Guiana, thought she saw Lord Lucan, and coined the word 'splodge' to describe turkey fricassee. Her late husband Bill, a Freemason, bequeathed me a Rolex watch and his signet ring. They had no children.*

7. *Very Rev James Edgar Atwell (b1946) [NR].*

Welham Street, Grantham, opposite the brewery, the first home of William Wand

Bishop Jacob Hostel ordinands: William Wand is standing centre, his future brother-in-law Herbert is sitting right.

Each Christmas Eve in my youth, the Haskins's would visit the Wands after Evensong at St Paul's Cathedral. 1952 was my first experience of a sulphurous 'peasouper' fog, not being able to see inches in front of me before we boarded a train home. The Wands shared their house with their daughter Kay and her husband Michael Addison[8]. Michael's father, Dr Christopher Addison, was the socialist minister who motivated the doyen of town planning, Raymond Unwin, to produce some of the first housing estates for working families, 'Homes for Heroes', and the 'Garden Cities' movement[9]. Dr Addison, the country's first Health Minister introduced the first Town and Country Planning Act[iv]. Not many planners realise their profession began as an initiative of the Ministry of *Health*.

At Fulham Palace on Christmas Eve, and later at Amen Court, we would be treated to Fuller's cake, especially bought at great expense from Harrods, where Kay's daughter Brigit Addison worked. Amy would present my mother with a box of crackers, very sought after in the 1950s. In my teens, Uncle Will would present me with a copy of his latest book. I remember commenting to him, in that way that only I could get away with, that his books would be easier to read if he didn't use a word on every page that needed a dictionary to work out its meaning. Now, I am similarly guilty. All in all, he wrote some 45 theological books, as well as pamphlets, entries to Encyclopaedia Britannica and newspaper columns[v]. *The History of the Early Church*, which he wrote during the six weeks his ship took to reach Australia in 1934, was perhaps the most celebrated, becoming a text-book in four volumes. It was used by students of theology for several decades. The present-day Haskins family (some of them) still make a pilgrimage to a great Cathedral church on Christmas Eve, but now we go to York Minister, and it is to our friends the Harpers we go after the service of Nine Lessons and Carols. York has a congregation of 5,000 over two nights – far larger than St Paul's in the 'Honest to God' 1960s[vi].

✳ ✳ ✳ ✳

Love and War

John William Charles Wand won a scholarship to Grantham Grammar School in 1897. In 1904, he scraped into St Edmund Hall Oxford, with the help of some outside funding arranged by his schoolmasters[vii]. He gained a First in Theology and undertook his theological training at Newcastle-upon-Tyne, occupying his first curacy there[viii]. There he met **Amy Wiggins.** She was looking after her brother, **Herbert Wiggins**, later surnamed **Denison**, who was also training to be a priest[10]. The picture of this Newcastle group was taken at about the time he was ordained deacon in 1908.

The Wiggins were none too pleased with Amy's choice of husband. Wand was the son of a tradesman; he was the grandson of a bricklayer. He'd no private income and no prospects – a poor catch, they thought. Will and Amy were forced to live apart for a year in the hope that Amy wasn't serious. Will was required to find a job earning £200 per annum.

8.   *Kathleen Amy Wand (1912-c2006) married Viscount Michael Addison (1914-1992) in 1936.*
9.   *Christopher Addison KC PC MD BSc FRCS (1869-1951), 1st Viscount Addison of Stallingborough; Sir Raymond Unwin Kt MA PRIBA (1863-1940) [NR] was involved in drawing out the plans for New Earswick in York, as well as Letchworth and Hampstead Garden Cities.*
10. *Amy Agnes Wiggins (1883-1966) was sister to Rev Herbert Bouchier Wiggins/Denison (1885-1966).*

£200 was too much for the parish of Benwell to find. Will and Amy moved to Lancaster Priory, marrying in 1911 and, in 1914, taking the post of a minor canon (Vicar Choral) at Salisbury. Processing into the Cathedral one Evensong that year, he counted twelve other priests at a time when the Army needed chaplains. He joined up, as a padre, as soon as he could.

Will saw service in Gallipoli in 1915 and spent nearly three years in Rouen in France, though he never went to the front. He'd been invalided out of Gallipoli.

Lighten our darkness!
Kneeling in the mud,
My hands still wet and warm with
human blood...

Some Less Rough Rhymes of a Padre
Woodbine Willie

St Mark's Vicarage, Salisbury, 1921

At Rouen, he ran a larger version of the wooden mission church at Benwell, though the congregation was rather different. These were nervous men on their way to the front, dedicated nurses caring for the wounded, and the superior distant headquarters staff. The church was conceived by Rev G A Studdert-Kennedy, a vicar's son from a poor part of Leeds[11].

Studdert-Kennedy, 'Woodbine Willie' as he was known, was a hero of the trenches. He could pack any hall from floor to ceiling. He handed out cigarettes ('Woodbines'), jumped on a table, and gave the men 'the straightest talk to which many of them had ever listened.[ix]' Woodbine Willie's books of poetry, one of which I read under the covers in my school dormitory, were full of good thoughts. Most people thought he spoke fresh from his head but Will used to vet his typewritten scripts so Kennedy could make sure every word shot through the heart.

Extempore sermons were something Uncle Will advocated in his book *Letters on Preaching* but, like Kennedy, he always prepared carefully, using a small folder to hold a 'crib sheet'.

The Wand family at Salisbury 1921. Amy and Will either side. Sitting: Paul and Kathleen (called Kay in later years); standing: Amy's eldest sister Mary Wiggins and their mother Annie

After Armistice was declared in 1918, Will was posted to Cologne and then back to Salisbury in March 1919. There he was offered the parish of St Mark's with its enormous vicarage. As well as his parish responsibilities, Will lectured on Church History and the Old Testament at Sarum Theological College. Students remember him shedding 'fresh light from his clear brain'[x]. The past came alive in his lectures.

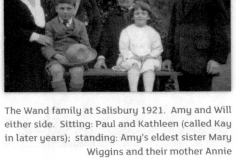

Courtyard of Oriel College, Oxford

✳ ✳ ✳ ✳

Oxford

Will's lectures at Sarum probably won him the job as Dean of Oriel, Oxford, in Michaelmas 1925. There, as deputy head of the college, he was in charge of discipline, as well as being head chaplain and a theological tutor. In Oxford, the family lived at lovely *Bartlemas*, a 1649 house rebuilt from older ruins. Amy, whose children Paul and Kay had been born in Lancaster, had her hands full with their upbringing[12]. Out of term time, they went on motoring holidays but, during the eight-week terms, Will often slept in college. He was responsible for what happened when the 'lights went out.' The college gates closed at midnight.

William Wand's churchmanship was clear for all to see when he became President of the Anglo-Catholic Oxford Church Union. He helped organise the centenary celebrations of the 'Oxford Movement'. The movement, which had begun with *Tracts for the Times* written by Newman and Pusey (1833-41), had called for the reinstatement of lost Christian traditions

Bartlemas, off Cowley Road, Oxford

---

11. *Rev Geoffrey Anketell Studdert-Kennedy MA MC (1883-1929) [NR] 'Woodbine Willie'. His father was Vicar of St Mary Quarry Hill, Leeds 1912-14.*

12. *Paul W Wand (1912-1934).*

Kay on board The Largs Bay (they travelled 3rd class) heading for Australia, July 1934

William and Amy Wand step off the boat in Brisbane Aug 1934

Mont Blanc

Swimming in Australia Christmas Day 1935. Michael & Kay Addison and William Wand

such as daily worship[13]. It encouraged a surge in church attendance during the Victorian period, not only in posh places but also in the East End of London. For example, St Nicholas in leafy Chislehurst had connections to a Rotherhithe mission in the darkest docklands and one on the north side of the river[xi]. It founded a number of churches including St Francis in Petts Wood, which I attended in my twenties[xii].

For a theological-optimist such as Wand, Anglo-Catholicism was more than 'smells and bells'. He identified six goals: the need to worship together; to work in society; to achieve unity between Christians; to reconcile science with religion; to find fresh expressions of worship; and with the Eucharist at its centre. Most traditions now accept all of these. An optimism fulfilled.

At Oxford, Will took up his pen. He published the *Golden String* which he'd prepared for his confirmation classes at Salisbury[xiii]. The publishers Methuen asked him to write further books – and they came thick and fast: *The Development of Sacramentalism (1928)*, *The History of the Modern Church from 1500 to the Present Day (1930)*, *The Old Faith and the New Age (1933)*. I even found a copy of *I and II Peter and Jude (1934)* in the cottage next-door to mine in Cornwall.

✳ ✳ ✳ ✳

Australia

Uncle Will was in his ninth academic year in Oxford when the Bishop of Salisbury was given the task of finding a new Archbishop for Brisbane, Australia. The Bishop, St Clair Donaldson, had been Brisbane's first Archbishop and knew the challenges of this vast and disparate Province[14]. He knew Will from his days in Salisbury and discerned that he had what it took to take up the mantle. He arranged to meet Will and Amy in a vicarage in Devizes, to offer Will the job. It was Christmas time and they thought about it over their plum pudding and party games. On 27 Dec 1933, Will sent a telegram: "Willing to accept – Wand."[xiv]

Will was allowed to see out the academic year, so Kay could finish her second year at Bedford Physical Training College and sail out to Queensland with them. Paul, their son who'd been taught by my grandfather Charles Haskins as a small boy, was heading for a first in Modern Greats and was to stay on at Balliol.

Sadly, not long after they stepped off the boat, they were greeted by a telegram. Paul had suffered a fatal climbing accident at Chamonix on the French-Swiss border near Mont Blanc[xv]. He and his friend had been mountaineering[15]. Staying on an extra day, 23 August, they were engulfed in an avalanche, and fell 1,800 feet to their death. Amy's brothers, Neville and Clare (see Chapter 12 for more on Clare), went out to search; the bodies weren't found until 22 Sep 1934. This was probably the worst moment of William Wand's life, and one he never really got over. It was ironic. Oxford was one of the happiest times of his life; if he hadn't gone to Australia, he'd have probably been offered a Chair (Professorship) in Church History[xvi]. Yet here he was on the other side of the world and he'd lost his only son. God has a way of testing his most trusted servants like that. He lost his only son. It reminds us how central the resurrection is to the Christian faith.

Emotion is a funny thing. For a grocer's son, Wand's Oxford education helped him walk amongst the great and the good but he still thought as the 'common man' thought. Yet some people considered him unemotional and distant. In a country which motored along

13. *Cardinal John Henry Newman CO DD (1801-1890) [NR] and Prof Edward Bouverie Pusey (1800-1882) [NR]*.
14. *The Rt Rev St Clair George Alfred Donaldson DD (1863-1935) [NR]*.
15. *John Doncaster Hoyland (1915-1934) [NR]*.

on matey comradeship, Will's academic analysis, his high standards and cool dispassion were too often perceived as signs of superiority, yet it was far from the truth. He had a loud laugh, a quick wit and the source of good jokes, often against himself. His face lit up when he recognised someone in the street. He was good with children, coming down to their level. People mirrored his joy when things went well.

Wand could be detached and balanced in his work, yet he was less equipped to deal with this loss. Having heard this news, he had to speak in public moments later – it took inner strength. 'Wand never forgot his son's energy and ideas. He saw them later in other young men, perhaps a bit in me. "To me," he wrote, "he was more than a son; of all my men friends, he was the closest.... We had even planned to write together."[xvii]

As Archbishop, Wand supervised four other dioceses as well as he own, Brisbane: the eastern coastal Dioceses of Rockhampton and North Queensland, Papua New Guinea and Carpentaria (now Northern Territory), which stretched all the way inland from the Gulf of Carpentaria to Alice Springs. The Bush Brothers were an essential part of that ministry. They reached out to Aborigine and lonely settler alike; they travelled miles. In fact, Uncle Will suggested that prospective Bush Brothers should spend a week or two in a garage before coming out. 'When you are all alone in the middle of nowhere your life may depend on your working knowledge of the innards of a car'[xviii]. One such Bush Brother was **Bryan Kay**, a former Oriel student, who later became his Chaplain[16].

Brisbane, an industrial town with a population then of 450,000, was capital of Queensland. The Cathedral of St John was still only half built in 1934. It was designed by John Pearson who was also responsible for Truro Cathedral[17]. The two are almost identical although Truro's was finished first. St John's Brisbane was only fully consecrated in 2008. Will was enthroned in the half-finished building in front of five Bishops and 190 clergy in September 1934, having been consecrated a Bishop at St Paul's London before he left England[xix].

Wand considered the principal skill of a Bishop's should be in administration – after all, 'that, I take it, is what the word *episcopus* (overseer) is meant to imply.'[xx] He was skilled at delegation, but only to reliable people – 'trust, thrust and competence' were his criteria. He steered people in a clear direction, even if that meant taking ruthless decisions. He issued some *ad clerums*, which shook the clergy up[18]. One was to forbid weddings during Lent. Lent was to be observed. This was not to be a go-as-you-please church life, which is what clergy too often reconcile themselves with today. Another was his move of the theological college to Bishopsbourne. He needed to supervise it: only 36 out of 136 of the clergy in his Diocese had degrees. At Wand's insistence, Brisbane developed a theology faculty, the first in Australia. But one of his first acts was to tell the clergy to buck up – in his opinion they were "mentally, morally and spiritually below standard." These high expectations and blunt words prompted Henry Le Fanu, Archbishop of Tasmania, to write to the Archbishop of Canterbury asking that Wand be sent home[19]. It wasn't the Australian way.

Yet Wand's church was expanding and Le Fanu's complaint was ignored. Fifty more churches were built in the Province in the next five years 1936-41. He consecrated the first Cathedral in New Guinea, St Peter and Paul at Dogura, in Oct 1939[xxi].

Bishopsbourne, the Archbishop's home, Brisbane, during the 1937 drought

Awaiting the arrival of Archbishop Wand for the consecration of Dogura Cathedral, Papua New Guinea

---

16. *Rev Prebendary Robert Bryan Hervey Kay (1912–1982) was with St Paul Bush Brothers of Charleville 1939-42; he married Barbara Hester Wiggins (1923-2011) in 1947.*

17. *John Loughborough Pearson RA RIBA (1817-1897) [NR] was a high churchman. He also designed St Michael's and All Angels church (1880) in West Croydon, near the Whitgift Centre where I worked 1973-87; and St Matthew-in-the-City (1896) in the centre of Auckland, New Zealand, where the author's wife Carolyn lived in 1979-80.*

18. *'To the clergy.'*

19. *Most Rev Henry Frewen Le Fanu (1870-1946) [NR].*

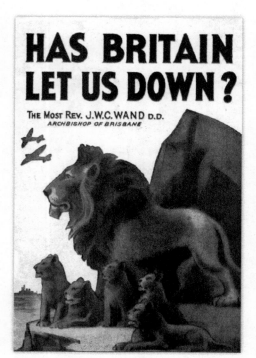

HAS BRITAIN LET US DOWN?

THE MOST REV. J.W.C. WAND D.D.
ARCHBISHOP OF BRISBANE

Throughout his career, Wand harnessed the power of the press. He took up the invitation to write weekly in the local paper, the Courier-Mail. He occasionally wrote for the Sydney Morning Herald. He broadcast every Sunday night – on commercial radio. He continued to write books but, with everything else he had to do, it took him 18 months to finish the last chapter of the book he started on the boat. One book he wrote, which he gave me when it was still around in the 1960s, was St Paul's *New Testament Letters*, which he rewrote in the style of a Bishop writing in a Diocesan magazine. It was one of the first attempts in the 20th century to modernise the language – years ahead of the *Philips* or the *Good News* bibles. It went through six reprints in those early years.

The publication which was to change William Wand's career was perhaps less than intentional. It was a defence of the British war effort. Everything was going badly. Hong Kong had fallen to the Japanese on Christmas Day 1941 and Singapore the following February. Australia, without a single army tank to defend itself, was threatened. Now he was invited to a St George's Society evening on 20 April 1942 at a time when the Australians were particularly jittery and blaming Britain for their woes. After Wand described the progress of the Navy, Army and Air Force in some detail (filched from the newspapers), he described the opinions of the Australian chattering classes as "the most dangerous piece of Fifth Column activity seen in this country."[xxii]

The fall of Singapore, he said, was as much Australia's fault as Britain's. It was Churchill who'd suggested the Aussie troops return to the Far East from the European front to defend themselves from the Japanese, not Australia. It was Australia that insisted its troops not be evacuated from Singapore. It was the Australian sector of Singapore defence that failed first. Wand attacked those who "would willingly stab Britain in the back" and hoped there were enough loyalists who would remain, "come weal or come woe, as for ever a British people."

Wand was astonished to receive one of those standing ovations that people seldom expect in their speaking careers. The talk was put into print as the pamphlet *Has Britain Let us Down?*, reprinted many times, and won the attention of Winston Churchill's Minister of Information, Brendan Bracken, who was eternally grateful for any support of that kind from the British Empire[20]. The Australian Prime Minister, Robert Menzies, was in England and one British Cabinet Minister thought Australia was 'the most dangerous obstacle facing this government'[xxiii]. Wand put the Australian Government on the defensive. By the time Menzies returned, he'd lost all support and was forced to resign[21]. It wasn't long before Wand received an invitation to become Bishop of Bath and Wells. Amy had no hesitation in having him accept.

England was different from Australia. For one thing, it was not brown – it was green – and Amy relished being near her family again. But England really was in the middle of a war, with bombs and rationing, with children evacuated across the country, and the women on the land and in the factories. After a safe passage across the Pacific and VIP treatment in San Francisco and New York, things got more miserable the nearer they were to home. An ex-Italian luxury yacht, the *Leonardo da Vinci* sailing in convoy, gave them comfort but no great protection. When they arrived at the docks in Glasgow, there was no one to meet them and no transport. With Amy sitting on the suitcases as the evening closed in, Will had to walk into town, eventually finding a taxi at a funeral parlour.

✳ ✳ ✳ ✳

20. *Brendan Bracken, 1st Viscount Bracken, MP PC (1901-1958) [NR].*
21. *Sir Robert Gordon Menzies KT AK CH FAA FRS QC (1894-1978) [NR].*

Bath and Wells

Wells is a sleepy Somerset town, one which I got to know slightly when visiting my great Uncle Bernard and Aunt Phyllis on the way back from Cornwall each year[22]. They lived at 14 New Street, a large old property showing its age but housing some wonderful furniture which they'd inherited or picked up on their travels. **Bernard,** Amy's brother, had met **Phyllis** when staying with the Wands in Salisbury. After service as a lawyer in Zanzibar and time in Cheltenham, Bernard and Phyllis worked with the Wands at both Wells and London. I liked Phyllis a lot. At the time, I knew nothing about her mother's pedigree which included a Lord Mayor of London or her family's natural aptitude with art – her daughter Barbara published poetry as 'Hester Kay' and her two children, my cousins, have spent their careers on the stage and with accomplished fine-art[23].

Uncle Will was enthroned at Wells in Nov 1943. Apart from its Cathedral, the 13th century Bishop's Palace is perhaps the biggest pull for tourists to the small Somerset town. There's a calm tranquillity about the Close. Its green trees and sand-grey walls plumb the depths of the dappled waters as their shadows stretch along the grassy sward.

The quirkiest aspect is the swans in the moat, which are trained to ring a bell near the Palace entrance. They do this to obtain food; consequently, for much of the day, the rope is kept out of reach of their beaks. Bishops come and Bishops go but the swans go on for ever. Not all the Bishops have been interested in this long-standing tradition, but Uncle Will took it upon himself to search high and low for a replacement swan when the pen (the female) died. He found one, wounded in one eye in the blitz, in Bristol. Within 36 hours she'd learnt to ring the bell and the next year produced four cygnets. Uncle Will even persuaded his Chaplain, who lived in, to join him for the occasional swim in the freezing waters of the moat. In his eighties, Uncle Will would still take a morning swim.

Because it was wartime, the Palace was accommodating St Brandon's School, from Bristol, which had been set up to educate Clergy Daughters in 1831[xxiv]. The previous Bishop, Frances Underhill, disliked the noise of the young people[24]. It disturbed his contemplative life but Will and Amy found the arrangement to their advantage. The large medieval building was well-heated in exchange for large quantities of fresh vegetables grown in their garden.

As this was his second diocese, Wand knew what to do to achieve results, and how to make those tough decisions. The Diocese had been motoring along without much direction under Frances Underhill – the popular Edmund Sara, the Assistant Bishop, doing most of the work[25]. Wand soon realised there could only be one gun in town, so to speak, and told Sara his

Bishop's Palace, Wells

Enthronement procession at Wells Cathedral

Amy and William Wand at the Bishop's Palace, Wells

---

22. *Bernard Henry Wiggins OBE CBSZ (1878-1972) and Phyllis Therese Mason (1889-1966).*

23. *Charles Farebrother (1783-1858). His father had been a ship's captain trading with China. His sons were priests. Rev Charles Farebrother (1821-1899) was chaplain to George II's youngest son Prince Adolphus, 1st Duke of Cambridge (1846), Rector of Irnham, and Corby in Lincolnshire (1851-99). Charles's daughter Theresa Emmerline Clara Farebrother (1859-1938) was Phyllis's mother. Phyllis's father was Charles Mason (1849-1929), Land Agent and Auctioneer from Louth in Lincolnshire and, before that, his father Thomas Mason (1808-1877) was farming at Healing, next door to Michael Addison's grandfather at Stallingborough; Barbara Hester Wiggins (1923-2011); Robert Jonathan Hervey Kay (b1950), Susan Hester Kay (b1948).*

24. *Rt Rev Francis Underhill (1878-1943) Dean of Rochester 1932-7, Bishop of Bath & Wells 1937-43, was cousin of the mystical author, Evelyn Underhill (1875 1941) [NR] He died in office. Evelyn Underhill had a marked influence on the author's Principal Lecturer at Christ Church College Canterbury: Dr Edith Lorna Kendall (1921-1995) [NR] was author of spiritual books such as: A City not Forsaken (1962), Watchmen upon thy Walls (1963) Contemplative Living in a Contemporary World (1970) and Michael Ramsey as Theologian (1995).*

25. *Rt Rev Edmund Willoughby Sara (1891-1965) [NR] born at Gwinear, near Hayle in Cornwall, was the son of a clerk at the Cordite Works in Camborne.*

services were no longer needed. He brought over the Oriel man who'd headed up the Brisbane Theological College and appointed him Suffragan Bishop of Taunton[26]. The Bush Brother, **Bryan Kay** who had been wounded in the war, was appointed domestic Chaplain, doubling as private secretary.

✻ ✻ ✻ ✻

After the blitz

In October 1944, seven months before the end of the war, one of our most respected of Archbishops of Canterbury, William Temple, died[27]. He was succeeded by Geoffrey Fisher[28]. I only once brushed up against the Fisher family in, of all places, Cornwall, in the 1950s when I was a child. The Fisher boys stayed at the Kendall's cottage at Portmellon. The family persuaded our farming hosts, the Grose's, to do them a big tea on the lawn at Penquarry, where we were staying. The Grose's lawn had the most tremendous view over the unspoilt coastline of south Cornwall – a place of outstanding natural beauty. We were kept well out of the way, that day.

The author's parents in the garden of Penquarry where the Archbishop's tea party took place

With Fisher at Canterbury, it meant that London was vacant. Brendan Bracken, the Information Minister, put forward William Wand for this position. "I know of no one who brings a better combination of gifts to the largest and most difficult Diocese in the world," he wrote[xxv].

The process of selection is different now but in Wand's day the Archbishop put four names to the Prime Minister and one was put to the Monarch. The process was less tedious but still a trial for all concerned. One stage involved a lunch with the Prime Minister at 10 Downing Street, at a time when Winston Churchill had his mind set on the war[29]. Eventually a date was found but the meal was to be held in Churchill's bunker so he could come straight from the business of the day. It was the last few days of the war in Europe. There were daily surrenders – Berlin, Italy, Rangoon, Czechoslovakia and the Channel Islands all in one month. There was the post-war occupation of Germany to think about, and food to be found. The Far East had yet to be won. It was difficult to persuade Churchill out of his reverie. Not one word was spoken about the appointment throughout the meal, but he reacted warmly to some of William Wand's 'Grantham' turns of phrase which seemed to put life in the old man or did he remember sitting on a train in British East Africa with Will's brother-in-law Clare? Something did the trick and the letter duly arrived. Subject to the King's approval, the appointment was to be announced in June 1945. The next stage should have been routine: the formal confirmation by the Vicar-General.

The confirmation for the Bath and Wells position had been a nightmare but nothing compared to this. A complaint was again made by the same group of evangelicals known as the National Union of Protestants. They objected to Wand's Anglo-Catholicism, seeing it as a take-over by the Roman Catholic church. But nothing was as bad as the enthronement itself. Like any new Bishop, Wand had to knock on the outside of the great West Doors of St Paul's Cathedral three times with his crozier (shepherd's crook). The police did their best as a howling mob of more than 200 members of the National Union bellowed 'Popery,' 'traitor,' 'liar,' and 'devil'. Percy Petter, a Baptist, was the founder of the 'National Union'[30]. He told a

26. *Rt Rev Harry Thomas (1897-1955) [NR], Principal St Francis Theological College, Milton, Brisbane and Archdeacon of Brisbane, 1936-44, Bishop of Taunton 1945-55.*

27. *Most Rev William Temple PC (1881-1944) [NR].*

28. *Most Rev Geoffrey Francis Fisher, Baron Fisher of Lambeth GCVO PC (1887-1972) [NR].*

29. *Sir Winston Leonard Spencer-Churchill KG, OM, CH, TD, DL, FRS, RA (1874-1965).*

30. *Percival Waddams Petter (1873-1955) [NR], Managing Director of Petters Ltd, an Engineering firm in Yeovil, was in fact a Baptist. Soon after this protest, in Dec 1945, he married Ruth Penson-Harris. They set out for Australia Sep 1947-Jun 1948 and made trouble there.*

50-strong protest outside the House of Commons later that day that he'd got into the service and after the Benediction, he'd walked up to the Chancel and announced: *'We have witnessed today the election of a bishop whose doctrine is not the doctrine of the Church of England. He is patron of the mass which our 31st Article condemns as a blasphemous fable and a dangerous conceit.'*[xxvi] The Union did not let up. They sent letters to the King and the Prime Minister.

I witnessed a similar protest 25 years later at Canterbury when Ian Paisley, with far fewer adherents, tried to spoil an outdoor Papal Mass at the 800th anniversary of Thomas à Becket's death[31]. It was the first hint of the 'Northern Ireland troubles' which were to decimate that beautiful country for nearly 30 years.

London needed a leader and Brendan Bracken had found one. Would morale be restored after the war? Wand's diocese was mainly north of the Thames (Southwark being to the south). It comprised 1,000 clergy, 28 deaneries and 700 churches – all but 70 churches had suffered war damage[xxvii]. Added to that, people had lost their church-going habit. Wand reckoned that the churches needed £1m to recover from the damage, and that St Paul's Cathedral alone needed £1m spending on it. It was a huge task, requiring huge personal resources, absolute resolution, and everybody pulling together. He combined strong leadership with sharp administration. On 25 Sep 1946, just two years before I was born, he sat on the steps of St Paul's all day and raised £26,000, the equivalent of several million pounds in today's money.

To start with, Will decided to make a personal visitation to the churches. This was normally done once a year by his three (soon to be four) Archdeacons but, to make a statement, he chose 11 big churches in 1947, invited over 13,000 lay leaders to them and made the ceremonies extra impressive with fanfares of bugles from the Church Lads and guards of honour from the Scouts and Guides. He called it 'Our Day of Opportunity', almost as if he had coined a term used in SWOT analysis[xxviii]. There were 543 parishes. 'Articles of Enquiry' went to each one. Churchwardens were asked to give their view of the spiritual condition of their parish. He spoke twice, in the service and afterwards, wearing his Bishop's gaiters[xxix]. The visitations brought people together in a new relationship. They provided hope. People said, "The church is not dead yet." He collected a further £36,000.

Wand didn't stop there. He organised a Lent course, called a *'School of Religion'* and rolled it out across three Dioceses. He organised an enormous Evangelistic mission which covered 122 centres and 155 leaders with a climax at the Albert Hall for 8,000 people. 750,000 attended other special events. It inspired two other missions, a whole-London Methodist initiative and a national crusade by Billy Graham, to which my father went. Three times the size of the normal Easter communion attendance attended Will's initiative and many more went to the others. The Christian church was back on the map.

The Education Acts of 1944 and 1945 had a big impact on the way church schools were funded, many Bishops letting things slide out of their control. Wand, who'd received his own education from a Church School, redoubled his efforts to finance schools and maintain spiritual control. He considered it his greatest triumph that he was able to retain their 'aided' status, which he thought "even more important than the rebuilding of churches."[xxx] He introduced the first Chaplaincy post for the University of London and in Sunbury-on-Thames there is now a Church of England High School (an Academy) in his memory.

Amongst the bombed out churches across London, there were the 46 churches in the square mile of the City itself, with hardly any population in their parishes. The architectural buffs wanted all these wonderful Wren and Hawksmoor churches to be fully restored[32]. Who was going to pay? In discussions, Wand hit on the saving formula. He invited 14 wealthy London Guilds and other organisations each to adopt a church, which became their 'chapel' and their

Demonstrators outside St Paul's Cathedral, London, during the the enthronement of Dr J W C Wand (formerly Archbishop of Brisbane) as Bishop of London. There were angry demonstrations, led by the Rev W St Clair Taylor, director of the National Union of Protestants, as Dr Wand left the cathedral. The protest concerned Roman Catholicism in the Anglican Church

Gift Day on the steps of St Paul's 25 Sep 1946 - £26,000 was raised, worth several million pounds in today's money

---

31. *Rev Ian Richard Kyle Paisley, Baron Bannside, PC MP MEP (1926-2014) [NR]. Archbishop St Thomas Becket (1120-1170) [NR] was murdered in the cathedral on the orders of Henry II.*

32. *Sir Christopher Michael Wren PRS (1632-1723) [NR]; Nicholas Hawksmoor (1661-1736) [NR].*

responsibility. He described it as a 'vast ecclesiastical laboratory'. There were links with city life and everything from the Air Force to an organisation promoting the Welsh language.

Wand was keen to bring all Christians together. Assisted by his first Bishop of Fulham, Basil Batty, he headed up the British Council of Churches' as the first Chairman of its Executive body[33]. He was at the 1948 foundation of the World Council of Churches in Amsterdam, which he'd heard described as having 'too much American money, too much German theology and too much Dutch bureaucracy.'

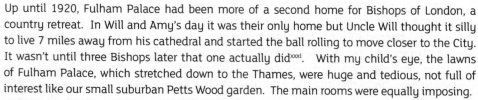

Fulham Palace

Up until 1920, Fulham Palace had been more of a second home for Bishops of London, a country retreat. In Will and Amy's day it was their only home but Uncle Will thought it silly to live 7 miles away from his cathedral and started the ball rolling to move closer to the City. It wasn't until three Bishops later that one actually did[xxxi]. With my child's eye, the lawns of Fulham Palace, which stretched down to the Thames, were huge and tedious, not full of interest like our small suburban Petts Wood garden. The main rooms were equally imposing.

Amy did much to make the ravaged 70-roomed building habitable[xxxii]. Few have their daughter's and brother's families living with them, let alone the chaplain, a niece, her friend and her cat, the chauffeur, his French wife and the head gardener. Nevertheless, everybody had their own space[xxxiii]. Amy brought in family members to help out. Her brother Bernard moved with them from Wells to take charge of the administration. Phyllis and their daughter Barbara helped with the household duties; Barbara was employed as cook[xxxiv]. Rationing stretched to steamed pudding once a week and fruit pie on Sundays, soup in the evenings with cheese for the Bishop.

Amy'd had practice at running problematic homes. In Brisbane, she'd taken over a place which hadn't been a family home for 50 years – half the rooms had never been occupied[xxxv]. In wartime Wells, sharing rooms with 150 schoolgirls, the visitors walked past rows of 'potties' to reach the Bishop's quarters.

Fulham Palace had suffered from the air raids and there was little heating. One occupant described the kitchen facilities in the same breath as Belsen. The large cold kitchen had little more than a small sink, a cold tap – no draining board. One of the 'dailies' fainted after seeing a rat 'the size of a cat'.

Like most of the Wiggins, Amy was an organiser and was good at dishing out jobs to others. As well as Central Vice-President of the Mothers' Union, she organised soup kitchens, the WRVS and stood on other committees at Mary Sumner House. Uncle Will depended on her for some Wiggins' magic, combined with its strategy and stamina.

Will kept up a punishing routine – breakfast at 8am, lunch at 1pm, tea at 4pm and supper at 7pm, prompt[xxxvi]. Morning started before breakfast with more than half an hour of devotion, followed by dealing with the morning mail. He ate his porridge standing up, 'like the Scots'. Yet he also found time for the cinema and detective novels, to take his mind off his work; otherwise he'd be haunted by migraines. He scheduled time with his family. A chaplain described a cheerful household. "Sunday breakfasts were always a hilarious affair. The family all came to the early service in the Chapel, after which we sat down to breakfast together, and the Bishop loved to hear from their own mouths of what the children had been doing over the past week. When they were younger, the meal usually finished with one or more of the party playing trains on the floor and it was with difficulty that the Bishop tore himself away from the dining room to get ready for his Sunday sermons."[xxxvii]

Fulham Palace, 1946, home of Bishops of London since AD700. Amy by the sundial. Paul Haskins with his uncle Will on the left.

33. *The Rt Rev Basil Staunton Batty OBE (1873-1952) [NR].*

Fulham was where Bryan Kay, his Chaplain, laid his eyes on the cook, the Bishop's niece, Barbara Wiggins. Unbeknown to the others, Bryan and Barbara would slip out of side doors and meet in the garden. They'd go for walks together along the tow-path, to Kew Gardens or to the cinema. Bryan shyly 'courted' her. Sometimes, when he said goodbye to Barbara, he'd stand in his cassock, twisting the end of his belt, running it towards the buckle and letting it go[xxxviii]. One day he took her rowing on the pond. He found it so difficult to pop the special question that the boat continued in circles, round and round, as he thought about what to say. They married at Fulham in 1947. My sister Barbara (same name) was a bridesmaid.

Regular senior staff meetings were held at Fulham every Monday. Afterwards, the Bishops and Archdeacons would move into another room so the women could join them for soup (they'd all bring their own sandwiches) followed by fruit and custard. I wonder how many of the decisions were taken in the second session, with the women present.

Uncle Will restored the chapel at Fulham – it was central to his life. A refuge for him to meet his God; a place he used each morning. I must have been one of the first to be baptised there before it was fully restored. The East window by Sir Ninian Comper (who was brought out of retirement) shows Wand alongside Bishop Creighton. At the architect's suggestion, his lost son Paul is shown in a small window at the top of the tracery[34].

Who's that big bear behind me? 1950.

Uncle Will with his granddaughters Ruth and Brigit Addison, and my sister Barbara (right), bridesmaids at Bryan Kay's marriage to Barbara Wiggins in 1947, in the Great Hall at Fulham Palace (the other bridesmaid was Caroline Kay) "The first splash of festivity of the post war years," said Barbara Kay

❋ ❋ ❋ ❋

Amen Court,

The tradition was for Bishops to die in office. Clergy pensions didn't exist, so money was very tight if you 'retired'. Uncle Will had his supplementary income from his books, of course. Wand was 60 when he took office as the 110th Bishop of London. Today there is a rule that clergy must stand down at 70, and can receive a pension at 65, but Wand led the way, much to everyone's surprise, when he announced his resignation at the age of 70 in 1955. There was talk of York, but Amy didn't want to live there.

It didn't exactly stop him working. Uncle Will was offered a minor Canonry at St Paul's Cathedral and in 1960 the job of Canon Treasurer came up. He stayed until the age of 84, in 1969.

One of his predecessors, Archbishop Laud, believed that the way of beauty was the pathway to heaven[35]. Wand was of the same frame of mind and his opinions must have won the day in those cathedral committee meetings. He would have championed his favoured design for the reconstruction of the bombed-out East End of the cathedral, a canopy over the altar, similar to the one that Sir Christopher Wren had designed in the 1670s but never implemented[36]. Its helical columns were modelled on Bernini's Renaissance baldacchino at Rome, themselves based on Solomon's original temple in Jerusalem. So after 3,000 years Solomon's temple had come to London[xxxix]. Today, after millions of pounds more have been spent wiping off the Victorian soot, the cathedral looks more like Wren conceived it than at any other time in history. When the East End was completed, Uncle Will stood with me beside the great west doors of St Paul's. We looked down the length of the nave at the finished product at the far end, resplendent in its gilded majesty. He asked for my opinion. That question from the great man meant a lot to me, a fourteen-year-old boy, even if I found it difficult to know what to say.

Living at 3 Amen Court, hidden behind the Cathedral, it was a comfortable existence. He was able to write some 19 books, edit the *Church Quarterly Review*, pen a weekly column in the *Church Times* and compose numerous articles and sermons, with the sun stippling light through the leaves of the trees outside the large plate-glass window[xl]. He still had contacts in

Chapel at Fulham Palace. Bishop Wand is pictured in the right-hand pane and his son Paul Wand (1912-1934) at the apex

34. *Sir John Ninian Comper RIBA (1864–1960) [NR].*

35. *Most Rev William Laud (1573-1645) [NR] Bishop of London 1628-33 Archbishop of Canterbury 1633-45.*

36. *Stephen Ernest Dykes Bower AA (1903-94) [NR],*

Amen Court, homes for the Canons of St Paul's

The baldacchino above St Paul's high altar

Fleet Street yet he wrote an article for me to place in a magazine that I had started up (with its own printing press) at *Dauntsey's* called, appropriately, *'The Mitre'*. From his enormous study, lined wall to wall with books (and over most other surfaces), he could stroll over to the Cathedral for his duties and devotions.

Canon Collins lived next door[37]. This straightforward, if abrasive, social activist started the 'Ban the Bomb' Campaign for Nuclear Disarmament (CND), still the world's largest peace movement, in that house.

Will and Amy's Kay and Michael Addison lived in what had been the 'servants' quarters'. They had their own back staircase joining the second floor bedrooms with the living rooms in the basement. After spending time in various government ministries, Michael resigned from the Treasury when he was 51 to take a job as a lecturer at the School of Management Studies at the Polytechnic of Central London. Kay did good works, in the family tradition, including holding the post of Commissioner of Guides. Of their children, Brigit married Michael Girling and moved out to Wimbledon[38]. Roo emigrated to New Zealand's South Island, marrying a sheep farmer, one John Wilding. After school at Bruton and the Essex Institute of Agriculture, Bill (as we called him) went to farm in Lincolnshire, not far from the 1st Viscount Addison's father's family farm at Stallingborough. He has since taken an interest in the environment, serving as a Vice President of National Parks and the British Trust for Conservation Volunteers[xli].

✳ ✳ ✳ ✳

Last Words

In 1968, two and a half years after Amy died, the Addisons moved with Uncle Will to the Old Stables, Maplehurst. There, Uncle Will had his own space, where he kept up his daily Mass, and swimming in the small (cold) swimming pool at the bottom of the garden. He moved into the *College of St Barnabas* at Lingfield, still writing for the *Church Times* in his nineties. He died on the same day in August 1977 as Elvis Presley.

It was at the *College of St Barnabas* that he wrote '*Letters on the Ministry*' addressed to me. He died before it was published. Thinking of me – the dilettante, the polymath – it sets out the role of a priest as someone 'hardly ever doing the same thing for a couple of hours together.' He links *Government* Ministry (where I worked at the time) with the *God's* Ministry – Wand felt that government office should never be wholly secularized. "Politics is simply the art of living together, and if the Church has nothing to say in that respect, what is her role to be?"[xlii] Christ's values have a part to play in whatever laws are made and however they are applied. Our current Queen sees it that way and several Prime Ministers have said the same[xliii]. Pope Gregory called himself *Servus servorum dei* – the 'Servant of the servants of God'. Ministers, of whichever sort, and 'obedient' civil servants (as they used to sign themselves), can't be above the law. They must humble themselves to the service of others, said Wand. Humility is an unfashionable word – Lord Longford wrote a book about it[xliv]. Sadly, I never fulfilled Uncle Will's expectations for me. I never became a priest.

'*Letters on the Ministry*' was written in the 'Age of Doubt'[xlv]. Would there be an age when Britain might no longer be called a Christian country, when we faced 'the reality of empty

---

37. *Canon Lewis John Collins MA (1905–1982) [NR] was the successor to William Wand as Dean of Oriel, in 1937. Canon of St Paul's London 1948-81. Chair of CND 1958-64 and of the Martin Luther King Foundation 1969-73. He also founded Christian Action in 1946, War on Want in 1951 and from 1950 supported the anti-apartheid movement in South Africa. He lived at 2 Amen Court.*

38. *Eleanor Brigit Addison (b1938) married Michael T Girling (b1934) from Ipswich in 1972; Caroline Ruth Addison (b1942) married John Hollis Wilding (b1942) in 1965; Viscount William Matthew Wand Addison (b1945) married Joanna May Dickinson in 1970, divorced her in 1990, and married Lesley Ann Mawer in 1991.*

churches', he pondered? Wand didn't rule that out. He went further, thinking of the 'poverty-stricken outcast existence' of the early church. He didn't recommend it though – giving up the church's buildings, ornaments, pomp or mystery – it invited defeat. He saw no future in "a desert of plain glass and kitchen tables…. We are not there yet…. Christianity was clothed in an organisation from the beginning, and was intended to be so at the very end. Disembodied ideals cannot last."[xlvi]   Uncle Will was an optimist with a true Wiggins wife, pressing him upwards and onwards. He combined his skills of organisation with his scholarship and learning, his people-management with oratory. He impressed Christ's authority on a badly beaten world and possessed a tenacity to overcome enormous odds. Yet he was a realist: 'It is the glorious tragedy of our profession that we must always strive to achieve the Kingdom of God whilst knowing that in this world we may never wholly achieve it.'[xlvii]

This grocer's son from Grantham had a place in many people's hearts. When speaking at the funeral of the offspring of another grocer from Grantham, from a pulpit where Uncle Will often stood, one of his successors said, 'Everything which has turned to love in our lives will be stored up in the memory of God.'[39]   Memories.

❋ ❋ ❋ ❋

William Wand still swimming in his unheated pool in his eighties

36.   College of St Barnabas, Lingfield c1906

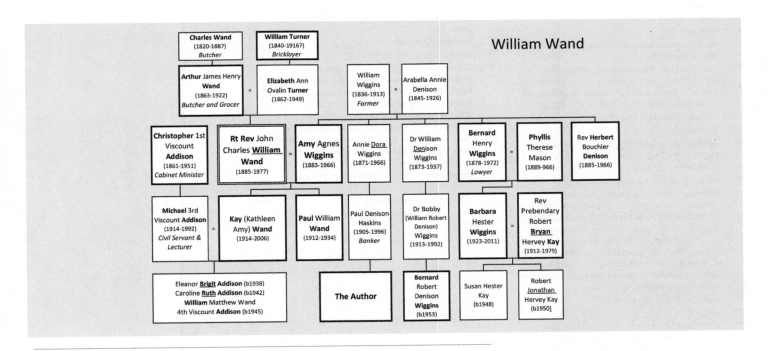

William Wand

39.   *Rt Rev Richard Chartres (b1947) [NR] Funeral oration for Baroness Margaret Thatcher [NR] 17 Apr 2013.*

Other Notes and References

i.   *Have I got News for You? BBC 7 Dec 2015. The author is not alone in having early memories – Alexander Armstrong (b1970), the Pointless Quiz show host (and President of Newcastle's Literary and Philosophical Society), remembers his early times including time in his mother's womb.*

ii.   *At a Coronation, the Bishop of London traditionally carries the paten (dish for wafers) and reads the epistle (1 Peter 2 v 13)*

iii. *Dauntsey's School, near Devizes, Wiltshire (1962-67)*

iv.   *http://rtpi.org.uk/media/895782/homes_for_ heroes_-_report.pdf accessed 3 Feb 2015. By 1924, it was estimated that the Addison Act style housing developments accounted for 62% of all new properties built.*

v.   *Wand, Letters on the Ministry p7. Who's Who 1976.*

vi.   *Bishop Robinson's book 'Honest to God' instigated a passionate debate about the nature of Christian belief at the start of a secular age.*

vii. *Ibid p27. He was part-funded by an Exhibition from the county education authority and helped by an ordination candidates' society.*

viii. *Bishop Jacob Hostel, Grainger Park Road, Newcastle (founded in 1901 and sold in 1925) and the Parish of Benwell. Ordained Deacon in 1908 at Newcastle Cathedral and Priest in 1909.*

ix.   *Wand, Changeful Page, p85.*

x.   *Peart-Binns p42.*

xi.   *In 1880, when the priest Rev Charles Lowder (1820-1880) [NR] Rector of St Peter's, London Docks, died, several thousand processed the 11 miles from Wapping to Chislehurst for a Requiem Mass.*

xii. *Haskins, Robert. A History of St Francis Petts Wood p3.*

xiii. *1926, Republished later as The Golden String: A Short Introduction to Christian Practice. The 'string' was the Catholic faith. Follow it, and like in the Minotaur's labyrinth, it will lead you out to safety and to heaven's gate.*

xiv. *Peart-Binns p56.*

xv.   *Hoyland. The accidfent occurred on the Innominata Ridge of Mont Blanc*

xvi. *Peart-Binns p56. Beresford Kidd (1864-1948) [NR], Warden of Keble, wrote to Wand on 26 Dec 1933 to say "... if, as we all hoped, you were to have been, and may still be, successor to the Chair of Ecclesiastical History...."*

xvii. *Brisbane Courier Mail, 6 Oct 1934.*

xviii. *The Mitre p3.*

xix. *Sydney Morning Herald, 6 Sep 1934. Consecration on 1 May 1934 at St Paul's Cathedral London; Enthronement at Brisbane, 5 Sep 1934.*

xx.   *Wand, Changeful Page, p131.*

xxi. *http://anglicanhistory.org/aus/png/dogura_ consecration1939.html accessed 6 May 2016 The new Cathedral held 800 and a further 500 stood outside during the Consecration. Wand began his sermon by giving a message to the Papuan Christians in the Wedauan language, having learnt enough to speak it.. Costing £4,000, it was built by 170 volunteers on a fighting ground where, 50 years previously, they followed battles with cannibal feasts.*

xxii. *Wand, Has Britain Let Us Down?*

xxiii. *Day p66.*

xxiv. *Originally in Gloucester, St Brandon's School moved to Bristol in 1833 and in 1945 to Clevedon Hall, Clevedon. It closed in 2004. More successful, Marlborough College was set up for the same the same reason to cater for sons of Clergy.*

xxv. *Letter from Bracken to Wand 22 Jun 1945 quoted by Peart-Binns p119f.*

xxvi. *The Morning Bulletin, Rockhampton 11 Oct 1945. Anglican clergy are expected to affirm the doctrine of the Church of England as set forth in the 39 Articles in the Book of Common Prayer.*

xxvii. *www.london.anglican.org/about/ accessed 25 Feb 2016. In 2013, 70 years later, the Diocese retains the same number of clergy.*

xxviii. *SWOT: Strengths, Weaknesses, Opportunities, Threats*

xxix. *Wand was one of the last prelates to wear Bishop's gaiters and spats, with buttons down the side of the leg – fastened with button hooks, as used in Jane Austen's day.*

xxx. *Episcopal letter 29 Oct 1955*

xxxi. *In 1973, the Palace was vacated by a Bishop for the last time. In 1975, it was leased to the local Council for 100 years. Since 2011, it has been run by the Fulham Palace Trust.*

xxxii. *In 1944 the ceiling of the main staircase had fallen in when a V2 bomb fell in the nearby allotments*

xxxiii. *Kay p43. The niece was Margot (Margaret Denison) Wiggins (1914-1993) and her friend Greta Fox, daughter of Rev John Thomas Fox, Vicar of Great Milton, Oxfordshire, near Watlington. Greta was thought of as a potential wife for the author's father Paul – Paul concluded she was 'too clever' for him.*

xxxiv. *Barbara Wiggins qualified in City & Guilds Cooking (1st class cert) and Household management (2nd class Dip) at North Gloucester Technical College.*

xxxv. *Courier-Mail, Brisbane, 1 Jan 1934*

xxxvi. *Kay p32.*

xxxvii. *London Churchman. Ven Anthony John Morcom (1916-1997) [NR] Bishop's Domestic Chaplain 1947-55*

xxxviii. *Kay p38.*

xxxix. *The canopy was conceived, designed and built 1958-62 after the exterior was complete.*

xl.   *Wand was editor of Church Quarterly Review 1956-68; he wrote Reflections from Amen Court, in the Church Times, 1957-73*

xli. *Hansard, 28 Apr 1999.*

xlii. *Wand, Changeful Page, p204.*

xliii. *Church Times 16 April 2014: David Cameron (b1966) [NR] wrote, 'I believe we should be more confident about our status as a Christian country, more ambitious about expanding the role of faith-based organisations, and, frankly, more evangelical about a faith that compels us to get out there and make a difference to people's lives.' Theresa May (neé Brasier b1956) [NR] normally worships at my nephew Luke's church, St Andrew's, Sonning.*

xliv. *Humility. Francis Aungier Pakenham, 7th Earl of Longford KG PC (1905-2001) [NR] was Government Minister 1947-51 and 1964-68.*

xlv. *Wand, Letters on Preaching p126.*

xlvi. *Wand, Letters on the Ministry p59.*

xlvii. *Ibid p51.*

I Love Driving West

Since the age of two – or minus six months, if I'm allowed to go back that far – I've been driving down to Cornwall at Easter. My mother, Jean, first went to *Penare Farm* over 100 years ago. Penare farmed the Dodman Point in South Cornwall. Jean was nine when she first went there with her mother Elsie in 1913.

Elsie's paintings now adorn my Cornish cottage walls. The coastline hasn't changed, thanks to the National Trust. Haymaking is no longer the job of boys absconding from school. In 1913, *Penare* was farmed by John and Edith Grose, a young couple just starting out[1]. John Grose had scraped together enough money, by house-painting, to buy the farm off the Mount-Edgcumbe estate at a time when farming was rock bottom and the estate was shedding some of its 13,000 acres because rents were so low. When Jean and Elsie revisited in 1918 and 1919, the Grose's daughter Betty had been born[2].

My parents renewed the connection with Cornwall in 1938, 1945 and 1947 and with the Grose's in 1948; after which we stayed with them every year from 1951-1966[i]. In 1943, John Grose had retired and passed his farm to the National Trust[ii]. He'd retained two fields for a few milking cows and had built a bungalow halfway down the hill towards the beach. The wind blew. Song thrushes chorused their love songs. Primroses and yellow hammers coloured the banks. There was an exquisite view from the garden. On the coastline between the Dodman and Nare Head, theirs was the only home to be seen.

With petrol rationing, it was amazing we ever reached Cornwall. It took about ten hours to drive from Petts Wood. We had to be up before light in order to be first on the road. We breakfasted at Stonehenge, stopped for a drink at the Rising Sun near Sticklepath and had a late lunch just past Launceston. It's even more incredible that we ever got back. When the Suez crisis erupted in 1956, there was petrol rationing again. Mr Grose agreed to give us (illegally) some of his agricultural fuel. I remember the pig being killed to celebrate our arrival. The squeal resonated round the valley – but lovely bacon!

There was the shock of drinking milk straight from the cow – it was warm! Of course: the cow's body heat! When aged thirteen, the nurse tested me for Tuberculosis (TB), I was immune because of that milk. John Grose and his fellow farmers conducted a perpetual war to keep the badger population from spreading TB. My brother-in-law, **Michael Burton** in Yorkshire was not so lucky[3]. When he caught TB, he spent a period in an adult isolation hospital, and carried on taking prescription drugs for some months before he was signed off.

Most afternoons were spent on Hemmick beach after a big lunch – normally home-made pasties unless Edith Grose had wrung the neck of another chicken. Most mornings we'd walk to Gorran Haven for a coffee. The Haven Café had a new-fangled machine they'd bought in Italy. It squirted steam through milk to froth it up. They called it espresso, but it was actually cappuccino. The noise of that machine still rings in my ears, reminding me of warmth and cheer after a headlong hike through driving rain across the Gruda.

When the Grose's grew too old, they sold their last fields to the National Trust in 1966 and moved to *Trenare* (my idea for a name) on Ruanhighlanes, to be near their now married daughter, Betty Julian. We found somewhere to stay in Mevagissey. First we stayed at the Headlands 'Hotel' at the top of Polkirt Hill, and then at Valley Park.

My most memorable experience at the Headlands was the mad sailor. The hotel had an annex with its own front door, which must have been left unlocked. I had the ground-floor bedroom with my sister Barbara upstairs. I woke in the middle of the night to be confronted

Elsie Tresidder (née Garden)
(1871-1950), the painter

John and Edith Grose, farmers
at Penare and Penquarry

Above Gorran Haven by Elsie Tresidder

---

1.   *John Nicholas Grose (1883-1968) [NR] married Mildred Edith Williams (1886-1976) [NR] in 1913.*
2.   *Gladys Betty Grose (1918-1986) [NR] married John F Julyan (1912-2007) [NR] in 1940.*
3.   *Michael Ian Burton (b1960).*

Valley Park, Mevagissey

John & Ann Harrison with Doll Gibson

Daily Express, 24 June 1964

by a slim young man in his twenties standing at the bedroom door, lecturing me in a guttural Eastern European language. By the door was the light pull, like in bathrooms. To stress what he was saying, and he was fairly stressed, he would pull the light cord on and off. The strobe effect has been more usually associated with Blackpool rather than Mevagissey at four in the morning. As I tried to calm him down, the volume increased. As the volume increased, and on and off went the light with more venom than the lighthouse in the harbour. Eventually the noise of the one-way conversation roused Barbara who woke my parents, and the lad was ushered away. He was last seen early that morning, by PC Plod, wandering down Polkirt Hill in his pyjamas. He was apprehended and taken back to his ship in Fowey. Was he being badly treated, missing his family or seeking asylum? I didn't speak the language.

Valley Park was much more salubrious. We stayed there each Easter from about 1969 to 1976, the year my mother died[iii]. The large house and grounds nestled behind the harbour with the access halfway up Tregony Hill on the hair-pin bend. Turning into Tregony Hill from Fore Street still presents a problem to this day – *wouldn't have it any different, now, would 'ee, my lovely?* The guest house had been extended. The grand staircase in the games room was supposed to have come from an Armada galleon, though it looked in too good a condition to have been sunk in battle. The lounge had a huge stone chimney-breast, which I copied in a small way for my cottage in Pentewan. The Harrisons who ran it (John, Ann and sister Doll) had come from Twickenham after being bombed out of Coventry in World War II[4]. John had been a draughtsman in the car factories – on the wall was a delightful painting of the golden stupas done during his war service in Burma.

✳ ✳ ✳ ✳

Bouncing Bombs

Ann and Doll were in the WRAF but applied their culinary arts wherever they went. Their family, the Gibson's, English 'White Russians', had moved back from Moscow when the Revolution took hold. Their businessman father lost all his shares, factories and property in 1917. The Gibsons were brought up in Porthleven alongside cousins, whose father was in the Forestry service in Simla, India. One of these, Guy Gibson, led the 'Dam Busters' raid, which broke the Mohne and Edersee dams and flooded the Ruhr valley, destroying the German war production[5]. Flying through heavy anti-aircraft fire, he delivered the 'bouncing bombs' devised by Barnes Wallace[6].

I once organised a Brain's Trust ('Question Time') and invited Sir Barnes Wallace to sit on the panel – he agreed – he had sent his sons to my school *Dauntsey's*. They were there before my time but one of Lord Tedder's sons was at school at the same time as me. Lord Tedder had been Eisenhower's deputy in the D Day landings and Operation Overlord[7]. Tedder was Chairman of the School Governors. Richard, his son, organised the infamous Food Strike[8]. I was Head of the 'Food Committee' of the 'School Council' while he was its President and as such was part of this minor revolution, which is still being re-evaluated in the bars of West

4. *John Rae Harrison (1909-1993) [NR] married Nancy Violet (Ann) Gibson (1909-2000) [NR] in 1937; Gwendoline Natalie (Doll) Gibson (1913-2000) [NR].*

5. *Wing Commander Guy Penrose Gibson VC DSO DFC (1918-1944) [NR] died in active service, aged 24, after 170 operations. Operation Chastise was carried out on 16–17 May 1943 by Royal Air Force No. 617 Squadron. He lived for a time at South View, Porthleven.*

6. *Sir Barnes Neville Wallis, CBE FRS RDI FRAeS (1887-1979) [NR].*

7. *Marshal of the Royal Air Force Arthur William Tedder, 1st Baron Tedder GCB (1890-1967) [NR] served as the Deputy Supreme Commander at Supreme Headquarters Allied Expeditionary Force under General (later President) Dwight David Eisenhower (1890-1969) [NR].*

8. *Prof Hon Richard S Tedder FRCP (b1946) [NR].*

Lavington, if nowhere else. The food was cheap, repetitive and boring. My main gripe was the way it was served. The two ex-sea cooks scooped the chips onto the plates with their greasy hands – probably crucial on the high seas but to this day I am not a fan of TV chefs (or anyone else) 'plating up' with their fingers.

In those days, the whole school sat down together. Richard stood at one door and I stood at the other. The word was out, and so the strike began. The duty housemaster said grace and we all sat down[9]. The kitchen staff brought out the food. Armfuls of it. Plates piled high with ground-meat pie. I can still see the lovely Fred Kelly, more than mightily challenged at the best of times, wandering up and down the aisles with plates of food which he could not deposit on the tables. Every time he tried, he was frustrated. Never in his life had he ever taken anything back to the counter. After a repeat performance for the second course, rice pudding, my housemaster stood up to say the final grace: "For what I have received may you be truly thankful."

There was a Governors' enquiry. They had to do something, for it had reached national press. William Hickey was on the case. I wonder who told him? The cooks were given the sack and the food has been great ever since. Richard was leaving that year but I had to die another day. Probably out of sympathy, the school elected me its President in his place.

※ ※ ※ ※

The Jago's

Mevagissey wasn't packed with too many people at Easter time. We enjoyed a semi-private existence at Valley Park with full evening meals and bar billiards in the games room afterwards. Drinks in the lounge before dinner were better than going to the Crown at St Ewe. It meant I didn't have to freeze in the car whilst the rest imbibed inside – I was underage and not allowed in. It is only recently that Cornish landlords have acquired the people skills needed to deal with families and children.

My sister Barbara introduced her new husband, Ian, to Valley Park. Being an outdoor sort of fellow, he liked to have a walk before breakfast. One morning, he didn't return at the usual time. Not only had he missed breakfast, he didn't appear for several hours. Just as we were starting to get really worried, he walked in through the door. The reason? Trying to brush it off as a minor detail, he was in fact pretty shaken up. He'd been stuck down a hole on the cliff path. He'd missed his footing and had dropped more than six feet. As he stared down, with the waves beneath his feet, his life passed before his eyes. How would he die? Battered on the cliffs? Drowned in the sea or would it be a lingering death from never being discovered? It was early. It was that time of year. There was no one around. Finally, he summoned up all the super-human strength that only Ian had. He pulled himself out of a hole – literally.

That year, the Harrisons received a letter from an Australian who'd visited Mevagissey the year before, one **Reginald Cory Jago**[10]. His forebears had lived in that same house, *Valley Park*. His story, how true I don't know, was that the family had once owned Mevagissey harbour. One night, probably during the Regency period, one of his forebears had gambled away the harbour to the Duke of Buckingham.

Jago – my mother knew of Jago's in her family. Perhaps we were related? We set off towards the Records Office in Truro which proved that we were. This was my first foray into family history.

50 Hallam Avenue
Lane Core 2066
NSW Australia

4 Sep 1969

Dear Mr Harrison

During my recent visit to England I called to see Valley Park, home of my grandparents which I had visited in my young days, the last occasion being 60 years ago. As promised I am sending a copy of the history of the family which my father set me in about 1916, with the exception of the last portion which I filled in, in red ink; so when you are reading it you must imagine my father is telling you the story. Instead of Valley Park being built about 100 years ago as stated in your brochure I would imagine it is nearer 200 years old. I can trace it back over 100. My sister has a photo of my father's grandparents taken over 100 years ago at Valley Park and one of my parents, myself, sister and brother taken in 1896, which I gave my sister recently. From the history and names given in my father's record you may be able to trace something more regarding the age of the old house.

I enjoyed my visit to see you and the chat we had, in fact the whole my visit to England was a memorable occasion, especially seeing my brother and sister after 57 years,

With kindest regards to yourself, your wife and Miss Gibson.

Yours sincerely

Reginald Cory Jago

John Sampson Jago
(1824-1889)

---

9.   David Duncan Burgess (1932-2008) [NR].
10.   Reginald Cory Jago (1891-1970).

Corran Farm, Gorran Highlanes, looking towards Heligan

Anne Jago née Courtis (1828-1909) and her daughter Annie (1851-1909) c1862

Richard Southwell Courtis (1795-1870)

Selina Courtis (1834-1896)

Ancient West Country Families in Exeter Museum records that the Jago's of Mevagissey and St Ewe were descended from a John Jago of Gorran and St Ewe. Tracking through the Jago's was interesting. There were some notorious clergy in the 17th century. One Robert Jago, Vicar of Wendron, was known for 'laying ghosts'. It didn't help that they all had the same name. Generations of our Jago's were called John Sampson Jago. A John Sampson Jago married a daughter of Nicholas Cory, vicar of Fowey[11]. Their son, also **John Sampson Jago**, was a Lieutenant RN at the time of Nelson[12]. His son, also John Sampson Jago, married one of the Mayor of Falmouth's, daughters, **Anne Courtis**, and settled at *Corran*, the farm off Gorran *Highlanes* adjoining Heligan[13]. He farmed 218 acres with the help of 4 men and 2 women. It was his grandson, **Reginald Jago**, who wrote the letter[14].

It was the Mayor of Falmouth who interested me. **Richard Southwell Courtis** has a tremendous ring to his name[15]. I discovered that my great grandfather, Surgeon-General John Nicholas Tresidder, married another of his daughters, **Emily Courtis**. There were three other daughters. **Ellen** married Dr Griffin and moved to Devon; **Caroline** married Rev Humphry Lowry Barnicoat, the Vicar of Landrake and St Erney near St Germans. **Selina** the youngest didn't marry. She lived at Tregerrick, also in Gorran Highlanes[16]. During the 1860s, my great grandfather returned to Falmouth and photographed people there, including the relatives you see on these pages.

Jean, my mother wrote to Reginald Jago and had a fulsome letter back. Sadly, he died the following year. When the naval lieutenant's eldest son, the one in the picture overleaf, died in Valley Park, Selina moved in with her sister Anne and daughter Annie, seen in the first picture.

✳ ✳ ✳ ✳

Jean's love for for Cornwall was innate. She knew no family there. She vaguely knew something of her ancestry. Her mother, the artistic Elsie, had been drawn there by the light but Elsie came from the Lake District. Jean was refreshed by the uncomplicated honesty of the Cornish people. She kept up a written correspondence with Edith Grose. It was only when she was aged 65 that she found a close family connection nearby. That stimulated me.

---

11. *John Sampson Jago (1754-1835) married Susanna Cory (1755-1823) in 1787.*
12. *Lt John Sampson Jago RN (1794-1871) Owner of 228 acres employing 5 men and 2 boys in 1861*
13. *John Sampson Jago (1824-1889) a Plymouth merchant, married Anne Courtis (1828-1909) in 1850.*
14. *Arundell Edward Cory Jago (1860-1931).*
15. *Dick (Richard Southwell) Courtis (1795-1870) married Nancy Hooton (1798-1835) in 1824. Their children were: Ellen (1824-1896), Annie (1828-1909), Caroline (1829-1911) Emily (1830-1917) and Selina (1834-1896), Nancy may have died after complications of the last childbirth.*
16. *The Rev Humphry Lowry Barnicoat (1820-1893) was brother of John Nicholas Tresidder's first wife Elizabeth Barnicoat (1816-1855). Humphry married Caroline Courtis (1829-1911) in 1853. She was John Nicholas Tresidder's second wife's sister.*

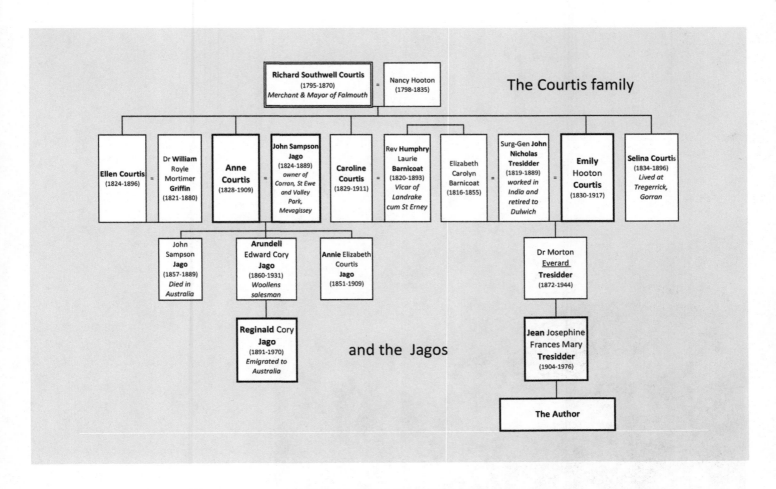

The Courtis family

Richard Southwell Courtis (1795-1870) *Merchant & Mayor of Falmouth* = Nancy Hooton (1798-1835)

Ellen Courtis (1824-1896) = Dr **William** Royle Mortimer **Griffin** (1821-1880)

Anne Courtis (1828-1909) = **John Sampson Jago** (1824-1889) *owner of Corran, St Ewe and Valley Park, Mevagissey*

Caroline Courtis (1829-1911)

Rev **Humphry** Laurie **Barnicoat** (1820-1893) *Vicar of Landrake cum St Erney* = Elizabeth Carolyn Barnicoat (1816-1855)

= Surg-Gen **John Nicholas Tresidder** (1819-1889) *worked in India and retired to Dulwich* = **Emily** Hooton **Courtis** (1830-1917)

Selina Courtis (1834-1896) *Lived at Tregerrick, Gorran*

John Sampson **Jago** (1857-1889) *Died in Australia*

Arundell Edward Cory **Jago** (1860-1931) *Woollens salesman*

Annie Elizabeth Courtis **Jago** (1851-1909)

Dr Morton Everard **Tresidder** (1872-1944)

Reginald Cory **Jago** (1891-1970) *Emigrated to Australia*

and the Jagos

Jean Josephine Frances Mary **Tresidder** (1904-1976)

The Author

Looking towards Nare Head with the Dodman in the distance

Other Notes and References

i. *The Haskins stayed with Mrs W E Richards at Tregenna Farm near Portholland in Summer 1947 and with the Groses in Easter 1948.*

ii. *National Trust Properties, 1961, p45: 58.7ha were given anonymously to the National Trust (NT) in 1919. 20.6ha were sold to the NT in 1943. A further 32.4ha including Lower Penare Farm were sold in 1964-66.*

iii. *Except 1970, when the author was studying for exams. He stayed after that on his own a couple of times before the Harrisons retired and then stayed at Trenare with Betty Julyan.*

Looking over Gorran Haven toward
Mevagissey, by Elsie Tresidder

The Lost House of Heligan

In the 1960s, my mother had two propositions to acquire houses in Cornwall. My father wasn't interested but I urged her on and she felt tempted – after all, one was a Round House in Veryan – offered to her one day in the Ship Inn, Portloe, for £50! Another was near Bodmin at Nanstallon (with a lovely church beautified by the Tractarians.) Neither house was suitable for someone so far from home, in days of poor roads, with all sorts of work to do – sewerage, water and electricity supplies. Before she died, I had taken up that passion. I was nearly 30, working in Croydon, living at home and it was high time I entered the property ladder.

We looked round *Heligan* together – the mansion house had just been converted into flats. The garden was a wilderness. After the First World War, when the Tremayne family had no direct successors, the place went downhill and the furniture was sold[1]. The dining room table and the red velvet dining chairs found their way to the 'parlour' of *Penare*, and later to Penquarry, the house where we stayed in Cornwall.

John Grose, the farmer, thought it a bit of a folly and left his wife Edith to fetch them home from the other end of Gorran Highlanes. She physically carried the chairs, two at a time, dropping them and going back for the next two, and so on, all the way home to Penare. The hour and a half walk took much longer that day.

It wasn't until Tim Smit arrived on the scene in 1990, with John Nelson, that Heligan gardens began to be won back from nature[2]. Up until then the grounds had been lying undisturbed, with only the knowledgeable locals haunting it. Tim had money, sense, time and enthusiasm. He provided the magic touch while John provided the building skills, which they coupled with the commitment of countless volunteers. Tim Smit went on to do something rather larger and more ambitious, the Eden Project, sometimes described as the 'eighth wonder of the world'. With loans, lottery money and the architect Nicholas Grimshaw, he transformed an old China Clay pit[3]. His two geodesic 'Biomes', which are based on a concept conceived by Buckminster Fuller, hold a rainforest in one and in the other a Mediterranean eco-climate. Featured in the James Bond movie *Die Another Day*, it is a rather more permanent outpost of the 'climate change' lobby than the Earth Centre in Doncaster that I was involved in[i].

It was my father's youngest cousin who persuaded me to buy. **Barbara** and **Bryan Kay** featured in the last chapter. I visited them in their retirement in Pentewan in Cornwall. Bryan went to Pennsylvania to help his daughter Susan build a chalet and never came back[4]. Sadly, on his first night there, he got up to go to the bathroom and fell through the unfinished stairwell. When the grief was finally over, I stayed with Barbara Kay. She proposed I should buy the cottage next door and introduced me to its owner. Providence stepped in. The vendor's name was made up of the first names of each of my parents combined - *Jean Paul*. I had to buy it. Barbara Kay lived next door for the rest of her life, pleading with me not to sell it in 1990 when we returned from Hong Kong.

I had a limited budget. Every surface, inside and out, had been painted magnolia and I had to make it my own. I began with the beams, which I painted black and decorated them with

Round Houses c1815 stand guard at each entrance to the village of Veryan to ward away evil – crosses on the roof and round so the devil has no place to hide.

Heligan House, near Mevagissey – built in 1692 in the William and Mary style with Victorian extensions, it was divided into flats 1971-74.

Eden Project biomes (Tropical and Mediterranean with café in the centre) opened in 2001.

Barbara and Bryan Kay outside their cottage in Pentewan c1977

---

1. *John Tremayne [NR] died in 1901 and his wife Mary Charlotte Martha neé Vivian [NR] died in 1917.*
2. *Sir Timothy Bartel Smit KBE (b1954) [NR]; Michael (John) Nelson (1939-2014) [NR].*
3. *Sir Nicholas Grimshaw KB CBE PPRA FIAA RIBA (b1939) [NR].*
4. *Susan Hester Kay (b1948) married Adrian Corbett (b1955) in 1999. Farm was at Wyalusing, north Pennsylvania.*

North Road, Pentewan

my Grandmother Elsie's pewter pots. Then I gutted the fireplace. As I knocked out the painted bricks, I threw them out of the window into the front garden. Not a lot happens in North Road, so the older residents came to watch, mostly old ladies, all now dead. There were the Barbery family (what an evocative name) whose forbears had bought cottages in 'the Row'. Vera Mills, two doors away, agreed to hold my door key – she'd been brought up at the end of the road[5]. Her father had been the village postman. She told me that my cottage had been an alehouse. She'd married a Mevagissey man (Mills is a Welsh name. Welsh coal miners came to Cornwall to mine for tin.) In her early married days, Vera had lived in Valley Park for a time. When my fireplace was finished, I invited all those people to a Housewarming party. The Harrisons came and their friend, Phyllis Kendall, who was the dowager of Bodrugan Farm (one of the Jago boys married a Kendall.)[6] She brought her silver teapot.

Some thirty-odd horse brasses later (one for every year), I am still in love with Cornwall. Here I am, putting down for posterity some of my memories, adding in facts I didn't know, weaving a tapestry of a colourful family which has one or two bright spots amongst its pastel shades.

Pentewan, Cornwall

Other Notes and References

1. Richard Buckminster Fuller (1895-1983) [NR] was a designer and independent thinker possessed of a 'world view'. The Earth Centre, funded by Millennium Commission and European funding lasted from 2001-4. Die Another Day was filmed in 2002.

5. Vera Louise Beard (1907-1995) [NR] married Fearnley Nicholls Mills (1906-1949) [NR] in 1938.
6. Frances Phyllis Trewhella (1905-1995) married Leonard Kendall (1899-1968) in 1930.

Cauldron of History

The Introduction to this book mentioned *Asketil* and '*God's Cauldron*'. Whatever the origins of my surname, the *ketil* has bubbled away throughout these pages covering many strands of my heritage. The dance is nearly over.

As the steam has risen from that ancestral cooking pot, the memories have quickened my mind. I can almost smell the Cornish cream thickening on the hotplate, the farmyard manure outside, the disinfectant permeating the military hospital, the pungent odours of a Dickensian street. I almost hear the blackbird's warbling song, the chime of the school bell, the chisel on stone, the rumble of a horse-drawn buggy on the beaten earth. I sense the heat radiating off the burning African veldt ....

Even as I drive down the high-banked Cornish lanes or survey an incarnadine sea, as my croquet ball aquaplanes across the dew, as I count the cash on the dining room table, or dress up as a Chinese potentate, there's a shiver down my spine .... Are these familiar sensations inherited, much like physical characteristics? The Chinese believe they are.

✻ ✻ ✻ ✻

Nature or Nurture?

There's a book entitled *The Son Also Rises*. It's a dense tome. What it says, however, challenges politicians who advocate equality of opportunity. It claims that throughout history – 16th century rural China or modern Metro-America; that whatever their policies – universal franchise, emancipation of women, comprehensive education, the NHS or the welfare state etc; that whatever one's wealth, or income or longevity, there is a magic formula – the surname. The pages of evidence measure samples of surnames over a dozen generations and conclude that, 'Social position is likely to be determined by innate inherited ability ... i.e. what we're born with – skills, energy, ambition, stamina, self-esteem and resilience.'[1]

The Son Also Rises generalises – whereas, in this book, for example, the Seccombes from Grampound and the Stephens from Scotland start as poor farmers and end up as knights of the realm. A mix of the gene pool and upbringing play their part ... but, if the *The Son Also Rises* is correct, the Haskins surname may take up to twelve generations, 300-450 years, to change its place in society.

In my case, dyslexia, numerical skills, thinking deeply and strategically; problem-solving and overcoming set-backs may be linked to my blood relatives. Physical traits, like sticky-out teeth, 'laid-back' posture, go-to-bed eyes ('Dreamboat' as the school's housekeeper Mrs Hopkins nicknamed me – what was she thinking?) and colour blindness; all inherited. Then there's the wandering mind, the going off at tangents, the mumbling, the hoarding, the muddle ... not forgetting the self-determination which is interpreted by those who like me as decisiveness and by those who don't as stubbonness; those must surely be inherited. Being charming one minute and grumpy the next – that certainly is.

The Son Also Rises would say that these traits have kept me in a social status similar to my parents. The Haskins surname has improved its standing only a little since the 1800s when they were immigrant artisans running their own business. I recall times when, if I'd played my cards differently, I could have soared – social situations, work opportunities – but I didn't; I somehow reverted to the norm.

Kindness is inherited from the Haskins family. Talking straight, a Cornish characteristic. Creativeness must come from the Garden side (Chapters 9 & 10). Short-term memory and speed of action I don't possess. In the next generation that will stem from my wife Carolyn's side.

Still no eyebrows. The author, aged 12.

Let still the woman take an elder than herself; so wears she to him, so sways she level in her husband's heart. For, boy, however do we praise ourselves, our fancies are more giddy and unfirm, more longing, wavering, sooner lost and worn than women's are.

Twelfth Night Act II Scene 4

It is a good idea to understand your innate strengths and weaknesses before you go too far in life. It might help your partner find out how best to cope with you. My father used to say to my future wife, "Don't expect to change him." Some of us stay being quirky. Some years ago I took a *Myers-Briggs* psychometric test[ii]. Amongst the many aspects (some too personal to mention) it discovered that I prefer logic and fair play, that I warm to those who have standards and respect deadlines. Because like many Cornish I like straight-talking (both ways), please don't take offence if I confront you directly about something. And just so you don't get the wrong end of the stick, and to be on the safe side, it's best to replay back to me what I've just said. Clever, these tests. Spot on, but not the whole answer. There's nurture as well as nature.

So what about upbringing? I have been blessed by not being brought up in the settings that some children are born into. Acute poverty or luxurious neglect; ignorance; pretension, or fuss; cruelty or coldness; sensation, sanctimony, hypocrisy or pettifogging dictate – I was lucky to avoid these. I didn't get beaten or abused. Smothered by love, perhaps. I went to a broadminded school which brought out the best in me. It encouraged freedom of thought, co-operation and service. It gave me self-confidence beyond my family traits. College with a girlfriend of the time brought out the analytical intellect[1]. No one taught me to make false compliments. And I had jobs that allowed me early on to exercise responsibility.

Pierre Bourdieu, the philosopher and sociologist, says that I am/we are defined not just by social class. It's not just about how much money I own (*economic* capital). I am shaped by every other sort of 'capital', *cultural, social,* and *academic*. My education, the groups I associated with, the civil service and armed forces for example, are 'social spaces' moulding my cultural attitudes and demeanour *('hexis')* such as accent, intonation, volume, gestures, diet. Indeed, how I smile, how I blow my nose, spit or fart; how I shine my shoes, hold my knife and fork, shake hands; the state of my fingernails, and my 'taste' in music, art or architecture, I've grown up inside a set of deep-seated unconscious beliefs and values *('doxa')*, which instinctively put me at ease in certain social networks. However, I suspect I've inherited a gene that 'ruptures' some of them. Whether it's seeking to question everything, like teaching in an East End overflow school, well out of my comfort zone, joining the unconventional 'Tadpoles' Society, marrying outside my social space, or 'stepping outside the box' in other ways, is it the 'non-conformist' *Huss kins* gene which stops me relaxing?

Marrying someone above one's social status helps in the surname stakes but Charles Haskins took a few knocks as a consequence and most other Haskins have avoided this risk. Many of my ancestors married late to younger brides. My great-grandmothers were 4, 9, 12 and 23 years younger than their husbands – however, most of us have found someone who's more screwed on than us. I was fortunate to find a wife nine years younger than me who has been able to manage my foibles. Carolyn and I are different in so many ways, yet she has an amazing ability to stay in balance and keep me straight. Was it because she came from a stable Yorkshire family or went to a grammar school? She has one leading advantage over me: no heavy expectations or stressful ambitions to join a legion of high-achieving ancestors.

So where did my unusual personality come from? My mother's eccentric friends? My liberal schooling? Or those ancestors?

❋ ❋ ❋ ❋

1.   *Catherine Anne Plummer (b1949) [NR]. Anne's sister Mary married an eccentric second son of Lord Longford.*

The future

A hundred years ago Hildebrand's, a chocolate firm, produced a series of forecasts[iii]. These included moving walkways (which we now call escalators), a theatre in your own home (TV), undersea boats (submarines) and a device to see through clothes and walls (X-rays). Too wacky said some but they sold lots of chocolate. Here are my 'fruit and nutty' ideas for the next 100 years, from the 'almost there' to the 'almost impossible':

- 'Internet of things' – the whole house and body is controllable from your smart phone
- 3D printers
- Reusable rockets (Elon Musk).
- Parcels delivered by drones (à la Hogwarts' owls)
- Controlled Nuclear Fusion, which leaves no nuclear waste and has no carbon impact
- Cars powered by hydrogen – or even water (separating out the H from the H_2O molecule)
- Artificial intelligence – algorithms that allow computers to think independently
- Chemical computers
- Perfect thought-transmission – as the Pollexfens had once believed[iv]
- Reforestation of the Sahara Desert – preventing world extinction[v]
- Living to 969 years[vi]

Not so nutty. Scientists are already working on most of these.

What of Britain's place in the world? The nation-state may well have risen in importance when Henry VIII declared his own 'Brexit' from Europe but it wasn't until the Regency period with William Pitt, Wellington and the East India Company, smarting from the loss of America, that the country secured any real significance through a network of captive markets world-wide. The British Empire was as its height the year my father was born but it was soon living on borrowed time – two world wars exhausted much of its capital. It may still have the fifth largest economy (once it was first) but average individual earning power in the UK (GDP per capita) is 27th in the world, below Hong Kong[vii]. What of the future? Its strengths were in the mastery of the seas, now dispersed, its natural resources, much of it closed down, and a fighting spirit, now frowned upon. Instead we survive on a services industry, a capacity for invention and a sense of fairness. Will they be enough to secure Britain's strength?

The wealth divide has been growing wider. I wonder whether continued polarisation, with an absence of faith, hope, or love, will result in social unrest not seen in England since William Wilberforce. Middle-order jobs are likely to be replaced by technology. I wonder when the middle classes will be squeezed out. As the UK's North-South divide grows larger, so does the health gap between rich and poor, despite the NHS being free at the point of service – and how long will that be for?[viii] Unbelievably, 85 individuals own more than that owned by 50% of the world's population[ix]. The number of millionaires in Britain has increased by 12% in one year alone[x]. The top 10% of the population owns 75% of the wealth and the other 90% owns 25%[xi]. Only 38% of 25-34 year olds owned their own homes in 2015-16, a 32% drop on the number ten years before[xii]. That number has been forecast to plummet to 16% by 2019-20[xiii]. Overseas investors are pushing out first-time UK buyers[xiv]. The greater the size of the private rental market, the fewer the chances to buy. Yet Property ownership and social status will always go hand in hand.

Ethos anthropos oaimon

Your character is your destiny

Heraclitus

What about your place in this world? My thoughts are Cornish. Will my descendants hold on to their Cornish roots? Or will they become economic migrants like the Gardens and Grants? Or move to America and back like the Genn's, or to Africa and back like the Wiggins, or to New Zealand and stay, like the Barnicoats and Morleys? Do these places offer more permanency? Not for me.

✳ ✳ ✳ ✳

There is no perfect life lived on this earth, just as there is no perfect golf swing.

Fred Haskins, golfer

Lessons of History

Fred Haskins the golfer who ended up in America said, 'After many years of searching, I reasoned that there is only an individual secret for each of us to find, and no secret as that will accomplish the goals for everyone in general. Everyone has to find his success best he can. There is no absolute way to do it. We're all different and react in different ways. There is no perfect life lived on this earth, just as there is no perfect golf swing.'[xv] However, like Dickens and some others have said, 'Those who fail to learn the lessons of history are destined to repeat the same mistakes.'[xvi] So here are some thoughts after stirring the cauldron one last time:

- Opportunities are precious. They come in unexpected forms, so be prepared. Anticipate. Like glowing Caribbean sunsets, full of reds and oranges, they don't happen that often, and they don't last for long. Seize the moment and say yes. But don't over-worry if you miss it: the world keeps revolving. There will be another glorious sunset, sometime.
- Over the generations, despite our genes, education has created opportunities and new attitudes. Opt for the teachers you prefer over the subject-matter, teachers who have a passion for their subject, who know it so well they can engage, challenge and intrigue you; who see your potential and maximise it, who give you genuine respect, those who have enlightened discipline and imaginative flair[xvii]. In the end it's about '*cultural*' attitudes.
- Do you think 'events happen to you' or do 'you change the world'? Be the latter like the Wiggins. For example, when the banking system developed thanks to the extravagant spending of George IV (ably assisted by Elizabeth Denison), the Elliotts and Freshfields exploited these new opportunities. Driven by the internet and globalisation, the financial system is in the process of being altered again out of all proportion. Banking as we know it is being replaced by FinTech, electronic trades, bit-coinage, peer-to-peer lending, crowd-funding; and world economics are no longer successfully controlled by individual governments. Investment involves risk. Investing spare resources is less risky. However, never use the equity in your home to invest in a business proposition. And buy a home you like, not as an investment.
- Managing money is important. Honesty goes hand in hand with good analytical skills. It's an attitude of mind, self-confidence and a correct assessment of situations and others. Like Micawber, live within your means[xviii]. Keep capital and revenue separate. Build capital. The semi-socialist 20th century ironically enabled the Haskins family (and others) to acquire freehold 'capital'. Hold onto it. William Joseph Denison told us to invest in property and never to part with it. It may not always come so easy. Bequeath your possessions to the next generation (and the one beyond).
- The power of patronage speeds success. Whether it be others helping you, or you helping others. Ultimately, though, it's you who'll make the difference. So be charitable and be magnanimous in victory[xix]. 'Authority' comes after you have earned 'respect', not the other way round. You can squeeze people so far: too far and they mutiny. Teamwork makes the dream work. Enemies have long memories. Being nice is not everything, as Frederick Evans found out, but it helps.
- Luck has a part to play, but you can plan for when luck comes your way. Lucky people

don't prevaricate or even aim for a rational decision; they back their hunches, secure in their *hexis*. If you can get into a mind-set that allows you to act confidently at speed, trust your intuition. Construct a social environment round your own disposition, your *habitus*[xx]. Of course, lucky people are busy people who leave the past behind, so they probably aren't reading this.

If we can live a little 'beyond ourselves' – whether it be Jean Haskins's ambition for a happy family, or the industry of Joseph Haskins; James Garden's craftsmanship or Douglas Smart's spatial skills; Willie Hodson's intuition or William Wand's God-given authority; William Thomas Haskins' polymath approach and, like Ann Gates and Renée Burton, a talent to inspire; John Nicholas Tresidder's sensitive concern for others, Ken Burton's sense of humour, Clare Wiggins's moral endeavour, Paul Haskins' integrity and analysis; or the organisational skills of Barbara Simpson and William Wiggins – can we attempt to give something more to the world than it had before we entered it?

Or, as one Bishop of London put it: "It is the 'attitude of mind' that is important. It's our instinctive reaction, or what dictates that reaction, that really matters …. On it depends in large measure our happiness or misery, our energy or sloth, our 'sense of being wanted' or loneliness amounting to despair."[xxi] As another Bishop of London said, "The ingredients of our civil society, our economy, our democratic institutions have to include truth-telling, mutual sympathy and inter-dependence – we all need to live 'beyond ourselves' …. The dominant note … after the memories is hope."[xxii]

This book will add to your memories. It's up to you how you handle hope.

> *It is our inner state of mind which is of first importance, not the estimate we put on things, but our instinctive reaction, or what dictates that reaction, that really matters."*
>
> William Wand

Caribbean sunset

Other Notes and References

i.   *Clark & others p15.*

ii.   *Some 50 years old, Katherine Briggs (1875–1968) [NR] and Isabel Myers (1897-1980) [NR] based their indicator on the theories of Carl Jung. The Myers & Briggs Foundation is based in Florida, USA. The author is an 'ENTJ'.*

iii.   *Hildebrand's Chocolates. c1900.*

iv.   *Murphy, Family Secrets, p386.*

v.   *Life Scientific, Episode 7, BBC Radio 4: Prof Georgina Mace, author of the Red list of Threatened Species, believes there is evidence of the planet being on the edge of a mass extinction, which will be world-wide and caused by people.*

vi.   *Methuselah's age in Genesis 5v27 was 969.*

vii.   *International Monetary Fund's World Economic Outlook database Oct 2015 – GDP per capita. http://www.imf. org/external/ns/cs.aspx?id=28 accessed 6 Oct 2015. Maddison p382 Table A7 shows UK as 1st in 20 major countries in the world for GDP per capita in 1870, 2nd in 1913 (USA cereal exports had damaged the UK) and 10th in 2003.*

viii.   *viz work of Profs Marmot (Queen Mary College, London) and Mayhew (Cass Business School)*

ix.   *Global Wealth Report 2013 and Forbes' The World's Billionaires as reported by Oxfam 2014*

x.   *Independent 8 Jun 2016. UK had 961,000 millionaires in 2015.*

xi.   *Office for National Statistics quoted by The Times 16 May 2014. In UK, the top 10% currently own 44% of the nation's capital and the bottom 50% own 9%. In Europe 1910, the top 10% owned 90% and the bottom 50% owned 5%. Piketty Table 7.2 p248, and Table 10.3 p344.*

xii.   *English Housing Survey 2016-17. A 34% drop to 37.3% from 10 years before, when home ownership by 25-34 year-olds was 56.5%. 45.7% of 25-34 yr olds are renting in the private sector, a 68% increase over 10 years previously.*

xiii.   *Hudson.*

xiv.   *Times 7 Apr 2017 quoting Valentine: 'Asian owners dominate new-build developments in East London and at One Cambridge Street Manchester.' 'Qatar now owns more of London than the Crown Estate.' 'The British, still accustomed to think of themselves as owners, are, in reality, increasingly a nation of tenants.'*

xv.   *Hyatt p222.*

xvi.   *'To be ignorant of the past is to remain ever the child.' Cicero BC46. 'People will not look forward to posterity, who never look backward to their ancestors.' Edmund Burke. 1729. 'It's in vain ... to recall the past, unless it works some influence upon the present.' Charles Dickens. 1849. 'Those who cannot remember the past are condemned to repeat it.' George Santayana 1905.*

xvii.   *Hattie: A synthesis of studies of some 80 million students supports this contention. It concludes that positive teacher-student interaction is the most important factor in effective teaching.*

xviii.   *Wilkins Micawber in David Copperfield by Charles Dickens said: "Annual income twenty pounds, annual expenditure nineteen pounds nineteen and six, result happiness. Annual income twenty pounds, annual expenditure twenty pounds nought and six, result misery." Dickens's father spent time in a debtor's prison.*

xix.   *Winston Churchill: 'In war, resolution; in defeat, defiance; in victory, magnanimity.'*

xx.   *Bourdieu.*

xxi.   *Wand, Letters on the Ministry p8.*

xxii.   *Rt Rev Richard John Carew Chartres KCVO FSA PC (b1947) [NR] Funeral oration for Margaret Thatcher 17 April 2013.*

Credits

My thanks to the following:

Andrew Allen – second cousin

Mark Allison – Robson Cruse's buttons and dagger

Susan Benson of the Cumbria Archive and local Studies Centre, Barrow, for introducing me to Walter Johnston and for permission to reproduce images

Birmingham Museums Trust © painting of Elizabeth Denison

Bunyan Meeting and the Rev Christopher Damp

British Library – permission to reproduce illustrations from its collection

Bruce W Clifton, from Australia

Shirley and Allen Garden, deceased, 2nd cousins from New South Wales, Australia,

Ann Gates – sister – family photographs

Ding Guang, Zhejiang University, Hangzhou, China – the Moule Evans brothers in China

Dik Lukman – Cmdr Webber RN

Bruce Edwards, Ravensden - editor

Julia Eales, for starting me on the journey using Ancestry.co.uk

Tony Farrar – illustration of Denby Dale home

Terry Greenwood from Toronto, a distant relation, who explained to me about the corn-millers of Wetherby

Shilpi Goswami Archivist at the Alkazi Foundation for the Arts, Delhi – John Nicholas Tresidder's photograph album which was acquired by the Foundation in 1997, and introducing me to Lorna Tresidder and Dr Sean Wilcock

The Haskins Commission and Paddy Blackmar, daughter of Fred Haskins

Will Hutton, Principal of Hertford College, Oxford – the painting of Rev William Denison DD

Liz Larsson, Manager of the Croquet Association, Cheltenham

Library of Congress, Washington

Michael Harvey, former Curator of Cinematography, National Media Museum, Bradford

Jeremy Irons – photographs of Hill House, Watlington

Walter M Johnston, local historian in Barrow-in-Furness

Susan and Jonathan Kay – second cousins – for their mother's unpublished life story manuscript

Ralph McTell and Cornish friends

Richard Meads – Blue Logic – graphic design

Sheila Mirczuk – starting the assembly of early photographs

Rev Allan Mitchell, Vicar of Dalton-in-Furness

Andrew and Kenneth Morley, 1st cousins by marriage once removed – photographs of the Grants and Morleys in New Zealand

Councillor Gordon Murray – Hamilton House, Dalton

Elise Naish, Collections Manager at Wardown Park Museum, Luton

National Maritime Museum, Greenwich, London © Bombardment of Algiers by George Chambers

National Museums Liverpool, Lady Lever Art Gallery © May Morning on

Magdalen Tower' by William Holman Hunt

Pamela Nottingham, author and lace-maker from Marlow

Northamptonshire Records Office – family photographs etc in Chapter 4

Annie Page – early help with graphic design

Michael Partridge, Archivist of Eastbourne College and the late Bill Bowden of the Eastbourne Local History Society

Husna Tara Prakash – Calcutta and Darjeeling

Mike Pratt, Chairman, Carlton & Chellington Historical Society

Sir Arthur Quiller-Couch Memorial Fund

Royal College of Surgeons of England

University of London Senate Library

Steve McKenna for inviting me to stay with him in Calcutta

Lottie Raby-Smith – 2nd cousin, 3 times removed – photograph of Elizabeth Carlyon Barnicoat

Barbara Simpson – sister – family photographs

Jean Spencer – 1st cousin by marriage – family papers and photographs

Sterling and Francine Clark Art Institute, Williamstown, Massachusetts

Shirley Thomas, lace-maker

Lorna Tresidder – second cousin –painting of J N Tresidder and photograph of his microscope

Sir Hereward and Lady Wake of Courteenhall – photographs and information

Anne Wallbank – photographs of Clare Wiggins and staff in Uganda

Christopher and Geoffrey Wiggins, cousins – Wiggins and Denison genealogy and pictures

Wikicommons/Creative Commons – some photographs are reproduced under licence by GFDL/CC BY-SA

Dr Sean Willcock – on J N Tresidder in India

David Wright – 3rd cousin – the golfing Haskins's

And to my wife, Carolyn for tolerating my wilder wackiness's with patience and good humour.

The Sir Arthur Quiller Couch Memorial Fund

BIBLIOGRAPHY

PRIMARY SOURCES

ARCHIVES

Barrow Records Office

Bedford Records Office

Bodleian Library, Oxford

Cornwall Records Office

The British Library: Boston Spa, Colindale and London Reading Rooms

National Archives

Northamptonshire Records Office

British Library Indian collection, Vibart letters, British India Office Ecclesiastical Returns, Parish register transcripts from the Presidency of Bengal, Delhi Commissioner's Office Mutiny Papers

GRAVESTONES

Charles Elliott, Tattingstone

William Ritchie, St Paul's Cathedral, Kolkata

DIARIES, PAPERS AND LETTERS

(JJFMT) Jean Haskins (née Tresidder): letters, diaries, postcard albums and address books

(EA) Letters from Ethel Allen (neé Tresidder) to Jean Haskins (neé Tresidder)

(EG) Ernest Gedge papers. Bodleian Library.

(GA) Gwendoline Allen's notes 21 Apr 1980

(HGG) H Gordon Garden. A voyage from England to San Francisco 1-15 Feb 1896. Hand-written, unpublished. 1896

(JG) Wills of James and Frances Garden and associated deeds, certificates and papers

(MET) Letters from M Everard Tresidder to his parents from Switzerland 1887-89, and to his future wife Elsie Garden

(NDH) Papers from Nancy Haskins

(PDH) Diaries, Postcard albums and Letters from Paul Denison Haskins to his wife Jean in the Second World War.

(RJH) Letters from Hong Kong and diaries by the author, 1987-1990.

(SPG) Letters from Macao from Simon Gates, 1982-4

Genealogy of the Bernau Family of Stolp. Charles Allan Bernau.

Hoyland, John S and Jessie M. Circular Letter dated 27 Sep 1934

Photograph album of John Nicholas Tresidder (Alkazi Foundation for the Arts, Delhi)

Photograph albums of Everard Tresidder, Jean Haskins (neé Tresidder), Mary Wiggins, Dora Haskins (neé Wiggins), Nancy and Paul Haskins

Pictures of Denisons

PRIVATE COLLECTIONS

Haskins, PD. The diary of P Denison Haskins from 26 July 1921 to 20 Sep 1921, written for the future references of what he expects to be but hopes not to be his last Summer Holidays as a School Boy at Brighton College.

Hatcher, Betty. History of the Wiggins Family compiled for the Rhodesian Branch. Private circulation. c1980.

Kay, Barbara Hester. Manuscript notes of a life. c2010.

Kendon, Margery. Ladies College Goudhurst. (Ashford: Private circulation, 1963)

Wand, William. Letters on the Ministry, c1976.

Wiggins, C A. Early Days in British East Africa and Uganda. (Private publication, 1960, revised with additions 1963)

PUBLISHED WORKS

Arnold, Thomas. Passages in a Wandering Life. (London: Edward Arnold, 1900)

Canning, Charlotte: A Glimpse of the Burning Plain: Leaves from the Indian Journals of Charlotte Canning. (London: Charles Allen., 1986)

Dickens: Interviews and Recollections Vol 1. Edited by Philip Collins. (London: Macmillan Press, 1981)

Forbes-Mitchell, William. The Relief of Lucknow, edited by Michael Edwardes. (London: Folio Society, 1962)

Forbes-Mitchell, William. Reminiscences of the Great Mutiny 1857-59: including the relief, siege, and capture of Lucknow, and the campaigns in Rohilcund and Oude. (London: Macmillan & Co, 1910. First published 1893)

HRH George, Prince of Wales. Memoirs of His Royal Highness the Prince of Wales in three volumes. Vol 1. (London: J F Hughes, 1808)

Frith, W P. My Autobiography and Reminiscences. (London: Richard Bentley & Son, 1888)

Hodson, W S R. Twelve Years of a Soldier's Life in India: being extracts from the letters of the late Major W S R Hodson BA, Trinity College Cambridge, First Bengal European Fusiliers, Commandant of Hodson's Horse, including a personal narrative of the siege of Delhi and Capture of the King and Princes. Second edition, edited by his brother George H Hodson. (London: John W Parker & Son, 1859)

Johnson, W T. Twelve Years of a Soldier's Life from the letters of Maj W T Johnson of the Native Regular Cavalry edited by his widow. (London: A D Innes & Co, 1897)

Knight, Charles. Passages of a Working Life during half a century. (London: Bradbury & Evans, 1865)

Moule, Arthur Evans. Half a century in China. (London: Hodder and Stoughton, 1911)

Napier, Lt-Gen Sir Charles James. Defects Civil and Military of the Indian Government, edited by Lt-Gen Sir William F P Napier (London: Charles Westerton, 1853)

Rees, L E Ruutz. A Personal Narrative of the Siege of Lucknow from its commencement to its relief by Sir Colin Campbell. (London: Longman, Brown, Green, Longmans & Roberts, 1858)

Roberts, F. Letters written during the Indian Mutiny. (London: Macmillan & Co Ltd, 1924)

Roberts, Field-Marshal Lord. Forty-One years in India: from Subaltern to Commander-in-Chief. (London: Richard Bentley & Son,., 1897)

Russell, William Howard. My Diary in India in the year 1858. Vols 1&2. (London: Routledge Warne & Routledge, 1860)

Shepherd, W J. A personal narrative of the outbreak and Massacre at Cawnpore during the Sepoy Revolt of 1857, second edition. (Lucknow: London Printing Press, 1879)

Sherer, John Walter. Thomson, Mowbray. Havelock's March on Cawnpore, 1857: A civilian's notes. (London: Thomas Nelson & Sons, 1910)

Sleeman, W H. Sleeman in Oudh: An abridgement of W H Sleeman's 'A Journey through the Kingdom of Oudh in 1849-50'. Edited with introduction. P D Reeves. (Cambridge: Cambridge University Press, 1971)

Storey, Graham and Tillotson, Kathleen, editors. The Pilgrim edition of Letters of Charles Dickens. (Oxford: Clarendon Press, 1995)

Terry, Ellen. Ellen Terry's Memoirs. Edited by Edith Craig & Christopher St John. (London: Victor Gollancz Ltd, 1933)

Thackeray, William Makepeace: The letters and private papers of William Makepeace Thackeray, edited by Edgar F. Harden. (New York & London: Garland, 1994)

Tresidder, M Everard. Disasters. Pigeon Racing 1912. A conscientious enquiry. (London: The Racing Pigeon Publishing Co Ltd, 1912)

Verney, G l. The Devil's Wind: The Story of the Naval Brigade at Lucknow, from the letters of Edmund Hope Verney and Other Papers concerning the Enterprise of the Ship's Company of HMS Shannon in the Campaign in India 1857-58. (London: Hutchinson, 1956)

Young, Keith. Delhi 1857: Its siege, assault and capture, as given in the diary and correspondence of the late Col Keith Young CB, Judge Advocate-General, Bengal. Norman, Henry Wylie and Yound, Mrs Keith, editors. (London: W & R Chambers Ltd, 1902)

Wand, J W C. Changeful Page: the autobiography of William Wand, formerly Bishop of London. (London: Hodder and Stoughton, 1965)

Yeats, W B. Autobiographies: Reveries over childhood and youth and the Trembling of the Veil. (London, Macmillan and Co, 1926)

SECONDARY SOURCES

NEWSPAPERS

African World and Cape-Cairo Express. 12 Sep 1903.

Allen's Indian Mail, 18 Oct 1851, 15 Apr 1857, 19 May 1857, 2 Jun 1857, 9 Jun 1857, 30 Jun 1857, 15 Jul 1857, 1 Oct 1857, 29 Oct 1857, 16 Nov 1857, 29 Oct 1859

Barrow-in-Furness, Ulverston and District Illustrated 1895; 1896

Bedfordshire Times and Independent, 10 May 1912

Berkshire Chronicle, 26 Sep 1846

The Blackheath Local Guide and District Advertiser. Vol XLIV No 12. Blackheath Press. 1932.

Bombay Times and Journal of Commerce, 19 Dec 1854, 5 Mar 1855, 11 May 1857, 15 Aug 1857, 17 Sep 1859.

Brisbane Courier-Mail, 1 Jan 1934, 6 Oct 1934

Bucks Herald, 11 Jun 1910, 16 Aug 1911, 27 Feb 1915, 14 May 1919

Chelmsford Chronicle, 9 May 1913

Courier-Mail, Brisbane, 1 Jan 1934, 6 Oct 1934

Daily Express, 24 June 1964

Daily Telegraph, 18 Feb 2013, 28 Mar 2013, 7 Sep 2013, 12 Oct 2013, 29 Dec 2013, 5 Apr 2014, 21 Apr 2014, 25 Feb 2016, 29 Mar 2016

Guardian, 12 Oct 2005, 21 Oct 2015

Hindu Patriot, Calcutta, 13 Jan 1873

Launceston Examiner, Tasmania, 19 Jan 1850

London Gazette, 24 Nov 1858, 29 Jun 1877

London Illustrated News, 23 Oct 1869

The Morning Bulletin, Rockhampton, 11 Oct 1945

Once a Week, 1859

Oriental Herald, Jun 1825

Soulby's Ulverston Advertiser and General Intelligencer 25 Dec 1856, 1 Oct 1857, 25 Oct 1860

South China Morning Post 27 Oct 2016

Sunday Times, 23 Nov 2014, 22 Mar 2015

Sydney Morning Herald, 6 Sep 1934

The Times (of London), 16 May 1797, 7 Jun 1858, 7 Jul 1893, 4&8 Mar 1912, 6 Feb 1924, 27 May 2013, 7 Nov 2013, 16 May 2014, 12 Jun 2014, 22 Dec 2015, 24 Dec 2015, 19 Apr 2016, 7 Apr 2017, 22 Sep 2017

Thames Advertiser, 6 Jan 1875

Wall Street Journal 12 Oct 2017

DICTIONARIES AND REFERENCE BOOKS

A Biographical Dictionary of 19th Century Photographers in South and South-East Asia. (India: Gazetteer of Central Asia, 1868)

Bengal Regulations 1851

The Children's Encyclopaedia. Edited by Mee, Arthur. (London: Amalgamated Press, 1908-64)

Complete Peerage of England, Scotland, Ireland, Great Britain and the United Kingdom; Extant, Extinct or Dormant; alphabetically arranged and edited by G E C. (London: George Bell & Sons, 1893)

Crockford's Clerical Directory

A Dictionary of English and Welsh Surnames. Charles Waring Bardsley, revised for the press by his widow. (London: H Frowde, 1901)

Dictionary of Evangelical Biography 1730-1860. Editor: Donald M Lewis. (London: Blackwell, 1995)

Dictionary of National Biography, various editions

Dictionary of nineteenth century journalism. (London: British Library, Academia Press, c2009)

Dulwich College Register 1619-1926. (Dulwich: Alleyn Club, 1926)

The Encyclopaedia of Early Photography. (London: Cassell & Company, 1911)

Encyclopaedia of Nineteenth-Century Photography. (New York & London: Routledge, 2008)

An English-Cornish Dictionary, compiled from the best sources. Fred W P Jago. (London: Simpkin Marshall & Co, 1887)

Harmsworth Encyclopaedia. (London: Amalgamated Press and Thomas Nelson & Son, 1905)

Hobson Jobson: A glossary of colloquial Anglo-India words and phrases, and of kindred terms, etymological, historical, geographical and discursive. Yule, Henry and Burnell, Arthur Coke, Editors. (London: John Murray, 1886)

Kelly's Directory, 1890

'Mannex': A history, topography and directory of Westmorland and the Hundreds of Lonsdale and Amounderness, Leyland and the town of Southport, &c.: with a history of Furness Abbey with Furness and Cartmel in Lancashire and an essay on the geology of the Lake District . P J Mannex & Co. 1866, 1882.

Oxford Dictionary of the Christian Church. Editor: Cross, Prof F L. (London: Oxford University Press, 1957)

Oxford Dictionary of National Biography. Editors: Patten, Robert L and Leary, Patrick. (London: Oxford University Press, 2014-15)

Oxford Convocation 1629.

'Parishes: Falmouth-Fowey', Magna Britannia: volume 3: Cornwall. 1814.

Parishes: Watlington, A History of the County of Oxford: Volume 8: Lewknor and Pyrton hundreds (1964)

Pigot's Directory, 1844 and others

Register of Baptisms, Marriages and Burials of the Parish of Falmouth in the County of Cornwall 1663-1812. Editors: Gay, Susan Elizabeth and Fox, Mrs Howard. (Exeter: Devon & Cornwall Record Society, 1914)

University of London General Register

Whitaker's Almanac

Who's Who

PERIODICALS, REPORTS & TV

Allen, Susan Heuck. American Journal of Archaeology. Vol 106. No 4. Book reviews. Minotaur: Sir Arthur Evans and the Archaeology of Minoan Myth. Archaeology Institute of America. Boston. 2002.

Association of Old Brightonians: List of Members. 1960.

Aspinall, A and Smith, E. Anthony, editors. English Historical Documents, XI, 1783-1832. (New York: Oxford University Press, 1959) Athey, T Whit and Nordveldt, Kenneth. 'Resolving the Placement of Haplogroup I-M223 in the Y-Chromosome Phylogenetic Tree, I-M223.' Journal of Genetic Genealogy 1: p54-55. 2005.

Barton, Nicholas. 'Rise of a Royal Furniture Maker.' Country Life. 10 &17 Feb 1966

Belchem, John (Editor). Liverpool 1800: Culture, Character & History. (Liverpool: Liverpool University Press, 2006)

Berman, Gavin & Dar, Aliyah. Prison Population Statistics. SN/SG/4334. (London: House of Commons Library. 29 Jul 2013)

Bowden, Bill. Alumni Records for Pupils and Masters – New College Eastbourne A Short Selected List from the 500 biographies. Eastbourne Local History Society. Also articles by other authors.

Britain in the Thirties. 22 minutes from London. BBC Film. Producer: Christopher Cook. Broadcast 9 Jun 1983.

Brown, Antony. She planted to perfection. (London: Reader's Digest, May 1993)

Collinge. J M. Office-Holders in Modern Britain: VIII Foreign Office Officials 1782-1870. (London: University of London, 1979)

Construction News: The Falklands Achievement. Mar 1986.

Cornwall Council: Technical Paper M1 China Clay. 2013.

Coldham, Peter Wilson. The Bristol Register of Servants sent to Foreign Plantations 1654-1686) (Baltimore: Genealogical Publishing Co Inc., 1988)

Crawford, D G. Roll of the Indian Medical Service 1615-1930. (London, W Thacker & Co, 1930)

Croquet Association Gazette, 2 Sep 1933, 26 May 1934

The Dauntseian. Dauntsey's School. Spring Term 1965.

Day, David. Has Britain Let Us Down? A Reconsideration. Journal of the Royal Historical Society of Queensland Volume 15 issue 1: pp. 62-66. (Brisbane, 1993)

Education at a Glance 2013: OECD Indicators. OECD Publishing. OECD. 2013

English Housing Survey 2017-18. Ministry of Housing, Communities and Local Government. Jan 2018.

Enterprise Neptune: A Fourth Progress Report on Enterprise Neptune, the National Trust Campaign to save the coast. National Trust. London. 1977.

Global Wealth Report 2013. (Zurich: Credit Suisse, 2013)

The Good Childhood Report 2015. (York: Children's Society in collaboration with the University of York, 2015)

Giumlia-Muir, Alessandra and Schiavo, Fulvia Lo. The Problem of Early Tin, Acts of the XIVth UISPP Congress, University of Liege, Belgium 2-8 Sep 2001. (Oxford: Archaeopress, 2003)

Evans, Arthur J. Stonehenge. Public lecture given in the Ashmolean Museum, Oxford 6 Dec 1888: Archaeological Review Vol 2 No 5 Jan 1889 pp312-330.

Farrar, W and Brownhill, J (Editors). Liverpool: Trade, population and geographical growth, A History of the County of Lancaster Vol 4. (London: Victoria County History. University of London, 1911)

Getty Images Gallery. Indian Treasures, Exhibition catalogue. London. 2017.

Hansard (the official report of the UK Parliament)

Have I got News for You? BBC 7 Dec 2015

Hawker 'The Gauger's Pocket.' Household Words Vol VI pp 515-7, 1853.

HEFCE: Global demand for English higher education: An analysis of international student entry to English higher education courses. April 2014 and May 2015.

Hildebrand's Chocolates. Life in the Year 2000. (Germany, c1900)

Home Office. Modern Slavery Strategy. (London, Nov 2014)

Horrocks, Lt Gen B G, Commander 30 Corps (Foreword) 30th Corps in Germany which tells who we are, where we are, why we're here and what happens next. (Germany, 1945)

Howitzer Herald (Nordhorn: 61st Medium Regiment,

1946)

Hudson, Neal. The Shifting Sands of Home Ownership, Residential Focus Q4 2014. Savills. Nov 2014.

International Labour Organisation and Walk Free Foundation in partnership with the International Organization for Migration. Global estimates of modern slavery: Forced labour and forced marriage. Geneva. 2017.

Kemp, Ross. 'Modern Slavery Strategy', This Week, BBC2, 17 Jan 2014.

Lee Ho Yin, DiStefano Lynne D, Tse Curry C K. Architectural Appraisal of Ho Tung Gardens. HTGAA. Hong Kong. 10 Oct 2011.

John Brown & Co Ltd: Atlas Works, Sheffield; Shipyard and Engineering Works, Clyde Bank. (London: Bedford Press, 1903)

Life Scientific, Episode 7, BBC Radio 4.

London Churchman.

Lutyens – the work of the English Architect Sir Edwin Lutyens 1869-1981. Exhibition Catalogue, Hayward Gallery 18 Nov 1981 - 31 Jan 1982. (London: Arts Council of Great Britain, 1981)

Micklethwait, John and Wooldridge, Adrian. We need a revolution. (London: Sunday Times Section 4. 18 May 2014)

The Mitre. Magazine of Dauntsey's School Christian Union. Dec 1966

Misra, Sanghamitra. The Nature of Colonial Intervention in the Naga Hills, 1840-80. (Mumbai: Economic and Political Weekly. 19 Dec 1998)

Mitchell, Brian Redman. International Historical Statistics 1750-2005. (Basingstoke and New York: Macmillan, 2007)

Moon, Norman S. Caleb Evans: Founder of the Bristol Education Society. The Baptist Quarterly 24 p175-190. Oct 1971.

Murray, John. On the Channels through which Cholera is Communicable. Read before the Public Medicine Section at the Annual Meeting of the British Medical Association. August 1873 and reprinted in the British Medical Journal 23 Aug 1873. (London: T Richards, 1873)

Murray, John. Report on the attack of Epidemic Cholera in Agra and Central India during the year 1861. (Agra: 1861)

National Trust Properties 1961. (London: National Trust, 1961)

O'Donoghue, Jim; Goulding, Louise; Allen, Grahame. Consumer Price Inflation Since 1750 (ISSN 0013-0400, Economic Trends No. 604, pp 38-46) 2004.

Once a Week! A Prospectus. (London: Bradbury and Evans, 1859)

Penhallurick, R D. Tin in Antiquity: its mining and trade throughout the ancient world with particular reference to Cornwall. London: The Institute of Metal, 1986.

Picard, Lisa of the British Library. Discuss your Ancestry Issue 1. (London: Ancestry, 2012)

Poliakoff, Miranda. Fulham and Gardens Palace: A Brief History. (London: Fulham Palace Trust, 2013)

Popović, Krsto Zrnov. Atlantic Jihad: The Untold story of White Slavery.

Pratt, Mike. 'History of Carlton & Chellington.' Carlton & Chellington Historical Society newsletter Vol 10 No

2 Jun 2012

QI Series K 'Kitchen Sink'. BBC 13 Dec 2013

Ramscar, M., Hendrix, P., Shaoul, C., Milin, P. and Baayen, H. The Myth of Cognitive Decline: Non-Linear Dynamics of Lifelong Learning. Topics in Cognitive Science, Vol 6 Issue 1 pp5-42 doi: 10.1111/tops.12078 (Cognitive Science Society, Jan 2014)

Royal Commission on the Sanitary State of the Army 1863

Schools Inquiry Commission 1868

Spread Eagle (Barclays' Bank house magazine) March 1965

Stephen, James. West India Slavery. A Review of the British West India Colonies Delineated, as it exists both in Law and Practice, and compared with the Slavery of other Countries, Ancient and Modern. Vol 1 being a delineation of the State in Point of Law. Extracted from the Edinburgh Review LXXXII (Aberdeen.: Aberdeen Anti-Slavery Society, 1825)

Story of the Cawnpore Mission. (Westminster: Society of the Propagation of the Gospel (SPG), 1923)

Thorne, Boydell and Brewer, editors. The History of Parliament: the House of Commons 1790-1820, (London, 1986)

Thomas, Ben and Wilson, Timothy. C D E Fortnum and the collecting and study of applied arts and sculpture in Victorian England (first published as Journal of the History of Collections Vol II No 2). (Oxford: OUP, 1999)

Vallance, Charles. Business Leaders who 'leave nothing to chance' attract bad luck and missed opportunities. (London: Daily Telegraph, 21 April 2014)

Valentine, Daniel Rossall. Solving the UK Housing Crisis. An analysis of the investment demand behind the UK's housing affordability crisis. Bow Group Nov 2015.

Viswanathan, Rashmi. The Tresidder Album: A Case Study of a Private 'Ethnography'. Trans Asia Photography Review Vol 7 Issue 1 'Self and Nation'. Michigan: Hampshire College, Oct 2016.

Ward, J T. East Yorkshire Landed Estates in the Nineteenth Century. Beverley: East Yorkshire Local History Society, 1967.

Whelan, Timothy D. Baptist Autographs in the John Rylands University Library of Manchester 1741-1907. Bulletin of the John Rylands University Library of Manchester. Vol 89; No 2 p203-226. Manchester. 2012.

Who wants to be a Millionaire? Paul Lashmar and Arleen Harris. The Independent. London. 1 Mar 1997.

Why Idi Amin Expelled the Asians. Agnes Asiimwe. New African magazine. London. 1 Oct 2012.

Wrigley, Tony. English county populations in the later eighteenth century: Male Occupational Change and Economic Growth 1750-1851. Cambridge Group for the History of Population and Social Structure, Department of Geography, University of Cambridge.

Wright, N T. Doubts about Doubt: Honest to God Forty Years On. Journal of Anglican Studies, 2005, Vol 3 (2), p181–96.

WEB SOURCES

http://en.wikipedia.org/wiki/Haplogroup_I-M438

www.blisworth.org.uk/images/Church/GFChurchnotes.htm

www.rootsweb.com/~genepool/genn/6-falmouth.html

www.goudhurstlocalhistorysociety.org/goudhurst-ladies-college/

https://archive.org/details/b20443559 accessed 22 Jun 2015

www.bartonhistory.wikispaces.com

http://www.historyofparliamentonline.org/

http://en.wikipedia.org/wiki/Iazyges.

http://www.oldbaileyonline.org/

http://butedock.demon.co.uk/cgs1919/ages.php accessed 25 Apr 2017

www.copinger.org.uk/1John28.html

www.geni.com

www.nottingham.ac.uk

www.sydenhamforesthillhistory.blogspot.co.uk/2008/11/kirkdale-learning-centre.html accessed 6 Sep 14

http://www.higherednwb.net/universityeducation.htm

http://www.british-history.ac.uk/report.aspx?compid=63826 accessed 5 Dec 2012

www.bl.uk/world-war-one/articles/the-indian-sepoy-in-the-first-world-war#sthash.XvIjIgWX.dpuf

https://hamidmahmood.co.uk/2012/11/01/the-dars-e-ni%E1%BA%93ami-and-the-transnational-traditionalist-madaris-in-britain/

http://himalaya.socanth.cam.ac.uk/collections/naga/record/r87694.html

www.chinworld.info/category/article/

http://spartacus-educational.com/DICbradleyEvans.htm

http://www.bbc.co.uk/scotland/history/land_and_votes/scottish_potato_blight/

http://exhibits.lib.byu.edu/literaryworlds/thackeray/

http://kindred.stanford.edu/#

www.chinesechurchvoices.com

www.amo.gov.hk/form/briefing/htgaa_report.pdf

http://www.nationalarchives.gov.uk/nelson/gallery8/

https://plus.google.com/112438254271931097551/posts accessed 4 Nov 2014.

www.wirksworth.org.uk/A04VALUE.htm

www.open.ac.uk/blogs/History-of-the-OU/?p=2250

www.marxists.org/history/england/combination-laws/luddites-1812.htm

http://www.newafricanmagazine.com/why-idi-amin-expelled-the-asians

http://wrap.warwick.ac.uk/34689/1/WRAP_THESIS_Kaijage_1975.pdf accessed: 23 Sep 2014

http://ntwrightpage.com/Wright_Doubts_About_Doubt.htm#_

http://rtpi.org.uk/media/895782/homes_for_heroes_-_report.pdf

http://anglicanhistory.org/aus/png/dogura_consecration1939.html

http://ntwrightpage.com/Wright_Doubts_About_Doubt.htm#_ftn1 accessed 3 Feb 2015

www.london.anglican.org/about/

http://www.imf.org/external/ns/cs.aspx?id=28

http://www.savills.co.uk/research_articles/141285/183883-0

https://publications.credit-suisse.com/tasks/render/file/?fileID=BCDB1364-A105-0560-1332EC9100FF5C83

http://www.independent.co.uk/news/business/news/the-number-of-british-millionaire-households-grew-by-12-in-2015-a7070591.html

http://www.forbes.com/billionaires/list/

http://www.savills.co.uk/research_articles/141285/183883-0 accessed 26 Feb 2015.

http://inflation.stephenmorley.org/ accessed 30 Apr 2017

https://quod.lib.umich.edu/t/tap/7977573.0007.104/--tresidder-album-a-case-study-of-a-private-ethnography?rgn=main;view=fulltext accessed 15 Dec 2017

Information for honours, rank, residence, births, deaths and marriages was gleaned through the National Archives and Parish Records, the Censuses, the London Gazette and Military records using www.ancestry.co.uk as well as www.familysearch.org and other websites. Some 6,000 family forebears are now kept together on Ancestry.co.uk for posterity.

BOOKS REFERRED TO IN THE TEXT

Adrian, Arthur A. Mark Lemon: First Editor of Punch. (London: Oxford University Press, 1966)

Allen, Percy. The Stage Life of Mrs Stirling: with some sketches of the Nineteenth Century Theatre. (London: T Fisher Unwin Ltd, 1922)

Banks, A G. H W Schneider of Barrow and Bowness. (Kendal: Titus Wilson, 1984)

Barnes, F. Barrow and District. (Barrow-in-Furness Corporation, 1968)

Best, Geoffrey. Shaftesbury (London: B T Batsford, 1964)

Bingham, Robert J. Photogenic manipulation: containing the theory and plain instructions in the art of photography or the production of pictures through the agency of light. (London: George Knight & Son, 1859)

Birch, Alan and Cole, Martin. Captive Years: The Occupation of Hong Kong 1941-45. (Hong Kong: Heinemann Educational Books (Asia) Ltd., 1982)

Blackmore R D. Lorna Doone: A Romance of Exmoor. (London: Sampson Low & Co. 1883) First published 1869.

Bradshaw, George. Bradshaw's Descriptive Railway Handbook [Britain], 1861. (Glasgow: Collins, Imprint 2004) Bradshaw's Continental Railway Guide [Europe] of 1863. (Glasgow: Collins, 2016)

Brandwood, Geoff and others. The Architecture of Sharpe, Paley and Austin. (Swindon: English Heritage, 2012)

Bourdieu, Pierre. Distinction: a social critique of the judgement of taste; translated by Richard Nice, with a new introduction by Tony Bennett. (London: Routledge, 2010; originally published in Paris in 1979)

Bowen, W H. Charles Dickens and his family. (Cambridge: W Heffer & Sons Ltd, 1956)

Carrol, Lewis. Through the Looking-Glass, and What Alice Found There. Illustrated by John Tenniel. (London: Macmillan & Co, 1950, first published 1871)

Chaudhuri, Binay Bhushan. Peasant History of Late Pre-colonial and Colonial India; History of Science, Philosophy and Culture in Indian Civilization. The Centre for Studies in Civilizations. (India: Pearson Longman, 2008)

Churchill, Winston Spencer. My African Journey. (London: Hodder & Stoughton, 1908)

Clark, Gregory and others. The Son also Rises: Surnames and the history of social mobility. (Princeton and Oxford: Princeton University Press, 2014)

Coates, Charles. The History of Antiquities of Reading. (London: J Nicholas & Son, 1802)

Collier, Richard. The Sound and Fury: an account of the Indian Mutiny. (London: Collins, 1963)

Copland, Ian; Mabbett, Ian; Roy, Asim; Brittlebank, Kate; Bowles, Adam. A History of the State and Religion in India (Abingdon & New York: Routledge, 2012)

Crawford, D G. A History of the Medical Service 1600-1913. (London: W Thacker & Co, 1914)

Cunliffe, Sir Barry. Iron Age Communities in Britain (fourth edition, extensively revised). (London: Routledge, 2004)

Dalrymple, William. The Last Mughal: The Fall of a dynasty, Delhi, 1857. (London: Bloomsbury, 2006)

Davies, K C and Hull, J. The Zoological Collections of the Oxford University Museum. A historical Review and General Account, with Comprehensive Donor Index to the year 1975. (Oxford: University Museum, 1976)

Davis, J F. Vizier Ali Khan or the Massacre of Benares: a chapter in British History. (London: John Murray, 1844)

Davis, Terence. John Nash, The Prince Regent's Architect. (London: Country Life Ltd, 1966)

Dent, Eileen and Geoffrey and others. A History of St Mary's Church and Parish Dalton-in-Furness. (Dalton-in-Furness, 2007)

Evans, Joan. Time and Chance. The story of Arthur Evans and his forebears. (London: Longmans, 1943)

Evans, Sir John. Ancient Bronze Implements, weapons and ornaments of Great Britain and Ireland. (London: Longmans, Green & Co, 1881)

Falconer, John. 'A pure labor of love': A publishing history of the People of India. Colonialist photography: imag(in)ing race and place. Editors Eleanor M Hight and Gary D Sampson. (Toronto: Routledge, 2002)

Ferrar, William John. The Proof of the Gospel, being the Demonstratio Evangelica of Eusebius of Cæsarea. Translations of Christian Literature. Series I: Greek Texts. (London: SPCK; New York: Macmillan, 1920)

Freeman, Douglas Southall. George Washington, a Biography, Vol 1. (London: Eyre and Spottiswoode, 1948)

Ganor, Nissim Raphael. Who were the Phoenicians? (Israel: KIP Katarim International Publishing Ltd, 2009)

Gay, Susan Elizabeth. Old Falmouth. The story of the town from the days of the Killigrews to the earliest part of the 19th century. (London: Headley Bros, 1903)

Gibbon, Edward. The History of the Decline and Fall of the Roman Empire: Volume 5. (London: Vernor, Hood & Sharpe, 1806)

Gordon, Peter. The Wakes of Northamptonshire. (Northampton: Libraries and Information Service, 1992)

Gupta, Pratul Chandra. Nana Sahib and the Rising at Cawnpore. (Oxford: Clarendon Press, 1963)

Harden, D B. Sir Arthur Evans 1851-1941 'A Memoir'. (Oxford: Ashmolean Museum, 1983)

Haskins, M Louise. The Desert. (London: Hodder & Stoughton, 1908)

Haskins, Robert. A History of St Francis Petts Wood. (Petts Wood: St Francis Church, 1984)

Haskins, Robert, Pirates of the Far East: A Pantomime. (Wetherby: Unpublished, performed 2007)

Haskins, Robert. The Stamp of Personality: Petts Wood a Garden Suburb. (Milton Keynes: Open University dissertation. Unpublished. 1980)

Hattie, John A C. Visible Learning: A synthesis of over 800 Meta-Analyses Relating to Achievement. (London: Routledge, 2008)

Hawker, Robert Stephen. Footprints of Former Men in Far Cornwall. (London: John Lane, 1893, first published as papers in 1870)

Hawksley, Lucinda. Katey: The Life and Loves of Dickens's Artist Daughter. (London: Doubleday, 2006)

Hawthorne, Nathaniel. Tanglewood Tales. (London: J M Dent & Sons, 1950. First published 1853)

Heathcote, T A. The Military in British India: The development of British land forces in South Asia 1600-1947 (Barnsley: Praetorian Press, 2013)

Heathcote, T A. Mutiny and Insurgency in India 1857-1858: The British Army in a Bloody Civil War. (Barnsley: Pen & Sword, 2007)

Hernon, Ian. Fortress Britain: All the Invasions and Incursions since 1066. (Stroud: The History Press, 2013)

Herodotus. The Histories. (Harmondsworth: Penguin Classics, 1954, 1971)

Hibbert, Christopher. The Great Mutiny: India 1857. (London: Allen Lane, 1978)

Hillcourt, William with Olave, Lady Baden-Powell. Baden-Powell: The Two Lives of a Hero. (London: Heinemann, 1964)

Hodges, Jim. How does your Garden Grow: An account of the developments at Dauntsey's School 1951-1991. (Warminster: Wessex Press, 1992)

Horwitz, Sylvia L. Find of a Lifetime: Sir Arthur Evans and the discovery of Knossos. (London: Weidenfeld and Nicholson, 1981)

Hughes, Thomas. Tom Brown's Schooldays. (London: Macmillan & Co, 1900, first edition 1857).

Hunter, William Wilson. Rulers of India: The Marquess of Dalhousie and final development of the Company's Rule. (Oxford: Clarendon Press, 1895)

Hyatt, Richard. Mr Haskins of Hoylake. (Columbus, Georgia, USA: The Haskins Commission, 2012)

Iliffe, John. East African Doctors: a history of the Modern Profession. (Cambridge: University Press, 1998)

Jones, Ken. The Wotton Tramway (Brill Branch). (Usk: Oakwood Press, 1974)

Kaijage, Frederick James. Labouring Barnsley, 1816-1856: A Social and Economic History. (Warwick: University of Warwick PhD Thesis, 1975)

Kaye, John William. Christianity in India. (London: Smith, Elder & Co, 1859)

Kaye, John William. A History of the Sepoy War in

BIBLIOGRAPHY

India 1857-1858. (London: W H Allen & Co. Vol 1 1864. Vol 2 5th Edition 1874)

Kellett, Jack. James Ramsden: Barrow's Man of Vision. Ulverston: Monksvale Press, 1990)

Kemp, David. The Pleasures and Treasures of Britain. Toronto: Dundurn Press Ltd, 1992)

King, Anthony & Crewe, Ivor. The Blunders of our Governments. (London: Oneworld Publications, 2013)

King, Frank H H, Editor. Eastern Banking: Essays in the History of the Hongkong and Shanghai Banking Corporation. (London: Athlone Press, 1983)

Jeffares, Alexander Norman. A New Commentary on the Collected Poems of W B Yeats. (London: Macmillan Press Ltd, 1968, 1984)

Kennedy, G A Studdert ('Woodbine Willie'). Lighten our Darkness: some less rough rhymes of a padre. (London: Hodder and Stoughton, 1925)

Lambot, Ian and Chambers, Gillian. One Queen's Road Central. (Hong Kong: Hongkong Bank, 1986)

Lear, Edward. The Complete Book of Nonsense. Editor: Holbrook Jackson. (London: Faber & Faber, 1967 first published in four volumes, 1846-1877)

Lee, Hermonie. Virginia Woolf: a biography. (London: Chatto & Windus, 1996)

Levy, M J. The Mistresses of King George IV. (London: Peter Owen, 1996)

Lobel, Mary D, Editor. A History of the County of Oxford Vol 8: Lewknor & Pyrton Parishes. (London: Victoria County History, 1964)

Low, Charles Rathbone. Memoir of Major-General J T Boileau RE FRS. (London: WH Allen &Co, 1887)

Madison, Angus. The Contours of the World Economy 1-2030 AD; essays in Macro-Economic History. (Oxford: University Press, 2007)

Macgillivray, Joseph Alexander. Minotaur: Sir Arthur Evans and the Archaeology of the Minoan Myth. (London: Jonathan Cape, 2000)

Mackenzie, Alexander. History of the Relations of the Government with the Hill Tribes of the North-East Frontier of Bengal. (Calcutta: Home Department Press, 1884)

Marsden, W E. Unequal Educational Provision in England and Wales: The Nineteenth-century Roots. (London: Woburn Press, 1987)

Mason, Philip. A matter of honour: an account of the Indian Army, its officers and men. (London: Jonathan Cape, 1974)

Maugham, Somerset. Strictly Personal. (New York. Arno Press. 1977)

McKibbens, Thomas R Jr. The Forgotten Heritage: A Lineage of Great Baptist Preaching. (Macon, Georgia, USA: Mercer University Press., 1986)

Milton, Giles. White Gold: The Extraordinary Story of Thomas Pellow and North Africa's One Million European Slaves. (Oxford: Hodder & Stoughton, 2004)

Misra, Amaresh. Mangal Pandey: the true story of an Indian Revolutionary. (New Delhi: Rupa & Co, 2005)

Misra, Amaresh. War of Civilisations: India and 1857. (New Delhi: Rupa & Co, 2008)

McCosh, John. Advice to Officers in India. (London: William H Allen & Co, 1856)

Murphy, William M. Family Secrets: William Butler Yeats and His Relatives. (New York: Syracuse University Press, 1995)

Murphy, William M. The Yeats Family and the Pollexfens of Sligo, with drawings by John Butler Yeats. (Dublin: The Dolmen Press, 1971)

Murray, J and Boileau J T. Picturesque Views in the North Western Province of India (London: J Hogarth, 1859)

Nayder, Lillian. The Other Dickens: A Life of Catherine Hogarth. (Ithaca & London: Cornell University Press, 2011)

Nightingale, Florence. Notes on Nursing: what it is and what it is not. (London: Harrison & Sons, 1859)

O'Connor, Mike. Cornish Folk Tales. (Stroud: The History Press, 2010. E-book edition 2011)

Pakenham, Frank, Earl of Longford. Humility. (London: Collins, Fontana Books, 1969)

Page, Norman (Editor). Charles Dickens: family history. (London: Routledge, 1999 reprinted 2001)

Palmer, J A B. The Mutiny Outbreak at Meerut in 1857. (Cambridge: Cambridge University Press, 1966)

Patten, Robert L. Charles Dickens and his publishers. (London: Clarendon Press, 1978)

Peart-Binns, John S. Wand of London. (Oxford: Mowbray, 1987)

Pevsner, Nikolaus. The Buildings of England: Lancashire: the Industrial and Commercial South. (Harmondsworth: Penguin Books, 1969)

Purvis, Malcolm. Tall Storeys. (Hong Kong: Palmer & Turner Ltd, 1985)

Pyle, Hilary. Jack B Yeats: a biography. (London: Routledge & Kegan Paul, 1970)

Ray, Gordon N. Thackeray: The Uses of Adversity. (New York: Octagon Books, 1972)

Ride, Lindsay and May, edited by Bernard Mello. An East India Company Cemetery: Protestant Burials in Macao. (Hong Kong: Hong Kong University Press, 1996)

Ridley, Jane. Edwin Lutyens. His Life, His Wife, His Work. (London: Pimlico, 2003)

Robinson, John A T. Honest to God. (London: SCM Press, 1963)

Roe, Nicholas. John Keats: A New Life. (New Haven and London: Yale University Press, 2012)

Ruskin, John. The Two Paths: being lectures on Art and its application to decoration and Manufacture delivered in 1858-9. (Orpington: George Allen, 1884)

Schreiner, Olive. The Story of an African Farm: a Novel. 2 Vols (London: Chapman & Hall, 1883) first published under the nom-de-plume Ralph Iron

Sherwood, Jennifer & Pevsner, Nikolaus. Oxfordshire. The Buildings of England. (Harmondsworth: Penguin Books, 1974)

Smit, Candy. Heligan History: Lost Gardens, Lost Gardeners. (Pentewan: Heligan Gardens Ltd, 2008)

Smith, Nicky. Queen of Games – A History of Croquet. (London: Weidenfeld and Nicolson, 1991)

Somerville, Christopher. Coast: A Celebration of Britain's Coastal Heritage. (London: BBC Books, 2005)

Spragg, Iain. London's Strangest Tales: The Thames. (London: Portico Books, 2014)

Springett, Christine & David. Success to the Lace Pillow: the Classification and Identification of 19th Century East Midland Lace Bobbins and Their Makers. (Rugby: C & D Springett, 1997)

Standiford, Les. The Man Who Invented Christmas: How Charles Dickens's A Christmas Carol Rescued His Career and Revived Our Holiday Spirits. (New York: Crown publishers, 2008)

Strickland, Agnes. The Lives of the Seven Bishops committed to the Tower in 1688, enriched with personal letters now first published from the Bodleian Library. (London: Bell & Daldy, 1866)

Thackeray, William Makepeace. The Rose and the Ring or the History of Prince Giglio and Prince Bulbo. A Fire-side Pantomime for Great and Small Children. (London: Smith Elder & Co, 1873) First published by Bradley and Evans. London. 1855.

Thompson, Flora. Lark Rise to Candleford. (London: Oxford University Press, 1945)

Tibbutt H G. Bunyan Meeting 1650-1950. (Bedford: The Trustees of the Bunyan Meeting. 1950)

Tomalin, Claire. The Invisible Woman: The Story of Nelly Ternan and Charles Dickens. (London: Viking, 1990)

Trescatheric, Bryn. How Barrow was built. (Barrow-in-Furness: Hougenai Press, 1985)

Trevelyan, Sir George Otto. Cawnpore. (London & Cambridge: Macmillan & Co, 1865)

Trotter, Lionel James. A Leader of Light Horse: Life of Hodson of Hodson's Horse. (London: William Blackwood and Sons, 1901)

Valentine, W. Intelligence Tests for Children. (London: Methuen & Co Ltd, 1945)

Wand, J W C. Has Britain Let Us Down? (London and Melbourne: Oxford University Press, May 1942)

Ward, Andrew. Our Bones Are Scattered –The Cawnpore Massacres and the Indian Mutiny of 1887. (New York: Henry Holt & Co Inc, 1996)

Wand, J W C. The New Testament Letters Prefaced and Paraphrased. (Oxford: Oxford University Press, 1944)

Waymark, Peter. A History of Petts Wood. (Petts Wood: Petts Wood and District Residents' Association, 1979)

Webb, Sidney and Beatrice. English Local Government: The Story of the King's Highway. (London: Longmans, Green & Co, 1920)

Wiggins, W Denison. Midwifery for Midwives. (London: Baillière, Tindall and Cox, 1904)

Wiggins, W R D. British Line Engraved Stamps: Repaired Impressions. 1855-1879 One Penny Die II. (London: Pall Mall Stamp Company for Robson Rowe Ltd. London. 1982. Limited edition (200) undated)

Wiggins, W R D. The Plating of Alphabet II: Plates 1 to 21: AA to TL. Penny Reds dated Mar-Dec 1855. (London: Robson Rowe, 1974)

Wilberforce, William. A Practical View of the Prevailing Religious System of professed Christians in the higher and middle classes of this country contrasted with real Christianity. (London: Swan Sonnenschein, Le Ba & Lowrey, 1886)

Willcock, Sean. The Aesthetics of Imperial Crisis: Image Making and Intervention in British India, c1857-1919. (York: University of York PhD thesis, 2013)

Williams, Charles. Caerhays Castle. (Falmouth: Pasticcio Ltd, 2011)

Winter, Gordon and Kochman, Wendy. Secrets of the Royals. (London: Robson Books, 1990)

Wiseman, Richard. The Luck Factor. (London: Arrow Books, 2004)

Woolf, Virginia. A Room of One's Own. (London: Hogarth Press, 1929)

Yadav, Kripal Chandra. The revolt of 1857 in Haryana. (New Delhi: Manohar Book Service, 1977)

OTHER BOOKS

Amhurst, Nicholas. Oculus Britanniæ: an heroi-panegyrical poem on the University of Oxford. Illustrated with divers beautiful similes, and useful digressions. (London, Covent Garden: R Francklin under Tom's Coffee House, 1724)

Ball, Charles. The History of the Indian Mutiny: a detailed account of the Sepoy insurrection in India; and a concise history of the great military events which have tended to consolidate the British Empire in Hindostan. 2 Vols. (London: Printing and Publishing Company, 1858)

Basu, Pernendu. Oudh and the East India Company. (Lucknow: Maxwell Company, 1943)

Bennett, Rev Joyce. Hasten Slowly. The First Legal Ordination of Women Priests. (Great Britain: Little London Associates, 1991)

Bright, William. The History of the Church from the Edict of Milan AD 313 to the Council of Chalcedon AD 451. (Oxford: Parker & Co, 1881)

Chapman, Leslie. Your Disobedient Civil Servant. (Harmondsworth: Penguin Books, 1978)

Cronin. A J. Dr Finlay's casebook omnibus. (Edinburgh: Birlinn, 2010)

Davis, Robert C. Christian Slaves, Muslim Masters — White Slavery in the Mediterranean, the Barbary Coast and Italy. (Basingstoke: Palgrave Macmillan, 2003)

Foster, R F. W B Yeats: A Life — The Apprentice Mage, 1865-1914. (Oxford: Oxford University Press, 1998)

Hancock, Christopher. Robert Morrison and the Birth of Chinese Protestantism. (London: T & T Clark, 2008)

Janis, Irving L. Victims of Groupthink: a psychological study of foreign-policy decisions and fiascos. (Boston: Houghton Mifflin Company, 1972)

Lewis, Bernard. Race and Slavery in the Middle East: An Historical Enquiry. (New York: Oxford University Press, 1990)

Nightingale, Florence. Suggestions for Thought: Selections and Commentaries edited by Calabria, Michael D and Macrae, Janet A. [Philadelphia: University of Pennsylvania Press, 1994]

Hall, H S and Knight, S R. Elementary Algebra. (London: Macmillan and Co Ltd, 1918)

Lake, William. A Complete Parochial History of the County of Cornwall complied from the best authorities and corrected and improved from actual survey. Vol 1. (Truro, 1867)

Moule, Arthur E. The Responsibility of the Church as Regards the Opium Traffic with China. (London: The Society for the Suppression of the Opium Trade, 1881)

Olive, George William. A School's Adventure. (The History of Dauntsey's School, West Lavington, from 1483 to 1950). (London: Sylvan Press, 1951)

Omissi, David. The Sepoy and the Raj: the Indian Army 1860-1940. (London: The Macmillan Press Ltd, 1994)

Palmer, Leonard R. Mycenaeans and Minoans. Aegean Prehistory in the Light of the Linear B Tablets. (London: Faber and Faber, 1961)

Palmer, Leonard R. A New Guide to the Palace of Knossos. (London: Faber and Faber, 1969)

Palmer, L R & Boardman, John. On the Knossos Tablets. (Oxford: Clarendon Press, 1963)

Piketty, Thomas, translated by Goldhammer, Arthur. Capital in the Twenty-First Century. (Cambridge Massachusetts: Belknap Press of Harvard University Press, 2014)

Ransome, Arthur. Missie Lee. (London: Jonathan Cape, 1941)

Ransome, Arthur. Peter Duck. (London: Collins, 1936)

Reid, Sir Robert. The History of the Frontier areas bordering on Assam 1883-1941. (Shillong: Assam Government Press, 1942)

Richards, Bob. Cornish Family Names. (Stroud: History Press, 2009)

Rouse, A L. A Cornish Childhood. (London: Jonathan Cape, 1942)

Sayers, Dorothy L and others. The Great Mystery of Life hereafter. (London: Hodder & Stoughton, 1957)

Segal, Farrar, Straus and Giroux. Islam's black slaves: the other black diaspora. (New York. 2002)

Seymour, J B. Postage Stamps of Great Britain: Part One: The Line-engraved Issues 1840-1853. (London: The Royal Philatelic Society, 1950)

Shafer, Elizabeth. Lilian Baylis: A Biography. (Hatfield: University of Hertfordshire Press, 2006)

Smith, Audrey Z. A History of the Hope Entomological Collections in the University Museum with lists of Archives and Collections. (Oxford: Oxford University Press, 1986)

Stephen, James. The Slavery of the British West India Colonies delineated as it exists both in law and practice and compared with the Slavery of other countries, ancient and modern. Vol 1. (London: Joseph Butterworth and Son, 1824)

Strickland, Agnes. The Lives of the Seven Bishops Committed to the Tower in 1688, enriched and illustrated with personal letters, now first published, from the Bodleian Library. (London: Bell and Daldy, 1866)

Unwin, Robert. Wetherby: The History of a Yorkshire Market Town. (Leeds: Leeds University Press & Wetherby Historical Trust, 1986)

Vickers, Hugh and McCullough, Caroline. Great Country House Disasters. (London: Arthur Baker Ltd, c1982)

Watson, J Forbes and Kaye, John William, editors. The People of India. A series of Photographic Illustrations, with descriptive letterpress, of the races and tribes of Hindustan originally prepared under the authority of the Government of India and reproduced by order of the Secretary of State for India in Council. (Original edition: London: India Museum & W H Allen, 1868. Facsimile: Bath: Pagoda Tree Press, 2007)

Williamson, George C. John Russell RA. (London: George Bell & Sons, 1894)

Woolf, Virginia. Moments of Being. (London: Pimlico, 2002)

Wood, Anthony A, Rivington, F C and J, and others. Athenae Oxonienses. An exact History of all the writers and Bishops who have had their education in the University of Oxford. To which are added the Fasti, or Annals of the said University. (London, 1815)

Yeats, W B. In Memory of Alfred Pollexfen. (Dublin: National Library of Ireland, c1916)

NOTES ON PRESENTATION

Footnotes refer mostly to people and their dates.

Endnotes, for each chapter, give sources or other information. They can, according to taste, be studied or skipped.

Familiar names have been used in the text where known. Many used their second names — these are underlined when listed in full.

[NR] — People 'Not Related'

Names of places in India, China and elsewhere normally use the spelling at the time when my forebears were there. On first mention, the current accepted spelling is shown in brackets.

Days and months are largely omitted for readability.

INDEX

A

Abbotswood, Furness, 140

Aberdeen Harbour, Hong Kong, 157

Abington House School, Northampton, 58

Adam, Robert (1728-1792). architect [NR], 166

Addenbrooke's Hospital, Cambridge, 120

Addison, Caroline Ruth, Mrs Wilding (b1942), 258

Addison, Christopher, 1st Viscount (1869-1951), 248

Addison, Eleanor Brigit, Mrs Girling (b1938), 248, 258

Addison, Michael, 3rd Viscount (1914-1992), 248, 258

Addison, William Matthew Wand, 4th Viscount (b1945), 258

Africa, 25, 32, 64, 68, 82, 107, 117, 136, 165, 175, 176, 177, 178, 180, 181, 182, 183, 184, 186, 187, 188, 197, 272

Aga Khan III (1877–1957) [NR], 179

Agra, 83, 88, 99, 102, 103

Akbar Shah II, Emperor, 79, 80

Algiers, 163

Allahabad, India, 83, 92, 102

Allen, Andrew (b 1945), 170, 171

Allen, James (1832-1936), 169

Allyghur, India, 83, 102

Amen Court, London, 248, 257

Amherst, Viscount William (1773-1857) [NR], 152

Anderson, Hans Christian (1805-1875) [NR], 126

Anson, General George (1797-1857) [NR], 90, 91

Antibes, 197

Ariadne, Princess of Crete, 214

Arles, Council of, 314, 26

Arwenack Manor, Falmouth, 26, 27

Ascot, Berkshire, 196, 240, 241

Ashfield House, Otley, 237

Ashmole, Elias (1617-1692) [NR], 212

Ashmolean Museum, Oxford, 211, 215, 216

Askari tribe, 183

Asketil, 11, 52, 269

Aspinall, Margaret (b1962), 69

Auckland, New Zealand, 243

Australia, 20, 59, 118, 139, 143, 248, 250, 251, 252, 254

Aylesford, Kent, 213

B

Baden-Powell, Lt Gen Robert, 1st Baron (1857-1941) [NR], 10, 175

Bahadur Shah Zafar, Emperor/King of Delhi (c1776-1862) [NR], 90, 96, 97, 102

Baji Rao, 86, 94

Baker, Sir Herbert (1862-1946) [NR], 77, 109, 221

Balfour, Francis (1851-1882) [NR], 211

Bank of England, 40, 221, 224, 230

Bank of India, 176, 177, 224

Barbary Coast, 163

Barclays Bank, 221, 225, 229

Barnicoat, Constance (1872-1922), 33, 129

Barnicoat, Elizabeth Carlyon (1816-1855), 32, 34, 83, 86

Barnicoat, Humphry (1788-1821), 32

Barnicoat, John Wallis (1814-1905), 33

Barnicoat, Thomas Humphry (b1952), 129

Barnsley, 59, 233, 235, 236, 238, 243, 244

Barnsley to Hull railway, 241

Barrackpore, India, 88

Barrington, Sir Eric (1847-1918) [NR], 178

Barrow Town Hall, 142

Barrow-in-Furness, 133, 138, 139, 140, 142

Bartlemas, Oxford, 249

Basoga tribe, 183

Bastard family, 11, 27

Batemans, 72

Bath, Somerset, 42, 252, 254

Baynes, Fanny (1820-1866), 139

Baynes, Thomas Carter (1823-1900), 139

Bazalgette, Sir Joseph (1819-1891) [NR], 115

Bedford, 14, 20, 22, 23

Behar, India, 88

Beijing (Peking), China, 148

Benares, India, 83, 102

Bennett, Rev Joyce (b1923) [NR], 152

Benwell, Newcastle-on-Tyne, 249

Bermondsey, 120

Bernau, Eliza (1842-1925), 149

Berry, Frederick L (1854-1922), 56

Bibighar, Cawnpore, 94, 95, 101

Bickland Water, Falmouth, 29

Bickley Hall Preparatory School, 172, 199, 200, 228

Bickley, Kent, 118, 120

Bird, Godfrey Vernon (1907-1979) [NR], 160

Bishop's Stortford, 65

Bithoor (Bithur), India, 84, 95

Black Water Fever, 182

Blackheath, 222, 224

Blackheath Concert Hall, 202

Blackheath Golf Club, 222

Blackheath High School, 50, 199, 200

Blackpool, Lancs, 121, 230

Blackwater estuary, Essex, 55, 222

Blagoveshchensk, Siberia, 157

Blake,William, (1757-1827) [NR], 15

Blankney Hall, Lincolnshire, 45

Bleak House, Broadstairs, 123

Blisworth, 53, 56

Boars Hill, Oxford, 216, 223, 224

Bodleian Library, Oxford, 65

Boileau, Alicia (1779-1851), 80

Boileau, Charles Elliott (1829-1857), 88

Boileau, Maj General John Theophilus (1805-1886), 103

Boler family, 207, 208

Boston Spa, Yorkshire, 11, 32

Boston USA, 65, 195, 223

Boulogne, France, 125, 208

Bowie, David (Robert Jones) (1947-2016) [NR], 200

Boxer Rebellion, 150, 151

Boy Scouts, 213, 217

Bradbury & Evans, 124, 125, 127, 128, 131

Bradbury, William (1800-1869) [NR], 123, 125

Bradshaw née Mellor, Dr Elsa Mary (1926-2016), 121

Bradshaw, Alison Rachel (b1989), 22

Bradshaw, Dr James David (b1927), 121

Bradshaw, Dr Louise Fiona (b1991), 22, 121

Bradshaw, Prof Jeremy Peter (b1959), 121

Brasenose College, Oxford, 211

Bray, John Graham (1912-1983), 195

Bridges, Robert Seymour (1844-1930), 130, 216

Brighton College, 222, 223, 224

Brighton or Brighthelmstone, 42, 43, 85, 120, 167, 202, 240

Brighton Pavilion, 42, 43, 240

Brisbane, Australia, 118, 250, 251, 254, 256

Bristol, 34, 55, 123, 167, 168, 172, 253

Bristol Baptist College, 168

Briting, Marie Julie (1892-1926), 201

British and Foreign Bible Society, 164, 187

British Archaeological Association, 45

British East Africa (Kenya), 175, 180, 181, 182, 184, 185, 186, 254

British South Africa Police, 175

Broadstairs, Kent, 123

Broadway Grammar School, Barnsley, 243

Bromley, Kent, 120, 200

Bronnert, Deborah (b1967) [NR], 160

Brontë family, 115, 116

Brown, Lancelot, (1715/16-1783) [NR], 134, 204

Brunel, Isambard Kingdom (1806 - 1859) [NR], 34

Brussels, 227

Buccleuch, 5th Duke of (1806-1884), 138, 140, 143

Buckingham Palace, 42

Buckland, Amy (1853-1908), 34

Budock, nr Falmouth, 25, 28

Bullers Wood, Chislehurst, Kent, 200

Bulmer, Matthew (1818-1979), 236

Bunyan, John (1628-1688), 14, 15, 20, 167, 168, 200

Burma (Myanmar), 85, 102, 104, 105, 107, 262

Burnley, Jonathan (1800-1870), 11

Burnley, Marcia (1830-1912), 11

Burton, Carolyn (b1957), 133, 137, 160, 207, 233, 234, 235, 236, 242, 243, 244, 245

Burton, Edith Annie (1910-1977), 235

Burton, Kenneth (b1924), 235, 236, 237, 238, 239, 242, 243

Burton, Lois Margaret (b1993), 60, 244

Burton, Michael Ian (b1960), 60, 243, 244, 261

Burton, Rowan Michael (b1991), 244

Burton, Thomas (1884-1925), 235

Butiaba, Uganda, 181

Buwanuka, Uganda, 183

C

Caerhays Castle, 42, 141, 221

Calais, France, 155, 208

Calcutta (Kolkata), India, 10, 34, 71, 77, 78, 79, 80, 81, 82, 83, 85, 88, 91, 98, 115, 116

Calmpthout (Kalmthout), Belgium, 201

Cambridge, 30, 50, 71, 72, 90, 120, 130, 156, 163, 167, 192

Camelford, Cornwall, 16, 17, 40

Cameron House, Leatherhead, 58, 59

Campaign for Nuclear Disarmament, 258

Candy, James Stuart (1902-1999) [NR], 216, 217, 218, 224, 241

Canning, Charles John, 1st Earl (1812-1862) [NR], 86, 91, 96, 102, 104, 109

Canning, George (1770-1827) [NR], 44

Canterbury, 44, 45, 101, 106, 107, 123, 135, 253, 254, 255, 257

Canton (Guangzhou), 147, 148

Cape Town University, 176

Cardiff, 55, 135

Carlton House, London, 42

Carlton, Bedfordshire, 71

Carlyon, Monmouthshire, 26

Carmichael Smyth, Maj George Munroe (1803-1890), 88, 89

Caroline Hill, Hong Kong, 157

Caroline of Brunswick, Queen, 42

Carr, John (1723-1807) [NR], architect, 52, 166

Carver, Canon Alfred James (1826-1909) [NR], 49

Case, 'The Misses' Kate and Marion [NR], 206

Castlereagh, Viscount Robert (1769-1822) [NR], 44

Cavell family, 207

Cawnpore, 81, 83, 84, 85, 86, 89, 91, 92, 93, 94, 95, 96, 97, 98, 99, 100, 102, 103, 105

Centre for the Study of Christianity in China, Oxford, 151

Chadwell Comprehensive School, 59

Chambers, Sir William (1723-1796) [NR], 166

Chamonix, France/Switzerland border, 250

Chapman & Hall, 124, 125

Charles I, 28

Charles II, 28

Charlestown, Cornwall, 27

Charnes Hall, Staffordshire, 204

Chekiang, China, 150

Cheltenham, 73, 81, 106, 120, 188, 253

Cheltenham Ladies College, 188

Childwall Hall, Liverpool, 141

Chillianwalla, Battle of (1849), 82

Chimes. The, 125

China Clay (kaolin), 161, 267

China Inland Mission, 149

Chippendale, Thomas (1718-1779) [NR], 166

Chislehurst, Kent, 144, 200, 250

Cholera, 34, 86, 96, 97, 98, 115, 121

Christ Church, Oxford, 243

Christmas Carol, 20, 124, 125

Chuki, China, 150

Chunar, India, 83

Chung Hom Kok, Hong Kong Island, 159

Church Missionary Society, 149, 150, 152, 164, 166, 167, 179, 187

Churchill, Sir Winston (1874-1965), 130, 179, 180, 188, 196, 204, 252, 254

Clapham Sect, 80, 164, 165, 166

Clapham, London, 164, 165, 166

Clayton, Mary (1891-1947), 118, 119

Clerkenwell, 13, 16

Clifton, Ann (1804-1880), 20, 22

Clifton, Benjamin, 20, 21

Coleridge, Samuel Taylor (1772-1834) [NR], 18

Collins, Canon Lewis John (1905-1985) [NR], 258

Collins, William (1721-1759) [NR], 18

Collins, William Wilkie (1824-1889), 126

Connaught Centre, Hong Kong, 158

Constance, Council of, 13

Constance, Germany, 13, 22, 25

Constantine Bay, Cornwall, 25

Constantine Corneu ap Conomar (St Constantine of Cornwall), 25

Constantine the Great (274 or 288-337) [NR], Roman Emperor, 25, 26

Constantine, Cornwall, 22, 25

Conyngham Hall, Knaresborough, 41

Conyngham, Francis Nathaniel, 2nd Marquess (1797-1876), 43, 44

Conyngham, Henry, 1st Marquess (1766-1832), 41, 43

Cooden Beach, Sussex, 72

Cookstown, N Ireland, 72

Cooper, Dr Peter (1854-1927), 194

Cooper, John Jekyn (1848-1905), 194, 195

Coppinger, 18, 19

Corfield, Thomas John Tresidder (1816-1887), 11

Corran, Gorran Highlanes, 264

Courteenhall, 49, 52, 53, 54, 55, 56, 58, 59, 60, 134

Courteenhall Grammar School, 49, 52, 53, 54, 56, 58, 60

Courtis, Anne (1828-1909), 264

Courtis, Caroline (1829-1911), 264

Courtis, Ellen (1824-1896), 264

Courtis, Emily Hooton (1830-1917), 88, 98, 105, 206, 264

Courtis, Richard Southwell (1795-1870), 264

Courtis, Selina (1834-1896), 264

Covent Garden, London, 42, 240

Crabb, Esther Anne (1848-1905), 136

Craddock, Sir Percy (1923-2010) [NR], 148

Craig Ellachie, West Horsley, Surrey, 240, 241

Crawford, Molly (1907-1992), 72, 221

Crawford, Walter Ruddell (1865-1927), 72

Crete, 25, 211, 213, 214, 215, 216, 218

Crimea, 87, 88, 100

Crimean War (1853-55),, 116

Cruse, Lt Robson RN (1785-1831), 31

Crystal Palace, 50, 196

Cullen, Moray, Scotland, 139

Culliford, Leonard Arthur (1888-1960) [NR], 225

Czechoslovakia, 13, 212, 254

D

da Gama, Vasco (c1460-1524) [NR], 180

da Vinci, Leonardo (1452-1519) [NR], 53

Dadford, Buckinghamshire, 56

Dagfield School, Southport, Lancs, 50

Dalhousie, James Andrew Broun-Ramsay, Marquess (1812-1860) [NR], 85, 86, 87, 109

Dalton Row or Terrace, Denby Dale, 239

Dalton-in-Furness, 138, 139, 142

Darby, John Nelson (1800-1882) [NR], 168

Darjeeling, 77, 107, 109

Dauntsey's School, 51, 53, 172, 229, 258, 262

David Brown Co Ltd, 238

Davis & Elliott, 166

Dawson, George (1888-1963), 239

Dawson, Prebendary Rev

Cooden Beach, Sussex, 72

William Rodgers (1871-1936) [NR], 222

de Fermery, Marie Anne Therese, 119

de Gaulle, Charles (1890-1970) [NR], 204

Delhi, 77, 78, 79, 80, 83, 88, 89, 90, 92, 93, 96, 97, 102, 103

Denbighshire Yeomanry, 21, 226

Denby Dale, 239, 242

Deng Xiaoping (1903-1997) [NR], 148, 153, 160

Denison, Albert, Baron Londesborough (1805-1860), 40, 44, 45

Denison, Arabella Annie (1845-1926), 46, 64, 65, 67, 68, 71, 73, 75

Denison, Bishop, 65

Denison, Elizabeth, Marchioness of Conyngham (1770-1861), 41, 42, 43, 44, 272

Denison, Henry George (1813-1879), 63, 65

Denison, Heywood, and Kennard, 40

Denison, John Law (1911-2006), 71

Denison, Joseph (1740-1832), 40, 166, 221

Denison, Rev Herbert Bouchier Wiggins (1885-1966), 64, 70, 71, 72, 248

Denison, Rev John (c1573-1629), 65

Denison, Rev William (1725-1786), 66, 67

Denison, Rev William (1763-1834), 65

Denison, Rev William (c1696-1755), 66

Denison, Rev William Henry (1848-1915), 46

Denison, William (1714-1782), 45

Denison, William Blethyn (1913-2010), 69, 71

Denison, William Francis Henry (1864-1917), 40

Denison, William Joseph (1769-1849), 40, 272

Detroit, USA, 156, 195

Devonshire, 6th Duke of (1748-1811), 11

Devonshire, 7th Duke of (1808-1891), 138, 140, 143

Dhankuta, Nepal, 108

Dharan, Nepal, 107, 108, 109

Dickens, Charles Culliford Boz (1837-1896), 126, 127

Dickens, Charles John Huffam (1812-1870), 49, 123, 124, 125, 126, 127, 128, 129, 130

Dickinson, Olive May (1925-2017), 242

Dillon & Co, 40

Doctrine of Lapse, 85, 86

Doddington Hall, Cheshire, 204

Dodman Point, South Cornwall, 19, 77, 261

Dolton (nee Hole), Joan (Peter) (1906-1998) [NR], 203

Dolton, Jack (1905-1981) [NR], 133, 203, 204, 224

Dombey & Son, 125

Dorking, Surrey, 40, 203
Drake, Sir Francis (1540-1596), 27, 156
Dreyfus, Lt Col Alfred (1859-1935) [NR], 186
Dublin, 44, 128, 136
Duke of Kent, Prince Edward (b1935), 188
Dulwich College, 49, 50, 53, 221, 243
Durham, 11, 150, 154, 167, 172, 243, 244

E

East India Company, 32, 33, 77, 78, 79, 80, 82, 83, 85, 90, 102, 103, 106, 147, 152
East Lake Golf Club, Atlanta, Georgia, USA, 22
Eastbourne College, 58
Edinburgh, 103, 121, 176, 221
Education Act 1870, 49, 54
Edward VII, 45
Edward VIII, 192
Elizabeth I (1533-1603), 25, 27, 63, 78, 234
Elliott, Charles (1752-1832), 133, 166
Elliott, Charles (1776-1856), 79, 80, 167
Elliott, Charlotte (1789-1871), 167
Elliott, Ethel Beatrice (1880-1978), 117, 130, 181, 184, 185, 187, 188
Elliott, Rev Henry Venn (1725-1797), 167
Entebbe, Uganda, 181, 184, 185, 186
Enterprise Neptune appeal, 206
Evans, Elizabeth Matilda Moule (1840-1907), 126, 127
Evans, Frederick Moule (1832-1902), 126, 127, 128
Evans, General Sir Horace Moule (1841-1923), 104, 105, 106, 108, 123, 127, 149, 168
Evans, Margaret Moule (1837-1909), 127
Evans, Mary Mullett (1801-1877), 167
Evans, 'Pater' Frederick Mullett (1804-1870), 123, 124, 125, 126, 128
Evans, Rev Caleb (1737-1791), 167, 168
Evans, Rev Hugh (1712-1781), 167, 168
Evans, Sir Arthur (1851-1941) [NR], 211, 212, 213, 215, 216, 217, 223, 224, 229, 231
Evans, Sir John (1823-1908) [NR], 211
Exmoor, 200, 203

F

Falkland Islands, 148, 234
Falmouth, Cornwall, 10, 25, 26, 28, 29, 30, 32, 33, 34, 35, 138, 163, 221, 264
Farningham, Kent, 202
Farrar, David (1732-1839), 11
Felstead School, 195
Fisher, Archbishop Geoffrey Francis (1887-1972) [NR], 254

Fitzherbert, Maria Anne née Smythe (1756-1837), 42
Forbes, Theodore (1788-1820), 80
Fortnum, Charles Drury Edward (1820-1899) [NR], 212, 213, 216
Foskett, Bernard (1685–1758) [NR], 168
Framfield, Sussex, 16
Franz Ferdinand, Archduke of Austria (1863-1914), 212
Freeman, Margaret (1848-1893), 212, 213, 216
Freemasonry, 29, 45, 69, 83, 86, 87, 128, 140
Freshfield, James William (1774-1864), 166
Freshwater, Isle of Wight, 224
Frieda Carr Hospital, Ngora, Uganda, 187
Fulham Palace, 247, 248, 256
Fulham, London, 143, 178, 247, 248, 256, 257
Fuller, Richard Buckminster (1895-1983) [NR], 267
Fung, Lady Ivy (1913-2000) [NR], 159
Furama Hotel, Hong Kong, 158
Futtehpore, India, 83, 94, 102

G

Gallipoli, Turkey, 249
Ganges river, India, 83, 92, 97, 98
Garden, Bertha Louisa (Bertie) (1877-1955), 50, 143, 144, 147, 154, 156, 161, 194, 205, 221
Garden, Elsie Annie (1871-1950), 50, 143, 144, 194, 195, 205, 261, 268
Garden, Henry Gordon (1875-1919), 143, 150, 156, 157
Garden, James (1822-1896), 139, 141, 142, 143
Garden, John (1793-1865), 139
Garden, Margaret Jane (1856-c1936), 194, 195
Garratt, Frances Ellen (1845-1930), 142, 143
Gates, Bridget Mary (b1962), 121, 136
Gates, John Thomas (1804-1908), 135
Gates, Michael John (1932-2009), 135, 136
Gates, Reginald Victor (1900-1979), 135
Gates, Ven Simon Philip (b1960), 136, 151, 152, 153, 154, 160
Gem, Grace Harvey, 188
General Strike 1926, 230
Genn, Ann (1783-1861), 29, 30
Genn, James (1782-1845), 29, 30, 33
Genn, Mary (1785-1868), 30
George III, 16, 41, 239
George IV, formerly Prince Regent, 41, 42, 43, 44, 85, 167, 169, 272
George V, 77, 192
George VI, 192, 194
Gereensboro, Maryland, USA, 29

Get Laid Beds, 134
Gherkin, 30 St Mary's Axe, London, 40
Gibson, Gwendoline Natalie (Ann) (1913-2000) [NR], 262
Gibson, Nancy Violet (Doll) (1909-?2004) [NR], 262
Gibson, Wg Cdr Guy Penrose (1918-1944) [NR], 262
Girling, Michael T (b1934), 258
Gladstone, William (1809-1898), 169
Glenn Innes, Australia, 118
Golden Jubilee 1887, 34, 56
Gondokoro, Sudan, 181
Goojerat, Battle of (1849), 82
Gordon, Maj Gen Charles George (1833-1885) [NR], 150
Gorran Churchtown, 56, 171, 172, 264
Gorran Haven, Cornwall, 261
Gorran Highlanes, 264, 267
Goudhurst College, 204, 205, 228
Gradwell, William (1820-1882) [NR], 139, 140, 143
Graham, Billy (1918-2018) [NR], 172, 255
Grampound, Cornwall, 78, 269
Grand Tour, 41, 45, 166
Grand Trunk Road, India, 83, 88, 101
Grant, 'Kitty' Kathleen May (1895-1982), 59, 240, 241, 243
Grant, Kenneth Henry (1896-1916), 241
Grant, Thomas (1858-1946), 241
Grantham, 222, 247, 248, 254, 259
Grantham Grammar School, 247, 248
Gregory, Sir Charles Hutton (1817-1898), 169
Grimston Park, Tadcaster, 44
Grose, Betty (1918-1986) [NR], 19, 261
Grose, John Nicholas (1883-1968) [NR], 19, 77, 254, 261, 267
Grose, Mildred Edith nee Williams (1886-1976) [NR], 261, 267
Grosse Isle Club, Dearborn, Michigan, USA, 22
Grylls, Thomas Reginald (1862-1953), 221
Guangzhou (Canton), 147, 148
Gutteridge, Michael (1842-1935), 71
Gutteridge, Prof Harold Cooke (1876-1953), 71
Gutteridge, Richard Joseph Cooke (1911-2000), 71, 72
Guy's Hospital, London, 118, 192

H

Haigh, Henry Bowman (1879-1947), 242
Hall, Sir John Hathorn (1894–1979) [NR], 188
Hamilton House, Dalton-in-Furness, 139, 142, 143
Hangchow (Hangzhou), 150, 151
Hangkow, 150, 156

Harpur Trust, Bedford, 20
Harriott, Matilda (1819-1877), 97, 102
Harris, Dr Horatio P (1824-1857) [NR], 88, 92
Harrison family, 262, 263, 268
Harrison, John Rae (1909-1993) [NR], 262
Hartwell's Motor Company, 223
Haskins, Albert (1877-1945), 21
Haskins, Ann Lorna (b 1934), 50, 59, 70, 120, 135, 136, 201, 204, 205, 206, 226, 228, 239, 273
Haskins, Annie (1866-1947?), 56, 57, 60
Haskins, Arthur (1810-1863), 14, 16
Haskins, Arthur (1855-1940), 222
Haskins, Arthur (1871-1947), 51, 56, 57, 59
Haskins, Arthur Robert (1826-1900), 20
Haskins, Barbara Pauline Margaret (b1937), 73, 120, 121, 123, 136, 137, 170, 196, 200, 204, 205, 207, 226, 257, 261, 262, 263, 273
Haskins, Bessie (1859-1930), 56
Haskins, Charles (1857-1934), 49, 50, 51, 52, 53, 54, 55, 56, 57, 58, 59
Haskins, Christopher James (b1989), 130, 208, 227
Haskins, David (1819-1912), 16, 17, 18, 32, 204
Haskins, Ellen (1837-1923), 20
Haskins, Emma (1843-1923), 20
Haskins, Frank (1862-1945), 55, 56, 135
Haskins, Frederick (1898-1981), 21, 22, 272
Haskins, George (1835-1872), 20, 21
Haskins, George (1851-1915), 51, 55, 56, 134, 240
Haskins, George (1892-1971), 21
Haskins, James Ebenezer (1816-1884), 15
Haskins, John (1834-1913), 16
Haskins, Jonathan Neil (b1986), 22, 53, 133, 153, 154, 208, 229, 234
Haskins, Joseph (1779-1855), 14, 15
Haskins, Joseph John (1803-1868), 15, 16, 21
Haskins, Joseph John (1826-1863), 21
Haskins, Joseph John (1859-1887), 50
Haskins, Lucie (1855-1931), 55, 56
Haskins, Lucy (1877-1945), 21
Haskins, Minnie Louise (1885-1957) [NR], 55
Haskins, Nancy Dora (1908-2000), 222, 224
Haskins, Paul Denison (1905-1996), 22, 39, 63, 73, 75, 133, 185, 200, 202, 203, 204, 207, 208, 211, 212, 213, 215, 216,

217, 218, 221, 222, 223, 224, 225, 226, 227, 228, 229, 230, 231, 273
Haskins, Thomas William (1882-1949), 21
Haskins, William (1804-1879), 15, 16, 19, 20, 21, 22
Haskins, William Thomas (1824-1898), 20, 49, 51, 53, 54, 58, 59, 60
Hastings, Warren (1732-1818) [NR], 78
Hatfield Peverel, Essex, 224
Hathorn, Mary (1860-1953), 118
Hawker, Rev Robert Stephen (1803-1875) [NR], 17, 18, 19, 125, 133
Hawksmoor, Nicholas (1661-1736) [NR], 255
Headingley, Yorkshire, 72
Heber, Bishop Reginald (1783-1826) [NR], 80, 81
Hehl, Mary Ann (Fanny Stirling) (1813-1895), 169
Heley, Mary A (1856-1940), 21
Heligan, Gorran Highlanes, 230, 264, 267
Hemmick Beach, Cornwall, 77, 200, 233, 261
Hepplewhite, George (1727-1786) [NR], 166
Hepworth, Barbara (1903-1975) [NR], 233
Heraklion, Crete, 213
Herodotus, 25
Hertford, Marchioness, Isabella Anne Seymour-Conway (1759-1834) [NR], 41
Hewitt, Maj-Gen William, 88, 89, 90
Hill House Epsom, 200
Hill House, Watlington, 63, 67, 70, 223
Hinchliffe, Harold (1893-1961) [NR], 242
Hinchliffe's mill, Denby Dale, 242
Hippopotamus, 180, 181
Ho Tung, Sir Robert (1862-1956) [NR], 155
Hodgson, Rebecca (1831-1902), 33
Hodson, Bvt-Maj William Stephen Raikes (1821-1858), 90, 91, 95, 96, 97, 100, 101, 102
Hoffman Manufacturung Company, 57
Hogarth, Catherine Thomson (1815-1879), 126, 127
Hogarth, Georgina (1827-1917), 125, 127
Holgate, Robert Archbishop of York (c1481-1555) [NR]., 235, 236
Holker Hall, Cumbria, 140
Horne, Mary (1887-1967) [NR], 207
Hong Kong, 22, 83, 98, 108, 147, 148, 151, 152, 153, 154, 155, 156, 157, 158, 159, 160, 234, 252, 267, 271
Hongkong and Shanghai Bank, 147, 152, 154, 155, 158, 221

Hooton, Nancy (1798-1835), 264
Hooton, William (1873-1956), 49
Household Words, 125, 126, 127
Howrah railway station, Calcutta, 78
Hudson Taylor, James (1832-1905) [NR], 149, 236
Hoylake, 21
Hunt, William Holman (1827-1910) [NR], 68
Huss, Rev John (1369-1415), 13, 14
Hutchings, William (1851-1933), 20

I

Illustrated London News, 124
India, 10, 28, 32, 33, 34, 35, 46, 50, 73, 77, 78, 82, 83, 84, 85, 87, 88, 109, 115, 116, 127, 134, 164, 165, 167, 179, 187, 236, 238
Irving, Sir Henry (1838-1905) [NR], 169
Isandlwana, Battle, South Africa, 32
Isle of Wight, 31, 224
Islington, 13, 14, 16, 149

J

Jacard's School, 3 Chemin de Longerai, Lausanne, 35, 191
Jago, John Sampson (1754-1835), 264
Jago, Lt John Sampson RN (1794-1871), 264
Jago, Reginald Cory (1891-1970), 263, 264
Jamaica Inn, Bodmin Moor, Cornwall, 16
James II, 19
James, Samuel (1846-1930), 244
Jardine Matheson, 158
Jarn Mound, Youlbury, 213
Jeffries Square, London, 40
Jhansi, India, 85, 102
Jinja, Uganda, 117, 181, 183
John Brown & Co, 34
Jones, 'Bobby' Robert Tyre Jr (1902-1971) [NR], 22
Jones, Joseph Walter (1857-1938) [NR], 192, 194
Jones, Sir Samuel (1610-1673) [NR], benefactor, 53
Juan le Pins, Antibes, 119, 197
Jubalpur, India, 191

K

Kampala, Uganda, 117, 181
Kathmandu, Nepal, 107, 108
Kavirondo (Luo) tribe, Kenya, 182, 183
Kay, Rev Prebendary Robert Bryan Hervey (1912–1982), 251, 254, 257, 267
Kay, Susan Hester (b1948), 46
Kean, Charles (1811-1868) [NR], 124, 169
Keats, John (1795-1851)

[NR], 18
Kennedy, Myles (1862–1928) [NR], 140
Kenya, 175, 176, 178, 182, 187, 188
Kenyon's mill, Barnsley, 242
Kewark, Eliza (c1795-?) [NR], 80
Khan Yusufzai, Azimullah (1830-1859) [NR], 86, 87, 88, 92, 94, 98, 100
Khan, Sarvur [NR], 94
Khartoum, Sudan, 150, 181
Kiangsu, China, 150
Kidbrooke Park, London, 203, 224
Killigrew, Elizabeth (1622-1680) [NR], mistress to Charles II, 28
Killigrew, John (1514-1567) [NR], 27
Killigrew, Sir Peter (1634-1704) [NR], 28
Kipling, Rudyard (1865-1936) [NR], 72
Kirk Deighton, 11
Kirkwood family, 159
Kisumu, British East Africa (Kenya), 180, 181, 182, 184, 185
Kitchener, Gen Horatio (1850-1916) [NR], 150
Knaresborough, 41
Knole Park, Sevenoaks, Kent, 130
Knossos, Crete, 211, 212, 213, 215, 218
Konstanz, Germany, 13
Kowloon, Hong Kong, 148, 151, 160
Kumi, Uganda, 187

L

Lake Albert, Uganda, 181
Lake Victoria, Africa, 117, 178, 181, 183, 185
Lambert, Edward (stage name Stirling) (1809-1894), 169
Lambert, Frances Mary (1842-1929), 169
Lancaster, 249
Lanhydrock House, Cornwall, 140
Lansdowne, Henry Petty-Fitzmaurice, 5th Marquess (1845-1927) [NR], 178
Lawrence of Arabia (1888-1935) [NR], 151
Lawrence, Sir Henry Montgomery (1806-1857) [NR], 90, 91, 95, 97
Laws, Amy Beatrice (1877-1935), 175, 176
Laws, Arthur Moore (1872-1927), 175, 187
Le Brasseur and Oakley, lawyers, 201
Leckford Road, Oxford, 187
Leeds, 40, 45, 46, 109, 221, 237, 244, 249
Legat, Arthur Alexander (1875-1959), 176, 221
Leicester, 182
Leighton Buzzard, 16, 21
Leighton Hall, Lancashire, 140
Lemon, Mark, (1809-1870) [NR], Editor of Punch, 126, 128

Leofric, Earl of Mercia (d1057) [NR], 52
Leprosy, 186, 187
Library of Congress, Washington DC, USA, 151
Lieven, Princess Dorothea von (1785-1857) [NR], 43
Lin Tse Hsu (1785-1850) [NR], Imperial High Commissioner, 148
Lindal-in-Furness, Cumbria, 140
Linear A, 218
Linear B, 217
Linen industry, 236
Linton, Yorkshire, 11
Little Dorrit, 125
Liverpool, 21, 40, 129, 136, 137, 141, 228, 236, 244
Liverpool Institute of Performing Arts, 244
Livingstone, Dr David (1813-1873) [NR], 175
Llandudno, Wales, 119
Lloyd, the Rt Rev Arthur Thomas (1844-1907) [NR], 67
Lockwood, George (1891-1956), 239
Lombard Lane, Whitefriars, 124
Lombard Street, City of London, 40, 229, 230
Lombard, Jean, 133
Londesborough Lodge, Scarborough, Yorkshire, 39, 40, 45
Londesborough Park, Yorkshire, 44, 45
London, 10, 13, 14, 15, 16, 19, 20, 30, 31, 32, 33, 34, 40, 42, 45, 49, 55, 71, 86, 103, 104, 107, 115, 116, 117, 118, 123, 124, 127, 128, 129, 133, 136, 137, 141, 143, 148, 151, 155, 157, 167, 168, 169, 170, 171, 176, 177, 185, 201, 221, 224, 241, 250, 253, 254, 255, 256, 257, 258
London city churches, 255
Longford, 7th Earl, Frank Pakenham, (1905-2001) [NR], 258
Longleat, Wiltshire, 229
Lorna Doone, 200, 204
Lucas Brothers, 240
Lucknow, 77, 84, 85, 91, 95, 96, 97, 98, 101
Lutyens, Sir Edwin (1869-1944) [NR], 77, 78, 109

M

MacArthur, Gen Douglas (1880-1964) [NR], 70
Macau, 152, 153, 154
Macaulay, Thomas Babington, 1st Baron (1800-1859), 86, 109, 130, 156, 223
Machen, Annie (1885-1952), 235, 236
Machen, Frank (1893-1950), 133
Machen, Harry (1881-1943), 133, 235, 236, 238
Machen, Willie (1853-1940), 133
Mackenzie, Dr Duncan (1861-1934) [NR], 215, 216

MacLehose, Baron Crawford (1917-2000) [NR], 157
MacNair, 'Masie' Mary Isabel (1907-1991), 185
Macpherson, Ethel Jane (née James) (1882-1975?) [NR], 57
Madras, 46, 79, 134
Magdalen College School, Oxford, 51, 68, 178
Magdalen College, Oxford, 66, 67, 243
Magdalen Hall, Oxford, 66, 67
Mahal, Begum Nawab Zinat (1821-1882) [NR], 94, 96, 101, 103
Maiden, Stewart (1886-1948) [NR], 22
Maidenhead, 34, 120, 202
Maldon, Essex, 57
Malindi, Kenya, 180
Malta, 34
Manchester, 126, 128, 142, 221
Manchester Guardian, 212
Manchuria, 156
Maplehurst, Sussex, 258
Marconi, Guglielmo (1874-1937) [NR], 57, 196, 237
Margate, Kent, 192, 208
Marlborough College, Wiltshire, 224
Marsden, Laura Peplow (1904-1994) [NR], 223
Maryland, USA, 29, 30, 33
Mason, Phyllis Therese (1889-1966), 70, 188, 253, 256
Masters, Francis (1821-?), 65
Masters, Mary (1825-1913), 65
Maugham, William Somerset (1874-1965) [NR], 197
May, George (1868-1884), 135
May, Nancy (1906-1984), 135, 136
May, William (1797-1864), 135
Mbale, Kenya, 181
McDouall, Laura Amelia (Millie) (1859-1938), 118
Meerut, India, 88, 89, 90, 91, 92
Mellor, Dr Elsa Mary (1926-2016), 121
Mevagissey, Cornwall, 31, 35, 261, 262, 263, 264, 268
Milton, John (1608-1674) [NR], 180
Minehead, 120
Minoan civilisation, 215, 218
Minos, King of Crete, 214, 215, 218
Minotaur, 211, 213, 214, 215
Mirzapore, India, 83
Mitchell, Andrew MP (b1956) [NR], 234
Mitchell, Sir David MP (1928-2014) [NR], 234
Mombasa, Kenya, 178, 179, 180, 181, 182, 187
Monk Bretton, Barnsley, Yorkshire, 235
Mont Blanc, 250
Moravian church, 14
Morley, Andrew (b1936), 243
Morley, Arthur (1888-1961),

239
Morley, Harold (1893-1961), 239, 240, 243
Morley, John (1833-1876), 242
Morley, Laura (1890-1955), 239
Morley, Reginald McGregor (1922-1998), 242
Morley, Renée Faith (1926-2017), 239, 242, 243, 273
Morley, Sarah (1886-1965), 239
Morley, Thomas (1801-1876), 242
Morley, Wallace Bramwell McGregor (b1932), 242
Morley, Wallace McGregor (1856-1927), 239
Morrison Chapel, Macau, 152, 153
Morrison, John Robert (1814-1843) [NR], 152
Morrison, Rev Robert (1782-1834) [NR], 149, 151, 152
Morwenstow, 17, 125, 133, 204
Mott, Melanie (b1950) [NR]., 208
Moule, Bishop George Evans (1828-1912), 149, 150, 151
Moule, Bishop Handley Carr Glyn (1841-1920), 150, 167, 172
Moule, Rev George Herbert (1876-1949), 151
Moule, Rev Henry (1801-1880), 116, 167
Moule, Rev Henry William (1871-1953), 151
Moule, Ven Arthur Evans (1835-1918), 149, 150, 151
Mount Elgon, Kenya/Uganda, 117, 181
Mount Homa, Kenya, 181
Mount Kenya, 184
Mount Kilimanjaro, Tanzania, 184
Mountain, Sir Edward Mortimer Bt (1872-1948) [NR], 191, 200
Mumias, Uganda, 182
Murray, Dr John (1809-1898) [NR], 116
Murray, Dr John (1809-1898) [NR]., 103
Murray, Lt Col James Harry Stewart (1866-1948), 73
Museveni, Yoweri (b1944) [NR], President of Uganda, 188
Musk, Elon (b1971) [NR], 53, 54, 271
MV Port Chalmers, 238
Mycenae Road, Greenwich, 194
Mycenae, Greece, 25, 213, 215, 218
Myers-Briggs psychometric test, 270

N

Nagpore (Nagpur), India, 85
Nairobi Golf Club, 184
Nairobi, Kenya, 176, 184, 185

Nana Govind Dhondu Pant (1824-c1857) [NR], 86, 87, 88, 92, 93, 94, 95, 97, 98, 99, 102
Nandi, Uganda, 182
Nare Head, Cornwall, 206, 261
Nash, John (1752-1835) [NR], architect, 42, 141
National Trust, 17, 58, 134, 206, 234, 261
National Union of Bank Employees (NUBE), 230
Nelson, Horatio, 1st Viscount Nelson, 1st Duke of Bronte KB (1758-1805) [NR], 166, 264
Nelson, New Zealand, 33
Nepal, 76, 77, 85, 88, 98, 106, 107, 108
Nestor, King of Pylos, 218
New College, Eastbourne, 58
New Sawley, 56
New Territories, 148, 158
New York, 252
New Zealand, 33, 70, 118, 129, 238, 243, 251, 258, 272
Newall, Air Chief Marshall Cyril (1886-1963) [NR], 238
Newcastle-upon-Tyne, 243, 244, 248, 249
Newlyn, Cornwall, 163
Newman, Cardinal John Henry (1801-1890) [NR], 249
Newton Aycliffe, County Durham, 244
Newton, Ernest (1856–1922) [NR], Architect, 187, 200
Newton, Rev John (1725-1807) [NR], 164
Newton, Sir Isaac (1642-1727) [NR], 247
Ngora, Uganda, 187, 188
Nicholson, Ben (1894-1982) [NR], 233
Nicholson, Simon (1934-1990) [NR], 233
Nicholson, Sir Sydney (1875-1947) [NR], 200
Nightingale, Florence (1820-1910) [NR], 100, 116, 124
Nimule, Sudan, 181
Ningpo (Ningbo), China, 148, 149, 151
Norbury Park, 200, 203, 210
Normandy, France, 242
North Atlantic convoys, 237
Northampton, 16, 51, 52, 56, 58
Northcote-Trevelyan Reforms, 49
Northern Territory, Australia, 251
Nozia River, 183
Numismatic Society, 45

O

Oare Manor, 200
Obote, Milton, President of Uganda (1925-2005) [NR], 188
Olympics 2012, 244
Operation Overlord, 262
Oriel College, Oxford, 249, 251, 254
Orlando, Florida, USA, 208
Orpington Bridge Club, 230

Oudh, 84, 85, 88, 93, 95, 97, 98, 101, 109
Outram, Lt-Gen Sir James (1803-1863), 84, 85, 91, 97, 101
Overseal, Derbyshire, 51, 55
Owletts Kent, 77
Oxford, 17, 50, 51, 55, 56, 63, 64, 65, 66, 67, 69, 71, 121, 131, 151, 176, 178, 181, 185, 187, 188, 192, 211, 212, 213, 223, 235, 240, 248, 249, 250
Oxford & Aylesbury Tramroad Company, 56
Oxford Museum of Natural History, 241
Oxford, Polstead Road, 151

P

Packet ships, 28, 29, 30, 32
Padstow to Wadebridge railway, 241
Paisley, Rev Ian (1926-2014) [NR], 255
Paley and Austin, 141
Palladio, Andrea (1508-1580) [NR], 166
Palmer & Turner, architects, 154, 158
Palmerston, Henry (1784-1865) [NR], 3rd Viscount, 148
Pande, Mangal (1827-1857) [NR], 88, 95
Pandora Inn, 28
Parker family, 207
Parrott, Joseph Philip (1905-1973) [NR], 230
Patrixbourne, Kent, 44
Pearson, Very Rev Hugh (1776-1856), 167
Peckham, 127, 137
Peking (Beijing), China, 148
Pell, Ruth Mary (1908-1999), 196
Penare Farm, 19, 261, 267
Pendennis, 125
Pendennis Castle, 26
Pender, Benjamin (1742-1812) [NR], 30
Pender, Francis (1778-1849) [NR], Mayor of Falmouth, 30
Penistone, Yorkshire, 238, 240, 242
Penquarry, Cornwall, 77, 254, 267
Pentewan, Cornwall, 10, 19, 26, 35, 168, 170, 171, 230, 233, 262
Perkins, George Frederick (1856-1934), 56
Perranzabuloe, Cornwall, 244
Peshawar, India, 83, 106
Petroc, Saint of Cornwall (6th century) [NR], 25
Pett, William (1552-1587) [NR], 234
Petter, Percy Waddams (1873-1955) [NR], 254
Petts Wood, 204, 207, 226, 229, 234, 250, 256, 261
Pickwick Papers, 124
Pilling, Lancs, 121
Pitt, William the Younger (1759-1806) [NR], 164, 165, 166
Plassey, Battle of (1757), 87
Plymouth Brethren, 170, 174

Poe, Edgar Alan (1809-1949) [NR], 18
Poldhu, Cornwall, 196
Polkerris, Cornwall, 27
Pollexfen, Charles (1838-1923), 129
Pollexfen, John Anthony (1840-1900), 129
Pollexfen, Muriel Alice (1876-1923), 35, 82, 129, 146, 154, 192
Pollexfen, Susan Mary (1841-1900), 128
Pollexfen, William (1811-1892), 128, 129
Polstead Road, Oxford, 187
Port Florence (Kisumu), Kenya, 181
Porthcurnick Beach, 211
Porthleven, Cornwall, 262
Porthluney, Caerhays Beach, 26
Portland, William, 6th Duke of (1857-1943) [NR], 241
Portloe, Cornwall, 225, 267
Portmellon, Cornwall, 254
Potomac River, USA, 30
Poulton, Prof Sir Edward Bagnall (1856-1943) [NR], 181, 216
Prague, 13
Prescelly hills, Pembrokeshire, Wales, 208
Property Services Agency, 107, 108, 233, 234
Punch, 124, 126, 128
Punjab, 83, 85, 116
Pusey, Prof Edward Bouverie (1800-1882) [NR], 249
Pylos, Greece, 218
Pyrton with Shirburn, Oxfordshire, 187

Q

Qing Dynasty, 149
Qualters & Smith Bros Ltd, 238, 242
Queensland, Australia, 250, 251

R

Radio Caroline, 207
Ragusa (Dubrovnik), 212
Raisina Hill, Delhi, India, 77
Raleigh, Sir Walter (1554-1618) [NR], 27
Ramsden, Sir James (1822-1896) [NR], 138, 140, 141, 143
Rana, Jang Bahadur (1817-1877) [NR], 107
Ranelagh School, Bracknell, 241
Rashleigh, John (1554-1624), 27
Ravenswood, Bromley, Kent, 200
Rawalpindi, Pakistan, 106
Reading, Berks, 63, 65, 120, 136, 137, 196, 241
Red Fort, Delhi, 77, 89, 96
Redbook's, Barnsley, 236
Redmore, Norah Ethel (1906-1985) [NR], 203
Reedham's School, Purley, Surrey, 50

Repulse Bay, Hong Kong Island, 158, 159
Reynolds, Emma (1862-1933), 240
Rhodes, Cecil (1853-1902) [NR]., 175, 176
Rhodesia (Zimbabwe), 69, 175, 176
Richie, Sir Richmond (1854-1912), 77, 78
Ride, Sir Lindsay (1898-1977) [NR] and Lady May (1915-1999) [NR], 159
Ridgeway, Eileen (1913-1986), 137
River Wey Navigation, 222
Robert I of Scotland 'the Bruce' (1274-1329), 139
Roberts, Emily (1846-1920), 244
Rockhampton, Australia, 251
Rotunda Museum, Scarborough, 39, 45
Rouen, France, 249
Royal Albert Bridge, River Tamar, 34
Royal Festival Hall, 71
Royal Naval College, 69
Royal Society, 45
Royal Society of Antiquaries, 45
Rugby School, 49, 53, 90, 100

S

Sackville-West, Vita (1892-1962), 130
Salisbury, Wiltshire, 46, 51, 65, 167, 224, 249, 250, 253
Salter, Doreen (b1927), 243
San Francisco, California, USA, 155, 156, 252
Sandringham, Norfolk, 192, 193
Sara Beattie Secretarial College, Hong Kong, 156
Sarajevo, 212
Sarum Theological College, Salisbury, Wilts, 249
Satara, India, 85
Saunders, Burslem Charles (1821-1888), 90, 96, 97, 102, 104
Saunders, Charles Alexander (1796-1864), 34, 90
Saunders, Robert Power (1831-1871), 34
Saunders, William Septimus (1803-1850), 34
Scarborough, 10, 39, 40, 45
Scargill, Arthur (b1938) [NR], 236
Schliemann, Dr Heinrich (1822-1890) [NR], 213
Schneider, Henry William (1817-1887) [NR], 138, 141, 143
Schreiner, Frederic Samuel (1841-1901) [NR], 58
Schreiner, Olive (1855–1920) [NR], 58
Scott, Sir George Gilbert (1811-1878) [NR], 141, 222
Scottish Institute of Bankers, 221
Screaming Lord Such (1940-1999) [NR], 207
Scruby, Basil (1875-1946)

[NR], 225
Seamer, East Yorkshire, 40
Seccombe, Henry Lawrence (1841-1910), 78, 178
Seccombe, Sir Thomas Lawrence (1812-1902), 78
Sevadah Kothi, Cawnpore, 94
Shaftesbury, 7th Earl of (1801-1885) [NR], 49, 240, 241
Shanghai, China, 147, 148, 150, 154, 155, 156, 157, 221
Sheffield, Yorkshire, 34, 121, 238
Shelley, Percy Bysshe (1792-1822) [NR], 18
Shenandoah Valley, Virginia, USA, 29
Shenzhen, China, 153, 154
Shepherd, Helen (b1967), 154
Shepley, Yorkshire, 242
Sheraton, Thomas (1751-1806) {NR], 166
Sherer, John Walter (1823-1911) [NR], 99, 100, 101, 102, 103, 154
Shivering Sands fort, 207
Shoreditch, London, 13, 14
Shrivenham, Berkshire (now Oxfordshire), 120
Simla, India, 90, 262
Simpson, Christopher (1875-1937), 136
Simpson, Hugh (b1973), 11, 137
Simpson, Ian (b1944), 136, 263
Simpson, James (1820-1894), 136
Simpson, James William (1846-1896), 136
Simpson, Luke (b1970), 10, 137, 167, 217
Simpson, Naomi (b1977), 137
Simpson, Ronald (1911-1980), 137
Simpson, Thomas (1777-1864), 136
Simpson, Wallis, born Betty Wallis Warfield, later Duchess of Windsor (1896-1986) [NR], 147
Slade School of Fine Art, London, 141
Slade, Felix (1790-1868). [NR], 141
Slane Castle, Ireland, 42
Sleeman, Maj-Gen Sir William Henry (1788-1856) [NR], 85
Sleeping Sickness, 117, 183
Sligo, Ireland, 27, 128
Slough, Berkshire, 127
Smart, George Douglas (1904-1971), 154, 155, 158, 159, 201
Smart, John Douglas (1863-1939), 147, 221
Smit, Sir Timothy Bartel (b1954) [NR], 267
Smith, Charlotte (1820-1899), 136
Society for the Propagation of the Gospel (SPG), 86
Soroti, Uganda, 187
Southampton, Hants, 32,

123, 136, 156
Spencer, George (1907-1995), 139
SS Empire Opossum, 238
SS Fort Chill Coating, 237
SS Grange Park, 237
SS Royal Sovereign, 208
St Alfege's Hospital, Greenwich, 69
St Brandon's School, 253
St Day, Cornwall, 11
St Ewe, Cornwall, 263, 264
St Ives, Cornwall, 30, 31, 33, 34, 137, 233
St Just-in-Roseland, Cornwall, 26
St Keverne, Cornwall, 163
St Luke's, London, 13
St Martin's-in-the-Fields, Trafalgar Square, 240
St Olave's, Bermondsey, London, 120
St Paul's Cathedral, London, 248, 255, 257
St Stephen's Chapel, Hong Kong, 159, 160
St Thomas's Hospital, 32
Staincross, Yorkshire, 235, 238
Stank Mine, Barrow, Cumbria, 138
Stanley Fort, Hong Kong, 159
Stephen, Adeline Virginia (1882-1941), 130, 165
Stephen, James (1733-1779), 165
Stephen, James (Jem) MP (1758-1832), 165
Stephen, Sir James (1789-1859), 165
Stephen, Sir Leslie (1832-1904), 130, 165
Stephens, Frances (Bunty) (1924-1978), 21
Stephenson, Helah (1883-1957), 242, 243
Sticklepath, Devon, 261
Stilwell, Mary Ann (1817-1910), 16
Stilwell, Richard (1797-1877), 16
Stirling, Fanny (Mary Ann Hehl) (1813-1895), 169, 171
Stonehenge, Wiltshire, 208, 218, 224, 261
Stowe, Buckinghamshire, 55, 56, 134, 135
Stratford House School, Bickley, Kent, 120, 200
Studdert-Kennedy, Rev Geoffrey Anketell (1883-1929) [NR], 249
Sudan, 150, 181, 182
Suez Canal, 82, 179, 238, 261
Switzerland, 13, 33, 35, 164, 191, 199, 207, 243, 245
Sydney, Australia, 107, 118, 170, 252
Sykes, Paul (b1943) [NR], 107
Syro-Phoenicians, 25, 208, 218

T
Tadpoles Society, 233
Taiping Rebellion, 149
Tanner, Mary (1838-1912), 16

Tate Gallery, 222
Tate, Sir Henry (1819-1899), 33
Taunton, Devon, 46, 58, 254
Taylor, Rev Samuel Benjamin (1841-1921), 71
Tedder, Air Chief Marshal Arthur William, 1st Baron (1890-1967) [NR], 238, 262
Tedder, Prof Hon Richard (b1946) [NR], 262, 263
Temple, Archbishop William (1881-1944) [NR], 254
Ternan, Ellen (1839-1914) [NR], 125, 126, 127
Terry, Dame Ellen (1847-1928) [NR], 169
Thackeray, Annie (1837-1919), 126
Thackeray, William Makepeace (1811-1863), 78, 81, 86, 88, 124, 125, 127, 130
Thames river, 14, 34, 69, 115, 255, 256
Thatcher, Baroness Margaret (1925-2013) [NR], 148, 233, 247
Theseus, Prince of Athens, 214
Thetford, Norfolk, 238
Tiananmen Square, Beijing, China, 153, 160
Tickner, Dorothy Gladys (née Denman) (1912-2005) [NR], 205
Tin, 26, 138, 244
Tito, Marshal Josip Broz (1892-1980) [NR], 212
Tolit and Dolby, architects, 67
Tom Brown's Schooldays, 49, 50
Tomusange, Bishop of Soroti [NR], 187
Tradescant, John the younger (1608-1662) [NR], 212
Travis, Sir Edward (1888-1956) [NR], 73
Treaty of Nanking 1842, 148
Treaty of Sergauli 1816, 107
Treaty of Tien-tsin (Tianjin) 1858-60, 148
Tregoneggie, nr Falmouth, Cornwall, 28, 29
Trelawny, Sir Jonathan, Bishop of Bristol, (1650-1721) [NR], 19
Trelissick, Cornwall, 58
Tremayne family, 230, 267
Tremearne, Fanny Newman (1809-1873), 30
Tremearne, Matilda (1847-1908), 31
Tresidder, Adrian Clive (1878-1923), 105, 128, 129, 195
Tresidder, Beryl Fergus (1899-1939), 118
Tresidder, Christiana Philoena (1784-1875), 31
Tresidder, Dr Edward Stanley (1859-1926), 118
Tresidder, Dr Harry Innes (1861-1922), 118
Tresidder, Dr Morton Everard (1871-1944), 191, 222
Tresidder, Dr Percy Edgar (1873-1942), 118, 119, 196, 197

Tresidder, Dr Tolmie Gordon (1898-1963), 119
Tresidder, Dr William Elliot (1864-1929), 118, 119
Tresidder, Elizabeth Anne (1846-1929), 34, 50, 168
Tresidder, Ethel (1862-1956), 170, 173
Tresidder, Frances Alice (1848-1851), 82
Tresidder, Jean (1904-1976), 50, 199, 200, 201, 202, 203, 204, 205, 206, 207, 224, 225, 226, 229, 230, 261, 267
Tresidder, John (1754-1810), 29
Tresidder, John Anthony Clive Pollexfen (1912-2001), 195, 196, 201, 203
Tresidder, Mary Rosamond (1847-1923), 50, 83, 221
Tresidder, Megan Sarah (1958-2001), 129
Tresidder, Nicholas (1718-1781), 27, 30, 35
Tresidder, Nicholas Tolmie (1782-1861), 29, 30, 31, 32
Tresidder, Rosemary Muriel Pollexfen (1911-1998), 203
Tresidder, Samuel (1730-1800), 28
Tresidder, Samuel (1791-1824), 32
Tresidder, Surgeon-General John Nicholas (1819-1889), 32, 35, 36, 77, 81, 82, 83, 84, 86, 87, 88, 98, 99, 100, 101, 102, 103, 105, 115, 116, 118, 120, 121, 264
Tresidder, Tolmie John (Jack) (1850-1931), 34, 49, 115
Tresidder, William Edward Walmsley (1796-1855), 30
Tresidder, William Tolmie (1817-1909), 31, 32
Tresidder. Dr Morton Everard (1871-1944), 10, 35, 69, 118, 119, 191, 192, 193, 194, 195, 196, 197, 200, 205
Tresuder, Nycholas (1550-1559), 25
Trevanion family, 42
Trewhiddle Manor, St Austell, Cornwall, 19
Trewinnard, Elizabeth, (1518-after 1582) [NR], 27
Twyford, Berkshire, 34, 120, 136

U
Uganda, 175, 177, 178, 179, 180, 181, 182, 183, 185, 186, 187, 188
Ulverston, Cumbria, 138, 140, 141
Umbala (Ambala), India, 83, 88
University of London, 58
Unwin, Sir Raymond (1863-1940) [NR], 248
Upton Grey, Manor House, Hants, 187

V
Venn, Nellie (Eling) (1758-1843), 166
Venn, Rev Henry (1725-

1797), 164
Venn, Rev John (1759-1813), 164
Ventris, Michael (1922-1956) [NR], 217
Versailles, France, 212
Vibart, Col Edward Daniel Hamilton 'Butcher' (1837-1923), 89, 90, 96, 116
Vibart, Maj Edward (1807-1857), 89, 92, 93, 96
Victoria, Queen, 34, 126
Villa Ariadne, Crete, 216
Virginia, USA, 29, 30, 216

W
Waddy, Elizabeth Mary (1917-2001) [NR], 172
Wadham, Edward (1828-1913) [NR], the Duke of Buccleuch's agent, 138, 140, 141, 142, 143
Wake, Rev Archibald (1856-1925) [NR], 52
Wake, Sir Charles, 10th Baronet (1791-1864) [NR], 52
Wake, Sir Herewald, 12th Bt (1852-1916) [NR], 20
Wake, Sir Hereward (1916-2017) [NR], 14th Baronet, 52
Wakefield, Yorkshire, 236
Waldorf Hotel, London, 201, 202
Wallace, Sir Barnes (1887-1979) [NR], 262
Walliswood, Surrey, The Spinney, 203
Wand, Kathleen, Viscountess Addison (1912-c2006), 248, 249, 250, 258
Wand, Paul (1912-1934), 249, 250, 251, 257
Wand, Rt Rev John William Charles (1885-1977), 118, 171, 222, 224, 247, 248, 249, 250, 251, 252, 253, 254, 255, 256, 257, 258
Washington, George (1732-1799) [NR], 29, 32
Watchfield, Berks/Oxon, 120
Watcombe Manor, Watlington, Oxon, 63, 178
Watlington, Oxfordshire, 63, 67, 70, 75, 178, 223, 224
Wellington, 1st Duke of (1769-1852) [NR], 41
Wellington, NZ, 243
Wells, Somerset, 252, 253, 254, 256
Wendron, Cornwall, 264
Wesley House, Cambridge, 72
Wesley, John (1703-1791) [NR], 167, 168
West Cornwall Bank, 221
West Horsley, Surrey, 164, 241, 243
West Kirby, The Wirral, 21
West Newton, Norfolk, 192
Westcombe Park, Blackheath, 194
Westgate-on-sea, Kent, 206, 207, 228
Westminster, 115
Westminster Abbey, 42, 247
Wetherby, Yorkshire, 11, 72, 118, 153, 229

Whale-headed stork, 181
Wheeler, Maj-Gen Sir Hugh Massey (1789-1857) [NR], 82, 84, 85, 91, 92, 98, 102
White House, Witham, Essex, 59, 222
Whitehead, Elizabeth (1828-1892), 51, 52, 54, 55, 56
Wiggins glacier, 185
Wiggins, Amy (1883-1966), 247, 248, 249, 250, 252, 256, 257, 258
Wiggins, Barbara Hester (1923-2011), 63, 68, 120, 136, 251, 253, 256, 257, 267
Wiggins, Bernard (1878-1972), 46, 70, 73, 177, 181, 253
Wiggins, Bernard (b1953), 247
Wiggins, Christopher (b1942), 72
Wiggins, David (b1954), 70
Wiggins, Denie (1905-1971), 185, 223, 224
Wiggins, Dora (1871-1966), 58, 73, 203, 204, 223
Wiggins, Dr Bobbie (1913-1992), 69, 70
Wiggins, Dr William Denison (1873-1937), 69, 70, 204
Wiggins, Dr William Robert Denison (1913-1926), 69
Wiggins, Ella Stevens (1908-1937), 176
Wiggins, George Francis (1880-1913), 176
Wiggins, Hugh (1911-1989), 222
Wiggins, Kathleen Eliza (1875-1963), 175, 176, 179, 188
Wiggins, Margaret Denison (1914-1993), 69, 71
Wiggins, Mary (1870-1946), 65, 73, 75, 216, 217, 218, 223, 224
Wiggins, Mervyn Clare (1911-1971), 188
Wiggins, Neville (1886-1970), 70, 72, 202, 221, 224, 250
Wiggins, Norah Clare (1909-2001), 187, 188
Wiggins, Philip (1874-1929), 64, 68, 175, 176
Wiggins, Phyllis Clare (1908-1989), 185, 187, 188
Wiggins, Rev Dr Clare (1876-1965), 107, 117, 175, 176, 177, 178, 179, 180, 181, 182, 183, 184, 185, 186, 187, 188, 250, 273
Wiggins, William JP (1836-1913), 63, 64, 67, 75, 175
Wilberforce, Sarah (1758-1816), 165
Wilberforce, William (1759-1833), 40, 80, 163, 164, 165, 166
Wilding, John Hollis (b1942), 258
Wilkinson, Edward (1761-1836), 46
Wilkinson, John later Denison (1759-1820), 46
William Denison & Co, 45
William Freeman Ltd, Barnsley, 242

William of Orange, William III of England, 14, 19
William the Conqueror, 52, 130
William, Duke of Cambridge (b1982), 80
Williams, John Michael (1813-1880) [NR], 221
Wilson, Baron David (b1935) [NR], 148
Wilson, Harriette, courtesan (1786-1845) [NR], 43
Wilson, Lt-Gen Sir Archdale (1803–1874) [NR], 90, 96
Witham Essex, 59, 222, 224
Witherow, Daniel (1807-1886), 21
Witherow, Susan (1828-1913), 21
Woburn, Beds, 21, 65
Wodehouse, Sir P G (1881-1975) [NR], 221
Wolsey, Cardinal Thomas (1473-1530) [NR], 247
Wolverston, Mary (c1535-1617) [NR], 27
Woodhead, Ann (1826-1893), 142
Woods, 'Tiger' (1902-1971) [NR], golfer, 22
Woolf née Stephen, Adeline Virginia (1882-1941), 130, 165
Wootton, Northants, 51
World Council of Churches, 256
Wren, Sir Christopher (1632-1723) [NR], 255, 257
Wright, Eleanor (1806-1831), 20, 22
Wyatt, Samuel (1737-1837) [NR], architect, 204
Wycliffe, Rev John (c1329-1384) [NR], 13

Y
Yarmouth, Isle of Wight, 224
Yeats, John Butler (1839-1922), 128
Yeats, William Butler (1865-1939), 128, 129, 130
Youlbury, Boars Hill, Oxford, 213, 216, 223, 224
Young '70s (later '80s), 59
Yugoslavia, 212

Z
Zanzibar, 177, 178
Zimbabwe, 69, 160, 175, 176

British possessions c1900